Communications
in Computer and Information Science 536

Editorial Board

More information about this series at http://www.springer.com/series/7899

Jemal H. Abawajy · Sougata Mukherjea
Sabu M. Thampi · Antonio Ruiz-Martínez (Eds.)

Security in Computing and Communications

Third International Symposium, SSCC 2015
Kochi, India, August 10–13, 2015
Proceedings

 Springer

Editors
Jemal H. Abawajy
Deakin University
Geelong, VIC
Australia

Sougata Mukherjea
IBM Research-India
New Delhi
India

Sabu M. Thampi
Indian Institute of Information Technology
    and Management
Kerala
India

Antonio Ruiz-Martínez
University of Murcia
Espinardo, Murcia
Spain

ISSN 1865-0929   ISSN 1865-0937   (electronic)
Communications in Computer and Information Science
ISBN 978-3-319-22914-0   ISBN 978-3-319-22915-7   (eBook)
DOI 10.1007/978-3-319-22915-7

Library of Congress Control Number: 2015946078

Springer Cham Heidelberg New York Dordrecht London

Springer International Publishing AG Switzerland is part of Springer Science+Business Media
(www.springer.com)

Preface

The International Symposium on Security in Computing and Communications (SSCC) aims to provide the most relevant opportunity to bring together researchers and practitioners from both academia and industry to exchange their knowledge and discuss their research findings. The third edition of the Symposium (SSCC 2015) was hosted by SCMS School of Engineering and Technology (SSET), SCMS Group of Institutions, Kochi, India, during August 10–13, 2015. SSCC 2015 was co-located with the 4th International Conference on Advances in Computing, Communications and Informatics (ICACCI 2015).

In response to the call for papers, 157 papers were submitted to the symposium. These papers were evaluated on the basis of their significance, novelty, and technical quality. Each paper was reviewed by at least three members of the Program Committee and 36 regular papers and 13 short papers were accepted.

There is a long list of people who volunteered their time and energy to put together the conference and who warrant acknowledgment. We would like to thank the authors of all the submitted papers, especially the accepted ones, and all the participants who made the symposium a successful event. Thanks to all members of the Technical Program Committee, and the external reviewers, for their hard work in evaluating and discussing papers.

We are grateful to the general chairs and members of the Steering Committee for their support. Our most sincere thanks go to all keynote and tutorial speakers who shared with us their expertise and knowledge. Special thanks to members of the Organizing Committee for their time and effort in organizing the conference.

Finally, we thank Alfred Hofmann and his team at Springer for their excellent support in publishing the proceedings on time.

August 2015

Jemal H. Abawajy
Sougata Mukherjea
Sabu M. Thampi
Antonio Ruiz-Martínez

Preface

Organization

General Chairs

Bharat Bhargava   Purdue University, USA
Chun-I Fan   National Sun Yat-sen University, Taiwan
Indrakshi Ray   Colorado State University, USA

Program Chairs

Sougata Mukherjea   IBM Research, India
Jemal H. Abawajy   Deakin University, Australia
Antonio Ruiz-Martínez   University of Murcia, Spain

Technical Program Committee/Additional Reviewers

Afrand Agah   West Chester University of Pennsylvania, USA
Pelin Angin   Purdue University, USA
Kai Bu   Zhejiang University, P.R. China
Feng Cheng   University of Potsdam, Germany
Saad Darwish   University of Alexandria, Egypt
Ashok Das   International Institute of Information Technology,
     Hyderabad, India
Apostolos Fournaris   University of Patras, Greece
Thomas Gamer   ABB AG, Germany
Fei Ge   Central China Normal University, P.R. China
Yiming Ji   University of South Carolina Beaufort, USA
Grzegorz Kolaczek   Wroclaw University of Technology, Poland
Jiguo Li   Hohai University, P.R. China
Wenzhong Li   Nanjing University, P.R. China
Marius Marcu   Politehnica University of Timisoara, Romania
Philippe Merle   Inria Lille - Nord Europe, France
Alex Morgan   Sunprogrammer Limited, UK
Mauricio Papa   The University of Tulsa, USA
Tuan-Minh Pham   HNUE, Vietnam
Sanjay Rawat   IIIT Hyderabad, India
Panagiotis Sarigiannidis   University of Western Macedonia, Greece
Piyush Shukla   UIT RGPV, India
Dimitrios Stratogiannis   National Technical University of Athens, Greece
Yong Wang   Dakota State University, USA
Andreas Wespi   IBM Zurich Research Laboratory, Switzerland
Ping Yang   Binghamton University, USA

Chau Yuen	Singapore University of Technology and Design, Singapore
Cristina Alcaraz Tello	University of Malaga, Spain
Dhananjoy Dey	DRDO, India
Alexandros Fragkiadakis	Institute of Computer Science, FORTH, Greece
Ming Li	Utah State University, USA
Flavio Lombardi	Third University of Rome, Italy
Gabriele Oligeri	Third University of Rome, Italy
SeongHan Shin	AIST, Japan
Sasan Adibi	Deakin University, Australia
Herath Mudiyanselage Nelanga Bandara	University of Moratuwa, Sri Lanka
Karima Boudaoud	University of Nice Sophia Antipolis, France
Sabrina Sicari	University of Insubria, Italy
Ha Duyen Trung	Hanoi University of Science and Technology, Vietnam
Avishek Adhikari	University of Calcutta, India
Honggang Hu	University of Science and Technology of China, P.R. China
Binod Kumar	JSPM's Jayawant Technical Campus, Pune, India
Thomas Lagkas	The University of Sheffield International Faculty, CITY College, Greece
Charalampos Patrikakis	Technological Educational Institute of Piraeus, Greece
Ulrich Schoen	Self-employed, Germany
Jonathan Tate	Private Sector, UK
Wei-Chih Ting	LoFTech, Taiwan
Francesco Tusa	University of Westminster, UK
Wei Yu	Towson University, USA
Abdalhossein Rezai	ACECR, Iran
Karim Al-Saedi	University of Mustansiriyah, Iraq
Aldar Chun-Fai Chan	Hong Kong Applied Science and Technology Research Institute, SAR China
Debashis De	West Bengal University of Technology, India
Gustavo Figueiredo	Federal University of Bahia, Brazil
K. Ganesh	SVECW, India
Gwo-Jiun Horng	Southern Taiwan University of Science and Technology, Taiwan
Sangeeta K.	Amrita Vishwa Vidyapeetham, India
Satyanarayan Reddy Kalli	Cambridge Institute of Technology, India
Praveen Khethavath	LaGuardia Community College, USA
Weizhi Meng	Institute for Infocomm Research (I2R), Singapore
S. Rajagopalan	Alagappa University, India
Sarbjeet Singh	Panjab University, Chandigarh, India
Vorapong Suppakitpaisarn	The University of Tokyo, Japan
Johnson Thomas	Oklahoma State University, USA
Bhushan Trivedi	GLS Institute Of Computer Technology, India
Chen Wang	Ericsson (China) Communications Co. Ltd., P.R. China

Bo Yan	University of Massachusetts Lowell, USA
Go Yun Ii	Inti International University, Malaysia
Purushothama Byrapura Rangappa	National Institute of Technology Goa, India
Pitipong Chanloha	Chulalongkorn University, Thailand
Raju Halder	IIT Patna, India
Lito Kriara	Disney Research Zurich, Switzerland
Muhana Muslam	Imam University, Saudi Arabia
Saibal Pal	DRDO, India
Anirban Sengupta	Jadavpur University, India
Artemios Voyiatzis	SBA Research, Austria
Mohamad Badra	CNRS/Zayed University, France
Yahaya Coulibaly	Universiti Teknologi Malaisia, Malaysia
Gr. Gangadharan	IDRBT, India
Panagiotis Georgopoulos	ETH Zurich, Switzerland
Shanmugasundaram Govindasamy	Sri Manakula Vinayagar Engineering College, India
David Kao	Time Warner Cable, USA
Massudi Mahmuddin	Universiti Utara Malaysia, Malaysia
Michael Rossberg	Technische Universität Ilmenau, Germany
Khairulmizam Samsudin	Universiti Putra Malaysia, Malaysia
Aris Skander	University of Constantine 1, Algeria
Mengjun Xie	University of Arkansas at Little Rock, USA
Mohammad AlOtaibi	Imam University, Saudi Arabia
Umesh Bhadade	SSBT College of Engineering and Technology, India
Amir Darehshoorzadeh	University of Ottawa, Canada
Sanjoy Das	Galgotias University, India
Makhlouf Hadji	IRT System X, France
Mounir Kellil	CEA LIST, France
Amad Mourad	University of Bejaia, Algeria
Cong Wang	City University of Hong Kong, SAR China
Suvrojit Das	National Institute of Technology, Durgapur, India
Marco Anisetti	Università degli Studi di Milano, Italy
José María de Fuentes	University Carlos III of Madrid, France
Paramate Horkaew	Suranaree University of Technology, Thailand
Nadeem Javaid	COMSATS Institute of IT, Pakistan
Christos Bouras	University of Patras CTI&P-Diophantus, Greece
Claude Carlet	University of Paris 8, France
Thomas Chen	City University London, UK
Chun-I Fan	National Sun Yat-sen University, Taiwan
Eduardo Fernandez	Florida Atlantic University, USA
Jiankun Hu	University of New South Wales, Australia
Nikos Komninos	City University London, UK
Chin-Laung Lei	National Taiwan University, Taiwan
Lau Lung	UFSC, Brazil

Turker Yilmaz	Koc University, Turkey
Pierpaolo Giacomin	Freelancer, Italy
Sandeep Kakde	Y.C. College of Engineering, India
Vishnu Pendyala	Santa Clara University, USA
Praveen Kumar Rajendran	Sathyabama University, India
Sachin Agrawal	SGBAU, India
Osama Attia	Iowa State University, USA
V. Balamurugan	Sathyabama University, India
Amol Bhagat	Prof Ram Meghe College of Engineering and Management, Badnera, India
Rama H.	SMVITM, India
Mohammed Kaabar	Washington State University, USA
Andreas Kliem	Technische Universität Berlin, Germany
Harish Kumar	Panjab University, India
Mahendra Kumar	UCE RTU KOTA, India
Jaemin Park	The Attached Institute of ETRI, Korea
Thaksen Parvat	Sinhgad Institute of Technology, Lonavala, India
Nadana Ravishankar	Valliammai Engineering College, India
Mohd Sadiq	Jamia Millia Islamia, India
Rajat Saxena	Indian Institute of Technology Indore, India
Ajay Shukla	Central Council for Research in Ayurvedic Sciences, India
Venkatasamy Sureshkumar	PSG College of Technology, India
Vinay Viradia	Charotar University of Science and Technology, India
Shiqiang Wang	Imperial College London, UK
Tarun Yadav	Defence Research and Development Organisation, India
Sarat Chettri	Assam Don Bosco University, India
Jignesh Doshi	L.J. Institute of Management Studies, Ahmedabad, India
Filippo Gandino	Politecnico di Torino, Italy
Kamal Gola	Teerthanker Mahaveer University, India
Asif Iqbal	Athena Labs, Zayed University, UAE
Ravi Kodali	National Institute of Technology, Warangal, India
Changqing Luo	Mississippi State University, USA
Arvind Rao	Defense Research & Development Organisation, India
Vaibhav Sharma	Teerthanker Mahaveer University, India
Chandra Vorugunti	Dhirubhai Ambani Institute of ICT, India
Amit Mishra	Jaypee Institute of Engineering and Technology, India
Sumesh S.	Amrita University, India
L.A. Akinyemi	University of Cape Town, South Africa
Balaji Badhrinarayanan	Manipal University, India
B. Borah	Tezpur Univertsity, India
Diego Tami	Federal University of Minas Gerais, Brazil
Anurag Tomar	Lovely Professional University, India
S. Vijaykumar	6TH SENSE, India

Rahul Waghmare	Indian Institute of Space Science and Technology, India
Ivan Pires	Instituto de Telecomunicacoes, University of Beira Interior, Portugal
Loris Corazza	University of Patras, Greece
Anderson da Silva	Federal University of Rio Grande do Sul (UFRGS), Brazil
Nikolaos Tsakiridis	Aristotle University of Thessaloniki, Greece
Mai Anh Do	Christopher Newport University, USA
Khalil Ibrahimi	University of IBN Tofail, Morocco
Yongsen Ma	College of William and Mary, USA
Girish Mishra	SAG, India
Chuong Ngo	College of William and Mary, USA
Alexis Olivereau	CEA LIST, France
Prompong Pakawanwong	The University of Tokyo, Japan
Atiqur Rahman	College of William and Mary, USA
Ram Ratan	SAG, DRDO, India
Mohammad Faridul Haque Siddiqui	The University of Toledo, USA
Jesse Victors	Utah State University, USA
Kyle Wallace	College of William and Mary, USA
Hanlin Zhang	Towson University, USA
Hongyang Zhao	College of William and Mary, USA
M. Archana	Annamalai University, India
Anuradha Dhull	ITM University Gurgaon, India
Supriya M.	Amrita Vishwa Vidyapeetham, India
Rajarajeswari Palaniappan	Anna University Chennai, India
Sunita Dhavale	Defence Institute of Advanced Technology, India
Latha Pillappa Hanumappa	Visvesvaraya Technological University, India
Preetha Prasanna	Thiagarajar College of Engineering, Anna University, India
Sugandha Sharma	Chandigarh University, India
Manisha Joshi	M.G.M.'s College of Engineering, India
Kriti Saroha	CDAC, India
Cli Dal Bianco	URI Universidade Regional Integrada, Brazil
Xue Li	Samsung Information Systems America R&D Center, USA
Meiqin Wang	Shandong University, P.R. China
Gulista Khan	TMU, India
S. Anandhi	PSG College of Technology, India
Deepa Krishnan	Pillai Institute of Information Technology, India
Aditi Sharma	MBM Engineering College Jodhpur, India
Kimaya Ambekar	K.J. SIMSR, India
Supriya Dubey	Motilal Nehru National Institute of Technology, Allahabad, India

Deepthi Haridas	Advanced Data Processing Research Institute (ADRIN), India
Vartika Srivastava	Jaypee Institute of Information and Technology, India
Kira Kastell	Frankfurt University of Applied Sciences, Germany
Jana Krimmling	IHP, Germany
Shilpa Mahajan	ITMU, India
S. Santhanalakshmi	Amrita School of Engineering, India
Suchithra M.	Amrita Vishwa Vidya Peetham, India
Priya R.	BSAU, India
Preeti Shivach	Gurukul Kangri Vishwavidyalaya Haridwar, India
Geethapriya Thamilarasu	University of Washington Bothell, USA
Ankita Wadhawan	DAV Institute of Engineering and Technology, India
Anjana Das	College of Engineering, Trivandrum, India
Shuo Qiu	Utah State University, USA
Alessandra Rizzardi	University of Insubria, Italy
André Stefanello	URI, Brazil
Athira U.	IIITM-K, India

ICACCI 2015 Steering Committee

Ravi Sandhu	University of Texas at San Antonio, USA
Sankar Kumar Pal	Indian Statistical Institute, Kolkata, India
Albert Y. Zomaya	The University of Sydney, Australia
H.V. Jagadish	University of Michigan, USA
Sartaj Sahni	University of Florida, USA
John F. Buford	Avaya Labs Research, USA
Jianwei Huang	The Chinese University of Hong Kong, SAR China
John Strassner	Software Labs, Futurewei, California, USA
Janusz Kacprzyk	Polish Academy of Sciences, Poland
Tan Kay Chen	National University of Singapore, Singapore
Srinivas Padmanabhuni	Infosys Labs, India, and ACM India
Suzanne McIntosh	New York University and Cloudera Inc., USA
Prabhat K. Mahanti	University of New Brunswick, Canada
R. Vaidyanathan	Louisiana State University, USA
Hideyuki Takagi	Kyushu University, Japan
Haibo He	University of Rhode Island, USA
Nikhil R. Pal	Indian Statistical Institute, Kolkata, India
Chandrasekaran K.	NITK, India
Junichi Suzuki	University of Massachusetts Boston, USA
Deepak Garg, Chair	IEEE Computer Society Chapter, IEEE India Council and Thapar University, India
Pascal Lorenz	University of Haute Alsace, France
Pramod P. Thevannoor	SCMS Group of Institutions, Kochi, India
Axel Sikora	University of Applied Sciences Offenburg, Germany
Maneesha Ramesh	Amrita Vishwa Vidyapeetham, Kollam, India
Sabu M. Thampi	IIITM-K, India

Suash Deb	INNS India Regional Chapter
Arun Somani	Iowa State University, USA
Preeti Bajaj	G.H. Raisoni COE, Nagpur, India
Arnab Bhattacharya	Indian Institute of Technology (IIT), Kanpur, India

ICACCI 2015 Organizing Committee

Patron

| G.P.C. Nayar (Founder and Chairman) | SCMS Group |

General Chairs

Jaime Lloret Mauri	Polytechnic University of Valencia, Spain
Dilip Krishnaswamy	IBM Research, India
Sabu M. Thampi	IIITM-K, India

Organizing Chair

| M. Madhavan (Director) | SCMS School of Engineering and Technology (SSET) |

Program Chairs

Michal Wozniak	Wroclaw University, Warsaw, Poland
Peter Mueller	IBM Zurich Research Laboratory, Switzerland
Neeli R. Prasad	Aalborg University, Denmark
Jose M. Alcaraz Calero	University of the West of Scotland, UK

Industry Track Chairs

Xinyu Que	IBM T.J. Watson Research Center, USA
Chung Shue (Calvin) CHEN	Alcatel-Lucent Bell Labs, France
Ashley Thomas	Dell Secureworks, USA

Workshop and Symposium Chairs

Joel Rodrigues	Instituto de Telecomunicaçoes, University of Beira Interior, Portugal
B.S. Manoj	Indian Institute of Space Science and Technology (IIST), India
Siby Abraham	University of Mumbai, India

Special Track Chairs

Ali Hessami   Vega Systems, UK
Robin Doss   Deakin University, Australia
Bhawna Mallick   Galgotias College of Engineering and Technology
                                (GCET), India

Panel Chair

Amitava Chatterjee   Jadavpur University, India

Demo/Poster Track Chairs

Vivek Ashok Bohara   IIIT-Delhi, India
Jiajian Chen   Qualcomm Research, USA

Doctoral Symposium Chairs

Ding-zhu Du   University of Texas, Dallas, USA
Christian Callegari   University of Pisa, Italy
Shivani Sud   Intel Labs, USA

Tutorial Chairs

Mukesh Taneja   Cisco Systems, Bangalore, India
Dhiya Al-Jumeily   Liverpool John Moores University, UK
Bob Gill   BCIT, Canada
Sergey Mosin   Vladimir State University, Russia
Edward Au   Marvell Semiconductor, USA

Publication Chair

Natarajan Meghanathan   Jackson State University, USA

Award Committee Chair

Donatella Darsena   University of Naples Parthenope, Italy

Publicity Chair

Tao Han   New Jersey Institute of Technology, USA

Organizing Secretary

Vinod P.   SCMS School of Engineering and Technology (SSET),
                                India

Contents

Cryptography and Steganography

System and Network Security

Application Security

Security in Cloud Computing

A Dynamic Multi-domain Access Control Model in Cloud Computing

Dapeng Xiong, Peng Zou[✉], Jun Cai, and Jun He

Science and Technology on Complex Electronic System Simulation Laboratory,
Academy of Equipment, Beijing 101416, China
{DapengXiongLNCS,PengZouLNCS,JunCaiLNCS,
JunHeLNCS}@Springer.com

Abstract. Access control technology is an important way to ensure the safety of the cloud platform, but the new features of cloud computation environment have brought new challenges to access control technology. Direct at the existing problems of flexibility, timeliness and other aspects in multi-domain access control in the current cloud, on the basis of task driving idea, this paper put forward a dynamic access control policy. New method combined the advantage of RBAC and task driving model, to implement a more flexible and efficient access control model. Through comparative experiment we draw that new policy was improved to be contributory in improving the flexibility and availability of role-based multi-domain access control model .

Keywords: Access control · Dynamic RBAC · Cloud · Multi-domain

1 Introduction

As a new computing model in the initial stage, cloud computation has brought great convenience to people in Internet era with its advantages of large scale, virtualization and high flexibility and so on. However, there is still much room left for improvement of cloud security. As the core technology to guarantee the safety of cloud computing system, access control technology ensures the protection of cloud computing resources to be accessed by legitimate users or programs, avoid unauthorized information leakage, so as to assure the safety and legal use of cloud computing resources. Cloud computing platform is a complex information system, characterized by large scale and distribution according to needs and so forth, these characteristics has brought new challenges to access control technology. Cloud computing environment is a virtual organization composed of various autonomous domains, users and resources are in different autonomous domains, and the relationship between users and resource providers is dynamic. Under these distributed multiple domains, access control mechanisms should be adequately flexible and dynamic in order to ensure the safety access in the multi-domain environment of cloud computing. However, there have been serious deficiencies of each existing product cloud in multi-domain access control. Therefore, the research of multi-domain access control model under cloud computing environment is of important scientific significance and application value.

© Springer International Publishing Switzerland 2015
J.H. Abawajy et al. (Eds): SSCC 2015, CCIS 536, pp. 3–12, 2015.
DOI: 10.1007/978-3-319-22915-7_1

Based on the analysis of requirements and difficulties of multi-domain access control under cloud computing environment, this paper extended and improved role-based multi-domain access control model, which introduced task-based driving mechanism and can dynamically adjust the inter-domain role mapping as needed, thus better solving the problem of inter-domain role mapping. Meanwhile, it solved the problem of policy conflict by the mean of inter-domain policy combination. Finally it completed the experiment on Openstack cloud platform, which proves that this model has advantages in safety and availability.

2   Related Work

2.1   Problem Analysis

Multi domain is one of the important features of the cloud computing environment. Before we discuss the multi-domain access control issues, we need to clarify the definition of domains in the cloud. Autonomous domain refers to "managerial authority of independence and autonomy, users and resources belonging to centralized management, physical organization or logical organization that has independent access control policy space and the only access control decision points" [1]. A typical cloud computing architecture is a distributed network environment made up of multiple autonomous domains. An example of multi-domain is as shown in the following figure (Fig. 1):

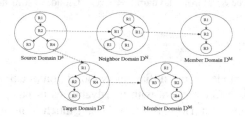

Fig. 1.   Structure schematic of multi-domain

Under the cloud computing multi-domain environment, a subject of a security domain should manage access authority of its own domain resource, and meanwhile apply to other security domains for resource access authorization. So, multi-domain access control is divided into intra-domain control and inter-domain control. Intra-domain control manages internal resources via the authority and policy established by itself, inter-domain control manages cross-domain resources operation through authorization control. To solve the multi-domain access control in cloud computation is to achieve inter-domain authorization and access control while ensuring intra-domain autonomy and security.

What is an ideal multi-domain model of cloud computation? To meet the needs of multi-domain authorization and the characteristics of the cloud, it is necessary to establish a general access control model, which should meet the following requirements:

(1) **Suitability**. Security interoperation should be able to better fit different security policies of each autonomous domain and should not cause security policy conflict or adjustment within each autonomous domain.

(2) **Responsive**. Reasonable response should be made to the request for cross-domain resource access. Under the premise of ensuring two-party security of interoperability, make a response to initiator's request for resource operation ASAP (authorized or rejected)

(3) **Scalable**. The model should be adapted to the characteristics of enormous amount, real-time change of intra-domain users and organization domains, which can flexibly expanded along with the change of the scale and structure of the domain. Here we tend to distributed access management, rather than centralized access decision.

(4) **Real-Time**. The model should have the ability to adjust in real time and can make a quick authorization decision according the adjustment of domain and users' access application, and cross-domain authority should be dynamically allocated and revoking.

(5) **Realizable**. A good security interoperation mechanism should be easily implemented, without introducing complex management support platforms.

2.2 Research Status

The most remarkable characteristic of multi-domain environment is distributed. Multi-domain access control technology in cloud computation has inherited and developed from the distributed multi-domain access control technology, and meanwhile we should also recognize that could computing system has great differences in multi-domain authorization compared to other distributed systems. Thus new characteristics of multi-domain access control under the cloud computing environment should be fully considered, to design access control model suitable for multi domains. At present, the research of multi-domain access control technology in cloud computation mainly focuses on the following aspects:

(1) **Designing of Multi-domain Access Control Model**. Mainly to solve synthesis problem of cross-domain access control strategy, to implement authorization access control of multi-domain coordination.

(2) **Policy Conflict Detection and Elimination.** To solve the problem of inconsistent access control rules introduced because of the synthetic strategies of multi-domain access control, detect and eliminate authentication and authorization that has conflicts.

(3) **Security Analysis of Strategies.** To prove that the designed access control model is safe and reliable and will not bring the authority leakage and other safety hazards.

The traditional multi-domain access control technology has been widely used in distributed information system. The common approaches of multi-domain access control mainly concentrate on the following categories: role-based access control, attribute-based access control, trust-based access control, or the enhanced combination of the above several strategies [2].

Difficulties in traditional multi-domain access control strategy. The dynamic, distributed, heterogeneous and autonomous multi-domain environment has presented new challenges to computational intra-domain and inter-domain security interoperability. The current multi-domain access control approach still has some deficiencies existing in the application in cloud computing platform in flexibility, security and availability and other aspects; it is mainly reflected in the following aspects:

- **Cross-Domain Interoperability.** How to construct multiple security domains for security policy of inter-domain interoperability, to ensure safe resource interoperability between security domains.
- **Policy Conflict**. How to coordinate and solve the problem of inconsistent security policy between intra domains and extra domains. The policy to assign access object tenant between users and tenants may conflict against each other. The policy decision point (PDP) should use the predefined algorithm, to solve the conflict.
- **Security of Policy**. The synthetic strategy should prevent permission leakage caused by cross-domain access. If the operation is prohibited in autonomous domain, it should also be forbidden in interoperability.
- **Management Mode**. Centralized cross-domain authorization is easy to avoid policy conflict and convenient for implementation, but it has poor expansibility and is easy to cause single point failure. While distributed cross-domain authorization is easy to extend and accord with the support of secure interoperability to local autonomy, but it's difficult to form a global view of strategies, prone to causing security conflict.
- **Moderate Control**. Excessive introducing various control mechanisms bring difficulties to achieve the access control policies, and also may affect the performance.

We took the OpenStack for example to analyze the implementation and existing problems of access control in a typical commercial cloud platform.

2.3   Access Control in OpenStack

OpenStack is the most representative open-source cloud computing platform. OpenStack (JUNO version) contains the following components: Nova, Neutron, Horizon, Swift, Glance, Cinder and Keystone etc., among which Keystone is an authorization control module of OpenStack, responsible for the authorization, service rules and service permission token, which implements Identity API in OpenStack.

Domains represent collections of users, groups, and projects in Keystone. A user, group or item can only belong to one domain, but they can be associated with other domains through authorization. Each domain has a namespace in Identity API, containing some unique attributes only visible to API. In the unique domain attributes of theses definitions, domain name and role name are visible to all domains, while project name, group name and user name can only be visible within the domains [3].

OpenStack Access Control (OSAC) module realizes the access control through the certification authority in Keystone; its core is the extension of typical role-based access control model. A brief description of OSAC' mechanism is as follows. As a role-based authorization model, the core part of OSAC is the role assignment. The user, group and item have a corresponding role, and permission is only related to the role, so all the items can get the authorization through the role. The user can be associated with item belonging to other domain by being authorized a user role of another item. The role-based access control model modifies the role of cross-domain users according to the permission of extra-domain resources in the service to achieve cross-domain authorization control, with great flexibility. The disadvantage of OpenStack authorization control is too coarse granularity of access control.

3   A Role-Based Multi-domain Access Control Policy in Cloud

In this section we focused on the features of cloud computing environment to construct and realize a security interoperability model suitable for distributed heterogeneous multi-domain environment. The design purpose of this model is to establish a multi-domain access control model based on dynamic role mapping, by means of role mapping, that is to realize resource access by constructing an inter-domain equivalence relation.

3.1   Task-Driving Dynamic Role Assignment

As role assignment based on role mapping is unchanged upon consultation, this way of authorization has disadvantages in permission timeliness and distribution on demand and other aspects. In RBAC model, another important concept, task, was introduced in this paper. The task (or activity) herein is the joint name of all cross-domain operating processes initiated by users. Task-role based access control (T-RBAC) solves security problems from the perspective of the user needs, which is an active security model based on task and using dynamic authorization. By adopting the viewpoint of task oriented, security model was established and security mechanism was implemented from the angle of tasks, and real-time security management was provided during the task processing, whose basic ideas are as follows (Fig. 2):

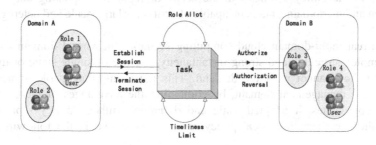

Fig. 2. Task-driving dynamic role assignment

(1) Combine access permission with task, the execution of each task is considered as a process that subject uses relevant access permission to access the object. During the task execution, the permission is consumed. The subject cannot access the object any more when the permission is exhausted,

(2) The access permission that the system grants to users is not only related to subject and object, but also associated with the current tasks of subject and task status. Object's access control permission is not stationary, but varies along with the change of tasks in this context. Due to the active, dynamic and other character-istics of T-RBAC, it has been widely used in decision making of information processing and transaction management system of workflow, distributed pro-cessing and multipoint access control.

This paper introduced task-driving mechanism, permission could be updated and overdue authorization should be revoked in real time according to the needs of current tasks. By combining the timeliness of task model and the flexibility of role model, it proposed a task-driving multi-domain access control model based on role mapping.

3.2   Real-Time Multi-domain Access Control Policy Synthesis

The main approach of RBAC-based multi-domain policy synthesis is the role mapping, which is to realize resource access by establishing an inter-domain role equivalence relation. The current role-based cross-domain policy synthesis approach can be divided into static mapping and dynamic mapping according to the question whether it can realize dynamic role mapping. The static mapping is a tightly coupled, global role mapping approach with a coordination center. One of the most classical frameworks of static mapping approach is the global role mapping method proposed by Shafiq [4]. The dynamic mapping is a loosely coupled approach based on request act with no coordination center. Smithi Piromruen et al. [5] proposed a dynamic interoperability framework between domains stand for Dynamic policy synthesis.

Two traditional synthesis methods have some limitations when applied in cloud computing environment. With the global efficiency, the static role mapping has an advantage in large-scale distributed intra-domain policy synthesis, but acts inefficiency in highly interactive conditions. With local flexibility, the dynamic role mapping has advantage in the policy synthesis in the scene of rapid role updating and frequent interaction among domains, but is incapable of action for large-scale and heterogeneous scene.

In the real multi-domain cloud computing scenario, the virtual domain has large scale, complex structure, and strong instantaneity, the use of single static or dynamic synthetic policy cannot meet the demand. This paper introduced role management engine in the management domain, by combining the advantages of these two role mapping approaches, it adopted static and dynamic synthetic policy separately in global policy synthesis and local policy renewal, as shown in the following figure (Fig. 3).

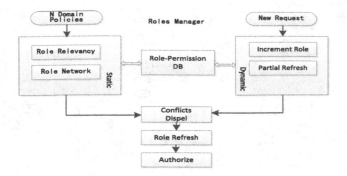

Fig. 3. Real-time multi-domain access control policy synthesis

Extending the idea of task-oriented, we combine static and dynamic synthesis method according to the task. Then provide real-time dynamic cross domain strategy synthesis to meet new request. The basic idea is as follows:

(1) Static strategy and dynamic policy updating models are managed by the engine of Role - permission manager, the two works together to maintain a role - permission Table

(2) Global synthesis module draw roles - permission map between domains in advance, then resolute conflicts uniformly. This process is time-consuming, but to ensure the safety and non - redundancy. Suitable for regular maintenance, such as in the access control engine initialization stage, take a long time to generate a global role authorization table, then to calculate and update it in the system idle time.

(3) Local strategy updating is task driving. Update related roles and permissions table in order to meet the new request. The domain map authorization requests from other domains to a part role set, which will be processed with permission mapping and conflicts resolution, so as to achieve the inter domain access.

The combined method can not only adapt to the global strategy for synthesis of large scale, heterogeneous multi domain environment, meanwhile to fulfill local strategy aroused by task. The synthetic methods have advantages in flexibility and availability compared with traditional multi-domain strategy.

4 Simulations and Performance Analysis

The experimental environment: 4 single CPU (each CPU4, frequency 1.6 GHz, memory 4G) servers. We set up a small cloud computing environment, which simulates a multi-domain environment consisted of 8 domains. Network topology of the cloud environment is as shown in Fig. 4.

Two simulation experiments have been designed in the multi-domain environment. One purposed to inspect the ability of Task driving RBAC model. Another aimed to observe the effect of the real-time multi-domain access control policies combination.

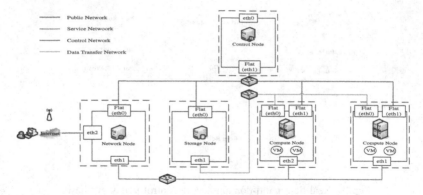

Fig. 4. Network topology of the experiment cloud

4.1   Task Driving RBAC Model

The purpose of the first experiment is to prove that, the task driving RBAC model which bring in the authorization mechanism of limited aging, will keep the risks of policies conflict low.

In order to illustrate the effect of Task driving and Aging Authorization, a contrast experiment was designed as follows. The experiment compared the history of policy conflicts along with cross-domain requests, in the case of RBAC bring in aging authorization or not. Experimental results as shown in Fig. 5.

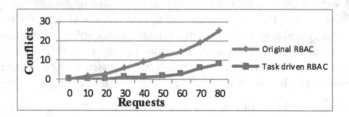

Fig. 5.   Experiment result of task driving RBAC model

By analyzing the experimental results, we can get the following conclusion. The original design of RBAC algorithm maintained in the given user role authorization, thus with the passage of time, newcomer of role authorization may cause conflicts against the existing authorization. While the new algorithm based on task driving RBAC bring in the aging control for each authorization, in which the manager will revoke the role authorization forwardly in a certain period of time after the session is completed, accordingly avoid unnecessary permission leakage due to expired license.

4.2   Real-Time Global Policy Synthesis

The purpose of the second experiment is to prove that, the real-time fusion method of global static synthesis and partial dynamic synthesis can improve the abilities of multi-domain access control policy synthesis.

In order to illustrate the effect of Real-time Global Policies Synthesis, a contrast experiment was designed as follows. The experiment compared the time consumption of policy synthesis, between Static synthesis method, Dynamic synthesis method and the new real-time synthesis method. We measured the relation between time consumption and real-time request and the scale of domains, in three test bed adopting different policy synthesis. Experimental results as shown in Fig. 6.

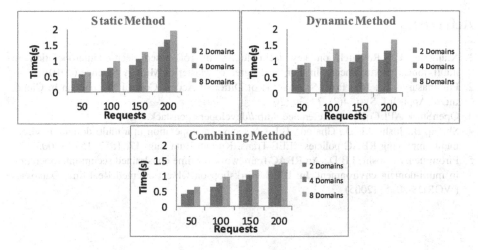

Fig. 6. Average time of policy synthesis

By analyzing the experimental results, we can get the following conclusion. Integrating real-time strategy synthesis method combines the advantages of two methods, using global synthetic strategy in large-scale initialization, using local dynamic update to meet the real-time request. Overall, the real-time strategy synthesis method saves synthetic time, has a certain degree of improvement on the flexibility and usability. We did not test its effect of our method in a much larger domain limited to environmental conditions.

5 Conclusion

On the basis of the analysis of technical defects existing in multi-domain access control in the current cloud computing platform, this paper improved the Role-based multi-domain access control model by bringing in aging control and policy synthesis manager, and the experiment showed that, this model has superiorities in certain conditions. (1) Compared with the general RBAC algorithm, this method can update the permissions according to task requirement timely, and revoke permissions at the end of the task, thereby reduce the possibility of permission leakage. (2) Dynamic updating role - access tables according to requests, to reduce the calculation time of global strategy of synthetic, and improve the efficiency of authorization. This paper also has some shortages in the following aspects worth further research. (1) How to determine the appropriate aging time. (2) A larger scale multi-domain test.

Acknowledgments. This research has been supported by National High Technology Research and Development Application of China (2012AA012902) and "HGJ" National Major Technological Projects (2013ZX01045-004).

References

1. Xiangran, C.: Research on key technologies of role-based secure interoperation in multi-domain environments. In: For the Degree of Master of Military Science (2010)
2. Punithasurya, K.: Jeba Priya S: Analysis of Different Access Control Mechanism in Cloud. Int. J. Appl. Inf. Syst. **4**(2), 34–39 (2012)
3. OpenStack API Complete Reference. http://developer.openstack.org/
4. Shafiq, B., Joshi, J.B.D., Ghafoor, B.E.: A secure interoperation in a multi-domain environment employing RBAC policies. IEEE Trans. Knowl. Data Eng. **17**, 1557–1577 (2005)
5. Piromruen, S., Joshi, J.B.D.: An RBAC framework for time constrained secure interoperation in multi-domain environment. In: IEEE Workshop on Object-oriented Real-time Databases (WORDS-2005) (2005)

Multilevel Threshold Secret Sharing in Distributed Cloud

Doyel Pal[1](✉), Praveenkumar Khethavath[2], Johnson P. Thomas[1], and Tingting Chen[3]

[1] Computer Science Department, Oklahoma State University,
Stillwater, OK 74075, USA
{doyelp,jpt}@cs.okstate.edu
[2] Mathematics, Engineering and Computer Science Department, LaGuardia
Community College, CUNY, Longisland City, NY 11101, USA
pkhethavath@lagcc.cuny.edu
[3] Computer Science Department, California State Polytechnic University,
Pomona, CA 91768, USA
tingtingchen@csupomona.edu

Abstract. Security is a highlighted concern in cloud and distributed cloud systems. Threshold secret sharing scheme is a widely used mechanism to secure different computing environments. We split secret into multiple shares and store them in different locations using threshold secret sharing scheme. In this paper we propose a multilevel threshold secret sharing scheme to enhance security of secret key in a distributed cloud environment. We create replicas of secret shares and distribute them among multiple resource providers to ensure availability. We also introduce dummy shares at each resource provider to realize the presence of any outside attacker. Our experiment results show that our scheme is feasible and secure.

1 Introduction

The Distributed cloud [16] makes use of resources provided by users in a P2P manner. In the distributed cloud resources are virtualized.. The existing cloud uses huge data centers where resources are provided using virtualization techniques. Some of the voluntary computing systems such as BOINC [14], SETI [15] and Planetlab [20] uses resources provided by users, but these are managed by a central entity and are completely different from either a centralized cloud or the distributed cloud. Unlike users of the existing cloud, who don't have control over the resources, in the distributed cloud users can choose resources of their choice. Moreover, in the distributed cloud, resources are provided by users. Since users of the distributed cloud have more control over resource selection, they can perform strong encryption to secure their data. The only issue will be managing these keys. We use secret sharing mechanism in this paper to protect secret keys in the distributed cloud.

Secret sharing schemes can mitigate the risks of managing these keys. Secret sharing schemes are used in many cryptographic protocols. Threshold secret

© Springer International Publishing Switzerland 2015
J.H. Abawajy et al. (Eds): SSCC 2015, CCIS 536, pp. 13–23, 2015.
DOI: 10.1007/978-3-319-22915-7_2

sharing scheme is the most widely used technique. The main ides behind the threshold secret sharing schemes was introduced by Shamir [1] and Blakley [2]. In the threshold secret sharing mechanism, information is split into multiple shares and these shares are distributed among multiple users. The only way to retrieve the information back is to have all the shares or a qualified number of shares available. This qualified number is the threshold. This means that any number of shares less than the threshold cannot retrieve the information. Shamir's secret sharing scheme is based on polynomial interpolation whereas Blakley's secret sharing scheme is based on geometry. Several secret sharing schemes has been introduced, e.g., threshold secret sharing scheme, ideal secret sharing, linear secret sharing, multi linear secret sharing, [1, 2, 4, 5] etc. The Asmuth and Bloom secret sharing scheme [17] uses the Chinese reminder theorem to reconstruct shares. Multi linear secret sharing schemes [18] uses monotone span programs. In these schemes, secret is a sequence of elements from a finite field and the share is derived using the secret and some random elements from the field. If the secret is of size one i.e. has only one element it is called linear.

In this paper we propose a multilevel threshold secret sharing scheme to provide security of secret key in the distributed cloud. In the first level of the proposed secret sharing scheme we split the secret key into multiple shares and distribute them among multiple resource providers. The second level consists of splitting each share into multiple numbers of sub-secrets at each resource provider. To make our scheme secure we make the determination of threshold value at the second level dynamic. We generate a share pool which is used to determine the number of shares at each resource provider using Chinese Remainder Theorem (CRT) [13]. The advantage of our proposed scheme is that in the distributed cloud, users provide resources and therefore user do not need to invest in the commercial cloud (e.g., Amazon AWS [22], EC2 [23], Windows Azure [24] etc.). Security in the distributed cloud has not been studied much and our scheme provides a way to get a secure way to protect the secret key. We perform the multilevel threshold secret sharing mechanism on the secret key itself as key plays an important role to encrypt or decrypt the file content. In our proposed scheme the secret is distributed over multiple resource providers therefore an attacker cannot have the original secret until and unless all the participating resource providers are compromised. We generate the replica of each secret shares to ensure the fact that if a provider is compromised then that particular share is available from other providers. Moreover the user can revoke the access of any resource provider if the provider is compromised. We increase the chance to detect if a provider is compromised by introducing dummy key shares at each resource provider.

The rest of the paper is organized as follows. In Sects. 2 and 3, we describe related work and present the problem statement respectively. In Sect. 4, we explain our proposed solution. In Sect. 5, we discuss the performance evaluations of our approach and in Sect. 6 we provide our conclusions.

2   Related Work

In this paper we use Shamir's threshold secret sharing scheme [1]. [1] is an ideal perfect secret sharing scheme as the size of shares are exactly same with the size of each share. A lot of work [5–7] has been developed based on [1]. A threshold ideal secret sharing has been proposed in [6] which uses only XOR operations to make shares and to recover the secret. The authors also show that this scheme is perfect and faster with reduced storage usage and computational cost compared to [1]. In [7] a multilevel threshold secret sharing scheme has been proposed with two modifications of [1]. The first modification allow the shareholders to keep both x coordinate and y- coordinate along with the share of secret and in the second modification a polynomial degree larger than the threshold value is used by the dealers to generate the share. In our scheme we perform splitting the secret twice, once by the user and the other by the resource provider. At resource provider along with the shares we also store dummy shares which improves security. Another type of secret sharing scheme, Linear secret sharing scheme [1, 2, 5] is based on linear algebra and it contains super polynomial lower bounds on the share size. Though [1] can only realize the access structure of the secret sharing scheme, [5] can design a secret sharing scheme from any given access structure. A multi linear secret sharing scheme which uses super polynomial bounds on the share size has been proposed in [4]. In [3] the authors introduce a hierarchical threshold secret sharing scheme. In this scheme secret is shared in a hierarchical structure among groups of participants which is further partitioned into levels.

Security is an important concern for cloud architecture as cloud storage is vulnerable to security threats. Protecting data storage and key management are two of the most important concerns among them. [8–12] concentrate on the cloud storage security and the secure key management scheme in different cloud environments. Cloudstash [8] concentrates on providing the security of the cloud storage. It considers the file as secret and applies secret sharing scheme directly on the multiple shares of secrets. This scheme hashes and signs each share of file and then distributes these signed multi shares into multi clouds. To overcome the limitations of single domain cloud a new second layer in the dependable cloud computing stack named Intercloud has been introduced in [9].This scheme performs symmetric encryption on the data and splits the key into shares using secret sharing scheme. It attaches the key shares as metadata to the pieces of data and distributes them to the clouds. The N cloud scheme [10] propose an improved cloud storage scheme in terms of availability, performance and confidentiality in cloud. It splits the file in many chunks and uploads the encrypted file chunks in geographically separated cloud storage's in parallel. It also replicates the chunks in non overlapping manner into many cloud storages. To reconstruct the file it downloads the chunks, decrypts them and reassembles them back to a file. This technique manages the encryption keys at client side and does not save them in clouds. To overcome the limitation of single cloud, the DepSky system [11] builds a cloud of clouds named Intercloud, on top of a set of storage clouds by using a combination of diverse commercial clouds. It uses the combination of

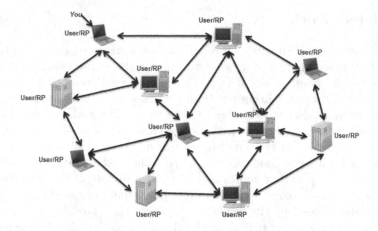

Fig. 1. Distributed cloud model

Byzantine quorum system protocols, cryptographic secret sharing, erasure codes and diversity of several clouds to improve the availability and confidentiality provided by commercial storage cloud. The CloudSeal scheme [12] provides an end to end content confidentiality protection mechanism for large scale content storage. It uses integrated symmetric encryption, threshold secret sharing, and proxy based re- encryption scheme to protect the content and to manage the user access. It also supports forward and backward security. In our multi-level threshold secret sharing scheme we provide security to protect secret key in the distributed cloud.

3   Problem Statement

In the distributed cloud model [16,21], users do computation and store data in resources provided by other users as shown in Fig. 1. Since users use resources provided by other users, there are obvious security concerns. Dependable Storage in the Intercloud [11], provides reasons why single cloud is not secure, namely, we need to have more than one cloud to make the system more secure. The Distributed cloud model by itself solves the problem of single domain cloud as it has more than one user who will be acting as a cloud provider. In distributed cloud, protecting data stored on other users' resources poses security issues, which is handled using standard encryption techniques, which in turn leads to key management issues and insider attacks. A resource provider can get access to the data stored on his resources with ease and can use brute force attacks on it. Security of data storage currently depends on how strong encryption keys a user has used or how effective the key management schemes used are. So instead of having a single key that gives access to the encrypted files, we propose using multiple shares. In our proposed secret sharing mechanism in the distributed cloud we use secure mechanisms to enhance the security of secret key shares.

We have a share pool that determines the number of shares for a particular key share.

In the distributed cloud, since users can join and leave the cloud, we need to make sure this resource pool is always available. So we make duplicates of this pool and store them for multiple resource providers in all clusters in the distributed cloud.

4   Proposed Solution

4.1   Preliminaries

In this section we discuss the basic preliminaries we use in this paper, that is, Shamir's threshold secret sharing scheme and Chinese Remainder Theorem.

Shamir's Threshold Secret Sharing. In this paper we use Shamir's (k, n) threshold secret sharing scheme [1]. Shamir's (k, n) threshold secret sharing scheme is based on polynomial interpolation. A secret S can be shared by n number of users and can be reconstructed as well, if the number of shares to reconstruct exceeds some threshold value k. This scheme uses a polynomial function of order $(k - 1)$ which can be constructed as,

$f(x) = d_0 + d_1 x + d_2 x^2 + \ldots d_{k-1} x^{k-1}$ Here d_0 is the secret S. Given any k shares $< x_0, f(x_0) >, .., < x_{(k-1)}, f(x_{(k-1)}) >$ the secret S can be reconstructed using Lagrange Interpolation formula as follows:

$$\sum_{i=0}^{k-1} (\Pi_{i \neq j} \frac{x_j}{x_j - x_i}) f(x_i)$$

Chinese Remainder Theorem. We use the Chinese Remainder Theorem (CRT) [13] to generate the threshold value at each resource provider at the second level of the threshold secret sharing scheme. Given the following system of equations,

$$x = a_1 mod p_1$$
$$x = a_2 mod p_2$$
$$\ldots\ldots\ldots\ldots$$
$$x = a_k mod p_k$$

There is one unique solution as

$$x = \sum_{(i=1)}^{k} \frac{P}{p_i} y_i a_i mod P$$

where $P = p_1 p_2 \ldots p_k$ and $\frac{P}{p_i} y_i mod p_i = 1$, if all moduli are pairwise coprime, i.e., $gcd(p_i, p_j) = 1$ for every $i \neq j$.

4.2   Proposed Scheme

The Distributed cloud is formed using the resource provided by users and can provide resource for free to everyone who is part of the system. The Distributed cloud makes use of virtualization to allocate resources to multiple users and shares available resources efficiently and it also avoids single point of failure. In this paper we propose a scheme to protect the secret key using a multilevel threshold secret sharing mechanism shown in Fig. 2 in the distributed cloud environment. Our proposed scheme encrypts the file using the secret key before distributing the key shares among participant resource providers whoom we assume to be honest. At the first level the user splits the key and distributes the shares among resource providers. Instead of attaching key shares as metadata to the pieces of data [9] we split the key shares at each resource provider again into multiple shares in the second level. The second level of our mechanism improves the security since to get the original secret the attacker has to have all the shares from the two levels. We generate the threshold value in the second level dynamically which enhances the security as the attacker cannot know about the threshold value beforehand. In addition to that at each resource provider we create dummy keys which increases the probability of knowing if a resource provider is compromised by any attacker. In Algorithm 1 we ensure the security of the secret key in a distributed cloud environment. To do that we use the multilevel threshold secret sharing scheme (t, n) in which the first level uses the threshold $t < n$ and the second level uses the threshold $t = m$.

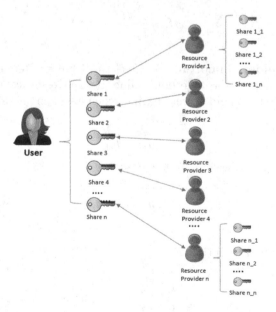

Fig. 2. Proposed multilevel threshold secret sharing scheme

First the user splits the secret key into n number of shares S_i,where $i \in (1, n)$ and distribute them among all resource providers (Algorithm 1.2. line 1 to 7). In this level the threshold value $t < n$ which indicates that to reconstruct the secret key at least t number of shares would be required. Each share of secret S_i is replicated into k numbers so that if one resource provider goes offline or compromised then that share can be accessed from other resource provider. At each resource provider we further split the share S_i into m number of shares S_{ij} (Algorithm 1.2. line 12). At this level, i.e., second level the threshold value m is generated dynamically. To determine the number of shares m each resource provider $R_i, i \in (1, n)$ selects a (P_i, N_i) pair from the share pool SP (Algorithm 1.2 line 9 to 12). The share pool is created beforehand (Algorithm 1.1. Generate share pool SP).The user saves the pair (i, P_i) for each provider R_i and the provider saves N_i. We intend to have multiple share pools and place one or two of them in each cluster of the distributed cloud. The CRT solution generates a number m which decides the number of shares to split and reconstruct in the second level. At each resource provider at least j number of dummy shares S_{ij}^D,where $i \in (1, n)$ and $j \geq m$, are generated (Algorithm 1.2 line 13). Whenever a resource provider is compromised, the user revokes the access of that particular resource provider. We intend to have a greater number of dummy shares than secret shares,i.e.,$j \geq m$, so that if any outside attacker tries to get the share, the probability that he ends up with the dummy share instead of a real share is greater than or equal to 0.5. This helps the user to take action (e.g., revoke the access of that resource provider) accordingly when some attacker selects a dummy key. To reconstruct the key sub shares, each resource provider need to have the P_i from the user to generate the threshold value m (Algorithm 1.3. line 2). The user reconstructs the secret S from t numbers of S_i shares.

Algorithm 1

Input: The secret key S, n number of resource providers in distributed cloud, threshold value $t \leq n$.

Algorithm 1.1. Generate share pool SP

From this share pool each resource provider generates a number out of a selected pair.

```
1: for i = 1 atleast n do
2:     Generate a random series of pairwise relatively prime positive integers,
       P_i = p_{i1}, p_{i2}, ., p_{im}.
3:     Generate a random series of m arbitrary integers N_i = n_{i1}, n_{i2}, ., n_{im}.
4:     Place these two series P_i along with N_i, represented as (P_i, N_i) in SP.
5: end for
```

Algorithm 1.2. Split Algorithm

1: User U encrypts the file f with secret key S.
2: Split the secret key S into n number of shares, $S_1, S_2, S_3, S_4, .., S_n$.
3: To reconstruct S at least t number of shares are required.
4: **for** *each share i of S, where $i \in 1, n$* **do**
5:     Replicate the share S_i into $k \geq 1$ number of replicas.
6:     Distribute the replicas among n number of resource providers.
7: **end for**
8: **for** *each resource provider, $R_i, i \in 1, n$* **do**
9:     Select a pair (P_i, N_i) from SP.
10:     User U saves (i, P_i) and R_i saves N_i.
11:     Get a unique solution $m = x_i$ from (P_i, N_i) using Chinese Remainder Theorem (CRT).
12:     Split the share of secret S_i into m number of shares, $S_{i1}, S_{i2}, S_{i3}, S_{i4}, .., S_{im}$.
13:     Generate j number of dummy shares S_{ij}^D, where $j \geq m$.
14: **end for**

Algorithm 1.3. Reconstruction Algorithm

1: **for** *each resource provider, $R_i, i \in 1, n$* **do**
2:     R_i asks for (i, P_i) pair from user U and R_i has N_i.
3:     Get a unique solution $m = x_i$ from (P_i, N_i) using Chinese Remainder Theorem (CRT).
4:     Reconstruct the share of secret S_i from m number of shares, $S_{i1}, S_{i2}, S_{i3}, S_{i4}, .., S_{im}$.
5: **end for**
6: **for** *each resource provider , $R_i, i \in 1, t$* **do**
7:     Collect the share S_i from each resource provider.
8: **end for**
9: Reconstruct the secret S from S_i where $i = 1, ..., t$.

5   Analysis

5.1   Experimental Analysis

We performed simulations using a distributed cloud model that is based on the P2P overlay Kademlia [19]. We implemented our algorithm for secret sharing on the distributed cloud. We assumed that resource providers have a minimum of 2 GB RAM up to 16 GB, 2 to 8 cores. First a node identifies available resource providers near him and then divides the key into multiple shares and distributes each share to an available resource provider. The Resource provider again creates more shares by using his share as the secret and stores it. User will maintain the list of providers who store the secret shares. When a user requires the key, he contacts other resource providers who have the shares. Once resource providers receive the request, they combine the shares they have and send the actual share to the user. Once the threshold numbers of shares are received by the user, he will reproduce the original key and use it. Figure 3 shows the average total time. The total time includes time taken to split the secret into shares at first level, find resources, distribute the shares to resource providers and split the shares at second level. We can see that as the number of nodes increases, the time to find nodes and distribute shares to nearby nodes decreases. Since the distributed cloud is formed by many users we can see our mechanism for secret sharing is feasible and efficient.

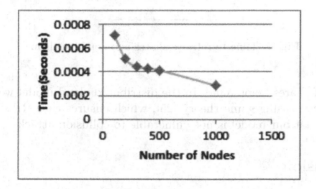

Fig. 3. Time to split shares and distribute them to other nodes

Figure 4 shows the time to retrieve the shares from resource providers and combine them to reproduce the secret. We see that the average time to retrieve shares from resource providers and to combine them takes significantly less time when compared to distributing the shares. In order to make sure that we have shares available to the user any time we will make replicas of shares and store them on multiple resource providers in the distributed cloud. This increases the chances of retrieving the share efficiently even when some of the nodes leave the network.

5.2   Security Analysis

In this paper since we are using a threshold secret sharing scheme and we are storing the shares and their replicas on multiple resource providers, compromising one or more resource providers will not disclose the secret. At the second level at each resource provider we generate equal or more dummy shares which an attacker may access as actual shares. If the resource provider is compromised by any outside attacker then the probability of using the dummy shares is greater than or equal to 0.5. This increases the chances for a resource provider to react to any security breach immediately. We create a share pool to reduce the user overhead in deciding the number of shares to be split. Since the resource provider selects (P_i, N_i) pairs randomly no eavesdropper can make a guess about

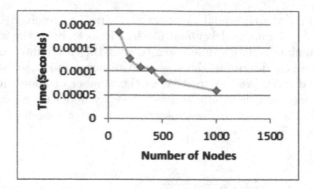

Fig. 4. Time to retrieve shares and combine them

the number of shares beforehand. In the distributed cloud model we have used, RP's are selected using game theory [25], which ensures that RP's are honest. This ensures that our model is not vulnerable to collusion attack

6   Conclusion

In this paper we propose a multilevel threshold secret sharing scheme to ensure the security of secret key in the distributed cloud environment. Our scheme can also be used for other distributed and P2P systems. Our findings show that a secret key, which plays a significant role to encrypt and decrypt the file content to be stored in cloud storage, can be stored securely in a distributed cloud environment. The increasing number of providers in the distributed cloud decreases the time to split and distribute the shares. Experimental and security analysis shows that our scheme is feasible and secure. Data replication is an other issue in distributed systems and we will look into new strategies to perform data replication to increase response time for finding data and making distributed cloud more robust.

References

1. Shamir, A.: How to share a secret. Commun. ACM **22**(11), 612–613 (1979)
2. Blakley, G.R.: Safeguarding cryptographic keys. In: International Workshop on Managing Requirements Knowledge. IEEE Computer Society (1899)
3. Tassa, T.: Hierarchical threshold secret sharing. J. Cryptol. **20**(2), 237–264 (2007)
4. Beimel, A., Ben-Efraim, A., Padró, C., Tyomkin, I.: Multi-linear secret-sharing schemes. In: Lindell, Y. (ed.) TCC 2014. LNCS, vol. 8349, pp. 394–418. Springer, Heidelberg (2014)
5. Ito, M., Saito, A., Nishizeki, T.: Secret sharing scheme realizing general access structure. Electron. Commun. Jpn. (Part III: Fundam. Electron. Sci.) **72**(9), 56–64 (1989)

6. Kurihara, J., Kiyomoto, S., Fukushima, K., Tanaka, T.: A New (k,n)-threshold secret sharing scheme and its extension. In: Wu, T.-C., Lei, C.-L., Rijmen, V., Lee, D.-T. (eds.) ISC 2008. LNCS, vol. 5222, pp. 455–470. Springer, Heidelberg (2008)
7. Lin, C., Harn, L., Ye, D.: Ideal perfect multilevel threshold secret sharing scheme. In: Fifth International Conference on Information Assurance and Security, IAS 2009, vol. 2. IEEE (2009)
8. Alsolami, F., Boult, T.E.: CloudStash: using secret-sharing scheme to secure data, not keys, in multi-clouds. In: 11th International Conference on Information Technology: New Generations, ITNG 2014. IEEE (2014)
9. Cachin, C., Haas, R., Vukolic, M.: Dependable storage in the intercloud. Research report RZ 3783 (2010)
10. Alsolami, F., Chow, C.E.: N-Cloud: improving performance and security in cloud storage. In: IEEE 14th International Conference on High Performance Switching and Routing, HPSR 2013. IEEE (2013)
11. Bessani, A., et al.: DepSky: dependable and secure storage in a cloud-of-clouds. ACM Trans. Storage (TOS) 9(4), Article No. 12 (2013)
12. Xiong, H., Zhang, X., Zhu, W., Yao, D.: CloudSeal: end-to-end content protection in cloud-based storage and delivery services. In: Rajarajan, M., Piper, F., Wang, H., Kesidis, G. (eds.) SecureComm 2011. LNICST, vol. 96, pp. 491–500. Springer, Heidelberg (2012)
13. Ding, C.: Chinese Remainder Theorem. World Scientific, Singapore (1996)
14. Anderson, D.P.: Boinc: a system for public-resource computing and storage. In: Proceedings of Fifth IEEE/ACM International Workshop on Grid Computing. IEEE (2004)
15. Anderson, D.P., et al.: SETI@ home: an experiment in public-resource computing. Commun. ACM 45(11), 56–61 (2002)
16. Khethavath, P., et al.: Introducing a distributed cloud architecture with efficient resource discovery and optimal resource allocation. In: IEEE Ninth World Congress on Services, SERVICES 2013. IEEE (2013)
17. Asmuth, C., Bloom, J.: A modular approach to key safeguarding. IEEE Trans. Inf. Theor. 30(2), 208–210 (1983)
18. Beimel, A.: Secret-sharing schemes: a survey. In: Chee, Y.M., Guo, Z., Ling, S., Shao, F., Tang, Y., Wang, H., Xing, C. (eds.) IWCC 2011. LNCS, vol. 6639, pp. 11–46. Springer, Heidelberg (2011)
19. Maymounkov, P., Mazières, D.: Kademlia: a peer-to-peer information system based on the XOR metric. In: Druschel, P., Kaashoek, M.F., Rowstron, A. (eds.) IPTPS 2002. LNCS, vol. 2429, pp. 53–65. Springer, Heidelberg (2002)
20. Chun, B., et al.: Planetlab: an overlay testbed for broad-coverage services. ACM SIGCOMM Comput. Commun. Rev. 33(3), 3–12 (2003)
21. Endo, P.T., et al.: Resource allocation for distributed cloud: concepts and research challenges. IEEE Netw. 25(4), 42–46 (2011)
22. Amazon AWS. http://aws.amazon.com/
23. Amazon EC2. http://aws.amazon.com/ec2/. Accessed on 22 July 2014
24. Microsoft Azure. http://azure.microsoft.com. Accessed on 22 July 2014
25. Praveen, K., Thomas, J., Liu, H.: Game theoretic approach to resource provisioning in a distributed cloud. In: International Conference on Data Science and Engineering, ICDSE 2014, pp. 51–56, 26–28 August 2014

Secure Sharing of Data in Cloud Computing

Deepnarayan Tiwari[1,2]($\boxtimes$) and G.R. Gangadharan[1]

[1] Institute for Development and Research in Banking Technology (IDRBT),
Hyderabad, India
{dtiwari,grgangadharan}@idrbt.ac.in
[2] School of Computer and Information Sciences (SCIS),
University of Hyderabad, Hyderabad, India

Abstract. Cloud computing is emerging as an increasingly popular computing paradigm. Sharing of data in the cloud environments raises the issues of confidentiality, integrity, and availability. In this paper, we propose a framework and methodology for sharing data over untrusted cloud, using proxy re-encryption based on elliptic curve discrete logarithm problem. The proposed methodology imperatively imposes the access control policies of data originator, preventing the cloud storage providers from unauthorized access and illegal authorization to access the data.

Keywords: Proxy re-encryption · Elliptic Curve Discrete Logarithm Problem (ECDLP) · Cloud computing · Data sharing

1 Introduction

Cloud computing is increasingly becoming a commercial trend because of its desirable properties, such as scalability, elasticity, fault-tolerance, and pay-per-use [1]. However, cloud infrastructure are still susceptible to internal threats (e.g., via virtual machines) and external threats (e.g., via system vulnerabilities) that may leak user sensitive data [12,13,15]. Therefore many organizations still hesitate to adopt cloud services [2].

Consider that a cloud service provider provides storage as a service, where users can store and access the data. Here the data kept on clouds could also be shared by a designated user (a user who is authorized by the data originator). The ideal privacy and security requirements of data sharing in the cloud are as follows [8,14]:

1. **Data Confidentiality -** The data should not be accessed by unauthorized users (including the cloud service provider). Data should remain confidential in transit, at rest, and on backup media.
2. **User Revocation -** If the access rights of an user are revoked, then the data should not be accessed. Ideally, user revocation should not effect other authorized users in the group.

© Springer International Publishing Switzerland 2015
J.H. Abawajy et al. (Eds): SSCC 2015, CCIS 536, pp. 24–35, 2015.
DOI: 10.1007/978-3-319-22915-7_3

3. **Collusion Between Entities** - During data sharing, even certain entities collude, they should still not be able to access the data without the data originator permission.

To the best of our knowledge, there exists no cryptographic models to satisfy the said properties in cloud environments [3,5,7,10,11]. We need a cryptographic system to impose the access control policies of the data originator, and to prevent the cloud storage providers from unauthorized access and making illegal authorization to access the data. We propose a model for sharing the data on cloud that satisfies the following objectives.

- A data originator outsources data to a third-party IT infrastructure. Therefore, the data originator must establish a mechanism to mandate the enforcement of data security by ensuring data confidentiality and integrity of the data over the cloud.
- A cloud service provider has ownership on computing and storage resources. Therefore the cloud service provider needs to formulate a system with strong privacy requirements and accessibility mechanisms over the data on cloud.

In this work, we present a novel mechanism using a trusted proxy agent for authorized sharing over an untrusted cloud service provider. This allows users to manage their data on any cloud storage providers and eliminates the dependency on the cloud provider for privacy preservation.

The organization of this paper is as follows Sect. 2 presents a literature review on related work. Section 3 proposes a framework that allow proxy based secure sharing of the data over the untrusted cloud storage. In Sect. 4, we describe the detailed construction of cryptographic protocol to achieve secure sharing of the data. Section 5 performs security analysis of the proposed scheme to prove security requirements. In Sect. 6, we analyze the performance of the proposed scheme, followed by concluding remarks in Sect. 7.

2   Related Work

A data originator may not fully trust on a cloud service provider because of various security related issues and concerns in cloud computing including data privacy, access control, availability, authentication, scalability, and so on [16–18].

The existing frameworks of secure sharing of the data in cloud computing [3–5,8,20] focus to achieve a fine grained access control to share the data over the untrusted cloud storage. The main intuition behind the current trend of secure sharing mechanism is that the data originator outsources the encrypted form of data to the cloud storage and then enforces self-resilient authorization by building a key management for access hierarchies. Following the said intuition, Kamara and Lauter [6] proposed a symmetric key based cryptographic cloud storage architecture. However, the scheme [6] does not support dynamic user configuration due to distribution of the symmetric key one by one to each requesting users. Further, this scheme results in higher computational and communication cost for the revocation as the owner has to retrieve the complete data and re-encrypt after republish.

To allow users to get secure and efficient access to outsource data files, both data and metadata must be properly protected. Zhao et al. [3] proposed a protocol for trusted data sharing over the untrusted cloud based on the progressive elliptic curve encryption scheme. But this scheme lacks authentication before storing and sharing of data in the untrusted cloud. Further, this scheme shares the secret key between the cloud provider and the data owner thereby affecting the privacy. Wang et al. [4] propose a methodology to encrypt data blocks with different keys so that flexible cryptography-based access control can be achieved. However, sharing of the encryption key to the users in [4] incurs more commutation and communication cost. Kumbhare et.al. [5] present an architecture for a secure storage repository for sharing scientific datasets using public clouds. However, the scheme does not support random sharing of the files.

Juels et al. [9] described a proof of retrivability mechanism focused on static data storage. This scheme pre-processes the data, in which sentinels blocks are randomly inserted into the file to detect corruption and the file is encrypted to hide these sentinels. However, this model does not support dynamic update and supports a limited number of queries.

Tysowki et al. [19] proposed a re-encryption-based key management towards secure and scalable mobile applications in clouds. This approach develops a model for key distribution based on the principle of dynamic data re-encryption that effectively utilizes the cloud for cryptographic computation while supporting a frequently-changing mobile user population that does not need to trust the cloud provider. However, the re-encryption task required in [19] during the change of a group member is an expensive operation. Also, it is more vulnerable that the manager maintains the database to store the secret key of the user to perform re-encryption.

In our work, we propose a new approach for secure sharing of data in cloud computing environments. The proposed model combines several coherent security components such as a public key cryptosystem based on ECDLP, authentication, authorization, and access control. Furthermore, this paper extends the schemes [3,7,19] by introducing a trusted proxy agent (TPA). The trusted proxy agent acts as a trusted mediator between the participating entities and preserves the privacy of the originator. The TPA reduces computation cost of the process and manages network and device heterogeneity. Further, the TPA presents the possibility for an organization to implement own security framework without depending upon the security solution of cloud providers.

3   A Framework for Secure Sharing of Data on the Cloud

In our proposed framework (see Fig. 1), the participating entities are data originator, trusted proxy agent, public untrusted cloud, and a set of authenticated shard entity. In Fig. 1, the bold line indicates trusted communication between the entities, the unidirectional line indicates communication between connecting entities, and the dotted line shows the conditional communication. The processing steps in the proposed framework for secure sharing of data on the cloud are as follows.

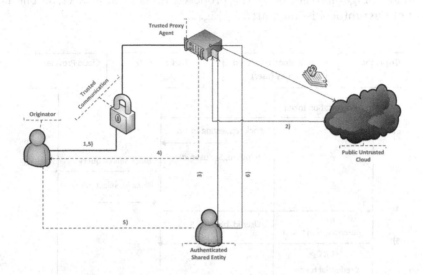

Fig. 1. A framework for secure sharing of data on the cloud

1. The originator constructs a message M. Before storing the encrypted form of the message M, the originator must confirm the authentication of the participating entity by calculating the authentication token. The originator sends the authentication token to the trusted proxy agent and to the authenticated shared entity. A participating entity can validate the authenticity of the originator before accepting the authentication token.
2. The authenticated shared entity makes a request to the trusted proxy agent for accessing the data. The trusted proxy agent verifies authentication of the requesting entity.
3. The trusted proxy agent constructs an efficient query to retrieve the encrypted form of the message from a public untrusted cloud. The public untrusted cloud performs the search operation for requesting encrypted data and sends back to the trusted proxy agent.
4. The trusted proxy agent makes a request to the data originator for the credential token to re-encrypt the message so that the requesting authenticated shared entity can decrypt the message.
5. The originator sends the credential token to the trusted proxy agent and the decryption token to the requesting authenticated shared entity.
6. The trusted proxy agent performs proxy re-encryption on the encrypted form of the message without compromising privacy of the message. The re-encrypted message is sent to the requesting authenticated shared entity.

4   A Methodology for Secure Sharing of Data on the Cloud

We propose the secure sharing protocol to achieve secure sharing of the data into cloud storage, implementing the proposed framework in Sect. 3. The flow control of the protocol is illustrated in Fig. 2.

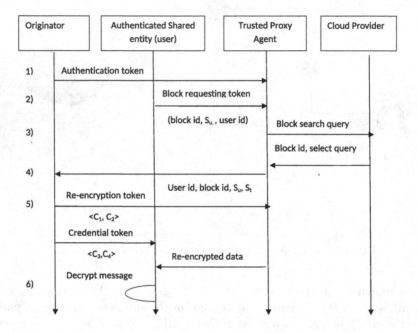

Fig. 2. Flow control of secure sharing of data on the cloud

The proposed secure sharing protocol consists of the following phases:

1. Initialization Phase

In this phase, the system generates public parameters to initialize the algorithm. The public parameters *params* are as follows.

$params = (\mathbb{G}_1, \mathbb{G}_2, e, n, g, P, H(.))$

Here $\mathbb{G}_1$ is additive subgroup of the group of points over an elliptic curve, $\mathbb{G}_2$ is an multiplicative subgroup of a finite field. $\mathbb{G}_1$ and $\mathbb{G}_2$ have same order n and are generated by P, $g = e(P, P)$, pairing function e from $\mathbb{G}_1 \times \mathbb{G}_1$ in $\mathbb{G}_2$, and $H(.)$ is an one-way function $h : E \to (0, 1)^l$ where E represents the finite data domain and l is the length of mapping context.

Each participating entity has a own derived public/private key pair. Here Pk_o, Pk_t, Pk_u, and Pk_a are the public keys of the data originator(o), trusted proxy agent(t), untrusted public cloud(u), and authenticated shared entity or users(a) respectively. The public key (pk) are calculated as follows:

Originator public key $pk_o = sk_oP$

Trusted proxy agent key $pk_t = sk_tP$

Untrusted public cloud key $pk_u = sk_uP$

Authenticated shared entity public key $pk_a = sk_aP$

where sk_o, sk_t, sk_u, and sk_a are random numbers consider as private key with $0 \leq sk_o, sk_t, sk_u, sk_a \leq n - 1$.

2. **Authentication and Signature Generation Phase**

   (a) The data originator makes a piece of the data m and a message warrant m_w. The message warrant m_w consists of the information such as fingerprint of the message m and the validity of the message m through timestamping.

   (b) The data originator generates authenticated signatures S_t and S_u to the trusted proxy agent and untrusted cloud provider. The signatures S_t and S_u are used as an proof to authenticate the identity of the data originator. S_t and S_u are computed as-
   $$S_t = H(m_w, x_s)sk_o + k_1$$
   $$S_u = H(m_w, x_s)sk_o + k_2$$
   where k_1 and k_2 are random numbers, $Q_1 = k_1P$, $Q_2 = k_2P$, and $Q(x_s, y_s) = Q_1 + Q_2$.
   The data originator sends (m_w, S_t, Q_1, Q) to the trusted proxy and (m_w, S_u, Q_1, Q) to the untrusted cloud provider in a secure manner.

   (c) The trusted proxy agent verifies the authenticity of the originator by computing
   $$S_tP \equiv H(m_w, x_s)pk_o + Q_1$$
   similarly, the untrusted cloud provider verifies as:
   $$S_uP \equiv H(m_w, x_s)pk_u + Q_2$$
   If the said equality holds then the further communication can be proceeded otherwise the communication is rejected.

3. **Encrypting and Metadata Generation Phase**

   In this phase the originator constructs the metadata of the message m and performs an encryption on the message m by using the following steps:

   (a) The originator divides the message m into n blocks.
   $$m = \{m_1, m_2, m_3, \ldots, m_n\}$$

   (b) The metadata of the message m includes the error detection code (edc) and message identification code (mic).

      i. Assume ψ is a function of error detection code are calculated as:
   $$e_i = \psi(m_i) \text{ where } 1 \leq 1 \leq n$$

      ii. Calculate message identification code(mic) as follows: $mic = H(\bigoplus_{i=1}^n e_i)$ where $\oplus$ is an exclusive OR operation.

   (c) The originator performs the encryption on the message m by using the following steps:

      i The data originator picks two random numbers r and k corresponding to the trusted proxy agent and the message block m_i, and then encrypts the message block m_i as follows.

   $$m_i' = m_i \oplus k(m, i)P \oplus rPk_t \oplus rP \oplus kP \tag{1}$$

where $k(m, i)P$ is a derived encryption key [4].

ii. Generate the signature on the encrypted message m_i' as

$$S_{m_i'} = H(m_i' \parallel mic)sk_o + pk_t$$

The encrypted form of the message block m_i', mic, and signature $S_{m_i'}$ are sent to the untrusted cloud for storage.

iii. Before storing the encrypted message m_i', the untrusted public cloud must be ensure about the identity of the data originator by performing the following operation on the signature $S_{m_i'}$.

$$PS_{m_i'} = H(m_i' \parallel mic)pk_o + sk_t$$

If this equation holds then the encrypted message m_i' is stored into the public cloud storage. Otherwise, the request for storing the data is rejected.

4. **Data Sharing Phase**

The authenticated shared entity or user makes a request with her public key for accessing the message block m_i to the trusted proxy agent (TPA). The following steps are executed to perform sharing of the message.

(a) The user prepares a block requesting token and sends to the trusted proxy agent. The block requesting token consists of block id, user signature S_u and user id.

(b) The trusted proxy agent authenticates the identity of the user (u) and constructs a select query to request the message block i to the untrusted cloud provider. The cloud provider returns the encrypted message block i to the TPA.

(c) The TPA makes a request to the originator to re-encrypt the message m_i' in respect of the user(u) so that the user (u) can obtain the original message m_i. The proxy re-encryption must ensure the privacy of the message without revealing the message of the originator to the TPA.

(d) For sharing data to the user(u), the originator issues the proxy re-encryption token $< C_1, C_2 >$ to the TPA and credential token $< C_3, C_4 >$ to the user(u). The credential token gives the permission to the user to decrypt the message block i. The re-encryption token and credential token are determined as follows.

i. The re-encryption token $< C_1, C_2 >$ is calculated and sent to the TPA, as follows.

$$C_1 = r \oplus e(pk_o, pk_a)^r \tag{2}$$

$$C_2 = e(pk_t, pk_a)^{rsk_o} \tag{3}$$

The calculated re-encryption token $< C_1, C_2 >$ is sent to the TPA to perform proxy re-encryption without revealing the privacy of the message block m_i.

ii. The credential token $< C_3, C_4 >$ is calculated as follows and sent to the user (u).

$$C_3 = k \oplus e(pk_o, pk_t)^k \tag{4}$$

$$C_4 = e(pk_t, pk_a)^{ksk_o} \tag{5}$$

The calculated credential token $< C_3, C_4 >$ is sent to the user(u) as an authorization to decrypt the message block m_i'

5. **Proxy Re-encryption and Decryption Phase**

After receiving the re-encryption token $< C_1, C_2 >$, the TPA re-encrypts the message block m_i' and sends m_i'' to the user(u). The user(u) uses the credential token $< C_3, C_4 >$ and $k(m, i)$ to decrypt the message m_i'' and accesses the message block m_i. The following steps are performed to re-encrypt the message m_i' and decrypt the message m_i''.

(a) The TPA computes the C_2^* to get extract the random value r.

$$C_2^* = (C_2)^{1/sk_t}$$
$$r = C_1 \oplus C_2^* \tag{6}$$

(b) The TPA performs re-encryption on the message m_i' as

$$m_i'' = m_i' \oplus rpk_t \oplus rP \tag{7}$$

The TPA sends the re-encrypted message m_i'' to the user. The user performs the encryption on the message m_i'' by performing the following steps.

(a) The user computes C_4^* to get the random value k.

$$C_4^* = (C_4)^{1/sk_a}$$
$$k = C_3 \oplus C_4^* \tag{8}$$

(b) The user performs the decryption process to access the message block m_i

$$m_i = m_i'' \oplus k(m, i)P \oplus kP \tag{9}$$

Thus, the user gets access to the message block m_i.

Correctness of the Algorithm: The verification of cryptographic operations in the encryption, proxy encryption, and decryption phases are demonstrated as follows. The correctness of decryption phase depends upon the derived value of the re-encryption token and the credential token. From Eqs. (6) and (7), we obtain the values of r and k as follows.

$r = C_1 \oplus C_2^*$

we calculate $C_2^* = (C_2)^{(1/sk_t)}$

where $C_2 = e(pk_t, pk_a)^{rsk_o}$

$C_2 = e(sk_t P, sk_a P)^{rsk_o}$

$$C_2^* = e(sk_t P, sk_a P)^{rsk_o(1/sk_t)}$$
$$C_2^* = (P, sk_a P)^{rsk_i}$$
$$C_2^* = (sk_o P, sk_a P)^r$$
$$C_2^* = (pk_o, pk_a)^r$$
$$C_1 = r \oplus (pk_o, pk_a)^r$$
So $r = C_1 \oplus C_2^*$

Similarly we calculate the value of k as: $C_4^* = (C_4)^{(1/sk_a)} = e(sk_t P, sk_a P)^{ksk_o\,(1/sk_a)}$

$$= e(sk_t P, P)^{ksk_o}$$
$$= e(sk_t P, sk_o P)^k = e(pk_t, pk_o)^k$$
So $k = C_3 \oplus C_4^*$

After getting the value of k and r, the user decrypts the message m_i using the Eq. (9).

5   Security Analysis

In this section, we propose the security analysis of the proposed algorithm under the real threat model.

5.1   Threat Model

We consider the real time threat model to prove the security of the proposed scheme by demonstrating the attacks against two types of adversaries.

1. Malicious user adversary- The attacker may have a secret key of the users to perform an unauthorized access of the data or may be a revoked users wants to access the data. The malicious user may act as a TPA, user, or data originator to prove himself as a legitimate entity and may make an attempt to find out secret information to access the data.
2. Curious but honest trusted proxy agent- The TPA performs the operation as defined in the proposed scheme but may be curious to make an attempt to gain the sensitive information of the message m.

5.2   Unauthorized Access to the Data (Data Confidentiality and User Authorization)

In our proposed scheme, neither the trusted proxy agent nor the users can participate in the process of sharing of the data without the credential token. The user cannot decrypt the data without the coordination of secure exchange of information between originator, trusted proxy, and user. The data originator can only issue the credential token and the proxy re-encryption token. The confidentiality of the message and authorization of the participating entity can be proven by considering the following lemmas.

Lemma 1. The unauthorized users cannot able to get proxy re-encryption token to re-encrypt the cipher text and pretend as a valid trusted proxy agent.

Proof. The validity of the assumption is based on the security of data sharing phase and proxy re-encryption phase. The unauthorized users may attempt to infer the security parameter r and k from an unbounded number of sessions. If the unauthorized user eavesdrops on the communication channel to capture the proxy re-encryption messages for determining the secret random value r, then the following operations are performed.

$$C_1^1 = r \oplus e(pk_o^1, pk_a^1)^r \tag{10}$$

$$C_2^1 = r \oplus e(pk_o^2, pk_a^2)^r \tag{11}$$

$$C_1^1 \oplus C_1^2 = e(pk_o^1, pk_a^1) \oplus e(pk_o^2, pk_a^2) \tag{12}$$

From Eq. (12), we observe that no polynomial time algorithm could deduce the random value r because solving the Computational Diffie-hellman Hardness (CDH) problem is computationally infeasible.

Lemma 2. The unauthorized users cannot obtain the credential token to decrypting the message.

Proof. The validation of the proof is based on the hardness to obtain the secret random value k. Consider that an unauthorized user eavesdrops on the communication channel to capture two or more credential messages for determining k. Following operations are performed to guess the value k.

$$C_3^1 = k \oplus e(pk_o^1, pk_t^1)^k \tag{13}$$

$$C_3^2 = k \oplus e(pk_o^2, pk_t^2)^k \tag{14}$$

$$C_3^1 \oplus C_3^2 = e(pk_o^1, pk_t^1) \oplus e(pk_o^2, pk_t^2) \tag{15}$$

From Eq. (15),we observe that no polynomial time algorithm could deduce the random value k because solving the Computational Diffie-hellman Hardness (CDH) problem is computationally infeasible.

6 Performance Analysis

In this section, we evaluate the performance analysis of the proposed scheme. Here, the cloud storage is implemented on the openstack swift (https://swiftstack. com/openstack-swift/). The openstack swift is an open source distributed storage system, that is used to store the objects and perform operations (get, put, and delete) on the data. Along with openstack swift, we use the cryptographic operation GMP library (https://gmlib.org), and Pairing Based Crypto (PBC) library (https://crypto.stanford.edu/pbc) to implement the proposed scheme.

We performed several experiments to upload and download the message and evaluated the performance of the proposed scheme in terms of communication and storage cost.

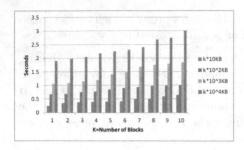
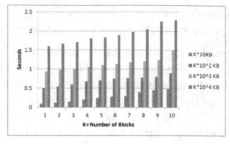

Fig. 3. Time to upload the file   **Fig. 4.** Time to download the file

6.1   Communication Cost

In our experiment, we consider k blocks with each block having the size as a power of 10 KB. We perform an upload operation to store the blocks into the cloud storage and a download operation to retrieve the block from the cloud storage.

The turnaround time for uploading and downloading of the blocks into cloud storage are illustrated in Figs. 3 and 4 respectively. The analysis shows that the communication cost of the proposed scheme does not increase in linear to the number of blocks.

6.2   Storage Cost

The storage cost is calculated as the sum of the storage overheads at the untrusted cloud and data originator. The storage overhead at the cloud is calculated as follows: $|m| * |k| * |i|$ where the size of the encrypted message m_i' is $|m|$, the size of the metadata is $|k|$, and the address of block is $|i|$. The storage overhead at the data originator depends upon the index table with the total number of block entries as $|b|$ and the size of the corresponding value within the block as $|k|$. Thus, the storage overhead on the data originator is $|b| * |k|$.

7   Conclusion

In this paper, we developed a framework and methodology for secure sharing of trusted data over untrusted cloud using proxy re-encryption based on ECDLP. The methodology is based on the proxy re-encryption scheme, allowing the data originator to store the encrypted data and share with different a authenticated shared entity. The proposed methodology can be further extended by including serachable encryption and the investigation of further improvements on the security and application in other scenarios.

References

1. Armbrust, M., Fox, A., Griffith, R., et al.: A view of cloud computing. Commun. ACM **53**, 50–58 (2010)

2. Subashini, S., Kavitha, V.: A survey on security issues in service delivery models of cloud computing. J. Netw. Comput. Appl. **34**, 1–11 (2011)

3. Zhao, G., Rong, C., Li, J., Zhang, F., Tang, Y.: Trusted data sharing over untrusted cloud storage providers. In: CloudCom-10, pp. 97–103 (2010)

4. Wang, W., Li, Z., Owens, R., Bhargava, B, K.: Secure and efficient access to outsourced data. In: CCSW, pp. 55–66 (2009)

5. Kumbhare, A.G., Simmhan, Y., Prasanna, V.: Designing a secure storage repository for sharing scientific datasets using public clouds. In:International workshop on Data intensive computing in the clouds (DataCloud-SC), pp. 31–40 (2011)

6. Kamara, S., Lauter, K.: Cryptographic cloud storage. In: Sion, R., Curtmola, R., Dietrich, S., Kiayias, A., Miret, J.M., Sako, K., Sebé, F. (eds.) RLCPS, WECSR, and WLC 2010. LNCS, vol. 6054, pp. 136–149. Springer, Heidelberg (2010)

7. Yang, Y., Zhang, Y.: A generic scheme for secure data sharing in cloud. In: International Conference on Parallel Processing Workshops (ICPPW), pp. 145–153 (2011)

8. Thilakanathan, D., Chen, S., Nepal, S., Calvo, R.A.: Secure data sharing in the cloud. In: Nepal, S., Pathan, M. (eds.) Security, Privacy and Trust in Cloud system, pp. 45–72. Springer, Heidelberg (2014)

9. Juels, A., Kaliski, B, S.: Pors: Proofs of retrievability for large files. In: CCS, pp. 584–597 (2007)

10. Xin, D., Jiadi, Y., Yuan, L., et al.: Achieving an effective, scalable and privacy-preserving data sharing service in cloud computing. Computers and Security **42**, 151–164 (2014)

11. Bharath, K.S., Yousef, E., Gerry, H., Sanjay, K.M.: A secure data sharing and query processing framework via federation of cloud computing. Inf. Syst. J. **48**, 196–212 (2015)

12. Deyan, C., Hong, Z.: Data security and privacy protection issues in cloud computing. In: International Conference on Computer Science and Electronics Engineering (ICCSEE), pp. 647–651 (2012)

13. Minqi, Z., Rong, Z., Wei Xie., et al.: Security and privacy in cloud computing: a survey. In: Semantics Knowledge and Grid (SKG), pp. 105–112 (2010)

14. Guiyi, W., Rongxing, L., Jun, S.: EFADS: Efficient, flexible and anonymous data sharing protocol for cloud computing with proxy re-encryption. J. Comput. Syst. Sci. **80**(8), 1549–1562 (2014)

15. Zhifeng, X., Yang, X.: Security and privacy in cloud computing. Commun. Surv. Tutorials **15**(2), 843–859 (2013)

16. Nyre, Å.A., Jaatun, M.G.: Privacy in a semantic cloud: what's trust got to do with it? In: Jaatun, M.G., Zhao, G., Rong, C. (eds.) Cloud Computing. LNCS, vol. 5931, pp. 107–118. Springer, Heidelberg (2009)

17. Younis, A.Y., Kashif, K., Madjid, M.: An access control model for cloud computing. J. Inf. Secur. Appl. **19**(1), 4560 (2014)

18. Raluca, A.P., Jacob, R.L., et al.: Enabling security in cloud storage SLAs with CloudProof. In: USENIX Annual Technical Conference (2011)

19. Tysowski, P.K., Hasan, M.A.: Re-encryption-based key management towards secure and scalable mobile applications in clouds. IACR Cryptology ePrint Archive (2011)

20. Tysowski, P.K., Hasan, M.A.: Hybrid attribute- and re-encryption-based key management for secure and scalable mobile applications in clouds. IEEE T. Cloud Comput. **1**(2), 172–186 (2013)

Comparing the Efficiency of Key Management Hierarchies for Access Control in Cloud

Naveen Kumar$^{(\boxtimes)}$, Anish Mathuria, and Manik Lal Das

DA-IICT, Gandhinagar, India
{naveen_kumar,anish_mathuria,maniklal_das}@daiict.ac.in

Abstract. This paper analyses the efficiency of user and resource-based hierarchies for read access control in cloud. It is shown that resource-based hierarchies are more efficient than user-based hierarchies in terms of communication and computation costs, when considering dynamic operations such as extending read authorization and user revocation.

Keywords: Access control · Resource hierarchy · Data outsourcing

1 Introduction

A major challenge to data outsourcing in cloud is keeping the data confidential from unauthorized entities including untrusted cloud service provider (CSP). The usual solution to enforcing data confidentiality involves encrypting each data file with a distinct key. A user authorized for accessing a set of data files needs to store the respective secret keys. To reduce the user's secret key storage, a *key management hierarchy* or simply a *hierarchy* is generally used [1,2]. A *hierarchy* is a directed acyclic graph where a key is assigned to each node using appropriate hierarchical key assignment scheme [1,2]. Data files are associated with the nodes and are encrypted with the respective node's key. The key assignment ensures that a user having a node's key can efficiently compute any descendant node's key in the hierarchy (and hence access the associated data files). Also, it is computationally infeasible to derive a key for any non-descendant node.

For key management, user tree hierarchy is proposed by Blundo et al. [3] where each node represents a group of users. Although tree hierarchies are easy to maintain, they require a variable amount of secret storage with each user to store access keys. In contrast to user trees, the user hierarchies proposed in [4,5,8] need single secret key storage with each user.

In a resource-based hierarchy, as the name suggests, every node represents a group of resources. A resource hierarchy has similar structure as that of *channel hierarchy* proposed by Wang et al. [9] for access control in *Pay-TV* application. In the same year, Vimercati et al. [5] have examined the suitability of user and resource-based hierarchies for enforcing access control policy in cloud scenario. They compared the number of nodes required by the two types of hierarchy. For a resource-based hierarchy, they estimated the number of nodes to be at most $2^{|R|}$,

© Springer International Publishing Switzerland 2015
J.H. Abawajy et al. (Eds): SSCC 2015, CCIS 536, pp. 36–44, 2015.
DOI: 10.1007/978-3-319-22915-7_4

where R is the set of resources. In general $|U| << |R|$ and $2^{|R|} >> 2^{|U|}$, where U is the set of users. The maximum number of nodes in a user hierarchy and resource hierarchy will be $2^{|U|}$ and $2^{|R|}$ respectively. Hence user hierarchy may appear to be more efficient than resource hierarchy in terms of public storage.

In this paper, we examine the suitability of resource-based hierarchies for key management. Our analysis shows that the storage complexity of $2^{|R|}$ nodes for resource hierarchy is a rudimentary estimation. A tighter analysis reveals that the storage complexity is $O(|R|)$ for both user and resource hierarchies in practical cases. We also show that resource hierarchy allows the dynamic operations such as extending read authorization and user revocation to be handled more efficiently than user-based hierarchy.

The rest of the paper is organized as follows. Section 2 reviews the existing types of key management hierarchy used for access control in cloud. Section 3 presents in detail the construction of resource-based hierarchy and compares it with the existing type of hierarchy. Section 4 describes how dynamic operations are handled in resource hierarchy and user hierarchy, and compares their performance.

2 Key Management Hierarchies Based on User Groupings

If o is the resource, then let $r[o]$ denote the ACL for o, that is, the set of users who are authorized to read o. In what follows, we assume that a suitable hierarchical key assignment scheme (for example, the schemes proposed in [1,2]) is used for key derivation. For the sake of readability, notations used in the subsequent sections are shown in Table 1.

2.1 User Graph

Following Blundo et al. [3], a user graph is defined as follows.

Definition 1. *(User Graph). A user graph over a given set of users U, represented as G_U is a graph $< V_U, E_U >$ rooted at node v_0, where V_U is the power set of U and $E_U = \{(v_i, v_j) | v_i.acl \subset v_j.acl\}$.*

Table 1. Notations used in subsequent sections

Notation	Description
$a, b, c, \ldots$	Resources
$A, B, C, \ldots$	End users
$v.acl$	An access control list for node v
$v.cpl$	A capability list for node v
(i, j)	A directed edge from node i to node j
K_i	Secret key assigned to node i
$\mathcal{E}$ and $\mathcal{D}$	A symmetric encryption and decryption operation
$\mathcal{C}$	A communication between data owner and CSP

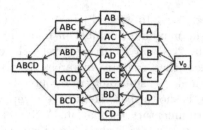

Fig. 1. A user graph over a set $\{A, B, C, D\}$.

For a node v, $v.acl$ is a set of users that can access the node v's key. Definition 1 ensures that v_0 is a common root node, there is a node corresponding to each subset of users and there is a directed path from each node v_1 to node v_2 with $v_1.acl \subset v_2.acl$. Also, there is an edge from root node to each single user node. Figure 1 shows a user graph with four users $\{A, B, C, D\}$. For simplicity, the edges that are implied by other edges are not shown in the figure.

We can enforce any authorization policy using user graph as follows. Every node x in the graph is assigned a distinct key K_x. The label of each node represents the node's authorization set i.e., each user in the label set can compute the node's key. For example, the key K_{AB} of node labeled AB can be derived by both the users A and B. The resources are encrypted with the keys of nodes whose labels correspond to the ACLs of resources.

In a user graph, each user stores just one secret key. This key can be used to derive all other authorized keys of that user. For example, knowledge of key K_A assigned to node A is sufficient to derive the keys $K_{AB}, K_{AC}, K_{AD}, K_{ABC}, K_{ABD}$ and K_{ABCD} assigned to nodes AB, AC, AD, ABC, ABD and $ABCD$, respectively.

A user graph is a worst case graph over a set U of users, i.e., it contains a node for every possible subset of U, other than the root node. In total, $2^{|U|}$ number of nodes are there in a user graph, over a user set U. To count the number of edges, consider all single user nodes as level 1 nodes, all double user nodes as level 2 nodes and so on. Maximum possible number of nodes at level 1 are $^{|U|}C_1$, at level 2 are $^{|U|}C_2$ and so on. Also, the number of incoming edges at each node in level 1 is 1 and in level 2 are 2 and so on. Therefore, the total number of incoming edges at level 1 are $1 \times {}^{|U|}C_1$, at level 2 are $2 \times {}^{|U|}C_2$ and so on. In total[1], it comes out as $2(\sum_{i=0}^{|U|/2} \frac{|U|!}{(|U|-i-1)!i!})$ i.e., $O(|U|^{|U|/2})$.

2.2   User Tree

A user tree is a subgraph of user graph, where each node can have at most one incoming edge. It contains all vertices whose keys are used for encrypting

---

[1] $= 1 \times {}^{|U|}C_1 + 2 \times {}^{|U|}C_2 + 3 \times {}^{|U|}C_3 + \ldots + (|U|-1) \times {}^{|U|}C_{|U|-1} + (|U|) \times {}^{|U|}C_{|U|}$
$= |U|/0! + |U|(|U|-1)/1! + |U|(|U|-1)(|U|-2)/2! + \ldots + |U|(|U|-1)/1! + |U|/0!$
$= 2\sum_{i=0}^{|U|/2} \frac{|U|!}{(|U|-i-1)!i!}$.

resources such vertices are called material vertices (denoted as $\mathcal{M}$). Following [3], a user tree can be defined as follows.

Definition 2. *(User Tree). Let $\mathcal{A}$ be a set of ACLs over a set U of users and set R of resources. A user tree $T =< V, E >$ for given $\mathcal{A}$ is a tree over U, subgraph of $G_U =< V_U, E_U >$, rooted at node v_0 with $v_0.acl = \phi$, where $\mathcal{M} \subseteq V \subseteq V_U$ and $E \subseteq E_U$.*

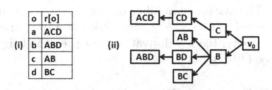

Fig. 2. (i) Ex. *ACLs* with read authorization, and (ii) User tree.

An example with four users $U = \{A, B, C, D\}$ and four resources $R = \{a, b, c, d\}$ is shown in Fig. 2, where (i) represents fixed set of ACLs, and (ii) represents an example user tree corresponding to the given ACLs. Here, there is a node for the read authorization set $r[o]$ for each resource o (material vertices). For example, there are nodes $ACD(r[a])$, $ABD(r[b])$, $AB(r[c])$ and $BC(r[d])$, in the user tree.

   Consider a set of ACLs in worst case i.e., each resource o has a distinct $r[o]$. There is a node for each $r[o]$, so at most $min(2^{|U|}, |R|)$ nodes are required. Since it is a tree hierarchy, the maximum number of edges will be of the order of the number of nodes i.e., $O(min(2^{|U|}, |R|))$. It is easy to see that a user may need more than one secret key. In the example tree of Fig. 2 (ii), user A should know the keys K_{ACD}, K_{AB} and K_{ABD}.

2.3   User Hierarchies

As in the case of a user tree, a user hierarchy is a subgraph of the respective user graph. The nodes of a user hierarchy can have more than one incoming edge. Following [4], a user hierarchy can be defined as follows.

Definition 3. *(User Hierarchy). Let $\mathcal{A}$ be a set of ACLs over a set U of users and set R of resources. A user hierarchy denoted $UH =< V, E >$ for given $\mathcal{A}$ is a subgraph of $G_U =< V_U, E_U >$ with $U \subseteq V$, $\mathcal{M} \subseteq V \subseteq V_U \setminus \{v_0\}$ and $E \subseteq E_U$.*

Definition 3 ensures that a user hierarchy includes root nodes representing the users. Consider the set of ACLs shown in Fig. 3 (i). A user hierarchy implementing the given ACLs is shown in Fig. 3 (ii).

   Since, each user has a dedicated node in the user hierarchy, a user requires only one secret key (i.e., the respective user node's key) storage, similar as in user graph. The maximum number of nodes in the worst case is $min(|R| + |U|, 2^{|U|})$ which is nearly the same as in case of corresponding user tree. The $|R| + |U|$

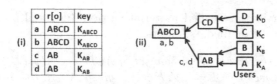

Fig. 3. (i) Example *ACLs* with read authorization, and (ii) A possible user hierarchy.

(instead of $|R|$ in the user tree) is due to the presence of a node for each user, in the user hierarchy. The maximum number of edges is however similar as in user graph in the worst case i.e., $O(|U|^{|U|/2})$, since it is not a tree. In every user-based hierarchy discussed above, the key derivation cost (i.e., the height of hierarchy) in worst case will be $O(|U|)$.

3   Hierarchies Based on Resource Groupings

If u is a user then let $cpl[u]$ denote the capability list ([6]) for u, that is, the set of resources for which u has read authorization.

3.1   Resource Graph

A resource graph can be defined in a similar fashion to as a user graph, as follows.

Definition 4. *(Resource Graph). A resource graph over a given set of resources R, represented as G_R is a graph $< V_R, E_R >$, where V_R is the power set of R and $E_R = \{(v_i, v_j)|v_j.cpl \subset v_i.cpl\}$.*

For a node v, $v.cpl$ is a set of resources that will be accessed using node v's key. An example resource graph with four resources $\{a, b, c, d\}$ is shown in Fig. 4. In the graph, each node is labeled as a possible capability list. There is a directed path from each node v_1 to node v_2 iff $v_2.cpl \subset v_1.cpl$. For example, the node abc with capability list $< a, b, c >$ has a path to each node with subset capability list such as ab, ac, bc, a, b and c.

In contrast to a user graph, a resource graph is a worst case graph over the set R. It contains $2^{|R|}$ number of nodes. Since $|R| >> |U|$ where U is the set of users, a resource graphs are not practical in implementation. However, we argue that in actual applications, we requires significantly less number of nodes, as compared to $2^{|R|}$.

3.2   Resource Hierarchy

A resource hierarchy can be viewed as a dual of user hierarchy.

Definition 5. *(Resource Hierarchy). Let $\mathcal{A}$ be a set of CPLs over a set U of users and set R of resources. A resource hierarchy RH for given $\mathcal{A}$, U and R is a graph $RH =< V, E >$, where $V = U \cup R \cup V'$ with $V' \subseteq V_R$ and $E = E' \cup \{(v_i, v_j)|v_i \in U \text{ and } v_j = v_i.cpl\}$ with $E' \subseteq E_R$.*

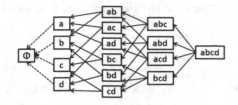

Fig. 4. A resource graph over a set $\{a, b, c, d\}$ of four resources.

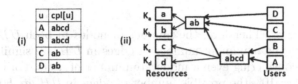

Fig. 5. (i) An example CPLs, and (ii) Corresponding resource hierarchy.

The above definition ensures that a resource hierarchy includes root nodes representing the users. There is an edge from each user node (u) to the node represents its capability list ($cpl[u] \in \mathcal{A}$). Ignoring the user nodes, there is a path from every node x to node y if $y.cpl \subset x.cpl$. An example resource hierarchy is shown in Fig. 5 where (i) represents an example set of CPLs and (ii) gives a corresponding resource hierarchy.

In a resource hierarchy, there is a leaf node for every resource. The later is encrypted by the key assigned to its leaf node. For example, in Fig. 5 (ii), the keys K_a, K_b, K_c, K_d are used to encrypt the resources a, b, c, d respectively.

In a resource hierarchy at most $min(|U|, 2^{|R|})$ (i.e., $|U|$ in practice since $|U| << 2^{|R|}$) nodes are required in the worst case. In total, $|U| + |R| + min(|U|, 2^{|R|})$ nodes are needed. Also, $|U| + |U|.|R|$ or $O(|U|.|R|)$ number of edges are needed in worst case, considering $|R| >> |U|$. In worst case, each intermediate node represents a subset of $O(|R|)$ resources i.e., from each such node there are $O(|R|)$ outgoing edges. These edges can be further reduced by increasing number of nodes in the hierarchy i.e., there is a tradeoff between the two. Also, the longest chain hierarchy created with all user authorization nodes are at most $O(|U|)$ and hence the key derivation cost.

Table 2 compares the Resource Hierarchy RH with existing user-based hierarchies (User Graph UG, User Tree UT and User Hierarchy UH) in worst case. We can see from the table that, maximum number of nodes in UH is $min(|R| + |U|, 2^{|U|})$ i.e., $O(|R|)$ when $|R| < 2^{|U|}$ for even a moderate number of users (considering $|U| << |R|$). For example, consider that we need to create an electronic health record management system for America, where approximately 1.5 lakh patients receive care every year (NHPCO Facts and Figures, [7]). Let, a central database is created to store the patient records. For 100 years and let 20 documents per patient per year, it requires $\sim 10^9$ data files to be stored. However, for a set of only 50 users, $2^{|U|} = 2^{50} \sim 10^{15}$, which is greater than the

Table 2. Comparison of resource hierarchy with existing user-based hierarchies

↓ features	User-based hierarchies			Resource-based hierarchy
	UG	UT	UH	RH
# of keys/users	Single	Multiple	Single	Single
# of nodes	$\Theta(2^{|U|})$	$O(min(|R|, 2^{|U|}))$	$O(min(|R|+|U|, 2^{|U|}))$	$O(|U| + |R| + min(|U|, 2^{|R|}))$
# of edges	$\Theta(|U|^{|U|/2})$	$O(min(|R|, 2^{|U|}))$	$O(|U|^{|U|/2})$	$O(|U|.|R|)$
key derivation cost	$\Theta(|U|)$	$\Theta(|U|)$	$\Theta(|U|)$	$\Theta(|U|)$

number of resources. Therefore, the number of nodes in both UH and RH is $O(|R|)$. However, the maximum number of edges in UH are significantly large than RH while considering even a moderate number of users. For example with $|U| = 50$ and $|R| = 10^9$, the possible number of edges in UH are 50^{25} which are much larger than 50.10^9 in case of RH.

4 Dynamic Operations

In the following, we evaluate the user and resource-based hierarchies in terms of computational and communication costs of the common dynamic operations such as extending read privileges and revoking a user.

4.1 Extending Read Privilege

User-Based Hierarchy. Here, if access authorization is extended for a resource o to a user u then $r[o]$ will be updated to $r[o]' = r[o] \cup \{u\}$. Now, since $r[o] \neq r[o]'$ (both represent different nodes in the hierarchy), resource o will be now encrypted with the key $K_{r[o]'}$. It requires the following steps by the data owner: (1) downloading the resource from the server $(1\mathcal{C})$, (2) decrypting it using the old key $(1\mathcal{D})$, (3) encrypting it with new key $(1\mathcal{E})$, and (4) storing it back to the server $(1\mathcal{C})$ (i.e., *total cost* $= 1\mathcal{E} + 1\mathcal{D} + 2\mathcal{C}$). For example, in the user hierarchy shown in Fig. 6 (i), extending read access for resource c to users C and D leads to the modified hierarchy shown in Fig. 6 (ii). In the modified hierarchy, resource c is now encrypted with K_{ABCD}.

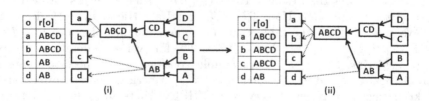

(i)   (ii)

Fig. 6. An example of user hierarchy (i) before, and (ii) after extending read access

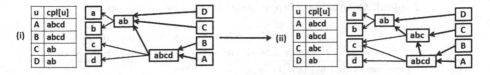

Fig. 7. An example of resource hierarchy (i) before, and (ii) after extending read access

Resource Hierarchy. Here, if access authorization is extended for a resource o to a user u then $cpl[u]$ will be updated to $cpl[u] \cup \{o\}$. Now, if the node for $cpl[u]$ does not exists, then the node is inserted in the hierarchy. It requires the following steps by the data owner: modify the resource hierarchy with respect to the updated cpl of the user and upload the updated public information at the server (*total cost* $= 1\mathcal{C}$). Consider the example hierarchy of Fig. 7 (i). Initially, user C has read access to the resources a and b (i.e., $cpl[C] = < a, b >$). Suppose, read access for resource c is given to the user C. The modified CPL and the hierarchy are shown in Fig. 7 (ii).

4.2   User Revocation

User-Based Hierarchy. Here, since each node represents a user grouping, a user revoke operation requires a modification to the hierarchy. The data owner will do the following: (1) delete the revoked user from each ACL, if exists, (2) delete user node and associated edges from the hierarchy, and delete each node previously accessible to the revoked user and replaced it by a new node (without revoked user label). For example, consider the user hierarchy given in Fig. 6 (i). Revoking user D from the hierarchy requires deletion of nodes CD and $ABCD$ (descendants) from the hierarchy and replace them with the nodes C and new node ABC (by deleting D) respectively. Since node C is already in the hierarchy, node CD is just deleted. Now, resources a and b are re-encrypted with new keys so that user D will not be able to access these resources. (3) re-keying procedure is executed corresponding to the nodes previously accessible to the revoked user, and (4) associated resources are re-encrypted with new keys.

Resource Hierarchy. Here, data owner will do the following: (1) delete the CPL for the revoked user, (2) delete user node and associated edges from the hierarchy, (3) re-keying procedure is executed in read hierarchy corresponding to the nodes previously accessible to revoked user, and (4) corresponding resources are re-encrypted with new keys.

4.3   Discussion

Table 3 compares the existing dynamic user-based hierarchy with the resource hierarchy. It compares with respect to the number of encryption (*Enc.*) or decryption (*Dec.*) operations needed at the data owner, communications (*Comm.*) needed with the service provider to extend one read access,

Table 3. Comparison of computation and communication cost

Scheme	# *Enc./Dec./Comm.* while extend read	modification in hierarchy structure while user revocation
User-based hierarchies [3,4,8]	$1\mathcal{E} + 1\mathcal{D} + 2\mathcal{C}$	Yes
Resource-based hierarchies	$1\mathcal{C}$	No

and whether revoking a user requires modification in the read hierarchy structure. An attractive property of the resource hierarchy is that it does not require any encryption or decryption operation while extending read access of a user. It requires single communication between data owner and the service provider (in comparison of two in other type) while extending a user' read access. Also, it does not require any modification in the read hierarchy structure when a user is revoked, unlike the user-based hierarchies.

References

1. Akl, S.G., Taylor, P.D.: Cryptographic solution to a problem of access control in a hierarchy. ACM Trans. Comput. Syst. **1**(3), 239–248 (1983)
2. Atallah, M.J., Frikken, K.B., Blanton, M.: Dynamic and efficient key management for access hierarchies. In: ACM Conference on Computer and Communications Security, pp. 190–202 (2005)
3. Blundo, C., Cimato, S., di Vimercati, S.D.C., Santis, A.D., Foresti, S., Paraboschi, S., Samarati, P.: Managing key hierarchies for access control enforcement: heuristic approaches. Comput. Secur. **29**(5), 533–547 (2010)
4. di Vimercati, S.D.C., Foresti, S., Jajodia, S., Livraga, G., Paraboschi, S., Samarati, P.: Enforcing dynamic write privileges in data outsourcing. Comput. Secur. **39**, 47–63 (2013)
5. di Vimercati, S.D.C., Foresti, S., Samarati, P.: Recent advances in access control. In: Gertz, M., Jajodia, S. (eds.) Handbook of Database Security - Applications and Trends, pp. 1–26. Springer, Heidelberg (2008)
6. Miller, M.S., Yee, K.-P., Shapiro, J.S.: Capability Myths Demolished. Technical Report SRL2003-02, Systems Research Laboratory, Department of Computer Science, Johns Hopkins University, March 2003
7. National Hospice and Palliative Care Organization. NHPCO Facts and Figures: Hospice Care in America (2013). http://www.nhpco.org/sites/default/files/public/Statistics_Research/2013_Facts_Figures.pdf
8. Raykova, M., Zhao, H., Bellovin, S.M.: Privacy enhanced access control for outsourced data sharing. In: Keromytis, A.D. (ed.) FC 2012. LNCS, vol. 7397, pp. 223–238. Springer, Heidelberg (2012)
9. Wang, S.-Y., Laih, C.-S.: Efficient key distribution for access control in pay-TV systems. IEEE Trans. Multimedia **10**(3), 480–492 (2008)

Adaptive and Secure Application Partitioning for Offloading in Mobile Cloud Computing

N.M. Dhanya[1](✉) and G. Kousalya[2]

[1] Department of Computer Science and Engineering,
Amrita School of Engineering, Coimbatore 641112, India
dhanyahari07@gmail.com
[2] Department of Computer Science and Engineering,
Coimbatore Institute of Technology, Coimbatore 641014, India
kousir@gmail.com

Abstract. Smart phones are capable of providing smart services to the users very similar to laptops and desktop computers. Despite of all these capabilities battery life and computational capabilities are still lacking. By combining mobiles with cloud will reduce all these disadvantages because cloud is having infinite resources for processing. But in cloud security is a major concern. Since mobile devices contain private data a secure offloading of application is necessary. In this paper we are proposing a secure partitioning of application so that the most sensitive or vulnerable part of the application can be kept in the mobile and rest of the application can be offloaded to the cloud.

1 Introduction

The introduction of cloud computing leads to a new era in utility computing, where the computing power is offered as a service [1]. The combination of Mobile technology with cloud computing radically changed the perspective of distributed application processing in mobile devices. The benefits that can be utilized by the end user are reduced cost, improved performance and higher scalability. The mobile devices having resource intensive components which will affect the battery charge. But we can't even offload the entire application to the cloud also. The total application offloading is not possible because majority of the applications are using the local resources like global positioning system, camera and other sensors [2]. So for offloading the application to cloud the application should be spitted into different groups according to some granularity levels. The parts which are highly resource intensive are offloaded to the cloud and system dependent parts are executed at the mobile device itself. The implementation of above model introduces the problem of communication cost between the components that reside at the mobile side and the components at the cloud side.

The deployment should be optimized based on both the mobile user and cloud provider perspective. All the remote components should be deployed to a virtual machine with enough CPU power while reducing the communication cost between the local and the remote components. One more constraint that is introduced is the security of the parts which are offloading. The partitioning should be such a way that the most

© Springer International Publishing Switzerland 2015
J.H. Abawajy et al. (Eds): SSCC 2015, CCIS 536, pp. 45–53, 2015.
DOI: 10.1007/978-3-319-22915-7_5

vulnerable parts are retained back in the mobile and the rest of the parts are offloaded to the cloud for remote execution. The major contribution of this paper include

1. We present algorithms to partition an application consisting of interconnected components which will reduce the communication cost between cloud and the mobile and at the same time reduces the security risk incurred due to offloading.
2. Considering the bandwidth as a dynamic variable an adaptive factor is included in the algorithm

2   Related Work

Graph partitioning is one of the fundamental issues in many domain such as task allocation on grid, network partitioning and VLSI design. The graph partitioning deals with cutting the graph into k parts while minimizing the number of edges that are cut. If the k = 2 it is called bi-partitioning which is needed in our problem. Finding a solution for this problem is NP-Hard [3] in nature. Kumar et al. [4] describes a series of offloading strategy and has done an extensive survey on the offloading strategy existing. Kernighan-Lin [5] One of the most popular local graph partitioning algorithm is Kernighan-Lin algorithm. The K-L algorithm starts with the partitioning of vertices in a balance manner that is each partition contain equal number of nodes. It proceeds in a series of passes. During each pass, the algorithm improves the initial solution by swapping pairs of vertices to create a new solution which is having smaller edge cuts if any. This process is repeated until no more subsets are found. This is the local minimum and no improvements can be done to this solution.

A simple min-cut algorithm by Stoer-Wagner [6] proposes a graph cutting those edges with minimum weights. This is one of the fastest algorithm. It works in different phases and at each phase it identifies a pair of vertices for min-cut. Multilevel k-way Partitioning Scheme for Irregular Graphs - Karypis and Kumar [7] introduced a new multilevel graph partitioning technique. It consists of three phases like coarsening, partitioning and un-coarsening. A graph G is initially coarsened into a smaller graph and then bisection is done on that graph. Then the coarsened graph is expanded back to the original graph by periodically refining the partition. Since this decreases the edge cut this is one of the popular methods used.

Graph partitioning - A survey- Ulrich Elsner [8]: this paper describes in detail about all the graph partitioning strategies. Hunt and Scott introduced an automatic distributed partitioning system called Coign, [12] which automatically transforms a program into distributed applications without accessing the source codes. Coign constructs a graph model of the application's inter-component communication through scenario-based profiling to find the best distribution. Later a graph cutting algorithm is executed to partition the application across the network. One of the advantages of this method is that an end user without source code can change the application into distributed applications.

The paper [13] deals with partitioning of programs in resources constrained devices to enable them to do distributed processing. This also deals with multiple constraints such as minimize energy and maximize performance. Here they are converting the application into Object Relational Graph (ORG) using static analysis and dynamic profiling. Later it is converted into Target Graph. This allows for uniform strategy for different constraints. Ou et al. [10] proposed a class level application partitioning strategy which improves the performance of offloading. It considers a multi-cost graph based model which is implemented in Java. It uses an online decision making strategy for splitting and offloading. the work is based on Heavy Edge Light Vertex Matching algorithm (HELVM). Expensive adaptation decision is the major disadvantage of this method. The work done by Tim et al. [14] proposes an algorithm which minimizes the time required for application execution. They are using Heavy Edge Matching (HEM) for coarsening and K-L for refinement. They uses Java and Adhoc framework for simulation.

3 Problem Statement

In our method the mobile application which is to be offloaded is partitioned into two for local and remote execution. First of all the application should be converted into graph called Weighted Object Relational Graph (WORG). Then taking the bandwidth changes into consideration the graph is broke dynamically. We are making the partition strategy as minimum data transfer and maximum security. So that the application is executed in a distributed manner with minimum transfer cost.

The Fig. 1 shows the architecture diagram for the proposed work. The Weighed object relational graph is calculated for the mobile application using the code analysis. Then the application is partitioned into two parts cloud partition and a local partition using genetic algorithm. The dynamic bandwidth due to mobility of the mobile node is also taken into consideration. Whenever there is a major change in the bandwidth correspondingly the partitions are changed.

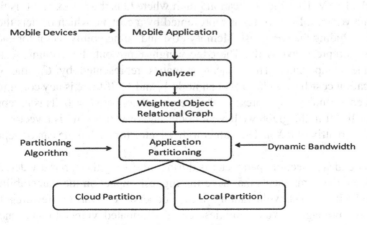

Fig. 1. System architecture

3.1   Weighted Object Relational Graph (WORG)

The application is converted into Weighted Object Relational Graph by using Soot Analysis frame work [9]. Figure 2 shows a sample WORG of a face recognition application. Each node is represented as a circle with weight which represents the memory cost for that node. En edge connecting two nodes represents the communication between the nodes with the corresponding costs. Static analysis and dynamic profiling techniques are used to create the WORG from the application. The example shows four classes Face preview, Image capture, Face Detection and Face detection library, where the face preview is the main class and from that image capture and face detection are called.

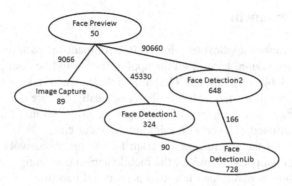

Fig. 2. Weighed object relational graph (WORG)

3.2   Application Partitioning Algorithm

Let a graph $G = (V, E)$ is the application graph where G is the vertex and E is the edges between the vertices. Each vertex is represented by a cost V_i, which depicts the cost of the vertex including the CPU cost, Memory cost and vulnerability factor for each node. The vector is represented as W_v. The edge weight represents the communication cost between the components. The adjacency matrix represented by C_{ij}, the value of communication cost(bandwidth) between node V_i and V_j. If there is any communication cost between V_i and V_j, C_{ij} represents the weight otherwise $C_{ij} = 0$. This is represented by a vector W_e. If in the graph we have n nodes and m vertices W_v is a vector of length *n and Cij* is a matrix of *n X n*. The vulnerability factor for each node can be represented as S_i.

The basic idea in security parameter is during offloading the app is divided in such a way that keep the components that have the biggest impact on the vulnerability to the local mobile itself. The vulnerability index depends on various features like call relationships, propagated vulnerabilities, cloud originated vulnerabilities and so on. Here we assume random values as vulnerability index for each node. In the optimized partitioning k modules are offloaded to the cloud. Our problem can be defined as an objective function *min (transmission cost) + max (security)*

Transmission cost: *Minimize* $\sum_{i=1}^{n} \sum_{j=1}^{k} C_{ij} \times (x_i \, XOR \, x_j) \times b$ where $x_i = 0$ if node i is executed on the local machine (mobile) and is equal to 1 if executed on remote machine.

Security cost: *Minimize* $\sum_{i=1}^{n} S_i \times (1 - x_i)$ Which will reduce the security risk of moving the more vulnerable nodes to the cloud. Here the security is preserved by moving less vulnerable nodes to the cloud. The total cost function can be represented as **Minimize** $\sum_{i=1}^{n} \sum_{j=1}^{k} C_{ij} \times (x_i \, XOR \, x_j) \times b + \sum_{i=1}^{n} S_i \times (1 - x_i)$

The above equation can be solved by Genetic algorithm is one of the evolutionary methods which can be used for graph partitioning [11]. The graph partitioning can be formulated as a multi-constrained optimization problem where the objective function can be formulated as above equation. The inputs to the algorithm can be *V - Number of nodes n, E - Number of edges, W_v - Node weight vector, W_e - Edge weight vector and S_n - Vulnerability index vector* and the output is formulated as a vector of length n with 0's and 1's where 0 represents local and 1 represent remote execution. The basic genetic algorithm can be stated as below.

The above algorithm works as follows. The optimized partition using genetic algorithm is calculated for the current bandwidth and the previous bandwidth. The following facts are considered for change partition

1. If the bandwidth is increasing the partitions which are there in the cloud remains the same and some of the local components are offloaded to the remote site. That is no change in S and some nodes in C will be shifting to S
2. If the bandwidth is decreasing the partition which is there in the mobile remains the same and some of the remote components are shifted back to the local site. That is no change in C and some nodes in S will be shifting to C.

Basic Genetic Algorithm
Input : WORG *(V, E, S_n , W_v, W_e)*

Output : Optimal partitioning solution $\overline{X}$ *where the local components are represented by 0 and remote components are represented by 1*
Algorithm :
      1. Initialize population X_0 with a random vector X with 0's and 1's
      2. Sort(X_0)
      3. While (gen!=maxGen)
          a.   *Use selection (Elitsm), mutation and crossover to generate children Q_i*
          b.   *$X_i = X_i \cup Q_i$*
          c.   *Sort(X_i in the descending order depending on the cost function)*
          d.   *$X_i = X_i[1..popsize]$*
          e.   *$X_{i+1} = X_i$*
          f.   *i++*
          g.   *gen++*
      4. End While

Bandwidth Adaptive Algorithm
Input : WORG (V, E, S_n, W_v, W_e) , b, b_p

Output : *Optimal partitioning solution* $\overline{X}$ *where the local components are represented by 0 and remote components are represented by 1*
compute the optimized partition (C_b, S_b) using current bandwidth b *using genetic algorithm*
Compute the optimized partition (C_{bp}, S_{bp}) using previous bandwidth bp *using genetic algorithm*
$V'=V-C_b-S_{bp}$
$m=| V' |$
while $m>1$ **do**
    $\{V_1, V_2, ... V_m\}$=order(V',WORG)
    $C=C_b \cup \{V_1, V_2, ... V_{m-1}\}$
    $S=\{V_m\} \cup S_{bp}$
    $X=(C,S)$
    if ($b-b_p>threshold$) **then** //Checking condition for change partition
        $\overline{X} =X$
    end
    $V'=V'-V_m$
    $m=m-1$
end

The application is partitioned according to the above algorithm and the dynamic and adaptive nature is calculated at each iteration of a bandwidth change. If the bandwidth changes the results are calculated and decision is taken on whether to shift the nodes from mobile to cloud or cloud to mobile depending on the above two conditions.

4   Application and Evaluation

The ORG constructed with the Dacapo Benchmark using soot framework and spark tool. The Table 1 specifies the graph which we considered for our experiments.

The ORG is constructed from the above data and adaptive splitting algorithm is applied onto the graph. The bandwidth is taken from a real time bandwidth trace obtained from a Samsung Galaxy phone.

Energy efficiency of graph partitioning algorithm The following is the evaluation of our algorithm with some standard methods. Stoer-Wagner is the basic graph

Table 1. - Sample application graph data

Programs	Classes	Methods	Nodes	Edges
avora	8812	22240	208	5430
H2	10264	14494	4912	11088
luindex	6530	8199	1027	6199
lusearch	7812	10148	1238	7148

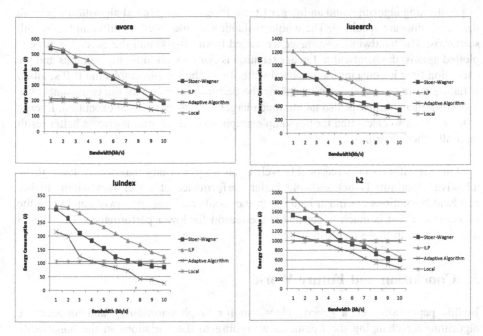

Fig. 3. Energy consumed for various graphs

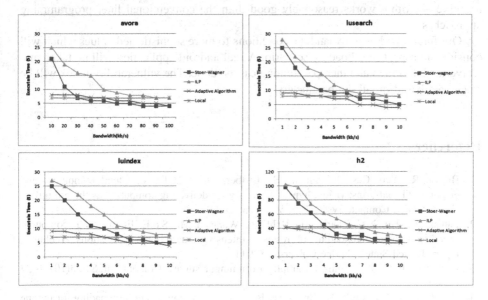

Fig. 4. Execution time for various graphs

bi-partitioning algorithm and an Integer Linear Programming based algorithm where all the constraints are specified. The whole evaluation is calculated on different bandwidth scenarios. The bandwidth parameter we varied from 10-100 and the execution time is plotted against the bandwidth. Local execution is done for all the sample graphs and the execution time is constant for any bandwidth. In all the sample graphs the ILP solution is taking more time because it is making the partition based on all the constraints. The Stoer-Wagner solution is also taking much larger time than the local execution. Energy efficiency is also calculated for the sample graph and our algorithm gives a better result than all other algorithms.

Our algorithm works reasonably well in all graphs at any bandwidth. Even if the adaptive algorithm is not showing better performance at lower bandwidth, higher bandwidth solutions are much better than the local solutions. At lower bandwidth the transmission cost is much larger that is the reason for lower performance. The Figs. 3 and 4 shows all these result .

5   Conclusion and Future Work

In this paper we used a genetic algorithm for graph partitioning and an adaptive algorithm for changing the fragments according to the variations in the bandwidth. Basically bandwidth is one of the most frequently changing components in offloading which will affect the decision a lot. Our algorithm is shifting the nodes dynamically depending on the current situations. Our experimental evaluation shows that the adaptive algorithm works reasonably good than the conventional liner programming approaches.

Our future work is to expand the conditions to more sophisticated values which will consider all aspect of offloading scenario. A real android application will be taken and converted into graph and then partitioning can be done. The vulnerability index will be calculated based on all the parameters.

References

1. Buyya, R., Yeo, C.S., Venugopal, S., Broberg, J., Brandic, I.: Cloud computing and emerging IT platforms: vision, hype, and reality for delivering computing as the 5th utility. Future Gener. Comput. Syst. **25**(6), 599–616 (2009)
2. Pathak, A., Hu, Y.C, Zhang, M., Bahl, P., Wang, Y.M.: S.o.E. Engineering, computer, enabling automatic offloading of resource-intensive smartphone applications. Technical report. United States, Purdue University (2011)
3. Fjallstrom, P.-O.: Algorithms for graph partitioning: a survey. Comput. Inf. Sci. **3**(10), 1–37 (1998)
4. Kumar, K., Liu, J., Lu, Y.H., Bhargava, B.: A survey of computation offloading for mobile systems. J. Mobile Netw. Appl. **18**(1), 129–140 (2013)
5. Kernighan, B.W., Lin, S.: An efficient heuristic procedure for partitioning graphs. Bell Syst. Tech. J. **49**, 291–307 (1970)

6. stoer, M., wagner, F.: A simple min-cut Algorithm. J. ACM (JACM) **44**(4), 585–591 (1997)
7. Karypis, G., kumar, V.: Multilevel k-way partitioning scheme for irregular graphs. J. Parallel Distrib. Comput. **48**(1), 96–129 (1998)
8. Elsner, U.: Graph partitioning - A survey
9. Einarsson, A., Nielsen, J.D.: Soot Framework: A Survivor's Guide to Java Program Analysis with Soot ΄ BRICS. Department of Computer Science University of Aarhus, Denmark (2008)
10. Ou, S., Yang, K., Liotta, A.: An adaptive multi-constraint partitioning algorithm for offloading in pervasive systems. In: Proceedings of the Fourth Annual IEEE International Conference on Pervasive Computing and Communications (PerCom 2006), pp. 25–116. IEEE, Pisa, Italy (2006)
11. Farshbaf, M., Feizi-Derakhshi, M.-R.: Multi-objective Optimization of Graph Partitioning using Genetic Algorithm. In: Third International Conference on Advanced Engineering Computing and Applications in Sciences, 2009. ADVCOMP 2009, 11–16 Oct 2009
12. Hunt, G.C., Scott, M.L.: The coign automatic distributed partitioning system. In: Proceedings of the 3rd Symposium on Operating Systems Design and Implementation (OSDI), pp. 187–200, Feb 1999
13. Wang, L., Franz, M.: Automatic Partitioning of Object-Oriented Programs for Resource-Constrained Mobile Devices with Multiple Distribution Objectives Parallel and Distributed Systems. In: ICPADS 2008, 14th IEEE International Conference on 8–10 Dec. 2008, pp. 369 – 376 (2008)
14. Verbelen, T., Stevens, T., De Turck, F.: Graph partitioning algorithms for optimizing software deployment in mobile cloud computing. Future Gener. Comput. Syst. **29**(2), 451–459 (2012)

Intelligent Intrusion Detection System
for Private Cloud Environment

Muthukumar B.[1($\boxtimes$)] and Praveen Kumar Rajendran[2]

[1] Faculty of Computing, Sathyabama University, Chennai, India
anbmuthusba@gmail.com
[2] Programmer Analyst Trainee,
Cognizant Technology Solutions, Chennai, India
praveenkumar558@gmail.com

Abstract. From the day cloud computing got its popularity, security and performance is the two important issues faced by the cloud service providers and the clients. Since cloud computing is a virtual pool of resources provided in an open environment (Internet), identifying intrusion of unauthorized users is one of the greatest challenges of the cloud service providers and cloud users. The artificial intelligence technique has been proposed in this paper in order to identify the intrusion of unauthorized user in a cloud environment. Application or research on cloud computing is always primarily focused upon any one of the issues. In our paper, the proposed algorithm satisfies the security aspects of cloud computing and the performance testing of the implementation satisfies the performance issues of cloud computing.

Keywords: Cloud computing · Intrusion · Intrusion detection system · Intelligence intrusion detection

1 Introduction

Cloud computing has made tremendous changes in the functioning and working in Information Technology sector As a result in exponential growth of data, the organization started to invest more on building their infrastructure which increased the capital expenditure of an organization. Cloud Computing has also changed the way in which business and personal data are being stored and accessed using computer, which has led to many kind of security issues [11]. Providing security for the data that has been stored in the cloud is one of the important responsibilities of the service provider. Although the infrastructure of the cloud is much more reliable, it faces lot of internal and external threats [12]. Hacking, Intrusion are the two major threat and security issues in cloud computing [3]. Activities of hacking can be easily identified on a network. Identification of intrusion in a network is quite tedious. An Intrusion Detection system that can identify the intrusion in an efficient manner and work as per the nature of cloud computing will give a solution for the security issue of cloud computing. An Intelligence Intrusion Detection system has been proposed in this paper, which would be another step in research on security aspects of cloud computing.

© Springer International Publishing Switzerland 2015
J.H. Abawajy et al. (Eds): SSCC 2015, CCIS 536, pp. 54–65, 2015.
DOI: 10.1007/978-3-319-22915-7_6

2 Cloud Computing

In cloud computing All the service are hosted via the Internet by service provider and used via Internet virtually, which leads to Internet intrusion [2]. Via cloud computing, the basic requirements of a customer are provided as a service. Software, Infrastructure, Platform are provided as a service by the service providers. In short, anything is provided as a service to the clients [15]. These Cloud services are provided in various manners such as "Public Cloud", "Private Cloud", and "Community Cloud". The main characteristic of the cloud service is "Pay as you go manner". It means the client has to pay only for the service which has been utilized.

Many research scholars and scientist have defined cloud computing at various occasions. Buyya et al. [1] has defined cloud computing as follows "Cloud is a parallel and distributed computing system consisting of a collection of inter-connected and virtualized computers that are dynamically provisioned and presented as one or more unified computing resources based on service-level agreements (SLA) established through negotiation between the service provider and consumers." From Buyya et al. [1] it can be inferred that cloud computing has the base of parallel computing, distributed computing, virtualization. Among these concepts, virtualization plays a major role in cloud computing. The major challenge before the research scholars is to provide a security for the transactions made and security for the data that is being stored [3, 7].

3 Intrusion and Intrusion Detection Systems

According to the Sundaram et al. [6], the term intrusion can be defined as "… the act of detecting actions that attempt to compromise the confidentiality, integrity or availability of a resource". The term Intrusion Detection is a field of research and development, which generally deals with intrusion and abnormal activity in a computer or in a network [4]. Intrusion, can be generally classified into two major categories such as Misuse Intrusion Detection and Anomaly Intrusion Detection. Intrusion Detection System can be classified as Network Based Intrusion Detection System and Host Based Intrusion Detection System.

Misuse Intrusion Detection is generally a signature based or rule based intrusion detection method. In misuse intrusion detection, the intrusion is identified when something happens apart from the set of rules that has been fixed by the administrator. The major drawback with this type of intrusion detection is, the rules have to be updated in a constant manner [7]. Iterative and Genetic are the two major types of Misuse intrusion detection method. Iterative detect intrusion in a continuous manner, where genetic method detects using previous history [13]. In anomaly intrusion, the intrusion is identified using the previous history of intrusion. Whenever an intrusion has been detected, the record of the intrusion will be stored in the database. If the same pattern of activity occurs in the future, using the stored pattern intrusion will be determined [7]. Static anomaly intrusion detection and dynamic anomaly intrusion are the two major types of anomaly intrusion detection method [14].

In general Intrusion detection system is either hardware or an application. If this hardware component of the application would be in the common place of a network and monitor the entire network's activity, it is said to be Network based Intrusion Detection System. David J. Weller-Fahy et al. [16] has defined network based intrusion detection system as an automated system that detects the intrusion in a network. The major drawback with the Network based Intrusion Detection System is, these systems cannot monitor the activities of each and every node that are present in the network In order to monitor the activities of each and every node in a network, Host Based Intrusion Detection System has been used. Host based Intrusion detection will not monitor the activities of the other host in the system or monitor the network [17].

3.1 Research Motivation

The main goal of research in Intrusion Detection System is to build an efficient intrusion detection system, which can detect any type of intrusion within the host as well as in the network. Patel et al. [7] describe, "Elasticity, Reliability, Agility and Adaptability, Availability", are some of the basic characteristics of cloud computing. Among the basic characteristics of cloud computing, the major challenge for implementing an intrusion detection system would be elasticity and adaptability. The intrusion detection system has to adopt it as per the nature of the cloud and also should work in an efficient manner even if there is any change in the nature of the cloud. Building an efficient intrusion detection system for an elastic environment is another major challenge for the researchers and developers. This can be possible, by embedding intelligent technique (Based upon Artificial Intelligence) within the intrusion detection system. In order to build such intelligent intrusion detection system with high security and performance, various research works have been studied.

3.2 Related Works

During our research work on intrusion detection and intrusion detection system, a detailed study on previous work was done and proposed a Hybrid Intrusion detection mode [5]. Our previous research work narrate that, intrusion detection system should be dynamic, self adaptive, scalable and efficient in nature.

Kleber Vieira et al. [8] have proposed a Hybrid Intrusion Detection System for Cloud computing and Grid computing environment. The proposed Intrusion detection system can detect only one type of intrusion i.e., either anomaly intrusion or misuse intrusion. The architecture and working of cloud computing and grid environment are completely different. Proposing a common intrusion detection system for two different concepts is contradictory. From our analysis we could infer that the proposed intrusion detection system is not efficient in terms of detecting new type of intrusion and hence it does not update the system. This system is more suitable for grid environment, than cloud based environment.

Tupakula et al. [9] have proposed a Virtual machine based Hybrid Intrusion Detection System for Infrastructure as a Service. From our analysis [19] we inferred that, this system cannot handle real time environment and implementing the intrusion detection system for other cloud services has not been defined. The system which has been narrated is quite complex and implementation steps (algorithm) for implementing the system has not been defined. The scope of implementing the system in a real time cloud based environment has not been discussed by the authors. And this system does not satisfy the characteristics of Hybrid Intrusion Detection system, which has been proposed in our earlier research work [5].

Kholidy et al. [10] have proposed a framework for Intrusion Detection in Cloud Systems. This framework isn't efficient as per our analysis and the same has been validated by Patel et al. [7]. As per our analysis, this system does not detect intrusion in fast and efficient manner.

As per our analysis made on earlier research works the following inferences were made.

1. Existing works are not Dynamic, Self adaptive, Efficient and Scalable in nature.
2. Proper algorithm for implementing the intrusion detection system has not been defined.
3. Existing intrusion detection systems are complex and difficult to implement.
4. Less efficient in detecting different types intrusion.
5. Performance has not been considered.

The following Intelligent Intrusion Detection Algorithm will overcome the drawbacks of the existing systems and also satisfy the characteristics of Intrusion Detection System proposed in our earlier research work [5].

4 Intelligent Intrusion Detection

The main goal of the Intelligent Intrusion Detection System is to detect the intrusion in an efficient manner with the help of previous history of intrusion and by updating the intrusion detection database in a constant manner. The purpose of introducing intelligence, technique is to detect intrusion in an efficient manner by predicting the intrusion using the training given to the system. The intelligence intrusion detection system has been proposed by combining hardware and an application to detect the intrusion. The 3 major phases of the proposed intrusion detection are.

1. Training the intrusion detection system.
2. Testing the intrusion detection system.
3. Implementation and updating intrusion detection system.

4.1 Muthu-Praveen Algorithm of Intelligent Intrusion

The above proposed Intelligent Intrusion Detection System can be implemented using the following algorithms. Each phase which has been discussed in Sect. 4 has been written as an algorithm.

Algorithm 1: Training the Intrusion Detection System

In the training phase, the hardware component and the application will be trained with sample intrusion data. If any such trace is found during the implementation phase, the application and the hardware will detect the intrusion based upon the training given. The sample intrusion data contains abnormal port number and protocol used by the end user, abnormal path through which the request has travelled.

```
1.    Start
2.    {
3.    Initialize the hardware component;
4.    Initialize the software component;
5.    {
6.    Fetch the sample intrusion data into the hardware component;
7.    {
8.    Store the data in the database of the hardware component;
9.    }
10. Fetch the sample intrusion data into the application;
11. {
12. Store the data in the database of the hardware component;
13. }
14. }
15. End
```

Algorithm 2: Testing the intrusion detection system

After training the intrusion detection system with the sample data, the system is tested to check whether the training has been done successfully. Testing phase of intrusion detection system can be implemented using the following Algorithm 2. In this phase, the system will be fetched with the similar kind of kind of data which has been used during the training phase. System should identify the trace of intrusion perfectly, if not the system will be trained once again.

```
1.    Start
2.    {
3.    Initialize the testing phase;
4.    Fetch the sample intrusion data to the hardware component and software
      component;
5.    If the system is able to detect the intrusion
6.    {
7.    Training is good and the testing is successful;
8.    }
9.    Else
10. {
11. Training is not good;
12. Testing phase is not successful;
13. System is recommended for training once again;
14. }
```

Algorithm 3: Implementing and Updating of Intelligent Intrusion Detection System

Once the training and testing is successful, the system will be exposed to the real time scenario. If the system identifies the similar kind of intrusion trace, the system will intimate the cloud admin and the users. If any new trace has been found, the trace will be stored in the database and will be used in the future training process. The following Algorithm 3 can update itself, without any human intervention (Intelligent mechanism).

```
1.  Start
2.  {
3.  For all the incoming request;
4.  Fetch the intrusion detection parameters from the request;
5.  For all the parameters
6.  {
7.  Check with the values stored in the database
8.  }
9.  If there is any deviation in the parameter
10. {
11. Intimate the cloud administrator about the intrusions;
12. }
13. If the deviation found is proved to be an intrusion trace
14. {
15. Pass the new intrusion trace to the data base;
16. Update the database;
17. }
18. If the deviation found is wrong
19. {
20. Store the traces in the database;
21. }
22. For all the proved intrusion traces
23. {
24. Use the trace that is stored in the database to train the system;
25. Intrusion alert will be made for such trace in the future;
26. }
27. For all the deviation which is found wrong
28. {
29. Use the trace that is stored in the database to train the system;
30. The system will not intimate about intrusion for such trace;
31. }
32. }
33. End
```

4.2   Implementation

In the above proposed algorithms software component is implemented using the.net as front end and SQL server as the back end. In order to implement the proposed intrusion detection algorithm in an open source environment such as open stack, it can be implemented using the open source languages PHP, Perl or Python with the same SQL server as the backend. Since the algorithm has been written in such a way that it will predict the deviations perfectly, the system will work more efficiently than earlier proposed systems. Index Page (Application Home Page), User Login Page, User Home Page, Admin Page has been created and the above proposed intrusion detection algorithm has been implemented in the above said pages.

4.3   Performance Evaluation

The performance of the implemented algorithm is measured using an open source performance testing tool, JMeter. In JMeter, the performance of the application is measured in terms of response time. In order to prove that application is functionally good, error criteria from the JMeter have been considered. Figure 1 shows the snapshot of Performance evaluation process (Aggregate Report), which is formed as Table 1.

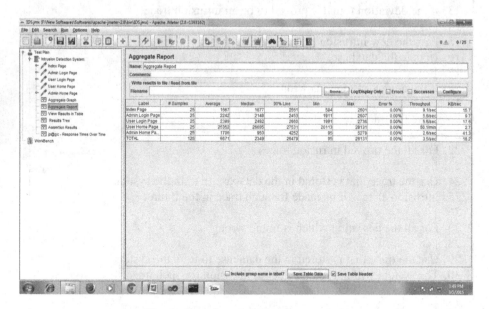

Fig. 1. Snapshot of performance analysis

4.4   Result of Performance Evaluation

The Fig. 2 and a Table 1 have been obtained to demonstrate the result of performance evaluation. In the Table 1, the term "label" indicates the pages which have been tested. "Sample" indicates the number of times (Users) the page has been tested. "Response time" will give the average time taken by each page. "Error %" indicates, whether the page has any functional error. Other parameters are included in the paper to show the originality, which are not considered in this paper. Future analysis and research can be carried out using those parameters. For readability purpose, the values derived from the tool are described with the respective units in the following Table 1.

Table 1. Performance evaluation for 5 users

Label	Samples (Count)	Average response Time (ms)	Median (ms)	90 % line (ms)	Min (ms)	Max (ms)	Error (%)	Throughput (Count/ms)	Data transfer (KB/ms)
Index Page	25	1667	1677	2551	584	2601	0	9.067827	15.74472
Admin Login Page	25	2242	2148	2453	1911	2607	0	5.581603	9.691494
User Login Page	25	2389	2492	2660	1991	2736	0	5.55679	17.64172
User Home Page	25	25352	26695	27531	20113	28131	0	0.835366	2.701071
Admin Home Page	25	1706	950	4252	95	5278	0	2.554409	41.26468
Total	125	6671	2349	26479	95	28131	0	3.494939	18.19826

4.5 Inference of Performance Evaluation

In the Fig. 2, Red line indicates Index page, Blue line indicates Admin Login Page, Pink color indicates User login page, Light blue color indicates Admin Home page and

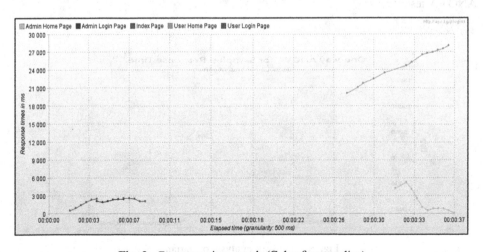

Fig. 2. Response time graph (Color figure online)

Green color indicates User home page. In the Fig. 2, X axis indicates the elapsed time and Y axis indicates the response time of each page that has been tested. The following are the inferences, which can be concluded from the Table 1 and Fig. 2.

1. The total Error percentage of the application is Zero percentage (0 %). Zero percentage 0 % of Error, shows that the application is functionally good (without any error, the application has passed in all the test cases).
2. The average response time of the application with 25 users is 6.67 s, which is less than 7 s. This indicates that 25 users can access the application within 7 s, from which we can infer that application holds good in terms of performance.
3. From the Table 1, we can infer that the response time range of 4 pages of the application is less than 2.6 s. From this result, we can conclude that 90 % of performance of the application holds good.
4. Range of response time for User Home page and Admin Home Page depends upon the content that has been created in that particular page. In our research, a sample Home page and admin page has been created and the testing has been carried out.
5. In the Fig. 2, the ranges of the response time between highest value and the lowest value are plotted. Highest and the lowest range of 4 pages (Index, Admin Login, User Login, Admin Home Page) are less than 6 s, and the range of User Home page is higher due to the content of the home page.

4.6   Statistical Analysis

In order to prove the correctness of the proposed algorithm, One-way Analysis of Variance test has been carried out using Minitab 17 (Trial Version). The main purpose of performing ANOVA test is to find the mean difference within the group and different group [19]. Here the mean difference within the group has been considered. One-way ANOVA test has been carried out between the mean values of Response time across the Sample value. Figure 3 and Table 2 is the result obtained from the One-way ANOVA test.

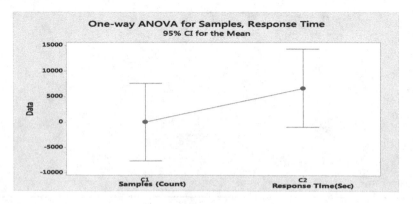

Fig. 3. One-way analysis of variance

In the Fig. 3, Samples are taken as the 1st factor and Response time is taken as the second factor and ANOVA test has been carried out. Table 2 has been derived as an output of one-way ANOVA process from Minitab 17 (trail version). Here F indicates the factor value, R indicates the Response value and CI indicates the confidence interval. For our research purpose, these parameters are considered. In our research, response is "Response time" and the factor that influences response time is "Samples". In the Table 2, C1 indicates the Response time and C2 indicates the sample.

Table 2. Result of one-way anova

<u>**Method**</u>

Null hypothesis   All means are equal
Alternative hypothesis At least one mean is different
Significance level $\alpha = 0.05$

Equal variances were assumed for the analysis.
<u>**Factor Information**</u>

Factor Levels Values
Factor   2   C1, C2
<u>**Analysis of Variance**</u>

Source DF   Adj SS   Adj MS   F-Value P-Value
Factor 1 110429936 110429936   2.02   0.193
Error   8 436622567   54577821
Total   9 547052503
<u>**Model Summary**</u>

 S   R-sq   R-sq(adj) R-sq(pred)
7387.68 20.19%   10.21%   0.00%
<u>**Means**</u>

Factor N   Mean StDev   95% CI
C1   5 25.00 0.00 (-7593.74, 7643.74)
C2   5 6671   10448 (-948, 14290)

Pooled StDev = 7387.68

4.7 Discussion

In the earlier research work, only the security aspects have been considered. In the proposed algorithm both security and performance aspect has been considered. The performance of the proposed algorithm may vary based upon the nature of the cloud. If the proposed algorithm is deployed in the public cloud, the security parameters and

Table 3. Comparison of proposed algorithm

S.no	Research work	Comparison criteria	
		Security	Performance
1	Kleber Vieira et al. [8]	Good	Not considered
2	Tupakula et al. [9]	Good	Not considered
3	Kholidy et al. [10]	Good	Not considered
4	Proposed Algorithm	Good	Considered

the performance parameters would vary at a large extent. The result of performance testing gives an overall impression, that the implementation is much efficient in terms of time and space (Table 3).

5 Future Scopes and Conclusion

In the private cloud environment, the proposed algorithm was able to detect all of new types of intrusion (100 %). The framework of the algorithm can be expanded and implemented in other cloud deployment models. Implemented application and the entire algorithm can be deployed in highly secured private cloud such as cloud that is being built for defense purpose, educational purpose etc. Nader Sohrabi Safa et al. [18] al has proposed a method to identify the customers using Artificial intelligence method; research using the concept proposed by Nader Sohrabi Safe et al. [18] would make the research on Intrusion detection much more interesting and also will make a new dimension in network security.

References

1. Buyya, R., Yeo, C.S., Venugopal, S., Broberg, J., Brandic, I.: Cloud computing and emerging IT platforms: vision, hype, and reality for delivering computing as the 5th utility. Future Gener. Comput. Syst. **25**(6), 599–616 (2009)
2. Zarrabi, A., Zarrabi, A.: Internet intrusion detection system service in a cloud. Int. J. Comput. Sci. **9**(1), 308 (2012)
3. Kandukuri, B.R., Paturi, R.V., Rakshit, A.: Cloud security issues. In: 2009 IEEE International Conference on Services Computing, Bangalore, 21–25 September 2009
4. Jabez, J., Muthukumar, B.: Intrusion detection system: time probability method and hyperbolic hopfield neural network. J. Theor. Appl. Inf. Technol. **67**(1), 65–77 (2014)
5. Rajendran, P.K., Muthukumar, B., Nagarajan, G.: Hybrid intrusion detection system for private cloud: a systematic approach. Procedia Comput. Sci **48**, 325–329 (2015)
6. Sundaram, A.: An introduction to intrusion detection. Crossroads **2**(4), 3–7 (1996)
7. Patel, A., Taghavi, M., Bakhtiyari, K., Júnior, J.C.: An intrusion detection and prevention system in cloud computing: a systematic review. J. Netw. Comput. Appl. **36**(1), 25–41 (2013)
8. Vieira, K., Schulter, A., Westphall, C., Westphall, C.: Intrusion detection for grid and cloud computing. It Prof. **4**, 38–43 (2009)

9. Tupakula, U., Varadharajan, V., Akku, N.: Intrusion detection techniques for infrastructure as a service cloud. In: 2011 IEEE Ninth International Conference on Dependable, Autonomic and Secure Computing (DASC). IEEE (2011)

10. Kholidy, H.A., Baiardi, F.: CIDS: a framework for intrusion detection in cloud systems. In: 2012 Ninth International Conference on Information Technology: New Generations (ITNG). IEEE (2012)

11. Stolfo, S.J., Salem, M.B., Keromytis, A.D.: Fog computing: Mitigating insider data theft attacks in the cloud. In: 2012 IEEE Symposium on Security and Privacy Workshops (SPW). IEEE (2012)

12. Wang, C., Wang, Q., Ren, K., Lou, W.: Privacy-preserving public auditing for data storage security in cloud computing. In: 2010 Proceedings IEEE INFOCOM, pp. 1–9. IEEE (2010)

13. Diaz-Gomez, P.A., Dean F.H.: Misuse detection-an iterative process vs. a genetic algorithm approach. In: ICEIS, vol. 2 (2007)

14. Govindarajan, M., Chandrasekaran, R.M.: Intrusion detection using neural based hybrid classification methods. Comput. Netw. 55(8), 1662–1671 (2011)

15. Jeba, L., Rathna, M.: Improving the quality of cloud service by ensemble prediction. Int. J. Appl. Eng. Res. 9(21), 9323–9326 (2014)

16. Weller-Fahy, D., Borghetti, B.J., Sodemann, A.A.: A survey of distance and similarity measures used within network intrusion anomaly detection. IEEE Commun. Surv. Tutor 17(1), 70–91 (2014). doi:10.1109/COMST.2014.2336610

17. Bai, Y., Kobayashi, H.: Intrusion detection systems: technology and development. In: 2003 17th International of Advanced Information Networking and Applications AINA 2003, vol. 27(29), pp. 710–715, March 2003

18. Safa, N.S., Ghani, N.A., Ismail, M.A.: An artificial neural network classification approach for improving accuracy of customer identification in e-commerce. Malays. J. Comput. Sci. 27(3), 171–185 (2014)

19. Rajendran, P.K., Muthukumar, B.: Hybrid intrusion detection algorithm for private cloud. WSEAS Trans. Comput. (2015, Accepted)

Design of an Efficient Verification Scheme for Correctness of Outsourced Computations in Cloud Computing

Ronak Vyas, Alok Singh, Jolly Singh,
Gunjan Soni, and B.R. Purushothama[(⊠)]

Department of Computer Science and Engineering,
National Institute of Technology Goa, Farmagudi, Ponda 403401, Goa, India
puru@nitgoa.ac.in

Abstract. As cloud computing allows consumers or clients to store and delegate their sensitive data, cloud service providers have a lot of power over this data. Hence, the service providers in cloud computing cannot be trusted. To protect itself from being cheated on, by the untrusted service provider, the client needs a way to verify the correctness of computations returned by the cloud server, on its own machine. This should have very low computational cost as compared to the original computational cost of the outsourced computations. Operation on vectors is one of the major computations performed by cloud servers as many applications hosted on it use vectors. One of the major operations on vectors is calculating the inner product of the vector and matrix multiplication extensively uses inner products. In this work, we present an efficient algorithm to verify the correctness of inner products of vectors, on the client side. Also, we efficiently apply this scheme to verify the product of matrices. We also present an extensive security analysis and prove mathematically that, the client can verify the correctness of the computations, with a significant probability of success. We also demonstrate the efficiency and correctness of the proposed algorithm.

Keywords: Cloud outsourcing · Computation correctness · Verification · Cloud computing

1 Introduction

Cloud Computing has many acceptable definitions. One of the widely used definition, "a model for enabling convenient, on-demand network access to a shared pool of configurable computing resources (e.g. networks, servers, storage, applications and services) that can be rapidly provisioned and released with minimal management effort or service provider interaction" is provided by National Institute of Standards and Technology [15]. Cloud computing model consists of a client (desktop computers, phones), a cloud server (Amazon EC2 [1], Microsoft Azure [4]) and a cloud service provider (Amazon [1], Microsoft [4], VMware [6],

© Springer International Publishing Switzerland 2015
J.H. Abawajy et al. (Eds): SSCC 2015, CCIS 536, pp. 66–77, 2015.
DOI: 10.1007/978-3-319-22915-7_7

Google [2]). Cloud computing is used by various clients to do a multitude of tasks, ranging from storing large amounts of data on the cloud (which the client cannot store on itself due to lack of storage) to delegating enormous computations to the cloud. In all cases, clients opt for cloud computing as they need a hefty number of resources, which are not available with them or they cannot afford the cost of purchasing the same.

Cloud computing provides three service models to its clients [15] viz., Cloud Software as a Service (SaaS), Cloud Platform as a Service (PaaS), and Cloud Infrastructure as a Service (IaaS). The SaaS are offered by cloud service provider like Amazon [1], Microsoft [4], Google [2] and IBM [3]. Red Hat's Openshift [5], Google's App Engine [2] and Windows Azure [4] are a few examples of PaaS providers and their PaaS services) and Windows Azure [4] and Google Compute Engine [2] are some of the examples of IaaS providers. By using these services for solving various problems, the clients can avoid the cost of building and maintaining a separate infrastructure and can choose to pay the service providers for the use of their services. Even with all the benefits related to cost, availability and reliability, cloud computing faces a major security hurdle. As the data or computations are kept on a cloud, which is being monitored and maintained by untrusted service provider, clients are skeptical about the security of their data or computation results. Cloud security is highly dependent on the trust between the two parties involved in the transaction. Client's trust on the service provider is highly dependent on the type of deployment model used by the cloud service provider. Deployment models are broadly classified into three: public cloud, private cloud and hybrid cloud [15].

With the increase in the popularity of the cloud computing, there is ever increasing deployment of applications on to the cloud computing platform. Significant fraction of the applications use computation of inner product of vectors. To highlight a few, in the computer science area research, the applications like, similarity document detection [17], determination of relative position for geometric objects [13] and association rule mining [22] use the inner product of vectors as fundamental operation. There is a possibility that the cloud server is compromised or is trying to save up computations, to maximize its profit. In this case, it may compute the results partially and return spurious results. If the client does not have a scheme to verify the returned results, it will not be able to detect the fraud and take the false results as the correct one, which could be dangerous as the client may need the correct results for sensitive and important tasks, for example, MRI tomography [8]. An important factor to be addressed while verifying the results on the client side is that the verification scheme on the client machine should not take as many computations as it took to compute results on the cloud. The concept of outsourcing becomes moot in such a situation. Most commonly outsourced computations include matrix multiplication using vector inner products [20] and batch modular exponentiation [14]. There is little work done in the area of verifying the results of the inner vector product computations. The focus of this work is to *design a verification scheme to verify the correctness of vector inner products returned by the cloud server on the client side.*

2   Related Work

In this section, we provide some insight into existing results on the verification of correctness of results returned by the cloud server. Ahn et al. [7] have provided the method for verification of the result based on the derivation of the signature based on the existing signatures. However, the scheme involves exponentiation computation at high cost for signature generation and verification. Also, the scheme is not applicable for large scale data and also there is an increase in the signature data. Numerous ideas have been proposed in the related exploration field of outsourced database services; methods based on verification trees [9,10,12,19], methods based on redundant data [11,23,24] and signature scheme based method [18]. In the methods of verification tree, numerous sorts of index trees are joined with the thought of Merkle Hash Tree [16] to develop new verification data structure. The scheme in [21] focuses on privacy preserving inner product computation using homomorphic encryption not on verification. Also, it is computation intensive. In the method of signature chain, data ordering is done first, and afterward every data is signed. The redundant data based methods involve regular and secret embedding of fake or duplicate data into the original data. In their corresponding application fields, all these verification schemes were proved to be effective. Few of the schemes such as, the verification tree or redundant data based scheme are also efficacious to be used for verifying the correctness of the inner product of vectors. However, the schemes are rendered inefficient or incur more extra cost when used with high dimension or large scale data due to the increase of burden in storage computation and transmission. There is a scheme by Gang Sheng et al. [20] to verify the results of inner vector product computations. The scheme require $O(mn)$ multiplications and $O(mn)$ additions. We seek to propose an effective and efficient verification scheme for the correctness verification of the inner product of vectors. We compare the proposed method with the method in [20], which contains one of the proposed efficient method and show that our proposed scheme is efficient.

3   Proposed Verification Scheme

In this section, we present an efficient scheme to verify the correctness of vector inner products on the client side.

3.1   System Model

The system model comprises of a cloud server (CS) and a client (C). CS is assumed to have "large" amount of resources at its disposal and C can generate computational requests $\mathcal{C}$ of any magnitude, at any time and CS will be available to process them. The term available indicates that the cloud server will be serving all the times when the client make any requests, i.e. it will never happen that the cloud server is not present to take any request or is offline as a result of this assumption. The generic protocol is as follows:

1. Client has a computationally intensive task $\mathcal{C}$, which has time complexity t for obtaining the result.
2. Client outsources the computation $\mathcal{C}$ to CS.
3. CS computes the result $\mathcal{R}$ and sends it to C.
4. C verifies the result $\mathcal{R}$ in time complexity $t_v < t$.

In the first step of the protocol, C will collect the data to be outsourced and will apply necessary privacy preserving measures to protect the integrity of the data. We assume that such a measure is addressed by the client. Client preprocesses the data in the first step if required by the outsourcing protocol. Preprocessing should take less computation cost as compared to the cost of actual computations done by CS. The second step involves outsourcing of the computation to CS. In the third step, CS carries out the required computations on the received data and sends the result of the computations to C. In the final step, C verifies the result in time $t_v < t$. Here, t is the time taken by CS to do the computations and t_v is the time taken by the client to verify the returned results.

Precisely, we define the problem we address. We focus on the following problem. Client, C has a dataset V such that,

$$V = \{\mathbf{v_i} \; ; \; i = 1, 2, 3 \ldots m\}$$

where $\mathbf{v_i}$ is a vector such that,

$$\mathbf{v_i} = \begin{bmatrix} v_{i1} & v_{i2} & \cdots & v_{in} \end{bmatrix}^T$$

The detailed representation of V is as follows :

$$V = \begin{bmatrix} v_{11} & v_{21} & \cdots\cdots & v_{m1} \\ v_{12} & v_{22} & \cdots\cdots & v_{m2} \\ \cdot & \cdot & \cdots\cdots & \cdot \\ \cdot & \cdot & \cdots\cdots & \cdot \\ \cdot & \cdot & \cdots\cdots & \cdot \\ v_{1n} & v_{2n} & \cdots\cdots & v_{mn} \end{bmatrix}$$

Each column in the above matrix V is a vector $\mathbf{v_i}$, where $1 \leq i \leq m$. There is another vector $\mathbf{u}$ such that,

$$\mathbf{u} = \begin{bmatrix} u_1 & u_2 & \cdots & u_n \end{bmatrix}$$

The server is expected to return a vector $\mathbf{r}$ which contains m elements. These elements are the vector inner product of each vector in V with $\mathbf{u}$. The resultant vector $\mathbf{r}$ is represented as:

$$\mathbf{r} = \begin{bmatrix} r_1 & r_2 & \cdots & r_m \end{bmatrix}^T = \begin{bmatrix} u.v_1 & u.v_2 & \cdots & u.v_m \end{bmatrix}^T$$

After CS returns the result vector $\mathbf{r}$, C needs to verify the correctness of $\mathbf{r}$ efficiently.

3.2   Proposed Verification Scheme

Our proposed verification scheme is divided into three phases:

1. Preprocessing deals with the processing the data to be outsourced by the client.
2. The computation phase involves the cloud server carrying out the required computations on the data outsourced by the client.
3. Verification phase is carried out on the client side, after the cloud server returns the results.

We make an assumption that the client will not discard the data to be outsourced from its storage unless it verifies the results returned by the server. This assumption is safe to make as the whole point of verification is to find whether the returned results are correct or not. This assumption is only for testing. In practical systems, clients can discard the data. If the results are found to be incorrect, the client will report the server as malicious and will need to outsource the computations to some other service provider. In the following sections, we explain each phase of the proposed verification scheme.

3.2.1   Preprocessing

Here, we elaborate the preprocessing phase of the verification scheme. The preprocessing algorithm is as follows:

1. Client chooses a random number p from the set of integers $[1, max]$, uniformly at random. We define max as the maximum possible integer that can be handled by the client machine. The probability of any arbitrary number being selected as p is $\frac{1}{max}$.
2. Client computes the sum vector $\mathbf{v_{m+1}}$ as follows:

$$\mathbf{v_{m+1}} = \left[(\textstyle\sum_{i=1}^{m} v_{i1}) \bmod p \quad (\textstyle\sum_{i=1}^{m} v_{i2}) \bmod p \quad \cdots \quad (\textstyle\sum_{i=1}^{m} v_{in}) \bmod p \right]^{\mathbf{T}}$$

3. Client chooses a number w from $[1, m+1]$, uniformly at random. Then client swaps $\mathbf{v_{m+1}}$ with $\mathbf{v_w}$.
4. Client stores (w, p) on its machine secretly from CS.

In the first step of preprocessing, C chooses a random number p, using a pseudo random number generator. In the second step, C computes the sum vector v_{m+1}. The ith element of the sum vector v_{m+1} contains the sum of ith elements of all vectors in V modulo p. Since, the sum vector needs to be appended in V, its position should be kept secret from CS. To do this, C chooses another random number w from $[1, m+1]$, uniformly at random. The set also includes $m+1$ because we are choosing a random position to keep the sum vector in V. Hence, we have $m+1$ positions which accommodate the sum vectors initial index, i.e. $m+1$. After choosing w, C swaps the sum vector $\mathbf{v_{m+1}}$ with $\mathbf{v_w}$ in V. So, the new position of sum vector in V will be at index w. Also, C stores (w, p) with itself.

3.2.2   Time Complexity of Preprocessing Phase

First, we analyze the time complexity of computing $\mathbf{r}$ given $\mathbf{u}$ and V. To compute a single vector inner product of two vectors of n elements each, n additions and n multiplications are required. So, the time complexity will be $O(n)$. To compute $\mathbf{r}$, m vector products need to be computed. So, it will take mn additions and mn multiplications. Thus, the required time complexity is $O(mn)$. Multiplication is computationally more intensive than addition. The preprocessing phase of our proposed algorithm computes the sum vector in mn additions, without any multiplications. Hence, the time complexity of preprocessing is $O(mn)$, which does not contain any multiplications. It should be noted that, the number of operations our proposed scheme performs is significantly less than $O(mn)$ multiplications and $O(mn)$ additions combined together. This is a significant improvement over the existing schemes.

3.3   Computation Phase

This phase involves outsourcing of the computations to the cloud server, computations of the results by the cloud server and sending of the results by the cloud server to the client. Client uploads $\mathbf{u}$ and V (which contains $m + 1$ vectors now) to the cloud server. Cloud server computes the inner products of all vectors in the matrix V with vector $\mathbf{u}$. The result returned by the server is the vector $\mathbf{r}$ such that,

$$\mathbf{r} = \left\{\, r_i \mid r_i = \mathbf{u}.\mathbf{v_i}\, ; \, \mathbf{v_i} \in V; i = 1, 2, 3 \cdots (m+1) \right\}$$

Here, i ranges from 1 to $(m + 1)$ instead of 1 to m because, the client has appended the sum vector to v during preprocessing and cloud server has no knowledge about its position in the matrix V.

3.3.1   Time Complexity of Computation Phase

Time complexity for computing $\mathbf{r}$ by the cloud server is $O(mn)$. It consists of mn multiplications and mn additions. The communication complexity is not considered, and it is assumed that client and server can communicate as much as they want, without affecting the computational complexity.

3.4   Verification

This phase verifies the results returned by the server on the client side. The vector $\mathbf{r}$ returned by the server contains $(m + 1)$ elements. Vector $\mathbf{r}$ can be represented as :

$$\mathbf{r} = \begin{bmatrix} r[1] & r[2] & \cdots & r[w] & \cdots & r[m] & r[m+1] \end{bmatrix}^T$$

$$= \begin{bmatrix} \mathbf{u}.\mathbf{v_1} & \mathbf{u}.\mathbf{v_2} & \cdots & \mathbf{u}.\mathbf{v_{m+1}} & \cdots & \mathbf{u}.\mathbf{v_m} & \mathbf{u}.\mathbf{v_w} \end{bmatrix}^T$$

The positions of $\mathbf{v_w}$ and $\mathbf{v_{m+1}}$ were exchanged in the preprocessing phase. This affects the positions of their inner products with $\mathbf{u}$, in the result vector $\mathbf{r}$, as shown in the above representation. The verification vector product $\mathbf{u}.\mathbf{v_{m+1}}$ is contained in $\mathbf{r}$. The *verification* algorithm is as follows:

1. Client computes $S_1 = (\sum_{i=1}^{m+1} \mathbf{r}[i]) \bmod p$ $(i \neq w)$ and $S_2 = \mathbf{r}[w] \bmod p$.
2. If $\mathbf{S_1} - \mathbf{S_2} = 0$ then, the client can conclude that the returned results are correct, with high probability.

It should be noted that, $\mathbf{r}[w]$ and r_w are different. $\mathbf{r}[w]$ is the wth element in the vector of result $\mathbf{r}$. Precisely, w is the index where the value of r_{m+1} will be found in $\mathbf{r}$. Verification phase takes $O(m)$ additions.

4   Correctness Proof and Security Analysis

In this section, we provide the proof of correctness of the proposed scheme and also analyze the security of the proposed scheme.

4.1   Proof of Correctness

In this section, we provide the proof of correctness of the proposed scheme. The dataset V is represented as,

$$V = \begin{bmatrix} v_{11} & v_{21} & \cdots\cdots & v_{m1} \\ v_{12} & v_{22} & \cdots\cdots & v_{m2} \\ \cdot & \cdot & \cdots\cdots & \cdot \\ \cdot & \cdot & \cdots\cdots & \cdot \\ \cdot & \cdot & \cdots\cdots & \cdot \\ v_{1n} & v_{2n} & \cdots\cdots & v_{mn} \end{bmatrix}$$

The sum vector $\mathbf{v_{m+1}}$ is represented as,

$$\mathbf{v_{m+1}} = \left[(\textstyle\sum_{i=1}^{m} v_{i1}) \bmod p \quad (\textstyle\sum_{i=1}^{m} v_{i2}) \bmod p \quad \cdots \quad (\textstyle\sum_{i=1}^{m} v_{in}) \bmod p\right]^{\mathbf{T}}$$

and

$$\mathbf{u}.\mathbf{v_{m+1}} = u_1(\sum_{i=1}^{m} v_{i1}) \bmod p + u_2(\sum_{i=1}^{m} v_{i2}) \bmod p + \cdots + u_n(\sum_{i=1}^{m} v_{in}) \bmod p$$

Theorem 1. $(\sum_{i=1}^{n} r_i) \bmod p = \mathbf{u}.\mathbf{v_{m+1}} \bmod p$

Proof. LHS can be written as

$(\sum_{i=1}^{n} r_i) \bmod p =$
$u_1(\sum_{i=1}^{m} v_{i1}) \bmod p + u_2(\sum_{i=1}^{m} v_{i2}) \bmod p + \cdots + u_n(\sum_{i=1}^{m} v_{in}) \bmod p$

We know that,

$$(x_1 + x_2) \bmod p = (x_1 \bmod p + x_2 \bmod p) \bmod p$$

Using the above equation, we can write,

$$(\sum_{i=1}^{n} r_i) \, mod \, p = (u_1(\sum_{i=1}^{m} v_{i1}) \, mod \, p + \cdots + u_n(\sum_{i=1}^{m} v_{in}) \, mod \, p) \, mod \, p$$

Hence,

$$(\sum_{i=1}^{n} r_i) \, mod \, p = \mathbf{u}.\mathbf{v}_{m+1} \, mod \, p.$$

4.2   What Ensures the Security of the Proposed Scheme?

The security of the proposed scheme depends on w and p which the client keeps as secret from the cloud server. If cloud server gains knowledge about w and p, it can modify the result and cheat the client.

Algorithm 1. Finding the value of w, p by cloud server

    Data : The modified matrix V containing $m + 1$ vectors
    Result: w, p
1 **for** $i = 1$ **to** max **do**
2     $sum = [0\,0 \cdots 0]$
3   **for** $l = 1$ **to** $(m+1)$ **do**
4   **for** $k = 1$ **to** n **do**
5   **for** $j = 1$ **to** $(m+1)$ **do**
6             $sum_k = sum_k + v_{kj} \; (j \neq l)$
          end
       end
    end
7   **if** $(sum = v_l)$ **then**
8        $w = l; p = i;$
9   **break;**
    end
 end

But, extracting the value of w and p is computationally infeasible from the given vectors. In the following algorithm, we show how a cloud server can attempt to gain insight on the value of w and p and why its attempts are ineffective. Cloud server has $m + 1$ vectors out of which one is a sum vector which the client hid in the matrix at wth position of matrix V. Server may execute Algorithm 1 to find the values of w and p. The complexity of Algorithm 1 is $O(max(l)(m + 1)2)$, where max is the maximum size of integer possible on the client machine. This algorithm seems to be exponential.

4.3   Security Analysis

In this section, we show how the proposed scheme deals with tampering of data by the cloud server and concludes that the results returned are incorrect.

4.3.1   Tampering with the Elements of r

Suppose an element of **r** is tampered as $r_i + t$. Assuming that all other elements in **r** are correctly computed, there are two possibilities.

1. If $i = (m + 1)$, then $S_2 = (S_2 + t) \bmod p$ and the probability of $S_1 = S_2$ is $\frac{1}{max}$ because, if server has knowledge about p then it can make t as a multiple of p and achieve success in making $S_1 = S_2$. But, guessing p correctly has a probability of $\frac{1}{max}$.
2. If $i \neq m + 1$, then $S_1 = (S_1 + t) \bmod p$ and the probability of $S_1 = S_2$ is likewise $\frac{1}{max}$.

4.3.2   Tampering with Elements of u and V

If server computes the results correctly after tampering with the elements of **u**, it has no motivation to tamper with its elements anymore as it is not saving any computations. If it tampers with elements of **V** as $v_{ij} + t$ then, the corresponding inner product will become $r_i + u_j t$. Here also there are two possibilities: $i = (m + 1)$ or $i \neq (m + 1)$. In both cases, the probability of server still cheating the client is $\frac{1}{max}$, as proved previously.

5   Application to Verification of Product of Two Matrices

The proposed scheme can be efficiently applied to verify the result of matrix multiplication. A large number of applications hosted on cloud use matrices, and matrix multiplication is a critical operation in these applications. The following algorithm shows how the scheme can be applied for verification of matrix multiplication.

1. **Input** : Two matrices A and B such that A is a $n \times m$ matrix and B is a $m \times k$ matrix. Precisely, A contains m vectors $\mathbf{v}_i$ ($1 \leq i \leq m$) of dimensionality m. Note that in matrix A, vectors are represented as their transpose for the ease of representation for our scheme.
2. **Output** : **Yes**: If the product is correct; **No**: otherwise.

5.1   Preprocessing

This phase of the scheme deals with the preprocessing carried out on the client side, prior to outsourcing the matrices to the cloud server. Algorithm 2 details the preprocessing. We detail the algorithm in the following steps:

1. Choose a random number p from the integer set $[1, max]$.
2. Append a vector $\mathbf{u_{k+1}}$ to B. $\mathbf{u_{k+1}}$ is calculated as follows :

$$\mathbf{u_{k+1}} = \left[(\textstyle\sum_{i=1}^{k} u_{i1}) \bmod p \ \ (\textstyle\sum_{i=1}^{k} u_{i2}) \bmod p \ \cdots \ (\textstyle\sum_{i=1}^{k} u_{in}) \bmod p \right]^T$$

3. Choose a random number w from the integer set $[1, k + 1]$ and swap $\mathbf{u_{k+1}}$ with $\mathbf{u_w}$.
4. Store w and p and outsource (A, B) to the cloud server.

Algorithm 2. Preprocessing done at client side

    Data : Matrix A and B such that A is a $n \times m$ and B is a $m \times k$ matrix.

1 $w \leftarrow Rand(1, max)$; $p \leftarrow Rand(1, max)$;

    // Choose uniformly at random w and p in the range 1 to max.;

2 **for** $j = 1$ **to** n **do**

3   **for** $i = 1$ **to** m **do**

       $u_j = u_j + u_i$;

     end

  end

4 $u_j = u_j \bmod p$;

5 $Swap(u_{k+1}, u_w)$;   // Swap u_{k+1} and u_w;

5.2 Computation

Computation phase is carried out by the cloud server. To carry out this, Cloud Server gets (A, B) from client, computes $C = A \cdot B$ and returns C to the client.

5.3 Verification

Client has matrix $C = AB$ which is represented as follows :

$$
C = \begin{bmatrix}
v_1.u_1 & v_1.u_2 & \cdot & v_1.u_{k+1} & \cdots & v_1.u_w \\
v_2.u_1 & v_2.u_2 & \cdot & v_2.u_{k+1} & \cdots & v_2.u_w \\
\cdot & \cdot & \cdot & \cdot & \cdots & \cdot \\
\cdot & \cdot & \cdot & \cdot & \cdots & \cdot \\
\cdot & \cdot & \cdot & \cdot & \cdots & \cdot \\
v_m.u_w & v_m.u_w & \cdot & v_m.u_{k+1} & \cdots & v_m.u_w
\end{bmatrix}
$$

Algorithm 3 gives the verification process.

Algorithm 3. Verification

    Data : Matrix C of dimension $m(n + 1)$ and w.

1 **for** $i = 1$ **to** m **do**

2   **for** $j = 1$ **to** n **do**

       $C_i = C_i + C_j$

     end

3     $C_i = C_i \bmod p$;

4   **if** $C_i \neq C_w$ **then**

       return "product is incorrect" ;

     else

       return "product is correct" ;

     end

  end

The details of the algorithm are as below.

1. **for** each row i in C, repeat the following step.
   (a) If $((\sum_{j=1}^{k+1} C[i][j] \, (j \neq w))) \, mod \, p \neq C[i][w] \, mod \, p$ then client can conclude that product is incorrect.
2. If Step 1 holds for all rows then product is correct.

Note that, the preprocessing phase has same time complexity in the case of matrix product verification and inner products verification. However, the *verification* in the case of matrices takes $O(mn)$ additions and $O(n)$ comparisons.

5.4   Comparison

Our proposed verification scheme performs better than the existing scheme by Gang Sheng et al. [20]. The existing scheme takes $O(mn)$ multiplications and $O(mn)$ additions whereas, our scheme takes only $O(mn)$ additions, while verifying the correctness of vector inner products. The verification phase, needs $O(m)$ additions only. The storage required in the proposed scheme is $O(1)$, whereas the existing scheme needs $O(n)$ storage. We also applied the proposed scheme to verify the correctness of product of matrix multiplication. An interesting observation to be made about verifying the product of matrix multiplication is that, it takes the same amount of time in the preprocessing step as it takes while verifying the correctness of vector inner products. The probabilistic bound for the server to break the security of the proposed scheme is $\frac{1}{max}$. The value of max normally on 64 bit systems is 2^{64}. So, $\frac{1}{max}$ is negligible. To support our claim of efficiency over Gang Sheng et al. [20], we implemented our proposed scheme in C++ using *long long int* type integers on a 64-bit Linux operating system. We tested the scheme, by using largest number of vectors possible in the system memory and the results were found to be correct.

6   Conclusion

We have proposed an efficient verification scheme for verifying the results of the vector inner products. The complexity of the preprocessing phase of the proposed scheme is $O(mn)$ without any multiplications and storage required is $O(1)$. The proposed scheme is shown to be efficient than the Gang Sheng et al. scheme. We have proved the correctness of the proposed scheme and discussed the security aspects of the proposed scheme. We have shown that, the probability with which the server can cheat the client is significantly low. Further, we have shown that, by using the proposed inner product verification scheme, the verification of outsourced matrix multiplication can be carried out efficiently. The proposed verification scheme can also be used as a subroutine to any computation which uses vector inner products, for example, similar document detection etc.

References

1. Amazon cloud service. http://aws.amazon.com/ec2/. Accessed 25 April 2014
2. Google cloud service. https://cloud.google.com/. Accessed 25 April 2014

3. IBM cloud service. http://www.ibm.com/cloud-computing/in/en/. Accessed 25 April 2014
4. Microsoft cloud service. http://azure.microsoft.com/en-us/solutions/. Accessed 25 April 2014
5. Red Hat openshift. https://www.openshift.com/. Accessed 25 April 2014
6. VMware cloud service. http://www.vmware.com. Accessed 25 April 2014
7. Ahn, J.H., Boneh, D., Camenisch, J., Hohenberger, S., shelat, A., Waters, B.: Computing on authenticated data. In: Cramer, R. (ed.) TCC 2012. LNCS, vol. 7194, pp. 1–20. Springer, Heidelberg (2012)
8. Barbour, R.L., Barbour, S.L.S., Koo, P.C., Graber, H.L., Chang, J., Aronson, R.: Mri-guided optical tomography: prospects and computation for a new imaging method. Comput. Sci. Eng. **2**(4), 63–77 (1995)
9. Devanbu, P., Gertz, M., Martel, C., Stubblebine, S.G.: Authentic data publication over the internet. J. Comput. Secur. **11**(3), 291–314 (2003)
10. Hequn, X., Dengguo, F.: An integrity checking scheme in outsourced database model. J. Comput. Res. Dev. **47**(6), 1107 (2010)
11. Ku, W.S., Hu, L., Shahabi, C., Wang, H.: A query integrity assurance scheme for accessing outsourced spatial databases. GeoInformatica **17**(1), 97–124 (2013)
12. Li, F., Hadjieleftheriou, M., Kollios, G., Reyzin, L.: Authenticated index structures for aggregation queries. ACM Trans. Inf. Syst. Secur. **13**(4), 32 (2010)
13. Yonglong, L., Liusheng, J.W.H., Weijiang, X.: Privacy protection in the relative position determination for two spatial geometric objects. J. Comput. Res. Dev. **43**(3), 410 (2006)
14. Ma, X., Li, J., Zhang, F.: Efficient and secure batch exponentiations outsourcing in cloud computing. In: 4th International Conference on Intelligent Networking and Collaborative Systems (INCoS), pp. 600–605, September 2012
15. Mell, P., Grance, T.: The nist definition of cloud computing. National Ins. Stand. Technol. **53**(6), 50 (2009)
16. Merkle, R.C.: A certified digital signature. In: Brassard, G. (ed.) CRYPTO 1989. LNCS, vol. 435, pp. 218–238. Springer, Heidelberg (1990)
17. Murugesan, M., Jiang, W., Clifton, C., Si, L., Vaidya, J.: Efficient privacy-preserving similar document detection. VLDB J. **19**(4), 457–475 (2010)
18. Pang, H., Tan, K.L.: Verifying completeness of relational query answers from online servers. ACM Trans. Inf. Syst. Secur. **11**(2), 5:1–5:50 (2008)
19. Papadopoulos, S., Wang, L., Yang, Y., Papadias, D., Karras, P.: Authenticated multistep nearest neighbor search. IEEE Trans. Knowl. Data Eng. **23**(5), 641–654 (2011)
20. Sheng, G., Wen, T., Guo, Q., Yin, Y.: Verifying correctness of inner product of vectors in cloud computing. In: Proceedings of the ACM International Workshop on Security in Cloud Computing, pp. 61–68. New York, NY, USA (2013)
21. Sheng, G., Wen, T., Guo, Q., Yin, Y.: Privacy preserving inner product of vectors in cloud computing. Int. J. Distrib. Sens. Netw. **2014**, 6 (2014). Article ID 537252
22. Vaidya, J., Clifton, C.: Privacy preserving association rule mining in vertically partitioned data. In: Proceedings of the Eighth ACM SIGKDD International Conference on Knowledge Discovery and Data Mining, pp. 639–644 (2002)
23. Wang, H., Yin, J., Perng, C.S., Yu, P.S.: Dual encryption for query integrity assurance. In: Proceedings of the 17th ACM Conference on Information and Knowledge Management, pp. 863–872 (2008)
24. Xie, M., Wang, H., Yin, J., Meng, X.: Integrity auditing of outsourced data. In: Proceedings of the 33rd International Conference on Very Large Data Bases, pp. 782–793 (2007)

FPGA Implementation of 128-Bit Fused Multiply Add Unit for Crypto Processors

Sandeep Kakde$^{(\boxtimes)}$, Mithilesh Mahindra,
Atish Khobragade, and Nikit Shah

Nagpur 440015, India
{sandip.kakde,mithileshmahendra}@gmail.com,
atish_khobragade@rediffmail.com,
NikitPrakash.Shah@utdallas.edu

Abstract. Fused Multiply Add Block is an important module in high-speed math co-processors and crypto processors. The main contribution of this paper is to reduce the latency. The vital components of Fused Multiply Add (FMA) unit with multi-mode operations are Alignment Shifter, Normalization shifter, Multiplier, Dual Adder by Carry Look Ahead Adder. The major technical challenges in existing FMA architectures are latency and higher precision. In order to reduce the latency, the Multiplier is designed by using reduced complexity Wallace Multiplier and the latency of overall architecture gets reduced up to 15–25 %. In this paper, the total delay of multiplier designed using reduced complexity Wallace Multiplier is found to be 37.673 ns. In order to get higher precision, we design explicitly Alignment Shifter and Normalization Shifter in the FMA unit by using Barrel Shifter as this Alignment Shifter and Normalization Shifter will have less precision, but since replacement of these blocks by Barrel Shifter will result into higher precision and the latency is further reduced by 25–35 % and the total delay of Alignment Shifter and Normalization Shifter using Barrel Shifter is found to be 5.845 ns.

Keywords: Floating point arithmetic · Latency · Fused multiply add · Barrel shifter · Crypto processors · Multimode operations

1 Introduction

In order to improve the precision and latency of floating-point results, higher precision floating-point computation is required. IEEE-754 floating-point double precision (64-bit) or extended double precision (80-bit) arithmetic has been implemented in modern processors, but they are becoming insufficient for today's large-scale applications due to the accumulation of errors in computations, this errors increased gradually after many times of floating-point arithmetic operation, resulting in imprecise and incredible computation results and also increased latency. The one promising approach to the precision problem is using the quadruple precision or QP floating-point data format also referred as binary128 as specified in the new IEEE-754-2008 standard [6], consisting of three fields as the 1-bit sign (S), the 15-bit exponent (E) and 112-bit fraction (T) (Refer Fig. 1). Another approach to increase the accuracy is using the

© Springer International Publishing Switzerland 2015
J.H. Abawajy et al. (Eds): SSCC 2015, CCIS 536, pp. 78–85, 2015.
DOI: 10.1007/978-3-319-22915-7_8

Fused Multiply Add. It combines improvements in performance (two operations in a single instruction) and improvements in accuracy (one single rounding) and is fundamental in many multimedia and scientific applications. The bias of exponent is 16383. The fraction of normalized data implies the integer bit as 1, which is not need to presented, so the precision is 113-bit.

2 Previous Work

Literature survey of the related work with reference to the requirements of high precision and high reliable floating-point arithmetic for technical computation shows the proposed architecture of a low-cost binary128 FMA design, which can perform a binary128 FMA operation with a latency of four cycles, or two binary64 FMAs fully pipelined operation with a latency of three cycles, or four binary32 FMAs fully pipelined operation with a latency of three cycles [1]. Another research shows flexible multimode embedded Floating - point unit for FPGAs with dual-precision floating-point adder and multiplier each can perform one double-precision operation or two single-precision operations in parallel [2]. This paper also presented a novel design for a dual-precision floating-point multiplier to show that the FPGA with embedded multimode FPUs provide considerable performance and area benefits in single-precision, double precision, fixed-point, and integer applications when implemented on the latest FPGAs, such as the Xilinx Virtex-5 FPGA. The paper [3] shows the high performance QPFMA with 7-stage pipeline satisfying the requirement of high performance processor. In this proposed work the complement of negative result by using the dual adder and the optimization LZA logic, reducing the data width of LZA and the level of normalization shifter, the hardware overhead and operation latency of the QPFMA is decrease. One more cascade design is proposed [4], which reduce the accumulation dependent latency by 2x over a fused design, at a cost of a 13 % increase in non-accumulation dependent latency. For more latency sensitive applications, a cascade design provides a number of parameters that can be optimized, and in particular, it allows one to create a design with very low effective latency between operations with sum dependence. The reduction in latency depends on two main optimizations: forwarding of unrounded results and tightening the accumulation bypass path by staggering the exponent and mantissa data path of the adder. The paper represents an architecture for the computation of the double-precision floating-point multiply-add fused operation to obtain the reduced latency floating-point addition, in which the alignment shifter, that is in parallel with the multiplier, is moved such that the multiplication can be bypassed, but this modification increases the critical path, a double-data path organization is implemented, in which the alignment shifter and normalization shifter are used in separate paths [5].

3 Proposed Work

In this proposed work, the multiple mode computation such as multiply- add, multiply-sub, multiply-multiply and add-sub has been consider for the implementation.

The major optimization proposed is to design and simulate the reduced latency and high performance multi mode SOC quadruple precision (binary128) floating-point FMA architecture for the FPGA with the decreased latency and high precision. Figure 1 shows the overall architecture of QPFMA with the major components as Multiplier-113 bit, 341 bit Alignment Shifter, 342 bit Normalization Shifter, 342 bit Dual Adder, 228 bit Leading Zero Anticipator and the rounding block. This architecture is computing Quadruple Precision floating-point data operation of $F = A*B + C$. In which alignment shifter is used to align the value of C as per the exponent difference obtain from the exponent difference block, this difference value can vary and cannot be fixed depending on exponent value of A, B and C i.e. E_A, E_B and E_C. To make a synthesizable shifter block we design a shifter by using barrel shifter concept and power of 2. The value of C will get shifted depending on the exponent calculation value. After every shifting the removed bits will generate sticky bit (st) as: If the operation is addition, then the first bit is produced by "OR"ing all the bits of C which is shifted out beyond 341, but if the operation is subtraction, then the sticky bit is produced by ANDing all the bits of C which is shifted out beyond 341 after C bit is inverted.

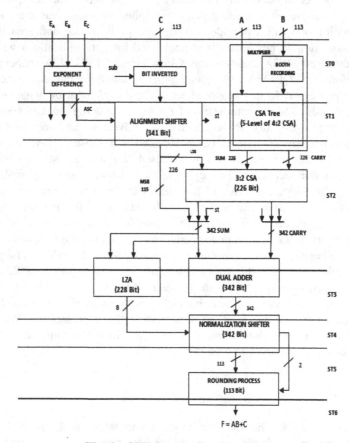

Fig. 1. QPFMA overall architecture

After the generation of sticky bit it is jointed to the least significant bit (LSB) of the Sum output from the 3:2 CSA as shown in Fig. 1, while a sticky bit produced from subtraction is jointed to the LSB of the Carry output from the 3:2 CSA. Then both the correct sticky bit and complement of the addend C can be recognize when Sum and Carry are added. The output of 3:2 CSA is the A and B input to the dual adder, which will add two numbers simultaneously and produce the sum output as the S0 and S1 and carry out (C_{out}). Considering the long latency of 342-bit adder, the dual adder is designed by using both the idea of end-around-carry adder and carry select adder. As in paper [3] it is divided into 3 segments, including two parallel 114-bit adders with the same addends and carry in as 0 and 1 in each segment. The dual adder can calculate out the absolute of (Carry, Sum) directly, avoiding the complement of negative result and reducing the latency of a 342-bit adder [7]. The latency of the dual adder is the latency of a 114-bit adder and a 2:1 multiplex. As the large area size will give very high delay and latency will get increased as observe in [3] the latency of the 342-bit adder is reduced to the latency of 114-bit adder and a 2:1 multiplex by using the dual adder. Therefore in this proposed design the 113-bit multiplier is made up by using reduced complexity Wallace multiplier which will generate two products output simultaneously (Carry, Sum) by multiplying two inputs A and B. This product AB obtained after the

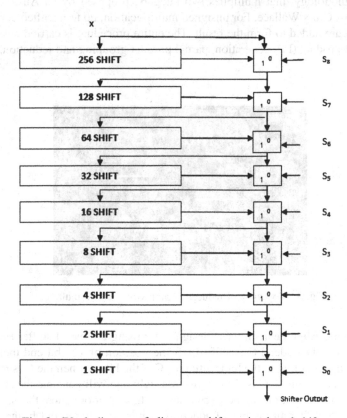

Fig. 2. Block diagram of alignment shifter using barrel shifter

multiplication is then added with the addend C which is available at the alignment shifter it will shift the addend C where as AB is fixed. This alignment shifter is designed by using the barrel shifter as shown in Fig. 2, where depending on the bit of addend C the select lines of MUX is activated and if the bit obtained is one it will shift the data otherwise it is kept as it is and forwarded for further operation to carry save adder and dual adder Due to this the hardware overhead is reduced and thus the delay required is reduced and hence the latency will get reduced.

4   Synthesis and Simulation of Sub-modules

The Multiplier and Alignment shifter are the important part of the fused multiply add architecture in this paper multiplier is designed by using the reduced complexity Wallace Multiplier which has 114 bits input x (0:113) and 114 bits input y (0:113) and will generate product output of 226 bits p (0:225) at a time.

Reduced complexity Wallace Multiplier is the modified version of Standard Wallace Multiplier [8]. The Fig. 3 shows the top view of Reduced Complexity Wallace Multiplier. The Fig. 4 shows the simulation waveform for the reduced complexity Wallace multiplier. A Wallace Multiplier is an easily hardware implementable and efficient methodology, that multiplies two integers, proposed by an Australian Computer Scientist Chris Wallace. For unsigned multiplication, up to n shifted copies of the multiplicand are added to form the result. The entire procedure is carried out into three steps: partial product (PP) generation, partial product grouping and reduction, and final addition.

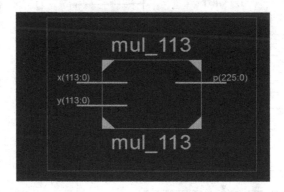

Fig. 3. Top view of reduced complexity Wallace multiplier

Whereas the Alignment shifter is designed by using the barrel shifter as shown in Fig. 5. in which the addend C is shifted left the position of 116 bit and then the C is shifted to right according to the bit position of C if the bit is 0 then the C is not shifted, else if the bit is 1 then the C is shifted towards right and will generate the sticky bit as following: If the operation to be performed is the addition; then the sticky bit is generated by "OR"ing all the bits of addend C which are shifted out further than 341

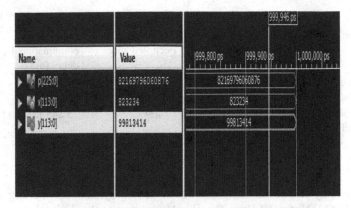

Fig. 4. Simulation result for reduced complexity Wallace multiplier

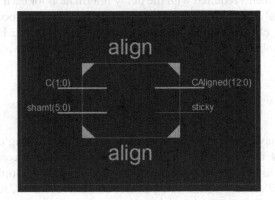

Fig. 5. Top view of alignment shifter using barrel shifter

and sticky bit thus generated is applied to the least significant bit (LSB) of the sum output from the 3:2 carry save adder. While if the operation is subtraction, then the C bit is inverted and the sticky bit is formed by "AND"ing all the bits of C shifted out beyond 341 and sticky bit thus generated is applied to the least significant bit (LSB) of the carry output from the 3:2 CSA. Then both the correct sticky bit and the addend C are applied to the dual adder for addition added. The critical part is to design an alignment shifter for fused multiply add unit.

5 Results

The synthesis result obtained from proposed design of multiplier by using the reduced complexity Wallace Multiplier and the Alignment shifter designed by using the barrel shifter for 128 bit Fused Multiply Add (FMA) unit is as shown in Table 1. All sub modules are first simulated for functional verification. Once all sub modules are simulated, the top level architecture is constructed using structural modeling. The input

Table 1. Compound adder synthesis result

Designed unit	Number of LUT uses as logic	Number of occupied slices	Maximum combinational path delay (ns)
Multiplier using Wallace multiplier	18208	10168	37.673 ns
Alignment shifter using barrel shifter	1236	469	5.845 ns

text file is read by test bench using test bench verilog syntax. The Verilog codes are dumped on FPGA Virtex-VI Kits. The simple way to test the design is to write a test bench that workout various features of the design. The simulation result and the number of logic elements required with the delay information for each design approach is reported and analyzed. The proposed Fused multiply add unit occupies 399 from 474,240 total logic elements which are corresponding to occupying 1 % of total logic elements. The number of bounded IOB's used is 514 from available 1200 thus occupying 42 %.

6 Conclusion

In this paper, we have implemented the design of dual adder using compound adder and emphasize that the total delay of dual adder designed using compound adder is found to be 5.776 ns. The delay for Multiplier using Wallace Multiplier is 37.673 ns and the delay for Alignment Shifter using Barrel Shifter is 5.845 ns. All the blocks are designed using Verilog HDL Language and simulated by Model-Sim 6.0 and Xilinx ISE 13.1 EDA simulators. The simulation and synthesis result indicates that the hardware overhead and the delay are reduced by this design. It will be further optimized by improvement in algorithm to decrease area and latency more. In order to expand this research further, converting the floating-point value into higher value of IEEE 754-2008 quadruple precision floating-point number can be designed automatically, as in this proposed works these values are converted manually. The design can be made in such a manner that it can accommodate any exponent and mantissa length. This will give the design more versatility to use any precision of IEEE binary format also; it can be designed for decimal floating point. The proposed architecture can be used in various embedded applications such as 3D graphics, Image Processing, Automotive Control, Robotics and Motion control.

References

1. Huang, L., Ma, S., Shen, L., Wang, Z., Xiao, N.: Low-cost binary128 floating-point FMA unit design with SIMD support. IEEE Trans. Comput. **61**(5), 745–751 (2012)

2. Chong, Y.J., Parameswaran, S.: Configurable multimode embedded floating-point units for FPGAs. IEEE Trans. Very Large Scale Integr. (VLSI) Syst. **19**(11), 1063–8210 (2011). © 2010 IEEE
3. He, J., Zhu Y.: Design and implementation of a quadruple floating-point fused multiply-add unit. In: Proceedings of the 2nd International Conference on Computer Science and Electronics Engineering (ICCSEE 2013)
4. Galal, S., Horowitz, M.: Latency sensitive FMA design. In: 2011 20th IEEE Symposium on Computer Arithmetic, 1063-6889/11 © 2011 IEEE. doi:10.1109/ARITH.2011.26
5. Bruguera, J.D., Lang, T.: Floating-point fused multiply-add: reduced latency for floating-point addition. In: Proceedings of 17th IEEE Symposium Computer Arithmetic, Hyannis, pp. 27–29. June 2005
6. IEEE Computer Society. IEEE Standard for Floating Point Arithmetic. IEEE Standard 754-2008, 3 Park Avenue New York, NY10016-5997, USA. 29 August 2008
7. Khan, S., Kakde, S., Suryawanshi, Y.: VLSI implementation of reduced complexity Wallace multiplier using energy efficient CMOS Full Adder. In: International Conference on Computational Intelligence and Computing Research-ICCIC 2013, 978-1-4799-1597-2/13©2013 IEEE
8. Khan, S., Kakde, S., Suryawanshi, Y.: Performance analysis of reduced complexity Wallace multiplier using energy efficient CMOS full adder. In: IEEE Sponsored International Conference on Renewable Energy and Sustainable Energy – ICRESE 2013, 978-1-4799-2075-4 © 2013 IEEE
9. Mahindra, M., Kakde, S., Somulu G.: HDL implementation of 128- bit fused multiply add unit for multi mode SoC. In: Proceedings of ICCSP 2013, pp. 451–454, 978-4799-3357-0 ©2013 IEEE

Authentication and Access Control Systems

A Fast Discrete Cosine Transform and a Cryptographic Technique for Authentication and Security of Digital Images

Quist-Aphetsi Kester[1,2,3(✉)], Laurent Nana[1], Anca Christine Pascu[1],
Sophie Gire[3], Jojo M. Eghan[3], and Nii Narku Quaynor[3]

[1] Lab-STICC (UMR CNRS 6285), European University of Brittany,
University of Brest France, Brest, France
Kester.quist-aphetsi@univ-brest.fr, kquist@ieee.org
[2] Faculty of Informatics, Ghana Technology University College, Accra, Ghana
[3] Department of Computer Science and Information Technology,
University of Cape Coast, Cape Coast, Ghana

Abstract. In a cyberspace where disparate applications are engaged in multimedia transmission, data compression is a key for maintaining bandwidth usage efficiency as well meeting the data requirements of the disparate applications. Security of data in such environment needed to be guaranteed. Cryptographic approaches engaged in the process have to be efficient enough to stand against attacks and also to maintain important visual continents after compression. In our work, we proposed a fast discrete cosine transform and a cryptographic technique for authentication and security of digital images. The cryptographic approach was applied to the image after compression, and before decompression, the image was successfully decrypted without significant loss of visual data. There was a loss in pixel values due to the compression process. The implementation of the proposed approach was done successfully and analysis of the output results was done using MATLAB.

1 Introduction

The rise of multimedia applications, ubiquitous systems, internet of things etc. has revolutionized the way development of applications are done as well as the development of devices. Disparate applications access multimedia contents via different media, nodes and through different service providers. Service and content providers ranging from cloud services, data warehousing to open source systems render different forms of multimedia data to users across different platforms and to disparate devices. This enables transmission of multimedia content data across different platforms and hence data security to these media transmitted signals and privacy is needed for ensuring

This work was supported by Lab-STICC (UMR CNRS 6285) Research Laboratory, UBO France, AWBC Canada, Ambassade de France-Institut Français-Ghana and the DCSIT-UCC

© Springer International Publishing Switzerland 2015
J.H. Abawajy et al. (Eds): SSCC 2015, CCIS 536, pp. 89–98, 2015.
DOI: 10.1007/978-3-319-22915-7_9

effective confidentiality. Data secure approaches must render denial of access to data compromisation over communications channels. Due to unauthorized surveillance and malicious activities over the internet, tech companies are challenged in rendering an effective security for the protection and privacy for their clients' data.

2 Review

In ensuring security and privacy for multimedia data storage for applications including images and video, fast and efficient cryptographic schemes are needed for security in both spatial and frequency domains. Transmission of multimedia images over com-munication channels requires compression techniques to reduce bandwidth consump-tion as well as the energy needed for transmission. There have been DCT techniques to security of digital images such as [1–5]. Lin, S.D. and Chin-Feng Chen in their work of a robust DCT-based watermarking for copyright protection proposed a technique for embedding watermarks into a host image in the frequency domain. Their approach embedded the watermark at low frequency and the weighted correction was used to improve the imperceptibility of the watermark. Their Experimental results demon-strated that the proposed method is resistant to some image-processing operations and JPEG compression to some degree [6]. A. Al-Haj in their work also Combined DWT-DCT Digital Image Watermarking. They described an imperceptible and a robust combined DWT-DCT digital image watermarking algorithm using a combination of the Discrete Wavelet Transform (DWT) and the two transforms improved the perfor-mance of the watermarking algorithms that are based solely on the DWT transform [7]. Fouzi Douak et al. in their work proposed Color image compression algorithm based on the DCT transform combined to an adaptive block scanning and in the work they designed a lossy image compression algorithm dedicated to color still images. The DCT transform was applied and followed by an iterative phase (using the bisection method) including the thresholding, the quantization, dequantization, the inverse DCT, YCbCr to RGB transform and the mean recovering [8]. The block diagram of their approach is shown below:

In our approach we proposed a fast discrete cosine transform and a cryptographic technique for authentication and security of digital images. The cryptographic approach

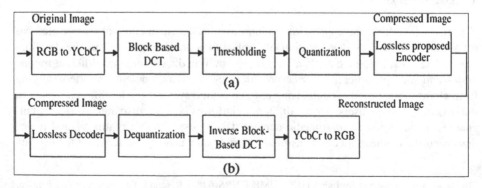

Fig. 1. Block diagram of compression algorithm scheme: (a) compression phase and (b) decompression phase

was applied to the image after compression, and before decompression, the image was successfully decrypted without significant loss of visual data. The proposed method yielded a fully recoverable image after the decryption and decompressing of the ciphered image in the frequency domain. This yielded a lossless operation and restored the image back to its decompressed state (Fig. 1).

3   Methodology

In our approach we first obtain the plain image and compressed it using the fast Discrete Cosine Transform process which yielded a compressed image at the end. After obtaining the compressed image, we engaged it in an encryption process with a key to get a ciphered but compressed image data with a lot of noise. We then reverse the process back to obtain the decompressed decrypted image at the end. The block diagram below illustrate the procedure used (Fig. 2).

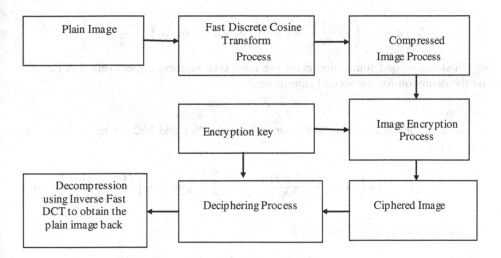

Fig. 2. Block diagram of the proposed approach

There was pixel value change as well as domain change during the compression procedure. This resulted in pixel loss. There was change in the compressed data during the encryption process as well.

3.1   The Fast Discrete Cosine Process

The DCT of a sequence
$$\{x[m], (m=0, \ldots, N-1)\}. \tag{1}$$
We define a new sequence using Fast Fourier Transform to yield,

$$\{y[m], (m=0, \ldots, N-1)\}. \tag{2}$$

$$\begin{cases} y[m] \overset{\Delta}{=} x[2m] \\ y[N-1-m] \overset{\Delta}{=} x[2m+1] \quad (i=0,\cdots,N/2-1) \end{cases} \tag{3}$$

Then the DCT of x[n] is as

$$\sum_{m=0}^{N-1} x[m] \cos\left(\frac{(2m+1)n\pi}{2N}\right)$$

$$\overline{\sum_{m=0}^{N/2-1} x[2m] \cos\left(\frac{(4m+1)n\pi}{2N}\right) + \sum_{m=0}^{N/2-1} x[2m+1] \cos\left(\frac{(4m+3)n\pi}{2N}\right)} \tag{4}$$

$$\sum_{m=0}^{N/2-1} y[m] \cos\left(\frac{(4m+1)n\pi}{2N}\right) + \sum_{m=0}^{N/2-1} y[N-1-m] \cos\left(\frac{(4m+3)n\pi}{2N}\right)$$

First and second summation is for even and odd numbers respectively. Let Eq. (5) be the definition for the second summation.

$$m' \overset{\Delta}{=} N-1-m \tag{5}$$

With the limits of 0 and N/2-1 for m becomes N-1 and N/2 for m' and we can rewrite (5) as

$$\sum_{m'=N/2}^{N-1} y[m'] \cos\left(2n\pi - \frac{(4m'+1)n\pi}{2N}\right) = \sum_{m'=N/2}^{N-1} y[m'] \cos\left(\frac{(4m'+1)n\pi}{2N}\right) \tag{6}$$

The summation in (4) now yields

$$X[n] = \sum_{m=0}^{N-1} y[m] \cos\left(\frac{(4m+1)n\pi}{2N}\right) \tag{7}$$

We then consider the DFT of y[m]:

$$Y[n] = \sum_{m=0}^{N-1} y[m] e^{-j2\pi mn/N} = \sum_{m=0}^{N-1} y[m] \left[\cos\left(\frac{2\pi mn}{N}\right) - j\sin\left(\frac{2\pi mn}{N}\right)\right] \tag{8}$$

Let

$$e^{-jn\pi/2N} = \cos\left(\frac{n\pi}{2N}\right) - j\sin\left(\frac{n\pi}{2N}\right) \tag{9}$$

The real part of the product of (8) and (9) will yield the following below

$$Re[e^{-jn\pi/2N}Y[n]] = \sum_{m=0}^{N-1} y[m] \left[\cos\left(\frac{2\pi mn}{N}\right)\cos\left(\frac{n\pi}{2N}\right) - \sin\left(\frac{2\pi mn}{N}\right)\sin\left(\frac{n\pi}{2N}\right)\right]$$

(10)

$$\sum_{m=0}^{N-1} y[m] \left[\cos\left(\frac{2\pi mn}{N}\right)\cos\left(\frac{n\pi}{2N}\right) - \sin\left(\frac{2\pi mn}{N}\right)\sin\left(\frac{n\pi}{2N}\right)\right] = \sum_{m=0}^{N-1} y[m]\cos\left(\frac{(4m+1)n\pi}{2N}\right)$$

(11)

Trigonometric Identity

$$\cos(\alpha + \beta) = \cos\alpha\cos\beta - \sin\alpha\sin\beta$$

(12)

Based on (13) we can rewrite (10) and (11) as

$$X[n] = Re[\,e^{-jn\pi/2N}Y[n]\,]$$

(13)

Y[n] is the DFT of y[m](defined from x[m]) which can be computed based on FFT using complexity of $O(N\log_2 N)$

3.2 The Encryption Process

For a given host signal defined by A as below in (15) and a given random key K as given in Eq. (16). The key was then used to encrypt the compresses data image

$$A = \begin{bmatrix} x_{11} & x_{12} & x_{13} & x_{14} & \cdots & & x_{1n} \\ x_{21} & x_{22} & & & \cdots & & x_{2n} \\ x_{31} & \cdot & \cdot & & \cdots & & x_{3n} \\ x_{41} & \cdot & & \cdot & \cdots & & x_{4n} \\ \cdot & & & & & & \\ \cdot & & & & & & \\ \cdot & & & & & & \\ x_{m1} & \cdot x_{m2} & x_{m3} & x_{m4} & \cdots & & x_{mn} \end{bmatrix}$$

(14)

For a given message E to be embedded in A we have,

$$K = \begin{bmatrix} x_{11} & x_{12} & x_{13} & x_{14} & \cdots & & x_{1n} \\ x_{21} & x_{22} & & & \cdots & & x_{2n} \\ x_{31} & \cdot & \cdot & & \cdots & & x_{3n} \\ x_{41} & \cdot & & \cdot & \cdots & & x_{4n} \\ \cdot & & & & & & \\ \cdot & & & & & & \\ \cdot & & & & & & \\ x_{m1} & \cdot x_{m2} & x_{m3} & x_{m4} & \cdots & & x_{mn} \end{bmatrix}$$

(15)

Where we obtain the channels of the image as R, G, B $\in$ A,K
(R o G)$_{ij}$ = (R)$_{ij}$. (G)$_{ij}$ and x $\in$ [i, j,m,n] and {x $\in$ I: 1 $\leq$ x $\leq$+∞}
For x $\in$ [R, G, B]: [a, b] = {x $\in$ I: a $\leq$ x $\geq$ b} where a = 0 and b = 255

$$R = r = A\,(m, n, 1)$$
$$G = g = A\,(m, n, 1)$$
$$B = b = A\,(m, n, 1)$$

(16)

Let [c, p] = s(R); is the size of R as [c, p] and s(R) = size of R be [row, column] = size (R) = R (c x p). Let the encrypting A with K will be

```
for i=1:1:cl
            for j=1:1:pl
            if(cl<c)
                        R(i,j)= f_R(Eij, Kij)
                        G(i,j)= f_G(Eij, Kij)
                        B(i,j)= f_B(Eij, Kij)
                  else
            end
      end
end
```

Finally the data will be converted into an image format to get the encrypted image and f_R(Eij, Kij) f_B(Eij, Kij) and f_B(Eij, Kij) are functions enciphering the image.

4   Results and Analysis

The image below of dimension 640 × 480 pixels obtained from a UAV, vertical and horizon resolution of 72 dpi and bit depth of 24was operated on by the proposed process and the following results were obtained from it (Figs. 3, 4, 5, 6, 7, 8, 9, 10, 11, and 12).

Fig. 3. The plain Image

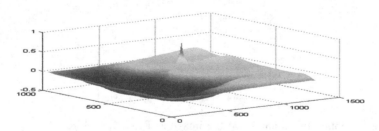

Fig. 4. The graph of the normalized cross-correlation of the matrices of the plain Image

Fig. 5. The compressed plain image

Fig. 6. The graph of the normalized cross-correlation of the matrices of the compressed image

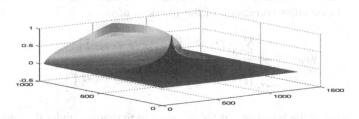

Fig. 7. The ciphered image

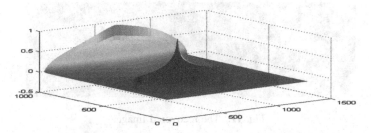

Fig. 8. The graph of the normalized cross-correlation of the matrices of the ciphered image

Fig. 9. The loss image

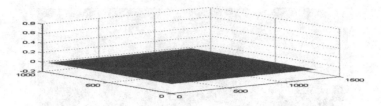

Fig. 10. The graph of the normalized cross-correlation of the matrices of the loss image

Fig. 11. The recovered Image

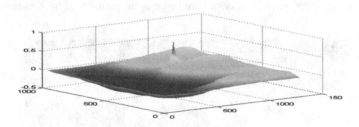

Fig. 12. The graph of the normalized cross-correlation of the matrices of the recovered image

The graph of the normalized cross-correlation of the matrices of the image
The normalized cross-correlation of the matrices of is

$$\gamma(u,v) = \frac{\sum_{x,y}\left[f(x,y)-\bar{f}_{u,v}\right]\left[t(x-u,y-v)-\bar{t}\right]}{\left\{\sum_{x,y}\left[f(x,y)-\bar{f}_{u,v}\right]^{2}\sum_{x,y}\left[t(x-u,y-v)-\bar{t}\right]^{2}\right\}^{0.5}} \tag{17}$$

f is the mean of the template, $\bar{t}$ is the mean of in the region under the template. $\bar{f}_{u,o}$ is the mean of $f(u,v)$ in the region under the template (Table 1).

PI = Plain Image
CI = Compressed Image
ECI = Encrypted Compressed Image
LI is the loss image.
DCI = Decompressed Image
RPI = Recovered Image

Table 1. Extracted features from the process.

Heading level	Entropy	Arithmetic mean
PI	7.1726	125.8132
CI	1.4686	5.74.26
ECI	1.1705	14.3430
DI	1.4686	5.7426
LI	2.3448	1.6031
DCI	7.8375	125.8132
RPI	7.8375	125.8132

5 Conclusion

The implementation showed to be very successful, the complexity time of the image cryptographic technique is O (N) with space complexity of O (1). The complexity of the DCT factoring fast furrier transforms is O (N log N) with complexity of O (1). From the table, it can clearly be seen that the arithmetic mean and the entropy values are comparatively good. The process was successful and fast and the decompressed image was successfully recovered from the ciphered image and compressed image. The approach showed to be effective against brute force attack.

Acknowledgments. This work was supported by Lab-STICC (UMR CNRS 6285) at UBO France, AWBC Canada, Ambassade de France-Institut Français-Ghana and the DCSIT-UCC, and also Dominique Sotteau (formerly directeur de recherche, Centre national de la recherche scientifique (CNRS) in France and head of international relations, Institut national de recherche en informatique et automatique, INRIA) and currently the Scientific counselor of AWBC.

References

1. Kang, H., Iwamura, K.: Information hiding method using best DCT and wavelet coefficients and itswatermark competition. Entropy **17**(3), 1218–1235 (2015)
2. Tomar, R., Patni, J.C., Dumka, A., Anand, A.: Blind watermarking technique for grey scale image using block level discrete cosine transform (DCT). In: Satapathy, S.C., Govardhan, A., Srujan Raju, K., Mandal, J.K. (eds.) Emerging ICT for Bridging the Future-Proceedings of the 49th Annual Convention of the Computer Society of India CSI Volume 2, vol. 338, pp. 81–89. Springer, Heidelberg (2015)
3. Dumas, J.G., Roch, J.L., Tannier, E., Varrette, S.: Foundations of Coding: Compression, Encryption, Error Correction. Wiley, New Jersey (2015)
4. Ji, X.Y., Bai, S., Guo, Y., Guo, H.: A new security solution to JPEG using hyper-chaotic system and modified zigzag scan coding. Commun. Nonlinear Sci. Numer. Simul. **22**(1), 321–333 (2015)
5. Furqan, A., Kumar, M.: Study and analysis of robust DWT-SVD domain based digital image watermarking technique using MATLAB. In: 2015 IEEE International Conference on Computational Intelligence and Communication Technology (CICT), pp. 638–644. IEEE, February 2015

6. Lin, S.D., Chen, C.-F.: A robust DCT-based watermarking for copyright protection. IEEE Trans. Consum. Electron. **46**(3), 415–421 (2000). doi:10.1109/30.883387
7. Al-Haj, A.: Combined DWT-DCT digital image watermarking. J. Comput. Sci. **3**(9), 740 (2007)
8. Douak, F., Benzid, R., Benoudjit, N.: Color image compression algorithm based on the DCT transform combined to an adaptive block scanning. AEU-Int. J. Electron. Commun. **65**(1), 16–26 (2011)

Anonymizing Classification Data
for Preserving Privacy

Sarat kr. Chettri[1(✉)] and B. Borah[2]

[1] Department of Computer Science Engineering and Information Technology,
Assam Don Bosco University, Guwahati, India
sarat.chettri@dbuniversity.ac.in
[2] Department of Computer Science and Engineering,
Tezpur University, Tezpur, India
bgb@tezu.ernet.in

Abstract. Classification of data with privacy preservation is a fundamental problem in privacy preserving data mining. The privacy goal requires concealing the sensitive information that may identify certain individuals breaching their privacy, whereas the classification goal requires to accurately classifying the data. One way to achieve both is to anonymize the dataset that contains the sensitive information of individuals before getting it released for data analysis. Microaggregation is an efficient privacy preservation technique used by statistical disclosure control community as well as data mining community to anonymize a dataset. It naturally satisfies k-anonymity without resorting to generalisations or suppression of data. In this paper we propose a new method named Microaggregation based Classification Tree (*MiCT*). In *MiCT* method data are perturbed prior to its classification and we use tree properties to achieve the objective of privacy preserving classification of data. To evaluate the effectiveness of the proposed method we have conducted experiments on real life data and proved that our method provides improved classification accuracy by preserving privacy.

Keywords: Microaggregation · Classification tree · Mixed data · Data privacy · Classification accuracy · Anonymity

1 Introduction

The concern about data security and privacy is growing day by day. With the advancement of computer technologies there is a huge paradigm shift in a way data are collected, stored and analysed. There is a large-scale data sharing among scientists, businesses organisations, governmental agencies, medical practitioners, data analysts etc. for different purposes. However, to manage this huge amount of data the tools and technologies that are being developed are not adequate to provide security or privacy measures. The reasons for this can be the adequacy of policies to ensure compliance with current approaches to security and privacy. Furthermore, there is either accidental or intentional breach in security or privacy of data, thus requiring to have efficient approaches to prevent data leakage. For example with Hadoop it is now easy for an

J.H. Abawajy et al. (Eds): SSCC 2015, CCIS 536, pp. 99–109, 2015.
DOI: 10.1007/978-3-319-22915-7_10

organization to manage the large volumes of data being generated every day, but at the same time it raises the problems related to security, data access, monitoring and their high availability. When dataset is being shared for analysis, it becomes an important issue to protect the privacy of individuals as information in the dataset may be personal and sensitive in nature. As shown in [1] there exist various kinds of threats to individuals' privacy with high risks of data disclosure. To this, many countries are enacting new laws and have strict legislation against such privacy breaches for example privacy regulation Health Insurance Portability and Accountability Act (HIPAA) in USA. Thus, the major challenge is how to perform various data analyses keeping the sensitivity of the information intact. So, there arises a need of a technique which can effectively protects individual's data and makes the released data useful for analyses.

Privacy preserving data mining (PPDM) aims at achieving a better trade-off between the quality of the mining result with improved privacy preservation. In this context Sweeney [2] has introduced the concept of k-anonymity which resists data linkage attack. The notion of k-anonymity is to make a dataset anonymous so that the probability of uniquely identifying an individual's record in the dataset is at most $1/k$. But k-anonymity method resorts to generalisation or suppression of data where generalization replaces a value with a less specific but semantically consistent value, and suppression does not release a value at all. There exists a drawback with generalisation, as the domain hierarchy tree has to be generated manually [3, 4] while suppression technique induces major information loss by suppressing the data value reducing its utility [5]. To overcome these drawbacks, Statistical Disclosure Control (SDC) method [6], microaggregation has been proposed naturally satisfying k-anonymity. The method modifies the dataset before its release and being perturbative in nature, the major challenge is to how to perform the modification so that both privacy risk and information loss caused due to data modification is low as possible. Maximum Distance to Average Vector 2 k (*MDAV2k*) [7] is an efficient multivariate variable-sized microaggregation method for protection of microdata i.e. protection of data related to individual or organization.

In this paper, we deal with the problem of anonymizing mixed data (continuous and categorical data) to preserve its privacy and perform the data anonymization in such a way that that we get a maximal accuracy while performing the data classification. To achieve the objective we propose a new method named Microaggregation based Classification Tree (*MiCT*) which uses tree properties and perturbs data. The anonymized dataset can be then shared to an analyst/user to train and develop classifier models using the anonymous data. There exist related methods in literature, namely Top Down Specialization (*TDS*) method [8] and its improved version Top Down Refinement (*TDR*) method [9] by Fung et al. Both the methods handle mixed data but it incurs huge loss in data utility due to data value suppression in the anonymous dataset. Friedman et al. [10] has proposed *KADET* where the author tried to combine k-anonymity concept with decision tree. Similar approach has been taken by Sharkey et al. [11] in *APT* method. But using the methods, we get an anonymous decision tree rather an anonymous dataset, this does not match our purpose. In this line, Kisilevich et al. has proposed a k-anonymity classification tree based suppression (*kACTUS*) [12] and its version *kACTUS 2* [13] builds an anonymous dataset by applying k-anonymity on decision tree, but it reduces the trade-off between the constraints of k-anonymity and classification accuracy. Typically both the methods uses suppression technique.

2 Related Concepts and Problem Formulation

The following are some of the related concepts to the article along with the formulation of the problem.

Definition 1 (Quasi-identifier). As shown in [14]. "A quasi-identifier (QI) is a set of attributes in a dataset D such that the combinations of attributes can be used to uniquely identify a particular record in D by linking with external information. E.g. zip code, age, designation etc.".

Definition 2 (k-anonymity). As shown in [14]. "A dataset D is said to satisfy k-anonymity for k > 1 if for each combinations of attributes of quasi-identifier (QI), there exist at least k records in D which cannot be distinguished from at least (k-1) other records".

Definition3 (Decision Tree). Decision tree builds a classification or regression model in the form of tree like structure, which mainly consists of decision nodes and leaf nodes. Based on certain score value the best attribute is selected for splitting and leaf node gives the value of the target attribute.

Table 1. Maximum distance to average vector 2k (*MDAV2k*) method

Algorithm : *MDAV2k*
1. Locate the most distant record x_r from the centroid x of the dataset D.
2. Find $2k$ nearest records of x_r, say $(y_1, y_2 ... y_{2k})$ and form a group g_i around x_r with the $(k-1)$ other nearest records.
3. Compute centroid x_i of the formed grouped g_i and compute distances d_1 from x_i to x_r and d_2 from x_i to y_j where $j = k$.
4. From y_j locate $(k-1)$ nearest records and find a centroid z of the grouped formed around y_j.
5. Get the distance d_3 from z to y_j and then find the gain factor $\gamma = d_3 = d_1$. Set $\gamma = 1 + 1/(5 + \gamma)$ if $\gamma > 1$.
6. Record y_j is inserted into group g_i if $(d_2 < \gamma\delta_3)$.
7. Check if group $|g_i| < 2k$ then go to step 3 taking next $(k+1)$ nearest record of x_r.
8. Repeat through step 1 if there remains at least $3k$ records to form any group.
9. If there remains at least $2k$ records not belonging to any group then repeat the steps 1 and 2.
10. Form a new group with the remaining records.

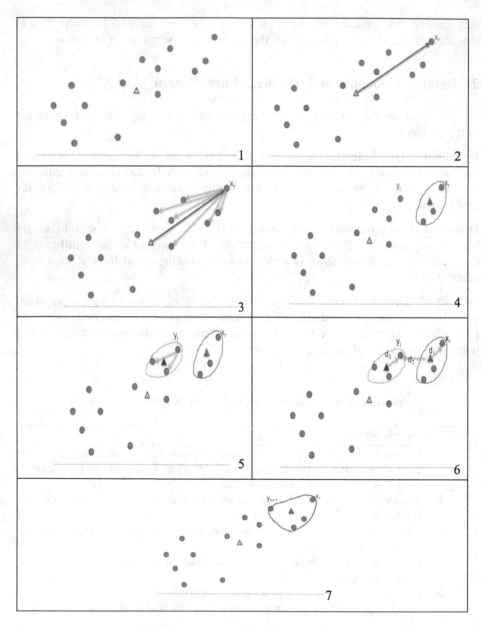

Fig. 1. Stepwise graphical representation of *MDAV2k* method where dots represents record, arrow represent distance measurement and triangle represents group's centroid ($k = 3$).

Definition 4 (Complying and Non-complying Nodes of Decision Tree). Given a decision tree T we construct a set S_1 with attributes by following the tree branch from the root node R_1 to leaf node L_1. If S_1 satisifies k-anonymity over quasi-identifier QI_1, we term it as complying node otherwise it is termed as non-complying node of decision tree.

2.1 Similarity Measurement

Let $X = \{x_1, x_2, x_3 \ldots x_q, x_{q+1}, x_{q+2} \ldots x_m\}$ and $Y = \{y_1, y_2, y_3 \ldots y_q, y_{q+1}, y_{q+2} \ldots y_m\}$ be two tuples with q numerical attributes and m categorical attributes. As shown in [14] the similarity comparison between mixed data is calculated as

$$d_m(X, Y) = d_n\left(x_{1 \ldots q}, y_{1 \ldots q}\right) + \gamma_b d_c\left(x_{q+1 \ldots m}, y_{q+1 \ldots m}\right) \tag{1}$$

Where, d_n represents Euclidean distance for numerical attributes and d_c gives the simple matching distance measure of categorical attributes. In order to have a balanced proportion of numerical and categorical attributes, we computed coefficient γ_b as the standard deviation of numerical attributes in D.

Our primary objective is to modify/transform the dataset D, so that classification performance of the classifier models built on the D and its modified version D' respectively is similar. With this as an objective, our proposed method *MiCT* produces a modified dataset D' from D by microaggregating only the non-complying nodes using *MDAV2k* method [7] (Table 1). The graphical representation of *MDAV2k* method is shown in Fig. 1. Given $k \in [2,n]$, a dataset D with attribute set $A = \{a_1, a_2, a_3 \ldots a_n\}$ with labeled instance C, the aim is to make an optimal modification $M{:}D \rightarrow D'$ such that records in D becomes k anonymous with better data utility in terms of classification.

3 Proposed Method

In our proposed approach we construct a classification tree using standard C4.5 algorithm with the quasi-identifiers (Definition 1) from the original dataset D. Once we have the classification model built on the original dataset, we build an equivalence class C of complying nodes and Q of non-complying nodes (Definition 4) for a given k value. We then perform the microaggregation on Q using *MDAV2k* method. If there does not exist any non-complying nodes in the tree then we can say that the dataset D is k anonymous (Definition 2) (Tables 2 and 3).

Table 2. Microaggregation based classification tree (*MiCT*) method

Algorithm : *MiCT*
Input: A classification tree T built over dataset D, virtual Quasi identifier $\{VQID_1, VQID_2 \ldots VQID_l\}$ and k
Output: Modified Dataset D'
1. For each attribute i in the $VQID_j$ do
2. Find the complying nodes C_n and non-complying nodes N_c for each hierarchical level l of T.
3. Construct two equivalence classes C with complying nodes and Q with the non-complying nodes.
4. End For
5. Using *MDAV2k* microaggregate Q to Q'
6. Compute D' as $C \cup Q'$
7. Return D'

Table 3. Classification tree construction algorithm.

Algorithm : Classification Tree Construction
Input: A dataset D
Output: A classification tree T
1. Find the Class frequency.
2. If there is only one class then return a leaf node.
3. For each attribute A in dataset D
4. Compute the Score (Eqn. 2) to find the attribute having highest score for splitting, let it be A_best .
5. Get a decision node obtained by splitting on A_best.
6. Add those nodes by performing a recourse on the sub lists obtained by splitting on A_best.

Given a classification tree T, and an anonymity requirement on virtual quasi-identifiers, $\{<VQID_1; k>; ::::; <VQID_p; K>\}$, for attributes in Q, microaggregate T. We used the concept of virtual identifier to find the non-complying nodes in each level of tree T (Fig. 2).

To determine the attribute A_best as a decision node, we have computed a Score as

$$Score(A) = \begin{cases} \frac{Infogain(A)}{Anonymity\_loss(A)} & if\ Anonymity\_loss \neq 0 \\ Infogain(A) & Otherwise \end{cases} \quad (2)$$

Where,

$$Infogain(A) = I(CurrentSet) - I(ChildSet)$$

$$I(Set) = -\frac{p}{p+n}log_2\left(\frac{p}{p+n}\right) - \frac{n}{p+n}log_2\left(\frac{p}{p+n}\right)$$

n = number of negative samples
p = number of positive samples

$$Anonymityloss(A) = min\sum_i N_{cl}$$

N_{cl} = number of non-complying nodes in level l

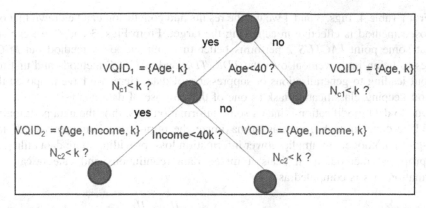

Fig. 2. Graphical representation of classification tree construction with virtual quasi-identifiers at every level.

4 Experimental Data and Results

For experimental purpose we have implemented the proposed method *MiCT* in C under Linux environment. The standard datasets used are the German Credit and Adult dataset form the UCI machine learning repository [15].

Adult dataset consist of two classes for classification which is used to predict whether income of an individual obtained from census report exceeds $50 thousand per year or not. German Credit dataset is used in finance domain where people are classified as good or bad credit risks. After cleaning the datasets, z-score method is used to normalize. Table 4 gives the description of the datasets and their original classification accuracy (C4.5 classifier) obtained using Weka tool (version 3.7.9).

Table 4. Datsets descritpion and their classification accuracy

Dataset	No. of instances	Continuous	Categorical	Original Classification Accuracy of C4.5
Adult	30162	8	6	85.66
German Credit	1000	7	13	71.67

The goals of our experimental study can be stated as follows:

1. To make a comparison of classification accuracies of the models built on original and anonymized datasets respectively.
2. To compare the effectiveness of the proposed method when compared to the existing methods based on classification accuracy made on the anonymized datasets.
3. To access the data utility in terms of information loss incurred due to data anonymization and the risk of data disclosure of the anonymized dataset once it gets released to public for analyses.

From Table 4, Figs. 3 and 4 we get the results and conclusion can be drawn that out proposed method is effective in achieving the target. From Figs. 3 and 4, we can see that at some point *kACTUS* 2 performs better than our proposed method but *MiCT* proves to be an improvement over the *TDR, TDS* and *kACTUS* methods and that too without leading to generalisations or suppression of data. Here, we have proposed the method keeping classification task as one of the purpose of data analysis.

Due to data modification it incurs some information loss, thus the data partitioning should be done in such a way as to maximize the intra-group homogeneity. Higher intra-group homogeneity implies lower information loss, providing more data utility. In our proposed method, as it deals it mixed data (continuous and categorical) the information loss is computed as

$$Information\ Loss(IL) = \frac{IL_n + IL_c}{2} \tag{3}$$

Where, IL_n is the ratio between sum of square error (SSE) and total sum of square (SST) of the continuous attributes in the dataset [17]. IL_c is the information loss incurred on categorical attributes, which is computed as

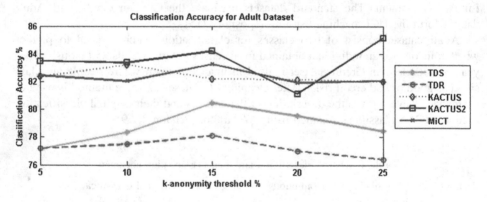

Fig. 3. Classification accuracy comparison on modified Adult dataset

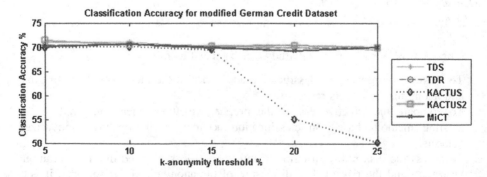

Fig. 4. Classification accuracy comparison on modified German credit dataset

$$IL_c = \frac{1}{g}\sum_{i=1}^{g} \frac{d_c(X_i, \bar{X}_i)}{|C_i|}.100 \qquad (4)$$

Where, g is the number of groups, X_i denotes the i-th categorical attribute, $\bar{X}_i$ is the mode of the group C_i, d_c denotes the simple matching distance measure among categorical attribute, $|C_i|$ denotes the number of categorical attributes in group C_i .

Figure 5 gives the information loss (Eq. 3) incurred by modifying/anonymizing the dataset D for different values of k. Now to access the security provided to the datasets by our proposed method we measured its data disclosure risk using the Distance Linkage Disclosure Risk (DLD) model [16]. As in [14], "it can be defined as for any anonymized record R' in an anonymized dataset D' if we compute a distance to the records in the original dataset D, we may get a nearest record R_1 and a second nearest record R_2. If either R_1 or R_2 turns out to be the original record R in the dataset D, then we call the record R a linked record". Let n_l be the number of records which can be linked in an anonymized dataset D' and N is the total number of records in D' then DLD is computed as

$$DLD = \frac{n_l}{N}.100 \qquad (5)$$

Figure 5 shows the percentage of risk of data disclosure (Eq. 5) even after anonymizing data for various k values. We also observe that for a given k-anonymity threshold value, with the increase in information loss, the risk of data disclosure of the anonymized datasets decreases and the reverse. A trade-off between these two parameters needs to be balanced.

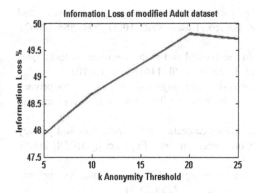
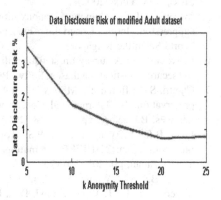

Fig. 5. Information loss and data disclosure risk of modified Adult dataset for different k threshold value.

5 Conclusions

In this paper, we have proposed a new method *MiCT* for privacy preservation of data during their classification using the concept of microaggregation. The method is based on multivariate data-oriented microaggregation method using tree concept, which anonymizes dataset prior to its release without resorting to generalization or suppression. The proposed method provides a good predictive performance using C4.5 classifier while comparing to the existing state of-the-art methods with less information loss and minimal risk of data disclosure. Experimental results on standard datasets shows that improved distance measurement for mixed data can partition the dataset effectively. As a future work, issues are regarding extensions of the proposed work in relation to data clustering and association rule mining and measuring the effectiveness of the proposed method in response to various attack techniques.

References

1. Aggarwal, C.C., Pei, J., Zhang, B.: On privacy preservation against adversarial data mining. In: 12th ACM SIGKDD International Conference on Knowledge Discovery and Data Mining - KDD 2006, pp. 501–516. ACM Press, New York (2006)
2. Sweeney, L.: k-anonymity: a model for protecting privacy. Int. J. Uncertainty, Fuzziness Knowl. Based Syst. **10**(5), 1–14 (2002)
3. Wang, K., Yu, P.S., Chakraborty, S.: Bottom-up generalization: a data mining solution to privacy protection. In: 4th IEEE International Conference on Data Mining, pp. 205–216 (2004)
4. Iyengar, S.V.: Transforming data to satisfy privacy constraints. In: 8th ACM SIGKDD International Conference on Knowledge Discovery and Data Mining, pp. 279–288. ACM Press, New York (2002)
5. Sweeney, L.: Achieving k-anonimity privacy protection using generalization and suppression. Int. J. Uncertainty Fuzziness Knowl. Based Syst. **10**(5), 571–588 (2002). World Scientific Singapore
6. Fayyoumi, E.: A survey on statistical disclosure control and micro-aggregation techniques for secure statistical databases. Softw. Pract. Experience **40**, 1161–1188 (2010)
7. Chettri, S.K., Borah, B.: MDAV2K : a variable-size microaggregation technique for privacy preservation. In: International Conference on Information Technology Convergence and Services, Bangalore, pp. 105–118 (2012)
8. Fung, B.C.M., Wang, K., Yu, P.S.: Top-down specialization for information and privacy preservation. In: 21st IEEE International Conference on Data Engineering (ICDE 2005), Tokyo, Japan, pp. 205–216 (2005)
9. Fung, B.C.M., Wang, K., Yu, P.S.: Anonymizing classification data for privacy preservation. IEEE Trans. Knowl. Data Eng. **19**(5), 711–725 (2007)
10. Friedman, A., Wolff, R., Schuster, A.: Providing k-anonymity in data mining. Int. J. Very Large Data Bases **17**(4), 789–804 (2008)
11. Sharkey, P., Tian, H., Zhang, W., Xu, S.: Privacy-preserving data mining through knowledge model sharing. In: Bonchi, F., Malin, B., Saygın, Y. (eds.) PInKDD 2007. LNCS, vol. 4890, pp. 97–115. Springer, Heidelberg (2008)

12. Kisilevich, S., Elovici, Y., Shapira, B., Rokach, L.: Efficient multidimensional suppression for k-anonymity. IEEE Trans. Knowl. Data Eng. **22**(3), 334–347 (2010)
13. Kisilevich, S., Elovici, Y., Shapira, B., Rokach, L.: kACTUS 2: privacy preserving in classification tasks using k-anonymity. In: Gal, C.S., Kantor, P.B., Lesk, M.E. (eds.) Protecting Persons While Protecting the People. LNCS, vol. 5661, pp. 63–81. Springer, Heidelberg (2009)
14. Chettri, S.K., Borah, B.: An efficient microaggregation method for protecting mixed data. In: Chaki, N., Meghanathan, N., Nagamalai, D. (eds.) Computer Networks and Communications (NetCom). LNEE, vol. 131, pp. 551–561. Springer, New York (2013)
15. Frank, A., Asuncion, A., Asuncion, A., Newman, D.J.: UCI Machine Learning Repository. University of California, School of Information and Computer Science, Irvine, CA (2010). http://mlearn.ics.uci.edu/MLRepository.html
16. Pagliuca, D.: Some results of individual ranking method on the system of enterprise accounts annual survey. Esprit SDC Project, Deliverable MI-3/ D (1999)
17. Domingo-Ferrer, J., Martinez-Balleste, A., Mateo-sanz, J.M., Sebé, F.: Efficient multivariate data-oriented microaggregation. VLDB J. **15**(4), 355–369 (2006)

An Optimal Authentication Protocol Using Certificateless ID-Based Signature in MANET

Vimal Kumar$^{(\boxtimes)}$ and Rakesh Kumar

Department of Computer Science and Engineering,
Madan Mohan Malaviya University of Technology, Gorakhpur 273010, U.P., India
{vimalmnnit16,rkiitr}@gmail.com

Abstract. Mobile Ad hoc Network (MANET) is a matter of great concern and an emerging research field of ubiquitous computing. Nowadays, security issues regarding MANETs are gaining remarkable research interest. MANET is more vulnerable to the security attacks by resource constraints. An ID based cryptography allows an user to generate their public keys without exchanging any certificates. In above scheme, public/private key can be construct without exchanging any certificate. The idea of bilinear pairings make the system efficient and easy to providing basic security. In order to provide secure communication in MANET, many researchers used different schemes to provide authentication. However, existing techniques have drawbacks such as forgery on adaptive chosen plain text message and back secrecy in traditional authentication schemes. In this paper, we work on an ID based signature scheme for achieving reliability and secure authentication in MANET. We show that proposed id based signature scheme is secure against forgery attack in the random oracle model under the Inverse-Computational Diffie-Hellman Problem (Inv-CDHP) assumption. Proposed scheme is more efficient in term of computation than other traditional schemes.

Keywords: MANET · ID-Based · Authentication · Digital signature · Bilinear pairing

1 Introduction

The main challenges of MANETs [1] are providing security for infrastructureless networks and more difficult to manage the cryptography key without use of any central authority (CA). Several mobile ad hoc network routing protocols such as Ad hoc On-Demand Distance Vector(AODV) [2] and Dynamic Source Routing (DSR)[3] were designed without use of any security mechanism. However, MANET routing systems face various security attacks from IP spoofing attacks to more complex rushing attacks. Providing good level of security to MANET with little consumption of bandwidth and low cost of computation has become an open challenge for security researchers. Designing a security protocol/algorithm for MANET is very difficult task due to their inherent characteristics [1], namely lack of central autority(CA), shared broadcast medium, insecure

© Springer International Publishing Switzerland 2015
J.H. Abawajy et al. (Eds): SSCC 2015, CCIS 536, pp. 110–121, 2015.
DOI: 10.1007/978-3-319-22915-7_11

operational environment, lack of association among nodes, physical vulnerability and limited resource constraints. MANETs are more vulnerable than wired network. Problem in distribution public/private key is another aspect of MANET Security [4, 5].

1.1 Taxonomy of Security Attacks

Figure 1 depicts taxonomy of security attacks [6, 7] in MANET. It is dividedinto two broad categories of security attacks, namely active and passive. A passive attacker cannot modify transmitted message while an active attacker attempts to insert or modify messages being exchanged between two nodes.

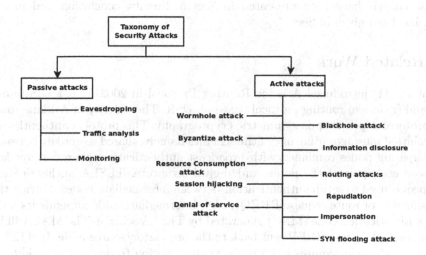

Fig. 1. Taxonomy of security attacks

Digital signature [8] is a popular scheme for information security. It is used for ensuring integrity, authentication and non-repudiation in MANET. Some security goals achieved by digital signature schemes are:

- **Integrity:** Transmitted message can not be altered by any malicious node. In other words, data sent by a sender node should reach without any modification to a recievier node.
- **Authentication:** It enables a node that must know the identity originator/peer node. Communicating without authentication can compromised with security measures and attacker could gain sensitive information and it could interfere with other nodes.
- **Non-repudiation:** Non-repudiation guarantees that sender/receiver of a message can not deny having sent/recieved of a message. Digital signature is most popular technique for ensuring non-repudiation.

Shamir [9] gave a most popular concept of Identity-based (ID-based) cryptosystem and ID based signature scheme. It reduces computational costs and this protocol enables public key to be used without exchanging certificates by the users. After discovery of this stream in cryptography, several ID based signature schemes have been proposed.

In this paper, we work on an ID based signature scheme which tackles the problems of forgery and computational costs in MANET. Security in proposed signature scheme under the inv-CDHP assumption [10].

The structure of the paper is organized as follows: The related works are explained in Sect. 2 while some preliminaries have been given under Sect. 3. Proposed scheme has been presented in Sect. 4. Proof of correctness and security analysis have been given under Sect. 5 while its performance evaluation and result analysis have been presented in Sect. 6. Finally, conclusion and future work has been given in Sect. 7.

2   Related Work

Hu et al. [11] introduced Ariadne Routing Protocol in 2002. It is a secure on-demand (reactive) routing protocol based on DSR. The sceurity of Aridane routing protocol depends upon symmetric cryptography. This protocol authenticates transmitted messages using one of the schemes namely, shared secret key between participating nodes combined with broadcast authentication, shared secret key between each pair of the nodes and digital signature. TESLA authentication protocol is used to setup authentication between intermediate nodes. During the transmission of route request(RREQ), each intermediate node appends its message authentication code (MAC) generated by TESLA scheme. The MAC will be authenticated when a RREP sent back to the originator/source node. In TESLA scheme, each node requires loose time synchronization to decide the validity of TESLA keys, which becomes major drawbacks of Aridane routing protocol.

Sanzgiri et al. [12] gave an authenticated routing protocol (ARAN) for MANET, which is based on AODV reactive routing protocols. In ARAN, each participating/intermediate node has a public key certificate signed by a trusted party, which associates its logical address with public key. ARAN uses asymmetric cryptography for ensuring authentication. It is more vulnerable to denial of service(DoS) attack due to flooding the harmfull packets in entire netwok.

Zapata et al. [13] gave a secure AODV (SAODV) routing protocol. It uses digital signature scheme to authenticate several fields such as RREP, RREQ and Hash chain used for authenticate hop count. Each originator/source node signs its own public key with transmitted message. The Key distribution problem in MANET is loosely solved by some compromise in security.

3   Preliminaries

In this section, we discuss bilinear pairing properties and also some realated problems [14–16].

Bilinear Pairing: Consider two groups G_1 and G_2 of same order q. Let $(G_1, +)$ be a additive cyclic group generated by P and $(G_2, *)$ be a multiplicative cyclic group generated by g.

Pairing: e: $G_1{}^*G_1 \rightarrow G_2$ with the following properties:

- **Bilinearity:** $\forall$ a, b$\in Z_{q*}$ and $\forall$P, Q$\in$G$_1$: $e(aP, bQ) = e(P,Q)^{ab}$.
- **Non-Degeneracy:** There exists $\forall P, Q \in$G$_1$ such that e(P,Q)$\neq$1, in other words all pairs of P,Q do not mapped to the identity in G_2.
- **Computability:** $\forall$P, Q$\in$G$_1$, there is an efficient algorithm to compute e(P,Q). It is computable in ploynomial time.

Computational Diffie-Hellman Problem(CDHP): $\forall$ a, b$\in Z_{q*}$, to compute abP for given P, aP, bP.

Inverse Computational Diffie-Hellman Problem (Inv-CDHP): $\forall$a$\in Z_{q*}$, to compute $a^{-1}P$ for given P, aP.

4 Our Proposed Scheme

In this section, we present an ID-based scheme for achieving reliability and secure authentication in MANETs. The proposed scheme consists of five phases:

- Setup Phase
- Join Phase
- Sign Generation Phase
- Verification Phase and finally
- Remove Phase

4.1 Setup Phase

In this sub section, the details of setup phase is demonstrated. The system parameters used in the proposed scheme are defined in Table 1.

Table 1. System parameters

S.N.	Definition
1.	G1 be a additive cyclic group of prime order q.
2.	G2 be a multiplicative group of prime order q.
3.	K is a system secret key.
4.	e is bilinear mapping e:G1*G2$\rightarrow$ G2.
5.	H is hash function, where H:0,1*$\rightarrow Z_{q*}$.
6.	p is a generator of group G1.
7.	q is a generator of group G2.
8.	Pub is a system public key.

In the setup phase clusterhead (CH) operation performs the following steps:

1. CH broadcasts the system parametrs (K,G1,G2,Pub,q,e,H,p) to set mobile nodes $\alpha = (M_1, M_2, ..., M_n)$.
2. A set of mobile node α receives the system parameters from CH, each mobile node sends own ID to their CH.
3. CH performs two basic operation namely, generation of public and private key:

   - Public Key Generation Phase(PU) :
     $Pu_1, Pu_2, ..., Pu_n = H(ID_1), H(ID_2), ..., H(ID_n)$
   - Private Key Generation Phase(Pr):
     $Pr_1, Pr_2, ..., Pr_n = Pu_1(P/s), Pu_2(P/s), ..., Pu_n(P/s)$

4. CH computes private key to the particular ID and sends back to the mobile node.

4.2   Join Phase

1. A set of new mobile node $\mu = M_{n+1}, -------------, M_{n+m}$ wants to join the running cluster. Then the new mobile node boradcasts a Join message in the entire cluster.
2. Upon receiving Join meaasge, CH upadates group member by $C_{update} = \mu \cup \alpha$ and broadcasts the system parameters in entire cluster.
3. Upon receiving the system parameters, new mobile sends their ID to corresponding CH.
4. CH generates the Public/Private keys to their corresponding ID and sends back to the new mobile node.

   - Generation of public key:
     $Pu_{n+1}, Pu_{n+2}, ..., Pu_{n+m} = H(ID_{n+1}), H(ID_{n+2}), ..., H(ID_{n+m})$
   - Generation of private key:
     $Pr_{n+1}, Pu_{n+2}, ..., Pu_{n+m} = Pu_{n+1}(P/s), Pu_{n+2}(P/s), ..., Pu_{n+m}(P/s)$

Round 1: Sign Genaration Phase

1. The mobile nodes choose random numbers $r_{n+1}, r_{n+2}, ..., r_{n+m} \in Zq^*$, computes $Vs_{n+1}, Vs_{n+2}, ..., Vs_{n+m} = g^{r_1}, g^{r_2}, ..., g^{r_n}$, where $1 \leq i \leq n$. It broadcasts Vs_i as public parametrs while r_i is kept as secret.
2. CH computes $h_{n+1}, h_{n+2}, ..., h_{n+m} = H(m_{n+1}), H(m_{n+2}), ..., H(M_{n+m})$ and $S_{n+1}, S_{n+2}, ..., S_{n+m} = (r_{n+1} + h_{n+1}), (r_{n+2} + h_{n+2}), ..., (r_{n+m} + h_{n+m})$. Here, (S_i, Vs_i) is known as signature of corresponding message(M_i), where $1 \leq i \leq n$.

Round 2: Verification Phase

1. The mobile node knows the system parameter and signature (S_i, Vs_i) on message m_i, the verifier firstly computes $h_i = H(m_i)$, where $n \leq i \leq m$.
2. The verifier accepts the signature when it holds following conditions:

   - $e(Pub, S_i) = (Vs_i.g^{h_i})Pu_i$, where $n \leq i \leq m$

4.3   Sign Generation Phase

1. The mobile node choose random numbers r_1, r_2,....,r_n $\in Zq^*$, computes Vs_1, Vs_2,......,$Vs_n = g^{r_1}, g^{r_2}$,....,g^{r_n}, where $1 \leq i \leq n$. It broadcasts Vs_i as public parametrs while r_i is kept as secret.
2. CH computes $h_1, h_2, ..., h_n = H(m_1), H(m_2)$,......,$H(m_n)$ and $S_1, S_2,....,S_n = (r_1 + h_1), (r_2 + h_2)$,....,$(r_n + h_n)$. Here, (S_i, Vs_i) is known as signature of corresponding message(M_i), $where$ $1 \leq i \leq n$.

4.4   Verification Phase

1. The mobile node knows the system parameter and signature (S_i, Vs_i) on message m_i, the verifier first computes $h_i = H(m_i)$, where $1 \leq i \leq n$.
2. The verifier accepts the signature on message m when holds following conditions:
   - $e(Pub, S_i) = (Vs_i.g^{h_i})Pu_i$, where $1 \leq i \leq n$

4.5   Remove Phase

1. Suppose that a set of mobile nodes $\lambda = M_{n-j},......,M_n$ leave the current cluster group.
2. Remaining mobile nodes can be calculated by $C_{rem} = C_{update}/\lambda$.
3. Each mobile node sends signed (remove message) to their CH.
4. CH verifies the signed message, if it is coming from authenticated mobile node, then CH removes mobile node from particular cluster.
5. Otherwiese, it is fake signed message.

5   Proof of Correctness and Security Analysis

In this section, we present our proposed scheme based on Inverse Computational Diffie-Hellman Problem(inv-CDHP). It shows correctness property and security analysis. There are two secnarios for checking the correctness of proposed scheme:

5.1   Proof of Correctness

Secnario 1: A set of mobile nodes running in the cluster:

$e(Pub, S_i) = (Vs_i, g^{h_i})Pu_i$ where $1 \leq i \leq n$
$e(Pub, S_i) = e(Pub, (r_i + h_i)Pr_i)$
$= e(sP, [(r_1 + h_1)Pr_1, (r_2 + h_2)Pr_2, ...,(r_n + h_n)Pr_n)])$
$= e(sP, [(r_1 + h_1)Pu_1(P/s), (r_2 + h_2)Pu_2(P/s), ...,(r_n + h_n)Pu_n(P/s)])$
$= e(sP, (P/s)[(r_1 + h_1)Pu_1, (r_2 + h_2)Pu_2, ...,(r_n + h_n)Pu_n])$
$= e(P, P[(r_1 + h_1)Pu_1, (r_2 + h_2)Pu_2, ...,(r_n + h_n)Pu_n])$
$= e(P, P)^{[(r_1+h_1)Pu_1,(r_2+h_2)Pu_2,.....,(r_n+h_n)Pu_n]}$
$= g^{[(r_1+h_1)Pu_1,(r_2+h_2)Pu_2,.....,(r_n+h_n)Pu_n]}$
$= g^{r_i Pu_i} g^{h_i Pu_i}$

$= (g^{r_i} g^{h_i})^P u_i$ where $1 \leq i \leq n$
$= (Vs_i, g^{h_i})$

Secnario 2: The correctness of our scheme, when a set of new mobile nodes μ join the runnig cluster.

$e(Pub, S_i) = (Vs_i, g^{h_i})Pu_i$ where $n+1 \leq i \leq m$
$e(Pub, S_i) = e(Pub, (r_i + h_i)Pr_i)$
$= e(sP, [(r_n + 1 + h_n + 1)Pr_n + 1, (r_n + 2 + h_n + 2)Pr_n + 2, \ldots\ldots, (r_n + m + h_n + m)Pr_{n+m}])$
$= e(sP, [(r_n+1+h_n+1)Pu_n+1(P/s), (r_n+2+h_n+2)Pu_n+2(P/s), \ldots\ldots, (r_n + m + h_n + m)Pu_{n+m}(P/s)])$
$= e(sP, (P/s)[(r_n + 1 + h_n + 1)Pu_{n+1}, (r_{n+2} + h_{n+2})Pu_{n+2}, \ldots, (r_{n+m} + h_{n+m})Pu_{n+m}])$
$= e(P, P[(r_{n+1} + h_{n+1})Pu_{n+1}, (r_{n+2} + h_{n+2})Pu_{n+2}, \ldots, (r_{n+m} + h_{n+m})Pu_{n+m}])$
$= e(P, P)^{[(r_{n+1}+h_{n+1})Pu_{n+1}, (r_{n+2}+h_{n+2})Pu_{n+2}, \ldots, (r_{n+m}+h_{n+m})Pu_{n+m}]}$
$= g^{[(r_{n+1}+h_{n+1})Pu_{n+1}, (r_{n+2}+h_{n+2})Pu_{n+2}, \ldots, (r_{n+m}+h_{n+m})Pu_{n+m}]}$
$= g^{r_i Pu_i} g^{h_i Pu_i}$
$= (g^{r_i} g^{h_i})^P u_i$ where $1 \leq i \leq n$
$= (Vs_i, g^{h_i})$

5.2   Security Analysis

In this section, we analyze the security of our proposed scheme. It shows that our proposed scheme is secure against forgery attack on adaptive chosen plain text message and ID attack. It also demonstrates our proposed scheme is unforgeable because hardness of inv-CDH problems.

Theorem 1 : Our proposed scheme is secure against forgery attack on adaptive chosen plain text message and ID attack in random oracle model because hardness of inv-CDH problems.

Proof : Suppose P be generator of Group G_1. We assume that attaker A captures a random instance (P, aP) of inv-CDH problem. The main goal of attacker is to compute $a^{-1}P$.

Adaptive Chosen Message Attack: Having knowledge of the Id and public key of the signer, an attacker can ask to signer to sign on any message that he wants. Pub and P are used as system parametrs for an algorithm A_1. We obtain signature (m, h', S_1, Vs) and (m, h', S_1, Vs), which are expected to be validity ones with respect to (w.r.t.) hash function H_1 and H_2 having differ value $h \neq h'$ on (m,s).
$e(Pub, s_i) = (Vs_i, g^{h_i})Pu_i$
$= (g^{r_i}, g^{h_i})Pu_i$
$= g^{(r_i+h_i)}Pu_i$
$= e(P, P)^{(r_i+h_i)}Pu_i$
$e(Pub, s_i) = e(sP, (r_i + h_i)Pr_i)$

$e(sP, s_i) = e(sP, (r_i + h_i))Pu_i(P/s)$
$= e(P, (r_i + h_i))Pu_iP$
$e(P, ss_i) = e(P, (r_i + h_i))Pu_iP$

$$e(P, ss_i - (r_i + h_i)Pu_iP) = 1 ....(1)$$

Similarly, $e(Pub, s_J) = (Vs_j, g^{h'_j})Pu_j$
$= (g^{r_j}, g^{h'_j})Pu_j$
$= g^{(r_j + h'_j)}Pu_j$
$= e(P, P)^{(r_j + h'_j)}Pu_j$
$e(Pub, s_j) = e(sP, (r_j + h'_j)Pr_j$
$e(sP, s_j) = e(sP, (r_j + h'_j))Pu_j(P/s)$
$= e(P, (r_j + h'_j))Pu_jP$
$e(P, ss_j) = e(P, (r_j + h'_j))Pu_jP$

$$e(P, ss_j - (r_j + h'_j)Pu_jP) = 1 ....(2)$$

From Eqs. (1) and (2)
$e(P, ss_i - (r_i + h_i)Pu_iP) = e(P, ss_j - (r_j + h'_j)Pu_jP)$
$e(P, (ss_i - ss_j) - P[(r_i + h_i)Pu_i - (r_j + h'_j)Pu_j]) = 1$
$e(P, (ss_i - ss_j) - P[(r_i + h_i)Pu_i - (r_i + h'_i)Pu_i]]) = 1$, where i= j *
$e(P, (ss_i - ss_j) - PPu_i[(r_i - r_i) + (h_i - h'_i)]]) = 1$
$e(P, (ss_i - ss_j) - PPu_i(h_i - h'_i)) = 1$
$s(s_i - s_j) - (h_i - h'_i)PPu_i = O$
where O is point at infinity. identity element is defined in elliptic-curve.
$s(s_i - s_j) = (h_i - h'_i)PPu_i$
$Pu_i(P/s) = \frac{(s_i - s_j)}{(h_i - h'_i)}$
$Pr_i = \frac{(s_i - s_j)}{(h_i - h'_i)}$

That means an attacker can find private key (P_r), an instance of inv-CDH problems in Group G_1. But inv-CDHP is hard in Theorem 1, so there is no efficient algorithm for forgery attack on adaptive chosen plain text message.

6   Performance Evaluation

In this section, we apply our proposed scheme to achieve optimal authentication, which is simulated using network simulator(ns-2.35) and it is compared with AODV and SAODV routing protocol with or without authentication.

6.1   Simulation Environment and Scenarios

The network topology is a rectangular area of 900 m height and 800 m width. All the fix links have speed in range from 10 m/s to 90 m/s. We use the IEEE 802.11 algorithms at physical and data link layer. AODV is used as routing algorithm in our scheme at network layer. Finally, user datagram protocol (UDP) packet is used in transport layer as traffic source. The simulation parameters are given in Table 2.

Table 2. Simulation parameters

Parameter	Value
Simulator	ns-2.35
Simulation time	900 s
No. of nodes	10 to 80
Routing protocols	AODV, SAODV
Traffic agent	TCP
Pause time	2 s
Node speed	2-10 m/s
Terrain area	9000m x800 m
Transmission range	250 m
Mobility Model	fixed waypoint mobility model
Each packet size	512 bytes

6.2   Performance Metrics

Below the various matrics that are used to evaluate the performance of these context are defined:

- Packet Delivery Fraction(PDF): Fraction of total number of packets generated by a traffic source to total number of packets recieved by a destination.
- End-to-End Delay : The average time taken by UDP data packets that successfully delivered to destinations.
- Throughput:The ratio of total number of UDP packets (data bits) successfully delivered to the destination node and time of simulation.

In Fig. 2, a comparision graph is drwan in between AODV without authentication, SAODV with authentication and our proposed scheme by considering average packet delivery fraction as a comparision parameter. The outcome represents that our proposed scheme carried 91.36 % while other two schemes such as AODV without authentication and SAODV having 90.12 % and 90.83 % respectively for average PDF. Hence proposed scheme is outperformed over others.

The outcome of simulation is calculated for average end to end delay for all given schemes in Fig. 3. AODV without authentication has 169.33 ms, SAODV with authentication has 152.127 ms while proposed scheme has 151.97 ms for average end to end delay parameter. Hence in our proposed scheme, average delay is lower in comparision with other two.

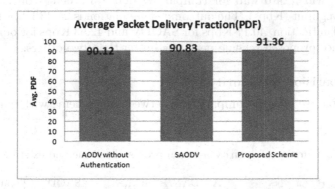

Fig. 2. Average packet delivery fraction

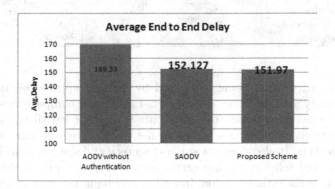

Fig. 3. Average end to end delay

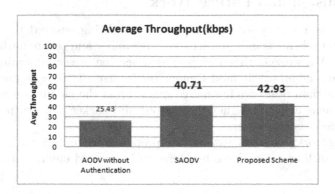

Fig. 4. Average throughput

In Fig. 4, which is drwan for compairing above 3 schemes on the basis of average throughput (Kbps). The outcome of simulation is 25.43 Kbps for AODV without authentication, 40.17 Kbps for SAODV and 42.93 Kbps for our proposed scheme. Hence proposed scheme performs better than two others.

6.3   Comparision of Security

In this section, we present comparisions between our scheme with existing ones [11–13]

Table 3. Comparision of security between proposed scheme and existing schemes

S.N.	Security Parameters	ARIDANE	ARAN	SAODV	Our Scheme
1.	Authentication	Yes	Yes	Yes	Yes
2.	Integrity	Yes	Yes	Yes	Yes
3.	Non-repudiation	No	Yes	Yes	Yes
4.	Secrecy	No	No	No	Yes
5.	Certificateless	No	No	No	Yes
6.	Time to generate digital signature	High	High	High	Low

Our Proposed scheme being compared by existing approaches in terms of time and security for generating digital signature. These comparisions are given in Table 3. In existing schemes, the certificate is used for key distribution management. However, all existing schemes do not ensure integrity, non-repudiation and authentication. It also does not support secrecy and slow in digital signature generation. In our scheme, we use certificateless cryptography under inv-CDH problems. It ensures authentication, integrity, non-repudiation, secrecy and slow in digital signature generation. It shows that proposed scheme is efficiently able to generate digital signature in terms of security and time.

7   Conclusion and Future Work

Authentication, integrity and non-repudiation is being ensured by the digital signature. Our scheme is used for achieving reliability and secure authentication in MANET. We showed that our proposed scheme is secure against forgery attack in the random oracle model under the inverse-CDHP assumption and is more efficient than other traditional schemes. From the simulation results, our proposed scheme achieves higher throughput and packet delivery fraction and end to end delay is also lesser.

In future work, we shall extend our proposed scheme in some important applications such as e-commerce business, authenticated email system and key distribution.

Acknowledgements. This research work is partially funded by the Technical Quality Improvement Programme Phase II (TEQIP-II).

References

1. Hu, Y.-C., Perrig, A.: A survey of secure wireless ad hoc routing. In: Proceedings of IEEE Security and Privacy, pp. 28–39. IEEE Press (2004)
2. Burmeste, M., de Medeiros, B.: On the security of route discovery in MANETs. In: Proceedings of IEEE Transactions on mobile computing, vol. 8, pp. 1180–1187. IEEE Press (2009)
3. Argyroudis, P.G., Mahony, D.O.: Secure routing for mobile ad hoc networks. In: Proceedings of IEEE Communications Surveys and Tutorials, Third Quarter, vol. 7, pp. 2–21. IEEE Press (2005)
4. Tian, B., Han, S., Hu, J., Dillon, T.: A mutual-healing key distribution scheme in wireless sensor networks. J. Netw. Comput. Appl. **34**, 80–88 (2011). Elsevier
5. Tian, B., Han, S., Parvin, S., Hu, J., Das, S.: Self-healing key distribution schemes for wireless networks: a Survey. Comput. J. **54**(4), 549–569 (2011). Oxford
6. Konate, K., Gaye, A.: attacks analysis in mobile ad hoc networks: modeling and simulation. In: Proceedings of IEEE International Conference on Intelligent Systems, Modeling and Simulation, pp. 367–372. IEEE Press (2011)
7. Zhang, Y., Lee, W.: Security in mobile ad-hoc networks. In: Mohapatra, P., Krishnamurthy, S.V. (eds.) Book Ad hoc Networks Technologies and Protocols, pp. 249–268. Springer, Heidelberg (2005)
8. Westhoff, D., Lamparter, B., Paar, C., Weimerskirch, A.: On digital signature in ad hoc network. Trans. Emerg. Telecommun. Technol. **16**, 411–425 (2005)
9. Shamir, A.: Identity-based cryptosystems and signature schemes. In: Blakely, G.R., Chaum, D. (eds.) CRYPTO 1984. LNCS, vol. 196, pp. 47–53. Springer, Heidelberg (1985)
10. Zhang, F., Safavi-Naini, R., Susilo, W.: An efficient signature scheme from bilinear pairings and its applications. In: Bao, F., Deng, R., Zhou, J. (eds.) PKC 2004. LNCS, vol. 2947, pp. 277–290. Springer, Heidelberg (2004)
11. Hu, Y.C., Perrig, A., Johnson, D.B.: Aridane: a secure on-demand routing protocol for ad hoc networks. In: Proceedings of International Conference on Mobile Computing and Networking (MobiCom 2002), pp. 12–23. ACM Press (2002)
12. Sanzgiri, K. et al. : A secure routing protocol for ad hoc networks. In: Proceedings of IEEE International Conference (INCP-02), pp. 78–87. IEEE Press (2002)
13. Zapata, M.G., Asokan, N.: Securing ad hoc routing protocols. In: Proceedings ACM Workshop on Wireless Security (WiSe), pp. 1–10. ACM Press (2002)
14. Wang, H., Zhang, Y.: Identity-based strong key-insulated ring signature scheme in the standard model. In: Seventh International Conference Mobile Ad-hoc Sensor Networks, pp. 451–455 (2011)
15. Mishra, S., Sahu, R.A., Padhye, S., Yadav, R.S.: An ID-based signature scheme from bilinear pairing based on k-plus problem. In: Proceedings of 3rd International Conference on Electronics Computer Technology (ICECT- 2011), Kanyakumari, India. IEEE, pp. 104–107 (2011)
16. Boneh, D., Lynn, B., Shacham, H.: Short signatures from the weil pairing. In: Boyd, C. (ed.) ASIACRYPT 2001. LNCS, vol. 2248, pp. 514–532. Springer, Heidelberg (2001)

Polynomial Construction and Non-tree Based Efficient Secure Group Key Management Scheme

Byrapura Rangappa Purushothama[1]([✉]) and B.B. Amberker[2]

[1] Department of Computer Science and Engineering,
National Institute of Technology Goa, Farmagudi, Ponda 403401, Goa, India
puru@nitgoa.ac.in
[2] Department of Computer Science and Engineering,
National Institute of Technology Warangal, Warangal 506004, Telangana, India
bba@nitw.ac.in

Abstract. Designing an efficient key management scheme for secure group communication is challenging. We focus on non-tree based group key management scheme as they provide flexible and practical mechanism for collaborative computing. In this paper, we propose a non-tree based secure group key management scheme based on polynomial construction method. In the proposed scheme, an user is supposed to store only two keys (private shared key and group key). When a new user joins the group, only one encryption is required for rekeying and when an existing user leaves the group, only one polynomial construction is required for rekeying. The storage at the key distribution center is reduced in the proposed scheme. We analyze the security of the scheme and show that collusion of any subset of users cannot obtain the secret key of any non-colluded user. We compare the proposed scheme with the non-tree based schemes relying on polynomial construction method and show that the proposed scheme is efficient.

Keywords: Secure group communication · Key management · Polynomial interpolation · Non-tree · Rekeying efficient

1 Introduction

Secure group communication (SGC) alludes to a situation in which the group of users can convey the messages among themselves in such a manner that outsiders even after intercepting the messages are not able to infer any information. Web has empowered the new era of utilizations to bolster collective work among topographically distributed users. Defending the security of the correspondence and guaranteeing the integrity of the applications is most extreme critical in such environment. With the outstanding development in present day communications, SGC has become greatly essential research territory. Applications like collaborative work, teleconferences, white-boards, distributed interactive simulation, video conferences, tele-medicine, and many others oblige SGC model [18].

© Springer International Publishing Switzerland 2015
J.H. Abawajy et al. (Eds): SSCC 2015, CCIS 536, pp. 122–133, 2015.
DOI: 10.1007/978-3-319-22915-7_12

The communications of the group can be secured with encryption technique utilizing a key called *group key*. The group key will be with only group members. Despite the fact that encryption is utilized to secure the messages traded among bunch of individuals, distributing the cryptographic keys to the users turns into an important issue.

Accordingly, the most essential issue confronting SGC is *key management*, that is, the procedure that empowers the group of users to establish and distribute the shared group keys. Generally, the groups are dynamic. The new individuals may join the gathering and existing individuals may leave the gathering amid the gathering correspondences. In this way, there is a need to change the group key when a new user joins the group and an existing member leaves the group. This raises to two security requirements that must be fulfilled by any secure group key management schemes: *backward secrecy* and *forward secrecy*. Providing backward secrecy intends to change the group key when a new user joins the group so that, the new user won't have the capacity to persue/read the past correspondences of the group. Forward secrecy means to change the group key when an existing user leaves the group so that he/she will no longer to read the future group messages. So, how to change the key, both efficiently and scalably is a considerable challenge. The process of changing the group key during these events is called *rekeying*. There are several key management schemes and the schemes are broadly categorized into centralized group key management schemes and they use key distribution center (KDC) to manage the group [4,5,16,17], De-centralized group key management schemes [12,13], and Distributed or contributory group key management schemes [3,6,10]. The survey of the schemes belonging to these categories is provided in [15].

In this work, we focus on the polynomial construction based group key management schemes. The existing polynomial group key management schemes provide a practical and flexible mechanism for collaborative computing. However, we show the limitations of the existing schemes and propose a group key management scheme based on polynomial construction and show that the scheme is more secure and efficient than the existing schemes. We analyze the security of the proposed scheme and show that the scheme is collusion resistant.

The rest of the paper is organized as follows. In Sect. 2, we give the details of the existing non-tree based key management schemes. Notations and definitions are given in Sect. 3. In Sect. 4, we elaborate the proposed scheme. The analysis of the proposed scheme for rekeying cost is in Sect. 5. In Sect. 6, we analyse the security of the proposed scheme and compare the scheme with the existing scheme along with performance evaluation followed by the conclusion.

2   Background

We categorize the existing group key management schemes as tree based group key management schemes and non-tree based group key management schemes. Several independent research groups have proposed tree based group key management schemes [4,11,16,17]. The rekeying cost (i.e., the number of key changes when an user joins/leaves the group or the number of messages required to communicate the changed keys to the group users when new user joins or leaves the group) is a function of the number of users in the group. In this work, we focus on the non-tree based key management schemes based on the polynomial construction method. Recently, Piao et al. [14] have proposed a centralized polynomial based key management scheme for secure group communication. Their scheme requires only one rekey message for rekeying. Each user has to store only one key and storage at KDC is less compared to tree based schemes. In a group with n users, $n + 1$ keys should be stored by KDC, whereas in Logical Key Tree [17] and binomial key tree [4] based schemes, KDC should store $2n - 1$ keys. However, despite possessing the appealing features, Piao et al. scheme is not secure as it does not satisfy forward and backward secrecy security requirements. Also, the Piao et al.'s scheme is not collusion resistant. In a group of n users, any $n - 1$ users can collude to get the secret key of other user [9]. So, the scheme by Piao et al. [14] cannot be used for secure group communication. The scheme by Zhou et al. [19] is similar to the Piao et al. scheme but it satisfies the security requirements. However, the scheme has computation overhead. We defer the details of these schemes till Sect. 6.1, since we find it appropriate to provide the details when we compare the proposed schemes with the schemes in [14,19]. Motivated by the appealing features exhibited by these schemes and efficiency achieved by the non-tree based key management schemes, we propose a secure and efficient key management scheme based on polynomial construction method, which is more secure and efficient than the schemes in [14,19].

3   Notations and Definitions

- $U = \{u_1, u_2, \ldots, u_n\}$ is the set (or group G) of n users and u_i is the identity of the user u_i.
- K_G is the group key of G.
- k_u: Secret key shared between user u and KDC.
- $x \to y : z$ denotes, sending a message z from user x to user y (or set of users y, utilizing unicast or multicast).
- $\{M\}_K$: Using key K encrypt the message M with semantically secure symmetric encryption scheme.
- $u \to KDC : (J, G)$, Join solicitation/request from a client u to KDC to join group G. When the context is clear, a solitary user u can be supplanted by a set of users $\{u_1, \ldots, u_t\}$.
- $u \to KDC : (L, G)$, It is a leave solicitation/request from a client u of group G to KDC.
- $userset(K)$: denotes the collection of users who are possessing the key K.
- $GF(p)$: Galois field, where p is a large prime.
- $x \in_R GF(p)$: Choosing uniformly at random x from $GF(p)$.
- $h : \{0, 1\}^* \to GF(p)$, a cryptographic hash function.

3.1   Lagrange's Polynomial Interpolation

Given a set of k points, $\{(x_1, y_1), \ldots, (x_j, y_j), \ldots, (x_k, y_k)\}$ where no two x_j are same, the *interpolation polynomial in the Lagrange's form* is the linear combination,

$$P(x) = \sum_{j=1}^{k-1} y_j l_j(x) \tag{1}$$

of Lagrange's basis polynomials

$$l_j(x) = \prod_{1 \le i \le k, i \ne j} \frac{x - x_i}{x_j - x_i}$$

The polynomial $P(x)$ will have a degree which is less than or equal to $k - 1$. There are polynomial interpolation algorithms to compute polynomial of degree k with complexity $O(k \log^2 k)$ [2,8].

4   Proposed Group Key Management Scheme Based on Polynomial Construction

In this section, we present a group key management scheme based on polynomial construction method. The scheme uses KDC. All the keys are chosen from $GF(p)$, where p is a sufficiently large prime.

4.1   Group Setup and Group Key Distribution

- Let $U = \{u_1, u_2, \ldots, u_n\}$ be the set of users in a secure group G.
- Initially, there are no users in group G.
- The users in U send the following request to KDC. W.l.o.g

$$\{u_1, u_2, \ldots, u_n\} \to KDC : (J, G)$$

- KDC chooses $K_G \in_R GF(p)$.
- KDC has a mechanism to authenticate a user u_i, $1 \le i \le n$ (we are not addressing the process of authentication as it is not objective of the work, anyway the KDC can utilize any of the current methods for authenticating the clients such as Kerberos, Strong three-way authentication, Station-to-station-protocol etc., [7]). KDC chooses a secret key $k_i \in_R GF(p)$ for u_i and securely sends (k_i, K_G) to u_i, $1 \le i \le n$. Initially, we assume the presence of a protected/secure channel between KDC and every client u_i (the secure channel can be realized by using the secure public key cryptosystem (with a note that public key cryptosystem is costly than symmetric key cryptosystem)) to communicate the shared secret key to the user by the KDC). Key k_i is the shared secret between u_i and KDC. The users in U can communicate securely using the group key K_G.

4.2   Join Protocol

In this section, we give the protocol for a new user join. The user u sends a join request to KDC to join the group G. KDC authenticates the user and generates k_u and sends securely to u (we assume the presence of a protected channel between KDC and user u initially). Trivially, to provide the backward secrecy for the group communications, KDC generates a new group key. The new group key is encrypted with the current group key of G and sent to all the existing users. All the existing users can decrypt the encrypted message with the old group key. Later, KDC encrypts the new group key with k_u and sends to u. This requires two messages to be sent for rekeying. One encrypted message intended for the existing group members and another for the new joining user. We give an improved join protocol which reduces the number of encryptions and the size of the rekey message transmitted for rekeying.

Protocol 1.1 elaborates the process of rekeying when a new user joins group G. The user u sends a join request to KDC to join G. KDC authenticates the user and generates k_u and sends securely to u (we assume the presence of a protected channel between KDC and user u initially). To ensure backward secrecy of the group communications, all the existing users obtain the new group key by computing the function h with current group key K_G as input. KDC computes $h(K_G)$, encrypts with k_u and sends to u. The new user obtains the new group key $h(K_G)$ by decrypting using k_u.

Protocol 1.1: Join Protocol

---
1 $u \rightarrow KDC : (J, G)$;
2 $KDC \Longleftrightarrow u$: KDC authenticates the user u and securely gives k_u;
            // k_u is the key shared between the user u and KDC;
3 Let K_G be the current group key of G;
4 KDC computes $h(K_G)$ and sets this as new group key;
5 All the existing users compute $h(K_G)$ and set this as new group key;
6 $KDC \rightarrow u : \{h(K_G)\}_{k_u}$;   // User u gets the new group key;

4.3   User Leave Event

Protocol 1.2 gives the process of rekeying when an existing user leaves the group G. Consider a group G of users $U = \{u_1, u_2, \ldots, u_n\}$ with the current group key K_G. Let $k_1, k_2, \ldots, k_n$ be the corresponding shared secret keys of the users in U with KDC. Suppose an user $u_l, l \in [1, n]$ wants to leave the group (or to be expelled from the group). To provide forward secrecy, KDC chooses a new group key K'_G. Also, KDC chooses a random key k_r which is distinct from all the keys it possesses. Also, it chooses a random key k_s which is distinct from K'_G. To communicate K'_G to the users in $U - \{u_l\}$, KDC constructs the polynomial $P_G(x)$ using Lagrange's polynomial interpolation Eq. 1 of Sect. 3.1 with the

points $\{(k_1, K'_G), (k_2, K'_G), \ldots, (k_{l-1}, K'_G), (k_{l+1}, K'_G), \ldots, (k_n, K'_G), (k_r, k_s)\}$
and broadcasts $P_G(x)$. Each user in $U - \{u_l\}$ obtains the new group key K'_G
by evaluating $P_G(x)$ at their respective private keys. For instance, u_1 obtains
new group key by computing $P_G(k_1)$. The leaving user u_l will not be able to
get the new group key K'_G as the point (k_l, K'_G) was not used in computing the
polynomial $P_G(x)$. Also, u_l does not know any of the private keys of other users
and the key k_r. So, the leaving user cannot get the group key K'_G.

Protocol 1.2: Leave Protocol

---

1 Let $\{u_1, u_2, \ldots, u_n\}$ be the current group users of G and $\{k_1, k_2, \ldots, k_n\}$ be the
  shared secret keys of the corresponding users of G with KDC;

2 $u_l \rightarrow KDC : (L, G)$, where $1 \leq l \leq n$;

3 Let K_G be the current group key of G;

4 KDC chooses a new group key $K'_G \in_R GF(p)$;

5 KDC chooses a new random key $k_r \in_R GF(p)$ such that it is distinct from all
  the keys it possesses;

6 KDC chooses a new random key $k_s \in_R GF(p)$ such that it is distinct from K'_G;

7 KDC constructs the polynomial $P_G(x)$ using Lagrange's polynomial
  interpolation Eq.1 of Sect. 3.1 with the points
  $\{(k_1, K'_G), (k_2, K'_G), (k_3, K'_G), \ldots, (k_{l-1}, K'_G), (k_{l+1}, K'_G), \ldots, (k_n, K'_G), (k_r, k_s)\}$.
  // $P_G(x)$ is the polynomial of degree n;

8 KDC broadcasts $P_G(x)$;

9 Each user u_i in $\{u_1, \ldots, u_n\} - \{u_l\}$ compute $P_G(k_i)$ to get new group key K'_G;

---

5   Analysis of the Proposed Scheme for Rekeying Cost

In this section, the proposed scheme is analyzed for rekeying and storage cost.

- *Storage cost at User:* User should store only *two* keys, the group key and
  his/her private shared key (with KDC).
- *Storage cost at the KDC:* For a group of size n, $n + 1$ keys must be stored by
  the KDC (i.e. group key and n keys shared with the users).
- *Number of encryptions upon user join event:* Only one encryption operation
  is required to communicate the changed group key to joining user.
- *Number of encryptions upon user leave event:* is 0. The cost of the user leaving
  is to compute the polynomial of degree in the order of number of existing users
  except leaving user.
- *Number of key changes upon user join event:* Only one key (group key).
- *Number of key changes upon user leave event:* Only one key (group key).
- *Number of Rekey messages upon user join activity:* One broadcast message of
  size $O(1)$.
- *Number of Rekey messages upon user leave activity:* One broadcast message
  which is a polynomial whose size is $O(n)$.

- *Server cost for rekeying on user join event:* Only one symmetric encryption and one hash operation is carried out by KDC.
- *Server cost on user leave event:* KDC constructs a polynomial of degree n for rekeying. Using FFT, the cost is $O(n \log^2 n)$ [2,8] .
- *User Computation cost for rekeying upon user leave:* Each user has to evaluate the polynomial which requires $O(n)$ cost.
- *User Computation cost during rekeying upon user join:* The existing users have to carry out only one hash operation and newly joined user has to carry out symmetric decryption operation.

6   Security Analysis and Comparison

In this section, we comment on the security of the proposed scheme and compare with the schemes proposed in [14,19].

Proposition 1 (Backward and Forward Secrecy). *The proposed group key management scheme satisfies backward and forward secrecy security requirements upon user join and leave activity respectively.*

Proof. Suppose KDC has setup a secure group of n users with the group key K. Let k_i be the shared key of u_i with KDC, for $i = 1, \ldots, n$. Consider the following cases:

1. *Backward Secrecy:* Consider a situation of user joining the group. By following Protocol 1.1 for rekeying, each user compute $h(K)$ and use as the new group key. KDC sends securely $h(K)$ to newly joining user. Since h is the cryptographic hash function, given $h(K)$ it is hard to get K. So, the newly joined user cannot get the old group key. So, the proposed scheme ensures the backward secrecy. New user gets the changed group key securely. New user cannot access the old group key as the encryption scheme used is secure. The probability with which the user can get the old group key is $\frac{1}{p}$, as keys are chosen from $GF(p)$. This probability is negligible for sufficiently larger p. So, the newly joining user cannot access the past communications.
2. *Forward Secrecy:* Consider a group of users $\{u_1, \ldots, u_l, \ldots, u_n\}$ with group key K. Suppose u_l is the leaving user. By following Protocol 1.2, KDC chooses a new group key K', constructs $P_G(x)$ using Eq. 1 of Sect. 3.1 with the points $\{(k_1, K'_G), \ldots, (k_{l-1}, K'_G), (k_{l+1}, K'_G), \ldots, (k_n, K'_G), (k_r, k_s)\}$. The random keys k_r and k_s are secret with KDC and these are distinct from all the keys that are held by KDC and also $k_s \neq K'_G$. KDC broadcasts polynomial $P_G(x)$. User u_l cannot get the new group key as he/she is not in possession of any of the secrets $k_1, \ldots, k_{l-1}, k_{l+1}, \ldots, k_n, k_r$. As all the keys are chosen from $GF(p)$, the probability the user u_l gets any of the required key is $\frac{n}{p}$. For sufficiently large p, $\frac{n}{p}$ is negligible. So, the scheme satisfies the forward secrecy requirement.

Proposition 2 (Secure Against Collusion). *The collusion of any $n-1$ users of the group does not reveal the secret shared key of the non-colluded n^{th} user.*

Proof. Consider n users u_i with $k_i, i = 1, \ldots, n$. Suppose that the KDC constructs the polynomial $P(x)$ with the points $\{(k_1, K_G), \ldots, (k_n, K_G), (r, s)\}$, where $k_i, K_G, r, s \in_R GF(p)$ and broadcasts $P(x)$. Suppose the users $u_i, i = 1, \ldots, n-1$ collude to get the $u'_n s$ secret key k_n. The colluded users have access to $k_i, i = 1, \ldots, n-1$, K_G and $P(x)$. The problem of obtaining k_n reduces to constructing the polynomial with the same set of points used by KDC to construct $P(x)$. The colluded users have $n-1$ points $(k_i, K_G), i = 1, \ldots, n-1$. These users can construct the polynomial $P'(x)$ of degree n by obtaining two more points. Let these points be $(k_r, P(k_r))$ and $(k_s, P(k_s))$ such that $k_r, k_s \in_R GF(p)$. So, $P(x) = P'(x)$ but $P(k_r) \neq K_G$. Since the colluded users know K_G, they can use the point (k_r, K_G) to construct $P'(x)$. Suppose, the polynomial $P'(x)$ is constructed with points $\{(k_1, K_G), \ldots, (k_{n-1}, K_G), (k_r, K_G), (k_s, P(k_s))\}$. $P'(x) = P(x)$ iff $k_r = k_n$. The probability that $k_r = k_n$ is $\frac{1}{p-n}$. For sufficiently larger p, the probability is negligible. So, the colluded users cannot get the private key k_n of the nth user u_n.

6.1 Comparison

In this section, the proposed scheme is compared with the schemes in [14,19] that are based on polynomial construction method. Table 1 gives the rekeying cost. We briefly explain the scheme by Piao et al. [14]. Consider a group of n users. Initially, KDC and each user u_i share securely a private key $k_i, i = 1, \ldots, n$. KDC chooses a group key K and constructs a polynomial

$$P(x) = (x - k_1)(x - k_2) \ldots (x - k_n) + K$$

and broadcasts $P(x)$. Each user u_i obtains the group key K by evaluating $P(x)$ at $x = k_i, i = 1, \ldots, n$. Suppose a new user u_{n+1} joins the group. KDC securely gives k_{n+1} to u_{n+1}. To ensure backward secrecy, KDC chooses a new group key K' and constructs the polynomial

$$P'(x) = (x - k_1)(x - k_2) \ldots (x - k_n)(x - k_{n+1}) + K'$$

and broadcasts $P'(x)$. Each user u_i (including u_{n+1}) obtain K' by evaluating $P'(x)$ at $x = k_i, i = 1, \ldots, n+1$. Suppose an existing user u_l, for some $l \in [1, n+1]$ leaves the group. To ensure forward secrecy, KDC chooses a new group key K'' and constructs the polynomial

$$P''(x) = (x - k_1)(x - k_2) \ldots (x - k_{l-1})(x - k_{l+1}) \ldots (x - k_{n+1}) + K''$$

and broadcasts $P''(x)$. Each user u_i (excluding the user u_l) obtain K'' by evaluating $P''(x)$ at $x = k_i, i = 1, \ldots, l-1, l+1, \ldots, n+1$. As shown below, the scheme does not satisfy forward and backward secrecy requirements.

– The newly joined user u_{n+1} knows $P(x)$ (might have stored the broadcasted $P(x)$). User u_{n+1} can obtain old group key K by computing $P(x) - \frac{P'(x) - K'}{(x - k_{n+1})}$.

Table 1. Comparison of the proposed scheme with the existing schemes

	Scheme in [19]	Scheme in [14]	Our Scheme
Key Derivation	$O(n)$	$O(n)$	$O(n)$
$P(x)$ Computation	$O(n^2)$	$O(n^2)$	$O(n \log^2 n)$
Forward Secrecy	Yes	No	Yes
Backward Secrecy	Yes	No	Yes
#Rekey messages on Join Event	1	1	1
#Rekey messages on Leave Event	1	1	1
#Key Changes on Join	1	1	1
#Key Changes on Leave	2	1	2
Size of Rekey message on Join	$O(n)$	$O(n)$	$O(1)$
Size of Rekey message on Leave	$O(n)$	$O(n)$	$O(n)$
SCC prior to $P(x)$	$O(nB)$	0	0
SCC on Join Event	$O(n^2)$	$O(n^2)$	c_E
SCC on Leave Event	$O(n^2)$	$O(n^2)$	$O(n \log^2 n)$
UCC Prior to Evaluation	$O(B)$	0	0
UCC on Join Event	$O(n)$	$O(n)$	c_D
UCC on Leave Event	$O(n)$	$O(n)$	$O(n)$
Communication Cost on Join	$O(n)$	$O(n)$	$O(1)$
Communication Cost on Leave	$O(n)$	$O(n)$	$O(n)$

- #SCC: Server Computation Cost
- #UCC: User Computation Cost

– As $P''(x)$ is sent in clear, the leaving user u_l knows $P''(x)$ and can get the group key K'' by computing $P''(x) - \frac{P'(x)-K'}{(x-k_l)}$.

Also, the Piao et al. scheme is not collusion resistant. Any $n-1$ users can collude to get the secret key of other user in a group of n users. W.l.o.g, suppose that the users $u_i, i = 1, \ldots n-1$ collude. They can get the $u'_n s$ secret key k_n by computing $\frac{P(x)-K}{(x-k_1)(x-k_2)\ldots(x-k_{n-1})}$. The newly joined user can get access to the past group key and the user who has left the group key can access the future group keys. Since, the scheme by Piao et al. [14] does not satisfy the security requirements (forward and backward secrecy) of SGC and is not collusion resistant, the scheme cannot be used for secure group communication.

The scheme in [19] is same as that of Piao et al. [14] with the following difference. Suppose that there are n users with each user sharing a secret with the KDC. To communicate the group key K, KDC constructs the polynomial

$$P(x) = (x - f(z, k_1))(x - f(z, k_2)) \ldots (x - f(z, k_n)) + K$$

where z is randomly chosen and $f : \{0,1\}^* \rightarrow \{0,1\}^p$ (is a public cryptographic hash function), where all the keys are chosen from F_p for large prime p. Also, $f(x,y)$ is the hash of $f(x||y)$ (|| being the concatenation operation). KDC broadcasts $(z, P(x))$. Each user u_i computes $f(z, k_i)$ and evaluates the polynomial

$P(x)$ at $f(z, k_i)$ to get the changed group key. Suppose a new user u_{n+1} joins the group, KDC securely shares a secret with new user and chooses new group key K' and new random value z', computes $f(z', k_i)$, $i = 1, \ldots, n+1$ and constructs polynomial $P'(x) = (x - f(z', k_1))(x - f(z', k_2)) \ldots (x - f(z', k_{n+1})) + K'$ and broadcasts $(z', P'(x))$. All the users including u_{n+1} compute $f(z', k_i)$, $i = 1, \ldots, n+1$ and evaluate the polynomial at their respective private key and obtain the changed group key. For user leave event the same procedure is carried out as join but excluding the point involving leaving user's private key. However, the KDC has to evaluate the function f, n times before computing the polynomial for a group of size n. Suppose that the running time of f is $O(B)$, then computing n times $f(z, k_i)$ has a cost $O(nB)$.

Table 2. Comparison of storage cost of proposed scheme with existing schemes

Schemes	Storage at KDC	Storage at user
Zou et al. [19]	$n + 1$	2
Piao et al. [14]	$n + 1$	2
Proposed Scheme	$n + 1$	2

In the proposed scheme, when a new user joins, only one encryption is required for rekeying. This cost is mentioned as c_E in Table 1. In the schemes of [14,19] the cost is $O(n^2)$ (the cost for constructing a polynomial). In [19], prior to polynomial construction, KDC incurs an additional cost $O(nB)$ during join and leave events. In Table 1, we have mentioned this cost as server computation cost prior to $P(x)$. Upon join event, the cost incurred by the user in [19] is $O(n)$ (for polynomial evaluation). In the proposed scheme, the user has to carry out one symmetric decryption operation. This cost is mentioned as c_D. In the proposed scheme, using FFT the polynomial can be constructed with the cost $O(n \log^2 n)$ [2,8] and there is no computation required prior to construction of the polynomial. In [19], the users have to evaluate the function f and the broadcasted polynomial to get the changed group key. In Table 1, this cost is mentioned as user computation cost prior to polynomial evaluation. In the proposed scheme, user has to evaluate only broadcasted polynomial and no prior computation is required. In [19], apart from the coefficients of the polynomial, an additional public value is broadcasted. Whereas, this is not required in the proposed scheme. As shown in Table 1, the proposed scheme is rekeying efficient upon group dynamic activities in comparison with the schemes in [14,19].

Table 2 gives the storage cost at the user and KDC. The storage cost at user and KDC is same for schemes in [14,19] and the proposed scheme.

6.2 Performance Evaluation

In the proposed group key management scheme, there is a need to carry out polynomial construction and polynomial evaluation for rekeying upon user leave event. We have implemented using pari cryptographic library [1]. The significant cost involved in the rekeying upon user leave is the polynomial construction by the KDC. The implementation is carried out with Ubuntu 10.4 OS, C language, Intel(R)Core(TM)2 Duo CPU E8400 (3.00 GHz) and 2 GB memory. Figure 1 shows the time taken for polynomial interpolation upon user leave event. We have considered 256 bit prime Galois Field. Figure 1 shows the time taken (in seconds) for rekeying for group with varied number of users.

The users after receiving the broadcasted polynomial have to evaluate it at their own key. The time taken to evaluate the polynomial of degree 20000 is 8 ms. So, the proposed scheme is rekeying efficient.

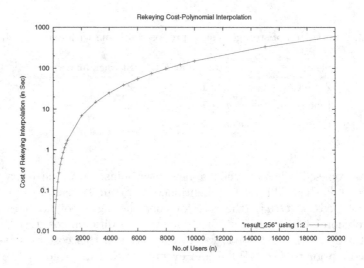

Fig. 1. Rekeying cost-polynomial construction

7   Conclusion and Future Work

We have proposed a group key management scheme based on polynomial construction method. The scheme is rekeying and storage efficient. The rekeying upon user leave event does not require any encryption operation but a polynomial broadcast. The user should store only two keys (private shared key and group key). When a user joins or leaves the group, only one rekey message is required for rekeying. Upon user join only one encryption operation and upon user leave only one polynomial construction is required for rekeying. The scheme is analyzed for security and is proved to be secure. Also, the scheme is proved to be collusion resistant. We have compared the proposed scheme with the existing schemes based on polynomial construction method and shown that the proposed scheme is efficient. As a future work, we want to make the proposed scheme secure against active attack model.

References

1. Pari c cryptography library. http://pari.math.u-bordeaux.fr/. Accessed on 06 April 2015
2. Aho, A.V., Hopcroft, J.E., Ullman, J.D.: The Design and Analysis of Computer Algorithms. Addison-Wesley, California (1974)
3. Amir, Y., Kim, Y., Nita-Rotaru, C., Schultz, J.L., Stanton, J.R., Tsudik, G.: Secure group communication using robust contributory key agreement. IEEE Trans. Parallel Distrib. Syst. **15**(5), 468–480 (2004)
4. Aparna, R., Amberker, B.B.: A key management scheme for secure group communication using binomial key trees. Int. J. Netw. Manage. **20**(6), 383–418 (2010)
5. Blundo, C., De Santis, A., Herzberg, A., Kutten, S., Vaccaro, U., Yung, M.: Perfectly-secure key distribution for dynamic conferences. In: Brickell, E.F. (ed.) CRYPTO 1992. LNCS, vol. 740, pp. 471–486. Springer, Heidelberg (1993)
6. Burmester, M., Desmedt, Y.G.: A secure and efficient conference key distribution system. In: De Santis, A. (ed.) EUROCRYPT 1994. LNCS, vol. 950, pp. 275–286. Springer, Heidelberg (1995)
7. Delfs, H., Knebl, H.: Introduction to Cryptography: Principles and Applications. Information Security and Cryptography. Springer, Berlin (2002)
8. Horowitz, E., Sahni, S.: Fundamentals of Computer Algorithms. Computer Science Press, New York (1978)
9. Kamal, A.A.: Cryptanalysis of a polynomial-based key management scheme for secure group communication. Int. J. Netw. Secur. **15**(1), 68–70 (2013)
10. Kim, Y., Perrig, A., Tsudik, G.: Tree-based group key agreement. ACM Trans. Inf. Syst. Secur. **7**(1), 60–96 (2004)
11. Ku, W.C., Chen, S.M.: An improved key management scheme for large dynamic groups using one-way function trees. In: Proceedings of International Conference on Parallel Processing Workshops, pp. 391–396, October 2003
12. Mittra, S.: Iolus: a framework for scalable secure multicasting. SIGCOMM Comput. Commun. Rev. **27**(4), 277–288 (1997)
13. Molva, R., Pannetrat, A.: Scalable multicast security in dynamic groups. In: ACM Conference on Computer and Communications Security, pp. 101–112 (1999)
14. Piao, Y., Kim, J., Tariq, U., Hong, M.: Polynomial-based key management for secure intra-group and inter-group communication. Comput. Math. Appl. **65**(9), 1300–1309 (2013)
15. Rafaeli, S., Hutchison, D.: A survey of key management for secure group communication. ACM Comput. Surv. **35**(3), 309–329 (2003)
16. Sherman, A.T., McGrew, D.A.: Key establishment in large dynamic groups using one-way function trees. IEEE Trans. Softw. Eng. **29**(5), 444–458 (2003)
17. Wong, C.K., Gouda, M.G., Lam, S.S.: Secure group communications using key graphs. IEEE/ACM Trans. Netw. **8**(1), 16–30 (2000)
18. Zou, X., Ramamurthy, B., Magliveras, S.S.: Secure Group Communications Over Data Networks. Springer, New York (2004). ISBN: 0387229701
19. Zou, X., Dai, Y.S., Bertino, E.: A practical and flexible key management mechanism for trusted collaborative computing. In: 27th IEEE International Conference on Computer Communications (INFOCOM), pp. 538–546 (2008)

Cryptanalysis and Improvement of ECC - Based Security Enhanced User Authentication Protocol for Wireless Sensor Networks

Anup Kumar Maurya[1,2]($\boxtimes$), V.N. Sastry[1], and Siba Kumar Udgata[2]

[1] Institute for Development and Research in Banking Technology, Hyderabad, India
anupmaurya88@gmail.com,{akmaurya,vnsastry}@idrbt.ac.in
[2] University of Hyderabad, Hyderabad, India
skudgata@gmail.com

Abstract. User authentication and secret session key exchange between a user and a sensor node are important security requirements of wireless sensor networks for retrieving the important, confidential and real time information from the sensor nodes. In 2014, Choi et al. proposed a elliptic curve cryptography based user authentication protocol with enhanced security for wireless sensor networks and after security analysis of their protocol we find that their protocol has some security drawbacks such as (1) no resilient against node capture attack, (2) insecure against stolen smart card attack (3) vulnerable to sensor node energy exhausting attacks. Based on the security analysis we propose a scheme to withstand the various security weaknesses of WSNs. Furthermore, the comparative security and computational performance analysis indicate that our proposed scheme is relatively more secure and efficient.

Keywords: User authentication · Session key establishment · Smart card · Elliptic curve cryptography(ECC) · Wireless sensor networks (WSNs)

1 Introduction

Wireless sensor networks (WSNs) involve a large amount of resource constrained (low computational capability, small memory, less transmission range, low communication bandwidth and low energy) tiny sensor nodes, a few powerful base stations, gateway and users. Each sensor node has sensing unit which senses the physical or environmental parameters (e.g. temperature, pressure, humidity etc.) and a processing and communication unit to communicate the measured real time data in a secure manner with its neighbor node or base station using wireless communication channel. The sensor nodes are generally scattered randomly in an ad hoc manner to complete certain task. Sensor nodes are susceptible to physical capture and uses insecure wireless communication medium. The head sensor node or base station may process the information gathered from the other sensor nodes, it may give control commands to the sensor node and finally it

© Springer International Publishing Switzerland 2015
J.H. Abawajy et al. (Eds): SSCC 2015, CCIS 536, pp. 134–145, 2015.
DOI: 10.1007/978-3-319-22915-7_13

can transmit the gathered information to a wired network. Authentic users can collect the information from sensor node, they can detect activities (e.g., possible attacks in battlefield, patient's body condition in mobile health-care system, natural disaster, landslide, forest fire, machine health condition etc.) and take appropriate decision. The security requirement for protecting the information and resources of WSNs includes: authentication, availability, authorization, confidentiality, integrity, non repudiation and freshness.

User authentication in WSNs is also known as user identification and it can be done using three factors, based on what you are (refers to behavioral and physical attributes like fingerprint, retinal pattern etc.), what you have (refers to documents or credentials like smart card, id card etc.) or what you know (encompasses passwords, personnel information etc.). The objective of the user authentication in WSNs is to resist impersonation attacks.

In recent years, several secure user authentication and session key establishment protocols for WSNs have been proposed in literature. In 2005, Benenson et al. [4] recommended a robust user authentication protocol implemented on the basis of ECC for authenticated querying of WSNs but Wong et al. [5] have shown that Benenson et al. [4] has some security pitfalls such as (i) impersonation attacks (ii) denial of service (DOS) attacks and proposed a efficient dynamic user authentication protocol for WSNs based on one-way hash function . Tseng et al. [6] found out that Wong et al.'s protocol [5] is susceptible to several security attacks such as replay, forgery, stolen-verifier and password guessing, then they suggested a scheme which can resist replay and forgery attacks and provides password modification phase. In 2009, Das et al. [7] have given a two factor strong authentication protocol for the user of WSNs. Latter, He et al. [8] pointed out that Das et al. [7] protocol has security pitfalls of impersonation attacks and does not provide easy password update facility and they suggested a improved two factor and cryptographic hash function based authentication protocol which can resist impersonation and insider attacks. Chen et al. [9] described that Das et al. protocol does not provide mutual authentication between sensor node and the gateway, and then presented a mutual authentication protocol. Yeh et al. [3] showed that Chen et al.'s [9] scheme does not provide easy password update phase and it is resistless to insider attack and they proposed a ECC - based user authentication scheme. In 2011, Han et al. [10] showed that Yeh et al. [3] scheme has various security pitfalls such as (i) no key agreement (ii) no mutual authentication. To overcome the vulnerability of Yeh et al.'s [3] protocol , in 2013 Shi et al. [2] elaborated a new user authentication protocol for WSNs which is efficient on the basis of communication and computation cost and more secure than Yeh.et al. [3] scheme. In 2014, Choi et al. [1] demonstrated that Shi et al. scheme is susceptible to several security pitfalls such as (i) session key attacks (ii) sensor node energy exhausting attacks and (iii) stolen smart card attacks. We observed that Choi et al.'s [1] scheme also has various security weaknesses such as (i) resistless against node capture attacks (ii) unsafe against stolen smart card attacks and as a result this scheme cannot be used for the WSNs which provides prominent and confidential information. Hence, we propose a scheme to withstand the various security defects of WSNs.

The remaining sections of the paper are organized as follow: we mention few basic mathematical functions, equations and notations in Sect. 2, which is essential for the security analysis of Choi et al.'s scheme. In Sect. 3, we demonstrate the Choi et al.'s scheme. After that, in Sect. 4, we report that Choi et al.'s scheme is vulnerable to several security attacks. In Sect. 5, we give a proposal to improve Choi et al.'s scheme which withstands existing security pitfalls of user authentication. We compare the computational performance of our proposed protocol with other existing protocol in Sect. 6. In Sect. 7, we elaborate security analysis of proposed scheme and its comparison with other scheme. At last, in Sect. 8, we conclude the paper.

2   Notations and Mathematical Preliminaries Used

The notations used for description and cryptanalysis of Choi et al.'s scheme are mention in Table 1.

The mathematical preliminaries required for the description and security analysis of Choi et al. protocol are as follows:

Table 1. Notations used

Notations	Description
p, q	Two large prime numbers
F_p	A finite field of characteristic p
E	Elliptic curve over finite field F_p
G	Group of points on E
P	A point on E with order q
U, V	Users
ID_U	The identity of U
S_n	n^{th} sensor node
pw_U	Password of U
ID_{Sn}	The identity of sensor node S_n
SC_U	Smart card of U
GW	The gateway node
x, y	Key generated by GW
$h(.)$	A collision resistant one - way hash function
P	Generator or basic point on E
$\|$	A string concatenation operator
$\oplus$	A bitwise XOR operator
$\times$	Elliptic curve scalar multiplication
$\mathcal{A}$	Adversary

2.1 Collision Resistant Cryptographic Hash Function

It is a function $h : I \rightarrow O$, where $I = \{0,1\}^*$ and $O = \{0,1\}^n$ which takes a binary string $c \in I$ of arbitrary length as input and provides output as a binary string $d \in O$ of length n such that $Adv_{\mathcal{A}}^h(t) \leq \tau$, for $\mathcal{A}$, for any sufficiently small $\tau > 0$. Where $Adv_{\mathcal{A}}^h(t) = Pr\left[(c,c') \leftarrow_R \mathcal{A} : c \neq c', h(c) = h(c')\right]$ is $\mathcal{A}$'s advantage in finding collision. Here, $(c,c') \leftarrow_R$ denotes that the pair (c,c') is randomly selected by $\mathcal{A}$ and Pr denotes the probability of the event $(c,c') \leftarrow_R \mathcal{A}$, if $c \neq c'$ and $h(c) = h(c')$. t is function execution time.

2.2 Elliptic Curve Cryptography (ECC)

ECC is asymmetric key cryptography and in comparison with other non-ECC based cryptography, it provides the similar security measures with smaller key size. For elliptic curve $E(F_p) : y^2 = (x^3 + ax + b) \pmod{p}$ over finite field F_p (where constant $a,b \in F_p$ and $4a^3 + 27b^2 \neq 0$) with $X, P \in E$ and $X = r \times P$ (where $r \in Z_q^*$), it is fairly simple to find X given r and P, however it is quite hard to calculate r given X and P [11].

3 Review of Choi et al.'s Protocol

In this section, we reproduce the Choi et al.'s protocol for clear understanding of our security analysis and proposal. This protocol assumes that the trusted gateway node generates x and y and shares a secret key $SK_{GS} = h(ID_{S_n}||y)$ with the sensor node. The protocol consists of three phases as discussed in following subsection.

3.1 User Registration

- At this stage, U chooses ID_U, pw_U, generates random number b_U, computes $\overline{pw_U} = h(pw_U \oplus b_U)$ and then sends ID_U and pw_U to GW through secure channel.
- GW computes $K_U = h(ID_U||x) \times P$, $A_U = \overline{pw_U} \oplus h(x \oplus y)$, $B_U = h(ID_U||\overline{pw_U} ||h(x \oplus y))$, $W_U = h(ID_U||\overline{pw_U}) \oplus K_U$ and generates a smart card SC_U for U which stores $\langle A_U, B_U, W_U, h(.) \rangle$
- U Stores b_U into SC_U.

3.2 User Login and Authentication Phase

The description of login and authentication phase involves following five steps:

1. U puts SC_U into the card reader and gives ID_U and pw_U. Then SC_U computes: $\overline{pw_U} = h(pw_U \oplus b_U), h(x \oplus y) = \overline{pw_U} \oplus A_U$. If $B_U' \neq h(ID_U||\overline{pw_U}||h(x \oplus y))$, aborts the protocol. Otherwise, SC_U computes $K_U = h(ID_U||\overline{pw_U}) \oplus W_U$, generates $r_U \in Z_s^*$, finds U_s' timestamp T_U, computes $X = r_U \times P, X' = r_U \times K_U, \omega = h(ID_U||h(ID_{S_n}||h(x \oplus y))||T_U), \alpha = h(ID_U||ID_{S_n}||X||X'||T_U||\omega)$. Then, U sends message $M_1 = (ID_U, ID_{S_n}, X, T_U, \alpha, \omega)$ to S_n

2. S_n retrieves current timestamp T'. If $T' - T_U > \Delta T$ or $\omega \neq h(ID_U||h(ID_{S_n}||h(x \oplus y))||T_U)$, S_n abort the protocol (where ΔT is the maximum transmission delay). Otherwise, S_n generates $r_s \in Z_q^*$, finds S_n's timestamp T_s, computes $Y = r_s \times P$, $\beta = h(SK_{GS}||\alpha||\omega||ID_U||ID_{S_n}||X||Y||T_U||T_s)$. S_n sends $M_2 = \langle X, \alpha, \omega, ID_U, ID_{S_n}, Y, T_U, T_s, \beta \rangle$ to GW.

3. GW retrieves current timestamp T''. Checks if $T'' - T_s > \Delta T$, GW abort this phase, otherwise calculates $X' = h(ID_U||x) \times X$. If $\beta \neq h(SK_{GS}||ID_U||X||\alpha||\omega||ID_{S_n}||Y||T_U||T_s)$ or if $\alpha \neq h(ID_U||ID_{S_n}||X||X'||T_U||\omega)$, GW abort this phase. Otherwise, find $GW's$ timestamp T_G and compute $\gamma = h(SK_{GS}||ID_U||X||\alpha||ID_{S_n}||Y||T_U||T_s||T_G)$,$\delta = h(ID_U||X||X'||T_U||ID_{S_n}||Y||T_s)$. Then, GW sends $M_3 = \langle T_G, \gamma, \delta \rangle$ to S_n.

4. S_n retrieves current timestamp T'''. If $T''' - T_G > \Delta T$ or if $\gamma \neq h(SK_{GS}||ID_U||\alpha||ID_{S_n}||Y||X||T_U||T_s||T_G)$, abort the protocol. Otherwise, S_n computes $K_{SU} = r_s \times X$ and retrieve r_s's timestamp T_s'. Then computes $\tau = h(Y||\delta||K_{SU}||T_s')$ and generate a session key $sk = h(X||Y||K_{SU})$. S_n sends $M_4 \langle Y, T_S, T_S', \delta, \tau \rangle$ to U.

5. U retrieves current timestamp T'''', computes $K_{US} = r_U \times Y$. If $T'''' - T_S' > \Delta T$ or $\delta \neq h(ID_U||X||X'||T_U||ID_{S_n}||Y||T_s)$ or $\tau \neq h(Y||T_s'||\delta||K_{US})$, U abort the protocol. Otherwise, U establishes session key $sk = h(Y||X||K_{US})$ with S_n.

3.3   User's Password Update Phase

In this stage, U puts its SC_U into card reader, gives ID_U, pw_U and then new password pw_U'. SC_U calculates $\overline{pw}_U = h(pw_U \oplus b_U), h(x \oplus y) = A_U \oplus \overline{pw}_U$. If $B_U \neq (B_U' = h(ID_U||\overline{pw_U}||h(x \oplus y)))$, abort this phase. Otherwise, SC_U computes: $K_U = h(ID_U||\overline{pw_U}) \oplus W_U, \overline{pw_U'} = h(pw_U' \oplus b_U), A_U' = h(x \oplus y) \oplus \overline{pw_U'}, B_U' = h(ID_U||\overline{pw_U'}||h(x \oplus y)), W_U' = h(ID_U||\overline{pw_U'}) \oplus K_U$. Replace A_U, B_U and W_U of SC_U with A_U', B_U' and W_U' respectively.

4   Cryptanalysis of Choi et al.'s Scheme

In this section, we first consider some assumptions under which the authentication protocol for WSN is analyzed. Then we show that Choi et.al.'s scheme is insecure against various known security attacks.

4.1   Assumptions

- Sensor node may not fix up with tamper - resistant hardware and if a node is captured by an adversary $\mathcal{A}$, all the prominent and confidential information saved in its memory can be accessed by the adversary. If the sensor nodes are tamper resistant, $\mathcal{A}$ can retrieve the information stored in the memory by measuring the power consumption of the captured sensor nodes.
- Base station or gateway cannot be compromised, by the adversary.

- Adversary can intercept the public communication channel, inject packets and reply the already transmitted information.
- Adversary can capture the smart card of user and it can extract the sensitive information like user identity and password stored in the card through a power analysis attack.

4.2   Attacks on Choi et al.'s Scheme

In this section, we elaborate that Choi et al.'s scheme has following security pitfalls:

Stolen Smart Card Attacks: Confidential information saved in stolen smart card can be retrieve by measuring its power consumption as described in Kocher et al.'s [12] scheme. The adversary $\mathcal{A}$ can capture two smart card SC_U and SC_V of user U and V respectively and then using power consumption attacks such as differential power analysis (DPA) and simple power analysis (SPA), $\mathcal{A}$ can find out the value of $\{A_U, B_U, W_U, h(.), b_U\}$ and $\{A_V, B_V, W_V, h(.), b_V\}$ from SC_U and SC_V respectively. Since, $A_U = \overline{pw_U} \oplus h(x \oplus y)$, $A_V = \overline{pw_V} \oplus h(x \oplus y)$, applying frequency analysis attacks on A_U, A_V and $A_U \oplus A_V = \overline{pw_U} \oplus h(x \oplus y) \oplus \overline{pw_V} \oplus h(x \oplus y) = \overline{pw_U} \oplus \overline{pw_V}$, the adversary $\mathcal{A}$ can find out the value of $h(x \oplus y)$.

Therefore, $\mathcal{A}$ can compute : $\overline{pw_U} = A_U \oplus h(x \oplus y)$, $B_U = h(ID_U||\overline{pw_U}||h(x \oplus y))$, $[ID_U$ is known by eavesdropping $M_1]$ and $K_U = W_U \oplus h(ID_U||\overline{pw_U})$. Now, $\overline{pw_U} = h(pw_U \oplus b_U)$ and b_U are known to $\mathcal{A}$, pw_U have low entropy and easy to break by dictionary attack. Therefore, with the help of off - line password attacks [13] on $\overline{pw_U}$, $\mathcal{A}$ can figure out user's password pw_U.

Resilience Against Sensor Node Capture Attack: It is evaluated by finding the fraction of total communication that are compromised by capturing m number of sensor node excluding the communication in which the captured m sensor nodes are involved. It measures the effect of m compromised sensor node on the rest of the network. The probability of decrypting the encrypted communication between S_j and user U can be denoted as $P_e(m)$. If $P_e(m) = 0$, the user authentication protocol will be secure against node capture attack.

Suppose $m = 1$ (i.e., one sensor node S_i is captured by $\mathcal{A}$). Then, $\mathcal{A}$ can find out $h(x \oplus y)$ which is store in the memory of S_i for computing the value of ω and also for verifying it with the ω of M_1. If $\mathcal{A}$ have smart card of U , $\mathcal{A}$ can extract $\{A_U, B_U, W_U, h(.), b_U\}$.Therefore, $\mathcal{A}$ can find out : $\overline{pw_U} = A_U \oplus h(x \oplus y)$, $B_U = h(ID_U||\overline{pw_U}||h(x \oplus y))$, $[ID_U$ is known by eavesdropping $M_1]$ and $K_U = W_U \oplus h(ID_U||\overline{pw_U})$. Now, $\overline{pw_U} = h(pw_U \oplus b_U)$ and b_U are known, pw_U have low entropy and easy to break by dictionary attack [13], so after executing off - line password attacks on $\overline{pw_U}$, $\mathcal{A}$ can figure out user's password pw_U. Then, A can get authenticated with sensor node $S_j(i \neq j)$ by sending $M_1 = \langle ID_U, ID_{S_j}, X, T_U, \alpha, \omega \rangle$ to S_j and receiving $M_4 = \langle Y, T_S, T'_S, \gamma, \tau \rangle$ from S_j. Therefore,$\mathcal{A}$ can establish a session key $sk_j = h(X||Y||K_{US_j})$ with S_j. It is clear that$\mathcal{A}$ can get authenticated and establish the session key between U and any other uncompromised sensor node S_j using a compromised sensor node S_i

and a stolen smart card. Thus, $P_e(m) \neq 0$. So, we can say that Choi et al.'s protocol is not resilient against node capture attack.

Sensor Node Energy Exhausting Attack: Sensor node has constrained resources, therefore the computational cost of sensor node is an important consideration. To increase the lifetime of sensor node we need to eliminate unnecessary computation on sensor node. Sometimes adversary's intension is to exhaust the energy of the sensor node in order to slow down or interrupt the network. This type of attack is also known as denial of service attack. In Choi et al. protocol S_n performs various operations such as one way hashing, random number generation and scalar point multiplication of ECC. The computational cost of point multiplication is more than performing one way hashing and generating random number.

Suppose $\mathcal{A}$ eavesdrops $M_1 = \langle ID_U, ID_{S_n}, X, T_U, \alpha, \omega \rangle$, extracts $h(x \oplus y)$ from captured sensor node S_i and $\mathcal{A}$ computes $\omega' = h(ID_U || h(ID_{S_j} || h(x \oplus y) || T_U))$. Then, $\mathcal{A}$ can send $M_1' = \langle ID_U, ID_{S_j}, X, T_U, \alpha, \omega' \rangle$ to S_j. Sensor node S_j computes $\omega'' = h(ID_U || h(ID_{S_j} || h(x \oplus y) || T_U))$, checks if $\omega' = \omega''$, generates $r_s \in Z_q^*$, retrieves S_j's timestamp T_s, computes $Y = r_s \times P$, $\beta = h(SK_{GS} || ID_U || \alpha || \omega' || ID_{S_j} || X || Y || T_U || T_s)$ and sends $M_2 = (ID_U, \alpha, \omega', ID_{S_j}, X, Y, T_U, T_S, \beta)$ to GW. In this way attacker can send more fake messages M_1'', M_1''', M_1'''' etc. to S_j and make S_j to perform unnecessary hashing, generating random number and scalar point multiplication in order to exhaust the battery power of S_j.

5   Discussions and Proposal

The security analysis of Choi et al.'s protocol clears that their protocol is vulnerable because of storing $h(x \oplus y)$ in sensor node (which helps in node capture attacks), storing $A_U = \overline{pw_U} \oplus h(x \oplus y)$ in smart card (it helps in stolen smart card attacks because the value of $h(x \oplus y)$ is same for different smart card which helps in frequency analysis attacks) and verification of ω on sensor node (it helps in sensor energy exhausting attacks). To overcome these security pitfalls, we propose a protocol involving three phases (1) User Registration (2) Login, authentication and session key establishment (3) Password Update Phase. We assume that (i) the trusted gateway node generates two 1024 bit secret key x, y and establishes a long term secret key $K_{GS_n} = h(ID_{S_n} \oplus y)$ with S_n (ii)$P \in E(F_p)$ is shared with U, S_n and GN. The three phase of our protocol are as follows:

5.1   User Registration

U needs to register with GW for retrieving real time and confidential data from the sensor node.

This phase has three steps as elaborated in following Table 2:

5.2   Login, Authentication and Session Key Establishment

This stage involves five steps in order to get login to GW, mutually authenticate U, S_n, GW and establish sk_{US_n} (a secret session key) between U and S_n. Each step checks validity of few conditions. If the condition is true the entity

Table 2. User registration

User	Gateway

1. U chooses ID_U, pw_U,
   generates a 1024 bit random number b_U,
   computes $\overline{pw_U} = h(pw_U \oplus b_U)$.

   U send $\langle ID_U, \overline{pw_U} \rangle$ to GW through secure channel
   $\longrightarrow$

2. GW computes $K_U = h(ID_U \| x) \times P$,
   $A_U = \overline{pw_U} \oplus h(ID_U \oplus y)$,
   $B_U = h(ID_U \| \overline{pw_U} \| h(ID_U \oplus y))$,
   $W_U = h(ID_U \| \overline{pw_U}) \oplus K_U$

   GW Issue SC_U to U which stores $\langle P, A_U, B_U, W_U, h(.) \rangle$
   $\longleftarrow$

3. U store b_U into SC_U

(U, S_n, GW) performs the next computation, otherwise it aborts the protocol. U performs step 1,5 and S_n execute step 2,4 and step 3 is performed by GW. The details of these steps are shown in following Table 3:

5.3 User's Password Update Phase

In this stage, the user U puts SC_U into the card reader, gives ID_U, pw_U and then new password pw'_U. SC_U computes $\overline{pw_U} = h(pw_U \oplus b_U)$, $h(ID_U \oplus y) = \overline{pw_U} \oplus A_U$, $B'_U = h(ID_U \| \overline{pw_U} \| h(ID_U \oplus y))$, Checks $B'_U = B_U$, Computes $K_U = h(ID_U \| \overline{pw_U}) \oplus W_U$, $\overline{pw_U} = h(pw'_U \| b_U)$, $A'_U = h(ID_U \oplus y) \oplus \overline{pw'_U}$, $B'_U = h(ID_U \| \overline{pw'_U} \| h(ID_U \oplus y))$, $W'_U = h(ID_U \| \overline{pw'_U}) \oplus K_U$. Replace A_U, B_U, W_U with A'_U, B'_U, W'_U.

6   Performance Comparison

We compare our protocol with Shi et al.'s [2] and Choi et al.'s [1] protocol on the basis of computational overhead of performing hashing, random number generation and elliptic curve scalar multiplication on smart card, sensor node and gateway node. Table 4 shows that the computational overhead of our protocol is more than Shi et al.'s protocol and less than Choi et al.'s protocol but through the security analysis, as described in Sect. 7, we find that our scheme is more secure than Choi et al.'s scheme. As Choi et al. analyzed that their scheme is more secure than Shi et al.s scheme therefore we can conclude that our scheme is more secure than Shi et al.'s scheme also.

Table 3. Login, authentication and session key establishment

User	Sensor	Gateway

Step1. U performs $\overline{pw_U} = h(pw_U \oplus b_U)$.
$h(ID_U \oplus y) = \overline{pw_U} \oplus A_U$,
$B'_U = h(ID_U||\overline{pw_U}||h(ID_U \oplus y))$,
Checks $B'_U = B_U$
Find $K_U = h(ID_U||\overline{pw_U}) \oplus W_U$,
Generate $r_U \in Z_q^*$
Find current timestamp T_U,
$X_U = r_U \times P$,
$X'_U = r_U \times K_U$,
$T'_U = P \oplus T_U$,
$\alpha = h(ID_U||ID_{S_n}||X_U||X'_U||T_U)$.
$\quad U$ send $M_1 = \langle ID_U, ID_{S_n}, X_U, D, T'_U, \alpha \rangle$ to S_n $\longrightarrow$

Step2. S_n computes $T_U = P \oplus T'$
Checks $T' - T_U \leq \Delta T$
Generates $r_S \in Z_q^*$
Find Current timestamp T_S,
$Y_S = r_S \times P$,
$\beta = h(K_{GS_n}||T_U||Y_S||T_S)$
S_n Send $M_2 = \langle ID_U, X_U, T'_U, \alpha, ID_{S_n}, Y_S, T_S, \beta \rangle$ to GW $\longrightarrow$

Step3. GW Checks $T'' - T_s \leq \Delta T$
Find $F_U = P \oplus T'$,
$X'_U = h(ID_U||x) \times X_U$
Checks
$\alpha = h(ID_U||ID_{S_n}||X_U||X'_U||T_U)$
Checks $\beta = h(K_{GS_n}||T_U||Y_s||T_s)$
Find current timestamp T_G
$\gamma = h(K_{GS_n}||\alpha||Y_s||T_s||T_G)$,
$\delta = h(X'_U||T_U||ID_{S_n}||Y_S||T_S))$.
$\quad GW$ Send $M_3 = \langle T_G, \gamma, \delta \rangle$ to S_n $\longleftarrow$

Step4. S_n Checks $T''' - T_G \leq \Delta T$
Checks
$\gamma = h(K_{GS_n})||\alpha||Y_s||T_s||T_G)$,
Find $K_{S_n U} = r_S \times X_U$,
current timestamp T'_S
$\tau = h(T'_S||\delta||K_{S_n U})$,
$sk_{S_n U} = h(K_{S_n U})$
$\quad S_n$ Send $M_4 = \langle Y_S, T_S, T'_S, \delta, \tau \rangle$ to U $\longleftarrow$

Step5. U Checks $T'''' - T'_S \leq \Delta T$,
$\delta = h(X'_U||T_U||ID_{S_n}||Y_S||T_S))$,
Find $K_{US_n} = r_S \times X_U$
Checks $\tau = h(T'_S||\delta||K_{US_n})$
$sk_{US_n} = h(K_{S_n U})$ [U Establishes session key sk_{US_n} with S_n]

Table 4. Computational overhead comparisons

Scheme	Computational Overhead on U, S_n, GW		
	U	S_n	GW
Shi et al.'s [2]	3M + 5H	2M +3H	1M + 4H
Choi et al.'s [1]	3M + 7H	2M + 4H	1M + 4H
Our Scheme	3M + 6H	2M + 3H	1M + 4H

Where, M and H are cost of performing elliptic curve scalar multiplication and hashing respectively.

7 Security Analysis and Comparison

In this section, we present that our scheme can resist various well known attacks of WSNs. The attacks which we resist through our protocol are as follow:

7.1 Stolen Smart Card Attacks

In case of Choi et al.'s [1] protocol the value $A_U = \overline{pw_U} \oplus h(x \oplus y)$ of smart card of user U and the value $A_V = \overline{pw_V} \oplus h(x \oplus y)$ of smart card of user V helps in frequency analysis attack because A_U and A_V consist of same parameter $h(x \oplus y)$. In case of our protocol A_U and A_V are not build with the same parameter. Therefore, frequency analysis attack is not easy in our scheme. So, even if the adversary $\mathcal{A}$ have smart card of U and V, $\mathcal{A}$ can not find out the password.

7.2 Resilience Against Sensor Node Capture Attack and Energy Exhausting Attack

Choi et al. [1] protocol suggest to store $h(x \oplus y)$ in sensor node's memory in order to resist energy exhausting attacks. But it is creating more insecurity because if $\mathcal{A}$ finds $h(x \oplus y)$ from a captured sensor node, $\mathcal{A}$ can find out the password associated with a stolen smart card and latter it can get authenticated and establish session key with any sensor node. In this way $\mathcal{A}$ succeeds in node capture attack. In order to resist energy exhausting attack we compute $T_U = P \oplus T'_U$ and checks the validity of $T' - T_U \leq \Delta T$. If $T' - T_U > \Delta T$, S_n aborts the protocol and avoid unnecessary computation to be safe from energy exhausting attacks. Since, we are not storing any secret parameter into the sensor node which helps in finding the user's password therefore our protocol is resilient against node capture attacks.

7.3 Other Security Attacks

Our protocol is secure against replay attack because each message which has been delivered through insecure channel contains a valid timestamp. We resist man-in-the middle attack by including authenticating parameter $\alpha, \beta, \gamma, \delta, \tau$ and unique long term secret key for each sensor node. User impersonation attack is not possible because attacker does not know the value of X'_U to find out the value of α. Since, we are using unique long term secret key for each sensor node therefore sensor impersonation attack is not possible. Our scheme yields mutual authentication and session key establishment which can help in resisting few more possible security attacks.

8   Conclusion and Future Work

In this paper, we have analyzed the security provided by Choi et al.'s user authentication protocol. We have found that their protocol has some security weakness such as (1) insecure against stolen smart card attack, (2) no resilient against node capture attack (3) vulnerable to sensor node energy exhausting attacks. Then, we have proposed an improved user authentication scheme using ECC to achieve desirable security requirement with effective computational cost. Our protocol withstands the security pitfalls of Choi et al.'s protocol and improved the computational performance also. In future, we aim to propose efficient three factor identification based mutual authentication protocol to withstand the security weakness of WSNs.

References

1. Choi, Y., Lee, D., Kim, J., Jung, J., Nam, J., Won, D.: Security enhanced user authentication protocol for wireless sensor networks using elliptic curve cryptography. Sens. **14**, 10081–10106 (2014)
2. Shi, W., Gong, P.: A new user authentication protocol for wireless sensor networks using elliptic curves cryptography. Int. J. Distrib. Sens. Netw. **2013**, 730–831 (2013)
3. Yeh, H.L., Chen, T.H., Liu, P.C., Kim, T.H., Wei, H.W.: A secured authentication protocol for wireless sensor networks using elliptic curves cryptography. Sens. **11**, 4767–4779 (2011)
4. Benenson, Z., Gedicke, N., Raivio, O: Realizing robust user authentication in sensor Networks. In: Workshop on Real-World Wireless Sensor Networks, Sweden June 2005
5. Wong, K.H.M., Zheng, Y., Cao, J., Wang, S.: A dynamic user authentication scheme for wireless sensor networks. In: Proceedings of the IEEE International Conference on Sensor Networks, Ubiquitous, and Trustworthy Computing (SUTC06), pp. 5–7, Taichung, Taiwan (2006)
6. Tseng, H.R., Jan, R.H., Yang, W.: An improved dynamic user authentication scheme for wireless sensor networks. In: Proceedings of the IEEE Global Communications Conference, GLOBECOM 2007, pp. 986–990, Washington (2007)
7. Das, M.L.: Two-factor user authentication in wireless sensor networks. IEEE Trans. Wirel. Commun. **8**, 1086–1090 (2009)
8. He, D., Gao, Y., Chan, S., Chen, C., Bu, J.: An enhanced two-factor user authentication scheme in wireless sensor networks. Ad Hoc Sens. Wirel. Netw. **10**, 361–371 (2010)

9. Chen, T.H., Shih, W.K.: A robust mutual authentication protocol for wireless sensor networks. ETRI J. **32**, 704–712 (2010)
10. Han, W.: Weakness of a Secured Authentication Protocol for Wireless Sensor Networks Using Elliptic Curves Cryptography. Cryptology ePrint Archive: Report 2011/293 (2011)
11. Miller, V.S.: Use of elliptic curves in cryptography. In: Williams, H.C. (ed.) CRYPTO 1985. LNCS, vol. 218, pp. 417–426. Springer, Heidelberg (1986)
12. Kocher, P., Jaffe, J., Jun, B.: Differential power analysis. In: Proceedings of the 19th Annual International Cryptology Conference on Advances in Cryptology, pp. 388–397, Santa Barbara (1999)
13. Nam, J., Paik, J., Kang, H.K., Kim, U.M., Won, D.: An off-line dictionary attack on a simple three-party key exchange protocol. IEEE Commun. Lett. **13**, 205–207 (2009)

Secure and Privacy Preserving Biometric Authentication Using Watermarking Technique

Doyel Pal[1(✉)], Praveenkumar Khethavath[2],
Johnson P. Thomas[1], and Tingting Chen[3]

[1] Computer Science Department, Oklahoma State University,
Stillwater, OK, USA
{doyelp,jpt}@cs.okstate.edu
[2] Mathematics, Engineering and Computer Science Department,
LaGuardia Community College, CUNY, Longisland City, NY, USA
pkhethavath@lagcc.cuny.edu
[3] Computer Science Department,
California State Polytechnic University, Pomona, CA, USA
tingtingchen@csupomona.edu

Abstract. Biometric authentication ensures user identity by means of users' biometric traits. Though biometrics is unique and secure, it can be still stolen or misused by any adversary. In this paper we propose a secure and privacy preserving biometric authentication scheme using watermarking technique. Watermarking is used for content authentication, copyright management, tamper detection, etc. We watermark the user's face image with finger print and encrypt the watermarked biometric to protect its privacy from adversary. The watermarked biometric technique has been used for privacy preserving authentication purpose. The analysis proves the correctness, privacy and efficiency of our scheme.

Keywords: Watermark · Biometric · Authentication · Secure · Privacy – preserving

1 Introduction

Authentication plays an important role to identify or authenticate any user. Authentication is primarily based on what user knows (e.g., password, PIN, etc.) or what user has (e.g., token, chip card, etc.) which can be disclosed, stolen, forgotten or lost. Biometric authentication is a secure way to authenticate any user since it is related to the uniqueness of what a user is, i.e. the physiological or behavioral characteristics of a user (e.g., finger print, iris, face image, handwriting etc.). Though biometric traits are unique and secure, unimodal biometric authentications that uses single biometric trait have some limitations [1, 8]. It is vulnerable to spoof attacks, noise in sensed data, distinctiveness, nonuniversality etc. One way to overcome the limitation is using more than one biometric traits of a user. In this paper we propose a secure and privacy

© Springer International Publishing Switzerland 2015
J.H. Abawajy et al. (Eds): SSCC 2015, CCIS 536, pp. 146–156, 2015.
DOI: 10.1007/978-3-319-22915-7_14

preserving biometric authentication scheme which uses more than one biometric trait that are, face image and finger print using watermarking technique.

Watermarking is a technique to embed specific data in a digital content. Watermarking scheme has enormous diversity. It can be categorized [9–11] based on embedding domain (Spatial domain, Transform domain, Feature domain), watermarking host signal (video signal, audio signal, IC design, etc.), availability of original signal during extraction (blind, semi–blind, non–blind) etc. The watermarking technique is advantageous because, to embed the watermark into the original data this technique does not create any separate file to store authentication information. Besides all the advantages of the watermarking technique, any modification on the embedded data can be manipulated easily. Therefore one important requirement of the watermark technique is to make it almost unrecognizable and robust so that watermark cannot be removed or modified by any attack.

To make the biometric watermarking technique more secure, encryption based privacy preserving techniques can be applied. Though watermarked biometrics is difficult to steal or forge but it is not secure when attacked by any determined attacker [2]. Few watermarking techniques (e.g., fragile, robust) becomes invalid or detectable if a slight modification or some image processing operations such as image scaling, cropping, bending is done on the watermarked image. As any individual's biometric features are unique therefore these biometric features should not be compromised or disclosed under any circumstances to any adversary. In this proposal we focus on the privacy preserving secure biometric watermarking scheme for authentication purpose. We preserve the privacy of users' watermarked biometrics using cryptography. To overcome the vulnerability of biometric authentications and to protect the privacy of user's watermarked biometrics, we use biometric authentication in conjunction with digital watermarking and cryptography. We embed the fingerprint on facial image as watermark to improve the security of user authentication and to achieve the privacy of users' biometric traits we encrypt the watermarked biometric before user verification.

The rest of the paper is organized as follows. In Sect. 2 we discuss about the existing related work. We describe the problem statement and preliminaries in Sects. 3 and 4 respectively. In Sect. 5 we explain the proposed solution. We discuss the system analysis and experimental analysis in Sects. 6 and 7 respectively. In Sect. 8 we give the conclusion.

2 Related Work

To authenticate the identity of any user biometric authentication is one of the most trustworthy techniques as it involves verification of users' biometric traits. Biometric authentication systems authenticate any user based on their physical traits, such as, fingerprint, face image, iris, signature etc. which are unique. Different biometric authentication mechanism has been used extensively in various domains. In [3] the authors proposed a framework for three – factor authentication scheme in a distributed system. A template protecting biometric authentication scheme to fingerprint data has been implemented in [4]. In this finger print based authentication mechanism the authors have presented an algorithm which identifies the reliable components of Gabor filtered fingerprint and applies quantization to make a binary representation of the fingerprint. Noise correction has been applied on the quantized binary representation. A multimodal biometric authentication scheme for adapting score–level fusion functions based on quality measures has been proposed in [5]. In [6] a novel and efficient facial image representation based on local binary pattern (LBP) has been proposed which extracts the LBP feature distributions by dividing the face image into several regions and concatenates them into an enhanced feature vector to be used as a face descriptor. Instead of using two different biometric traits a personal identification scheme using palm print and hand geometry which can be acquired from the same image has been proposed in [7]. The authors have integrated the hand geometry on the palm print to improve the performance of the verification system.

Ample of biometric watermarking techniques has been proposed. In [9] the authors proposed a semi – blind biometric watermarking scheme using both watermarking technique and face image recognition. The face features are embedded in the non-overlapping blocks of host image using Singular Value Decomposition (SVD). A robust hybrid biometric watermarking approach for offline handwritten signature has been proposed in [10]. The authors amalgamate the lifting wavelet transform (LWT) and SVD to make the biometric watermarking technique robust. In [11] a watermarking scheme in spatial domain for color image using SVD technique has been introduced. Three dimensions of color iris images are used to embed into color face image to make the technique robust and reliable. An image ownership and tampering authentication scheme based on watermarking techniques has been proposed in [12]. The watermarking technique is used here to detect the malicious manipulation over embedded images and to protect the rightful ownership. In [13] the authors proposed an efficient and secure encryption scheme to transmit the biometric data over unsecured data channel. An asymmetric watermarking technique has been proposed in [18]. In [19] a layered architecture for watermarking technique has been proposed which provides security by using cryptography primitive on top of the watermarking algorithm.

3   Problem Statement

In this paper, we verify the authentication of a user in a privacy preserving secure manner using user's biometrics, watermarking scheme and cryptography. The problem can be framed formally as follows. There are n number of users $U_1, U_2, \ldots., U_i, \ldots, U_n$ and a server S which holds a database D_{fv} with all users' encrypted watermarked feature vector $WSDB_{fv}$. Given a user $U_i's$ biometrics, i.e., face image (I) and fingerprint (F), the user's face image $'I'$ will be watermarked with fingerprint $'F'$ and will be denoted as WB_{fv}. The Euclidean distance ∂ between the user's encrypted watermarked feature vector WB_{fv} and the encrypted watermarked feature vectors $WSDB_{fv}$, in D_{fv} decides the user's authentication (Eq. 1).

$$\partial(E(WB_{fv}), E(WSDB_{fv})) \leq \tau \dots\dots \tag{1}$$

τ denotes the threshold value and if $\partial \leq \tau$, the algorithm determines that user is an authentic one.

4 Preliminaries

4.1 Homomorphic Encryption

In this paper we calculate the Euclidean distance between two cipher texts and to do that we use homomorphic property based encryption scheme. Homomorphic encryption technique allows specific types of arithmetic computations on cipher text and when decrypted the plaintext matches with the result of arithmetic operations on plaintexts without seemingly inherent loss of the encryption. In ring theory, homomorphism is a mapping $\varphi : R \rightarrow S$ that respects both addition and multiplication. Therefore,

$$\forall x, y \in R, \quad \varphi(x + y) = \varphi(x) + \varphi(y) \ and \ \varphi(xy) = \varphi(x) \, \varphi(y)$$

The homomorphic encryption which preserves a single operation such as addition or multiplication is known as partially homomorphic encryption and those which preserves both of the addition and multiplication is known as fully homomorphic encryption. For example, RSA and ElGamal [14, 15] supports the multiplicative homomorphic property, i.e., if $E(x)$ denotes the ciphertext of plain text x then according to multiplicative homomorphism,

$$E(x_1) \cdot E(x_2) = E(x_1 \cdot x_2)$$

Whereas the additive homomorphic property of Paillier cryptosystem [16] denotes that,

$$E(x_1) \cdot E(x_2) = E(x_1 + x_2)$$

4.2 Singular Value Decomposition

In Linear Algebra, Singular Value Decomposition [17] is a factorization technique of a real or complex matrix. In signal processing SVD has been used in applications, e.g., watermarking, noise reduction, image compression, etc. According to SVD theorem any rectangular matrix A of m $\times$ n dimension can be decomposed into the product of three matrices: an orthogonal matrix U of size m $\times$ m, a diagonal matrix S of size m $\times$ n and the transpose of a orthogonal matrix V of size n $\times$ n.

$$A_{m \times n} = U_{m \times m} S_{m \times n} V_{n \times n}$$

The original matrix can be obtained by multiplying U, S, V^T.

$$A = U_{m \times m} S_{m \times n} V_{n \times n}^{T}$$

SVD based watermarking techniques can be categorized into many categories [9], such as, by modification right/left singular vectors of the host images, modification of all singular vectors, hybrid transformation techniques which combines SVD with other transformations(DWT, DFT, DCT, etc.), etc.

5 Proposed Solution

We propose a solution for privacy preserving secure biometric authentication scheme using watermarking technique in this paper. We consider two biometric traits, face image (I) and fingerprint (F) for biometric watermarking authentication purpose and extract the feature vectors from both of these biometrics. To make the entire authentication procedure secure we perform some specific transformations on the real biometric feature vectors instead of using the original biometric feature vectors. The reason behind distorting the feature vectors is to make the authentication more secure. So even if any adversary manages to get the water marked feature vector, they will not be able to get the transformed matrices to be worked on. Since nowadays anyone's face image can be captured by any adversary we will watermark the transformed face image with transformed finger print image to make it more secure. We use linear transformation, i.e., rotation on the actual feature vectors and denote it as transformed feature vector afterwards in this paper. We watermark the transformed feature vector of face image (TSI) with transformed feature vector of fingerprint (TSF) using SVD based watermarking technique. On the watermarked biometric we perform all the further computation for authentication. The watermarked feature vector is stored in the server to authenticate any user. To preserve the privacy of user's watermarked biometrics we encrypt the watermarked biometrics using homomorphic encryption scheme at both the server end and user end. A user is authenticated by calculating the Euclidean distance

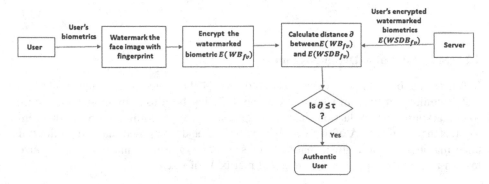

Fig. 1. Overall flow of the authentication mechanism

between the encrypted watermarked biometric provided from user end and the encrypted watermarked biometric from server end. Since Euclidean distance between cipher texts will be calculated we use one of the homomorphic encryption techniques as it allows computation on cipher texts. The distance less than some threshold value τ indicates that the user is an authenticate one. The overall flow of the entire authentication procedure is given in Fig. 1 below.

Algorithm 1
Input: User's finger print F, user's face image I
Steps:

1. The system generates private key – public key pair (x, y) where x is the private key and y is the public key.
2. The server S keeps a database DB for all users water marked biometrics $WSDB_{fv}$
3. Get the feature vector matrix F_{fv} of finger print F.
4. Get the feature vector matrix I_{fv} of face image I.
5. Perform rotation on face image feature vector, $RI_{fv} = \text{Rotation}(F_{fv})$
6. Perform rotation on finger print feature vector, $RF_{fv} = \text{Rotation}(I_{fv})$
7. Perform SVD based watermarking method to watermark RI_{fv} withRF_{fv}. The resulting biometric for user U_i becomes WB_{fv}
8. $for\ i = to\ n$
9. $for\ j = to\ m$
    a. Compute $E(g^{WB_{fv}[i,j]})$and $E(g^{WB_{fv}[i,j]^2})$ and sends them to the server.
10. $end\ for$
11. $end\ for$
12. Server computes
$$C = \prod_{i,j=1}^{m,n} E(g^{WB_{fv}([i,j]^2)}) E(g^{WB_{fv}[i,j]})^{-2(WSDB_{fv}[i,j]} E(g^{WSDB_{fv}[i,j]^2})$$
13. Server decrypts C with private key x and obtain
$$D(C) = g^{\sum_{i,j=1}^{m,n}(WB_{fv}[i,j] - WSDB_{fv}[i,j])^2}$$
14. $if\ D(C) \leq \tau$
    The user is authenticated.
15. $else$
    Discard the user
16. $end\ if$

5.1   Algorithm

In this section we describe the algorithm (Algorithm 1) for the proposed solution. At first the feature vectors of user's face image and finger print will be extracted. The feature vectors will be distorted using some linear transformation, e.g., rotation

(Algorithm 1 line 4–5). To watermark the transformed face image, RI_{fv} with transformed finger print, RF_{fv} we use SVD based watermarking technique [21] (Algorithm 1 line 6). The rest of the computations will be performed on watermarked feature vector WB_{fv}.

We use the ElGamal encryption scheme to encrypt the watermarked feature vector WB_{fv}. Algorithm 1 at the user end computes $E(g^{WB_{fv}[i,j]})$ and $E(g^{WB_{fv}[i,j]^2})$ and sends them to the server (line 7–10). The server has the watermarked transformed feature vector for all users beforehand. To check the authentication the server computes the Euclidean distance between the encrypted feature vectors $WSDB_{fv}$ and WB_{fv} for a particular user (Algorithm 1 line 11). The server computes

$$C = \prod_{i,j=1}^{m,n} E(g^{WB_{fv}([i,j]^2)})E(g^{WB_{fv}[i,j]})^{-2(WSDB_{fv}[i,j])}E(g^{WSDB_{fv}[i,j]^2})$$

which is the Euclidean distance between the encrypted feature vectors. The decrypted Euclidean distance $D(C) = \partial \leq \tau$ denotes that the user is an authenticate one.

6   System Analysis

In this section we analyze the proposed solution in terms of correctness, privacy and performance.

6.1   Correctness Analysis

To proof the correctness of Algorithm 1 it should be proved that server and the user computes the Euclidean distance without knowing the plain text of the feature vectors. The line number 13 of Algorithm 1 can be proved by the homomorphic property of ElGamal algorithm. Figure 2 depicts the correctness of our algorithm.

6.2   Privacy Analysis

In this section we will discuss about the privacy of the proposed solution. We assume that the server is secure. Algorithm 1 is secure in a semi honest model [23]. The user sends the encrypted biometrics to server therefore any adversary will learn nothing but the encrypted watermarked feature vector. Moreover the server does the computation on the cipher texts to get the distance, which implies that Algorithm 1 is secure in a semi honest model. The only decrypted text is the encrypted distance from which no one can learn about the user's biometrics which indicates privacy is preserved in our proposed solution.

$D(C)$

$$= D(\prod_{i,j=1}^{m,n} E(g^{WBfv([i,j]^2)}) \, E(g^{WBfv[i,j]})^{-2(WSDBfv[i,j])} E(g^{WSDBfv[i,j]^2}))$$

$$= D(E(\prod_{i,j=1}^{m,n} g^{(WBfv([i,j])^2} \, g^{(WSDBfv[i,j]^2)}) \prod_{i,j=1}^{m,n} (E(g^{(WBfv[i,j])})^{-2(WSDBfv[i,j])}))$$

$$= D(E(\prod_{i,j=1}^{m,n} g^{(WBfv([i,j])^2} \, g^{(WSDBfv[i,j])^2} \, g^{(WBfv[i,j])^{-2(WSDBfv)}}))$$

$$= D\left(E\left(g^{\sum_{i,j=1}^{m,n}(WBfv[i,j] - WSDBfv[i,j])^2}\right)\right)$$

$$= g^{\sum_{i,j=1}^{m,n}(WBfv[i,j] - WSDBfv[i,j])^2}$$

Fig. 2. Correctness analysis

7 Experimental Analysis

7.1 Experiment Setup

To test the performance we consider different face images sizes varying from 3 KB–7 KB and embed different finger prints on them using watermarking technique. Before watermarking the face image we extract the feature vectors of face image and finger print and transform them by linear transformation technique. To extract the feature vector of biometrics we use PCA - based Face Recognition System package using Matlab [20]. For watermarking purpose, we use the SVD based watermarking technique proposed in [21]. To implement our technique we use the Java programming language and JAMA package [22], since feature vector comes as a form of matrix. We use the SVD based watermarking technique, but because of the constraint of JAMA package for SVD calculation we modified the library so that it can work for any type of feature vector matrix. Existing JAMA package works correctly only for full rank $m \times n$ matrices with $m \geq n$.

7.2 Performance Analysis

We evaluate the performance of our technique in terms of time for different modules that are, watermarking time, encryption time and distance calculation time.

Figure 3 shows the computation time to watermark the face image with finger print image using SVD based watermarking technique at the user end for different file sizes. We vary the file sizes from 10 KB to 100 KB with 10–20 KB interval. Figure 3 shows that if we increase the face image size then the time to watermark the biometrics increases linearly.

We encrypt the watermarked face image with ElGamal encryption technique. Figure 4 depicts the time to encrypt the watermarked feature vector at the user end for different size of face images. The time to encrypt the watermarked face images increases linearly with the increasing face image sizes.

The user is an authenticate one if the distance between the encrypted watermarked biometric at the user end and at the server end is below some threshold value τ.

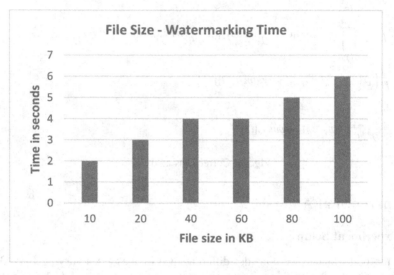

Fig. 3. Computation time of watermarking for different file sizes

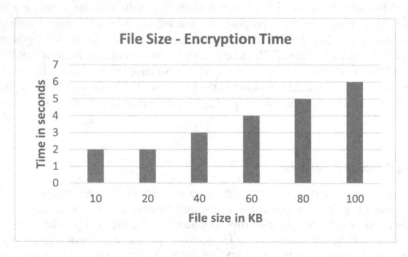

Fig. 4. Computation time of encryption for different file sizes

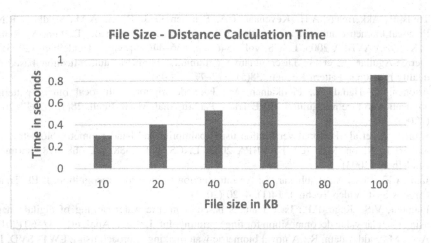

Fig. 5. Computation time to calculate distance for different file sizes

Figure 5 shows the computation time to calculate distance for a particular user at the server side. From Fig. 5 it is evident that with the increasing face image size the time to calculate distance increases linearly.

8 Conclusion

In this paper we propose a secure privacy preserving technique to authenticate a user in a system using user biometrics. We transform the user biometric and watermark the face image with finger print to secure the authentication technique. To preserve the privacy of users watermarked biometric we encrypt it using homomorphic encryption technique. The analysis of our system proves the correctness and privacy of our scheme. The performance analysis shows the efficiency of our technique since the time to authenticate a particular user is less than 11 s where the face image size is 100 KB. For the average face image of less than 10 KB size the proposed technique takes less than 5 s time.

References

1. Riha, Z.: Toward reliable user authentication through biometrics. IEEE Secur. Priv. **1**(3), 45–49 (2003)
2. Katzenbeisser, S.: On the integration of watermarks and cryptography. In: Kalker, T., Cox, I., Ro, Y.M. (eds.) IWDW 2003. LNCS, vol. 2939, pp. 50–60. Springer, Heidelberg (2004)
3. Huang, X., et al.: A generic framework for three-factor authentication: preserving security and privacy in distributed systems. IEEE Trans. Parallel Distrib. Syst. **22**(8), 1390–1397 (2011)

4. Tuyls, P., Akkermans, A.H., Kevenaar, T.A., Schrijen, G.-J., Bazen, A.M., Veldhuis, R.N.: Practical biometric authentication with template protection. In: Kanade, T., Jain, A., Ratha, N.K. (eds.) AVBPA 2005. LNCS, vol. 3546, pp. 436–446. Springer, Heidelberg (2005)
5. Fierrez-Aguilar, J., et al.: Discriminative multimodal biometric authentication based on quality measures. Pattern Recogn. 38(5), 777–779 (2005)
6. Ahonen, T., Hadid, A., Pietikainen, M.: Face description with local binary patterns: application to face recognition. IEEE Trans. Pattern Anal. Mach. Intell. 28(12), 2037–2041 (2006)
7. Kumar, A., et al.: Personal verification using palmprint and hand geometry biometric. In: Kittler, J., Nixon, M.S. (eds.) AVBPA 2003. LNCS, vol. 2688, pp. 668–678. Springer, Heidelberg (2003)
8. Jain, A.K., Ross, A., Prabhakar, S.: An introduction to biometric recognition. IEEE Trans. Circuits Syst. Video Technol. 14(1), 4–20 (2004)
9. Inamdar, V.S., Rege, P.P.: Face features based biometric watermarking of digital image using singular value decomposition for fingerprinting. Int. J. Secur. Appl. 6(2), 47–60 (2012)
10. Arya, M., Siddavatam, R.: A novel biometric watermaking approach using LWT- SVD. In: Das, V.V., Thomas, G., Lumban Gaol, F. (eds.) AIM 2011. CCIS, vol. 147, pp. 123–131. Springer, Heidelberg (2011)
11. Dogan, S., et al.: A robust color image watermarking with singular value decomposition method. Adv. Eng. Softw. 42(6), 336–346 (2011)
12. Chang, C.-C., Yih-Shin, H., Tzu-Chuen, L.: A watermarking-based image ownership and tampering authentication scheme. Pattern Recogn. Lett. 27(5), 439–446 (2006)
13. Mehta, G., Dutta, M.K., Kim, P.S.: An efficient & secure encryption scheme for biometric data using holmes map & singular value decomposition. In: 2014 International Conference on Medical Imaging, m-Health and Emerging Communication Systems (MedCom). IEEE (2014)
14. Rivest, R.L., Shamir, A., Adleman, L.: A method for obtaining digital signatures and public-key cryptosystems. Commun. ACM 21(2), 120–126 (1978)
15. Elgamal, T.: A public key cryptosystem and a signature scheme based on discrete logarithms. IEEE Trans. Inform. Theory 31(4), 469–472 (1985)
16. Paillier, P.: Public-Key Cryptosystems Based on Composite Degree Residuosity Classes. In: Stern, J. (ed.) EUROCRYPT 1999. LNCS, vol. 1592, pp. 223–238. Springer, Heidelberg (1999)
17. Golub, G.H., Reinsch, C.: Singular value decomposition and least squares solutions. Numer. Math. 14(5), 403–420 (1970)
18. Furon, T., Duhamel, P.: An asymmetric watermarking method. IEEE Trans. Signal Process. 51(4), 981–995 (2003)
19. Cox, I.J., Doërr, G., Furon, T.: Watermarking is not cryptography. In: Shi, Y.Q., Jeon, B. (eds.) IWDW 2006. LNCS, vol. 4283, pp. 1–15. Springer, Heidelberg (2006)
20. http://www.mathworks.com/matlabcentral/fileexchange/17032-pca-based-face-recognition-system
21. Satish Chandra, D.V.: Digital image watermarking using singular value decomposition. In: The 2002 45th Midwest Symposium on Circuits and Systems, MWSCAS 2002, vol. 3. IEEE (2002)
22. http://math.nist.gov/javanumerics/jama/
23. Lindell, Y., Pinkas, B.: Privacy preserving data mining. In: Bellare, M. (ed.) CRYPTO 2000. LNCS, vol. 1880, pp. 36–54. Springer, Heidelberg (2000)

Reducing Vulnerability of a Fingerprint Authentication System

A. Athira Ram$^{(\boxtimes)}$ and T.S. Jyothis$^{(\boxtimes)}$

Jyothi Engineering College, Trissur, India
athiraram@gmail.com, jyothis@jecc.ac.in

Abstract. A fingerprint authentication system usually suffers from privacy problem. A third party intruder can steal the information stored in the database and try to recreate the original fingerprint. Here a system is proposed which prevents the possibility of generating fingerprints from the information in the database. Two different fingerprints are acquired from a person. Then the orientation of ridges is calculated from the first fingerprint and minutiae points are extracted from a reference area in second fingerprint. They are combined to form a mixed template which is encrypted using blowfish cipher. The encrypted template serves as a virtual biometric. This prevents the revealing of original fingerprints to third party intruders. Moreover the attacker may not be aware that it is a mixed template that is used rather than the original fingerprint.

Keywords: Authentication · Biometric · Enrollment · False acceptance rate · False rejection rate · Feistel network · Ridge · Skeletonization

1 Introduction

A fingerprint authentication system is the most commonly used Biometric Authentication systems. A fingerprint is an impression left by the friction ridges found on the inner surface of human fingers. A friction ridge is a raised portion of the epidermis on the surface of the palms [1]. The ridges and the furrows constitute the fingerprint pattern. Fingerprints are one of the unchangeable and infallible means of human identification because the ridge patterns are detailed, unique, never repeat, difficult to alter and persist throughout life. It is because of these characteristics fingerprint technology is widely used in authentication systems. The uniqueness of fingerprint patterns made it to be used as to differentiate the legitimate users with frauds. Certain features from fingerprint are extracted during authentication and they are stored on databases. As time moved on, people started even to fool these systems by making an artificial pattern of fingerprints from the stolen data stored in the database. The issue that arises in this type of system is protection of fingerprint privacy [2]. The work in [3] proposes a bio-hashing method in which a pseudo random number is mixed with fingerprint features. The accuracy of this approach depends on key which is assumed to be never stolen. In [4] some transformation which uses a key is proposed. Here use of key reduces the matching accuracy. A fuzzy vault is used to secure fingerprint in [5]. But this method is vulnerable to key inversion attack. In [6] a biometric mixing method is proposed where each person gives two fingerprints. Minutiae points from them are

© Springer International Publishing Switzerland 2015
J.H. Abawajy et al. (Eds): SSCC 2015, CCIS 536, pp. 157–167, 2015.
DOI: 10.1007/978-3-319-22915-7_15

found and superimposed. Combined minutiae list becomes the combined biometric ID. Compared with other techniques, combined biometric is more secure since the attacker may not be aware that a combined template is stored in database. Here a system is proposed such that it is capable to provide privacy to the stored fingerprints. In the proposed system instead of using a single fingerprint, two different fingerprints are used. From both of them different features are extracted and then a combined template is formed which is then encrypted using a private key.

2   Proposed System

Two different fingerprints are to be acquired from two different fingers of a person during the enrollment process. From the first fingerprint, orientation of ridges is estimated. Then from the second fingerprint, a reference area is selected and from there minutiae points are extracted. Then using these, a combined fingerprint sample area is created. This combined fingerprint sample is undergone encryption using a secret key.

2.1   Fingerprint Sensing

Fingerprint Sensing is the process of acquiring fingerprint of a person through either live scan method or inked fingerprint method. For the proposed system, two fingerprints are to be obtained from two different fingers.

2.2   Pre-processing of Fingerprints

Fingerprints are pre-processed before processing them to enhance poor fingerprint patterns. The very first step in the pre-processing of fingerprints is the conversion to black and white images. In this step all the pixel values in the fingerprint images are converted either to 0 or 1. The bi-level conversion of image is depicted in Fig. 1.

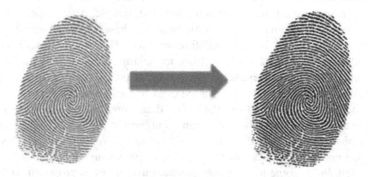

Fig. 1. Conversion to bi-level image

The next pre-processing step is to skeletonize the fingerprints. Fingerprint skeletonization is the thinning of ridges in fingerprint to one pixel width. The thinning process is shown in Fig. 2.

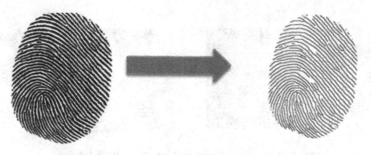

Fig. 2. Thinning of fingerprint

In the proposed system, both the fingerprint images are to be made bi-level and to be thinned.

2.3   Orientation Estimation

The first step is to find the orientation of the first fingerprint. Orientation is the direction of ridges [7].Orientation is not estimated for a pixel alone but for a block of pixels. For that the fingerprint image is divided into N x N set of non-overlapping block of pixels. An example orientation image is shown in Fig. 3.

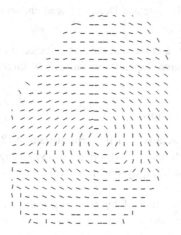

Fig. 3. Orientation image

2.4 Reference Area Detection

Next step is to detect the reference area in the second fingerprint patterns. Basically there are four different fingerprint patterns which are shown in Fig. 4.

Fig. 4. Fingerprint patterns: Arch, Tent, Whorl, Loop

Based on the fingerprint patterns, certain points can be detected which is called as singular points. They are the points where there is a sudden change in ridge direction. There are two types of singular points: Core and Delta points shown in Fig. 5

Fig. 5. Core and Delta in fingerprint patterns

In the proposed system, a reference area is selected around the singular point in second image. The size of area depends on the size of fingerprint image.

2.5 Minutiae Point Extraction

Minutiae are small precise details of a fingerprint pattern [8]. They are of two types: Ridge endings and Ridge bifurcations which are shown in Fig. 6. Ridge endings are the points where the ridges end abruptly and ridge bifurcations are the points where the ridges split into two ridges.

The minutiae points are obtained by scanning the local neighbor pixels of each pixel in the skeletonized fingerprint image, using a 3 × 3 window. The crossing number is calculated which is the sum of pixel value and its neighbouring pixel values as shown in Fig. 7.

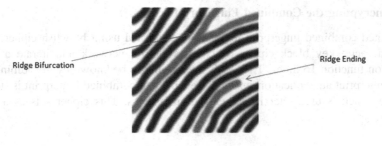

Fig. 6. Minutiae points

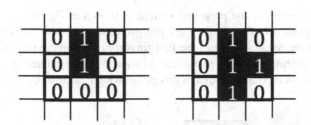

Fig. 7. Crossing number calculation

If the crossing number equals 2, then it is a ridge ending and if it equals 4 then it is a ridge bifurcation.

A minutiae m_i is described by four parameters: $m_i = (x_i, y_i, \Theta_i, t_i)$ where x_i, y_i are coordinates of the minutiae point, Θ_i is minutiae direction and t_i is type of the minutiae point (ridge ending or ridge bifurcation)

2.6   Combined Fingerprint Generation

Using the orientation of first fingerprint and the minutiae points in the reference area of second fingerprint, a combined fingerprint template is generated as in Fig. 8. The minutiae point $(x_i, y_i, \Theta_i, t_i)$ in the second fingerprint originally has an orientation of value Θ_i which is rotated to value α_i, the orientation value at the (x_i, y_i) point in first fingerprint.

Fig. 8. Combined template generation

2.7   Encrypting the Combined Fingerprint

The created combined fingerprint template is encrypted using blowfish cipher. Blowfish is a secret key block cipher which uses Feistel network and iterate a simple encryption function 16 times. The key is meant only to be known by the administrator of the fingerprint authentication system. The cipher of combined fingerprint is stored in database which is used later in authentication process. This cipher acts as a virtual biometric.

3   Enrollment and Authentication

The enrollment process of the proposed system is shown in Fig. 9

After fingerprint acquisition, they are pre-processed in order to enhance the fingerprints and to reduce noise. From the first fingerprint orientation is found and from the second fingerprint minutiae points are extracted in the reference area detected. A quality estimation module is added in this phase which calculates the trustiness value

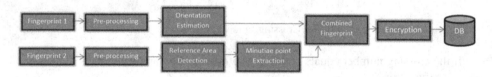

Fig. 9. Enrollment phase

of estimated orientations and minutiae points. If the difference between orientation value of a pixel and that of its neighbor's is more than 30, then the orientation is considered spurious. Similarly if the number of minutiae points in a particular area is more than normal then minutiae points detected at that area are considered as false points. If the total number of spurious orientation and minutia points so detected are less than 30 % of total area of fingerprint then enrollment is done. Using orientation values and minutia points, a combined template is generated which is encrypted and stored in database.

The authentication process has the same steps and is shown in Fig. 10. Two query fingerprints are needed. From the first fingerprint orientation is estimated and from the second fingerprint a reference area is detected and then within that area minutia points are detected. These are compared with the decrypted fingerprint templates stored in database. If matching occurs more than to a particular threshold value then the fingerprints are authenticated.

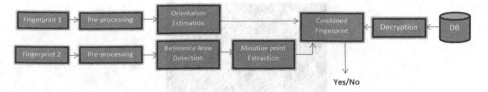

Fig. 10. Authentication phase

4 Simulation Results

The proposed system is simulated using Java 7. The Database used is MySql. The experiment is conducted on a collection of 50 different fingerprint patterns from which 2^{50} different combinations can be made. Both live scan and inked fingerprints are included in the collection.

During the enrollment process, after fingerprints acquisition, they are converted to bi-level images and are thinned. From the first fingerprint the orientation is estimated. The block size used for orientation estimation is block of 16 pixels. This can be varied according to the size of fingerprint image used. The reference area is detected around the singular point which is illustrated in Fig. 11

Fig. 11. Reference area detected

Here in the experiment the radius is taken as the one-third of the total width of fingerprint image pattern. Then the minutiae points are found out. But if the reference area concentrates over any edge area of the pattern then some unwanted endpoints will be detected by the system. An example is in Fig. 12.

To avoid this, a feature selection module is added to the system during the enrollment. There the system minutiae point extraction can be enhanced using manually selecting the minutiae points as shown in user interface shown in Fig. 13.

Fig. 12. Non minutiae points detected

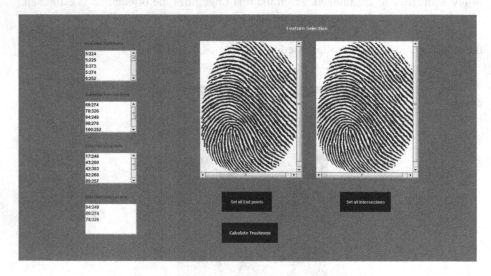

Fig. 13. User interface to manually select minutiae points

After selecting the genuine minutiae points a combined template is generated. The combined template is a java object of class fingerprint.

```
class fingerprint
{
Point referencepoint;
ArrayList minutiae;
ArrayList orientation;}
```

After creating the combined template it is encrypted using blowfish cipher. The cipher of combined cipher is stored in database which is used later in authentication process. This cipher acts as a virtual biometric.

During the authentication phase also two different fingerprints are required. The query fingerprints are pre-processed. Then from the first query fingerprint the orientation is estimated. From the second query fingerprint, a reference area is found out and within which the minutiae points are detected. The virtual biometrics stored in database are taken one by one and decrypted. The original templates thus obtained are compared with the query template.

The orientation values of query fingerprint are directly compared with the orientation values in the template. The minutiae points in query are compared with Euclidean distance between the points and the reference points to that in templates in database.

The percentage of total number of matched minutiae point and percentage of total number of orientation values are calculated. The average of these two is taken as the match score.

To find the threshold value of match score, a randomly selected fingerprint is combined with all other fingerprints to form 49 combined templates. The match score-frequency obtained during 49 genuine tests is shown in Fig. 14.

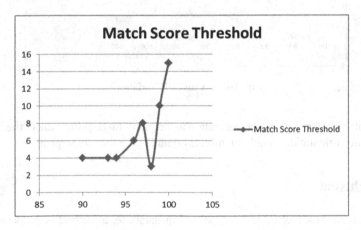

Fig. 14. Match score-frequency

Match score obtained during different genuine and imposter test are shown in Fig. 15.

The False Acceptance and False Rejection in a range of threshold, 90–100 is shown in Fig. 16.

Equal Error Rate (EER) is obtained at 95 %. The threshold value can be set to 95 % to minimize the false acceptance. During the experiments the threshold value is set to 90 % to optimize false acceptance rate and false rejection rate.

If matching occurs above 90 % it is authenticated. The matching score is set in accordance with the quality and size of image quality and size of image.

From the encrypted templates stored in database the intruder cannot recreate any fingerprint templates. If somehow an intruder obtains the encryption key and decrypts

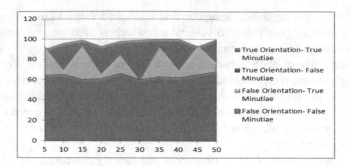

Fig. 15. Match score threshold

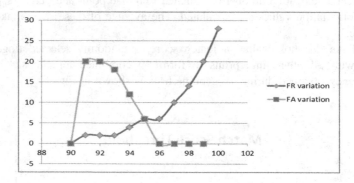

Fig. 16. FA and FR variations

the template, he/she can never recreate the original fingerprints since the template contains only orientation details or minutia details of either fingerprint.

5 Conclusion

To protect the privacy of fingerprints stored in database, a method is proposed which encrypts a mixed template formed of orientation of one fingerprint and minutiae points of other fingerprints. The system prevents intruders from recreating the original fingerprint from the virtual biometric stored. The system is able to provide low error rate also.

References

1. Lee, H.C., Gaensslen, R.E: Advances in Fingerprint Technology, 2nd edn., p. 426. CRC Press, New York (2001)
2. Nagar, B., Nandakumar, K., Jain, A.K: Securing Fingerprint Template: Fuzzy Vault with Minutiae Descriptors (2008)

3. Chen, H., Chen, H.: A novel algorithm of fingerprint encryption using minutiae-based transformation. Pattern Recognit. **32**(11), 305–309 (2011)
4. Teoh, B.J.A., Ngo, C.L.D., Goh, A.: Biohashing: two factor authentication featuring fingerprint data and tokenised random number. Pattern Recognit. **37**, 2245–2255 (2004)
5. Yanikoglu, B., Kholmatov, A.: Combining multiple biometrics to protect privacy. In: Proceedings ICPR- BCTP Workshop, Cambridge, U.K. (2004)
6. Ratha, N., Connell, J., Bolle, R.: Enhancing security and privacy in biometrics-based authentication systems. IBM Syst. J. **40**, 614–634 (2001)
7. Liu, L., Dai, T.: A reliable fingerprint orientation estimation algorithm. J. Inf. Sci. Eng. **27**, 353–368 (2011)
8. Łukasz, W.: A minutiae based matching algorithm in fingerprint recognition systems. J. Med. Inf. Tech. **13**, 1642–6037 (2009)
9. Li, S., Kot, A.C.: Attack using reconstructed fingerprint. In: Proceedings of the IEEE International Workshop on Inform. Forensics and Security (WIFS), Foz do Iguacu, Brazil (2011)

Heart Rate Variability for Biometric Authentication Using Time-Domain Features

Nazneen Akhter[1(✉)], Hanumant Gite[1], Gulam Rabbani[2],
and Karbhari Kale[1]

[1] Department of Computer Science and Information Technology,
Dr. Babasaheb Ambedkar Marathwada University, Aurangabad, MS, India
{getnazneen,hanumantgitecsit,kvkale91}@gmail.com
[2] Department of Physics and Electronics,
Maulana Azad College of Arts, Science and Commerce,
Dr. Rafiq Zakaria Campus, Aurangabad, MS, India
dr_grabbani@yahoo.com

Abstract. Heart Rate Variability (HRV) is a natural property found in heart rate. Medical science since last two decades has been beholding on it as a diagnostic and prognostic tool. This study is intended towards harnessing the HRV property of heart for authentication purpose. For measuring the RR-Interval for HRV analysis, we used photoplethysmography (PPG) based pulse sensor and in-house designed microcontroller based RR-Interval measurement system. Data acquisition is done on PC via serial-to-USB bridge adaptor. Seven Time domain features are generated using standard statistical techniques. Out of 10 samples of each subject, five are used for template creations and other five are used for testing. The system resulted in 17 % EER. The FAR & FRR graph against threshold and the ROC curve are presented.

Keywords: Heart Rate Variability · PPG signals · Time-domain features · Euclidean distance

1 Introduction

In security research domain there is a recent trend towards the use of biosignals for biometric recognition [1], which focuses on identifying and authenticating an individual based on his heart signal or brain signal properties. Biosignals are known to contain strong subject-specific signal patterns that are hard to forge and can only be assessed if the user is present and alive [2]. Traditional biometrics can be easily manipulated [3], on the contrary biosignals are much harder to manipulate and also they inherently come with liveness detection [4], the data generated by biosignals is so intrinsic to an individual that it is hard to steal and even much harder to mimic or forge. Therefore, biosignals based biometric is robust enough against spoofing attacks or falsification. Heart signals being very specific to a particular individual [5], were under investigation from the point of view of person identity thus brisk research activities went into examining these signals.

© Springer International Publishing Switzerland 2015
J.H. Abawajy et al. (Eds): SSCC 2015, CCIS 536, pp. 168–175, 2015.
DOI: 10.1007/978-3-319-22915-7_16

Today the most important research direction in biometric domain is the characterization of novel biometric modalities. HRV is one such heart beat property that can be explored for uniqueness of a person, up till now HRV has been found to be associated with a wide variety of health disorders [6]. In one of our previous article [7] we used five different wrapper algorithms to identify useful features from a large feature set having 101 features. The wrapper algorithms proposed time domain features to be more reliable and effective in recognition systems. Therefore in this article we utilize time domain features obtained from HRV time series data for authentication purpose.

2 HRV Background

Heart Rate Variability is naturally occurring variation in the time gap between two consecutive heartbeats. Figure 1 shows the schematic representation of an ECG showing the prominent components. The highest spike is called as the R peak which represents the occurrence of heartbeat. The time interval between two adjacent R-R peaks is known as R-R interval. The beat-to-beat variation is popularly known as Heart rate variability (HRV). HRV analysis helps in assessing overall cardiac health and the state of the autonomic nervous system (ANS) responsible for regulating cardiac activity [8]. In 1996, a task force of the European Society of Cardiology and the North American Society of Pacing and Electrophysiology developed and published standards for the measurement, physiological interpretation, and clinical use of HRV analysis [9].

3 Methodology

In the proposed system as seen in Fig. 2, initially the biometric data of subjects is collected in this case it is the raw HRV time series data i.e. the RR-Interval sequence. For data acquisition we designed and developed a RR-Interval measurement hardware

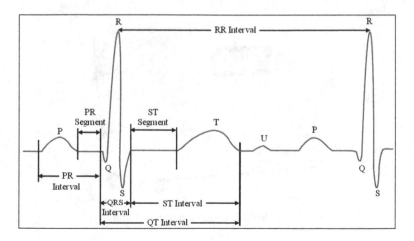

Fig. 1. Prominent components of an ECG signal.

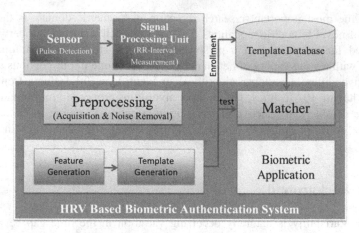

Fig. 2. Proposed system workflow

that is equipped with a pulse sensor to detect the heartbeats. This gave us the freedom to generate our own KVKHRV database, as there is no such specific standard HRV database available for biometric purpose.

3.1   Sensor and Signal Processing Unit (Data Acquisition)

The Sensor shown in Fig. 3 is basically a PPG signal based pulse sensor, and the Signal processing unit is a microcontroller based processing unit which is not only a low cost user friendly device but is also very portable and can be interfaced with a computer via USB or Serial port. The sensor is reflection type and makes use of the reflected red light from the finger tissues. When a finger is placed on the light transmitter-receiver pair, the red light reflected from finger gets modulated in synchronism with the heartbeat and blood flow. This signal is detected and preprocessed in the processing unit and produces

Fig. 3. Sensor & signal processing unit

a square pulse of 100 ms with every heartbeat. The heart beat pulse is derived after signal conditioning through a microcontroller and the output pulse is TTL compatible that can be interfaced with standard microcontrollers or any other TTL circuit. There are more details to the design and development of this unit which is beyond the scope of this article and hence not elaborated further. Details of the design and development of this unit along with working is presented in [6, 10].

3.2 Preprocessing

Preprocessing is done in the data acquisition software which is a GUI designed in Visual Basic 6 as shown in Fig. 4. It is responsible for four specific tasks i.e. collect incoming RR intervals at serial/USB port, remove ectopy (noise) from the RR data, and convert the received RR interval from milliseconds to seconds and finally store a sequence of RR intervals of fixed duration in a text file for further processing. Ectopy or noise in RR time series may originate due to several reasons like: inherent variability of the heartbeats, improper threshold detection of the beats, amplitude variation, missing beat, double triggering due to beat shape, and electronic noise including pickup. All real time systems are prone to this problem to different extent and therefore ectopy removal from RR time series is a standard practice. Detailed ectopy removal process is presented in [11]. Keeping in line with the convention the RR interval sequence i.e. the RRI file is stored in format with two columns with the first column representing the time from the commencement of the measurement when the RRI is measured and the second column contains the actual RRI measured at that instant of time. The data acquisition software works in four modes the smallest mode is most suitable for bio-metric purpose while the other modes can be used for short term HRV based medical diagnosis.

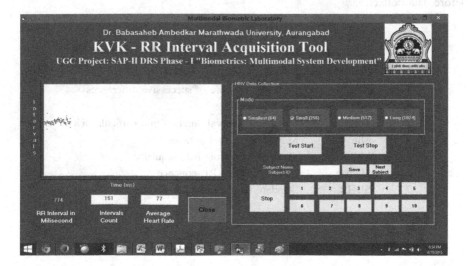

Fig. 4. GUI of the data acquisition system

3.3   Feature Generation

Time-domain measures are the simplest techniques that can be applied on RR-Interval sequence. Standard statistical techniques like mean, median, etc. can be applied on the RR-Interval sequence and time domain measures can be ascertained. These may be separated into two classes: (1) those got from direct estimations of RR- Intervals and (2) those derived from the differences between RR-Intervals [12]. All the features used in experiments are enlisted in the Table 1. These features were selected on the bases of the selected features proposed by five feature selection algorithms proposed in [7].

3.4   Database Specification

At present our KVKHRV database consists 2430 sequences of RR-Intervals of 81 subjects (47 males and 34 Females) whose 10 samples each of 64 RR-Intervals were measured continuously for 1 min approximately, in three different sessions spread over nine months with time interval of three months between each session. The ages of the individuals varied from 18 to 69 years, with mean and standard deviation of 31 and 11 respectively. As it would be natural in any physiological based biometric recognition system, some subjects would have health issues, we too have few samples of this sort around 9 % of subjects reported hypertension and other diseased conditions. Any biosignal based biometric system is susceptible to effects of mental, physical, physiological and even emotional state of the subject. Hence subjects were first relaxed then data was collected in sitting relaxed position for all the sessions. No psychological stimuli was given and neither any physiological restrictions were applied like not taking of caffeine products and no other similar kind of considerations were adhered since this data is specifically collected only for biometrics applications otherwise such considerations are mandatory if we need to make medical analysis of the HRV data so collected. The subjects were informed of the purpose and their consent was taken before data collection.

Table 1. Time-domain feature obtained from RR-interval sequence

Sr. no.	Feature name	Features description
1	RMSSD	Root mean square of successive differences
2	MeanHR	Mean Heart Rate
3	Max	Maximum Interval duration in a particular RRI
4	Min	Minimum Interval duration
5	Mean	Mean of the whole RRI sequence
6	Median	Median of the RRI sequence
7	SDHR	Standard Deviation of Heart Rate

Table 2. FAR & FRR along with the corresponding thresholds and recognition rates

Threshold	FAR	FRR	Recognition rate
0.02	0.0	100.0	0
0.03	3.3	93.3	6.7
0.04	5.0	80.0	20
0.05	6.6	60.0	40
0.06	11.6	30.2	69.8
0.07	18.3	13.3	86.7
0.08	36.6	6.6	93.4
0.09	43.3	5.0	95
0.10	56.6	5.0	95
0.11	66.6	3.3	96.7
0.12	80.0	3.3	96.7
0.13	86.6	0.0	100

4 Results and Discussions

For this experiment, we randomly chose 60 subjects of out of 81. We used four samples from session one and three each from session two and three making total of ten samples per subject. Then we partitioned the samples in two groups of five each. With first group samples we created the enroll template, by taking mean of all five samples and similarly we the other group we created the test template. We calculate the Euclidean distances between the two templates (enroll & Test) for all the subjects, the test template having the smallest Euclidian distance with enroll template is considered to belong to that same subject. From the distance matrix so obtained we calculated the

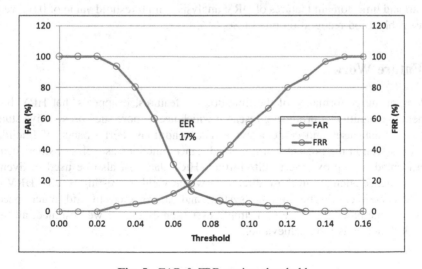

Fig. 5. FAR & FRR against threshold

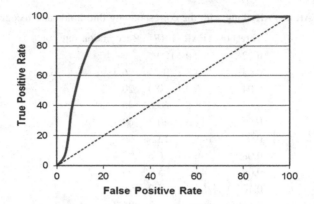

Fig. 6. ROC curve of the proposed system

maximum and minimum value to decide the threshold. As we increased the threshold, FAR is increased and FRR is decreased, both FAR and FRR are inversely proportional. If we keep threshold value too loose we get recognition rate 100 % but we can't accept this 100 % recognition rate because FAR is more therefor we have to select recognition rate where false acceptance and rejection are low. At a given threshold a biometric system that gives low FAR and Low FRR is good one in our case its 0.07 as can be seen in Table 2 and Fig. 5. Also the ROC Curve can be seen in Fig. 6.

5 Conclusion

One of the important characteristic of the heart is its heart rate variability (HRV) that has been used for different applications including diagnosis and prognosis. We attempted biometric authentication of 60 subjects in this article using the HRV property of heart and time domain features of HRV analysis, with threshold value of 0.07 we got a reasonably good recognition rate of 86.7 %.

6 Future Work

Looking at the performance of the time-domain features, it appears that HRV based biometric recognition is promising research which needs more such prospective studies with larger databases and context aware data conditions. Performance of Euclidean distance is seen in the present work, more distance functions as well classifiers can be experimented to improve the results further. HRV data can also be used in liveness detection hence attempts in those directions would yield interesting results. HRV can also be experiment in multimodal system and is expected to add much needed robustness and efficiency. Due to a simple user friendly device we designed, all these research dimensions look achievable.

Acknowledgement. This work was carried out in Multimodal System Development laboratory established under UGC's SAP scheme SAP (II) DRS Phase-I F. No.-3-42/2009 & SAP (II) DRS Phase-II F. No.4-15/2015. This work was also supported by UGC under One Time Research Grant F. No. 4-10/2010 (BSR) & 19-132/2014 (BSR).The authors acknowledge UGC for the same. The authors also acknowledge UGC for providing BSR fellowship.

References

1. da Silva, H.P., Lourenço, A., Fred, A., Raposo, N., Aires-de-Sousa, M.: Check your biosignals here: a new dataset for off-the-person ECG biometrics. Comput. Methods Programs Biomed. **113**, 503–514 (2014)
2. Singh, Y.N., Singh, S.K., Ray, A.K.: Bioelectrical signals as emerging biometrics: issues and challenges. ISRN Signal Process. **2012**, 1–13 (2012)
3. Ross, A.: An introduction to multibiometrics (2007)
4. Agrafioti, F.:. ECG in biometric recognition: time dependency and application challenges (2011)
5. Khandait, P., Bawane, N., Limaye, S.: Features extraction of ECG signal for detection of cardiac arrhythmias. Int. J. Comput. Appl. **8**, 6–10 (2012)
6. Akhter, N., Mahdi, J.F., Manza, G.R., Registrar, D.: Microcontroller based data acquisition system for heart rate variability (HRV). Measurement **1**, 576–583 (2012)
7. Akhter, N., Tharewal, S., Kale, V., Bhalerao, A., Kale, K.V.: Heart based biometrics and use of heart rate variability in human identification systems. In: 2nd International Doctoral Symposium, 23–25 May 2015
8. Acharya, U.R., Joseph, K.P., Kannathal, N., Lim, C.M., Suri, J.S.: Heart rate variability: a review. Med. Biol. Eng. Comput. **44**, 1031–1051 (2006)
9. Malik, M., Bigger, J.T., Camm, A.J., Kleiger, R.E., Malliani, A., Moss, A.J., Schwartz, P.J.: Heart rate variability. Eur. Heart J. **17**, 354–381 (1996)
10. Akhter, N., Tharewal, S., Gite, H., Kale, K.V.: Microcontroller based RR-interval measurement using PPG signals for hear variability based biometric application. In: International Symposium on Emerging Topics in Circuits and Systems, 10–13 August 2015
11. Akhter, N., Gite, H., Tharewal, S., Kale, K.V.: Computer based RR-interval detection system with ectopy correction in HRV data. In: International Conference on Advances in Computing, Communications and Informatics, 10–13 August 2015
12. Miyamoto, M., Ichimaru, Y., Katayama, S.: Heart rate variability. Nippon Rinsho. **50**, 717–722 (1992)

Modeling Fuzzy Role Based Access Control Using Fuzzy Formal Concept Analysis

Chandra Mouliswaran Subramanian[1]([⊠]), Aswani Kumar Cherukuri[1], and Chandrasekar Chelliah[2]

[1] School of Information Technology and Engineering,
VIT University, Vellore, India
scmwaran@gmail.com, cherukuri@acm.org
[2] Department of Computer Science, Periyar University, Salem, India
ccsekar@gmail.com

Abstract. Role based access control (RBAC) is the widely accepted and used access control model. However, mappings among the set of users, roles and permissions in RBAC is a major challenging task. This leads to errors in practical applications. Incorporating human decisions on mappings of RBAC could resolve this issue. But, in real time, human decisions are fuzzy in nature. So, fuzzy techniques can be incorporated into RBAC through fuzzy role based access control (FRBAC). Fuzzy formal concept analysis (FFCA) is a mathematical model for representation of uncertain information in the form of formal context. However to the best of our knowledge, there are no works on modelling fuzzy RBAC through fuzzy FCA. The objective of this paper is to propose the model of representing FRBAC in the form of FFCA. The initial results of our experiments show that the proposed model could implement the major features of RBAC.

Keywords: Access control · Fuzzy FCA · FRBAC · RBAC

1 Introduction

Role based access control is the highly sophisticated predominantly used policy neutral access control model for online enterprise application [1–3]. The major relationships among the components of RBAC are mappings of role with permission, user with role and user with permission. It has extensively reduced the complexity of security administrator in terms of managing the access permissions of users. By implementing the important security principles of RBAC such as least privilege, separation of duty and data abstraction, it has further simplified the task of security administrator and made it easier. In the recent times, with the massive growth of the number of users in online enterprise applications, the mappings on user with role becomes complicated and error prone. The error in user with role mapping leads to escape the frauds and creates the conflict of interest in assigning dynamically mutually exclusive roles. It leads to the involvement of human decisions on user with role mapping become essential. But, in real time scenario, human decisions on mapping user with role are fuzzy. In this mapping, the crisp set of objects or users are assigned with fuzzy role strength while

© Springer International Publishing Switzerland 2015
J.H. Abawajy et al. (Eds): SSCC 2015, CCIS 536, pp. 176–185, 2015.
DOI: 10.1007/978-3-319-22915-7_17

mapping with different set of roles. So that, the application of fuzzy role based access control (FRBAC) in user with role mappings become essential. Martínez-García et al. [4] have successfully introduced the FRBAC model with its complete formalism in the form of core FRBAC, hierarchical FRBAC and constrained FRBAC.

Fuzzy formal context is the mathematical representation of uncertain information in the form of formal context and it incorporates the fuzzy set theory into formal concept analysis (FCA). Fuzzy formal concept analysis (FFCA) has been successfully applied in evaluation of clustering quality [5]. In the recent time FFCA has been applied in distributed creation of model in cloud environment [6]. The literature [7] shows the various applications of FFCA in knowledge discovery in databases (KDD) such as discovery of semantic web services, user behavioural model from web usage logs etc. Concept lattices have been extensively used in implementation of access control policies [8]. Sergei et al. [9] have used an interactive technique to construct lattices for access control models with the help of attribute exploration process in FCA. Dau and Knechtel [10] have designed the triadic formal context for RBAC and further discussed the steps to derive dyadic formal context. FFCA has also been adapted in fuzzy descriptive logics [11].

Motivated by the fruitful results of Martínez-García et al. [4], Sergei et al. [9] and Dau and Knechtel [10], we propose fuzzy role based access control model using fuzzy formal concept analysis. In this paper, we have formalized a model for user with role mapping of FRBAC using one-sided threshold method of FFCA. Our intensive literature shows that this is the first attempt in formalizing FRBAC using FFCA. The initial results of our experiments show that the proposed model could implement the user with role mappings of FRBAC. The rest of the paper is organized as follows. Sections 2.1 and 2.2 provides the brief background of FRBAC and FFCA respectively. The related work is described in Sect. 2.3. We present the proposed modeling of FRBAC using FFCA in Sect. 3 and the demonstration of experimental results in Sect. 4.

2 Background

2.1 Fuzzy Role Based Access Control

FRBAC is suitable for risk based environments where the uncertain authorization related information exists. Here, the action on the data resources gets fractional meaning. Access decisions are based on the level of imprecision and get the fuzzy value in the range of zero to one. Incorporating fuzzy decisions in the mappings of user with role, role with permission and user with permission derives the FRBAC model. Some of the FRBAC system [11] defines the mapping of user with role based on the comparison of trustworthiness of user and role. A user is fixed to a role only when the trustworthiness of the user is greater than or equal to the role required trustworthiness. It gives the comparison between role and trust degree. In addition to this, permissions are assigned to trust degree rather than roles.

To describe the RBAC model, we use the notation and model definition given by Martínez-García et al. in [4]. FRBAC has been divided into three parts namely core FRBAC, hierarchical FRBAC and constrained FRBAC. The basic functionalities are dealt in Core FRBAC. Hierarchical FRBAC is the extension of the core FRBAC with hierarchies of roles. Constrained FRBAC incorporates the separation of duty constraints. The main functionality of core FRBAC is the assignment of user with role and role with permission fixed through the fuzzy relation of the form UA: U x R $\rightarrow$ [0, 1] and PA: R x P $\rightarrow$ [0, 1]. Here, UA represents the mappings of user (U) with role(R) and PA represents the mappings of roles (R) with permissions (P). The user with role mapping represents how the individual user (u) associated with the individual role (r) with the mapping function (μ_{UA}) which represents the strength of user with role. Similarly, the role with permission mapping represents how the individual role (r) associated with different permission (p) with the mapping function (μ_{PA}) which represents the strength of role with permission. The readers are suggested to refer [4] to find the study on active assignment relation, user with permission mapping and access function. Hierarchical FRBAC defines the hierarchical relation between roles. Here, the permissions of high priority role are derived from the low priority role and the users of high priority role are the users of the low priority role. Here, the high priority role represents the senior role in role hierarchy and low priority role represents the junior role in role hierarchy. Constrained FRBAC describes the constraints on static separation of duty and dynamic separation of duty in FRBAC. The detailed study on hierarchical FRBAC and constrained FRBAC is available in [4]. To understand the real time application scenarios of FRBAC, consider the example described in [4] that the database of a hospital is accessed by an external party in order to perform the epidemical research. Here, the external party user is allowed to get a role with a relational strength to access the hospital database based on the trustworthiness. This is an example of user with role mapping in FRBAC.

2.2 Fuzzy Formal Concept Analysis

Formal concept analysis (FCA) is a mathematical theory which makes the knowledge in terms of formal concepts. The formal concept is an ordered pair with extents and intents. The extents are the subset of all objects in the context. The intents are the subset of all attributes in the context. The partial ordering among the set of all formal concepts with super-sub relationship is known as concept lattice.

Fuzzy formal concept analysis (FFCA) is a mathematical model to represent the uncertain information in the precise formalism of FCA. It works on uncertain values. It integrates the fuzzy set theory and formal concept analysis. It is a fuzzy valued relation in which an object can have the attribute in a certain conceptual scaling. We can define the fuzzy relationship (R) between objects (OBJ) and attributes (ATT) as R: OBJ x ATT $\rightarrow$ [0,1]. FFCA has the membership value in the range of zero and one. Fuzzy formal concept is a pair < A, B > where A is a set of objects with crisp values and B is a set of attributes with fuzzy values such that $A^\uparrow = B$ and $B^\downarrow = A$.

$$A^\uparrow = \{a \, / \, \mu_A(a) \mid \mu_A(a) = \min_{b \in B}(\mu_R(a,b))\} \tag{1}$$

$$B^\downarrow = \{b \in B \mid \forall a \in A : \mu_R(a,b) \geq \mu_A(a)\} \tag{2}$$

In the above Eqs. (1) and (2), the operators (↑) and (↓) represents the concept forming operators. Similarly, fuzzy formal concept can be defined with fuzzy set of objects and crisp set of attributes. The alpha cut is a common approach to fuzzification of FCA. It is to reduce the fuzzy value into crisp calculation. There are two methods to represent the fuzzy formal concepts. They are one-sided threshold and fuzzy closure operator based on residuated implication. The one sided threshold holds either intents or extents as fuzzy and not the both. The other method is the fuzzy closure operation based on residuated implication holds both intents and extents as fuzzy. In real time scenario, there are practical applications for one sided threshold as like user with role mapping in FRBAC. It is difficult to represent the practical applications for the FFCA method based on residuated implications. The method based on alpha-cut becomes crisp, once the particular choice of threshold is met. The literature [7] shows the various applications of FFCA in KDD such as discovery of semantic web services, user behavioural model from web usage logs etc.

2.3 Related Work

The basic RBAC policy, model, components and their interactions are available in [1]. Sandhu et al. have introduced the unified model for RBAC called NIST RBAC model [2, 3]. Temporal-RBAC (TRBAC) [12] was introduced as the extension of the RBAC to meet the interest of individuals in terms activating and disabling the roles periodically. Distributed RBAC (dRBAC) [13] mechanism was evolved to meet the requirements of multiple domain environments. Based on the concept of classification of tasks, Task-role based access control (T-RBAC) [14] was introduced to suit the requirements of enterprises and industrial applications. Unal and Cagalyan [15] modeled the FPM-RBAC to solve major issues of multiple domains RBAC such as location and mobility constraints, inter domain services and separation of duty. Baracaldo et al. [16] have recommended a RBAC framework to support the temporal and separation of duty constraints for the secure inter operation among multiple domains. Kumar and Newman [17] introduced a new approach called STRBAC to deal with spatio-temporal aspects of RBAC. Zhou et al. [18] have introduced the cryptographic RBAC system for the storage system in cloud environment. Lee et al. [19] have introduced the XACML based RBAC model for substation automation system in smart grid environment. Ni et al. [20] have introduced framework for privacy aware RBAC. Martino et al. [21] have introduced the Multi-domain and privacy aware RBAC in eHealth. Takabi et al. [22] have proposed a model to introduce separation of duty policies in RBAC using fuzzy set theory. Nawarathna and Kodithuwakku [23] have presented a new FRBAC model for database security with Fuzzy policy evaluator. Wang and Liu [24] have proposed a user-role assignment model based on user trustworthiness in the system. Knechtel [25] have formalized the access control matrix of RBAC as a triadic context with the support of descriptive logic. Aswani Kumar [26] has used the formal concept analysis to model the access permission of RBAC. Further, Aswani Kumar [27] has used fuzzy K-means clustering to reduce the formal context and used the FCA for association rule mining. Chinese wall security policy has been modeled using formal concept analysis [28]. Singh et al. [29] have proposed an algorithm for fuzzy formal concepts generation based on the interval values. Based on our thorough literature survey, this is the first attempt to achieve FRABC using fuzzy FCA.

3 Fuzzy Role Based Access Control Using Fuzzy FCA

In the access control matrix of FRBAC, rows represent subjects, columns represent the objects and the entries in this matrix are the fuzzy values ranges from zero to one. So, it is called as fuzzy access control matrix. Generally, these fuzzy access control matrix represents the three different mappings in FRBAC. Those mappings are user with role, role with permission and user with permission. In this proposed model, we present the fuzzy access control matrix which represents the mappings of the user with role only. In this matrix, rows are the crisp set of users and the columns are the fuzzy set of roles and the entries are the fuzzy values which represents the relational strength of crisp users on different fuzzy roles. Based on the application dependent and authorization-related information such as the trustworthiness of the user, seniority level of the user and the purpose of need to know by user, the fuzzy relational strength values is assigned in user-role assignment. The user-role relation strength also represents the risk associated to the fact that a user belongs to a role. The value of relational strength is derived from user trustworthiness. To derive the user and role matrix as the context, the set of users are identified as the formal objects and the set of roles as the formal attributes.

The steps given below describe the procedure to derive the user with role mappings of fuzzy role based access control using fuzzy formal concept analysis.

1. Identify the set of users (U), the set of roles (R) and the relational strength (I) of individual users on different roles. Here, the relational strengths are the fuzzy values.
2. Derive the matrix (M_{UxR}) of identified users (U) and roles (R) by assigning the fuzzy relational strength value between users and roles.
3. Transform the matrix (M_{UxR}) derived in step 2 as the fuzzy formal context $K_{U,R} = K (U, R, I^{U,R})$ as the mappings the users with roles in FRBAC.
4. Obtain the different fuzzy concepts from the fuzzy formal context ($K_{U,R}$) derived in step 3.
5. Construct the fuzzy concept lattice from the fuzzy formal concepts obtained in step 4. Here, the formal objects or users are organized in various levels of the lattice depends upon how the various users are associated with the different formal attributes or roles.

In the next section, we demonstrate the proposed modeling of FRBAC using FFCA with a practical example.

4 Experimental Results

To demonstrate our proposed work, we consider the scenario of FRBAC on mapping user with role. To bring the clarity in our discussion, we consider only the four users and four roles. The four users are identified as U1, U2, U3 and U4 and the four roles are identified as R1, R2, R3 and R4. The mapping of these users with roles is the fuzzy values from zero to one. Here, the users are considered as the crisp objects and the roles are considered as the fuzzy attributes. The association of individual users U1, U2, U3 and U4 with fuzzy roles R1, R2, R3 and R4 are described as UA1, UA2, UA3 and UA4 respectively and they are mentioned below.

$$UA1 = \{1, 0.7, 0, 0\} \quad UA2 = \{0, 1, 1, 0.6\}$$
$$UA3 = \{0.4, 0, 1, 0.8\} \quad UA4 = \{0.8, 0, 0.4, 1\}$$

By merging the UA1, UA2, UA3 and UA4, we can derive the matrix (M_{UxR}) of user with role mapping in FRBAC. Then, extract the fuzzy values from the above mentioned associations and formalize the fuzzy formal context as described below in the Table 1.

Next, derive the various fuzzy concepts from the fuzzy formal context of users with roles mapping of FRBAC described in Table 1. Here, we use fuzzy concept generation algorithm described in [30].

The generated fuzzy formal concepts under the fuzzy formal context described in Table 1 are shown in Table 2. From the Table 2, we can understand the fuzzy concepts as follows. The concept C2 represents the users U1, U3 and U4 and they are related to the role R1 with the role strength of 0.4. The concept C3 represents the users U2, U3 and U4 and they are related to the roles R3 and R4 with the role strength of 0.4 and 0.6

Table 1. A fuzzy formal context of FRBAC.

	R1	R2	R3	R4
U1	1	0.7	0	0
U2	0	1	1	0.6
U3	0.4	0	1	0.8
U4	0.8	0	0.4	1

Table 2. Fuzzy concepts of the FRBAC fuzzy formal context given in Table 1.

Concept No.	Concepts
C1	{[U1,U2,U3,U4], [Ø] }
C2	{[U1,U3,U4], [R1/0.4]}
C3	{[U2,U3,U4], [R3/0.4, R4/0.6] }
C4	{[U1,U2], [R2/0.7] }
C5	{[U1,U4], [R1/0.8]}
C6	{[U3,U4], [R1/0.4, R3/0.4, R4/0.8] }
C7	{[U2,U3], [R3, R4/0.6] }
C8	{[U1], [R1, R2/0.7] }
C9	{[U4], [R1/0.8, R3/0.4, R4] }
C10	{[U2], [R2,R3, R4/0.6] }
C11	{[U3], [R1/0.4, R3, R4/0.8]}
C12	{[Ø], [R1,R2,R3,R4]}

respectively. Similarly, the concept C4 represents the users U1 and U2 and they are related to R2 with the role strength of 0.7. In this way, we can understand all the concepts listed in Table 2, by the way in which the set of user at individual concepts are associated with the set of roles along with their role strength.

Totally, we have achieved twelve different concepts. This formal analysis on user-role assignment helps to classify the various concepts and helps to understand how the individual user is associated with different roles and more than one user are associated with different common roles with their relational strength.

Then, we construct the fuzzy concept lattice structure as shown in Fig. 1 from the fuzzy formal concepts listed in Table 2. In this lattice structure, the nodes are representing the concepts and the concepts are representing the association of set of users along with the set of roles with their role strength. The addition and deletion of users into the fuzzy formal context or the updates into the role strength will bring the necessary updates into the resultant concept lattice as per the concept forming operator function. In this lattice structure, we can visualize that concepts containing all of the four users U1, U2, U3 and U4 at the top level or level 1 and the concepts associated with three users U1, U2 and U3 are at the level 2. Similarly, the concepts associated with two users, single user and none of the users are at the level 3, level 4 and level 5

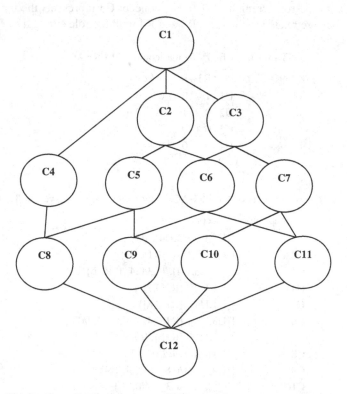

Fig. 1. Fuzzy lattice structure of FRBAC fuzzy concepts in Table 2.

respectively. This represents that least privilege and user hierarchy is achieved in mapping of users with role in FRBAC. It represents the user hierarchy with their least privilege based on the relational strength on different roles. In addition to this, user-role assignment lattice help to visualize how many roles with which every individual user is associated. This lattice structure is required to be experimented further to test whether it satisfies the other security features such as static and dynamic separation of duty. Similarly, the experimentation on other mappings of FRBAC such as role with permission and user with permission in fuzzy formal context is left for the future work.

5 Conclusion

In this paper, we have modeled FRBAC using fuzzy FCA. To demonstrate this, we have formalized the set of users as the crisp objects and the set of roles as fuzzy attributes in FRBAC. The entries into this fuzzy formal context represent the relational strength of the set of users with different roles in FRBAC based fuzzy formal context. This fuzzy formal context exactly represents the mapping of user with role in FRBAC. Then, we generate the list of fuzzy concepts for the FRBAC based fuzzy formal context. Next, we construct the model of FRBAC based fuzzy concept lattice from the fuzzy concepts generated. The resultant FRBAC based fuzzy concept lattice satisfies the two main security features of FRBAC such as least privilege and user hierarchy.

References

1. Sandhu, R.S., Coyne, E.J., Feinstein, H.L., Youman, C.E.: Role-based access control models. Computer **29**(2), 38–47 (1996)
2. Sandhu, R., Ferraiolo, D., Kuhn, R.: The NIST model for role based access control: towards a unified standard. In: Proceedings of the 5th ACM Workshop on Role Based Access Control, July 26–27, Berlin, pp. 47–63 (2000). Initial proposal for the current INCITS 359-2004 RBAC standard
3. Ferraiolo, D.F., Sandhu, R., Gavrila, S., Richard Kuhn, D., Chandramouli, R.: Proposed NIST standard for role-based access control. ACM Trans. Inf. Syst. Secur. (TISSEC) **4**(3), 224–274 (2001)
4. Martínez-García, C., Navarro-Arribas, G., Borrell, J.: Fuzzy role-based access control. Inf. Process. Lett. **111**(10), 483–487 (2011)
5. Sassi, M., Touzi, A.G., Ounelli, H.: Clustering quality evaluation based on fuzzy FCA. In: Wagner, R., Revell, N., Pernul, G. (eds.) DEXA 2007. LNCS, vol. 4653, pp. 639–649. Springer, Heidelberg (2007)
6. Sarnovsky, M., Butka, P., Pocsova, J.: Cloud computing as a platform for distributed fuzzy FCA approach in data analysis. In: 16th IEEE International Conference on Intelligent Engineering Systems (INES), pp. 291–296. IEEE (2012)
7. Poelmans, J., Elzinga, P., Viaene, S., Dedene, G.: Formal concept analysis in knowledge discovery: a survey. In: Croitoru, M., Ferré, S., Lukose, D. (eds.) ICCS 2010. LNCS, vol. 6208, pp. 139–153. Springer, Heidelberg (2010)
8. Crampton, J.: Authorization and antichains. Ph.D. diss.: Birkbeck College (2002)

9. Sergei, A.O., Kourie, D.G., Eloff, J.H.P.: Building access control models with attribute exploration. Comput. Secur. **28**(1–2), 2–7 (2009)
10. Dau, F., Knechtel, M.: Access policy design supported by FCA methods. In: Rudolph, S., Dau, F., Kuznetsov, S.O. (eds.) ICCS 2009. LNCS, vol. 5662, pp. 141–154. Springer, Heidelberg (2009)
11. Takabi, H., Amini, M., Jalili, R.: Enhancing role-based access control model through fuzzy relations. In: Third International Symposium on Information Assurance and Security, IAS 2007, pp. 131–136. IEEE (2007)
12. Bertino, E., Bonatti, P.A., Ferrari, E.: TRBAC: A temporal role-based access control model. ACM Trans. Inf. Syst. Secur. (TISSEC) **4**(3), 191–233 (2001)
13. Freudenthal, E., Pesin, T., Port, L., Keenan, E., Karamcheti, V.: dRBAC: distributed role-based access control for dynamic coalition environments. In: Proceedings of the 22nd International Conference on Distributed Computing Systems, pp. 411–420. IEEE (2002)
14. Oh, S., Park, S.: Task-role based access control (T-RBAC): an improved access control model for enterprise environment. In: Ibrahim, M., Küng, J., Revell, N. (eds.) DEXA 2000. LNCS, vol. 1873, p. 264. Springer, Heidelberg (2000)
15. Unal, D., Caglayan, M.U.: A formal role-based access control model for security policies in multi-domain mobile networks. Comput. Netw. **57**, 330–350 (2013)
16. Baracaldo, N., Maasoumzadeh, A., Joshi, J.: A secure constriant aware role based access conrol interoperation framework. IEEE (2011). 978-1-4577-0460-4/11
17. Kumar, M., Newman, R.E.: STRBAC - an approach towards spatio-temporal role-based access control. In: Proceedings of the 3rd IASTED International Conference on Communication, Network, and Information Security, pp. 150– 155 (2006)
18. Zhou, L., Varadharajan, V., Hitchens, M.: Secure administration of cryptographic role-based access control for large-scale cloud storage systems. J. Comput. Syst. Sci. **80**(8), 1518–1533 (2014)
19. Lee, B., Kim, D.-K., Yang, H., Jang, H.: Role-based access control for substation automation systems using XACML. Inf. Syst. **53**, 237–249 (2015)
20. Ni, Q., Bertino, E., Lobo, J., Brodie, C., Karat, C.-M., Karat, J., Trombeta, A.: Privacy-aware role-based access control. ACM Trans. Inf. Syst. Secur. (TISSEC) **13**(3), 1–31 (2010)
21. Martino, L.D., Ni, Q., Lin, D., Bertino, E.: Multi-domain and privacy-aware role based access control in eHealth. In: Second International Conference on Pervasive Computing Technologies for Healthcare, Pervasive Health 2008, pp. 131–134. IEEE (2008)
22. Takabi, H., Amini, M., Jalili, R.: Separation of duty in role-based access control model through fuzzy relations. In: Third International Symposium on Information Assurance and Security, IAS 2007, pp. 125–130. IEEE (2007)
23. Nawarathna, U.H.G.R.D., Kodithuwakku, S.R.: A fuzzy role based access control model for database security. In: Proceedings of the International Conference on Information and Automation, pp. 313–318 (2005)
24. Wang, C., Liu, S.: Study on fuzzy theory based web access control model. In: International Symposiums on Information Processing (ISIP) 2008, pp. 178–182. IEEE (2008)
25. Knechtel, M.: Access restrictions to and with description logic web ontologies, pp. 1–139. Dresden University of Technology (2010)
26. Aswani Kumar, Ch.: Designing role-based access control using formal concept analysis. Secur. Commun. Netw. **6**(3), 373–383 (2013)
27. Aswani Kumar, Ch.: Fuzzy clustering-based formal concept analysis for association rules mining. Applied artificial intelligence **26**(3), 274–301 (2012)

28. Mouliswaran, S.C., Aswani Kumar, C., Chandrasekar, C.: Modeling Chinese wall access control using formal concept analysis. In: International Conference on Contemporary Computing and Informatics (IC3I), pp. 811–816. IEEE (2014)
29. Singh, P.K., Aswani Kumar, C., Li, J.: Knowledge representation using interval-valued fuzzy formal concept lattice. Soft Comput., 1–18 (2015). doi:10.1007/s00500-015-1600-1
30. Martin, T., Majidian, A.: Finding fuzzy concepts for creative knowledge discovery. Int. J. Intell. Syst. 28(1), 93–114 (2013)

An Efficient Fingerprint Minutiae Detection Algorithm

Y. Prashanth Reddy[1], Kamlesh Tiwari[1]([✉]),
Vandana Dixit Kaushik[2], and Phalguni Gupta[3]

[1] Department of Computer Science and Engineering,
Indian Institute of Technology Kanpur, Kanpur 208016, India
{yeredla,ktiwari}@iitk.ac.in
[2] Department of Computer Science and Engineering,
Harcourt Butler Technological Institute, Kanpur 208002, India
vandanadixitk@yahoo.com
[3] National Institute of Technical Teachers' Training and Research Kolkata,
Salt Lake, Kolkata 700106, India
pg@iitk.ac.in

Abstract. Fingerprint is one of the most preferred biometric traits for automatic human authentication. Similarity between two fingerprints is determined by matching, which is mostly dependent on the properties of minutiae points. A false minutiae that can be induced due to bad quality of fingerprint or erroneous evaluation of localization algorithm adversely affects the performance of the system. This paper proposes an algorithm to extract the true minutiae from fingerprint images. Extraction of minutiae points involves background suppression, image enhancement, binarization, thinning, minutiae localization, and cleaning. Experimental results on two databases have shown that the proposed algorithm has higher accuracy of being true.

1 Introduction

Fingerprint is one of the widely accepted biometric trait. Major reason for this is that it is easy to acquire. The fingerprint of a person does not vary throughout his lifetime but it is not the case with some other biometrics traits such as face. Fingerprints of even two identical twins are found to be different. Also, fingerprint acquisition with the help of a scanner is simple. A fingerprint contains two major types of characteristics namely ridges and valleys. Ridges are solid line present in the fingerprint. Valley is the space between two ridges. The flow of the ridges and valleys categorizes the fingerprint of a person.

Minutiae are the points on the fingerprint which satisfy certain properties. There are around 150 different types of minutiae in a fingerprint. However, two types of minutiae, namely ridge ending and bifurcation points are commonly used in most of the fingerprint matching algorithms. The point where three ridges meet is termed as bifurcation and the place where a ridge ends is called a ridge ending. These minutiae are commonly used to determine whether two

© Springer International Publishing Switzerland 2015
J.H. Abawajy et al. (Eds): SSCC 2015, CCIS 536, pp. 186–194, 2015.
DOI: 10.1007/978-3-319-22915-7_18

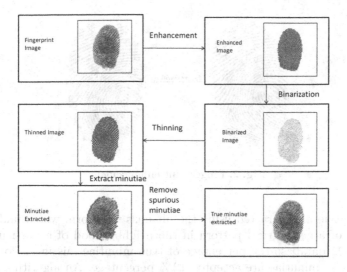

Fig. 1. Flow chart of the proposed algorithm

fingerprints are matched or not. It determines the similarity between the minutiae patterns of two fingerprints. In this mechanism, at the time of enrollment, the minutiae, termed as features are stored in the database. When the person provides the fingerprint again for matching, the minutiae of the fingerprint are used to find the similarity with those available in the database. However, it is not always possible to extract true minutiae from a fingerprint image. This is due to the noise appeared at the time of the acquisition of the fingerprint. Also a fingerprint may have a cut ridge because of dry fingers. It is a challenging task to extract only the true minutiae from a fingerprint image. The accuracy of the fingerprint system mainly depends upon the extraction of true minutiae.

This paper consists of five sections. Next section presents a brief review on the problem of extracting true minutiae from fingerprints. The proposed approach of extracting true minutiae has been presented in Sect. 3. Experimental results are discussed in the next section. Finally conclusions are given in the last section.

2 Literature Review

The algorithm proposed in [7] works on the gray scale fingerprint and extracts the minutiae based on adaptive tracing of the gray level ridge. Another algorithm in [9], works directly on the gray scale images for the extraction of minutiae. The algorithm has worked on a personal database and the percentage of false minutiae is around 6 % on good quality images. In [11], a minutiae extraction algorithm based on run length encoding has been proposed. Algorithm in [12], has claimed that extracting the minutiae extraction from valleys provides a better set of minutiae than the extraction with the help of ridges. On a private database is has extracted 12 % of the true minutiae and 15 % of false minutiae.

Fig. 2. Fingerprint enhancement

In [2], minutiae are extracted using the hit-miss transform which finds out the occurrence of a geometrical pattern in the neighborhood of a particular pixel. On FVC2002 database the percentage of true minutiae missing is found to be 10 % and false minutiae are accepted 12 % percentage. An algorithm proposed in [4], works on the binary version of fingerprint to detect minutiae in the fingerprint image. In [1], a pipe-lined algorithm for the detection of minutiae has been proposed. Minutiae extraction algorithm in [8], works on region masks where each pixel in the image is looked for the patterns in the ridge mask and based on that, the minutiae are extracted. On a private database the number of true minutiae missing reported are around 8 % which is also very large. In [5], minutiae extraction is based on the Gabor phase of the fingerprint. In [6], a fingerprint enhancement algorithm has been proposed. It have been tested on FVC2000 database and gives EER of 5.3 %. An algorithm to extract minutiae based on the application of fuzzy logic on fingerprint images has been proposed in [10]. It has 20 % of the minutiae which are detected true on its database.

3   Proposed Algorithm

This chapter proposes an efficient algorithm to extract true minutiae. The steps involved in the algorithm are fingerprint enhancement and orientation estimation, binarization, thinning, preliminary minutiae extraction, and false minutiae removal. The flowchart of the proposed algorithm is shown in Fig. 1

3.1   Fingerprint Enhancement

Performance of any fingerprint minutiae detection algorithm mainly depends on the quality of the fingerprint. The fingerprint may have discontinuities in the ridge flow because of the bruises, wounds in the fingerprint area, dust on the fingerprint scanner etc. In some cases, the finger of a person may be dry due to which the ridge thickness would be very thin. Hence fingerprint enhancement is required to extract minutiae.

Short time fourier transform is an enhancement technique [3] which works in the frequency domain of the given image. The fingerprint is being taken to

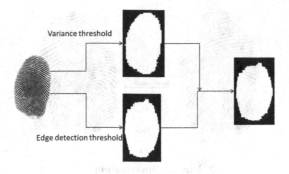

Fig. 3. Bounding box

the frequency domain and is divided into blocks of fixed size. Consecutive blocks of the fingerprint are overlapped by a certain number of pixels from the adjacent blocks, thereby maintaining the continuity of the ridges in the fingerprint across various blocks. Energy of a particular block is the highest frequency in the particular block. Based on the energy present in a block of the frequency image, the ridge and valley regions are separated and false ridge discontinuities are connected. In the process, the orientation of each block is also estimated. It returns the orientation of the block as well as the enhanced fingerprint image. The enhanced image is shown in Fig. 2.

3.2 Foreground and Background Segmentation

A non fingerprint area in a fingerprint image is called as background. A minutiae point detected in background region are certainly the false ones. To mark the background area, the fingerprint is divided into smaller blocks and in each block, the variance is calculated. First, the square of each pixel value of each block is calculated. Now, this square of the mean pixel intensity of the block is subtracted from each squared pixel and the mean of the resultant is calculated. This is called as the variance of the block. It is observed that the background regions have very less variance as compared to the fingerprint blocks. Regions having variance less than a threshold are marked as background.

There can be some regions which are not fingerprint but still have high variance due to noise. These regions are identified by applying Sobel operator to highlight edges. Threshold is applied on the edge detected image and all pixels having higher intensity than the threshold are marked as white and others are marked as black and then a bounding box of the white pixels is calculated. In each row of the fingerprint, the first and the last white pixels in the fingerprint are found and all intermediate pixels in the row are marked as white.

If a pixel is white in both the above methods then it is called as foreground pixel; otherwise it is a background pixel. This is applied as a mask for the minutiae extracted and all pixels which are outside the bounding box are deleted. The bounding box of a fingerprint image is shown in Fig. 3.

Fig. 4. Binarization

3.3 Binarization

The enhanced image is binarized *i.e.* the areas of the ridge are marked as 0 and the other areas are marked as 1. To do so, the fingerprint is divided into blocks. If the intensity of the pixel in a block is greater than the average intensity of the block, the pixel is marked as 1; otherwise it is set to be 0. The result of binarization applied on an image is shown in Fig. 4.

3.4 Thinning

The thinned image contains the outline of the ridge flow in the image which helps to detect the minutiae points. Thinning preserves the continuity of the ridge flow in fingerprint image. The thinning operation is performed until the ridge thickness is 1 pixel wide. In an image, for each pixel other than the boundaries, the 3×3 neighborhood pixels are considered for thinning. The process of thinning is repeated until there is no change in the image from one iteration to another. Small ridges may appear in the thinned fingerprint image due to noise. These ridges are called island and are removed to prevent the detection of spurious minutiae. To do so, each ridge having the length less than a threshold are removed from the thinned image. The result of the thinning is shown in Fig. 5.

3.5 Minutiae Extraction

Minutiae extraction is based on the concept of crossing number of a pixel which is the number of changes from 0 to 1 while taking a round in clockwise direction within 3×3 neighborhood of the pixels. The crossing number of a termination point is 1 and bifurcation point is 3. Crossing number is determined for each pixel. A pixel whose crossing number is 1 is termed as preliminary ridge ending and is stored in a list. The pixels having crossing number 3 are called preliminary bifurcation points and are collected in another list. All such detected ridge endings and bifurcation points are termed as preliminary minutiae points (PMP).

Fig. 5. Thinning

3.6 Spurious Minutiae Cleaning

There can be few spurious minutiae in the list of preliminary minutiae points (PMP). These spurius minutiae may lie in the list of PMP because of the noise and dry fingerprints that may cause false discontinuities, breaks and holes, hooks, minutiae outside the boundary and minutiae at the end of foreground region. All the noisy minutiae in PMP should be removed to retain only true minutiae.

Cleaning Outside Fingerprint Foreground. Noise in fingerprint may induce some candidate minutiae outside the fingerprint region. The fingerprint boundary is used for removing the candidate minutiae outside the foreground. Each candidate minutia's location is checked to find if it is in foreground region or background region by using the bounding box as constructed in Sect. 3.2. If the minutiae is present in the background region, then the minutiae is removed from the list of PMP.

Cleaning at Foreground Boundary. Every ridge ends at the end of fingerprint foreground. The probability of having a true minutiae at this point is very low. Removal of those candidate minutiae is being done in the following way. For every minutiae, we have to check in the thinned image if there are any minutiae in the 4 directions *i.e.* top, bottom left and right. If there are ones in all directions then we can say that the minutiae is not in the boundary. Otherwise, we need to check it in four diagonal directions and if there are ones in all directions, even then it is not in the boundary. In both the cases, if there is no one in any one direction each, then the minutiae is said to be in the boundary and hence it is removed.

Cleaning of Very Near Minutiae Points. A cut in a ridge results in false candidate minutiae in preliminary minutiae list. Hence, if two minutiae are very close to each other then there is a fair chance of both being false. It is also observed that the two minutiae occurring due to false discontinuity has very low orientation difference. Therefore, any two candidate minutiae lying in narrow neighborhood with similar orientation are deleted from preliminary minutiae list. Also, when two bifurcations are very close to each other with a minimum difference in their orientations, then such bifurcations are also removed from the list of candidate minutiae.

Table 1. Results of manual verification-IITK database

Subject	PROPOSED			NIST (MINDTCT)		
	AMD	ATMM	AFMD	AMD	ATMM	AFMD
1	45.33	0.33	4.17	55.17	1	12.67
2	33	0.33	0	47.33	2	12
3	49.83	1.17	1	68.17	0.67	17.5
4	69	1.17	2.17	84.83	0.33	16.5
5	54.83	1.17	0.67	66.33	0.33	10.67
6	47.17	2	0	60.5	0.5	10.83
7	62.33	0.17	2.83	72.33	0.83	11.83
8	34.17	2.17	0.33	43.83	1	6.83
9	27.83	0.33	0.5	48.17	0.33	20.17
10	50.83	2.5	1.33	69.33	2.67	14.67
11	52	0.5	2.5	65.17	0.17	15
12	28.33	0	1	48.33	0.67	20.33
13	56.83	0.83	1.17	70.67	0.5	13.67
14	60	0.5	3.33	61.83	2	2.67
15	50.83	0.83	1	57.67	2	5
16	35.5	0	2.67	45.5	0.17	12.5
17	48.5	1.17	2.67	56.33	0.5	8.83
18	41.17	0.5	1.83	52.33	1	11.5
19	59.83	1.17	6	68.17	0.5	12.67
20	67.17	1.83	2	79.67	1.17	11.5
21	49	0	2.33	64	0.5	16.83
22	51	0.5	1	65.17	0.33	14.33
23	35	0.5	0.33	42.83	0.5	7.17
24	25.67	0.83	0	38.17	0.17	11.5
25	50.33	0.33	2.33	61.33	0	13
Avg	49	0.83	1.7	60	0.8	12.3

Cleaning Minutiae Due to False Joining. Noise between two ridge lines may falsely connect them. It gives rise to some hook like structure in between the ridges. They create false bifurcations. If a ridge and a bifurcation are very close to each other with a minimum orientation difference, they are false candidate minutiae with a very high probability and hence, they are removed.

4   Experimental Results

The proposed minutiae extraction algorithm is tested on two databases *viz*. IITK and FVC2006. Minutiae are plotted on the fingerprint and are manually verified

Table 2. Results of manual verification-FVC database

Subject	PROPOSED			NIST (MINDTCT)		
	AMD	ATMM	AFMD	AMD	ATMM	AFMD
1	48.67	0	6.67	68.33	0	26.33
2	29.33	0	5.33	43	0.67	18.33
3	52	0.67	4.33	84.33	1.67	32.99
4	61	0	3	97.33	0.67	38.67
5	28.33	0.33	1.67	47.67	0.67	19.34
6	38	2	0	75.33	0	31.33
7	32.33	1.33	0.67	53.67	1.33	16.67
8	57.67	0	3.67	81	1	26
9	38.33	0.67	0.33	68	1.33	26.66
10	43.67	0.67	1.33	63.67	0	19.33
11	37	0.67	1	54.67	2	14.66
12	31.67	0.67	3	69	0.33	37.99
13	43.33	0	1	68	2	23.67
14	39.33	2.67	0.33	58	1	9.99
15	46	0	1.67	72.67	0.33	28
16	56	1	2.33	88.67	0.33	31.67
17	54.33	0.33	2.67	82.33	1.33	28.34
Avg	43.35	0.64	2.3	69.15	0.83	26.5

for correctness by visualization and three parameters are calculated, namely total number of minutiae detected per image, total number of true minutiae missing per image and the number of false minutiae detected per image. The first database is collected from 25 IITK students with 6 images per person in total it contains 150 fingerprint images. Table 1 shows the parameters namely average number of minutiae detected (AMD), average of true minutiae missing (ATMM) and average number of false minutiae detected (AFMD) per fingerprint image. Average number of true minutiae missing and that of false minutiae detected are 0.8 and 1.7 respectively. The proposed algorithm is also compared against the minutiae extractor of NIST (MINDTCT). The second database is a subset of FVC2006 which contains 51 images from 17 subjects. It has been found that the average number of true minutiae missed and that of false minutiae detected are 0.6 and 2.3 respectively. Table 2 shows the parameters calculated and the comparison with respect to the NIST (MINDTCT).

5   Conclusion

The paper has proposed a new minutiae extraction algorithm which reduces the number of false minutiae extracted on a fingerprint image. The algorithm has been tested on two databases namely IITK student database which consists of

25 subjects with six images per subject. The algorithm has also been tested on a subset of FVC2006 database that contains 51 fingerprint images of 17 subjects. Fingerprints from both the databases are checked manually and the average number of false minutiae detected and the average number of true minutiae missing per image are calculated. On IITK database, the average number of true minutiae missing and that of false minutiae detected are 0.8 and 1.7 respectively. Also, on FVC2006 database, it has been found that the average number of true minutiae missed and that of false minutiae detected are 0.6 and 2.3 respectively.

References

1. Alibeigi, E., Rizi, M.T., Behnamfar, P.: Pipelined minutiae extraction from fingerprint images. In: Canadian Conference on Electrical and Computer Engineering, CCECE 2009, pp. 239–242. IEEE (2009)
2. Bansal, R., Sehgal, P., Bedi, P.: Effective morphological extraction of true fingerprint minutiae based on the hit or miss transform. Int. J. Biometrics Bioinform. (IJBB) 4(2), 71–85 (2010)
3. Chikkerur, S., Cartwright, A.N., Govindaraju, V.: Fingerprint enhancement using STFT analysis. Pattern Recogn. 40(1), 198–211 (2007)
4. Gamassi, M., Piuri, V., Scotti, F.: Fingerprint local analysis for high-performance minutiae extraction. In: IEEE International Conference on Image Processing, ICIP 2005, vol. 3, pp. 265–272. IEEE (2005)
5. Gao, X., Chen, X., Cao, J., Deng, Z., Liu, C., Feng, J.: A novel method of fingerprint minutiae extraction based on gabor phase. In: 17th IEEE International Conference on Image Processing (ICIP), 2010, pp. 3077–3080. IEEE (2010)
6. He, Y., Tian, J., Luo, X., Zhang, T.: Image enhancement and minutiae matching in fingerprint verification. Pattern Recogn. Lett. 24(9), 1349–1360 (2003)
7. Jiang, X., Yau, W.-Y., Ser, W.: Detecting the fingerprint minutiae by adaptive tracing the gray-level ridge. Pattern Recogn. 34(5), 999–1013 (2001)
8. Kaur, R., Sandhu, P.S., Kamra, A.: A novel method for fingerprint feature extraction. In: International Conference on Networking and Information Technology (ICNIT) 2010, pp. 1–5. IEEE (2010)
9. Maio, D., Maltoni, D.: Direct gray-scale minutiae detection in fingerprints. IEEE Trans. Pattern Anal. Mach. Intell. 19(1), 27–40 (1997)
10. Sagar, V.K., Alex, K.J.B.: Hybrid fuzzy logic and neural network model for fingerprint minutiae extraction. In: International Joint Conference on Neural Networks, IJCNN 1999, vol. 5, pp. 3255–3259. IEEE (1999)
11. Shin, J.-H., Hwang, H.-Y., Chien, S.-I.: Detecting fingerprint minutiae by run length encoding scheme. Pattern Recogn. 39(6), 1140–1154 (2006)
12. Zhao, F., Tang, X.: Preprocessing and postprocessing for skeleton-based fingerprint minutiae extraction. Pattern Recogn. 40(4), 1270–1281 (2007)

Cryptography and Steganography

An Improved Substitution Method for Data Encryption Using *DNA* Sequence and *CDMB*

Ravi Gupta$^{(\boxtimes)}$ and Rahul Kumar Singh

Department of Computer Science and Engineering, Chandigarh University,
Gharuan 140413, India
{ravigupta9088, rahulsinghcse25}@gmail.com

Abstract. Cryptography provides the solution in fields such as banking services, digital certificate, digital signature, message and image encryption etc. In this paper, we propose an improved data encryption approach based on the Deoxyribonucleic acid that exploits two different techniques: Substitution technique and Central Dogma of Molecular Biology. It transforms the message into protein (cipher text) using various complementary rules. Deoxyribonucleic acid provides robust *DNA* sequence for the substitution technique from approximately 163 million huge *DNA* database, where Central Dogma of Molecular Biology support the encrypted output of substitution method using transcription and translation technique.

Keywords: Cryptography · Deoxyribonucleic acid (*DNA*) sequence · Central Dogma of Molecular Biology (*CDMB*)

1 Introduction

Data hiding is taking as an approach for transforming confidential data into an unreadable format on online and offline. Data hiding provides security in the various areas like banking services, digital certificate, digital signature, message and image encryption etc. Data transactions and uses of data on the internet are growing every second. For handling, this growing data various symmetric and asymmetric cryptographic algorithms such as DES, RSA, TDES, and AES are available, but these are not enough to provide security on the fast growing internet in the fields like Banking services, Information sharing, Defence, and Social networking etc where hackers are active for stealing the information. Need of new cryptography algorithm raised for the better security on online and offline for vast data. *DNA* computing is selected by various researchers as a remedy for security on a large amount of data in the recent years and has been proposed various *DNA* based cryptographic approaches [1–3]. *DNA* contains some fascinating properties such as high storage capacity, vast parallelism, and high energy efficiency etc that are a boon for the data hiding and for the solution of applications such as an optimization problem, image and signal processing, clustering and forecasting etc [5, 6]. A gram *DNA* can contain 10^8 TB of data which is equal to 10^{21} *DNA*-bases.

In this paper, *DNA* sequence is taken from *DNA* database (like GENBANK) for the proposed algorithm. The *DNA* sequence is converted into fake *DNA* sequences as

© Springer International Publishing Switzerland 2015
J.H. Abawajy et al. (Eds): SSCC 2015, CCIS 536, pp. 197–206, 2015.
DOI: 10.1007/978-3-319-22915-7_19

information carrier because *DNA* sequence contains two exciting attractive features such as there is almost no difference between right *DNA* sequence and fake *DNA* sequence, and second is 163 millions *DNA* sequences publically available on *DNA* database.

2   Related Work

Researchers are trying to find better result in the fields like data and image encryption, automata theory, optimization and scheduling problem etc by *DNA* computing. Shiu *et al.* [1] introduced three cryptographic approaches such as Insertion method, Complementary pair method, and Substitution method using the properties of *DNA* sequences. There is nearly no difference between fake and original *DNA* sequence and around 163 million *DNA* sequence available in *DNA* database. They showed that substitution method is better than other two approaches. Liu et al. [2] proposed a new data hiding approach using *DNA* sequence and encrypted each character of cipher text in the word file. Taur et al. [3] improved the substitution method of Shiu using the table lookup substitution. Huang et al. [8] also improved Shiu's work and proposed new reversible data hiding method using the histogram technique. Abbasy et al. [7] introduced a novel data hiding algorithm where message hide in *DNA* sequence using software point of view.

3   Background

3.1   Biological Study

DNA is germ plasm in all the surviving life. *DNA* contains four different bases (or Nucleotides) such as Adenine (A), Guanine (G), Cytosine (C), and Thymine (T). In the *DNA*, A only pairs with T using double-hydrogen bonds and G with C using triple-hydrogen bonds using Complementary rules discovered by Watson-Crick [6]. *DNA* contains two nitrogen bases: Purines and Pyrimidines. Where A and G bases are double-ring molecules called purines and C and T bases are single-ring molecules called pyrimidines.

Same as *DNA*, *RNA* also contains four bases except that Thymine (T) replaced by Uracil (U) in the *RNA* sequence. Proteins are large molecules formed by amino acids (Fig. 1).

3.2   Central Dogma of Molecular Biology

Transformation of *DNA* sequence to protein sequence is called Central Dogma of Molecular Biology discovered by Watson-Crick [9]. They also proposed two different techniques: Transcription and Translation. Conversion of *DNA* sequence to *RNA* sequence is happened by Transcription, whereas *RNA* to protein is called Translation. Combination of any three *RNA* bases out of four bases makes codon. Table 1 shows 64-*RNA* codon made by $4 \times 4 \times 4$ possibilities where corresponding amino acid for it in

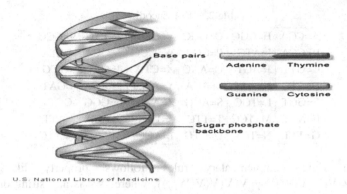

Fig. 1. *DNA* Structure [11]

DNA⟹RNA⟹Protein

Fig. 2. Central Dogma of Molecular Biology

Table 1. Codon table of *RNA* for representing Amino acids [10]

Nucleotide codon	Amino acid name	Amino acid code
UUU	Phenylalanine	F
UUC		F1
CCU	Proline	P
CCC		P1
CCA		P2
CCG		P3
.	.	.
.	.	.
.	.	.
ACU	Threonine	T
ACC		T1
ACA		T2
ACG		T3

the table. One amino acid has been referred by more than one codon. Hence amino acid for each codon will be formed by the suffix with integer in the amino acid first letter [9] (Fig. 2).

4 Proposed Scheme

Proposed scheme uses a *DNA* encoding Table 2 for plaintext to *DNA* sequence conversion. In the table, each character is formed by a combination of three *DNA* bases. Proposed algorithm also uses various complementary rules for boosting the cipher text

Table 2. *DNA* Encoding [2]

A=CGA	H=CGC	O=GGC	V=CCT	2=TAG	9=GCG
B=CCA	I=ATG	P=GGA	W=CCG	3=GCA	=ATA
C=GTT	J=AGT	Q=AAC	X=CTA	4=GAG	,=TCG
D=TTG	K=AAG	R=TCA	Y=AAA	5=AGA	.=GAT
E=GGT	L=TGC	S=ACG	Z=AAT	6=GGG	:GCT
F=ACT	M=TCC	T=TTC	0=TTA	7=ACA	;=ATT
G=TTT	N=TCT	U=CTG	1=ACC	8=AGG	_=ATC

because a right complementary rules follows property like $V(W) \neq V(V(W)) \neq V(V(V(W))) \neq V(V(V(V(W))))$, where 'W' is any string or alphabet. Following complementary rules for the proposed approach are used: (AT) (CA) (GC) (TG), Means V (A) = T.

For the *DNA* sequence, A(00), T(11), C(01), and G(10) are used to binary conversion, is called binary coding scheme. For example, 00110110 are binary bits for "ATCG" *DNA* sequence.

The receiver knows *DNA* encoding table, complementary rules, binary coding scheme and *RNA* codon table using a secure channel made by the sender.

Limitation of Proposed Algorithm. In the proposed approach, Left one and two *RNA* nucleotides will be same in the final cipher text (Protein) for *RNA* to Protein conversion, because there is no amino acid code for left one and two *RNA* nucleotides.

Encryption Process:

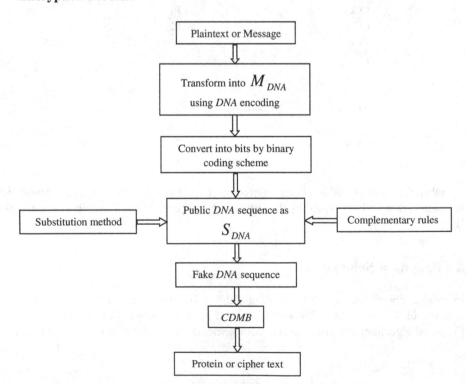

In the encryption process, get a plaintext and convert it into the artificial *DNA* sequence using *DNA* encoding. Binary coding scheme will transform artificial *DNA* sequence into bits. Select a long *DNA* sequence (from GENBANK), where length should be greater or equal to the number of bits. After that, a set of random integers is generated, where number of elements in the set equal to binary bits and range of each element should be from 1 to length of *DNA* sequence. Now apply substitution method using complementary rules to the *DNA* sequence, it will provide fake *DNA* sequence. *CDMB* will convert fake *DNA* sequence to protein sequence. Send protein sequence to receiver end.

Decryption Process:

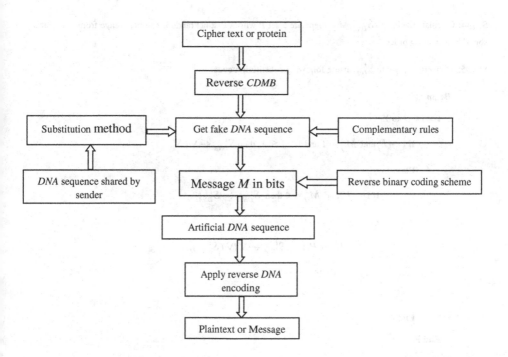

In the decryption process, received protein sequence will be converted into the fake *DNA* sequence using inverse *CDMB* technique. Now apply the substitution method to the fake *DNA* sequence using the sender's shared *DNA* sequence and complementary rules, it will generate a binary sequence. After that, use reverse binary coding into the binary sequence, it will produce another fake *DNA* sequence. At last, inverse *DNA* encoding will generate final plaintext to the fake *DNA* sequence.

4.1 Proposed Algorithm

Proposed algorithm exploits substitution method from Shiu et al. [1].

Encryption Algorithm:

Input: Message M

Output: Cipher text C

Step-1: Get message M and convert into DNA sequence as M_{DNA} using DNA encoding table 1.

Step-2: Convert M_{DNA} into bits using binary coding scheme as M' and calculate the length of M' as X.

Step-3: Select a DNA sequence as S_{DNA} from publically available DNA database (Like GENBANK) where $S_{DNA} \geq X$.

Step-4: Calculate the length S_{DNA} as Y. Generate a set P with X distinct random numbers range from 1 to Y and sort P in increasing order.

Step-5: Convert S_{DNA} into S'_{DNA} using following substitution code:

   Begin

      For i ← 1 to Y

            If i $== P_j$ and $M'_j == 1$ and $1 \leq j \leq X$, then $S^i_{DNA} \leftarrow$ V (S^i_{DNA})

         Else

              If i $== P_j$ and $M'_j == 0$ then $S^i_{DNA} \leftarrow S^i_{DNA}$

            Else

                  If i $\neq P_j$ then $S^i_{DNA} \leftarrow$ V (V $(S^i_{DNA}))$

                End If

            End If

         End If

      End For

   End

Step-6: Convert fake DNA sequence S'_{DNA} into RNA sequence by replacing T with U.

Step-7: By the amino acid code convert RNA sequence into PROTEIN sequence.

Step-8: Send protein sequence to receiver end.

Decryption Algorithm:

Input: Cipher text C as Protein, DNA sequence as S

Output: Plaintext P

Step-1: Convert cipher text C (Protein) into RNA sequence using RNA codon table.

Step-2: Get fake DNA sequence as S' by replacing U with T in RNA sequence.

Step-3: Calculate the length of S' and S as X and Y respectively.

Step-4: Get message M from S' using following substitution code:

> **Begin**
>
> $d \leftarrow 1$
>
> For $c \leftarrow 1$ to X
>
> > **If** $S'_c = S_c$ then $M_d \leftarrow 0$ and $d \leftarrow d + 1$
> >
> > **Else**
> >
> > > **If** $S'_c = V(S_c)$ then $M_d \leftarrow 1$ and $d \leftarrow d + 1$
> > >
> > > **End If**
> >
> > **End If**
>
> **End For**
>
> **End**

Step-5: Convert M into DNA sequence using reverse binary coding.

Step-6: Get plaintext by convert DNA sequence into P using reverse DNA encoding.

5   Result and Discussion

Encryption process of proposed approach has been explained using plaintext "AB" and public *DNA* sequence "AAGCTTACAGACTCCAGGTATGGACTTCAAGT". Result of the encryption process is generated in the form of protein that will be finally sent to the receiver.

ORIGINAL MESSAGE M: **AB**

$$M_{DNA} : CGACCA$$

$$M' : 100100101000$$

$$S_{DNA} : AAGCTTACAGACTCCAGGTATGGACTTCAAGT$$

$$P : \{2, 3, 5, 7, 8, 11, 13, 15, 17, 19, 20, 23\}$$

$$S'_{DNA} : GTGTTCTCGAATGTCGCATACAG$$

$$RNA\,sequence : \ GUGUUCUCGAAUGUCGCAUACAG$$

$$PROTEIN : \ V3F1S3N1V1A2Y1AG$$

Possibility of Attack in Proposed Approach. For a successful attack in the proposed approach, intruder must have to attempt successful guess for the following terms:

For (1): $\frac{1}{1.63 \times 10^8}$ = right *DNA* sequence from 163 million *DNA* sequence
For (2): $\frac{1}{6}$ = right complementary rules in the 6 possibilities given below:
(AT) (TC) (CG) (GA),
(AT) (TG) (GC) (CA),
(AC) (CT) (TG) (GA),
(AC) (CG) (GT) (TA),
(AG) (GT) (TC) (CA), and (AG) (GC) (CT) (TA)
For (3): $\frac{1}{64}$ = correct guess of *DNA* encoding table possibilities.
For (4): $\frac{1}{24}$ = correct guess of binary coding scheme possibilities.
For (5): $\frac{1}{x}$ = right match of *RNA* codon code.

For Example. GCU, GCC, GCA, and GCG codons come in Alanine group, where A, A1, A2, and A3 are Amino acid codes respectively for codons. Therefore, we have 4! Possibilities for Amino acid code for Alanine codons. Hence, value of X depends on the number of codons in the specified Amino acid, here $X = 4!$ (Table 3).

Table 3. Shows the comparison between the Shiu et al. and proposed approach.

Factor	Shiu et al. approach [1]	Proposed approach
Security	Lesser than proposed approach	More secure, because use of *DNA* encoding and *CDMB* technique
Cryptographic strength	Lesser than proposed approach	More because *CDMB* strengthen the encrypted output
Complexness of algorithm	Lesser than our approach	More complex by inclusion of *CDMB* and *DNA* encoding
Compactness of cipher text	Fewer compresses than proposed approach	More compress using *CDMB* technique
Possibility of attack	$\frac{1}{1.63 \times 10^8} \times \frac{1}{6}$ or $\frac{1}{3^n}$	$\frac{1}{1.63 \times 10^8} \times \frac{1}{6} \times \frac{1}{64} \times \frac{1}{24} \times \frac{1}{X}$

6 Conclusion

This paper proposes an improved data hiding approach based on Deoxyribonucleic acid that exploits two different techniques: *Substitution technique* and *Central Dogma* of Molecular Biology. It transforms the message into protein (cipher text) using various complementary rules. Compared to Shiu et al. approach, the proposed approach showed compact encrypted output and complex possible attack for breaking cipher text. Using Tables 1, 2 in the proposed scheme, it is observed that it provides complex calculation than Shiu et al. approach.

References

1. Shiu, H.J., Ng, K.L., Fang, J.F., Lee, R.C.T., Huang, C.H.: Data hiding methods based upon *DNA* sequences. Inf. Sci. **180**, 2196–2208 (2010)
2. Liu, H., Lin, D., Kadir, A.: A novel data hiding method based on deoxyribonucleic acid coding. Comput. Electr. Eng. **39**, 1164–1173 (2013)
3. Taur, J.S., Lin, H.Y., Lee, H.L., Tao, C.W.: Data hiding in *DNA* sequences based on table lookup substitution. Int. J. Innovative Comput. Inf. Control **8**(10), 6585–6598 (2012)
4. Gehani, A., LaBean, T., Reif, J.: *DNA*-based cryptography. Dismacs Ser. Discrete Math. Theor. Comput. Sci. **54**, 233–349 (2000)
5. Kar, N., Majumder, A., Saha, A., Jamatia, A., Chakma, K., Pal, M.C.: An improved data security using *DNA* sequencing. In: Proceedings of the 3rd ACM MobiHoc workshop on Pervasive wireless healthcare, pp. 13–18 (2013)
6. Mandge, T., Choudhary, V.: A *DNA* encryption technique based on matrix manipulation and secure key generation scheme. In: IEEE International conference on Information Communication and Embedded Systems (ICICES), pp. 47–52 (2013)
7. Abbasy, M.R., Nikfard, P., Ordi, A., Torkaman, M.R.N.: *DNA* base data hiding algorithm. Int. J. New Comput. Architect. Appl. (IJNCAA) **2**(1), 183–192 (2012)
8. Huang, Y.H., Chang, C.C., Wu, C.Y.: A *DNA*-based data hiding technique with low modification rates. Multimedia Tools Appl. **70**, 1–13 (2012)

9. Hussain, U.N., Chithralekha, T., Raj, A.N., Sathish, G., Dharani, A.: A hybrid *DNA* algorithm for *DES* using Central Dogma of Molecular Biology (*CDMB*). Int. J. Comput. Appl. **42**(20), 1–4 (2012)
10. *RNA* codon table. http://en.wikibooks.org/wiki/Proteomics/Protein_Primary_Structure/Genetic_Code
11. *DNA* structure. http://ghr.nlm.nih.gov/handbook/basics/DNA

Analysis of Neural Synchronization Using Genetic Approach for Secure Key Generation

S. Santhanalakshmi[1($\boxtimes$)], Sangeeta K.[1], and G.K. Patra[2]

[1] Department of CS&E, AmritaVishwa Vidyapeetham, School of Engineering,
Bangalore Campus, Bangalore, India
{s_lakshmi, k_sangeeta}@blr.amrita.edu
[2] Council of Scientific and Industrial Research, 4 PI, Bangalore 560037, India
gkpatra@csir4pi.in

Abstract. Cryptography depends on two components, an algorithm and a key. Keys are used for encryption of information as well as in other cryptographic schemes such as digital signature and message authentication codes. Neural cryptography is a way to create shared secret key. Key generation in Tree Parity Machine neural network is done by mutual learning. Neural networks receive common inputs to synchronize using a suitable learning rule. Because of this effect neural synchronization can be used to construct a cryptographic key-exchange protocol. Faster synchronization of the neural network has been achieved by generating the optimal weights for the sender and receiver from a genetic process. In this paper the performance of the genetic algorithm has been analysed by varying the neural network and genetic parameters.

Keywords: Key agreement · Synchronization · Best fit · Neural network · Mutual learning

1 Introduction

The technological progress and inevitable dependency on electronic systems for e-commerce and communication today, increases concern related to privacy and fraud. Although there can be various ways to protect information from undesired access, it is most useful to safeguard data so that it can be transmitted over internet without fear of compromise. Cryptographic methods are used to maintain the confidentiality and integrity of information. Cryptography relies upon two components, an algorithm and a key – ideally a strong algorithm and a key combination should be difficult to break. Thus the cornerstone of secure cryptosystems is *key establishment* which is the process by which two (or more) entities establish a shared secret key for subsequent secure communications [1]. Key establishment includes both key agreement and key transport [2]. Key agreement is a method of key establishment in which the resultant shared secret key is derived by two (or more) parties as a result of mutual information exchange/communication between the sender and receiver. Most of the protocols currently being used for key agreement fall into two wide categories – (i) those based on public-key cryptography and practically implemented with number theory, (ii) those based on symmetric key generation and a trusted agent, implemented with some form

© Springer International Publishing Switzerland 2015
J.H. Abawajy et al. (Eds): SSCC 2015, CCIS 536, pp. 207–216, 2015.
DOI: 10.1007/978-3-319-22915-7_20

of polynomial or integer arithmetic [3]. Diffie -Hellman [4] in 1970 designed a protocol to securely exchange the keys –"security of which depends upon the difficulty of computing discrete logarithms", that assumes to be computationally infeasible to calculate the shared secret key given the public values. Security issues related to the DH protocol have been addressed in [5]. Since then, many public key cryptosystems have been presented which are based on number theory, and they demand large computational power [6]. Moreover the processes involved in generating public key are very complex and time consuming.

Neural cryptography is a recent approach that aims to solve the key exchange problem with non classical computing through neural networks training on the same input patterns [7]. In 2002, Kanter et al. published a series of papers related to neural networks and cryptography [8, 9]. They demonstrated that when two artificial neural networks are trained by suitable learning rules, on their mutual outputs, then these networks can develop equivalent states of their internal synaptic weights, i.e., the networks synchronize to a state with identical time dependent weights. These synchronized weights are then used as a key for encryption and decryption process. In [10], the simulation shows that the synchronization time increases logarithmically with N (input neurons). Ruttor et al. in [11] proved the dependence of synchronization on the synaptic depth of the neural network. Security analysis of neural cryptography presented in [12] describes the geometric attack and Majority Flipping Attack (MFA) as the vulnerabilities. Furthermore, it was shown in their work that the number of networks needed for a majority/cooperative attack to be successful grows exponentially with increasing synaptic depth [12, 13]. Thus, a larger synaptic depth with a lower synchronization time is the need for secure neural cryptography.

Synchronization of the Tree Parity Machine using genetic algorithm is described in [14]. A best fit weight vector found using a genetic algorithm is considered as input to train the network using the feed forward process. As the optimal weights lead to faster convergence of the neural network than the random weights, this allows for a larger synaptic depth L to be considered. However the process of synchronization, now also depends the genetic factors like Crossover rate (P_c), Mutation rate (P_m) in addition to its dependence the number of neurons in the hidden layer and the input layer. In this paper a performance analysis of the protocol proposed in [14] is carried out for varying number of neurons in the input and the hidden layer.

In Sect. 2 we describe the generation of genetic weights which are then used as inputs for the Tree Parity machine network described in Sect. 3. Results are presented in Sect. 4

2 Genetic Algorithm

A genetic algorithm (GA) [15] is a method for solving both constrained and unconstrained optimization problems based on a natural selection process that mimics biological evolution. GA's simulate the survival of the fittest among individuals over consecutive generation for solving a problem. In order to generate initial weights for the TPM we represent each individual by a binary string so that a generation comprises of a population of binary strings that are analogous to the chromosomes that we see in our DNA. The algorithm randomly selects individuals from the current population and uses them as parents to produce the children for the next generation. Each successive generation will contain better 'partial solutions' than previous generations and once the offspring are not noticeably different from those in previous generations, the algorithm is said to have converged. Steps followed are:

   i. Generate random population x (i.e. random weights) of n binary strings of size 5 representing the initial weights.

   ii. Evaluate the fitness f(x) of each weight using the function in the population

$$f(x) = \begin{cases} -L & x < -L \\ x2 & -L \leq x < L \\ L & x \geq L \end{cases}$$

   iii. Create a new population by repeating following steps until the weights converge [16].

      a. "Select two parent chromosomes from a population according to their fitness.

      b. With a crossover probability(P_c) cross over the parents to form a new offspring. If no crossover isperformed, offspring is an exact copy of parents.

      c. With a mutation probability (P_m) mutate new offspring at each locus. Place new offspring in anew population".

   iv. Use new generated population for a further run of algorithm

   v. If the end condition (Number of iterations) is satisfied, stop, and return the best solution in current population

   vi. Go to step ii.

The performance of a genetic-search depends on the amount of exploration (population diversity) and exploitation (selection pressure).To have an effective search, there must be a proper balance between them and to ensure this, the GA parameters, such as population size, crossover probability P_c and mutation probability P_m are to be selected in the optimal sense [17]. The crossover probability and mutation probability are considered in the range of (0.6 to 1.0) and (0.001-0.04) respectively.

In order to identify the optimal GA-parameters (Fig. 1), P_c is varied keeping for a fixed $P_m = 0.04$ and maximum number of generations $G_{max} = 100$ as shown in Fig. 1a. The best fitness here corresponds to $P_c = 0.9$. Next, for a fixed value P_c and G_{max}, fitness is plotted for varying P_m in Fig. 1b. Here fitness is maximum from $P_m = 0.03$ onwards. Finally, by fixing P_c and P_m the maximum number of generations required for the population size 12 is decided based on the convergence of weights as shown in (Table 1a and 1b).

Thus the optimal GA parameters are found to be Pc = 0.9, Pm = 0.03, and $G_{max} = 50$ for the population size of 12. With the above optimal GA parameters the initial weight vectors w are generated for the sender and the receiver.

Genetic Algorithm can be combined with neural networks (NN) to develop the combined GA-NN approach [17].

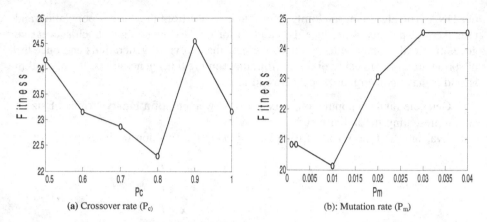

Fig. 1. Results of the parametric study conducted for determining the optimal GA-parameters.

Table 1. a: Maximum number of generations (Gmax)-Sender

Initial weights	−2	−2	5	−5	−5	6	−3	−6	6	0	−3	−1
10th iteration	5	−5	0	5	5	−5	−5	0	5	0	0	−5
20th iteration	5	−5	0	5	−5	−5	−5	0	−5	0	0	−5
25th iteration	−5	−5	0	−5	5	5	5	0	5	0	0	−5
50th iteration	5	−5	0	5	−5	−5	−5	0	−5	0	0	−5

Table 1. b: Maximum number of generations (G$_{max}$)-Receiver

Initial weights	−4	−2	5	−5	2	−2	3	5	1	6	6	1
10th iteration	5	5	0	0	−5	−5	−5	0	−5	0	0	5
20th iteration	5	5	0	0	−5	−5	−5	0	−5	0	0	5
25th iteration	−5	5	0	−5	5	5	5	0	5	0	0	5
50th iteration	5	5	0	0	−5	−5	−5	0	−5	0	0	5

Since TPM that is a fixed architecture NN its performance is dependent on the weights connecting the neurons of input and hidden layer. In this work GA have been utilized to determine optimal weights in a fixed architecture NN.

3   Synchronization of Tree Parity Machine

Two tree parity machine neural networks shown in Fig. 2 are trained on their mutual output bits, the networks synchronize to a state with identical time dependent weights [19]. Both the communicating networks receive an identical input vector x_i and weight vector w_i generated from $\sigma_i = w_i x_i$ the genetic process, to generate an output bit $\tau = \pi \sigma_i$ used for training. The hidden neurons are obtained from as shown in Fig. 2. This process is repeated till coincident weights are obtained in the successive iterations.

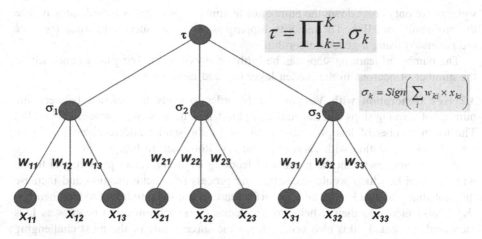

Fig. 2. Tree parity machine

When synchronization is achieved, the weights w_i of both tree parity machines are same; they become the secret keys for communication between A and B. In this work we have shown that the process of synchronization can be further improved by varying the number of hidden neurons.

4 Results and Analysis

4.1 Generation of Keys: As described in previous section the TPM network uses optimal weights obtained from the genetic algorithm as initial weight vectors to generate the synchronized weights as keys. It has been shown in Fig. 3 that the optimal

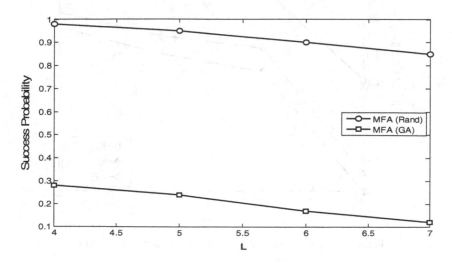

Fig. 3. Success rate of MFA with Random weights and GA weights

weights not only bring down the number of learning steps but also considerably reduce the probability of MFA. The majority flipping attack is not successful when the keys are generated using a genetic algorithm.

The number of learning steps can be further reduced by studying its dependence on the number of neurons in the hidden layer (K) and input layer (N).

4.2 Key Generation with Varying K: In order to study the relation between the number of learning steps and the number of hidden neurons K, we considered N = 100. The mean number of learning steps required by the sender and receiver to achieve weight synchronization with varying K and L is illustrated in Fig. 4.

It has been known that the number of learning steps is directly proportional to the weight range L, which would decelerate the process of synchronization and increase the probability of attack. But, along with increase in L if the number of hidden neurons (K) is also increased then it helps to accelerate the synchronization process as L is increased. Eventually this also brings down the success rate of the most challenging attack in neural cryptography. The probability percentage success rate of Majority Flipping Attack (MFA) with M (100) attackers is shown in Fig. 5, where it is seen that the success of attack reduces as the number of hidden neuron increases. Thus, faster synchronization with genetic weights allows for a larger value of L which in turn increases the security.

4.3 Key Generation with Varying N: The tree parity machine in Fig. 1 was also analysed by varying the weight range L and the number of input neurons N. Here the number of hidden neurons K is fixed as 4. Figure 6 shows the plot of mean learning steps for the sender and receiver for varying N and L. It is seen that the

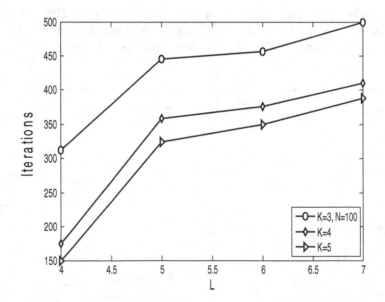

Fig. 4. The mean synchronization steps with different K and L

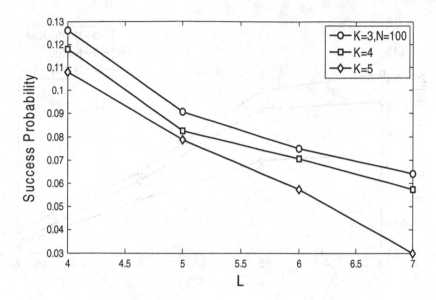

Fig. 5. Success probability rate of MFA for M = 100 attackers

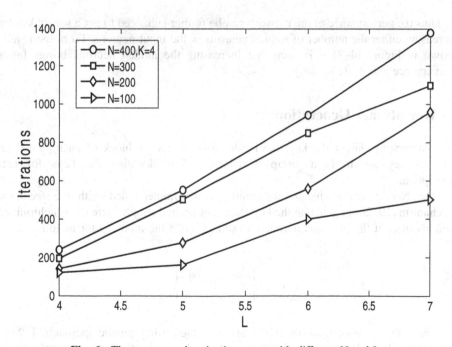

Fig. 6. The mean synchronization steps with different N and L

number of learning steps considerably increase as N increases, due to which the probability of success of MFA with M (number of attackers) increases as seen in Fig. 7.

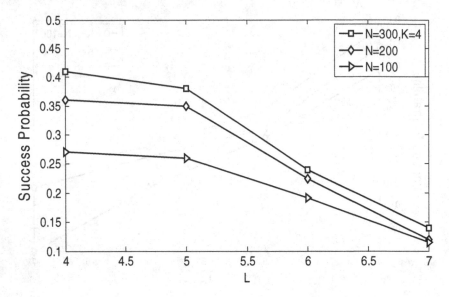

Fig. 7. Success probability rate of MFA for M = 100

Thus the performance of the network can be further enhanced to get a secure key by increasing either the number of hidden neurons or the input neurons. From the results shown in Figure [4–7] it is seen that increasing the hidden neurons brings faster convergence and more security.

5 Key Stream Generation

In cryptography, larger the key, the harder it is to crack a block of encrypted data. [18]. A key stream is a group of characters/bits denoting the keys for text encryption.

The Neural key exchange algorithm can be implemented with the feedback mechanism [19, 20] to generate the key stream of desired length. Here the synchronized weights (w_{in}) of the previous iteration would generate the input vector as follows:

$$x_i = \left\{ \begin{array}{l} -1, w_{in} < 0 \\ 1, w_{in} > 0 \end{array} \right\}$$

The new sets of optimal weights w are generated using genetic approach. TPM is synchronized for this new set of inputs and weights and a fresh set of synchronized weights is obtained which is appended to the previous set of synchronized weights to obtain a key of desired length.

6   Conclusions

Neural cryptography can be used for key generation over secured channels. Incrementing the synaptic depth of the neural networks increases the synchronization time of the networks, but the replacement of random weights with optimal weights helps to reduce this time. Further an increase in the number of hidden/input neurons accelerates convergence and also reduces the probability of success of MFA attack. Neural cryptography using soft computing promises to revolutionize secure communication by providing more security based on the neural networks.

References

1. Boyd, C., Mathuria, A.: Protcols For Authentication and Key Establishment, ISBN 3- 540-43107-1 Springer Verlag-540-43107-1 Springer Verlag, Berlin Heideberg, New York
2. Barker, E., Roginsky, A.: Recommendation for Cryptographic Key Generation, National Institute of Standards and Technology Special Publication 800-133, Natl. Inst. Stand. Technol. Spec. Publ. 800-133, pp.26 (December 2012)
3. Leighton, T., Micali, S.: Secret-Key Agreement without Public-Key Cryptography. In: Stinson, D.R. (ed.) CRYPTO 1993. LNCS, vol. 773, pp. 456–479. Springer, Heidelberg (1994)
4. Diffie, W., Hellman, M.E.: New directions in cryptography. IEEE Trans. Inf. Theory **22**, 644–654 (1976)
5. Raymond, J.-F., Stiglic, A.: Security Issues in the Diffie-Hellman Key Agreement Protocol. http://crypto.cs.mcgill.ca/ ~ stiglic/Papers/dhfull.pdf
6. Neal, K.: A Course in Number Theory and Cryptography. Springer, New york (1994)
7. Kinzel, W., Kanter, I.: Neural Cryptography In: Proceedings of the 9th International Conference on Neural Information Processing (ICONIP'02) vol. 3, pp. 1351–1354 (2002)
8. Rosen-Zvi, M., Kanter, I., Kinzel, W.: Cryptography based on neural networks—analytical results. J. Phys. **35**(47), L707 (2002)
9. Kanter, I., Kinzel, W., Kanter, E.: Secure Exchange of Information by Synchronization of Neural Networks. Europhys. Lett. **57**, 141–147 (2002)
10. Klimov, A., Mityagin, A., Shamir, A.: Analysis of neural cryptography. In: Zheng, Y. (ed.) Advances in Cryptology ASIACRYPT 2002. LNCS, vol. 2501, pp. 288–298. Springer, Heidelberg (2002)
11. Klein, E., Mislovathy, R., Kanter, I., Ruttor, A., Kinzel, W.: " Synchronization of Neural Networks by Mutual Learning and its Application to Cryptography", Advances in Neural Information Processing Systems, vol. 17, pp. 689–696. MIT Press, Cambridge, MA (2005)
12. Ruttor, A., kinzel, W.: Genetic Attack on Neural Cryptography. Phys. Rev. E **73**(3), 036121 (2006)
13. Shacham, L.N., Klein, E., Mislovaty, R., Kanter, I., Kinzel, W.: Cooperating attackers in neural cryptography. Phys. Rev. E: Stat., Nonlin, Soft Matter Phys. **69**(6), 066137 (2004)
14. Santhanalakshmi, S., Sudarshan, T.S.B., Patra, G.K.: Neural synchronization by mutual learning using genetic approach for secure key generation. In: Thampi, S.M., Zomaya, A.Y., Strufe, T., Alcaraz Calero, J.M., Thomas, T. (eds.) SNDS 2012. CCIS, vol. 335, pp. 422–431. Springer, Heidelberg (2012)
15. Goldberg, D.E.: Genetic Algorithms in Search, Optimization and Machine Learning, Addison- Wesley, Boston (1989)

16. Karlik, B.: Soft computing methods in bioinformatics: a comprehensive review. Math. Comput. Appl. **18**, 176–197 (2013)
17. Pratihar, D.K.: Soft Computing. Narosa Publishing House, New Delhi (2008)
18. Ruttor, A.: Neural Synchronization and Cryptography, Dissertation, Bayerischen Julius-Maximilians-Universitat Wurzburg (2006)
19. Kessler, G.C.: An Overview of Cryptography, Handbook on Local Area Networks. Auerbach, New York (1998)
20. Santhanalakshmi, S., Sangeeta, K., Patra, G.K.: Design of Stream cipher for text encryption using soft computing based techniques. IJCSNS Int. J. Comput. Sci. Netw. Secur. **12**(12), 149–152 (2012)

CLCT: Cross Language Cipher Technique

Laukendra Singh$^{(\boxtimes)}$ and Rahul Johari

University School of Information and Communication Technology,
Guru Gobind Singh Indraprastha University, New Delhi, India
laukendrasingh.ipu@gmail.com, rahul@ipu.ac.in

Abstract. Information Security has become an important issue in data communication. In modern world, internet and network applications are growing fast. So the importance and the value of the exchanged data over the internet or other media types are increasing. Any loss or threat to information can prove to be huge loss to the organization. Encryption technique is the best solution against the intruder. In this paper we formalize a new symmetric cryptographic cipher technique which is easy to understand and implement. This introduced cipher technique's name is Cross Language Cipher technique (CLCT). In this technique we use the concept of cross language which plays an important role in data security. Today most of the cipher techniques work with English language but we use two languages English and Hindi in our cipher technique. Basically, here are two functions in CLCT; first replaces/converts the English text data to Hindi text data and second function encrypt the Hindi text data. The encryption function is similar to Caesar cipher's function. To find the actual plaintext by intruder is not an easy task because CLCT uses diffusion property. So, CLCT is more reliable and powerful cipher technique. Most of cipher techniques have issue of higher performance and good security feature. Advantages of CLCT are that its performance is high and is less vulnerable to network attack.

Keywords: Cryptography · Encryption · Decryption · Security · Cipher · CLCT · Diffusion

1 Introduction

1.1 Cryptography

Security is the most challenging aspects in the internet and network applications. We need to secure the data in data communication whether the mode of communication is wired or wireless. Basically data security means protecting its confidentiality, integrity, and availability [1]. The consequences of a failure to protect any of the three aspects will incur loss in business, loss of company's goodwill. Organizations are spread across states and countries. Organizations use internet as a backbone to carry out their day to day operations including sensitive data transfer. There is a need to protect customer data as mandated by security controls. So organizations have to pay a huge price in case of compromise of data, especially customer's confidential data. With the rapid growth of information technology and science of encryption, an innovative area for cryptographic products has evolved. The better solution to offer the necessary

© Springer International Publishing Switzerland 2015
J.H. Abawajy et al. (Eds): SSCC 2015, CCIS 536, pp. 217–227, 2015.
DOI: 10.1007/978-3-319-22915-7_21

protection regarding data is cryptography. Many definitions of cryptography are given by authors in their research papers and text books. For the sake of completeness and clarity some of them are listed as follows: "Cryptography is the science that studies the mathematical techniques for keeping message secure and free from attack" [2]. "Cryptography is the subdivision of cryptology in which encryption/decryption algorithms are designed to guarantee the security and authentication of data" [3]. Figure 1 provides a better understanding regarding cryptography. Cryptography is further classified into private key cryptography and public key cryptography.

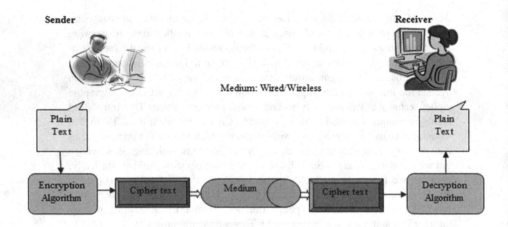

Fig. 1. Concept of cryptography

Private Key Cryptography. In private key cryptography system sender and receiver share a single private key which is used to encrypt and decrypt messages. The algorithm used for private key cryptography is called symmetric key algorithm. Symmetric key algorithm is also divided in two types; stream cipher and block cipher. Stream ciphers encrypt the information bit by bit and Block ciphers encrypt the bits of information block by block.

Public Key Cryptography. Public key cryptography uses the pair of keys one is secret key and other is public key in which one is used for encrypting the message and other is used for decrypting the message.

1.2   What is Cipher?

In cryptography, a cipher is an algorithm for performing encryption or decryption – a series of well-defined steps that can be followed as a procedure [4]. Most of modern ciphers can be categorized in several ways:

- By whether they work on blocks of symbols usually of a fixed size called Block Cipher, or on a continuous stream of symbols called Stream Cipher.
- By whether same key is used for both encryption and decryption called symmetric algorithm, or if a different key is used for each called asymmetric key algorithm. Key must be known to sender and recipient and no one else. Asymmetric key algorithm has public-private key property and one of the key may be made public without loss of confidentiality.
- Ciphers are also categorized as follows [Fig. 2]:

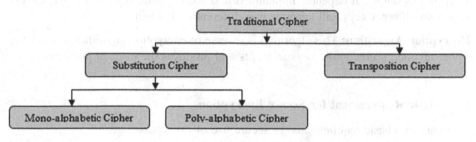

Fig. 2. Categories of ciphers

1.2.1   Substitution Cipher
In Substitution Cipher, one symbol is substituted by other symbol.

Mono-alphabetic Cipher: In mono-alphabetic, a symbol or character in the plaintext is always changed to the same symbol or character in the cipher text regardless of its position in the text. The relationship between symbols in plaintext and cipher text is one-to-one.

Poly-alphabetic Cipher: Whereas in the Poly-alphabetic Cipher, each occurrence of symbol in plaintext can have a different substitute in cipher text. The relationship between the symbols in plaintext and symbols in cipher text is one-to-many.

1.2.2   Transposition Cipher
There is no substitution of characters in transposition cipher; instead their location change. In other words, a transposition cipher reorders or permutes the symbols in a block of symbols.

1.3   Architecture of Cipher

An encryption scheme has five ingredients:

Plaintext: This is the actual readable text or message that is fed into the algorithm as input.

Encryption Algorithm: The algorithm performs various transformation and substitution on the plain text.

Secret/Public Key: Secret key is also an input to the symmetric encryption/decryption algorithm and private-public key combination is used in a asymmetric encryption/decryption algorithm. The key value is independent of the plaintext and cipher text. The algorithm produces the result as output depending on that particular key being used at that time.

Cipher Text: This is an unreadable text or message produced from Encryption algorithm as output. It depends on plaintext and secret/public keys. For a given message, two different keys will generate two different cipher text.

Decryption Algorithm: This algorithm is reverse of encryption algorithm. It takes the cipher text and secret/public keys as inputs and produces the original plaintext.

1.4   Basic Requirement for Secure Encryption

There are two basic requirements for secure use of encryption:

- Sender and receiver must have exchanged copies of the secret/private key in a secure fashion and must keep the key secure.
- We need a strong encryption algorithm. We would like an algorithm to be such that an opponent should be unable to decrypt the cipher text or discover the key.

2   Related Work

In [3] author(s) demonstrate the comparative performance analysis of MD5, DES and AES encryption algorithms on the basis of execution time, LOC (Lines of Code) over a web application. In [5] author(s) discusses and analyses the current developments in online authentication procedures including one-time-password systems, biometrics and Public Switched Telephone Network for cardholder authentication. The author(s) proposes a complete new framework for both onsite and online (Internet shopping) credit card transactions. In [6, 9] author(s) presents a detailed review on various types of vulnerabilities, Structured Query Language Injection attacks, Cross Site Scripting Attack, and prevention techniques. The Author(s), also proposes future expectations and possible developments of countermeasures against Structured Query Language Injection attacks. In [7] author(s) presents an integrated model to prevent reflected cross site scripting attack and SQL Injection attacks in applications which are made in PHP. These models work in two modes which are production and safe mode environment. They create sanitizer model for reflected cross site scripting attack and security query model for SQL Injection attack in safe mode. They validate user input text against sanitizer model and input entries which create SQL queries are validated against security query model in production mode. In [8] author(s) demonstrates the vulnerabilities and network attacks pertaining to cryptographic algorithms such as AES, DES and MD 5 et al. In [10] author(s) also proposes a similar technique to handle the security of the alphabets and numbers but without any detailed comparison. In [11] author(s) proposes a technique to encrypt and decrypt the Alphabets, Numbers and Alphanumeric data in minimum span of time with minimum lines of code, designed logic of which has been coded in JAVA In [12] author(s) have designed a Java based tool to show the exploitation of Injection using SQL Injection attack and Broken Authentication using Brute Force Attack and Dictionary Attack and the prevention of all these attacks by storing the data in our database in encrypted form using AES algorithm. In [13] author(s) have explored prevalent system vulnerabilities such as Password Ageing, Empty String Password, Empty Catch Block Problem etc. and network attacks such as Brute force attack, Denial of service Attack and Dictionary Attack etc.

3 Proposed Work

In modern World, web and network applications are growing fast. So security is the most challenging aspects in the web and network applications. By keeping it in mind, we introduce a new cipher technique. This new introduced cipher technique is known as Cross Language Cipher Technique (CLCT). CLCT is easy to understand and implement. Mostly cipher techniques work with English language. So, in this cipher technique we use the concept of cross language which provides an important role in data security. We use two languages like English and Hindi in our cipher technique. CLCT uses multiple functions at both the side sender and receiver. The actual input text is written in English language. First function of CLCT encodes the characters of English language into their corresponding ASCII value. Second function represents the corresponding ASCII value of English language characters to ASCII value of Hindi language characters. The representation of characters is manually defined. Third function is the actual encryption function which encrypts the particular data or information with the help of key. Fourth function starts to work when it gets output from the encryption function. It decodes the received data or information into Hindi language text. The output from the decode function is the actual cipher text which is sent to the receiver. The reverse steps are applied at receiver side to get the actual plain text.

3.1 Description of Algorithm

Working steps of the algorithm at both side sender and receiver are defined in following.

3.1.1 Sender Side

Steps that are performed at sender side are defined as follows:

1. Take the input text from a text file (MY.txt) in English language.
2. Encode the text into ASCII value.
3. Represent/convert the encoded text into ASCII value text of Hindi language.
4. Store the converted text into MY1.txt file.

5. Split the string (text) into characters.
6. Applying encryption algorithm.
7. Merge the characters into string after encryption.
8. Decode the string (text) into Hindi language text.
9. Store the actual cipher text (decoded text) into MY2.txt file.
10. Send the cipher text to the receiver.

Flow diagram of desired CLCT technique at sender side is shown in Fig. 3.

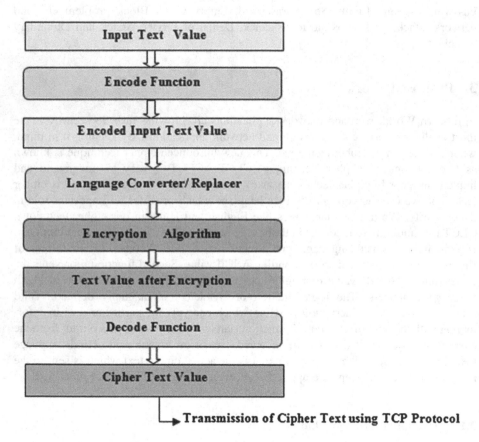

Fig. 3. CLCT cipher encryption at sender side.

Input Text Value: The value of this field is simply a text which is written in English language format. This is the actual input text.

Encode Function: Encode function encodes the input text data into their corresponding ASCII value.

Encode Input Text Value: This is a ASCII value received from the output of Encode Function and saved in a file.

Language Replacer/Converter: This body of the CLCT algorithm plays an important role. Function of this body represents the ASCII value of English language text data to the ASCII value of Hindi language text data. This is a manual representation.

Encryption Algorithm: This is the actual encryption function which is similar to Caesar cipher. Input text data to this function is encrypted to another text data which is known as cipher text. But this is not the actual cipher text of CLCT cipher technique.

Text Value After Encryption: This field defines the cipher text value which is obtained after performing encryption algorithm.

Decode Function: This function decodes the received text data into Hindi text data.

Cipher Text Value: This is the actual cipher text data/value is stored in a file.
Now Sender sends the cipher text data to the Receiver.

3.1.2   Receiver Side
Steps that are performed at receiver side are defined as follows:

1. Take the cipher text as input.
2. Encode the received text data into their corresponding ASCII value.
3. Store the encoded text data.
4. Split data text into characters.
5. Apply the decryption algorithm.
6. Merge the characters into string after decryption.
7. Decode the string into Hindi language text.
8. Replace/Convert the Hindi text data to the required English text.

Flow diagram of desired CLCT cipher technique at receiver side is defined in Fig. 4.

Example: Encrypt the message "CRYPTOGRAPHY" using CLCT.

Solution: Table 1 illustrates the concept of CLCT technique for the given input text.

Sent from Sender

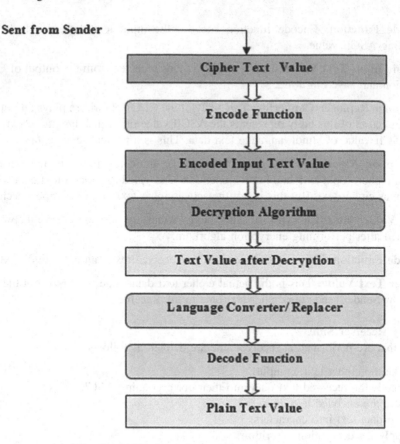

Fig. 4. CLCT cipher decryption at receiver side.

Table 1. CLCT algorithm with Encryption and Decryption at Sender side and Receiver side respectively

Sender Side	Receiver Side
1. Plain Text: CRYPTOGRAPHY	**6.** Plain Text: CRYPTOGRAPHY
2. Input text to Encode Function: CRYPTOGRAPHY	**5.** Decode Function decodes the received text from Language Replacer/Converter into English language text format. This is the actual plain text of CLCT technique.
3. Output text from Encode Function and input to Language Replacer/Converter: CRYPTOG RAPHY	**4.** Output text from Decryption Function and input to Language Replacer/Converter: चरयपतो गरअपहय
4. Output text from Language Replacer/Converter and input to Encryption Function: चरयपतो गरअपहय	**3.** Output text from Encode Function and input to Decryption Function: तऺहऴमॕ डऺएऴृह
5. Decode Function decodes the received text from Encryption Function into Hindi language text format. This is the actual cipher text of CLCT technique.	**2.** Input text to Encode Function: तப्हक़मப्डப्एक़्ह
6. Cipher Text: तப्हक़मப्डப्एक़्ह	**1.** Cipher Text: तப्हक़मப्डப्एक़्ह

4   Simulation

We have used NetBeans IDE 7.1 as simulator for implementation of CLCT technique. The reason for using the NetBeans IDE is that, it is open source. The code has been written entirely in java programming language because besides being open source it offers the flexibility of easy to code cryptographic functions. The snapshots are illustrated in Figs. 5 and 6.

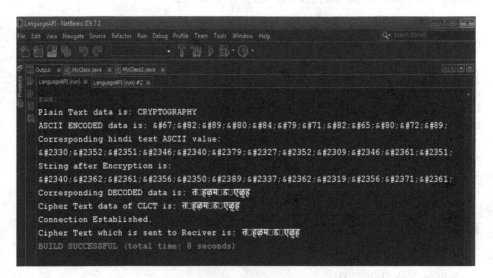

Fig. 5. CLCT at sender side

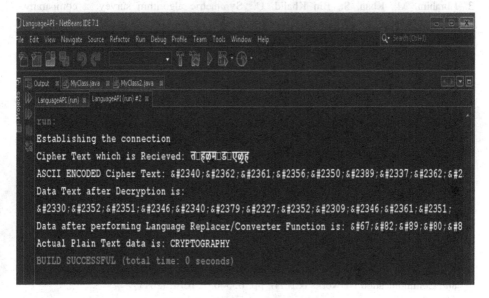

Fig. 6. CLCT at receiver side

5   Analysis

Today most of the cipher techniques in the literature are designed and developed in the English Language, but the introduction of this new cross language cipher technique of converting plaintext from the English to Hindi language would make the resultant cipher text robust, computationally strong and more secure to various attacks such as BruteForce Attack, Man in the Middle Attack, Birthday Attack, Replay attack et al. making it difficult for the hackers and crackers to decode it.

6   Conclusion and Future Work

We have successfully implemented our proposed CLCT technique. The cipher Text obtained is safe, reliable and secure. In future work, instead of converting Plain Text (in English language) to Cipher Text (in Hindi language) it can be mapped/converted to other regional languages like Assamese, Bengali, Oriya, Tamil and Telugu. Also we propose to compare other results of CLCT technique with other cryptographic techniques such as Additive cipher, Affine cipher, Vigenere cipher, Rail Fence cipher, Hill cipher et al. on the parameters such as LOC (Line of Code), space and time complexity etc.

References

1. Forouzan, B.A.: Cryptography and Network Security. Mc. Graw-Hill, Special Indian Edition, New Delhi (2007)
2. Chaudhari, M.P., Patel, S.R.: A survey on cryptography algorithms. Int. J. Adv. Res. Comput. Sci. Manage. Stud. 2(3), 100–104 (2014)
3. Ebrahim, M., Khan, S., Bin Khalid, U.: Symmetric algorithm survey: a comparative analysis. Int. J. Comput. Appl. 61(20), 12–19 (2013)
4. Johari, R., Jain, I., Ujjwal, R.L.: Performance analysis of MD5, DES and AES encryption algorithms for credit card application. In: International Conference on Modeling and computing (ICMC – 2014) (2014)
5. Gupta, S., Johari, R.: A new framework for credit card transactions involving mutual authentication between cardholder and merchant. In: 2011 International Conference on Communication Systems and Network Technologies (CSNT), pp. 22–26. IEEE (2011)
6. Johari, R., Sharma,P.: A survey on web application vulnerabilities (SQLIA, XSS) exploitation and security engine for SQL injection. In: 2012 International Conference on Communication Systems and Network Technologies (CSNT), pp. 453–458. IEEE (2012)
7. Sharma, P., Johari, R., Sarma, S.S.: Integrated approach to prevent SQL injection attack and reflected cross site scripting attack. Int. J. Syst. Assur. Eng. Manage. 3(4), 343–351 (2012). Springer
8. Ahuja, S., Johari, R., Khokhar, C.: CRiPT : cryptography in penetration testing. In: Springer's AISC Series for International Conference on Computer and Communication Technologies - IC3T (to appear 2015)
9. Johari, R., Gupta, N.: Secure query processing in delay tolerant network using java cryptography architecture. In: 2011 International Conference on Computational Intelligence and Communication Networks (CICN), pp. 653–657. IEEE (2011)

10. Ruby, L., Johari, R.: Designing a secure encryption technique for web based application. Int. J. Adv. Res. Sci. Eng. (IJARSE) **3**(7), 159–163 (2014)
11. Ruby, L., Johari,R.: SANE :Secure encryption technique for alpahamuneric data over web based applications. Int. J. Eng. Res. Technol. (IJERT) 3(8) (2014)
12. Jain, I., Johari, R., Ujjwal, R.L.: CAVEAT: credit card vulnerability exhibition and authentication tool. In: Second International Symposium on Security in Computing and Communications (SSCC 2014), pp 391–399 Springer (2014)
13. Ahuja, S., Johari, R., Khokhar, C.: EAST: Exploitation of Attacks and System Threats in Network. In: Mandal, J.K., Satapathy, S.C., Sanyal, M.K., Sarkar, P.P., Mukhopadhyay, A. (eds.) Information Systems Design and Intelligent Applications. Advances in Intelligent Systems and Computing (AISC Series), vol. 339, pp. 601–611. (2015)

A Hybrid Cryptographic and Steganographic Security Approach for Identity Management and Security of Digital Images

Quist-Aphetsi Kester[1,2,3(✉)], Laurent Nana[1], Anca Christine Pascu[1],
Sophie Gire[1], Jojo M. Eghan[3], and Nii Narku Quaynor[3]

[1] Lab-STICC (UMR CNRS 6285), European University of Brittany,
University of Brest, Brest, France
`Kester.quist-aphetsi@univ-brest.fr`, `kquist@ieee.org`
[2] Faculty of Informatics, Ghana Technology University College, Accra, Ghana
[3] Department of Computer Science and Information Technology,
University of Cape Coast, Cape Coast, Ghana

Abstract. Privacy and security of image data are of paramount importance in our ever growing internet ecosystem of multimedia applications. Identity and security of image content play a major role in forensics and protection against media property theft. Copyright issues and ownership management as well as source identification within today's cyberspace are very crucial. In our work, we proposed a hybrid technique of ensuring security of digital images as well as owner Identification by combining cryptographic and steganographic approaches. The steganography was used to embed a secret identification tag into the image which was engaged using a secret key. This was applied directly on the pixel values of the image used. The cryptographic technique was used to encrypt the image to conceal its visual contents. The implementation was done successfully and analysis of the output results was done using MATLAB.

1 Introduction

Identity management [1, 2] for data storage and transmission is a key security feature for confidentiality, integrity, authentication and non repudiation [3, 4]. These features reassure the sources and the recipients during communications. Their usage can lead to copyright protection issues, forensics investigations, etc. [5–7]. These processes are achieved via embedding processes that disguises or hides the data. Security and Information hiding play a major role in safety and security of electronic data exchange. These can be seen in its subsidiary field: Steganography, Cryptography and Watermarking approaches [8]. Steganography involves the hiding of plaintext or data without disguising the visual understanding of it. This means once it is uncovered, the data hidden can easily be understood [9]. Cryptography is a process of hiding data via data

This work was supported by Lab-STICC (UMR CNRS 6285) Research Laboratory, UBO France, AWBC Canada, Ambassade de France-Institut Français-Ghana and the DCSIT-UCC.

J.H. Abawajy et al. (Eds): SSCC 2015, CCIS 536, pp. 228–237, 2015.
DOI: 10.1007/978-3-319-22915-7_22

transposition, replacement or advanced computational procedures that changes the entire structure of the data and rendering it into garbage. It can easily be detected but cannot easily be understood visually or in its raw states but one can engage cryptanalytic procedures that at the end can only produce a probable answer out of a set of infinite or fine uncertainties [10]. Watermarking is the process of embedding data into a carrier signal via different approaches with the hope of detecting it and using it to confirm the authenticity of the carrier [11]. This can affect the data quality of the carrier itself or not. All the three approaches of security and information hiding are crucial in securing data in cyber space.

2 Review

With today's advanced technologies in computation based on intelligence approaches and computational power, security approaches becomes weak and susceptible to attacks [12–14]. With advancements in artificial intelligence text based cryptographic approaches can be attacked using brute force attacks and then analyzed using formal methods for text mining [15, 16] and also multimedia contents can easily be analyzed using signal processing techniques in detecting additional embed contents [16]. Off-the-shelf software can easily remove some watermarking from data hence advanced approaches are needed to boost robustness, reduce visibility and cause less visual defects to the carrier signal. Therefore hybrid approaches are currently one of the most effective ways for providing security for digital images. Savita Badhan and Mamta Juneja in their work proposed an approach for data hiding in color images using lsb based steganography with improved capacity and resistance to statistical attacks. Their process engaged RGB 24 bit bitmap image that carried the secret DES encrypted message that was embedded by utilizing the different pixel intensities of the cover RGB image [17]. In our work, we proposed a hybrid technique for ensuring security of digital images, authentication, owner Identification by combining cryptographic and steganographic approaches. The steganography was used to embed a secret identification tag into the image by process of engagement of a secrete key together with the image. The secret key can be used in retrieving the hidden data image from the image. This was applied directly on the pixel values of the image. The cryptographic technique was used to encrypt the image to conceal its visual contents. The process is described below.

3 Methodology

The entire methodology is summarized in the Fig. 1 below. In our approach we first obtain the plain image, PI, and then embed the message, M, in the image using a secret key, K, with the steganographic approach, S = f (PI, K, M). The key and the message were combined to embed the message in the pixel values of the image. Features, IF = f (S, K), were then extracted from the image and then used to engage the ciphering process. The features extracted were the geometric mean and the entropy, since they are conserved for the pain image containing the embed data and its ciphered image.

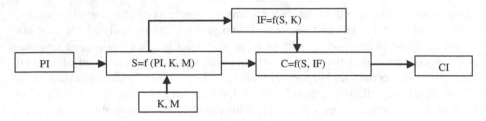

Fig. 1. The summary of the process engaged

Fig. 2. The developed application for the process using visual basic

The features were then used to encrypt the, S, which is the image containing the data based on the cryptographic approach, C = f(S, IF), to produced the ciphered image, CI. The figure below showed the block diagram used in the entire process (Fig. 2).

3.1 The Steganography Process

Let the host signal be defined by PI as below. The following approach was used to embed the data into the image, PI. For a given Image, we have

$$
PI = \begin{bmatrix}
x_{11} & x_{12} & x_{13} & x_{14} & . & . & . & x_{1n} \\
x_{21} & x_{22} & . & . & . & . & . & x_{2n} \\
x_{31} & . & . & . & . & . & . & x_{3n} \\
x_{41} & . & . & . & . & . & . & x_{4n} \\
. & . & . & . & . & . & . & . \\
. & . & . & . & . & . & . & . \\
. & . & . & . & . & . & . & . \\
x_{m1} & x_{m2} & x_{m3} & x_{m4} & . & . & . & x_{mn}
\end{bmatrix} \tag{1}
$$

For a given message M to be embedded in PI we have,

$$
M = \begin{bmatrix}
x_{11} & x_{12} & x_{13} & . & . & . & x_{1n} \\
x_{21} & x_{22} & & . & . & . & x_{2n} \\
x_{31} & . & & . & . & . & x_{3n} \\
. & . & . & . & . & . & . \\
. & . & . & . & . & . & . \\
. & . & . & . & . & . & . \\
x_{m1} & x_{m2} & x_{m3} & . & . & . & x_{mn}
\end{bmatrix}
\tag{2}
$$

For a given K to be embedded in PI we have,

$$
K = \begin{bmatrix}
x_{11} & x_{12} & x_{13} & . & . & . & x_{1n} \\
x_{21} & x_{22} & & . & . & . & x_{2n} \\
x_{31} & . & & . & . & . & x_{3n} \\
. & . & . & . & . & . & . \\
. & . & . & . & . & . & . \\
. & . & . & . & . & . & . \\
x_{m1} & x_{m2} & x_{m3} & . & . & . & x_{mn}
\end{bmatrix}
\tag{3}
$$

Where we obtain the channels of the image as R, G, B $\in$ PI
$(R \circ G)_{ij} = (R)_{ij} \cdot (G)_{ij}$ and $x \in [i, j, m, n]$ and $\{x \in I: 1 \leq x \leq +\infty\}$
For $x \in [R, G, B]$: $[a, b] = \{x \in I: a \leq x \leq b\}$ where $a = 0$ and $b = 255$

$$
R = r = PI(m, n, 1)
$$
$$
G = g = PI\ (m, n, 1)
$$
$$
B = b = PI\ (m, n, 1)
\tag{4}
$$

The following steps were used in the embedding process:

(a) Initialize the random number generator to select positions to store the message based on the key, K.
(b) Translate a password into an offset value.
(c) Process the message, M, for embedding.
(d) Pick a random pixel and RGB component based on the key.
(e) Get the pixel's color components.
(f) Get the value we must store.
(g) Update the color.
(h) Set the pixel's color.

3.2   The Feature Extraction

Features extracted from the image were the entropy and the geometrical mean.

Let PI = an image = f (R, G, B)

I is a color image of m x n x 3 arrays

$$
PI = \begin{bmatrix}
x_{11} & x_{12} & x_{13} & x_{14} & . & . & . & x_{1n} \\
x_{21} & x_{22} & . & . & . & . & . & x_{2n} \\
x_{31} & . & . & . & . & . & . & x_{3n} \\
x_{41} & . & . & . & . & . & . & x_{4n} \\
. & . & . & . & . & . & . & . \\
. & . & . & . & . & . & . & . \\
. & . & . & . & . & . & . & . \\
x_{m1} & .x_{m2} & x_{m3} & x_{m4} & . & . & . & x_{mn}
\end{bmatrix}
\tag{5}
$$

$x \in PI : [a, b] = \{x \in I: a \le x \le b\}$ a = 0 and b = 255 I = set positive integers

The geometric mean is

$$
m = \left[\prod_{i=1}^{n} x_i \right]^{\frac{1}{n}}
\tag{6}
$$

Where $x \in b\_i1 : [a, b] = \{x \in I: a \le x \le b\}$

$\delta(xi)$ = entropy(I) which is the entropy of the plain and it is a scalar value representing the entropy of grayscale image The entropy is a statistical measure of randomness that can be used to characterize the texture of the input image. Entropy is defined as follows:

$$
\delta(xi) = - \sum_{\eta=0}^{\varepsilon-1} \psi(xi). \ \log 2 \ (\psi(xi))
\tag{7}
$$

Where:

δ = Entropy of image

ε = Gray value of an input image (0-255).

$\Psi (\eta)$ = Probability of the occurrence of symbol η

3.3   The Visual Cryptographic Process

The image encryption process engaged C = f(S, IF) in ciphering the image and displacing the pixel values using a visual cryptographic technique.

Engagement k was used encrypt the plain image.

```
Start
Reading the image data,
Let PI= f (R, G, B)
new_image=imread(PI);
PI is a color image of m x n x 3 arrays
(R, G, B) =   m x n
Where R, G, B ∈PI
(R o G) i j = (R) ij. (G) ij
Where r_11 = first value of R
             r= [ri1] (i=1, 2… m)
               x ∈ r_i1 : [a, b]= {x ∈ I: a ≤ x ≤ b}
               a=0 and b=255
             R= r= I (m, n, 1)
  Where g_12 = first value of G
             g= [gi2] (i=1, 2... m)
             x ∈ g : [a, b]= {x ∈ I: a ≤ x ≤ b}
            a=0 and b=255
             G= g= I (m, n, 1)
And       b_13 = first value of B
             g= [bi3] (i=1, 2... m)
             x ∈ b_i1 : [a, b]= {x ∈ I: a ≤ x ≤ b}
             a=0 and b=255
             B=b= I (m, n, 1)
k=abs (mod ((c*(δ(xi)* m)), p))
   for i: Δi:kn
  Let t'(i,j) =Transpose of r(i,j)
      t'(i,j)=  f(r',c,p);
  Let y'(i,j) =Transpose of  y(i,j)
  y'(i,j)=  f(g',c,p);
  Let u'(i,j)  =Transpose of u(i,j)
  u'(i,j)=  f(b',c,p);
end
Transformion of t'(i,j) into  f(t'(i,j),c,p))
r= f(t'(i,j),c,p))=f(r, c, p)
Transformion of y'(i,j)into  f(y'(i,j),c,p))
g= f(y'(i,j),c,p))=f(g, c, p)
Transformion of u'(i,j) into  f(u'(i,j),c,p))
b= f(u(i,j),c,p))=f(b, c, p)
CI= f (3,r,g,b);
end
```

4 Results and Analysis

The image below of dimension 640 × 480 pixels image with vertical and horizontal resolution of 72 dpi and bit depth of 24was operated on by the proposed process and the following results were obtained from it (Figs. 3, 4, 5, 6, 7, 8).

Fig. 3. The plain Image

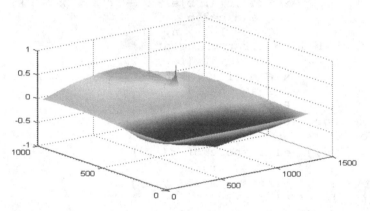

Fig. 4. The graph of the normalized cross-correlation of the matrices of the plain image

Fig. 5. The stega plain image

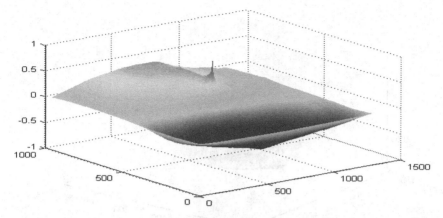

Fig. 6. The graph of the normalized cross-correlation of the matrices of the stega image

Fig. 7. The ciphered-stega image d image

The graph of the normalized cross-correlation of the matrices of the image
The normalized cross-correlation of the matrices of is

$$\gamma(u,v) = \frac{\sum_{x,y} \left[f(x,y) - \bar{f}_{u,v} \right] \left[t(x-u, y-v) - \bar{t} \right]}{\left\{ \sum_{x,y} \left[f(x,y) - \bar{f}_{u,v} \right]^2 \sum_{x,y} \left[t(x-u, y-v) - t \right]^2 \right\}^{0.5}} \tag{8}$$

f is the mean of the template, $\bar{t}$ is the mean of in the region under the template. $\bar{f}_{u,o}$ is the mean of $f(u,v)$ in the region under the template (Table 1).

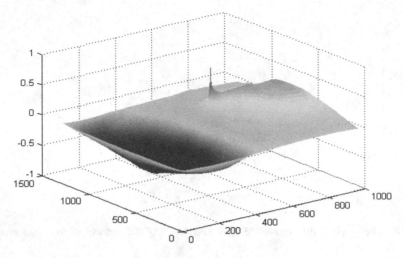

Fig. 8. The graph of the normalized cross-correlation of matrices of ciphered-stega Image

Table 1. Extracted features from the process.

Heading level	Entropy	Arithmetic mean
PI	7.7234	126.6555
SI	7.7234	126.6554
CI	7.7234	126.6554

PI = Plain Image
SI = Stega Image
CI is the loss image.

5 Conclusion

The implementation showed to be very successful and effective. The data was successfully embedded in the plain image and there was only a slight difference in the change in entropy vale and highly undetectable in the arithmetic mean due to value approximation. The data embedded was retrieved successfully after a successful decryption of the encrypted image. The approach showed to be effective against brute force attack.

Acknowledgments. This work was supported by Lab-STICC (UMR CNRS 6285) at UBO France, AWBC Canada, Ambassade de France-Institut Français-Ghana and the DCSIT-UCC, and also Dominique Sotteau (formerly directeur de recherche, Centre national de la recherche scientifique (CNRS) in France and head of international relations, Institut national de recherche en informatique et automatique, INRIA) and currently the Scientific counselor of AWBC.

References

1. Abbasi, A., Chen, H.: Writeprints: A stylometric approach to identity-level identification and similarity detection in cyberspace. ACM Trans. Inf. Syst. (TOIS) **26**(2), 7 (2008)
2. Hung, J.-F., Rau, H.-H., Hsu, C.-Y., Chen, S.-C., Tsai, D.-J., Fann, Y., Park, J., Eng, J.: Implementing globally unique identifier architecture in date collection for a health management study in taiwan aboriginal tribe. In: Park, J.J(.J.H)., Pan, Y., Kim, C., Yang, Y. (eds.) Future Information Technology-II. LNEE, vol. 329, pp. 121–127. Springer, Heidelberg (2015)
3. Sun, J., Zhang, C., Fang, Y.: An Id-based framework achieving privacy and non-repudiation in vehicular ad hoc networks. In: IEEE Military Communications Conference, MILCOM 2007, pp. 1–7. IEEE, October 2007
4. Neuman, B.C., Ts'o, T.: Kerberos: An authentication service for computer networks. IEEE Commun. Mag. **32**(9), 33–38 (1994)
5. Acquisti, A., Gritzalis, S., Lambrinoudakis, C., di Vimercati, S. (eds.): Digital Privacy: Theory, Technologies, and Practices. CRC Press, Boca Raton (2007)
6. Bidgoli, H.: Handbook of Information Security: Information Warfare, Social, Legal, and International Issues and Security Foundations. Wiley, New York (2006). Vol. 2
7. Lazzez, A., Slimani, T.: Forensics investigation of web application security attacks. Int. J. Comput. Netw. Inf. Secur. (IJCNIS) **7**(3), 10 (2015)
8. Cox, I., Miller, M., Bloom, J., Fridrich, J., Kalker, T.: Digital Watermarking and Steganography. Morgan Kaufmann, San Francisco (2007)
9. Raggo, M.T., Hosmer, C.: Data Hiding: Exposing Concealed Data in Multimedia, Operating Systems Mobile Devices and Network Protocols. Newnes, Oxford (2012)
10. Rebeiro, C., Mukhopadhyay, D., Bhattacharya, S.: Modern cryptography. In: Rebeiro, C., Mukhopadhyay, D., Bhattacharya, S. (eds.) Timing Channels in Cryptography, pp. 13–35. Springer, Heidelberg (2015)
11. Ren, N., Wang, Q., Zhu, C.: GIS spatial data updating algorithm based on digital watermarking technology. In: Bian, F., Xie, Y. (eds.) GRMSE 2014. CCIS, vol. 482, pp. 143–150. Springer, Heidelberg (2015)
12. Schneier, B., Fredrikson, M., Kohno, T., Ristenpart, T.: Surreptitiously Weakening Cryptographic Systems (2015)
13. Farash, M.S.: Cryptanalysis and improvement of 'an improved authentication with key agreement scheme on elliptic curve cryptosystem for global mobility networks'. Int. J. Netw. Manage. **25**(1), 31–51 (2015)
14. Mourouzis, T.: Optimizations in Algebraic and Differential Cryptanalysis (Doctoral dissertation, UCL (University College London)) (2015)
15. Duan, H., Luo, Q.: New progresses in swarm intelligence–based computation. Int. J. Bio-Inspired Comput. **7**(1), 26–35 (2015)
16. Husien, S., Badi, H.: Artificial neural network for steganography. Neural Comput. Appl. **26**(1), 111–116 (2015)
17. Badhan, S., Juneja, M.: A novel approach for data hiding in color images using LSB based steganography with improved capacity and resistance to statistical attacks. In: Jain, L.C., Patnaik, S., Ichalkaranje, N. (eds.) Intelligent Computing, Communication and Devices, vol. 309, pp. 183–190. Springer, Heidelberg (2015)

A Coupled Chaos Based Image Encryption Scheme Using Bit Level Diffusion

P. Devaraj and C. Kavitha[(⊠)]

Department of Mathematics, College of Engineering Guindy,
Anna University Chennai, Chennai 600025, India
devaraj@annauniv.edu, kavistha@gmail.com

Abstract. A chaos based image encryption scheme with bit level operation and nonlinear chaotic map is proposed in this paper. The bit plane permutation and diffusion using bits from neighboring pixel and other two colour channels introduce confusion and diffusion within the colour components as well as between the colour components. Simulation results show that the security of the scheme is enhanced when compared with certain known existing schemes.

Keywords: Couple nonlinear chaotic map · Pixel permutation · Bit level diffusion · Chaos

1 Introduction

Image encryption is one of the topic that addresses multimedia security. Recently, many chaos based image encryption algorithms are developed [1–4]. To improve the security, some of these schemes now focus on bit level operations. In [5], Fu et.al. has implemented two stage chaos-based bit-level permutation in which diffusion effect is also incorporated in permutation. In [6], bit level permutation and pixel diffusion is implemented. Zhou et.al. [7], has used the bit plane of source image as the security key bit plane to encrypt the image. In [8] heterogeneous bit-permutation and expanded XOR is used in diffusion. The proposed scheme permutes the bit planes between the colour channels considering four bits as a unit along with pixel permutation. Diffusion process is designed to depend on the bits of the neighbouring pixel values as well as the other colour components. To increase the security of the scheme, coupled nonlinear chaotic map is used to generate the key sequences.

2 Coupled Nonlinear Chaotic Map

Coupled nonlinear chaotic map is a three dimensional nonlinear chaotic map designed by combining the standard map and logistic map. The standard map and logistic map are chaotic in nature when their corresponding parameters

© Springer International Publishing Switzerland 2015
J.H. Abawajy et al. (Eds): SSCC 2015, CCIS 536, pp. 238–246, 2015.
DOI: 10.1007/978-3-319-22915-7_23

takes the values $|K| > 18$ and $\mu = 4$. Hence, the coupled nonlinear chaotic map is defined as:

$$x_{n+1} = (z_n + x_n + y_n) \bmod 2\pi$$
$$y_{n+1} = (y_n + K.\sin(x_{n+1})) \bmod 2\pi$$
$$z_{n+1} = (y_{n+1} + 4.z_n.(1 - z_n)) \bmod 1$$

where the initial values x_0, $y_0 \in (0, 2\pi)$ and $z_0 \in (0, 1)$ and the parameter $|K| > 18$. The lyapunov exponent of the coupled nonlinear chaotic map is plotted with the values $x_0 = .4$, $y_0 = .3 * 2 * pi$, $z_0 = .777$ and K varying from 1 to 1000. The lyapunov exponent in Fig. 1 is positive and hence the sequence generated by this map is chaotic in nature. Figure 2 shows that the distribution of the map is uniform. Hence, the map is secure and well suited for image encryption.

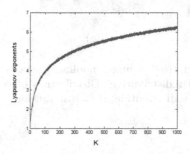

Fig. 1. Lyapunov exponents of the coupled nonlinear chaotic map

3 Proposed Scheme

Consider the 24 bit colour image as plain image that is stored in three two-dimensional arrays R, G, B that represent red, green and blue colour channels respectively, each of dimension $H \times W$.

3.1 Key Generation

Let X_0, $Y_0 \in (0, 2\pi)$ and $Z_0 \in (0, 1)$ and the parameter $|K| > 18$. The map is iterated $H \times W$ times to generate an array of keys of size $H \times W \times 3$. The permutation also uses two random sequences. The keys and the random sequences are generated as follows. The random integers u_1, u_2, s_1 and s_2 such that $\gcd(u_1, H) = 1$ and $\gcd(u_2, \frac{W}{4}) = 1$ are used for random sequences generation. Initialize $N = 255$; $X(1) = X_0$; $Y(1) = Y_0$; $Z(1) = Z_0$; $t = 1$.

> $for\ I = 1 : H \times W$
> $\quad X(I+1) = (Z(I) + X(I) + Y(I)) \bmod 2\pi$
> $\quad Y(I+1) = (Y(I) + K.\sin(X(I+1))) \bmod 2\pi$
> $\quad Z(I+1) = (Y(I+1) + 4.Z(I).(1 - Z(I))) \bmod 1$
> end

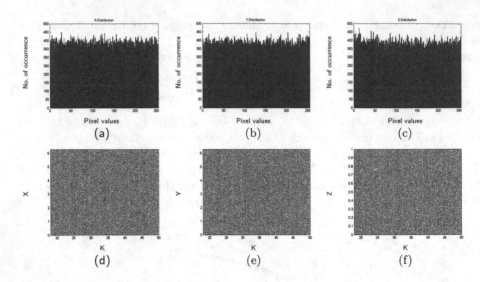

Fig. 2. Histogram of discretized coupled nonlinear chaotic map(a) x_distribution, (b) y_distribution, (c) (b) z_distribution, Distribution of coupled nonlinear chaotic map(d) x_distribution, (e) y_distribution, (f) z_distribution

$$for\ I = 1 : H$$
$$for\ J = 1 : W$$
$$key(I, J, 1) = \left\lfloor \frac{X(t)}{2\pi}.N \right\rfloor + 1;\ \ key(I, J, 2) = \left\lfloor \frac{Y(t)}{2\pi}.N \right\rfloor + 1;$$
$$key(I, J, 3) = \lfloor Z(t).N \rfloor + 1;\ \ t = t + 1$$
$$end$$
$$end$$
$$for\ I = 1 : H$$
$$KR(I) = (u_1.I + s_1)\ mod\ H + 1$$
$$end$$
$$for\ I = 1 : W/4$$
$$KC(I) = (u_2.I + s_2)\ mod\ (W/4) + 1$$
$$end$$

3.2 Encryption

Pixel Permutation: Pixel permutation groups the pixels in each colour component into four blocks of size $H \times \frac{W}{4}$ within which permutation is done using the key KR and KC and its values are modified by adding the key, 'key'. Here, $+$ is addition modulo 256 and $A(I, J, :)$ represents the Ith row and J^{th} column of the array A of size $H \times W \times 3$. Initialize $i1 = ones(1, 4)$; $j1 = ones(1, 4)$.

$$for\ I = 1 : H$$
$$for\ J = 1 : W$$
$$t = (I + J)\ mod\ 4 + 1$$
$$PI1(KR(i1(t)), (t-1).\frac{W}{4} + KC(j1(t)), :)$$
$$= (PI(I, J, :) + key(I, J, 1))\ mod\ 256$$
$$if\ j1(t) < \frac{W}{4}$$
$$j1(t) = j1(t) + 1$$
$$else$$
$$i1(t) = i1(t) + 1; j1(t) = 1$$
$$end$$
$$end$$
$$end$$

Bit-Plane Permutation: In a 24-bit colour image, there are three colour channels, R, G, B. The intensity of each colours in a pixel is represented using 8 bit integer i.e. values from 0 to 255, where each bit corresponds to a bit plane. Modifying these bit planes have significant changes in the image. In the scheme, the four Most Significant Bits (MSB) and four Least Significant Bits (LSB) are separated and permuted between channels. To make the resulting image key dependant and impose nonlinearity, the array of keys, 'key', generated using the coupled nonlinear map is added and a circular shift operation is applied to the pixel values. Here, $\|$ represents concatenation and $\ggg$ represents the circular right shift. Initialise t_1, t_2, t_3 to an integer value between 0 and 8.

$$PI1 = [R, G, B]$$
$$R = [R_{MSB}, R_{LSB}]; G = [G_{MSB}, G_{LSB}]; B = [B_{MSB}, B_{LSB}]$$
$$R1 = R_{LSB}\|G_{MSB}; G1 = R_{MSB}\|B_{MSB}; B1 = G_{LSB}\|B_{LSB}$$
$$R1 = ((R1 + key(:, :, 1))\ mod\ 256) \ggg t_1$$
$$G1 = ((G1 + key(:, :, 2))\ mod\ 256) \ggg t_2$$
$$B1 = ((B1 + key(:, :, 3))\ mod\ 256) \ggg t_3$$
$$PI = [R1, G1, B1]$$

Inter Component Bit Plane Diffusion: In this scheme, bit level diffusion is incorporated. Bits from neighbouring colour channels and the neighbouring pixels are combined to introduce a new 8 bit value that is XORed with the current pixel value. Moreover, the diffusion process is also designed to depend on the previously modified pixel value and the key. This process produce highly diffused image in which a slight change in one component affects all the components. Hence, this scheme is secure against linear and differential attack. Here, in $PI(I, J, K)_s$, s represents the bit plane s of the pixel value $PI(I, J, K)$.

$Initialise\ temp = PI(H, W, 3)$

$for\ K = 1 : 3$

   $for\ I = 1 : H$

      $for\ J = 1 : W$

         $t = PI(I, J - 1, K)_1 || PI(I + 1, J, K)_2 || PI(I, J + 1, K)_3 ||$

           $PI(I - 1, J, K)_4 || PI(I + 1, J - 1, K + 1)_5 || PI(I + 1, J + 1, K + 1)_6$

           $|| PI(I - 1, J - 1, K - 1)_7 || PI(I - 1, J + 1, K - 1)_8$

          $PI(I, J, K) = PI(I, J, K) \oplus t \oplus temp \oplus key(I, J, 2)$

          $temp = PI(I, J, K)$

      end

   end

end

3.3 Decryption

Decryption includes all the processes involved in encryption with inverse operations using same keys.

4 Security Analysis

4.1 Information Entropy Analysis

Information entropy is a measure of uncertainty or unrevealed information contained in the message. The alphabet set for the colour image contains 256 values (0 to 255).Therefore, entropy image is computed using the formula

$$H(m) = -\sum_{i=0}^{255} p(m_i) \log_2 p(m_i)$$

where $p(m_i)$ is the probability that the symbol m_i occurs in the message m. Table 1 shows the entropy of the cipher image is close to desired value i.e. 8 bits.

Table 1. Information entropy of cipher images

	Proposed Scheme			[8]			[9]		
Ciper Image	Red	Green	Blue	Red	Blue	Green	Red	Blue	Green
Lena	7.9993	7.9992	7.9993	7.9974	7.9970	7.9971	7.9993	7.9993	7.9993
Pepper	7.9993	7.9995	7.9994	7.9972	7.9972	7.9968	-	-	-
Baboon	7.9993	7.9994	7.9993	7.9972	7.9969	7.9969	-	-	-

4.2   Statistical Analysis

The histogram of the original image and the corresponding cipher image depicted in Fig. 3 shows that the distribution of the pixel values for the cipher image is uniform delivering no information about the plain image.

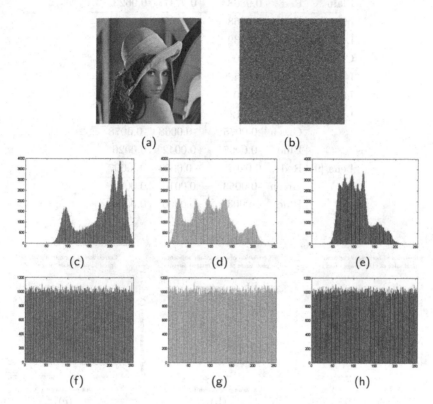

Fig. 3. (a) Plain Image, (b) Cipher Image, Histogram of plain image: (c) Red Channel, (d) Green Channel, (e) Blue Channel, Histogram of cipher image: (f) Red Channel, (g) Green Channel, (h) Blue Channel (Color figure online)

4.3   Correlation Analysis

Correlation analysis is used to examine the relation of the pixel values with its adjacent pixels. The correlation coefficient is calculated using the formula:

$$r = \frac{N(\sum XY) - (\sum X)(\sum Y)}{\sqrt{[N\sum X^2 - (\sum X)^2][N\sum Y^2 - (\sum Y)^2]}}.$$

For a randomly chosen pixel its horizontally adjacent, vertically adjacent and diagonally adjacent pixels values are considered for calculating correlation. The correlation coefficient for the plain and cipher image is given in the Table 2 and it shows that the cipher image is highly uncorrelated (Fig. 4).

Table 2. Correlation coefficients between adjacent pixels of plain image and cipher images

Image		Horizontal	Vertical	Diagonal
Plain	Red	0.9868	0.9747	0.9623
Image	Green	0.9868	0.9739	0.9628
Lena	Blue	0.9739	0.9543	0.9344
Cipher	Red	0.0009	-0.0030	0.0069
Image	Green	0.0043	-0.0005	-0.0027
Lena	Blue	0.0001	-0.0040	0.0030
Lena [8]	Red	-0.0127	0.0067	0.0060
	Green	-0.0075	-0.0068	-0.0078
	Blue	-0.0007	0.0042	0.0026
Lena [9]	Red	0.0207	-0.0023	-0.0007
	Green	-0.0053	0.0016	0.0000
	Blue	0.0003	0.0000	0.0000

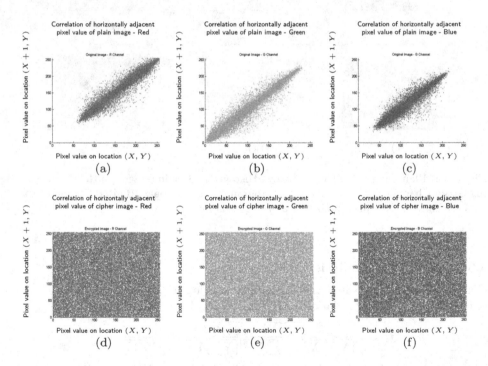

Fig. 4. Correlation analysis: frames (a), (b) and (c) shows horizontally adjacent pixel of the plain image, frames (d), (e) and (f) shows horizontally adjacent pixel of the cipher image

4.4   Differential Analysis

The plain image sensitivity examines the resistance of the encryption scheme against differential attack. The diffusion process in this scheme spreads the changes made in one component to all components, which makes it highly sensitive. Two measures for differential analysis: number of pixel change rate (NPCR) and the unified averaged changed intensity (UACI) are computed for the cipher images $C1$ and $C2$ corresponding to the two plain images, say $P1$ and $P2$, that vary in one pixel value. For each colour component, an array of dimension $H \times W$ is initialised with $V(i,j) = 1$ if pixel value at (i,j) location of the images $C1$ and $C2$ are different, else, $V(i,j) = 0$. Table 3, shows the NPCR and UACI values computed using the formulae:

$$NPCR_{R/G/B} = \frac{\sum_{i=1}^{H} \sum_{j=1}^{W} V_{R/G/B}(i,j)}{H \times W} \times 100\%$$

$$UACI_{R/G/B} = \frac{[\sum_{i=1}^{H} \sum_{j=1}^{W} \frac{|C1_{R/G/B} - C2_{R/G/B}|}{2^8 - 1}]}{H \times W} \times 100\%$$

are greater than 99.6094% and 33.4635% respectively. Hence, the scheme is highly sensitive and is secure against differential attack.

Table 3. NPCR% and UACI% Values

Cipher Image	NPCR			UACI		
	Red	Green	Blue	Red	Blue	Green
Lena (R channel modified)	99.6006	99.6014	99.5930	33.5284	33.4903	33.3815
Lena (G channel modified)	99.6243	99.6117	99.6002	33.4881	33.5169	33.4137
Lena (B channel modified)	99.5972	99.6258	99.6067	33.5163	33.5105	33.4572
Lena [8]	99.6124	99.6134	99.6192	33.4438	33.5232	33.5010
Lena [9]	99.61			33.48		

Table 4. Key Sensitivity

Modified Key Value	NPCR%			UACI%		
	Red	Green	Blue	Red	Blue	Green
$X_0 = .4 + 1.0000e^{-14}$	99.6117	99.6006	99.6098	33.5114	33.4191	33.4744
$Y_0 = .3 \times 2 \times \pi + 1.0000e^{-14}$	99.6063	99.5827	99.6254	33.4726	33.4810	33.4440
$Z_0 = .777 + 1.0000e^{-14}$	99.5941	99.6094	99.5922	33.4234	33.5894	33.3921
$K = 22 + 1.0000e^{-14}$	99.6132	99.6082	99.5922	33.4156	33.4848	33.4466

4.5   Key Sensitivity

Key sensitivity of the encryption scheme is examined in this section. A test image of size 512×512 is encrypted with the keys : $K = 22, X_1 = .4, Y_1 = .3*2*\pi, Z_1 = 0.777, u_1 = 7, u_2 = 17, s_1 = 19, s_2 = 99$. The sensitivity is analysed using $NPCR$ and $UACI$ calculated from the cipher image with modified keys and the original cipher image. From the Table 4, it is clear that the cipher image is highly sensitive even for small change in the keys.

4.6   Key Space Analysis

This scheme is highly secure against brute force attack with a key space of ≈ 194 bits, considering the precision of 10^{-14}.

5   Conclusion

In this paper, an image encryption scheme is proposed and analysed using various tests. Two well known maps, namely logistic map and standard map are coupled together and a new chaotic map is obtained. This map is used for the present encryption scheme. The scheme includes the confusion using pixel permutation and bit plane permutation along with diffusion, operating at bit level and nonlinear diffusion using the key stream. Statistical analysis, differential analysis, key space analysis and entropy analysis have been carried out to demonstrate the security of the new image encryption procedure. These types of analysis show that the scheme is secure.

References

1. Sam, I.S., Devaraj, P., Bhuvaneswaran, R.S.: A novel image cipher based on mixed transformed logistic maps. Multimedia. Tools Appl. **56**(2), 315–330 (2012). doi:10.1007/s11042-010-0652-6
2. Sam, I.S., Devaraj, P., Bhuvaneswaran, R.S.: Transformed logistic block cipher scheme for image encryption. In: Meghanathan, N., Kaushik, B.K., Nagamalai, D. (eds.) CCSIT 2011 Part II. CCIS, vol. 132, pp. 70–78. Springer, Heidelberg (2011)
3. Lian, S., Sun, J., Wang, Z.: Security analysis of a chaos-based image encryption algorithm. Physica A **351**, 645–661 (2005)
4. Tong, X.: Design of an image encryption scheme based on a multiple chaotic map. Commun. Nonlinear Sci. Numer. Simul. **18**, 1725–1733 (2013)
5. Fu, C., Lin, B., Miao, Y., Liu, X., Chen, J.: A novel chaos-based bit-level permutation scheme for digital image encryption. Opt. Commun. **284**, 5415–5423 (2011)
6. Zhu, Z., Zhang, W., Wong, K., Yu, H.: A chaos-based symmetric image encryption scheme using a bit-level permutation. Inf. Sci. **181**, 1171–1186 (2011)
7. Zhou, Y., Cao, W., Philip Chen, C.L.: Image encryption using binary bit plane. Sig. Process. **100**, 197–207 (2014)
8. Wang, X., Zhang, H.: A color image encryption with heterogeneous bit-permutation and correlated chaos. Opt. Commun. **342**, 51–60 (2015)
9. Zhang, W., Yu, H., Zhu, Z.: Color image encryption based on paired interpermuting planes. Opt. Commun. **338**, 199–208 (2015)

Secure Communication Using Digital Watermarking with Encrypted Text Hidden in an Image

M. Sundari[✉], P.B. Revathi[✉], and S. Sumesh[✉]

Department of CS and IT, Amrita School of Arts and Sciences Kochi,
Amrita Vishwa Vidyapeetham, Coimbatore, India
{sundari1551,revathybalagopal}@gmail.com,
ssumesh@hotmail.com

Abstract. Increased data transmission through the network has led to the need for greater security in order to protect against different attacks. To transfer data safely, there are many techniques in use, such as digital watermarking, fingerprinting, cryptography, digital signature and steganography. The aim of this paper is to propose a method to send text data securely over the network using digital watermarking, steganography and cryptography techniques together in combination, to provide greater security. First, the cover image will be compressed using JPEG Compression Algorithm. The message to be sent is then encrypted using the improved RSA algorithm. Then the encrypted message bits and the bits of watermark image are embedded into the compressed cover image.

Keywords: Cryptography · Steganography · Digital watermarking · DCT · Improved RSA · JPEG compression

1 Introduction

Secure transmission of data over a network has become a major concern due to the enormous growth in the use of the internet for all communications. The data transmitted over the network may be used by any persons, who are not intended to receive the data, for any malicious purposes. There are many techniques introduced to transmit data securely over the internet or a network. In this paper, techniques such as digital watermarking, cryptography, and steganography are used together to achieve a robust system.

1.1 Cryptography

Cryptography is the art of achieving security by converting the data into an unreadable form. The data that can be read and understood without any difficulty is called plain text while the encrypted text is called cipher text. The method of encoding plain text is called encryption and the process of reversing cipher text to its original plain text is called decryption. Cryptography offers the means for protecting the data by encoding it into an unreadable form thus providing confidentiality [1].

© Springer International Publishing Switzerland 2015
J.H. Abawajy et al. (Eds): SSCC 2015, CCIS 536, pp. 247–255, 2015.
DOI: 10.1007/978-3-319-22915-7_24

1.2   Steganography

Steganography is the art of hiding the digital information in any other digital cover media. A steganographic system hides the content by embedding in a cover media so as not to arouse an eavesdropper's suspicion. The stego object should always preserve the quality of the original cover media. The data transmitted will be a secret between two parties, thus providing confidentiality and protection against security threats [1].

1.3   Digital Watermarking

Digital watermarking is a process of embedding digital watermarks into a multimedia file. A digital watermark can be any signal or pattern embedded into any multimedia file which can be used for copyright protection and authentication, as it cannot be altered or modified. This provides message integrity [2].

2   Literature Review

The system is based on cryptography and steganography. The cover image for hiding the secret image is encrypted using a pseudo randomly generated key. The secret image is embedded into the cover image using Adaptive Pixel Pair Matching (APPM) algorithm. The extraction procedure is similar to that of the embedding procedure. The use of APPM improves the Peak-Signal-Noise-Ratio (PSNR) value for the given data and the extraction is also as simple as embedding in which we can reveal the precise secret image [1].

Nested watermarking is done using Least Significant Bit (LSB) technique with blowfish encryption. The watermark will be encrypted first and then embedded into another watermark. The nested watermark is again encrypted and embedded in the cover image. At the receiver end, watermark is extracted from the cover image and decrypted and the watermark embedded inside the watermark is extracted and decrypted and it is then used for authentication [2].

A combination of steganography and cryptography is used to take advantage of both the techniques. Blowfish Encryption Algorithm is used for encrypting the message to be hidden inside the image for making it non readable and secure. After encryption, LSB technique of steganography is applied for further enhancing the security [3].

A new symmetric encryption algorithm is developed and used along with LSB steganography [4].

A data hiding system based on audio steganography and cryptography is proposed to secure data transfer between the source and destination. Audio medium is used as the cover media and a LSB algorithm is employed to encode the message inside the audio file [5].

A new algorithm is proposed for invisible digital watermarking in which the cover image is zoomed to twice its original size using row-column duplication scheme and the entire target image will be hidden in the cover image starting from the first byte position of the cover image [6].

A text watermarking algorithm is proposed using combined image and text watermark to fully protect the text document. Then the text document is encrypted using RSA algorithm. In this algorithm double letters in the text are used for embedding the watermark [7].

A new algorithm for digital watermarking is proposed, which is based on image segmentation and Discrete Cosine Transform (DCT) is proposed. The image is segmented using Expectation Maximization Segmentation algorithm. Each segment is divided into 8*8 blocks and zigzag reordering is applied to each block of each segment [8].

This paper uses the singular value decomposition technique and quantization-based watermarking technique for protecting the copyrights of digital images. From the experimental analysis, it has been found that the quality of the watermarked image is better and the extracted watermark can be easily identified [9].

New block based embedding of the encrypted watermark using the Singular value decomposition algorithm is proposed. For encryption, two algorithms are used, RC6 and chaotic Baker map encryption algorithm. Four modes of RC6 are performed and chaotic Baker map are used and compared [10].

The system is proposed as a solution for enhancing security level using image compression and DCT based watermarking together. A new algorithm is proposed based on adaptive Huffman encoding for image compression. Compared to adaptive Huffman and static Huffman, the new algorithm has less storage space and reduced number of passes for encoding [11].

The system proposes an improved DCT based image watermarking technique by adjusting the low frequency coefficients by concept of mathematical remainder and embedding the watermark into these coefficients [12].

This system uses three prime numbers instead of two prime numbers. Public key and a new variable are generated using the three numbers and key length (n). The message is encrypted using the public key and the new variable is transmitted instead of n thus reading the encrypted text is difficult. The private key is calculated using the new variable transmitted along with the message and this private key is used for decrypting the message [13].

3 Proposed System

The proposed system is based on digital watermarking, cryptography and steganography. The purpose of this system is to send the text data securely over the network. The cover image is compressed using JPEG Compression algorithm. The message is encrypted using improved RSA and the encrypted message and watermark image are converted into bit streams and embedded in each 8×8 DCT blocks of the cover image. This embedding process is done on the sender side as shown in the Fig. 1(a) and its extraction process is done at the receiver side as shown in the Fig. 1(b).

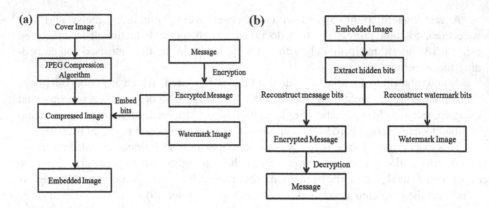

Fig. 1. (a) Flowchart for embedding process, and (b) Flowchart for extraction process

3.1 Embedding Process

The cover image for hiding the message is compressed using JPEG Compression that helps to reduce the bandwidth usage. A plain text is taken as the input and encrypted using the improved RSA algorithm. The encrypted text is converted into bits. The length of the message is stored in first DCT block and every 8-bits of the message are stored in each DCT block until the bit stream runs out. Similarly, the watermark image also will be converted into bits and the length of the watermark will be stored in the next immediate block and every 8-bits of the watermark image are stored in each DCT block until the bit stream runs out.

3.2 Extraction Process

The hidden bits will be extracted from the received image. Thus we get the message bits and watermark bits. The watermark bits are reconstructed back to the image. The reconstructed image will be authenticated against the original watermark image to ensure that it is from the legitimate party. Now the message bits extracted will be reconstructed and decrypted using the private key.

3.3 Module Wise Description

Compress Module. JPEG compression algorithm is used for compressing the image. JPEG Compression is a lossy compression method as it discards the unimportant data during its encoding phase. It is not just a single algorithm, but rather a combination of different algorithms. First, the image is transformed to YCbCr format as it helps to attain the best compression ratios. The next step is to downsample the chrominance components by averaging groups of pixels together. Then apply DCT for each 8×8 block of pixels, so that the redundant data can be avoided. Quantize each 8×8 block by dividing the 64 DCT coefficients with 64 quantization matrix coefficients. This is the lossy step which cannot be reverted back to get the original image. Quantization matrix coefficients are chosen based on a scaling factor called quality factor. The quality factor can take any value between 0 and 100. The image quality and compression rate depend on this quality factor. The resulting coefficients are encoded using Huffman compression, which is a lossless compression method and converts the data, rendering it even smaller thus it requires less storage space [14].

Crypto Module. In this module, the text data is encrypted using the RSA algorithm. The RSA algorithm is a public key cryptosystem named after its inventors namely, Ron Rivest, Adi Shamir, Len Adleman in 1977. RSA, which provides a reliable and safe system, can be used for both public key encryption and digital signatures. Key generation, Encryption, Decryption are the three steps followed and this algorithm uses a pair of keys for encryption and decryption. The message will be encrypted using a public key which can be accessed by anyone but can be decrypted using the private key only known to the receiver. In this paper, an improved version of the RSA algorithm has been proposed [15]

RSA is basically based on two distinct primes chosen at random. In improved RSA, five prime numbers of variable bit length are chosen at random, i.e., One prime number will be of bit length 8 while others will be of size 2, 4 or 6. Usually, prime numbers of same bit length is used in RSA but in improved RSA, different bit length are used for each prime number because of which, key length may not grow too long, whereas if we use 8 bit length for each prime number the key length might grow longer. And, also the passes for generating five small prime numbers is very less than that required for generating two large prime numbers. When an attacker tries to get the prime numbers from the key length due to small key length he may not be aware of the use of five prime numbers. This makes it difficult for the attacker to find the prime numbers and trace the private key.

Step 1: Key Generation. Generate 5 distinct primes at random of varying bit length in which one number will be of eight bit length, one number of 6 bit length, two numbers will be of 4 bit length and other one of 2 bit length.

Compute key length n by multiplying all 5 prime numbers.
Compute Euler's Totient, φ (n), where, φ is Euler's totient function,

$$\varphi(n) = (p-1)(q-1)(r-1)(s-1)(t-1). \tag{1}$$

Choose an integer e, the public key exponent, such that, e and φ(n) are co prime.

$$1 < e < \varphi(n) \text{ and } \gcd(e, \varphi(n)) = 1. \tag{2}$$

Compute a value for d, the private key exponent, such that, d is the multiplicative inverse of e (modulo φ(n)).

$$d \equiv e^{-1}(\mod \varphi(n)). \tag{3}$$

The public key is (E, N) and the private key is (D, N).

Step 2: Encryption. Receiver transmits the public key to the sender and keeps the private key secret. Sender encrypts the message m to be send using public key, such that $0 \leq m < n$.

$$c = m^e (\text{mod } n). \tag{4}$$

Step 3: Decryption. Receiver decrypts the message using the private key,

$$m = c^d (\text{mod } n). \tag{5}$$

Stego module. In this module, the encrypted message and the watermark image are hidden into the compressed image and extracted from it and reconstructed back as follows:.

Step 1: The encrypted message and the watermark image are converted into bit streams.

Step 2: The length of the encrypted message is embedded in the first 8×8 block of the compressed image.

Step 3: Every 8 bits of the encrypted message are embedded in each successive 8 × 8 block of the image. This is repeated until the bits run out.

Step 4: The length of the watermark image bits is embedded in the succeeding block after the message bits are embedded.

Step 5: Every 8 bits of the watermark image are embedded in each successive 8 × 8 block. This is repeated until the bits run out.

Step 6: For extraction, the length of the encrypted message is extracted from first 8 × 8 block.

Step 7: Then the bits are extracted from each block until the specified length.

Step 8: Then watermark image length is extracted from the succeeding block and the bits are extracted from each block until the length specified has been reached.

Step 9: The bits are reconstructed to get the encrypted message and watermark image.

Step 10: The watermark image is authenticated against the original watermark image and the reconstructed message is decrypted.

4   Implementation

The proposed system is implemented in java. The image is first compressed using JPEG compression algorithm with different quality factor values and then the message is encrypted using improved RSA algorithm and the watermark image is embedded into the compressed image. The compression leads to reduced bandwidth usage and also loss of some pixels. The PSNR value and compression rate is calculated against the original image and the stego image. The encryption and decryption time of the improved RSA algorithm is compared with the original RSA algorithm.

The Table 1 shows the encryption and decryption time of improved RSA and original RSA algorithm in which the improved RSA has very less encryption time but the decryption time is greater than the original one.

The Table 2 shows the time taken for compression, embedding and extracting the information, PSNR value and Mean Square Error (MSE) of stego image against the original image and the compression rate of the image based on different quantization scaling factor (quality factor).

Figure 2(a) shows a graph illustrating that the PSNR value increases as the quality factor increases whereas, Fig. 2(b) shows that the compression rate decreases on increasing quality factor.

Table 1. Comparison of improved RSA and original RSA

Algorithm	Encryption Time(sec)	Decryption Time(sec)
RSA	0.00998112	0.00087567
Improved RSA	0.00367728	0.00101462

Table 2. Comparison of original image and Stego image

Quality factor	Time (sec)			PSNR (dB)	MSE	Compression rate (%)
	Compression	Embedding information	Extracting information			
0	0.0317	0.0676	0.0890	21.53	457.0	90.8
25	0.0322	0.0677	0.0699	30.49	58.0	88.67
50	0.0303	0.0679	0.0694	32.11	40.0	86.88
75	0.0553	0.0678	0.0694	33.22	31.0	84.03
100	0.0592	0.0667	0.0901	37.71	11.0	43.5

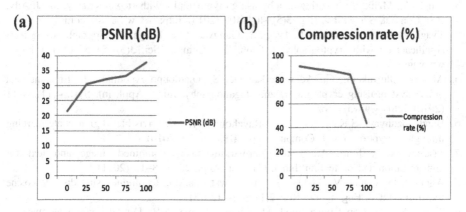

Fig. 2. (a) A graph showing PSNR value against the quality factor, and (b) A graph showing compression rate against the quality factor

5 Future Work

The time taken for encryption and decryption of improved RSA and original RSA is calculated. From the calculated results, the encryption time of the improved RSA is much less than the original RSA but the decryption time is slightly greater. So in future we are trying to improve the decryption time. Also, the compression rate decreases as the quality of the image increases, therefore the compression algorithm can also be improved to achieve better compression rate and PSNR value in a certain quality factor for achieving greater security.

6 Conclusion

In this paper, we have proposed a solution to transfer the data securely through the network using an improved RSA algorithm, JPEG Compression and image watermarking, all together. In our improved RSA algorithm the encryption time is much lesser than the original RSA algorithm. The watermarking process helps to authenticate the data. This combined approach provides more security by offering confidentiality, message integrity, and authentication.

References

1. Rosaline, S.I., Rengarajaswamy, C.: A Steganographic substitution technique using APPM for encrypted pixels. In: International Conference on Information Communication and Embedded Systems (ICES), 21–22 February 2013. IEEE Explore (2013)
2. Bhalla, J.S., Nagrath, P.: Nested digital image watermarking technique using blowfish encryption algorithm. Int. J. Sci. Res. Publ. 3(4), 1–6 (2013)
3. Singh, A., Malik, S.: Securing data by using cryptography with steganography. Int. J. Adv. Res. Comput. Sci. Softw. Eng. 3(5), 404–409 (2013). http://www.ijarcsse.com
4. Tyagi, V., kumar, A., Patel, R., Tyagi, S., Gangwar, S.S.: Image steganography using least significant bit with cryptography. J. Glob. Res. Comput. Sci. 3(3), 53–55 (2012). http://www.jgrcs.info
5. Abikoye Oluwakemi, C., Adewole Kayode, S., Oladipupo Ayotunde, J.: Efficient data hiding system using cryptography and steganography. Int. J. Appl. Inf. Syst. 4(11), 6–11 (2012). http://www.ijais.org
6. Bandyopadhyay, S.K., Paul, T.U., Raychoudhury, A.: Invisible digital watermarking through encryption. Int. J. Comput. Appl. 4(8), 18–20 (2010)
7. Jaseena, K.U., John, A.: Text watermarking using combined image and text for authentication and protection. Int. J. Comput. Appl. 20(4), 8–13 (2011)
8. Agrawal, D., Gupta, V., Mehta, G.: Digital watermarking technique using discrete cosine transform. Int. J. Eng. Innov. Res. 2(1), 9–14 (2013)
9. Thapa, M., Sandeep Kumar Sood, Meenakshi Sharma, A.P.: Digital image watermarking technique based on different attacks. International Journal of Advanced Computer Science and Applications, Vol. 2, No. 4, pp. 14–19 (2011)

10. Ghazy, R.A., Amoon, M., Abdallah, H.A., El-Fishawy, N.A., Hadhoud, M.M., Dessouky, M.I., Alshebeili, S.A., Abd El-Samie, F.E.: Block based embedding of encrypted watermarks using singular value decomposition. Optik **125**(20), 6299–6304 (2014)
11. Singh, A., Gahlawat, M.: Secure data transmission using watermarking and image compression. Int. J. Adv. Res. Comput. Eng. Technol. (IJARCET) **2**(5), 1705–1724 (2013)
12. Lin, S.D., Shie, S.-C., Guo, J.Y.: Improving the robustness of DCT-based image watermarking against JPEG compression. Comput. Stan. Interfaces **32**(1–2), 54–60 (2010)
13. Choudhary, V., Praveen, N.: Enhanced Rsa Cryptosystem Based On Three Prime Numbers. Int. J. Innovative Sci. Eng. Technol 1(10), pp. 753–757 (2014). ISSN 2348 – 7968
14. Swaminathan, A., Agarwal, G.: A Comparative Study Of Image Compression Methods, Digital Image Processing
15. Nizar, F., Latheef, F., Jamal, A.: RSA based encrypted data embedding using APPM. Int. J. Eng. Trends Technol. **9**(15), 777–782 (2014)

A Novel Image Encryption Scheme Using an Irrevocable Multimodal Biometric Key

M. Suchithra[✉] and O.K. Sikha

Amrita School of Engineering, Amrita Vishwa Vidyapeetham, Coimbatore, India
{suchithra.ragam, sikhakrishnanunni}@gmail.com

Abstract. In today's digital world the use of secret key is inevitable to any secure communication through the network. But human beings feel hard to recollect the lengthy cryptographic key. One solution to this would be the use of biometric characteristics of human beings which are unique in nature, that makes the attacker difficult to guess the key generated from these features. Here we propose a new scheme for multimodal biometric key generation to secure cryptographic communication. Initially, the feature points of fingerprint and iris image are extracted using SLGS feature extraction algorithm followed by which chaotic mechanism is applied to shuffle the feature vectors and finally fused them to produce a single biometric key. In this paper we also present a new image encryption technique using the multimodal biometric key, where we are able to reconstruct the secret image without any pixel quality loss.

Keywords: Multimodal biometrics · Biometric cryptosystem · Image encryption

1 Introduction

Due to the rapid change in computer technology and the heavy use of electronic and social media, the protection of data has become more challenging task. As days passed, the security issues in various fields such as military applications, mobile phone communication, online transaction is becoming more difficult and is a matter of serious concern [1]. So providing security to the data from unauthorized access should be a great problem taken into consideration. Different techniques have been developed to hide secret data from unauthorized users in which encryption is the most prominent one. Encryption is the process of changing the appearance of original data by using some mathematical models and a secret key. At the receiver side decryption: which is the inverse of encryption is carried out to retrieve the original data. Conventional symmetric and asymmetric encryption schemes like DES, AES, etc. are restricted only to text files and are unable to process high amount of data such as images and videos [2]. The main reason is that the image size is always greater than that of text, so the conventional cryptographic schemes will take more time to encrypt an image. The other reason is that the decrypted image can have small level of acceptable distortion due to the characteristics of human perception, where as in text encryption the decrypted and original text should be the same.

© Springer International Publishing Switzerland 2015
J.H. Abawajy et al. (Eds): SSCC 2015, CCIS 536, pp. 256–264, 2015.
DOI: 10.1007/978-3-319-22915-7_25

The security of a crypto system is fully depends on the strength of the secret key which is used to encrypt the data. Normally the key used for encryption will be random and is very difficult to memorize, so people will tempt to write or store the key somewhere else which is vulnerable to attack [3]. Incorporating biometrics with cryptography can solve this problem effectively. Biometrics refers to unique human traits which can be used to identify a person. The identifiers are measurable and distinctive feature set that will help to describe and label a person. Biometric traits like iris, fingerprint, face, ear etc. can be used to identify an authorized individual [4, 5]. But single attribute based biometric systems are no longer in use because of some practical problems like: spoofing attacks, lack of universality and distinctiveness [6]. Several researches have been done to solve this problem and came up with the idea of multimodal biometric systems, which combines features acquired from various resources [7, 8]. Multimodal biometric systems uses multiple modalities like face, gait, voice, iris, fingerprint which will improve the recognition rate and reduce the probability of spoofing attacks since the attacker feels it difficult to get access to multiple traits of an individual. Now a day's studies on the fusion of multiple biometric traits acquired greater importance since it provide more security [9–11].

Researchers have made an attempt to combine biometrics and cryptography together which results in the development of Biometric Cryptosystem [12]. This resolves the problem of memorizing passwords and PIN and provides better security [13–16]. Studies proved that it is impossible to break the cryptographic key generated from biometric traits of a person since the key is enduringly associated with the characteristics of the corresponding individual. Additional level of security can be added by incorporating multimodal based key generation into cryptographic applications [6].

In this paper we introduce an efficient method for generating a n bit cryptographic key from multiple biometric modalities like face, iris, and fingerprint. Initially features are extracted from iris and fingerprint, which is then shuffled using chaos systems to provide randomness to the key. Obtained features are then fused and a 256 bit key is generated. We have also introduce a new image encryption scheme using the generated multimodal key.

The rest of the paper is organized as follows. Section 2 demonstrates the generation of multimodal biometric key. The proposed method of image encryption using the generated key is explained in Sect. 3. Section 4 includes the experimentation results of the proposed approach and conclusions are summed up in Sect. 5.

2 Proposed System

The proposed system contains two modules, key generation and image encryption.

2.1 Key Generation

The proposed scheme uses iris and fingerprint traits to generate an irrevocable cryptographic key. Use of multiple biometric traits makes the system more secure as the intruder won't get access to multiple traits of a person simultaneously. Key generation module has three major steps involved:

(1) Feature extraction from fingerprint and iris
(2) Fusion of feature vectors
(3) Cryptographic key generation

Figure 1 shows key generation scheme.

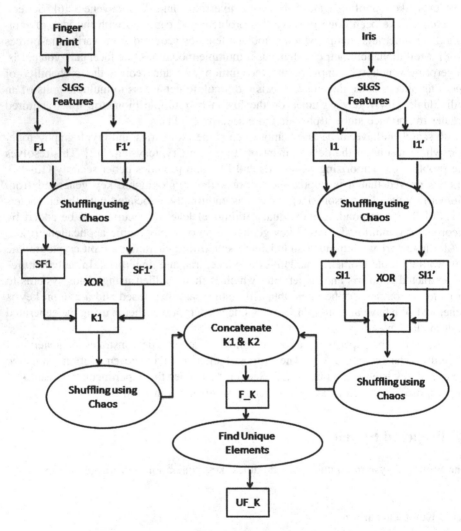

Fig. 1. Key generation scheme using multimodal biometric traits

2.1.1 Feature Extraction

This subsection describes the process of extracting features from preprocessed iris and fingerprint images. We chose fingerprint and iris as the biometric traits because of their permanence and uniqueness. SLGS [symmetric local graph structure] method has been used to extract features from these traits. SLGS operator is capable of extracting texture information of images, this method gives a better representation of local features for each neighboring pixels [17].

Feature Representation

F_1 and I_1 represents feature vectors obtained from fingerprint and iris respectively, F_1' and I_1' contains the bit complement of corresponding feature elements of F_1 and I_1

$$F_1 = \{x_1, x_2, x_3 \ldots x_n\} \qquad |F_1| = n$$

$$F_1' = \left\{x_1', x_2', x_3' \ldots x_{n_n}'\right\} \qquad |F_1'| = n$$

$$I_1 = \{y_1, y_2, y_3 \ldots y_m\} \qquad |I_1| = m$$

$$I_1' = \left\{y_1', y_2', y_3' \ldots y_{m_n}'\right\} \qquad |I_1'| = m$$

The four vectors: F_1, I_1, F_1' and I_1' are given as input into the fusion stage. The fusion process includes the following steps:

2.1.2 Shuffling of Feature Vectors Using Chaos Theory

The first stage of multimodal biometric fusion is the shuffling of individual feature vectors. The proposed system uses a chaos based fusion since it permutes [confusion] feature elements based on the initial condition of the chaotic system. We have used the random behavior of Lorenz attractor to permute the four feature vectors; here the initial condition and the control parameters of the Lorenz system will act as a secret key [18]. The vectors SF_1, SF_1', SI_1, SI_1' represent shuffled feature vectors.

2.1.3 Concatenation of Shuffled Feature Vectors

The shuffled feature vectors SF_1, SF_1', SI_1, SI_1' are concatenated together to generate multi modal biometric template as follows.

   I. Convert all elements of the vectors SF_1, SF_1', SI_1, SI_1' into binary form
  II. Binary XOR operation is performed between the components of SF_1 *and* SF_1' and SI_1 *and* SI_1'. The resultant binary values are then convert back to decimal and is stored in K_1, K_2 respectively.
 III. Elements of K_1, K_2 are shuffled again using Lorenz attractor.
 IV. Concatenate K_1 and K_2, result is stored in F_K which will serve as the multi-modal biometric key.

2.1.4   Generation of K Bit Cryptographic Key from Multi Modal Biometric Features

The final key vector can be represented as:

$$F\_K = \{fk_1, fk_2, \ldots\ldots fk_l\}$$

The set of unique elements from the key vector F_K is identified and stored in UF_K which will serve as the multimodal biometric template.

$$UF\_K = \{uk_1, uk_2, \ldots\ldots\ldots uk_d\} \ : \ d \leq l$$

3   Image Encryption Using Multimodal Biometric Key

Step1: Take a secret image X and resize it into $n \times n$.

Step2: Input Key selection of $n/8$ bytes or n bits:

Take any consecutive $n/8$ values from the generated multimodal biometric key and convert each value to its 8 bit binary form to make n bit binary key K.

$K = [K_1, K_2, K_3, \ldots K_{n/8}]$, each K_i has 8 bit binary representation.

$\quad K_1 = [b_1, b_2, b_3, \ldots b_8]$,

$\quad K_2 = [b_9, b_{10}, b_{11}, \ldots b_{16}]$,

ie $\ldots\ldots\ldots\ldots\ldots\ldots\ldots\ldots\ldots$,

$\quad K_{n/8} = [b_{n-7}, b_{n-6}, b_{n-5}, \ldots b_n]$

and each $b_i \in \{1.$, where $i = 1.2.3\ldots$

$$K = [b_1, b_2, b_3, \ldots, b_8, b_9, b_{10}, b_{11}, \ldots b_{16}, \ldots\ldots, b_{n-7}, b_{n-6}, b_{n-5}, \ldots b_n]$$

Step3: Repeat steps 4 to 6 for 3 times.

Step4: Do the column wise pixel shuffling

4.1 if $b_i = 1$ and $(index(b_i)\%2) > 0$

4.1.1 Take the ith column C_i of the image X and divide into $\frac{n}{4}$ blocks of size 4×1. $C_i = [Cb_1, Cb_2, Cb_3 \ldots Cb_{n/4}]$ and each C is of size 4×1, where $i = 1, 2, 3, \ldots, n/$

4.1.2 Reverse each $\frac{n}{4}$ sub blocks column wise.

4.1.3 Then divide the column vector C_i of size $n \times 1$ into two half. $C_i = [C_{half1} \ C_{half2}]$, Where C_{half1} is the first $n/2$ values of the column and C_{half2} is the next $n/2$ values starting from the index $n/2 + 1$ to n.

4.1.4 Then shuffle the column vector C_i in the following way:

The first element in C_{half2} is shifted to index 1 and the first element in C_{half1} is shifted to index 2. Then the second element in C_{half2} is shifted to index 3 and the second element in C_{half1} is shifted to index 4. Repeat the same procedure until all elements are shifted.

4.2 if $b_i = 0$ and $(index(b_i)\%2) > 0$

4.2.1 Take the ith column C_i of the image X and divide into $\frac{n}{2}$ blocks of size 2×1.

$$C_i = [Cb_1, Cb_2, Cb_3 \ldots Cb_{n/2}]$$

and each C is of size 2×1, where $i = 1, 2, 3, \ldots, n/$

4.2.2 Reverse each $\frac{n}{2}$ sub blocks column wise

4.2.3 Then divide the column vector C_i of size $n \times 1$ into two half . As similar to step 4.1.3

4.2.4 Then shuffle the column vector C_i in the following way:

The first element in C_{half1} is shifted to index 1 and

the first element in C_{half2} is shifted to index 2. Then the second element in C_{half1} is shifted to index 3 and the second element in C_{half2} is shifted to index 4. Repeat the same procedure until all elements are shifted.

4.3 if $b_i = 1$ and $(index(b_i)\%2) == 0$

4.3.1 Divide the column vector C_i of size $n \times 1$ into two half as similar to step 4.1.3.

4.3.2 Then shuffle the column vector C_i as similar to step 4.1.4

4.4 if $b_i = 0$ and $(index(b_i)\%2) == 0$

4.4.1 Divide the column vector C_i of size $n \times 1$ into two half as similar to step 4.1.3.

4.4.2 Then shuffle the column vector C_i as similar to step 4.2.4

Step5: Repeat the shuffling rules for all n columns.

Step6: Do row wise pixel shuffling using the method mentioned in step 4 and 5.

Step7: End

Decryption:

Step1: Take the encrypted image and the same n bit binary key.

Step2: Repeat the steps 3 to 4 for 3 rounds.

Step3: Do the row wise shuffling of the pixels using the reverse of the procedure explained in the encryption side. Repeat the same for all the n rows.

Step4: Do the column wise shuffling of the pixels using the reverse of the procedure explained in the encryption side. Repeat the same for all the n columns.

Step5: End

4 Results and Discussions

This section describes the results of the proposed system. The secret image shown in Fig. 2(b) of size 256×256 is taken for testing the proposed method. The corresponding multimodal biometric key of length 256 bits is shown in Fig. 2(a). The encrypted image

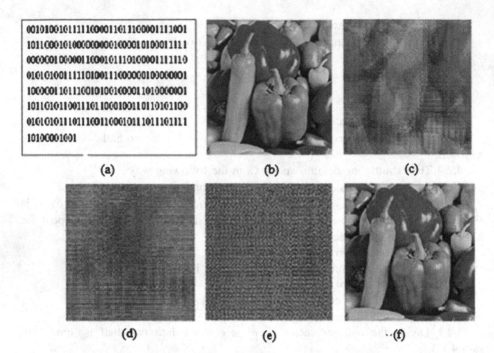

Fig. 2. (a) 256 bit key generated from multimodal biometric traits, (b) Secret image (c) Encrypted image after round 1, (d) Encrypted image after round 2, (e) Encrypted image after round 3, (f) Decrypted image

after round 1, 2, and 3 are shown in Fig. 2(c), (d) and (e) respectively. Figure 2(f) shows the decrypted image which is exactly same as the secret image shown in Fig. 2(b).

4.1 Key Space Analysis

The proposed encryption algorithm is enduringly depends on the multimodal biometric key. So we have to make sure that the obtained key is secure and the key space is large enough to prevent the brute force attack. Since the key is generated from human traits the security of the key will never fails. Also the system uses an n bit binary key for encrypting an image of size $n \times n$. So the total number of possible combinations of secret key is 2^n, which makes an intruder difficult to attack the system by brute force method. The rules applied for shuffling pixels of the input image is fully depend on the bit value and corresponding position which will make the system more secure.

4.2 Time Analysis

The average times taken for encryption and decryption techniques are shown in Table 1. The codes are tested on a system running on INTEL i5 processor (2.40 GHz) with 4 GB RAM, and Matlab 2014(b) for the time analysis.

Table 1. Time analysis

Image size	Time taken for encryption/ decryption (in seconds)
256 × 256	0.9–0.13
1024 × 1024	1.2–1.5
2048 × 2048	5.3–5.9

4.3 Correlation Analysis

Correlation coefficient measures the similarity between two vectors or two images. The Pearson correlation coefficient takes a value between +1 and −1 where the values 1, 0, −1 indicates total positive correlation, no correlation, total negative correlation respectively. The correlation coefficient value between the secret image (Fig. 2(b)) and encrypted image (Fig. 2(e)) is obtained as 0.0046. This implies that the two images are less similar.

5 Conclusion

In this work, a new method for image encryption technique has been proposed which uses a highly secured multimodal biometric key of larger size. Using this method it is observed that the secret image can be recovered from the encrypted image without any pixel quality loss. The security of the proposed system is fully depends on the multimodal biometric key. A chaotic based mechanism is used to shuffle the extracted features which provide randomness to the generated key.

The proposed framework may produce overhead, since a lot of encryption calculations have to be done for each block of data. This overhead can be reduced by incorporating parallel computing to the system.

References

1. Acharya, B., Panigrahy, S.K.: image encryption using advanced hill cipher algorithm. Int. J. Recent Trends Eng. **1**(1), 663–667 (2009)
2. Öztürk, I., Sogukpınar, I.: Analysis and comparison of image encryption algorithms. World Acad. Sci. Eng. Technol. **3**, 26–30 (2005)
3. Zhang, L., Liao, X., Klein, D.V.: Foiling the cracker: a survey of, and improvements to, password security. In: Proceedings of the 2nd USENIX Workshop Security, pp. 5–14 (1990)
4. Rabuzin, K., Baca, M., Malekovic, M.: A Multimodal biometric system implemented within an active database management system. J. Softw. **2**(4) (2007)
5. Baca, M., Rabuzin, K.: Biometrics in network security. In: Proceedings of the XXVIII International Convention MIPRO 2005, pp. 205–210, Rijeka (2005)
6. Jagadeesan, A., Duraiswamy, K.: Secured cryptographic key generation from multimodal biometrics: feature level fusion of fingerprint and iris. (IJCSIS) Int. J. Comput. Sci. Inf. Secur. **7**(2), 28–37 (2010)

7. Hong, L., Jain, A.K., Pankanti, S.: Can multibiometrics improve performance? In: Proceedings of IEEE Workshop on Automatic Identification Advanced Technologies, NJ, USA, pp. 59–64 (1999)
8. Jain, A., Nandakumar, K., Ross, A.: Score normalization in multimodal biometric systems. Pattern Recogn. **38**, 2270–2285 (2005)
9. Wang, R., Bhanu, B.: Performance prediction for multimodal biometrics. In: Proceedings of the IEEE International Conference on Pattern Recognition, pp. 586–589 (2006)
10. Jing, X., Yao, Y., Zhang, D., Yang, J., Li, M.: Face and palm print pixel level fusion and Kernel DCV-RBF classifier for small sample biometric recognition. Pattern Recogn. **40**(11), 3209–3224 (2007)
11. Zhang, T., Li, X., Tao, D., Yang, J.: Multi-modal biometrics using geometry preserving projections. Pattern Recogn. **41**(3), 805–813 (2008)
12. Arul, P., Shanmugam, A.: Generate a key for AES using biometric for VOIP network security. J. Theor. Appl. Inf. Technol. **5**(2), 107–112 (2009)
13. Goh, A., Ngo, D.C.L.: Computation of cryptographic keys from face biometrics. In: Lioy, A., Mazzocchi, D. (eds.) CMS 2003. LNCS, vol. 2828, pp. 1–13. Springer, Heidelberg (2003)
14. Hao, F., Chan, C.W.: Private key generation from on-line handwritten signatures. Inf. Manage. Comput. Secur. **10**(2), 159–164 (2002)
15. Chen, B., Chandran, V.: Biometric based cryptographic key generation from faces. In: Proceedings of 9th Biennial Conference of the Australian Pattern Recognition Society on Digital Image Computing Techniques and Applications, pp. 394–401, December 2007
16. Lalithamani, N., Soman, K.P.: An effective scheme for generating irrevocable cryptographic key from cancelable fingerprint templates. Int. J. Comput. Sci. Netw. Secur. **9**(3), 183–193 (2009)
17. Abdullah, M.F.A., Sayeed, M.S., Muthu, K.S., Bashier, H.K., Azman, A., Ibrahim, S.Z.: Face recognition with symmetric local graph structure (SLGS). Expert Syst. Appl. **41**, 6131–6137 (2014)
18. Prasad, M., Sudha, K.L.: Chaos image encryption using pixel shuffling. In: Wyld, D.C., et al. (eds.) CCSEA 2011, CS & IT 02, pp. 169–179 (2011)

Dual Stage Text Steganography Using Unicode Homoglyphs

Sachin Hosmani, H.G. Rama Bhat$^{(\boxtimes)}$, and K. Chandrasekaran

National Institute of Technology, Mangalore, Karnataka, India
{sachinhosmani,ramabhathg1993}@gmail.com, kchnitk@ieee.org

Abstract. Text steganography is hiding text in text. A hidden text gets hidden in a cover text to produce a plain looking stego text. This plain looking stego text is posted as the message which no one suspects to contain anything concealed. Today, text messages are a common mode of communication over the internet and it is associated with a huge amount of traffic. Steganography is an added layer of protection that can be used for security and privacy. In this paper, we describe a text steganography approach that provides a good capacity and maintains a high difficulty of decryption. We make use of approaches of space manipulation, linguistic translation and Unicode homoglyphs in our algorithm. Our implementation is in Python. Also, we explain a parallel approach for hiding large hidden text messages in large cover text messages.

Keywords: Steganography · Information hiding · Text steganography

1 Introduction

Steganography is the art of writing messages that contain hidden messages in such a way that no one suspects the presence of the hidden messages. While cryptography tries to prevent an adversary from decrypting the contents of a message, steganography tries to prevent the adversary from suspecting the message to be of interest in the first place. When one sends a hidden message concealed in another message, no one will suspect that the outer message contains anything of interest outside its plain meaning. Steganography has had a high prevalence in history, well before the era of computers and internet.

Steganography can be well explained with an example. [1] Two accomplices in crime Alice and Bob are imprisoned and are allowed to communicate only via a monitored communication channel. Alice and Bob want to hatch an escape plan. Obviously, they don't want the prison warden to know about this. They cannot speak in a language foreign to the warden because the warden will suspect something fishy and will block their communication. They can, however speak in plain English, which the warden understands well, but also hide pieces of information in their plain English that the warden couldn't possibly suspect. The general model of Steganography is shown Fig. 1 where the sender embeds the hidden text in the cover text and the receiver deciphers it.

© Springer International Publishing Switzerland 2015
J.H. Abawajy et al. (Eds): SSCC 2015, CCIS 536, pp. 265–276, 2015.
DOI: 10.1007/978-3-319-22915-7_26

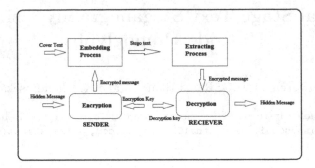

Fig. 1. Steganography model

In this section we introduce the concept of steganography and its applications. In the Related works section, we present different works that have been done in the field of steganography. In the next section we present our approach to steganography with detailed descriptions of our steganography algorithms. Under the Experiments and Results section, we give examples and analyze different steganography algorithms and compare them with our algorithm using different parameters. Finally we conclude and suggest future work that can be done.

2   Literature Survey

People have been hiding information using different methods and variations throughout history. For example ancient Greeks wrote text on wax-covered tablets. To pass a hidden message, a person would scrape wax off a tablet, write a message on the underlying wood and again cover the tablet with wax to make it appear blank and unused [2,3]. During World war 2, invisible inks were used for hiding information. With invisible ink, a seemingly innocent letter could contain a very different message written between the lines [4]. Document layouts are also used for hiding important information. Documents were also marked and identified by modulating the position of lines and words [5].

Text steganography is an important type of steganography that is used. There are many approaches that have been used for text steganography. Some the of popular approaches that have been used for steganography are briefly described here.

Line shift method is a method in which the lines of the cover text are shifted vertically up or down depending on the encountered bits in the hidden text [6]. This method has a lot of limitations. It cannot be used in situations where there is no control over how lines are vertically spaced before rendering. It cannot be used in situations where lines are to be sent as a single string across the medium. This approach also has very low ratio (HCR). Also this approach has a high decoding probability since the number of lines a message might span across is usually less compared to the size of the message.

White steganography is another text steganography method which involves using one or two spaces after every word in the cover text depending on whether the current bit in the hidden text is 0 or 1. This method provides a higher HCR and also provides a lower DP because of the large number of combinations possible for a hidden text [7].

Linguistically-driven generation methods are methods where a context free grammar is written to generate natural like text [10]. Each production in the grammar tells us how to expand a part (or whole) of the message being sent. If a production has multiple possibilities, the choice gives us an opportunity to hide bits. Depending on the choices we make while choosing the productions, the hidden message get covertly written. Since the generated text is completely generated from the grammar, it isn't possible to control it.

Linguistic translation involves replacing certain or all words of the cover text with synonyms so that the meaning of the cover text remains the same but gets modified to contain the secret message [9]. This method offers an HCR that depends on the kind of words in the cover text, but for regular English usage it offers a good HCR. DP is also known to be low.

Unicode is a character set that is internationally recognised as a standard for encoding characters. Since it has to cater to a large number of languages, the set is very large. A character set is a set of code points that unambiguously define characters and their scripts or groups. Code points are rendered as glyphs. A glyph can be thought of as the visual representation of a character. Homoglyphs are glyphs that cannot be quickly identified as different glyphs with visual inspection. Unicode has many homoglyph sets [8]. Unicode homoglyphs can be used in steganography because an adversary will not be able to tell if a character is replaced by its homoglyph or not.

3   Text Steganography

Text steganography is hiding text inside text. Some of the main components that are involved as shown in Fig. 2 are:

- Hidden text: The text to hide.
- Cover text: The outer text to hide the hidden text in.
- Stego text: The text created after hiding the text.
- Encoder: The algorithm that encodes the hidden text inside the cover text.
- Decoder: The algorithm that decodes the hidden text from the stego text.

3.1   Evaluation Criteria

- Hidden text Cover text Ratio (HCR):
  If the number of bits in the hidden text is n1 and the number of bits in the cover text is n2, and the two are chosen such that the cover text is used completely for hiding purposes, HCR = n1 / n2. A greater HCR means greater efficiency.

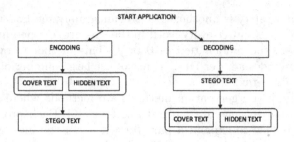

Fig. 2. Flow chart for text steganography

– Difficulty of decoding/Probability of a hidden text guess to be correct (DP: Decoding Probability):
  If the adversary finds out that a message contains a hidden text and knows the approach used for hiding the message, for a message of size constant k, if there are m possibilities of hidden text, then the probability of a correct guess the first time is $1/m$. Lower the probability, greater the security of steganography.
– Tamper Resistance:
  An attacker may try to alter the data embedded in a cover, rather than destroy it. A tamper resistant steganographic algorithm makes it extremely hard to alter the hidden data or to erase them and embed a different message.

4   Our Proposed Approach

We decided on an approach that makes use of white steganography (space manipulation), linguistic translation and Unicode homoglyphs. Combining all these approaches into our algorithms has given us a more superior algorithm in terms of HCR and DP.

4.1   Algorithm

There are two algorithms involved. One for producing a steganographed text from a cover text and a hidden text and another for retrieving the hidden text from a steganographed text.

Encoding. (See Algorithm 1) The hidden text is encoded as binary using Huffman coding. This gives us efficiency in number of bits needed to represent the given hidden text. An MD5 checksum of this is found and appended to it with a special delimiter bit combination (specially reserved in the Huffman encoding) in between. It is then encrypted using a key. A simple symmetric stream cipher like XOR can be used for the encryption. This adds an extra layer of security. The cover text is tokenized into spaces and words. Each token in the cover text has to be dealt with depending on whether it is a word or a space. If it is a word, it has to be replaced with a synonym. If it is a space, it has to replaced with two spaces, possibly. Depending on how many words there are in a synonym list, we can hide some number of bits with this process for words and a constant of 1 bit per space. These many number of bits from the hidden text are extracted from the hidden bit sequence and they are treated collectively as a number and indexed into the synonym list.

Algorithm 1 Encoding

1: **Input:** Cover text (C), Hidden Text (H), Key (K)
2: **Output:** Steganographed text (S)
3: **procedure** ENCODE(COVER(C), HIDDEN(H), KEY(K))
4:     HB = huffman_encode(H)
5:     HB = HB + delimiter + MD5(HB)
6:     HB = encrypt(HB, K)
7:     S = ""
8:     tokens = tokenize(C)
9:     **while** token_count(tokens) != 0 and remaining_bit_count(HB) != 0 **do:**
10:         token = get_next_token(tokens)
11:         **if** token is a word: **then**
12:             synonyms = get_synonyms(token)
13:             bit_size = largest_bit_size(synonyms.length)
14:             index = get_next_bits(HB, bit_size)
15:             synonym = synonyms[index]
16:             S += synonym
17:         **if** token is space: **then**
18:             **if** get_next_bits(HB, 1) == 1: **then**
19:                 S += " "
20:             **else**
21:                 S += ""
22:     S += "\a"
23:     **if** token_count(tokens) == 0: **then**
24:         **while** token_count(tokens) != 0: **do**
25:             token = get_next_token(tokens)
26:             s += token
27:     **if** remaining_bit_count(HB) != 0: **then**
28:         **for** c, i in S: **do**
29:             **if** remaining_count(HB) == 0: **then**
30:                 break
31:             homoglyphs = get_homoglyphs(c)
32:             bit_size = largest_bit_size(homoglyphs.length)
33:             index = get_next_bits(HB, bit_size)
34:             homoglyph = homoglyphs[index]
35:             S[i] = homoglyph
36:     S[i] = "\a"
37:     **return** S

For spaces, if the next bit is 1, a pair of spaces are substituted for a space, if the next bit is 0, a single space is kept. At the end, we append a '\a' character. While decoding, this will help us know when to stop. If at the end of this process, all the bits are hidden, the process is done. Otherwise, for every character in our stego text, we find a list of Unicode homoglyphs for it. Like with synonyms, we choose a homoglyph depending on the bit sequence. We replace the character with the chosen homoglyph. Again, at the end of process, we append a '\a' character to mark that the hiding of bits has ended in the second phase. If we are going through the second phase, it means the first phase completely used the cover text and hence the first '\a' will be only at the end of the stego text. So, the second '\a' will always be before the first one. '\a' is a non-printable character and hence will not affect the visual output of the text.

Decoding. (See Algorithm 2) If the last character of the stego text is "\a", it means that both stages of steganography were involved, the outer stage being Unicode homoglyphs. So, first we have to retrieve bits hidden using Unicode homoglyphs. For every character in the stego text until "\a" is encountered, we find the list of its homoglyphs and find its position in the list. This position tells us the bit sequence hidden in it. This position is converted into binary and appended to H2. At the end of this iteration, we'll have the bit sequence hidden using Unicode homoglyphs. After this stage, we tokenize the stego text as during encoding and iterate through it until "\a" is found. For every token, if it is a space, we check if the next token is also a space. If it is, that means there are two consecutive spaces and this means that the bit hidden is 1. If not, the bit hidden is 0. If we encounter a word, we find the list of its synonyms. We then find the position of this word in the list. This position tells the bit sequence hidden in the word. The position is converted to binary and appended to H1. At the end of this process, we have the bit sequence hidden with the first stage of steganography. Now we have to combine the two pieces of bit sequences to get the complete bit sequence. This is an encrypted bit sequence. We have to decrypt this using the same symmetric cipher and key we used for encryption. Converting this decrypted sequence to characters using Huffman decoding gives us back the original hidden text.

Parallel Processing of Large Texts. (See Algorithm 3) This algorithm tries to allow parallel processing of large strings. The first step is to split the cover text into chunks of MAX_SIZE and processing them individually and parallely. The problem here is that, a chunk may get modified after synonym substitution and space manipulation to contain greater characters than the allowed limit. Hence we need to expand each chunk to the maximum possible size it can take. We are essentially finding an upper bound.

Once we have an upper bound for each chunk's size, we again split the cover text with its expanded state in mind. Each chunk we create will always be containable in a chunk because it is an upper bound. Since we have now partitioned the cover text, we just have to partition the hidden text. It can be simply done by finding the next sequence of hidden text (in bits) that can be hidden in the chunk. We need to consider a lower bound for this, because we can't say beforehand, what synonyms will get used and hence how many bits we can hide using Unicode homoglyphs. Once we have the cover text and hidden text bits split into chunks like this, we can simple parallely process pairs of them for steganography.

Algorithm 2 Decoding

1: **Input:** Steganographed Text (S), Key (K)
2: **Output:** Hidden text (H)
3: **procedure** DECODE(STEGANOGRAPHED TEXT(S),KEY(K))
4:     H1 = H2 = ""
5:     if S[S.length - 1] == "\a": **then**
6:         **for** each c in S: **do**
7:             **if** c == "\a": **then**
8:                 break
9:             homoglyphs = get_homoglyphs(c)
10:            index = homoglyphs.index_of(c)
11:            binary_index = number_to_binary(index)
12:            H2 += binary_index
13:     tokens = tokenize(S):
14:     **for** each token in tokens: **do**
15:         **if** token == "\a": **then**
16:             break
17:         **if** token == "": **then**
18:             next_token = get_next_token(tokens)
19:             **if** next_token == "": **then**
20:                 H1 += "1"
21:             **else**
22:                 push_back_token(tokens, next_token)
23:                 H1 += "0"
24:         **if** token is a word: **then**
25:             synonyms = get_synonyms(token)
26:             index = synonyms.index_of(token)
27:             binary_index = number_to_binary(index)
28:             H1 += binary_index
29:     HB = H1 + H2
30:     HB = decrypt(HB, K)
31:     checksum = HB.split(delimiter)[1]
32:     if checksum != MD5(HB.split(delimiter)[0]): **then**
33:         discard_message()
34:         return null
35:     H = huffman_decode(HB)
36:     **return** H

4.2   Synonym Storage and Retrieval

In real languages, the set of synonyms is not a closed set. Since the semantics of a language are subjective, there is a lot of grayness involved in interpreting the closeness of two words. When we decide to replace a word in the cover text with a synonym, we must ensure that to decode it successfully afterwards, the synonym set we chose the synonym from, is a closed set.

Algorithm 3 Parallel processing for large cover and hidden text

---

1: **Input:** Cover text (C), Hidden text (H), MAX SIZE: the maximum chunk size
2: **Output:** Array of cover text index (Ci), hidden text index (Hi) tuples
3: **procedure** SPLITTEXTS(COVER TEXT (C), HIDDEN TEXT (H), MAX SIZE)
4:     chunk_count = C.length / MAX_SIZE
5:     chunks = []
6:     **for** i from 0 to chunk_count - 1 **do**
7:         chunks.push(C.substr(i*MAX_SIZE, MAX_SIZE))
8:     syn_size_cache = {}
9:     **for** each chunk in chunks in parallel: **do**
10:         **for** each word in chunk: **do**
11:             synonyms = get_synonyms(chunk)
12:             max_syn_size = 0
13:             **for** each synonym in synonyms: **do**
14:                 **if** max_syn_size <synonym.length: **then**
15:                     max_syn_size = synonym.length
16:             syn_size_cache[word] = max_syn_size
17:     running_size = 0
18:     new_chunks = []
19:     running_chunk = ""
20:     **for** each word in C: **do**
21:         running_size += syn_size_cache[word] + 2
22:         **if** running_size >MAX_SIZE: **then**
23:             new_chunks.push(running_chunk)
24:             running_size = 0
25:             running_chunk = word
26:         **else**
27:             running_chunk += word
28:     **for** each chunk in new_chunks in parallel: **do**
29:         chunk_capacity[chunk] = get_lower_bound(chunk)
30:     tuples = []
31:     hidden_text_start = 0
32:     chunk_start = 0
33:     **for** each chunk in chunks: **do**
34:         tuples.push([chunk_start, hidden_text_start])
35:         hidden_text_start += chunk_capacity[chunk]
36:         chunk_start += chunk.length
37:     **return** tuples

This is our approach when we need to search for a synonym of a word:

- Check if plain text file with that word as title exists
- If it does (each line of it is a synonym belonging to that synonym set):

  - Read the synonym at the required index (line number in the file)

- If it doesn't (this word is a new one encountered):

  - Consult a dictionary for a list of synonyms of the word.
  - For every synonym, create a file with the synonym as the title.

- Populate the file with a synonym in each line.
- Read the synonym at the required index.

This way, we ensure that every synonym set is closed.

5   Results and Analysis

In this section we discuss the results measured in terms of the metrics we explained earlier. We also discuss the specifics of implementation of our algorithms.

5.1   Analysis

Here are the criteria that we considered for the analysis of our steganography algorithm.

1. Hidden text Cover text Ratio (HCR)
   A greater HCR implies more text can be hidden in the given cover text.
   HCR for our steganography algorithm is given by:

   $$N = N_1 + \log_2(N_2) + (\log_2(N_3) * N_4) \tag{a}$$

   where,
   N - Average Number of bits that can be hidden per word
   N_1 - Average number of spaces per word
   N_2 - Average number of synonyms per word
   N_3 - Average number of homoglyphs per character
   N_4 - Average number of characters per word

   This follows from the fact that there can be one bit hidden for per space, $log(N_2)$ bits hidden for a word with N_2 synonyms and $log(N_3) * N_4$ bits hidden for a word with N_4 characters and N_3 homoglyphs per character. Assuming, $N_1 = 1$, $N_2 = 4$, $N_3 = 2$, $N_4 = 5$ we get, N = 8.
   For space manipulation alone, $HCR = N_1$ and for linguistic translation, $HCR = log_2(N_2)$.
   HCR for different algorithms are shown in the Fig. 3. for a large cover text.
2. Decoding Probability (DP)
   Decoding Probability is the probability that an adversary guesses the hidden text, if he knows the approach used for hiding the message and also knows that the message contains the hidden message. As DP decreases, the security of the steganography increases.
   If a space was used for hiding text, then there were only 2 possibilities of hidden text, i.e. "0" or "1". If synonym list was used then there are as many possibilities as there are words in the given synonym set. For e.g. If a set has 4 words, then no. of possibilities are 4.

So in our algorithm which uses the combination of these two along with homoglyphs the possibilities will be the product of possibilities of these two and the homoglyphs.

DP for our steganography algorithm is given by:

$$DP = 1/(X * Y * Z) \tag{b}$$

where,

$$X = 2 \tag{1}$$

$$Y = \prod_{i=1}^{Nw} x_i \tag{2}$$

$$Z = \prod_{i=1}^{Nc} k_i \tag{3}$$

where,

DP - Decoding Probability
X - Number of possibilities for spaces
Y - Number of possibilities for synonyms
Z - Number of possibilities for homoglyphs
Nw - Number of words
Nc - Number of characters
x_i - Number of synonyms for $i_t h$ word
k_i - Number of homoglyphs for $i_t h$ character

This is simply one divided by the number of possibilities. Each component of our algorithm provides a certain number of possibilities and the total is the product of all of them. For the semantics of space, the adversary has to make just 2 guesses. For synonyms, for each word in the text, the number of synonyms of that word have to be multiplied to get the total number of possibilities. The same logic applies to homoglyphs too.

For space manipulation alone, $DP = 2$
For linguistic translation alone, $DP = Y$
DP for different algorithms are shown in the Fig. 4. for a large cover text.

3. Tamper Resistance

As per our algorithm, in our approach, we find a checksum of our hidden text bits and append it to the hidden text with a delimiter in between. The delimiter is a special bit combination reserved in our Huffman coding. If the message is intercepted in between and is tampered with, it will be impossible for the adversary to tamper the message and yet keep the checksum correct. Note that checksum is done after encryption and so that is an additional level of protection. Also, since the adversary will not have access to the homoglyph

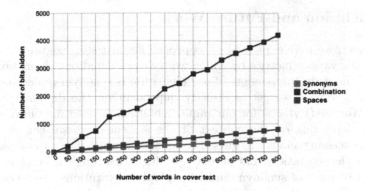

Fig. 3. HCR for different algorithms

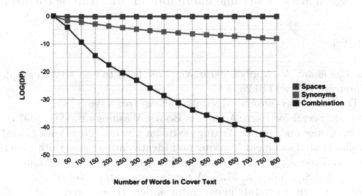

Fig. 4. DP for different algorithms

index table or the synonym table, he will only be able to tamper the message by making random modifications which will necessarily get detected due to the checksum.

Table 1 summarizes comparison of our algorithm with the rest of the algorithms.

Table 1. Comparison of different steganography techniques

Criteria	White	Linguistic	Combination
HCR	1	1	8
DP	Very High	Medium	Very low

6   Conclusion and Future Work

In this paper, we have explained an approach for text steganography. We have discussed the various metrics by which we have evaluated our algorithm.

One of the main components of our algorithm is synonym replacement. The quality of synonyms we get is directly dependent on the dictionary we use. We used Wordnik(Python) for our implementation. A word may have multiple synonyms depending on the context of the sentence. So, we can do natural language processing and try to guess the context in which a word was used. This will reduce the semantic errors we may get due to a wrong choice of synonyms. Also, the frequency of synonym and homoglyph substitutions can be controlled in order to preserve the originality of the cover text to the desired extent.

Our work is limited to an ASCII character set containing alphabets, numbers and special characters. We can extend this to a larger character set, but we need to address the availability of synonyms for these words. Also since our algorithm works for English alone, a suitable internationalization can be carried out.

References

1. Nechta, I., Fionov, A.: Applying statistical methods to text steganography (2011). arXiv preprint arXiv:1110.2654
2. Kahn, D.: The Codebreakers. Macmillan, New York (1967)
3. Norman, B.: Secret Warfare. Acropolis Books, Washington, D.C. (1973)
4. Zim, H.S.: Codes and Secret Writing. William Morrow, New York (1948)
5. J. Brassilet et al., Document Marking and Identification using Both Line and Word Shifting. In: Proceedings of Infocom 1995. IEEE CS Press, Los Alamitos (1995)
6. Shahreza, M.H.S., Shahreza, M.S.: A new synonym text steganography. In: International Conference on Intelligent Information Hiding and Multimedia Signal Processing, pp. 1524–1526 (2006)
7. Bender, W., Gruhl, D., Morimoto, N., Lu, A.: Techniques for data hiding. IBM Syst. J. **35**, 313–336 (1996)
8. Roshanbin, N., Miller, J.: Finding homoglyphs - a step towards detecting unicode-based visual spoofing attacks. In: Bouguettaya, A., Hauswirth, M., Liu, L. (eds.) WISE 2011. LNCS, vol. 6997, pp. 1–14. Springer, Heidelberg (2011)
9. Chapman, M., Davida, G.I., Rennhard, M.: A practical and effective approach to large-scale automated linguistic steganography. In: Davida, G.I., Frankel, Y. (eds.) ISC 2001. LNCS, vol. 2200, pp. 156–165. Springer, Heidelberg (2001)
10. Chapman, M., Davida, G.: Hiding the hidden ciphertext in innocuous text. In: Han, Y., Quing, S. (eds.) ICICS 1997. LNCS, vol. 1334. Springer, Heidelberg (1997)

Securing Database Server Using Homomorphic Encryption and Re-encryption

Sarath Greeshma[✉] and R. Jayapriya

Deparment of Computer Science and Engineering,
Amrita Vishwa Vidyapeetham (University), Amritapuri, Kollam 690525, India
greeshmasarath@am.amrita.edu, jayapriyar81@gmail.com

Abstract. A problem with organizations for shifting their storage to cloud or remote server is maintenance of confidentiality, integrity and availability of outsourced data,especially if the remote server is not trusted. Encryption can be used as a solution to these security concerns. But it should be possible for the data owner and other authenticated users of the data to perform queries (especially statistical queries) over data in encrypted domain. Usage of symmetric encryption will create another security concerns like management of key, denying a user from querying data etc. The problem with asymmetric encryption technique is only owner of the data is allowed to decrypt the data with his private key.

In this paper we proposed a solution to all these problems by designing an asymmetric fully homomorphic encryption algorithm to encrypt the data. Encryption is done using public key of the owner. So that only owner can decrypt it with his own private key. If owner wants to allow a third party or delegate to perform query over encrypted data then owner will calculate a re-encryption key for him, so that authorized delegates can submit queries to database server and re-encrypt the query result with this re-encryption key so that delegate can decrypt it with his own private key.

Keywords: DBaaS · Homomorphic encryption · Re-encryption

1 Introduction

Data owners can outsource their data to remote servers or cloud, providing database as a service to reduce the overhead of storing large amount of data in their local system is called Database as a service(DBaaS). All the transaction management, access control, data backup, recovery mechanism, fault tolerance and disaster management is done by the storage server. DBaaS removes much of the pain of database administration and management task from the owners. DBaaS is user friendly, cost -effective and easily deployable. Entities involved in DBaaS are dataowner, delegates authorized to read and manipulate the data and data storage server. The data owner is responsible for loading the data in the storage server. The data owner can permit or deny the users for querying the database using GRANT and REVOKE. The ultimate goal of DBaaS is that

© Springer International Publishing Switzerland 2015
J.H. Abawajy et al. (Eds): SSCC 2015, CCIS 536, pp. 277–289, 2015.
DOI: 10.1007/978-3-319-22915-7_27

the owner does not think about the storage and security of the data in database. That is why we are experiencing the rapid increase in popularity of DBaaS. But security of the outsourced data is very important. Data should be protected from outside attackers and from the storage server. So encryption is found to be an inherent option for the security of the outsourced data.

Data owner can encrypt the data before outsourcing the data to the storage server. There are methods to access the data from the storage server. In download-decrypt approach, when a user query to access the data entire data should be downloaded in the users system. User has to decrypt the data and execute query over the data. Disadvantage of the method is high computation and communication overhead. Second method is temporarily decrypting data in the storage server, performing the query and encrypt the whole data again, but it does not guarantee data confidentiality because all data can be viewed by the server. Another method is the partial decryption of data in the server and remaining by the user. This method also leads to overhead. Another method is decrypt and then encrypt approach. In this method data is decrypted and then encrypted using user's public key when user is requested to access the data. Disadvantage of this method is computation overhead and does not guarantee confidentiality of the data.

Data encryption can be either symmetric or asymmetric. In symmetric encryption method owner can encrypt and decrypt the data using his own private key. Only using this private key delegates can decrypt the data. Key management and distribution are very difficult in symmetric encryption. In asymmetric encryption method owner can encrypt the data using the public key and can decrypt the data using his private key. But if a delegate want to access the data, data server should decrypt the data by contacting the owner and encrypt it using delegate's public key so that he can decrypt it using his own private key. But this method is not efficient as it creates a bottleneck in owner when each time data server approaches the owner for decrypting the data.

Problem with the method of using shared secret by both owner and authorized delegates is, if the shared secret key is lost or if we want to remove a compromised delegate then entire system has to be changed for security which is an overhead. Executing queries over the encrypted data is also leads to confidentiality problem. Attack may occur while transferring the encrypted data.

In order to overcome these problems we design a structure preserving asymmetric homomorphic encryption. Homomorphic encryption will allow to perform operations on the encryption domain itself without decryption. Homomorphic encryption are of two types, partial homomorphic encryption and fully homomorphic encryption. In partial homomorphic encryption we can only perform some operations on encrypted data. But in fully homomorphic encryption we can perform operations on the encrypted data while preserving the structure. In asymmetric fully homomorphic encryption method owner can encrypt the data using his public key and decrypt the query result using his own private key. But users other than owner want to perform query then he has to contact the owner for the decryption of query result which is an overhead.

In this paper we also introduce a re-encryption key calculation mechanism. Owner will calculate the re-encryption key for each user. User can then re-encrypt the query result using this re-encryption key in such a way that each user can decrypt the result using their own private key rather than owner's private key.

2 Related Work

In [1] author gives an overview of database outsourcing, general security requirements and security technique of outsourced data. This paper achieves the security requirements by encryption based approaches. Encryption can be applied at different granularity levels depending on the data to be accessed is mentioned in [2]. This paper also deals with symmetric and asymmetric encryption schemes. One problem specified in this paper is execution of query on the stored data.

In [3] deals with the combined use of fragmentation and encryption. This paper specifies that not all data items are sensitive so it should not be encrypted and in many situations data themselves are not sensitive rather their association is sensitive. Vertical or horizontal fragmentation is used to fragment the data and non sensitive data items are not encrypted. The major problem in this work is the execution of query over the stored data. The encryption of whole database through some standard encryption algorithms does not allow to execute any SQL operation directly on the encrypted data. An initial solution presented in [4] is based on data aggregation technique that associate plain text metadata to sets of encrypted data. But plaintext metadata may leak sensitive information and introduces unnecessary network overheads.

In [5–7] deal with homomorphic encryption to execute queries directly over the encrypted data without decrypting it. The proxy re-encryption schemes are proposed by Mambo and Okamoto [8] and Blaze et al. [9]. Proxy re-encryption is a cryptographic primitive which translates ciphertexts from one encryption key to another encryption key. It can be used to forward encrypted messages without having to expose the cleartexts to the potential users. Paillier algorithm is additive homomorphism. RSA and Elgamal are multiplicative homomorphism. Brakerski-Gentry-Vaikuntanathan (BGV) [11,12], Algebra Homomorphic Encryption scheme based on updated ElGamal (AHEE), Non-interactive Exponential Homomorphic Encryption algorithm (NEHE) are fully homomorphic encryption schemes.

In [10] introduces an approach for data forwarding which is based on the Elgamal based cryptosystem called atomic proxy re-encryption. In this system a re-encryption key $RK_{A \to B}$ is used for data forwarding. The re-encryption key is generated by the owner using the secret key of other entity which is not secure. Drawback of this method is that the proxy can compute re-encryption key $RK_{B \to A}$, which would enable bidirectionality.

This paper also proposes an improvement of atomic proxy re-encryption. Unidirectionality of data is provided in this method. Here the re-encryption key is generated by the owner using the public key of other entity. So no prior arrangement or secret sharing is necessary. Unidirectionality directionality is obtained by Inverse Exponent Assumption.

3   Proposed Solution Approach

Data is encrypted before outsourcing using the homomorphic encryption. Public key of the owner is used to encrypt the data and stored in storage server. So that owner can send their query to storage server with encrypting data part in the query. Then encrypted query is executed over encrypted data and the result is also transformed in encrypted form. Owner can decrypt the result using his own private key (Fig. 1).

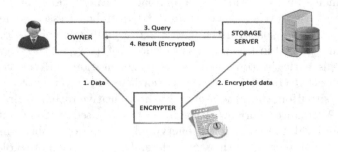

Fig. 1. Proposed system for owner

4   Algorithm

Owner Encryption

1. Select two prime numbers say p and q.
2. Calculate N=p×q , p is public q and N are confidential.
3. Select a generator g of group Z_p^*
4. Select a random number x such that $g^x \neq 1$
5. Calculate y=g^x mod p, use this y for encryption.
6. Encryption will be performed in the following two steps.

   (i) Select a random number r and perform homomorphic encryption as.

$$E(M) = (M + r * p) mod N$$

   (ii) Select a random number k such that $g^k \neq 1$, encryption as follows:

$$E_r(m) = (a, b) = (g^k mod p, y^k E(M) mod p)$$

7. Decryption is as follows:

$$M = b * (a^x)^{-1} mod p$$

5   Proof of Algorithm

Let m be the message to be encrypted. Choose a large prime number p and a random number r.

$$E(m) = (m + r * p) mod N$$

$$E_r(m) = (g^k mod p, y^k E(m) mod p)$$

$$E_r(m) = (g^k mod p, y^k(m + r * p) mod N mod p)$$

Decryption can be done as follows:

$$\frac{y^k(m + r * p) mod N mod p}{(g^k mod p)^x} mod p$$

$$\frac{y^k(m + r * p) mod N mod p}{(g^x mod p)^k} mod p$$

$$((g^k mod p)^x) mod p = ((g^x mod p)^k) mod p \text{ as } g^k mod p \text{ and } g^x mod p \neq 1.$$

$$\frac{y^k(m + r * p) mod N mod p}{y^k mod p} mod p = m$$

5.1   Example 1

Let message $m = 2345$. In these examples instead of division we take multiplicative inverse of second number and the result is multiplied with the first number. Here we take small prime numbers p and q. Normally 1024 bit prime numbers are taken for security. Encryption and decryption of message is shown below.

p = fca682ce8e12caba26efccf7110e526db078b05edecbcd1eb4a208f3ae1617ae01f35b91a4
7e6df63413c5e12ed0899bcd132acd50d99151bdc43ee737592e17

q = AADD9DB8DBE9C48B3FD4E6AE33C9FC07CB308DB3B3C9D20ED6639CCA703
308717D4D9B009BC66842AECDA12AE6A380E62881FF2F2D82C68528AA6056583
A48F3

N = 118416040752516504387034582856884136717529498795710111216702413080701047
786396170618715614987709627624787186815214801362666827727853735266159103307 2
794646299081180024140071675418820006818110456545198317813593912160247604588 8
557204348145140493066806965902615898213293188512009321894016105442894694946 5
340852181

$g = 6, k = 7, x = 7, r = 3$

Encryption can be done as below:

$$E(m) = (2345 + 3 * p) mod N$$

= 396971306855958372226437921548023072731855810888702266167354681192731390871
091061574393565581236127120515653557210111462562143883948190118069387103323 8
0014

E_r(m)=(279936,3159032659424786203680270605117629346611120)

Decryption can be done as below:

$$\frac{3159032659424786203680270605117629346611120}{(279936)^7} modp$$

$$= 2345$$

5.2   Security Analysis

Public parameter of the algorithm is p and N. Confidential parameters are q and y. Public key is g^x used for encryption and private key x is used for decryption. Security of the algorithm relies on the use of 1024 bit prime numbers p and q. Security of the cryptosystem is also based on mathematical problem called discrete logarithmic problem. Discrete logarithmic problem provides security while computing y=g^xmodp. Here even if the y and g value are known it is difficult to calculate x value. i.e., difficult to find the private key of owner. The difficulty of solving the discrete logarithm problem yields secure cryptosystem.

Since the algorithm is fully homomorphic encryption statistical queries can be directly executed over the encrypted data. Homomorphic encryption can provide the results after calculations as working directly on the raw data. So there is no intermediate decryption in the storage server which provides more security for the data. Here the encrypted query is executed over the encrypted data and the result is also in encrypted form. The owner can decrypt the data using his private key. Then the data is secure in the storage server and during the transmission.

5.3   Proof of Additive Homomorphism

Let m_1 &m_2 are two messages.

$$C_1 = (g^{k_1} modp, y^{k_1}(m_1 + r_1 * p)modN modp)$$

$$C_2 = (g^{k_1} modp, y^{k_1}(m_2 + r_2 * p)modN modp)$$

$$C_1 + C_2 = (g^{k_1} modp, y^{k_1}(m_1 + m_2 + r_1 p + r_2 p)modN modp)$$

$$= (g^{k_1} modp, y^{k_1}(m_1 + m_2)modp)$$

Decryption:

$$\frac{y^{k_1}(m_1 + m_2)modp}{(g^{k_1} modp)^x} modp = m_1 + m_2$$

Algorithm realizes the property of additive homomorphic encryption.

5.4   Proof of Multiplicative Homomorphism

$$C_1.C_2 = (g^{2k_1}modp, y^{2k_1}(m_1m_2)modp)$$

Decryption:

$$\frac{y^{2k_1}(m_1m_2)modp}{(g^{2k_1}modp)^x}modp$$

$$\frac{y^{2k_1}(m_1m_2)modp}{(g^x modp)^{2k_1}}modp = m_1m_2$$

Algorithm realizes the property of multiplicative Homomorphic encryption.

5.5   Example 2

Let message $m_1 = 12345$, p = 2531249999 , q = 23737511

$$E_r(m_1) = (279936, 134823799)$$

Let message $m_2 = 23451$

$$E_r(m_2) = (279936, 27165587)$$

Additive Homomorphism

$$12345 + 23451$$

$$E_r(m_1) + E_r(m_2) = (279936, 161989386)$$

Decryption:

$$\frac{161989386}{(279936)^7}modp = 35796$$

Multiplicative Homomorphism

$$12345 * 23451$$

$$E_r(m_1).E_r(m_2) = (78364164096, 3662567641405013)$$

Decryption:

$$\frac{3662567641405013}{279936^7}modp = 289502595$$

Drawback of the system is the overhead in the owner while authorized users want to access the stored data. User must approach the owner for the decryption of the query result. Decryption can be performed only using owner's private key.

6   Multiuser System

We design a new algorithm such that each user can decrypt the data using their own private key. when a user wants to access the data in the storage server, user will first contact the owner with his public key. Owner will compute the re-encryption key using the public key of the user and private key of the owner. This re-encryption key is given to the user as a token of authorization. Once the re-encryption key is calculated user will store it so that next time user can re-encrypt the query result without contacting the owner. User can submit the query to the storage server and retrieve the query result. User had to re-encrypt the query result using his re-encryption key and then he can then decrypt the result using their own private key rather than the owner's private key (Fig. 2).

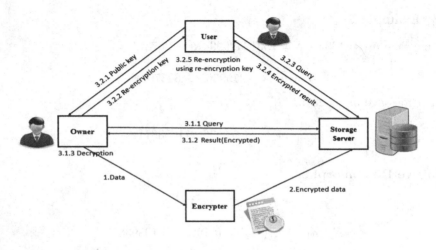

Fig. 2. Proposed system for multiple users

7   Algorithm

1. Select two prime numbers say p and q.
2. Calculate product of these prime numbers N=p*q, p is public and N is confidential.
3. Select a random number x, k and g where x, k and g are smaller than p.
4. Encryption will be performed in the following steps.
5. Select a random number r and perform following homomorphic encryption.

$$E(M) = (M + r * p) mod N$$

$$E_r(M) = (a, b) = (g^{xk} E(M), g^k)$$

(i) Delegate selects a random number t and compute g^t and sends it to owner

(ii) Owner will compute re-encryption key $k_{re} = g^{tk}/g^{xk}$ and sends it to delegate.

(iii) Delegate will re-encrypt the query result as follows:

$$E_r(M) = (a, b) = (g^{xk}E(M)\frac{g^{tk}}{g^{xk}}, g^k)$$

$$E_r(M) = (a, b) = (g^{tk}E(M), g^k)$$

6. Decryption is M= $a*(b^x)^{-1}$(modp) by owner.
   Decryption is M= $a*(b^t)^{-1}$(modp) by user.

Public parameter of owner is g^x and private key are k and x. Public parameter of delegate is g^t and private key is t.

8   Proof of Algorithm

8.1   Proof of Owner Encryption and Decryption

Let m be the message to be encrypted.

$$E(m) = (m + r * p)modN$$

$$E_r(m) = (g^{xk}E(m), g^k)$$

$$E^r(m) = (g^{xk}(m + r * p)modN, g^k)$$

Decryption can be done as follows:

$$\frac{g^{xk} * (m + r * p)modN}{(g^k)^x} modp = m$$

8.2   Proof of User Encryption and Decryption

$$E_r(m) = (g^{xk} * (m + r * p)modN, (g^k)^x)$$

$$E_r(m) = (g^{xk} * (m + r * p)modN * \frac{g^{tk}}{g^{xk}}, g^k)$$

$$E_r(m) = (g^{tk} * (m + r * p)modN, g^k)$$

Decryption can be done as follows:

$$\frac{g^{tk} * (m + r * p)modN}{(g^k)^t} modp = m$$

8.3   Proof of Additive Homomorphism

$$C_1 = (g^{xk}(m_1 + r_1 * p)modN), g^k modp$$
$$C_2 = (g^{xk}(m_2 + r_2 * p)modN), g^k modp$$
$$C_1 + C_2 = (g^{xk}(m_1 + m_2 + r_1p + r_2p)modN), g^k modp)$$
$$= (g^{xk}(m_1 + m_2 + r_1p + r_2p), g^k modp)$$

Decryption:

$$\frac{g^{xk}(m_1 + m_2 + r_1p + r_2p)}{(g^k)^x} modp = m_1 + m_2$$

Algorithm realizes the property of additive homomorphism.

8.4   Proof of Multiplicative Homomorphism

$$C_1.C_2 = ((m_1m_2 + m_1r_2p + m_1r_1p + r_1r_2p^2) * g^{2xk}, g^{2k})$$

Decryption:

$$\frac{g^{2xk}(m_1m_2 + m_1r_2p + m_2r_1p + r_1r_2p^2)modN}{(g^{2k})^x} = m_1m_2$$

Algorithm realizes the property of multiplicative homomorphism.

8.5   Example 3

Let message $m_1 = 245$ is to be encrypted.
   p=253124999,q= 23737511, g=25, x=7

Owner Encryption and Decryption Given Below

$$E_r(M) = (123182572774945044, 28515649)$$

Decryption:
$$\frac{123182572774945044}{28515649^7} modp = 245$$

User Encryption and Decryption Given Below

$$E_r(M) = (42705144193779578, 28515649)$$

Decryption:
$$\frac{42705144193779578}{28515649^{25}} modp = 245$$

8.6   Security Analysis

Public parameter of the owner is g^x and private parameters are x and k. Public parameter of the user is g^t and private parameters is t. Security of the algorithm relies on the use of 1024 bit prime numbers and discrete logarithmic problem. Here k value is only known to the owner. Both the k value and private key is used for decryption which provides more security.

9   Experimentation and Analysis

We implemented the proposed method in Corei3 processor with 4 GB RAM using Java Platform. Time needed for server, owner and user for processing the query and result in milliseconds is listed in Table 1. While comparing with other homomorphic encryption techniques, time taken for each query execution is reduced as decryption-encryption replaces a single re-encryption.

Table 1. Time needed for query processing

Query	Time taken by the server for processing the query(ms)	Time taken by the owner for decrypting the result(ms)	Time taken by the user for decrypting the result(ms)
Select (n tuples)	1373	1066	1170
Select (single tuple)	22	33	70
Update(Sum)	246	6	61
Update(Mul)	169	6	65
Count	336	113	210
Sum	1121	215	302
Average	2100	331	411

9.1   Time Complexity

Encryption of a message 'M' requires $\frac{M}{2^{1024}}$ steps. Re-encryption key computation requires one exponentiation and one multiplication as $g^{xk^{-1}}$ can be precomputed. One Inverse calculation and one multiplication is used in the decryption phase which requires $O(\log(p^2))$ where p is the public parameter of the owner.

9.2   Security Analysis

Owner Security: Owner can encrypt the data using asymmetric homomorphic encryption and stored in the storage server. Owner can encrypt the data using his public key g^x and decrypted using his private key x. Owner can calculate the re-encryption key k_{re} for each user securely using owner's private key and user's public key. Owner can control the access to the data storage server using Access Control List (ACL) or capability list. If the owner found any user as untrustworthy, then owner can easily remove the user from ACL.

User Security: Once the user entered into the system,it's re-encryption key is computed by the owner and stored in the user's file. Re-encryption key is used to re-encrypt the query result so that each user can decrypt the result using his own private key.

10 Conclusion

Database as a service has lot of advantages but security of the outsourced data is very important. Encryption is the ultimate approach to protect the data from outsiders. In our work, we implement an algorithm which provides security of the outsourced data and explore technique to query over the encrypted database with minimum cost. Normal encryption techniques will not allow to execute statistical queries (for example AVG, SUM) over encrypted domain. Encryption technique proposed in this paper is fully homomorphic i.e., addition and multiplication can be performed in encrypted data itself avoiding extra encryption and decryption thereby reducing the cost. Re-encryption key acts as a token for authentication as the data owner will calculate it only for the authorized users. It also reduces the overhead of owner such a way that each user can decrypt the result using their own re-encryption key rather. Re-encryption key calculation is also secure as owner needs only the public key of delegates for calculating it. As the whole technique relies on asymmetric cryptosystem it is easy for the owner to remove an authenticated user from accessing the database when a malpractice is detected.

Acknowledgement. Our sincere gratitude to Dr. M.R Kaimal, Chairman, Department of Computer Science, for his valuable suggestions. Our special thanks to Dr. Jyothisha J Nair, Vice Chairperson, Computer Science and Engineering, and Mrs.Sandhya Harikumar, for their guidance and coordination.

References

1. Pathak, A.R., Padmavathi, B.: Survey of confidentiality and integrity in outsourced databases. Int. J. Sci. Eng. Technol. (IJSET) **2**(3) (2013)
2. Iyer, B., Mehrotra, S., Mykletun, E., Tsudik, G., Wu, Y.: A framework for efficient storage security in RDBMS. In: Bertino, E., Christodoulakis, S., Plexousakis, D., Christophides, V., Koubarakis, M., Böhm, K. (eds.) EDBT 2004. LNCS, vol. 2992, pp. 147–164. Springer, Heidelberg (2004)
3. Ciriani, V., et al.: Combining fragmentation and encryption to protect privacy in data storage. ACM Trans. Inf. Syst. Secur. (TISSEC) **13**(3), 1–33 (2010)
4. Hacigumus, H., Iyer, B., Mehrotra, S.: Providing database as a service. In: 18th International Conference on Data Engineering, February 2002
5. Fontaine, C., Galand, F.: A survey of homomorphic encryption for nonspecialists. EURASIP J. Inf. Secur. **2007**, 10 (2007)
6. Tebaa, M., El Hajji, S., El Ghazi, A.: Homomorphic encryption applied to the cloud computing security. In: Proceedings of the World Congress on Engineering, vol. 1 (2012)

7. Singh, N., Ahuja, R.: Fuzzy based fully homomorphic encryption scheme for security in cloud computing. Int. J. Sci. Res. (IJSR) (2012)
8. Mambo, M., Okamoto, E.: Proxy cryptosystems: delegation of the power to decrypt ciphertexts. IEICE Trans. Fundamentals of Electronics, Comm. and Computer Sciences 80(1), 54–63 (1997)
9. Blaze, M., Bleumer, G., Strauss, M.J.: Divertible protocols and atomic proxy cryptography. In: Nyberg, K. (ed.) EUROCRYPT 1998. LNCS, vol. 1403, pp. 127–144. Springer, Heidelberg (1998)
10. Ateniese, G., Fu, K., Green, M., Hohenberger, S.: Improved proxy re-encryption schemes with applications to secure distributed storage. ACM Trans. Inf. Syst. Secur. (TISSEC)
11. Brakerski, Z., Vaikuntanathan, V.: Efficient fully homomorphic encryption from (standard) LWE. SIAM J. Comput. 43(2), 831–871 (2014)
12. Gentry, C., Halevi, S.: Implementing Gentry's fully-homomorphic encryption scheme. In: Paterson, K.G. (ed.) EUROCRYPT 2011. LNCS, vol. 6632, pp. 129–148. Springer, Heidelberg (2011)

A Robust and Secure DWT-SVD Digital Image Watermarking Using Encrypted Watermark for Copyright Protection of Cheque Image

Sudhanshu Suhas Gonge[1(✉)] and Ashok Ghatol[2]

[1] Faculty of Engineering and Technology,
Sant Gadge Baba Amravati University, Amravati, India
sudhanshu1984gonge@rediffmail.com
[2] KJ's, Educational Institute, Kondhwa, Pune, India
vc_2005@rediffmail.com

Abstract. Digital watermarking is a process of embedding a data/additional information into exiting data. This additional data/information are used for embedding called as watermark. With this watermark, if the file or data get copied, this is then used to identify the originality of data. As, Digital communication facilitates transfer of digital data such as text, audio, image, video, etc. The un-authorized user can copy this data & can use anywhere they want. However, this creates the problem of security, ownership and copyright protection. To overcome this problem, digital watermarking is used. During transmission of data, there are many attacks occurring either intentionally or non-intentionally on digital watermarked image. These results into degradation of image quality and watermark may get destroyed. To provide security to watermark private key encryption and decryption is used. This encrypted watermark is used further for digital watermarking process using combined DWT-SVD transform. In this Paper, it is going to discuss *"A Robust and Secure DWT-SVD Digital Image Watermarking Using Encrypted Watermark for Copyright Protection of Cheque Image."* Digital Watermarking Technique is used to provide ownership & copyright protection for cheque image and private key encryption & decryption technique used for security of bank watermark.

Keywords: Digital watermarking · DWT · SVD · Encryption and decryption technique

1 Introduction

21st century is an era of internet technology. Internet Technology facilitates data communication from source to destination. It helps in transferring data like text, audio, video, or in image format. It is widely used in every sector and application. As, we know, banking system provides facility of money withdrawal through ATM application with the help of Internet Technology [1]. Nowadays, in banking sector, all banks are connected with the help of this technology. It helps in transfer of money in form of demand draft, bank cheque, or through NEFT. However, to transfer bank cheque it uses an application with help of internet technology called as cheque truncation system.

© Springer International Publishing Switzerland 2015
J.H. Abawajy et al. (Eds): SSCC 2015, CCIS 536, pp. 290–303, 2015.
DOI: 10.1007/978-3-319-22915-7_28

This application avoids the physical transfer of bank cheque images from drawer bank account to drawee bank account. It reduces the physical work of an employee. It transfers money faster as compare to previous method of clearing cheque. In this case of CTS, bank cheque is scan and image is created. This bank cheque image is sent from drawer account to drawee account for clearing process through cheque truncation system. Due to this reason there is need of copyright protection to bank cheque image.

In order to overcome this issue, Digital watermarking technique can be used. There are different types of watermark that can be used for the watermarking application depending upon the type of data such as, public watermark, private watermark, fragile watermark, visible watermark, invisible watermark, etc. In this paper invisible watermarking scheme is used. However, there is a flow of bank cheque images from drawer bank account to drawee bank account through communication channel with help of internet technology [2].

There are many possibilities of different attack on this bank cheque image. It may damage the watermark embedded in bank cheque image. To overcome this problem, private key algorithm is used to provide security to the watermark. Attacks on the digital data from piracy point of view can be of two types: active and passive. These are also classified as simple, synchronization, and deadlock attack [3]. To overcome this issue researchers have identified and demonstrated a number of techniques like Fourier Transform, Discrete cosine Transform, Wavelet Transform [Hartung, 1999]. A lot of research has been carried out during last few years in the area of digital watermarking [Eugene, Mohanty, 1999; Chiou, 1999].

In This paper, it is going to discuss *"A Robust and Secure DWT-SVD Digital Image Watermarking Using Encrypted Watermark for Copyright Protection of Cheque Image."* Digital watermarking technique is used to provide ownership & copyright protection for cheque image and private key encryption & decryption technique is used for security of bank watermark.

2 Digital Watermarking Lifecycle and Its Methods

Digital watermarking life cycle consists of three phases:

- Embedding Phase,
- Attack Phase, and
- Extraction Phase.

The following Fig. 1 shows the lifecycle of digital watermarking process.

2.1 Frequency Domain Watermarking

It is a sinusoidal function having periodic nature of images. The aim of this domain is to represent an image as a weighted sum of sinusoidal function. In this domain, there is a space in which image value at image position X represents the amount that intensity values in image I vary over a specific distance related to image position X [4]. There are different frequency transforms such as DCT, DWT, FFT, SVD, or combination of

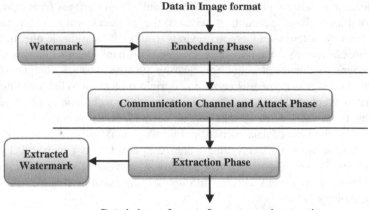

Fig. 1. Digital watermarking life cycle process.

one or more transform can be used for digital image watermarking. In this paper, combination of DWT-SVD transform watermarking principal is implemented [4, 5].

2.2 Discrete Wavelet Transform

Discrete wavelet transform decomposes a signal into a set of basic function. This basic function of signal called as wavelets [5, 6]. These wavelets are obtained from single prototype wavelet Y (t) called mother wavelet by using dilation and shifting parameters shown in following equation:

$$\psi_{a,b}(t) = \frac{1}{\sqrt{a}}\psi(\frac{t-b}{a}) \qquad (1)$$

where,
   a is the scaling parameter and b is the shifting parameter.
   DWT allows good localization both in time and spatial domain. It also helps in complete transformation of whole image [4, 5, 6]. It also provides better identification of which data relevant to human perception. DWT has higher flexibility. Thus, it provides good performance for watermark embedding & extraction procedure without affecting quality of bank cheque image [6].
   In this paper 2D- discrete wavelet transform is used. The 2D-Discrete wavelet transform divides the host image into four sub-bands as shown in Fig. 2. The four sub-bands are LL approximate sub-band which has lower resolution version of image. LH sub-band contains horizontal edge data of image. HL sub-band contains vertical edge data of image and HH sub-band contains diagonal edge data of image. Most of the time DWT watermarking algorithms embed only in the HL, LH, or HH sub-bands. In this paper, encrypted watermark is going to embed in LL approximate sub-band [5, 6].

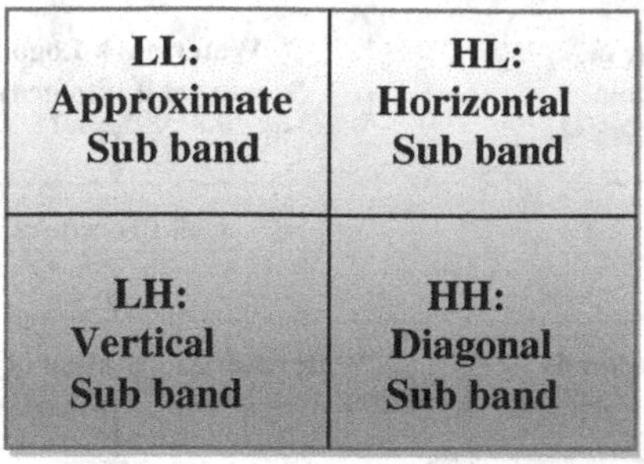

LL: Approximate Sub band	HL: Horizontal Sub band
LH: Vertical Sub band	HH: Diagonal Sub band

Fig. 2. Discrete wavelet transform Sub-bands.

2.3 Singular Value Decomposition Transform

A SVD transform is a technique used for handling matrices which contain sets of equation that do not have an inverse. This includes square matrices whose determinant is zero and all other are rectangular matrices [7, 14, 15, 18]. A common usage of SVD transform includes computing the least square solutions, range i.e. (column Space) of matrices, null space and pseudo inverse of matrices [7, 8].

Mathematically, it is expressed as:-
The SVD of mxn matrix A is given by formula:-

$$A = U.W.V^T \tag{2}$$

Where,

- U is an mxn matrix of orthogonal Eigen vectors of $A.A^T.$
- V^T is transpose of an nxn matrix containing the orthogonal Eigen vectors of $A^T.A$.
- W is an nxn diagonal matrix of the singular values which are the square roots of Eigen values of AT.A.

The SVD transform is packed with energy in a given number of transformation coefficient is maximized [7, 8]. It has property of noise reduction. It is easy to calculate and have sufficient and most optimal in given image processing [9, 10].

In this paper, SVD transform is used along with discrete wavelet transform for digital watermarking application using encrypted watermark [9, 11–13, 17].

3 Proposed Combined DWT-SVD Digital Watermarking Algorithm Using Encrypted Watermark

The Proposed method is shown in Fig. 3. It explains the working of combined DWT-SVD transform used for watermarking of bank cheque images and private key encryption and decryption is explain for security of bank watermark used for embedding and extraction process [9–18].

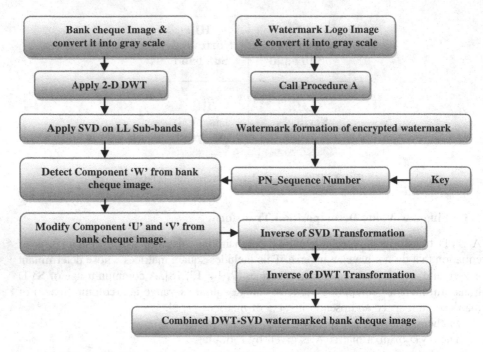

Fig. 3. Working of combined DWT-SVD watermark embedding algorithm.

3.1   Combined DWT-SVD Watermark Embedding Process Algorithm

Step 1: Read bank cheque image and convert it into grayscale image.
Step 2: Select the watermark logo for embedding process and convert it into grayscale watermark logo.
Step 3: Call procedure A.
Step 4: Apply 2-D discrete wavelet transform and divide bank cheque image into four sub-bands i.e. (LL, LH, HL, and HH).
Step 5: After obtaining encrypted watermark, use this watermark for embedding purpose.
Step 6: Perform SVD transform on LL sub-band of bank cheque image.
Step 7: Generate two pn_sequence i.e. w_0 & w_1 which is not similar to each other for embedding encrypted watermark logo bit by selecting greater complexity block by using the attributes of components W.
Step 8: Apply the following equation it watermark bit is 1 then:-

$$Ww = W + \alpha * w_0 = Uw_0 * Ww_0 * Vw_0^T \tag{3}$$

Otherwise,

$$Ww = W + \alpha * w_1 = Uw_1 * Ww_1 * Vw_1^T \tag{4}$$

Step 9: Modify the component of U & V with the help of step 7 and step 8.
Step 10: Take the inverse of SVD transform.
Step 11: Take the inverse of DWT transform.
Step 12: Finally, Combined DWT-SVD watermarked bank cheque image is obtained.

3.2 Procedure A

- Select Watermark logo.
- Provide the valid key of 256 bit along with the gain factor. The value of gain factor varies between 0 & 1.
- Read the size of watermark logo image.
- Generate matrix of random values.
- Make round value for these random values.
- XOR operation is performed on rounded values.

Finally, encrypted watermark logo image is obtained.

3.3 Combined DWT-SVD Watermark Extraction Process Algorithm

Step 1: Read watermarked bank cheque image.
Step 2: Apply 2-D discrete wavelet transform & divide watermarked bank cheque image into 4 sub-bands.
Step 3: Apply SVD transform on LL sub-band of watermarked bank cheque image.
Step 4: Determine the complexity of the block by calculating the non-zero co-efficient in 'W' component for each block.
Step 5: The same seed of image pixel are used to create again two pn_sequence w_0 & w_1 which were used for embedding process.
Step 6: Extract the watermark bit '1' if, the correlation with w_0 is less than w_1, if not extracted bit of watermark is consider as 0.
Step 7: Call Procedure B.
Step 8: Similarity between original watermark and extracted decrypted watermark from bank cheque image is calculated by reconstruction of watermark with help of extracted watermark bits of decrypted watermark [9, 11, 14, 16].

3.4   Procedure B

- Select extracted watermark which is in encrypted form.
- Provide the same valid key which has been used for encryption process.
- Generate random numbers.
- Make round value for generated random values.
- Apply XOR operation on rounded values.

Show extracted and decrypted watermark. Fig. 4 shows Watermark extraction process.

4   Experiments and Results

In this paper, research is discussed on the basis of following parameters explain in 4.1 and 4.2. It is used to perform experiments on host image and watermark used for experiment purpose which is explained in 4.3. The aim of selecting combined DWT-SVD transform is due their properties. Such as, DWT is kernel technique of JPEG-2000. It have higher flexibility. It gives better identification of which data relevant to human perception by providing high compression ratio [9]. SVD transform has noise reduction property. SVD transform is packed with energy which has maximized number of co-efficient. In paper [7], explain the integration of encryption and watermarking technique. But, DCT fails to achieve robustness of watermark even after security is provided [7]. In paper [9], combined DWT-DCT watermarking is explained.

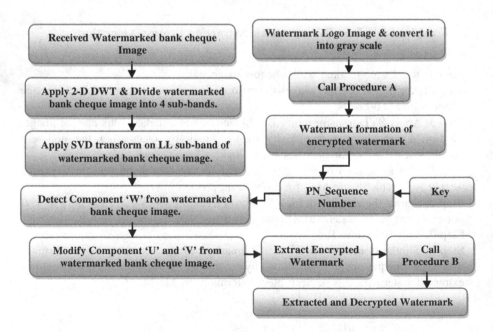

Fig. 4. Working of combined DWT-SVD watermark extraction algorithm.

In which, peak signal to noise ratio remain constant for all levels of DWT even after increase in gain factor. Thus, it is decided that by combining SVD along with DWT provides better performance.

4.1   Imperceptibility

Imperceptibility is calculated for measurement of peak signal to noise ratio of water-marked bank cheque images. Mathematically it can be expressed as:-

$$
\begin{aligned}
PSNR_{db} &= 10Log_{10}\left\{Max_1^2/\ MSE\right\} \\
&= 10Log_{10}\left\{Max_1/\ MSE^{(1/2)}\right\}
\end{aligned}
\tag{5}
$$

4.2   Robustness

Robustness is a measure of the immunity of the watermark against attempts to remove or degrade it, intentionally or unintentionally, by different types of digital signal pro-cessing attacks [10, 12]. In this paper, salt & pepper noise is considered. Mathemati-cally, robustness can be calculated as:-

$$
\rho(W, \hat{W}) = \frac{\sum\limits_{i=1}^{N} W_i * \hat{W}_i}{\sqrt{\sum\limits_{i=1}^{N} (W_i)^2}\sqrt{\sum\limits_{i=1}^{N} (\hat{W}_i)^2}}
\tag{6}
$$

4.3   Discussion on Experimentation

For experimental purpose, we consider bank cheque image having dimensions 600 x 310 and 24 bit depth. The format used for images is in bitmap format for both bank image and watermark logo image used for embedding process. These both images are converted into grayscale image. After conversion in grayscale, bit depth of both image reduced to 8 bit. Figures 5 and 6 show the original bank cheque image and watermark logo image. Figure 7 shows grayscale conversion of original watermark and Fig. 8 shows grayscale conversion of watermark logo.

Figure 9 shows the encrypted watermark obtained after execution of procedure A.

Figure 10 shows watermarked grayscale bank cheque image before attack. Fig. 11 shows the watermarked grayscale bank cheque image after applying salt & pepper noise attack for 0.5 noise density. The value of noise density varies from 0 to 1. Since watermark embedding process is done in approximate sub-bands i.e. LL sub-bands

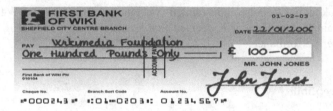

Fig. 5. Original bank cheque image.

Fig. 6. Original watermark logo image.

Fig. 7. Grayscale bank cheque image.

Fig. 8. Grayscale watermark logo image.

Fig. 9. Encrypted watermark logo image.

after applying DWT-SVD. Figure 12 shows the decrypted watermark after extraction from watermarked cheque image. Figure 13 explains the bank cheque image after extraction of watermark is shown above.

Fig. 10. Watermarked bank cheque image.

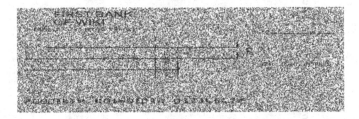

Fig. 11. Watermarked bank cheque image after salt and pepper noise attack for 0.4 noise density.

Fig. 12. Decrypted watermark image after extraction from watermarked bank cheque image after attack.

Fig. 13. Bank cheque image after extraction of encrypted watermark.

4.4 Observation Table

Above observation table shows the reading of peak signal to the noise ratio for different gain factors. The gain factor is used for controlling the embedding power of the watermark. The value of gain factor is considered between 1 and 8 because embedding process is done in LL approximate sub-band after applying DWT with the help of SVD transform and bit depth of bank cheque image is 8 bit. The private key value also used

Table 1. PSNR values for (a) encrypted watermark (b) embedded watermark (c) extracted watermark cross correlation co-efficient values and elapsed time for different values of gain factor and key values used for encryption.

Gain factor α	Key used for encryption.	Encrypt-ion of watermark PSNR value in dB.	Elapsed time for watermark encrypt-ion process.	Embedded watermark using DWT-SVD PSNR value in dB.	Elapsed time for embedding process.	Extracted watermark using DWT-SVD PSNR value in dB.	Elapsed time for extraction Process.	NC Value after salt & pepper noise attack for (0.4)
1	0.01	51.263	1.433	−4.379	0.253	−5.980	0.267	−0.6775
2	0.02	51.248	1.423	−10.402	0.213	−12.004	0.248	−0.6701
3	0.03	51.258	1.389	−13.925	0.216	−15.527	0.253	−0.6750
4	0.04	51.238	1.392	−16.425	0.250	−18.026	0.263	−0.6689
5	0.05	51.267	1.425	−18.363	0.230	−18.363	0.277	−0.6670
6	0.06	51.227	1.461	−19.947	0.216	−21.548	0.249	−0.6754
7	0.07	51.265	1.499	−21.286	0.266	−22.887	0.305	−0.6608
8	0.08	51.264	1.490	−22.446	0.215	−24.047	0.274	−0.6672

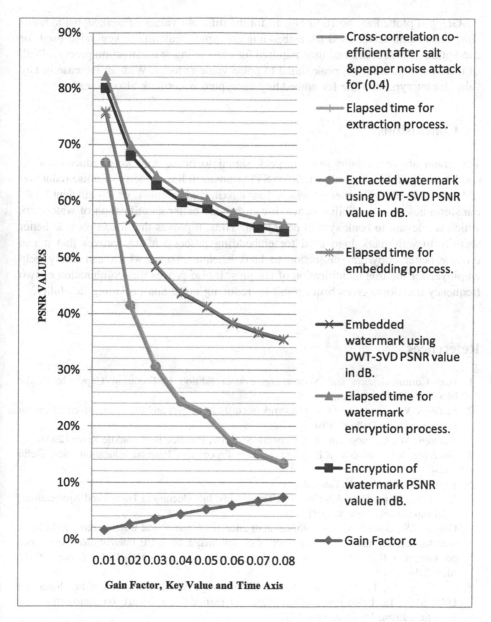

Fig. 14. % PSNR for (a) encrypted watermark (b)embedded watermark (c)extracted watermark, cross correlation co-efficient values and elapesd time for different values of gain factor and key values used for encryption.

between 0 and 1 because bit depth of watermark image is 8 bit. It helps to control encryption power of signal. Above figures from Figs. 9 to 13 are output for the gain factor value 4 and key value 0.04 (Table 1).

Graph is plotted as shown in Fig. 14 for the different values of peak signal to noise ratio versus gain factor used for embedding encrypted watermark, key value used for encryption of watermark and time required for embedding and extraction process. With an increase in gain factor, peak signal to noise value reduces. With an increase in key value for encryption, time for embedding encrypted watermark also increases.

5 Conclusions

The graph above explains that the peak signal to noise ratio gets reduced due to combined DWT-SVD transform. Since SVD transform has property of noise reduction and has packed with energy which has maximized number of co-efficient.DWT transform has more flexibility hence, it can provide better identification of watermark which is relevant to bank system perception. Thus, it proves that it can provide better security to watermark logo used for embedding process. It also proves that it can provide better copyright protection to bank cheque images which can easily help employee for the true identification of cheques. It also proves that combination of two frequency transform gives better result by reducing noise and providing flexibility.

References

1. Data Communication and Networking, Fourth Edition by-Forouzan Copyright © the McGraw-Hill Companies, Inc
2. Stallings, W.: Cryptography and Network Security Principles and Practices, 4th edn. Pearson Education, New Delhi (2006)
3. Stallings, W.: Cryptography and Network Security. Prentice Hall, Saddle River (2003)
4. Gonzalez, R.C., Woods, R.E.: Digital Image Processing. Pearson Education, New Delhi (2004)
5. Polikar, R.: TheWaveletTutorial
6. Rao, R.M., Bopardikar, A.S.: Wavelet Transforms: Introduction to Theory and Applications. Addison-Wesley, New York (1998)
7. Gonge, S.S., Ghatol, A.A.: Combination of encryption and digital watermarking techniques used for security and copyright protection of still image. In: IEEE International Conference on Recent Advanced and Innovations in Engineering (ICRAIE-2014), Jaipur, 09–11 May 2014
8. Yin, C.-q., Li, L., Lv, A.-q., Qu, L.: Color image watermarking algorithm based on DWT-SVD. In: Proceedings of the IEEE International Conference on Automation and Logistics, Jinan, 18–21 August 2007
9. Gonge, S.S., Ghatol, A.A.: Combined DWT-DCT digital watermarking technique software used for CTS of bank. In: 2014 IEEE Conference on Issues and Challenges in Intelligent Computing Techniques (ICICT-2014), Ghaziabad, 7th and 8th February 2014
10. Kundur, D., Hatzinakos, D.: A Robust Digital Image Watermarking Method Using Wavelet-Based Fusion
11. Luo, T.: Mutual information based watermarking detection in wavelet domain for copyright protection. In: IEEE. School of Computer Science and Technology(HUST)

12. Shnayderman, A., Gusev, A., Eskicioglu, A.M.: An SVD-Based gray scale image quality measure for local and global assessment. IEEE Trans. Image process. 15(2), 422–429 (2006)
13. Chung, K.-L., Yang, W.-N., Huang, Y.-H., Wu, S.-T., Hsu, Y.-C.: On SVD-based watermarking algorithm. Appl. Math. Comput. 188(1), 54–57 (2007)
14. Kaladharan, N.: Unique key using encryption and decryption of image. Int. J. Adv. Res. Comput. Commun. Eng. 3(10) (2014). ISSN: 2278-1021, 2319-5940
15. Liu, R., Tan, T.: An SVD-based watermarking scheme for protecting rightful ownership. IEEE Trans. Multimed. 4, 121–128 (2002)
16. Wen-ge, F., Lei, L.: SVD and DWT zero-bit watermarking algorithm. In: 2nd International Asia Conference on Informatics in Control, Automation and Robotics, 2010, 2nd March 2011
17. Golub, G.H., Van Loan, C.F.: Matrix Computations, 3rd edn. John Hopkins University Press, Baltimore (1996)
18. Golub, G., Kahan, W.: Calculating the singular values and pseudo-inverse of a matrix. SIAM J. Numer. Anal. 2(2), 205–224 (1965)

System and Network Security

Occlusion Detection Based on Fractal Texture Analysis in Surveillance Videos Using Tree-Based Classifiers

J. Arunnehru$^{(\boxtimes)}$, M. Kalaiselvi Geetha, and T. Nanthini

Speech and Vision Laboratory, Department of Computer Science and Engineering,
Annamalai University, Annamalainagar, Tamilnadu, India
{arunnehru.aucse,geesiv}@gmail.com

Abstract. Occlusion detection in video has been an active research for decades. This interest is motivated by numerous applications, such as visual surveillance, human-computer interaction, and sports event analysis. In this paper, an occlusion detection approach based on fractal texture analysis is proposed. Texture features are extracted from the segmented images using Segmentation-based Fractal Texture Analysis (SFTA) algorithm. The experiments are carried out using a PNNL-Parking-Lot dataset and the various tree-based classifiers such as random forest, random tree, decision tree (J48), and REP tree are used for classification. In the experiment results, random forest classifier showed the best performance with an overall accuracy rate of 98.3 % for SET-1, 98.2 % for SET-2, and 83.7 % for SET-3, which outperforms other algorithms.

Keywords: Video surveillance · Occlusion detection · Texture analysis · Feature extraction · Tree based classifiers

1 Introduction

Multiple object detection has been an active research in computer vision application. It plays an important role in human-computer interaction, smart video surveillance, image retrieval and robot navigation, etc. The goal of object detection is to find an object is present in an image or not [1]. Object tracking is the process of accurately tracking moving objects across successive frames in an image sequence. It is difficult to track the objects in surveillance videos due to occlusion. Occlusion occurs when the view of the foreground object is completely or partially blocked by other objects. Occlusion can be caused by various reasons such as other moving objects, static scene's background and when two or more objects occlude each other. Sometimes, one part of the object occludes another part, this is called as self-occlusion. Inter-object occlusion occurs when two tracked objects occluded each other. Background occlusion occurs during the background structure occludes the moving foreground object. Occlusions can be

© Springer International Publishing Switzerland 2015
J.H. Abawajy et al. (Eds): SSCC 2015, CCIS 536, pp. 307–316, 2015.
DOI: 10.1007/978-3-319-22915-7_29

classified by three types: full-occlusion, partial occlusion and non-occlusion. Full-occlusion would happen when an object is completely blocked by another object. Partial occlusion occurs when the part of the moving foreground object is partially blocked by a background structure or other object. During non-occlusion the object being tracked is having all tracking features and appears as a single blob. Many approaches have been proposed, yet it remains a challenging task because the occlusion may occur with the different appearance in different scenarios.

2   Related Work

A lot of approaches have already been proposed for occlusion handling. Eum et al. [2] proposed a new approach for face recognizability with Exceptional Occlusion Handling (EOH). The recognizability evaluation is conducted based on local regions of the facial components. Chen et al. [3] proposed a novel 3D object tracking method using image sets and depth-based occlusion detection. Training and testing example, contains a set of image instances of an object. Each image set is represented by natural second-order statistic. Kernel partial squares are used for object representation. Occlusion is detected using the depth information obtained from binocular video data. Min et al. [4] has presented an efficient approach to detect occlusion for robust face recognition. The presence of occlusion is analyzed on a face and then the non occluded facial regions are recognized based on selective local Gabor binary patterns. He et al. [5] proposed a novel approach for occlusion detection based on integral region with covariance based feature descriptor and has been proven to be robust and versatile. Trueba et al. [6] proposed a novel method to handle occlusion and complexity in World in Miniature (WIM). This method is used for handling occlusion by selecting the regions of a scene from the exocentric point. Sharma et al. [7] proposed a novel and efficient approach for face recognition system to handle partial occlusions. Gabor filter with Eigen faces are used for occlusion handling. Park et al. [8] has presented a 3D model from depth images with self occlusion. This model considers self occlusion from 2.5D depth video with multi-modal interactions to provide broadcasting applications. It presents a series of techniques for an actor to construct a smooth mesh model with self-occluded regions. He, et al. [5] proposed a novel Adacov (Adaptive covariance tracking) approach for efficient and robust tracking region covariance is computed based on integral region. They applied Log-Euclidean Riemannian Metric to find the Manifold distance for the covariance matrices. Occlusion is detected using the distance in the tracking. When the object reappears, it regresses into generalized adaptive covariance tracking. The search window size can be tuned differently according to the tasks need. Roy et al. [9] presented a new method for gait recognition during occlusion. The occlusion is detected and the clean and unclean gait cycles are extracted from the whole input sequence. Then the occluded gait silhouette frames are reconstructed using BGPDM (Balanced Gaussian Process Dynamic Model), PCA (Principal Component Analysis) is applied to map training gait silhouette images in Eigen space. K-means clustering is applied to obtain the key poses. Arunnehru and Kalaiselvi Geetha [10] presented a survey on real time analysis of object tracking algorithms for surveillance video applications. The performances of the major tracking algorithms for different video sequences are analyzed. Visual Tracking Decomposition algorithm (VTD), Multiple Instance Learning Tracker (MILT), and Track-Learning-Detection method (TLD) algorithms are tested on video sequences.

2.1 Outline of the Work

This paper deals with occlusion detection that aims to detect the occlusions from the video sequences. The proposed method is evaluated using a PNNL parking Lot dataset with crowded scenes. Object present in the video is identified by using ground truth information provided in the dataset itself. The detected foreground of the moving object is segmented by identifying the Region of Interest (ROI). The texture features are extracted from the segmented objects using SFTA [11, 12] algorithm with feature vector $n_t = 8$. The extracted texture features are fed into the tree-based classifiers [13] such as random forest, random tree, decision tree (J48), and REP tree. The rest of this paper is organized as follows. Section 3 explains the feature extraction method and related discussions. Section 4 illustrates the workflow of the proposed approach. Section 5 presents the experimental results. Finally, Sect. 6 concludes the paper.

3 Feature Extraction

A feature set consists of distinct characteristic which represents the meaningful data extracted from an image or video sequences that are vital for further analysis. The following subsection describes about the feature extraction procedure.

3.1 Object Detection

Object detection is the process of finding objects present in an image or video sequences. In this section the objects present in the video frames is identified using the ground truth information provided in the dataset itself. The ROI of the identified objects is extracted from the video frame for the feature extraction process. Region of Interest (ROI) is the selected subset of samples identified for a particular purpose within a dataset. Figure 1 shows the ROI of the identified objects and Fig. 2 shows the extracted ROI of the objects.

3.2 Segmentation-Based Fractal Texture Analysis (SFTA)

SFTA is an efficient texture feature extraction method. Texture feature plays an important role in understanding and image analysis. These are intended to capture the repetitive patterns and granularity of regions within an image. This method is divided into two parts:

Fig. 1. ROI of the identified objects

Fig. 2. Extracted ROI from PNNL-Parking Lot dataset

1. The input grayscale image is decomposed into a set of binary images using Two - Threshold Binary Decomposition (TTBD) algorithm.
2. Fractal dimension, mean gray level, and size are computed from the resulting binary image.

3.3   Two-Threshold Binary Decomposition (TTBD)

The TTBD algorithm uses a grayscale image as input and decomposes the image into a set of binary images. The first step of TTBD is to compute a set of threshold values by selecting an equally spaced gray level value from the input image. In the next step, it decomposes the input grayscale image into a set of binary images by selecting the pairs of threshold values and applying two-threshold segmentation of the input image as follows:

$$I_b(x, y) = \begin{cases} 1 & if \ \ t_l < I(x, y) \le t_u \\ 0, & otherwise \end{cases} \tag{1}$$

In Eq. 1, $I_b(x, y)$ is the input grayscale image, t_l and t_u are the lower and upper threshold values. Figure 3(a) illustrates the decomposition of non-occluded image. The set of binary images obtained using feature vector $n_t = 8$.

3.4   SFTA Extraction Algorithm

After applying the TTBD algorithm to the input image, the SFTA features are computed from the obtained binary images. The feature vector dimension is based on the number of binary images obtained by TTBD multiplied by three. As explained in Algorithm 1, fractal dimension, mean gray level and size are computed from each binary is shown in Fig. 3(b).

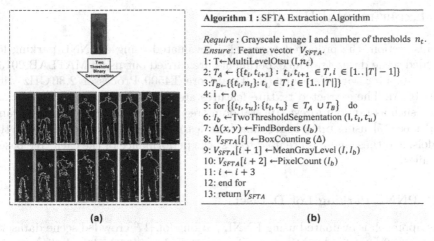

Algorithm 1 : SFTA Extraction Algorithm

Require : Grayscale image I and number of thresholds n_t.
Ensure : Feature vector V_{SFTA}.
1: T←MultiLevelOtsu (I,n_t)
2: T_A ← $\{\{t_i, t_{i+1}\} : t_i, t_{i+1} \in T, i \in [1..|T|-1]\}$
3: T_B←$\{\{t_i, n_t\}: t_i \in T, i \in [1..|T|]\}$
4: i ← 0
5: for $\{\{t_l, t_u\}: \{t_l, t_u\} \in T_A \cup T_B\}$ do
6: I_b ←TwoThresholdSegmentation (I, t_l, t_u)
7: $\Delta(x, y)$ ←FindBorders (I_b)
8: $V_{SFTA}[i]$ ←BoxCounting (Δ)
9: $V_{SFTA}[i + 1]$ ←MeanGrayLevel (I, I_b)
10: $V_{SFTA}[i + 2]$ ←PixelCount (I_b)
11: $i \leftarrow i + 3$
12: end for
13: return V_{SFTA}

(a)   (b)

Fig. 3. (a) The resulting set of binary images was obtained using $n_t = 8$ for non-occluded objects, (b) SFTA Extraction algorithm

4 Workflow of the Proposed Approach

PNNL parking lot crowded scene datasets are used for experimental purpose. The video is processed at 29 frames per second. It is essential to preprocess the video sequences to remove the noise. The object is identified from the video sequences using ground truth information. The ROI of the objects is extracted from the video sequences and texture features are extracted as discussed in Sect. 3. The extracted features are fed into the tree based classifiers for occlusion detection. The workflow of the proposed approach is shown in Fig. 4. In this approach, different tree based classifiers such as random forest, random tree, decision tree (J48) and REP tree are used in order to evaluate the effectiveness of these classifiers on the PNNL parking lot crowded scene datasets.

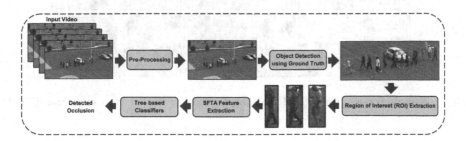

Fig. 4. Workflow of the proposed approach

5 Experimental Results

In this section, the proposed approach is evaluated using a PNNL parking lot crowded scene datasets. The experiments are carried out using MATLAB 2013a on a computer with Pentium (R) Dual-Core T4500 Processor 2.30 GHz with 4 GB RAM. The extracted texture features are fed to different tree based classifiers such as random forest [16], random tree, and decision tree (J48) [14] and REP tree [15] using open source machine learning tool WEKA to develop the models, and these models are used to test the performance of the each tree based classifier.

5.1 PNNL Parking Lot Dataset

This approach is evaluated using PNNL parking lot [17] crowded scene datasets. It contains 2 sets of videos. Sequence 1 is a crowded scene, which including groups of pedestrians walking in queues. This set contains long-term inter-objects occlusions, and similarity of appearance among the people present in the scene. There are 1000 frames in this sequence and it is a crowded scene with 14 pedestrians. The resolution of the frames in this data set is 1920 × 1080, and the frame rate is 29 fps. Sequence 2 includes abrupt motion, similarity of appearance and long-term inter-objects occlusions among the people in the scene. This sequence contains 1500 frames with 13 pedestrians. The frame resolution in this data set is 1920 × 1080, and the frame rate is 30 fps. The PNNL parking lot crowded scene dataset is divided into three sets: SET-1 is sequence 1, SET-2 is sequence 2 and SET-3 is the combination of SET-1 and SET-2. The sample frames from the PNNL parking lot are shown in Fig. 5.

Fig. 5. Sample frames from PNNL parking lot dataset SET-1 (top row) and SET-2 (bottom row)

5.2 Quantitative Evaluation

As explained in Sect. 3, the 48-dimensional feature vectors are extracted. The performance is evaluated using 10-fold cross-validation approach. The extracted features are fed to the tree-based classifier. The statistical measures of Precision (P), Recall (R), F-measure (F) and Accuracy (A) are defined as $P = tn + tp/tp + tn + fp + fn$, $R = tp/tp + fn$, $F - measure = 2P \times R/P + R$ and $A = tp + tn/tn + fp + tp + fn$. Where, tp and fp is the number of true positive and false positive predictions of the class. tn and fn is the number of true negative and false negative predictions. Precision is a measure of exactness. Recall gives how good a class is identified correctly and F-measure is the harmonic mean of precision and recall.

5.3 Experimental Results on Tree-Based Classifiers

The experiments are carried out using an open source machine learning tool WEKA [18]. Three types of occlusions are considered (non-occlusion, partial occlusion, and full-occlusion). The performances of the classifiers are measured using 10-fold cross-validation model.

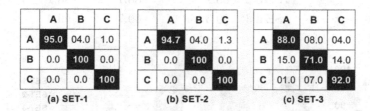

	A	B	C
A	95.0	04.0	1.0
B	0.0	100	0.0
C	0.0	0.0	100

(a) SET-1

	A	B	C
A	94.7	04.0	1.3
B	0.0	100	0.0
C	0.0	0.0	100

(b) SET-2

	A	B	C
A	88.0	08.0	04.0
B	15.0	71.0	14.0
C	01.0	07.0	92.0

(c) SET-3

Fig. 6. Confusion matrices (%) for random forest classifier on PNNL parking lot dataset, where A = non-occlusion, B = partial occlusion and C= full-occlusion

The quantitative evaluation results for SET-1, SET-2 and SET-3 are tabulated in Table 1, which shows that the proposed method has a higher precision, recall and F-measure for the random forest classifier on PNNL parking lot datasets. From the results, it shows that the random forest classifier gives the best accuracy rate of 98.3 % for SET-1, 98.2 % for SET-2, and 83.7 % for SET-3, the random tree shows the accuracy rate of 95.4 % for SET-1, 95.8 % for SET-2, and 78.2 % for SET-3, the accuracy of J48 is 94.3 % for SET-1, 94.4 % for SET-2, and 75.8 % for SET-3, and REP tree shows the accuracy of 89.5 % for SET-1, 88.1 % for SET-2, and 69.7 % for SET-3. Finally, the random forest classifier shows the highest accuracy rate when compared to other tree based classification algorithms. Figure 6 shows the confusion matrices of the random forest classifier on a PNNL parking lot dataset (SET-1, SET-2 and SET-3), where the correct response defines the main diagonal, the majority of classes are correctly classified in SET-1 and SET-2. In SET-3, partial occlusion is misclassified as non-occlusion and full-occlusion respectively. The overall performance of the proposed approach with different tree-based classifiers on PNNL parking lot dataset is shown in Fig. 7. From this figure, random forest shows the excelled performance in accuracy among other tree based algorithms.

Table 1. Performance measures of the PNNL Parking lot dataset using tree based classifiers

Classifiers	Dataset	Precision (%)	Recall (%)	F-measure (%)
Random forest	SET 1	98.4	98.3	98.3
	SET 2	98.3	98.2	98.2
	SET 3	83.7	83.7	83.5
Random tree	SET 1	95.7	95.4	95.3
	SET 2	96.0	95.8	95.7
	SET 3	78.1	78.2	77.7
Decision tree (J48)	SET 1	94.5	94.3	94.2
	SET 2	94.6	94.4	94.3
	SET 3	75.7	75.8	75.5
REP tree	SET 1	89.5	89.5	89.3
	SET 2	88.2	88.1	88.1
	SET 3	69.5	69.7	69.4

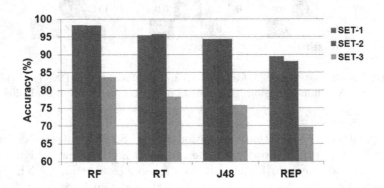

Fig. 7. Performance measure of the different tree-based classifiers

6   Conclusion

This paper presented a method for occlusion detection in surveillance videos using fractal texture analysis. Experiments are conducted on PNNL parking lot datasets with crowded scenes. The ROI of the object is extracted from the video sequences in order to extract the texture features. This approach evaluates the performance of texture feature in video sequences using tree-based algorithms such as random forest, random tree, REP tree, and decision tree (J48). The recognition results are obtained by the proposed approach on PNNL parking lot datasets. It shows that the average recognition result was 98.3 % for SET-1,

98.2 % for SET-2, and 83.7 % for SET-3, and that the random forest classifier performs best, when compared with random tree, REP tree, and decision tree (J48) classifiers.

References

1. Hsia, C.H., Guo, J.M.: Efficient modified directional lifting-based discrete wavelet transform for moving object detection. Signal Process. **96**, 138–152 (2014)
2. Eum, S., Suhr, J.K., Kim, J.: Face recognizability evaluation for ATM applications with exceptional occlusion handling. In: IEEE Computer Society Conference on Computer Vision and Pattern Recognition, pp. 82–89 (2011)
3. Chen, Y., Shen, Y., Liu, X., Zhong, B.: 3D object tracking via image sets and depth-based occlusion detection. Signal Process. **112**, 146–153 (2014)
4. Min, R., Hadid, A., Dugelay, J.L.: Efficient detection of occlusion prior to robust face recognition. Sci. World J. (2014)
5. He, R., Yang, B., Sang, N., Yu, Y., Bai, G., Li, J.: Integral region-based covariance tracking with occlusion detection. Multimedia Tools Appl. **74**, 1–22 (2014)
6. Trueba, R., Andujar, C., Argelaguet, F.: Complexity and occlusion management for the world-in-miniature metaphor. In: Butz, A., Fisher, B., Christie, M., Krüger, A., Olivier, P., Therón, R. (eds.) SG 2009. LNCS, vol. 5531, pp. 155–166. Springer, Heidelberg (2009)
7. Sharma, M., Prakash, S., Gupta, P.: Face recognition system robust to occlusion. In: Huang, D.-S., Gan, Y., Premaratne, P., Han, K. (eds.) ICIC 2011. LNCS, vol. 6840, pp. 604–609. Springer, Heidelberg (2012)
8. Park, J.-C., Kim, S.-M., Lee, K.-H.: 3D mesh construction from depth images with occlusion. In: Zhuang, Y., Yang, S.-Q., Rui, Y., He, Q. (eds.) PCM 2006. LNCS, vol. 4261, pp. 770–778. Springer, Heidelberg (2006)
9. Roy, A., Sural, S., Mukherjee, J., Rigoll, G.: Occlusion detection and gait silhouette reconstruction from degraded scenes. SIVIP **5**, 415–430 (2011)
10. Arunnehru, J., Kalaiselvi Geetha, M.: Maximum intensity block code for action recognition in video using tree-based classifiers. In: Suresh, L.P., Dash, S.S., Panigrahi, B.K. (eds.) Artificial Intelligence and Evolutionary Algorithms in Engineering Systems, vol. 325, pp. 715–722. Springer, India (2014)
11. Costa, A.F., Humpire-Mamani, G., Traina, A.J.M.: An efficient algorithm for fractal analysis of textures. In: Proceedings of Graphics, Patterns and Images (SIB-GRAPI), pp. 39–46 (2012)
12. Nanthini, T., Kalaiselvi Geetha, M., Arunnehru, J.: Occlusion detection and handling based on fractal texture analysis in surveillance videos using neural network classifier. Int. J. Appl. Eng. Res. **9**(20), 4631–4635 (2014)
13. Arunnehru, J., Kalaiselvi Geetha, M.: Quantitative real-time analysis of object tracking algorithm for surveillance applications. Int. J. Emerg. Technol. Adv. Eng. **3**(1), 234–240 (2013)
14. Kumar, Y., Upendra, J.: An efficient Intrusion detection based on decision tree classifier using feature reduction. Int. J. Sci. Res. Publ. **2**(1), 1–6 (2012)
15. Singh, S., Gupta, D.L., Malviya, A.K.: Performance analysis of classification tree learning algorithms. Int. J. Comput. Appl. **55**(6), 39–44 (2012)
16. Breiman, L.: Random forest. Mach. Learn. **45**(1), 5–32 (2001)

17. Shu, G., Dehghan, A., Oreifej, O., Hand, E., Shah, M.: Part-based multiple-person tracking with partial occlusion handling. In: Proceedings of Computer Vision and Pattern Recognition (CVPR), pp. 1815–1821. IEEE (2012)
18. Witten, I.H., Frank, E.: Data Mining: Practical Machine Learning Tools and Techniques with Java Implementations. Morgan Kaufmann Publishers, Burlington (1999)

A Modus Operandi for Social Networking Security Solutions Based on Varied Usages

R. Kamatchi[✉] and Kanika Minocha

KJ Somaiya Institute of Management Studies and Research, Mumbai, India
{kamatchi,kanika.m}@somaiya.edu

Abstract. The popularity of social networking sites is increasing beyond belief. There is no disagreement about the effectiveness of sites such as Facebook, LinkedIn and Twitter. These sites can be used for professional networking and job searches, as a tool to keep the public informed about the safety and other issues, as a means to increase sales revenue or as a way to reconnect with friends. There is a rapid increase in the number of social media users. However, with the increase in number of users there is also an increase in the security threats affecting the users' privacy, personal data, identity and confidentiality. In this paper we have aimed at categorising security and privacy threats based on the kind of usage of social media. We have also presented an algorithm to find the appropriate solution to address the security and privacy related issues as per the usage category. This paper helps in improving security and privacy of SNS (Social Networking Sites) users without compromising the benefits of sharing information through SNSs.

Keywords: Security and Privacy · Social networks · Social media · Anonymity · Information security solutions

1 Introduction

Social Networking sites such as Facebook, LinkedIn and Twitter (Big 3) are defined as interactive web-based applications that provide users with an opportunity to communicate with friends, colleagues and family, join groups, form social communities, chat, meet new people, share photos, and also to organize events and to network with others in a manner similar to real life. The number of users of Social Networking Sites (SNS) has been growing at an incredible rate. They have become a major platform for communication and interaction between users.

These SNS provide significant advantages for personal, general and business use. Some of the benefits worth noting for social networks are

- Users can stay connected to their peers very conveniently, irrespective of their geographical location.
- Like-minded individuals can interact with each other by forming groups and communities.
- Creates a virtual space for innovative modes of online collaboration, education, trust-formation and experience-sharing.

© Springer International Publishing Switzerland 2015
J.H. Abawajy et al. (Eds): SSCC 2015, CCIS 536, pp. 317–328, 2015.
DOI: 10.1007/978-3-319-22915-7_30

- Can be used for marketing, branding and promotion of the businesses. Furthermore SNS can also engage a broad range of people in a company in the strategic planning process.

The success of a SNS is measured by the number of users attracted by it, therefore SNS focus on design and features appropriate for increasing the number of members and their connections. Since security and privacy is not the upmost priority for the development of SNS, so the security and access control mechanisms of SNS are relatively weak. Resultantly, these SNS are vulnerable to security and privacy related threats for their members. A user may have a couple of close friends and thousands of distant friends, but a SNS may simply categorize them all as "friends". In an era where our actual identity is overshadowed by our online identity, the potential security risks associated with these social networks cannot be ignored.

1.1 Organization

The remainder of this paper is organized as follows:
In Sect. 2 we have summarized the related work in privacy and security of online social networks. In Sect. 3 we describe different uses of online network and information security issues that needs to be ensured in each use. In Sect. 4 we discuss various security threats and the security issues it impacts. In Sect. 5 we provide solutions for resolving the security issues. In Sect. 6 we have given a step by step procedure to reach the appropriate solution. In Sect. 7 we have discussed various cases in support of the proposed algorithm. In Sect. 8 we offer future research directions along with conclusion

2 Background Study

The growth of social media in organizations worldwide has been phenomenal in the recent years. Its impact is evident in different areas of interest. The extent of social networking aspects among today's generation has created an open platform wherein users exchange all their personnel and sensitive data unintentionally. Osterman Research has discovered that the web has been growing as a threat vector for the past several years, as shown in Fig. 1 for the period 2007 through 2013 [1].

These new Internet-based communications tools such as Facebook, Twitter and Skype have already achieved widespread penetration inside organizations [2]. This aspect of Social media has opened up many serious challenges for the business organizations. A paper by Gross and Acquisty reveals that 71 % of the Facebook users have the tendency to provide large amounts of sensitive personal information such as image, birthdates, in their profile. This data expose themselves to various kinds of security risks [3] which varies from simple authenticity issues to severe confidentiality issues.

Michael Fire has proposed a thorough review of the different security and privacy risks which threaten the users in general and children in particular [11]. Javier Echaiz highlights the benefits of safe use of SNSs and emphasizes the most important threats to members of SNSs, the main factors behind these threats and present policy and

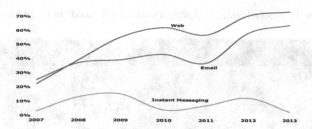

Fig. 1. Growth of web as a threat vector

technical recommendations in order to improve security [4]. Fernand Almeida presents the most common security risks faced by the major Web 2.0 applications, most relevant paths and best practices to avoid these identified security risks in a corporate environment.

2.1   Our Contribution

This paper is an attempt to identify the different security and privacy threats that culminate in different usage perspectives of social network. More Specifically the study offers the following contributions. Firstly we outline the different usage perspectives of social network that covers all the major uses of SNS with an additional focus on information security issues that needs to be addressed rigorously in each usage category. Secondly we also categorize each SN threat according to information security issue it effects. Thirdly, we categorize each security solution as per the security issue it resolves. Fourthly we have devised a step by step procedure to be followed in order to reach an appropriate solution as per the individual use. Lastly we tested the algorithm with 2 different live cases.

3   Uses of Online Social Network and the Security Threat Dimension

The online uses of social network discussed includes, for what purpose do they use social networks and how are they engaged with content online. A diverse range of reasons for using social media can be categorised as Personal, General and business purposes. This reveals that all individuals adapt social media platforms for their unique needs and interests.

Professional or Business.   Use of social media in the workplace is important to achieving business objectives. Professional or Business usage of SNS considers uses from an organizational point of view. Social Media is used for Marketing, Branding, Promotion, Team Work, Surveillance, Customer Service etc.:

Table 1. General usage and security issues that needs to be addressed

	Confidentiality	Privacy	Authenticity	Data Integrity	Access Rights	Availability	Non Repudiation
Networking		✓	✓				
Entertainment			✓	✓		✓	
ContentCreation		✓	✓			✓	
Fun			✓	✓		✓	
News Media			✓	✓			✓

Table 2. Personal usage and the security issues that needs to be addressed

	Confidentiality	Privacy	Authenticity	Data Integrity	Access Rights	Availability	Non Repudiation
Learning			✓				
Communication	✓	✓			✓	✓	✓
Research			✓	✓			
Job Seeking		✓					✓
User Grouping	✓	✓	✓				

Table 3. Business usage and the information security issues that needs to be addressed

	Confidentiality	Privacy	Authenticity	Data Integrity	Access Rights	Availability	Non Repudiation
Marketing		✓	✓	✓		✓	✓
Team Work			✓		✓		
Surveillance	✓	✓	✓	✓	✓		✓
Promotions			✓	✓	✓		✓
Customer Service			✓	✓	✓	✓	

Personal. Social Media is also used for personalized purposes including learning from blogs and postings, Personalized Communication, Research, Job Seeking, Educational purposes and for joining personalized user groups.

General. Social Media is also used for general purposes like Networking, Entertainment, Information creation, Fun, News Media etc.: where privacy and personalization is not the concern.

3.1   Information Security and Its Key Issues

Information security, is the practice of shielding information from unauthorized access, use, disclosure, disruption, perusal, modification, inspection, recording or destruction. The issues related to the same can be classified into the following seven categories [6].

- Authentication—verification of identity of users.
- Authorization— deciding whether or not to allow action on a resource.
- Data confidentiality— guarding the secrecy of sensitive data.
- Data integrity— detection of tampered data
- Non-repudiation — assuring that neither the sender nor the receiver can deny the message they have sent or received.
- Protection against attacks—ensuring that attackers cannot gain control over applications.
- Privacy—ensuring that the application is not violating the privacy of the users.

Varied usage scenarios and the various security issues that need to be addressed are specified in Tables 1, 2 and 3.

4   Security Threats in Social Media and Security Threat Dimension It Impacts

- **Eavesdropping:** - Eavesdropping refers to secretly listening to a private conversation without the consent of the user. An online conversation between users can be recorded by third party applications without the expressed consent of users.
- **Information Spoofing:**-At times Social Media users accidently alter their privacy settings and inadvertently release their information and unauthorized users get to view and misuse this information.
- **Identity Theft:** - The verification of identity of a user can be an issue. The identity of a user can be stolen by social engineering techniques or by using key logging software.
- **Vandalism, Harassment and Stalking:** A social media user can reveal his personal information including phone number, location, schedule, home address, etc.: in his profile which can be misused by an attacker for social stalking i.e. to intimidate the victim through physical proximity, through e-mails, or even phone calls, instant messengers or messaging on SNSs.
- **Defamation and Slandering:**- It refers to the communication of false and misleading information about an individual person, business, religion, or nation product, group, government.
- **Profile Squatting:** An attacker can create a fake profile in order to impersonate a renowned brand or a renowned person. Such profiles are generally created by the people who are aware of the personal details of a user and they create a profile to impersonate him or her thus causing all sorts of difficulties for the victim

- **Malwares and Computer Virus:** [11] Malware is a malicious software that is developed to interrupt a computer operation to gain access to the private information of the user and aso to collect user credentials.
- **Digital File of Personal Information:** With the development of data mining technology and with reduction in cost of disk storage, third party can generate a digital dossier of personal data with the information that has been revealed on the profiles of SNSs.
- **Face Recognition:** social network users often add images to their individual profiles that can be used to identify the corresponding profile holders. Hence a stranger can make use of this data source to correlate the profiles across services by using face recognition
- **Cross Site Scripting (XSS):** This is an assault against web applications. The attacker using XSS exploits the trust of the web client in the web application and a malicious code is run by a web client capable of collecting sensitive information. An adversary can make use of this defenselessness to compromise the account, to perform a phishing attack and also to spread the unwanted content to the email as well as instant Messaging (IM) traffic.
- **Phishing:** [13] In this attack the information available on social network is exploited to increase the success rate of a phishing attack. Phishing can expose the sensitive information, such as passwords and credit-card details or bank account numbers and thus causing financial and reputation damage.
- **SNS Aggregators:** Some of the upcoming applications such as Snag, ProfileLinker, TwitterFeed, SocialMediaPop, NameBeeNameBee etc. offers read/write access to several SNS accounts so as to integrate the data into a single web application. However such applications use very weak authentication mechanisms and thus increasing the vulnerability
- **Corporate Espionage:** It refers to social engineering attacks where psychological manipulation of people is done to divulge confidential information
- **Spam:-** Spammers create the unsolicited and massive messages to produce traffic to their sites and to gain better ranks at search engines that leads to overloading of social networks.
- **Clickjacking:-** [10] It is a malicious technique that makes the user click on something different from what they actually intended to click. Clickjacking helps the attacker to manipulate the user into posting some spam messages, user performs likes to link unknowingly and also opens webcamera and microphone for user recording.
- **De-anonymization Attack:** In this attack, attacker learns about the social network group the victim belongs to. Since the number of social network groups are much less than the number of social network individual user, thus it is easier to first focus on the group and then to reach the individual user via group. Attacker uses history stealing method to obtain the urls visited by victim in past to figure out the victim's group.

Table 4 indicates various threats and the security issues it impacts.

Table 4. Threats and the security issues it impacts

	Confidentiality	Privacy	Authenticity	Data Integrity	Access Rights	Availability	Non Repudiation
Eavesdropping	✓	✓					
Info Spoofing	✓	✓		✓			✓
Stalking	✓	✓	✓				
Defamation			✓	✓			✓
Spam and cyber Squatting		✓	✓				
Malware and virus		✓		✓		✓	
Replay				✓			✓
Digital Doiser of Personal Information	✓	✓			✓		✓
Cross Content Scripting	✓			✓	✓		
Phishing	✓	✓	✓				
SNN aggregators			✓				
Baits in SNS			✓				
Deanonymization	✓	✓	✓				✓

5   Solutions to the Security Threat

- **Authentication Mechanisms:** SNS operators use authentication mechanisms such as captcha, photos of friend's identification, two factor authentication. Two factor authentication can be chosen requiring user to enter password when logging in along with a verification code that is sent to the user's mobile device. This ensures that the user logging in is an authentic user and his account has not been compromised.
- **Security and Privacy Settings:** SNS users can configure their privacy settings in a way that enables users to protect their personal data from other users. Users can customize their privacy settings and can choose the other users in the network that have access to their personal details, pictures, posts etc.:
- **Internet Security Solutions:** A number of security companies such as McAfee and Symantec AVG offer software suits that typically includes antivirus and firewall that shields social media users against malware, phishing and clickjacking attacks.
- **FB Phishing Protector:** It is an add-on for firefox which warns social media users against a suspicious activity such as script injection attacks in turn providing immunity to phishing attack.

Table 5. Security solutions and security issues they resolve

	Confidentiality	Privacy	Authenticity	Data Integrity	Access Control	Availability	Non Repudiation
Internet Security Solution	✓		✓			✓	✓
AVG Privacy Fix		✓					
Phishing Protector		✓				✓	
Norton Safeweb			✓				
Mcafee Social protection		✓			✓		✓
MyPermissions		✓			✓		
NoScript Security suit			✓		✓		
Privacy Scanner		✓			✓		
Defensio	✓						✓
Zone Alarm Privacy Scan		✓			✓		
Netnanny		✓	✓		✓		
Minor Monitor	✓						
Socware Detection						✓	
Improving Privacy Setting Interface		✓					
Security appliances		✓	✓				
IPS software			✓				

- **Norton Safe Web:** [12] It is a facebook application that scans the news feeds for facebook users and warns the user about both unsafe links and unsafe sites.
- **AVG Privacy Fix:** It is an add on that offers a user to simply manage their privacy settings on SNS.
- **MyPermissions:** It is a web service that provides option for users to revoke the permissions they had given in the past to various applications thus reassuring their privacy. It also sends periodic reminders to the users to check their SNS permission settings.
- **McAfeee Social Protection:** It is a mobile application that enables facebook users to protect their uploaded photos by precisely controlling who can view and download their images.

- **Net Nanny [5]:** This software assists parents in safeguarding their kids from harmful content. It lets the parents monitor their children activity on various SNS.
- **Zone Alarm Privacy Scan:** It is a facebook application that can identify the posts that expose the user's private information.

Table 6. Summary table for solutions, threats, security issues and applicability of solution to social media platform

	Threats	Security Issue it Resolves	Applicability to Social Media Platform
Internet Security Solution	Malware, Phishing and Clickjacking attacks	Confidentiality, Authenticity and Availability	Facebook,Linkedin, Google
AVG Privacy Fix	Information Spoofing, Vandalism and Stalking, Profile Stalking	Privacy	Facebook,Linkedin, Google
Phishing Protector	XSS and Phishing attack	Privacy and Availability	Facebook
Norton Safeweb	Spam, malware and clickjacking attacks	Authenticity	Facebook
Mcafee Social protection	Face Recognition, Information Leakage and Location leakage	Privacy, Access Control and Non Repudiation	Facebook
MyPermissions	Information Spoofing, Vandalism and Stalking, Profile Stalking	Privacy and Access Control	Facebook,Twitter and LinkedIn
NoScript Security suit	Clickjacking and XSS attack.	Authenticity and Access Control	Facebook,Twitter and LinkedIn
Privacy Scanner	Information Spoofing, Vandalism and Stalking, Profile Stalking	Privacy and Access Control	Facebook
Defensio	Malware links and Information leakage	Confidentiality and Non Repudiation	Facebook
Zone Alarm Privacy Scan	Information Spoofing, Vandalism and Stalking, Profile Stalking	Privacy and Access Control	Facebook
Netnanny	Profile Squatting	Privacy, Authenticity and Access Control;	Facebook,Twitter and Flickr

- **Defensio:** It protects SNS users from threats like malware links that are posted on facebook page of the user. It also assists in preventing information leakage.
- **Privacy Scanner:** It is an application for facebook that aids in identifying and fixing the risky settings of the user which may lead to privacy concerns.
- **NoScript Security Suit:** It is an extension to Mozilla based web browsers that allows executable content such as flash, java and javascript only from trusted domains of the user's choice hence protecting user from click jacking and XSS attack.

Table 5 indicates the security solutions and the security issues they resolve while Table 6 is a summary table for Solutions, Threats, Security Issues and Applicability of solution to social media platform.

6   Algorithm to Choose the Appropriate Solution for the Threat Faced

S1: Choose the usage level from the three usage categories $U_i = \{1.....3\}$
S2: Identify the Sub category in the selected usage U_{ij} where $i = 1....3$
$J = 1....5$
S3: Identify the common security issues $Sec_i = \{1.......7\}$
S4: Prioritize the issue listing as per your need
S5: Realize the Security threats from Table 4
S6: Select the security solution Sol_{ij} where i defines the threat and j defines the solution
S7: Implement the security solution from the given list and evaluate the effectiveness of the same.

7   Results and Discussions

Case Analysis:

Case I: "Alice was an outgoing 12-year-old girl who had a lot of friends at school. At sleepovers, she and her friends used to take photographs of each other dancing, doing each other's hair and makeup and many other silly, but fun things, including one in just the front of Alice's house.

One of her friends somehow shared some of the photos of the party with another student, who was not invited to the party. That student made a fake social media page having pictures of Alice and her house and then sent the link to some other school mates who weren't at the party either. On that fake page, some kids posted some mean statements about Alice and also encouraged other students to play a prank her at home. The next weekend, Alice and her family found trash discarded in their yard, toilet paper thrown on their trees and eggs strewn at their front door.

Alice discovered about the fake social media page and told this to her parents who reached out to other school parents, notified school authorities and also notified the social media site that the profile was a fake. Eventually, the pranks stopped and also page was taken down." [14]

S1: The usage level of this case could be categorized into **General**.

S2: The sub category of usage level could be defined as **Fun**.

S3: This category can face Authenticity, Data integrity, Availability issues. The above mentioned case addresses more on Authenticity and Data integrity issues.

S4: As the fake profile page is the basic issue of the above mentioned case, the priority issue could be mentioned as Authenticity. If the authenticity of the page could have been ensured, then the message from the unidentified people would have been detected.

S5: The security threats can be finalised as **Profile Squatting and Defamation**. The Profile Squatting is the basic problem which then led to the defamation of the account holder. So, the Profile Squatting is the main problem which needs to be addressed primarily.

S6: Norton Safeweb, NoScript Security suit and Net nanny are the various solutions which addresses the Authenticity problem and Net Nanny is the unique solution to the problem of Cyber squatting.

Case II: Alice was holding an account with Twitter. Once he was navigating through his page and was going through various links sent by his friends. While doing so, he came across an advertisement page which was displaying various accessories with a bulk discount. He was going through the same. He wanted to know more details about the products. So he clicked on the button "Follow us on Facebook – Like" button. It was an inadvertent action by Alice. But the content was posted on his wall with the remark that Alice liked the page and forwarded to his friends.

It was an unauthorized site which has been circulated all the friends of Alice. The friends were shocked to get such a message from Alice. They started enquiring Alice about the same. Then only Alice came to know about this ill posting in his wall. He sent an apologising message to all.

S1. The usage level of this case could be categorized into **Personal**.

S2: The sub category of usage level could be defined as **Learning**. Alice wanted to learn more about the advertised product.

S3: This category can face Authenticity issues. As the reliability of the source is not clear, this category can also lead to repudiability issues.

S4: The originality of the content and the source is not verified. This is the main root cause for the entire problem.

S5: The security threat can be finalised as **ClickJacking** and **Cross site scripting**. The wrong selection made by Alice is the main root cause for the problem. So the main issue can be finalized as **ClickJacking.**

S6: **Norton Safeweb, NoScript Security suit and Net nanny** are the various solutions which addresses the Authenticity problem. All the three solutions can be used for the **ClickJacking** problem. Based on the platform support for Twitter, **NoScript Security suit** would be more appropriate.

8 Conclusion and Future Scope

This study has been performed with the limited samples of three major usage categories with 5 subcategories each. As the social networking sites are cropping up rapidly, this study can be further extended by including more and more subcategories. This paper relates the different threats with the major security issues classification which can be further extended. As a whole, this study provides a successful modus operandi towards a smooth ride in a social networking environment. It is realized that the extension of SNS will inculcate more issues, On the other hand the solutions can also be developed easily by relating itself to the security issues.

References

1. Best Practices in Email, Web and Social Media Security, An Osterman Research White Paper, 2–4 January 2014
2. Jaokan, A., Sharma, C.: Mobile VoIP – approaching the tripping point (2010). http://www.futuretext.com/downloads/mobile_voip.pdf
3. Gross, R., Acquisti, A.: Privacy and information revelation in online social networks. In: ACM Workshop on Privacy in the Electronic Society (WPES) (2005)
4. Echaiz, J., Ardenghi, J.: http://lisidi.cs.uns.edu.ar. Accessed 20 November 2014
5. Amin, T., Okhiria, O., Lu, J., An, J.: Facebook: a comprehensive analysis of phishing on a social system (2010). https://Courses.ece.ubc.ca/412/term_project/reports/2010/facebook.pdf. Accessed 01 February 2014
6. Landeen, R., Ou, J., Rhodes, T.: New ways in going to hack your web app. Blackhat, AD (2011)
7. Baltazar, J., Costoya, J., Flores, R.: The real face of koobface: the largest web 2.0 botnet explained. Trend Micro Res. 5(9), 10 (2009)
8. Symantec. Norton Safe web. https://www.facebook.com/appcenter/nortonsafeweb. Accessed 14 November 2014
9. Contentwatch. Net Nanny. http://www.netnanny.com/. Accessed 14 November 2014
10. Cheng, Z., Caverlee, J., Lee, K.: Your are where you tweet: a content based approach to geo-locating twitter users. In: Proceedings of the 19th ACM International Conference on Information and Knowledge Management, CKIM 2010, pp. 759–768. ACM (2010)
11. Fire, M., Goldschmidt, R., Elovia, Y.: Online social networks: threats & solutions. IEEE Commun. Surv. Tutorials, 8–20 (2014)
12. Echaiz, J., Ardenghi, J.: http://lisidi.cs.uns.edu.ar. Accessed 20 November 2014
13. Leitch, S., Warren, M.: Security issues challenging facebook. In: Proceedings of the 7th Australian Information Security Management Conference, pp. 137–140, December 2013
14. www.growingwireless.org. Accessed 14 November 2014

A Secret Common Information Duality
for Tripartite Noisy Correlations

Pradeep Kr. Banerjee[✉]

Indian Institute of Technology Kharagpur, Kharagpur, India
pradeep.banerjee@gmail.com

Abstract. We explore the duality between the simulation and extraction of secret correlations in light of a similar well-known operational duality between the two notions of common information due to Wyner, and Gács and Körner. For the *inverse* problem of simulating a tripartite noisy correlation from noiseless secret key and unlimited public communication, we show that Winter's (2005) result for the key cost in terms of a conditional version of Wyner's common information can be simply reexpressed in terms of the existence of a bipartite protocol monotone. For the *forward* problem of key distillation from noisy correlations, we construct simple distributions for which the conditional Gács and Körner common information achieves a tight bound on the secret key rate. We conjecture that this holds in general for non-communicative key agreement models. We also comment on the interconvertibility of secret correlations under local operations and public communication.

Keywords: Information-theoretic security · Secret key agreement · Common information · Monotones

1 Introduction

Information-theoretic (IT) or unconditional security—widely acknowledged as the strictest notion of security has witnessed a renaissance since the 90's, arguably following Maurer's seminal work on secret key (SK) agreement by public discussion from correlated source sequences [1,2]. Compared to computational complexity-based approaches, IT-security provides a framework for *provable security* by bounding the adversary's total information. Assumptions are made neither on the latter's computational or memory resources nor on the unproven computational hardness of certain problems. By harnessing noise and appropriate coding and signaling strategies at the *physical layer* (the lowest layer in the protocol stack), IT-security potentially complements conventional upper layer cryptographic protocols (e.g., RSA, Diffie-Hellman key exchange) and is an important component of future communication networks [18]. The paradigm is especially valuable for improving security in large-scale wireless networks and distributed networks with minimal infrastructure (e.g., mobile *ad hoc* sensor

© Springer International Publishing Switzerland 2015
J.H. Abawajy et al. (Eds): SSCC 2015, CCIS 536, pp. 329–341, 2015.
DOI: 10.1007/978-3-319-22915-7_31

networks) where the broadcast nature of the transmission medium makes it particularly vulnerable to attacks, and key distribution and management is difficult and computationally expensive [18].

But for all its advantages, unconditionally secure key distribution is impossible to realize from scratch, for instance, if the legitimate parties are only given access to a noiseless public communication channel [1–3]. This pessimism can however be relativized if the parties are additionally given access to simple auxiliary devices (e.g., noisy correlations or communication channels) that are not completely under the control of an adversary [14]. Thus, information-theoretic reductions between such primitives are of great interest.

Interconvertibility of noisy tripartite correlations and a uniformly distributed, noiseless SK have been studied under the rubric of SK agreement by public discussion (called the *forward problem* [1,2]) and the dual problem of simulating a noisy correlation from noiseless SK and public communication (called the *inverse problem* [3–6]). In general, there are irreversible losses in exchanging noisy correlations in that, going from one noisy correlation to another and back is not lossless (even asymptotically) [3,16]. In light of the resource character of noisy correlations in enabling SK agreement, and that of SK in simulating a tripartite correlation, quantifying such resources are of interest.

To make things precise, consider three distant parties, honest Alice and Bob, and an adversary Eve who observe sequences $X^n = (X_1, \ldots, X_n)$, $Y^n = (Y_1, \ldots, Y_n)$, and $Z^n = (Z_1, \ldots, Z_n)$ respectively, where the sequence triple $(X^n Y^n Z^n)$ has the generic component variables $(XYZ) \sim p_{XYZ}$. Starting with no initially shared SKs, and using only local operations and unlimited public communication (LOPC) over a noiseless, authenticated (but, otherwise insecure) channel, what is the maximum rate at which Alice and Bob can distil a SK (i.e., the maximum possible *SK rate*), such that Eve's information (Z^n and the entire public discussion) about the generated SK is arbitrarily small? Conversely, starting with perfect SKs, what is the *SK cost* of approximately simulating the correlated triple XYZ using only LOPC?

We explore this duality between the secrecy extractable from p_{XYZ} and that required to simulate p_{XYZ} in light of a similar well-known operational duality between the two notions of common information (CI) due to Gács and Körner [7] and Wyner [8]. For the *inverse* problem of simulating p_{XYZ} from noiseless SK and unlimited public communication, Winter [4] gave a single-letter characterization of the asymptotic minimal SK cost of formation in terms of a conditional version of Wyner's CI. We first show that the SK cost of formation can be simply reexpressed in terms of the existence of a bipartite protocol monotone. For the *forward* problem of key distillation from p_{XYZ}, we construct simple distributions for which the conditional Gács and Körner CI captures the "explicit" secret CI, thus achieving a tight bound on the SK rate. We also comment on the interconvertibility of secret correlations under LOPC.

2   CI Duality and Secret CI

Random variables (RVs) and their finite alphabets are denoted using uppercase letters X and script letters $\mathcal{X}$. X^n denotes the sequence $(X_1, \ldots, X_n)$.

$p_X(x) = \Pr\{X = x\}$ denotes the distribution (pmf) of a discrete RV X. $X - Y - Z$ denotes that X, Y, Z form a Markov chain satisfying $p_{XYZ} = p_{XY}p_{Z|Y}$. Likewise, X, Y, Z is said to form a conditional Markov chain given U if $X - UY - Z$. The entropy of X is defined as $H(X) = -\sum_{x \in \mathcal{X}} p_X(x) \log p_X(x)$ and the mutual information of X and Y is given by $I(X; Y) = H(X) - H(X|Y)$. The total variational distance between p_X and $p_{X'}$ is defined as $\mathsf{TV}(p_X, p_{X'}) = \frac{1}{2}\sum_{x \in \mathcal{X}} |p_X(x) - p_{X'}(x)|$.

The zero pattern of p_{XY} can be specified by its characteristic bipartite graph B_{XY} with the vertex set $\mathcal{X} \cup \mathcal{Y}$ and an edge connecting two vertices x and y iff $p_{XY}(x, y) \geq 0$. If B_{XY} contains only a single connected component, we say that p_{XY} is *indecomposable*. An *ergodic decomposition* of $p_{XY}(x, y)$ is defined by a unique partition of the space $\mathcal{X} \times \mathcal{Y}$ into connected components. The following double markovity lemma [12] (also see Problem 16.25, p. 392 in [11]) is useful.

Lemma 1. *A triple of RVs* (X, Y, Q) *satisfies the double Markov conditions*

$$X - Y - Q, \quad Y - X - Q \tag{1}$$

iff there exists a pmf $p_{Q'|XY}$ *such that* $H(Q'|X) = H(Q'|Y) = 0$ *and* $XY - Q' - Q$. *Furthermore, (1) implies* $I(XY; Q) \leq H(Q')$ *with equality iff* $H(Q'|Q) = 0$.

Proof. Given $p_{Q|XY}$ such that $X - Y - Q$ and $Y - X - Q$, it follows that $p_{XY}(x, y) > 0 \Rightarrow p_{Q|XY}(q|x, y) = p_{Q|X}(q|x) = p_{Q|Y}(q|y) \; \forall q$. Given an ergodic decomposition of $p_{XY}(x, y)$ such that $\mathcal{X} \times \mathcal{Y} = \bigcup_{q'} \mathcal{X}_{q'} \times \mathcal{Y}_{q'}$, where the $\mathcal{X}_{q'}$'s and $\mathcal{Y}_{q'}$'s having different subscripts are disjoint, define $p_{Q'|XY}$ as $Q' = q'$ iff $x \in \mathcal{X}_{q'} \Leftrightarrow y \in \mathcal{Y}_{q'}$. Clearly $H(Q'|X) = H(Q'|Y) = 0$. Then, for any $Q = q$ and for every q', $p_{Q|XY}(q|\cdot, \cdot)$ is constant over $\mathcal{X}_{q'} \times \mathcal{Y}_{q'}$. This implies that $p_{Q|XY}(q|x, y) = p_{Q|Q'}(q|q')$ so that $XY - Q' - Q$. The converse is obvious. Thus, given (1), we get Q' such that $I(XY; Q|Q') = 0$ so that $I(XY; Q) = I(XYQ'; Q) = I(Q'; Q) = H(Q') - H(Q'|Q) \leq H(Q')$. $\square$

Gács and Körner (GK) [7] defined CI as the maximum rate of common randomness (CR) (R) that Alice and Bob, observing X^n and Y^n separately can *extract* without communication $(R_0 = 0)$, i.e., $C_{GK}(X; Y) = \sup \frac{1}{n} H(f_1(X^n))$ where the sup is taken over all sequences of pairs of deterministic mappings (f_1^n, f_2^n) such that $\Pr\{f_1^n(X^n) \neq f_2^n(Y^n)\} \to 0$ as $n \to \infty$ (see setup in Fig. 1(a)). GK showed that

$$C_{GK}(X; Y) = \max_{Q: \, H(Q|X) = H(Q|Y) = 0} H(Q) = H(Q_*) \tag{2}$$

where Q_* is the *maximal common RV* of the pair (X, Y) induced by the ergodic decomposition of p_{XY}. For all X, Y, we have $I(X; Y) = H(Q_*) + I(X; Y|Q_*)$. We say that p_{XY} is *resolvable*, if $I(X; Y|Q_*) = 0$. An alternative characterization of $C_{GK}(X; Y)$ follows from Lemma 1 [12].

$$C_{GK}(X; Y) = \max_{Q: \, Q-X-Y, \, Q-Y-X} I(XY; Q), \quad |\mathcal{Q}| \leq |\mathcal{X}||\mathcal{Y}| + 2 \tag{3}$$

$C_{GK}(X;Y)$ is identically zero for all indecomposable distributions. For example, a binary symmetric channel with non-zero crossover probability is indecomposable and hence $C_{GK}(X;Y) = 0$. Thus, CR is a far stronger resource than correlation, in that the latter does not result in common random bits, in general. Nevertheless, when Alice communicates with Bob ($R_0 > 0$), they can unlock hidden layers of potential CR [9]. With a high enough rate of communication (that is independent of Bob's output), the CR rate *increases* to $I(X;Y)$ [9].

A conditional version of GK CI is defined as follows.

$$C_{GK}(X;Y|Z) = H(Q_*|Z) = \max_{\substack{Q:H(Q|XZ)=0 \\ H(Q|YZ)=0}} H(Q|Z) = \max_{\substack{Q-XZ-Y \\ Q-YZ-X}} I(XY;Q|Z) \quad (4)$$

Conditioning always reduces GK CI, i.e., $C_{GK}(X;Y|Z) \le C_{GK}(X;Y)$. We say that p_{XYZ} is *conditionally resolvable*, if $I(X;Y|ZQ_*) = 0$.

Wyner [8] defined CI as the minimum rate of CR (R) needed to *generate* X^n and Y^n separately using local operations (independent noisy channels: $Q \to X^n$, $Q \to Y^n$) and no communication ($R_0 = 0$) (see setup in Fig. 1(b)).

$$C_W(X;Y) = \min_{Q:X-Q-Y} I(XY;Q), \quad |\mathcal{Q}| \le |\mathcal{X}||\mathcal{Y}| \quad (5)$$

Likewise, a conditional version of Wyner's CI is defined as follows.

$$C_W(X;Y|Z) = \min_{Q:X-QZ-Y} I(XY;Q|Z) \quad (6)$$

$C_W(X;Y)$ quantifies the resource cost for the distributed approximate simulation of p_{XY}. When Alice communicates with Bob ($R_0 > 0$), with a high enough rate of communication (independent of Bob's output), the CR rate *reduces* to $I(X;Y)$ [9]. Reversing the direction of Alice's operation ($X^n \to Q^n$) (see Fig. 1(c)) leads to a two-stage simulation of a noisy channel via the Markov chain $X - Q - Y$. Now Alice and Bob can use the reverse Shannon theorem [10] to simulate a first stage, with Alice mapping X^n to some intermediate RV Q^n which she sends noiselessly to Bob. In the second stage, Bob locally maps Q^n to get Y^n. This gives a nontrivial tradeoff between the (noiseless) communication rate R_0 and CR rate R leading to an alternative characterization of Wyner's CI as the communication cost of distributed channel simulation without any CR ($R = 0$). With unlimited CR, the cost reduces to $I(X;Y)$ [9]. Finally, to complete the duality, we note the following well-known relation between the different notions of CI [12]: $C_{GK}(X;Y) \le I(X;Y) \le C_W(X;Y)$ with equality holding iff p_{XY} is resolvable, whence $C_{GK}(X;Y) = I(X;Y) \Leftrightarrow I(X;Y) = C_W(X;Y)$.

The setup for the standard SK agreement scenario [1–3,14,15] shown in Fig. 1(d) is a generalization of the GK setup (see Fig. 1(a)) that now allows for interactive communication. Consider the following distributed communication protocol, Π_{KA}. Alice (X) and Bob (Y) communicate interactively over an authenticated (noiseless) public discussion channel (transparent to an adversary, Eve (Z)). Both have independent access to an infinite stream of private randomness. The protocol proceeds in rounds, where in each round each party flips private coins, and based on the messages exchanged so far, publicly sends a message to the other party. At the end of the protocol, Alice (Bob) either accepts

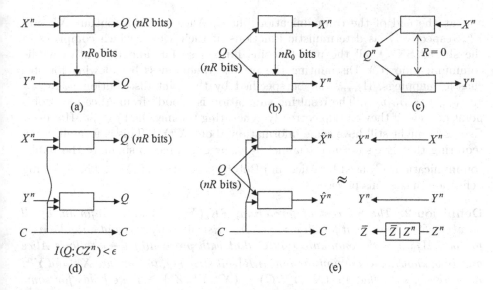

Fig. 1. *Common information duality (with communication):* (a) Gács and Körner's setup ($R_0 = 0$) [7] (b) Wyner's setup ($R_0 = 0$) [8] (c) Inverting Alice's channel gives an alternative characterization of Wyner's CI as the communication cost of channel simulation without any CR ($R = 0$) [9,10] (d) Setup for SK agreement [1–3] (e) Setup for distributed simulation of p_{XYZ} from SK and public communication [3–6]

or rejects the protocol execution, and outputs a key Q_X (Q_Y) depending on her (his) view of the protocol, which comprises of X^n (Y^n), all local computations, and the entire public communication (encapsulated in the RV C). The asymptotic maximum rate of SK distillation is called the *SK rate* [1–3].

Definition 1. *The SK rate, $S(X;Y\|Z)$ is defined as the largest real number R such that for all $\epsilon > 0$, there exists an integer n and a randomized protocol Π_{KA} with communication C that with probability $1 - \epsilon$, allows Alice (knowing X^n) and Bob (knowing Y^n) to compute Q_X and Q_Y, respectively, satisfying $\Pr\{Q_X = Q_Y = Q\} \geq 1 - \epsilon$, $H(Q) = \log|Q| \geq n(R - \epsilon)$, $I(Q;CZ^n) < \epsilon$.*

Analogously, there exists an inverse protocol Π_{form}, and a dual measure, the asymptotic minimal *SK cost of formation* of the triple $(X, Y, Z) \sim p_{XYZ}$ [3–6]. While the distributed channel synthesis problem [9] (setup in Fig. 1(b)) explores the role of CR and one-way communication in the formation of bipartite correlations p_{XY} shared between honest Alice and Bob, the setup in Fig. 1(e) explores the role of *secret CR* (i.e., SK) and public communication in the distributed simulation of tripartite correlations p_{XYZ}, now additionally shared with an adversary Eve [3–6]. To start with, Alice and Bob share a SK in the form of R perfectly correlated bits, i.e., Alice has Q_X and Bob, Q_Y such that $Q_X = Q_Y = Q$ and $H(Q) = R$. The goal is to approximately simulate correlated sequence triples of the form (X^n, Y^n, Z^n), upto a local degrading of Z^n. Both parties have independent access to sources of private randomness. The protocol proceeds in rounds and at the end of the communication phase, Alice and Bob output $\hat{X}^n$ and $\hat{Y}^n$, respectively, as deterministic functions of their views, which comprises of the shared SK Q, all the private coins flipped so far, and the entire public communication (C). Discounting the private randomness by allowing for stochastic mappings, Π_{form} can be specified by the joint distribution $p_{\hat{X}^n\hat{Y}^nCQ} = p_{\hat{X}^n|CQ,\hat{Y}^n|CQ}p_{CQ}$. The resulting simulation is "good" from Alice and Bob's point of view, if they end up correctly generating the marginal $p_{X^nY^n}$. However, Eve (Z^n) might still have some information about X^nY^n. This is formalized by requiring that Eve's optimal channel $p_{\bar{Z}|Z^n}$ is only able to simulate the public communication (C) used by Alice and Bob to generate $(\hat{X}^n, \hat{Y}^n)$. The following definition makes this precise [3].

Definition 2. *The SK cost of formation, $SK_c(X;Y|Z)$ is the infimum of all numbers $R \geq 0$ such that for all $\epsilon > 0$, there exists an integer n and a randomized protocol Π_{form} with communication C that with probability $1 - \epsilon$, allows Alice and Bob, knowing a common random $\lfloor nR \rfloor$-bit string Q, to compute $\hat{X}^n$ and $\hat{Y}^n$, respectively, such that $\Pr\{(\hat{X}^n, \hat{Y}^n, C) = (X^n, Y^n, \bar{Z})\} \geq 1 - \epsilon$ holds for some correlated sequence triple (X^n, Y^n, Z^n) that has generic component variables $(X, Y, Z) \sim p_{XYZ}$ and some channel $p_{\bar{Z}|Z^n}$.*

p_{XYZ} contains secret correlations iff it cannot be generated by LOPC, i.e., $SK_c(X;Y|Z) > 0$ [17]. Both the SK cost of formation and the SK rate are measures of the secrecy content of p_{XYZ} and admit a clear operational interpretation: $SK_c(X;Y|Z)$ quantifies the *minimum* amount of SK bits required to (approximately) *simulate* p_{XYZ}, whereas $S(X;Y||Z)$ quantifies the *maximum* amount of SK bits that one can *extract* from p_{XYZ}.

Winter used resolvability-based arguments [4] to arrive at the full secret correlation vs. public communication trade-off for the inverse problem and defined the SK cost of formation with unlimited public communication as

$$SK_c(X;Y|Z) = \min_{\substack{Q:X-Q\bar{Z}-Y \\ \bar{Z}:XY-Z-\bar{Z}}} I(XY;Q|\bar{Z}) \tag{7}$$

where the minimum is taken over all RVs Q and $\bar{Z}$. Cardinalities of the corresponding alphabets are bounded as $|\mathcal{Q}| \leq |\mathcal{X}||\mathcal{Y}|$, and $|\bar{\mathcal{Z}}| \leq |\mathcal{Z}|$ respectively. $SK_c(X;Y|Z)$ is bounded from below by the *intrinsic information* [3], that intuitively speaking, measures the correlation shared between Alice and Bob that Eve cannot access or destroy [2].

$$I(X;Y \downarrow Z) = \min_{\bar{Z}:XY-Z-\bar{Z}} I(X;Y|\bar{Z}) \tag{8}$$

where the cardinality of the alphabet $\bar{\mathcal{Z}}$ of RV $\bar{Z}$ is bounded as $|\bar{\mathcal{Z}}| \leq |\mathcal{Z}|$ [13]. Both $I(X;Y \downarrow Z)$ and $SK_c(X;Y|Z)$ are known to be *lockable* [3,4], i.e., can fall sharply by an arbitrary large amount on giving away a single bit to Eve.

3 Main Contributions

3.1 Wyner's Conditional CI and the SK Cost of Formation

$C_W(X;Y)$ can be interpreted as the SK cost of creating a product distribution with Eve. Now consider Eve's optimal channel $p_{\bar{Z}|Z}$. To create a (public) correlation, Alice randomly samples $\bar{Z}$ and publicly announces the value of $\bar{Z}$ over a symmetric broadcast channel to Bob and Eve. Then the SK cost of creating the product distribution $p_{XY|\bar{Z}}$ is $C_W(X;Y|\bar{Z})$. In this section, we introduce the concept of protocol monotones [6,14–16] for axiomatizing the general properties of upper bounds on the SK rate and show that $C_W(X;Y|\bar{Z})$ qualifies as such an upper bound and is a natural candidate for quantifying the SK cost of formation.

When distant parties wish to establish a SK by manipulating some set of private and public resources, it is natural to restrict attention to LOPC operations. Since the "resourcefulness" or "secrecy content" of the state is a non-local property that cannot increase under LOPC, this set of transformations is deemed as a *free* resource. Mathematically, resources can be quantified by *monotones*, real-valued functions of joint distributions that cannot increase under LOPC. LOPC monotones were first introduced in [16] as classical counterparts of entanglement or LOCC (local operations and classical communication) monotones to study the rate of resource conversion under LOPC. A resource cannot increase under LOPC operations by Alice and Bob. Since Eve, in her role as a malicious adversary is always assumed to operate optimally against Alice and Bob, the same resource cannot decrease under her LOPC operations [6,16]. We define a monotone as follows.

Definition 3. *For all jointly distributed RVs (X, Y, Z), let $\mathcal{M}(X;Y|Z)$ be a real-valued function of p_{XYZ}. Then $\mathcal{M}$ is a monotone if the following hold:*

(1) Monotonicity under local operations (LO) by Alice and Bob: *Suppose Alice modifies X to $\bar{X}$ by sending X over a channel, characterized by $p_{\bar{X}|X}$. Then $\mathcal{M}$ can only decrease, i.e., for all jointly distributed RVs $(X, Y, Z, \bar{X})$ with $\bar{X} : YZ - X - \bar{X}$, $\mathcal{M}(\bar{X};Y|Z) \leq \mathcal{M}(X;Y|Z)$, and likewise for Bob.*

(2) Monotonicity under public communication (PC) by Alice and Bob: *Suppose Alice publicly announces the value of $\widetilde{X}$. Then $\mathcal{M}$ can only decrease, i.e., for all jointly distributed RVs $(X, Y, Z, \widetilde{X})$ with $H(\widetilde{X}|X) = 0$, $\mathcal{M}(X;Y\widetilde{X}|Z\widetilde{X}) \leq \mathcal{M}(X;Y|Z)$, and likewise for Bob.*

(3) Monotonicity under local operations (LO) by Eve: *Suppose Eve modifies Z to $\bar{Z}$ by sending Z over a channel, characterized by $p_{\bar{Z}|Z}$. Then $\mathcal{M}$ can only increase, i.e., for all jointly distributed RVs $(X, Y, Z, \bar{Z})$ with $\bar{Z} : XY - Z - \bar{Z}$, $\mathcal{M}(X;Y|\bar{Z}) \geq \mathcal{M}(X;Y|Z)$.*

(4) Monotonicity under public communication (PC) by Eve: *Suppose Eve publicly announces the value of $\widetilde{Z}$. Then $\mathcal{M}$ can only increase, i.e., for all jointly distributed RVs $(X, Y, Z, \widetilde{Z})$ with $H(\widetilde{Z}|Z) = 0,$, $\mathcal{M}(\widetilde{Z}X; \widetilde{Z}Y|Z) \geq \mathcal{M}(X;Y|Z)$.*

(5) Additivity and Continuity: $\mathcal{M}$ *is additive on tensor products and is a semi-positive, continuous function of p_{XYZ}. A stronger notion of asymptotic continuity requires that for two pmfs p_{XYZ}, q_{XYZ}, if* $\mathsf{TV}(p_{XYZ}, q_{XYZ}) = \epsilon$, *then* $|\mathcal{M}(p_{XYZ}) - \mathcal{M}(q_{XYZ})| \leq \epsilon \log d + \delta(\epsilon)$, *where d is some constant that depends on $|\mathcal{X}|$, $|\mathcal{Y}|$ and $|\mathcal{Z}|$ and $\delta(\epsilon)$ is any function that depends only on ϵ with $\delta(0) = 0$.*

If $\mathcal{M}$ satisfies the conditions in Definition 3, then $\mathcal{M}$ is an upper bound on the SK rate [14]. Upper bounds on the rate at which instances of a target primitive can be realized per invocation of the source primitive can be obtained by comparing the value of the monotone on the source and target states. Given the class of LOPC operations, suppose that the parties are able to convert n copies of p_{XYZ} into some realization of a distribution q'_{XYZ} which is close to m independent realizations of the target distribution q_{XYZ}, i.e., $p^{\otimes n} \overset{LOPC}{\to} q' \simeq q^{\otimes m}$. Then by virtue of Property (5) in Definition 3, we have, $\mathcal{M}(p^{\otimes n}) = n\mathcal{M}(p) \geq \mathcal{M}(q') \simeq m\mathcal{M}(q)$, so that the optimal rate $R(p \to q)$ at which transformations $p^{\otimes n} \overset{LOPC}{\to} q^{\otimes m}$ are possible is upper bounded as $\frac{m}{n} \leq \frac{\mathcal{M}(p)}{\mathcal{M}(q)}$ [16]. Thus if $p^s_{SS\Delta}$ denotes the distribution of a perfect secret bit with $p^s_{SS\Delta}(0, 0, \delta) = p^s_{SS\Delta}(1, 1, \delta) = \frac{1}{2}$, then for any pmf q_{XYZ}, $S(X; Y || Z) = R(q \to p^s) \leq \frac{I(X;Y\downarrow Z)}{I(S;S\downarrow\Delta)} = I(X; Y \downarrow Z)$, since $I(S; S \downarrow \Delta) = 1$, and $I(X; Y \downarrow Z)$ is a monotone [3]. Likewise $R(p^s \to q) \leq \frac{I(S;S\downarrow\Delta)}{I(X;Y\downarrow Z)} = \frac{1}{I(X;Y\downarrow Z)}$. Hence $SK_c(X; Y|Z) = \frac{1}{R(p^s \to q)} \geq I(X; Y \downarrow Z)$ [3].

$C_W(X; Y|Z)$ violates monotonicity under LO by Eve[1] and thus fails to achieve an upper bound on the SK rate. To preserve monotonicity under LO by Eve, an additional minimization is required over all stochastic maps $p_{\bar{Z}|Z}$ that can be chosen by Eve for locally processing her observations. This implies a minimization over all Markov chains $XY - Z - \bar{Z}$ which is tantamount to the simulation approximation of $(X^n Y^n Z^n)$ upto a local degrading in Z^n in Definition 2 of the SK cost of formation. This yields a new quantity called *Wyner's intrinsic conditional CI* that satisfies monotonicity under Eve's LOPC operations.

$$C_W(X; Y \downarrow Z) = \min_{\bar{Z}: XY - Z - \bar{Z}} C_W(X; Y|\bar{Z}) = \min_{\substack{Q: X - Q\bar{Z} - Y \\ \bar{Z}: XY - Z - \bar{Z}}} I(XY; Q|\bar{Z}) \quad (9)$$

The cardinality of the alphabet $\bar{\mathcal{Z}}$ of $\bar{Z}$ is bounded as $|\bar{\mathcal{Z}}| \leq |\mathcal{Z}|$. This can be shown following similar arguments as in [13] using Carathéodory's theorem. From (6), we have $|\mathcal{Q}| \leq |\mathcal{X}||\mathcal{Y}|$. We now show that $C_W(X; Y \downarrow Z)$ is indeed a monotone and hence a valid upper bound on the SK rate.

Lemma 2. $C_W(X; Y \downarrow Z)$ *is a monotone.*

Proof. Let $p_{\bar{Z}|Z}$ be the minimizer in $C_W(X; Y \downarrow Z)$. Then it suffices to show that $C_W(X; Y|\bar{Z})$ satisfies monotonicity under Alice and Bob's LOPC operations.

---

[1] Given jointly distributed RVs $(X, Y, Z, \bar{Z})$ with $\bar{Z} : XY - Z - \bar{Z}$, it does not hold in general that $C_W(X; Y|\bar{Z}) \geq C_W(X; Y|Z)$.

We shall require the following monotonicity inequalities: (a) $H(Z|f(Y)) \geq H(Z|Y)$, (b) $I(X;Y|f(X)Z) \leq I(X;Y|Z)$. For all jointly distributed RVs $(XY\bar{Z}Q\bar{X})$ such that $Y\bar{Z} - X - \bar{X}$ and $\bar{X} - Q\bar{Z} - Y$, monotonicity under LO by Alice holds since,

$$I(\bar{X}Y;Q|\bar{Z}) = H(Q|\bar{Z}) - H(Q|\bar{X}Y\bar{Z}) \overset{(a)}{\leq} H(Q|\bar{Z}) - H(Q|XY\bar{Z}) = I(XY;Q|\bar{Z}),$$

and likewise for Bob. Similarly, for all jointly distributed RVs $(XY\bar{Z}Q\tilde{X})$ such that $H(\tilde{X}|X) = 0$, monotonicity under PC by Alice holds since,

$$I(XY\tilde{X};Q\tilde{X}|\bar{Z}\tilde{X}) = I(XY;Q|\bar{Z}\tilde{X}) \overset{(b)}{\leq} I(XY;Q|\bar{Z}),$$

and likewise for Bob.

Additivity and continuity are valuable properties if the monotone is to provide information on the rate of transformations $p^{\otimes n} \overset{LOPC}{\to} q^{\otimes m}$ in the asymptotic limit $n, m \to \infty$. It is easy to show that for independent triples $(X_1 Y_1 \bar{Z}_1)$ and $(X_2 Y_2 \bar{Z}_2)$, $C_W(X_1 X_2; Y_1 Y_2|\bar{Z}_1 \bar{Z}_2) = C_W(X_1; Y_1|\bar{Z}_1) + C_W(X_2; Y_2|\bar{Z}_2)$. We do not target the stronger notion of asymptotic continuity since it is already known that the SK cost fails this property and admits locking [4].   □

Theorem 3 gives the main result of this section.

Theorem 3. *With unlimited public communication,* $SK_c(X;Y|Z) = C_W(X;Y \downarrow Z)$. *Furthermore, if $p_{\bar{Z}|Z}$ is the optimal stochastic map achieving the minimum in the characterization of $C_W(X;Y \downarrow Z)$, then $C_W(X;Y \downarrow Z) = I(X;Y \downarrow Z)$ iff there exists a pmf $p_{Q'|XYZ\bar{Z}}$ s.t. $H(Q'|X\bar{Z}) = H(Q'|Y\bar{Z}) = 0$ and $X - \bar{Z}Q' - Y$.*

Proof. From (7), (9) and Lemma 2, the first equality is obvious. For the second equality, the "only if" part is trivial. For the "if" part, first note that

$$C_W(X;Y \downarrow Z) = \min_{\substack{Q:X-Q\bar{Z}-Y \\ \bar{Z}:XY-Z-\bar{Z}}} I(XY;Q|\bar{Z}) = \min_{\substack{Q:X-Q\bar{Z}-Y \\ \bar{Z}:XY-Z-\bar{Z}}} (I(Y;Q|X\bar{Z}) + I(X;Q|\bar{Z}))$$

$$\overset{(a)}{=} \min_{\substack{Q:X-Q\bar{Z}-Y \\ \bar{Z}:XY-Z-\bar{Z}}} (I(X;Y|\bar{Z}) + I(Y;Q|X\bar{Z}) + I(X;Q|Y\bar{Z})),$$

where (a) follows from writing $I(X;Q|\bar{Z})$ as $I(X;Y|\bar{Z}) + I(X;Q|Y\bar{Z}) - I(X;Y|Q\bar{Z})$, and noting that $I(X;Y|Q\bar{Z}) = 0$. Then given jointly distributed RVs $(XYZ\bar{Z}Q)$ achieving the minimum in (9), if $I(Y;Q|X\bar{Z}) = I(X;Q|Y\bar{Z}) = 0$, then by Lemma 1, there exists a pmf $p_{Q'|XYZZ}$ such that $H(Q'|X\bar{Z}) = H(Q'|Y\bar{Z}) = 0$, $XY - Q'\bar{Z} - Q$ and $I(XY;Q|\bar{Z}) \leq H(Q'|\bar{Z})$, with equality iff $H(Q'|Q\bar{Z}) = 0$. Finally note that $H(Q'|\bar{Z}) \leq I(X;Y|\bar{Z})$ with equality iff $X - \bar{Z}Q' - Y$.   □

3.2   Gács and Körner (GK) Conditional CI and the SK Rate

For the general source model (with arbitrary public discussion), calculation of the exact SK rate remains an open problem [1–3,15]. Without any communication, the problem is still more complicated in that even the determination of probability distributions that allow for the distillation of SK remains an unsolved problem. GK showed that in a non-communicative model, common codes of a pair of discrete, memoryless correlated sources cannot exploit any correlation beyond a certain deterministic interdependence of the sources. Remarkably, they showed that the asymptotic case is no better than the zero error case and that $C_{GK}(X;Y)$ depends only on the zero pattern of the underlying joint distribution p_{XY}. Intuitively, $C_{GK}(X;Y|Z)$ captures the most "explicit" form of secret CI, i.e., the maximum amount of SK that can be extracted without any communication. In this section, we construct simple distributions for which $C_{GK}(X;Y|Z)$ achieves a tight bound on the SK rate. We conjecture that $C_{GK}(X;Y|Z)$ quantifies the achievable SK rate for non-communicative key agreement models. We also comment on the lossless interconvertibility of secret correlations.

Example 1. Consider the distribution p^1_{XYZ} with $\mathcal{X} = \mathcal{Y} = \mathcal{Z} = \{0, 1, 2, 3\}$. We write $p^1_{XYZ}(a, b, c) = (abc)$. Given $(000) = (011) = (101) = (110) = \frac{1}{8}$, and $(222) = (333) = \frac{1}{4}$. Graphically, p^1_{XYZ} is shown in the following table (with Z's value given in parentheses): $p^1_{XYZ} = \frac{1}{8} \begin{pmatrix} 1(0) & 1(1) & . & . \\ 1(1) & 1(0) & . & . \\ . & . & 2(2) & . \\ . & . & . & 2(3) \end{pmatrix}$. Alice, Bob and Eve each have access to this table and many independent copies of X, Y and Z, respectively. For each independent random experiment generating $(X, Y, Z) \sim p^1_{XYZ}$, Eve can infer Alice and Bob's values with complete certainty, when she receives either 2 or 3. When she receives either 0 or 1, she can only infer that Alice's and Bob's symbols are restricted to the upper left quadrant (i.e., the set $\{0, 1\}$), but then in this range, X and Y are uniformly distributed. Clearly, Alice and Bob can share no secret. Now, consider the distributions

$$p^2_{XYZ} = \frac{1}{8} \begin{pmatrix} 1(0) & 1(1) & . & . \\ 1(1) & 1(0) & . & . \\ . & . & 2(2) & . \\ . & . & . & 2(2) \end{pmatrix}, \text{ and } p^3_{XYZ} = \frac{1}{8} \begin{pmatrix} 1(0) & 1(1) & . & . \\ 1(1) & 1(0) & . & . \\ . & . & 2(0) & . \\ . & . & . & 2(1) \end{pmatrix}, \text{ where Eve's}$$

symbol set is successively depleted to $\mathcal{Z} = \{0, 1, 2\}$ and $\mathcal{Z} = \{0, 1\}$, respectively. In the latter case, Alice and Bob can realize one perfect SK bit, since Eve can no longer infer anything about their quadrant information (upper left or lower right). This intuition is borne out by $C_{GK}(X;Y|Z)$, which evaluates to 0, 0.5 and 1, respectively, for p^1, p^2 and p^3. p^3 is *resolvable* but not *conditionally resolvable*. A distribution p^4 that is *conditionally resolvable* but not *resolvable* is the following: $(000) = (100) = (010) = (110) = \frac{1}{18}$, $(001) = (101) = (011) = (111) = \frac{1}{21}$, $(032) = (042) = \frac{1}{15}$, $(252) = \frac{1}{5}$, $(220) = \frac{1}{9}$, $(221) = \frac{1}{7}$. Finally, $C_{GK}(X;Y|Z) = 1$ for the following more general distribution p^5 that is neither *resolvable* nor *conditionally resolvable*: $(000) = (011) = (020) = (101) = \frac{1}{10}$, $(110) = (121) = \frac{1}{20}$, $(230) = (331) = \frac{1}{4}$, where using arguments similar to the ones for p^3, Alice and Bob can be shown to achieve one perfect SK bit.

Example 2. Consider the following sequence of distributions:

$$(p_{XYZ})_n(x,y,z) = \begin{cases} \frac{1}{2n^2}, & \text{if } x,y \in \{0,\ldots,n-1\},\ z = x+y \ (\mathrm{mod}\, n), \\ \frac{1}{2n}, & \text{if } x \in \{n,\ldots,2n-1\},\ y = x,\ z = x \ (\mathrm{mod}\, n). \end{cases}$$

$$(q_{XYZ})_n(x,y,z) = \begin{cases} \frac{1}{\log n}(p_{XYZ})_n, & \text{if } x \neq \Delta,\ y \neq \Delta,\ z \neq \Delta, \\ 1 - \frac{1}{\log n}, & \text{if } x = y = z = \Delta, \end{cases}$$

where $(q_{XYZ})_n$ is derived from $(p_{XYZ})_n$ by extending the symbol sets $(\mathcal{X},\mathcal{Y},\mathcal{Z})$ to include an extra symbol Δ. Renner and Wolf [3] showed that $(q_{XYZ})_n$ has *asymptotic bound information*, i.e., $(q_{XYZ})_n$ is asymptotically non-distillable $(S(X_{(n)};Y_{(n)}\|Z_{(n)}) = \frac{1}{\log n} \to 0$, as $n \to \infty)$, and yet cannot be created by LOPC, since $SK_c(X_{(n)};Y_{(n)}|Z_{(n)}) \geq I(X_{(n)};Y_{(n)} \downarrow Z_{(n)}) = \frac{1}{\log n}(1 + \frac{1}{2}\log n) > \frac{1}{2}$ [3]. Omitting the index n, for a given Z, the maximal common RV of the pair (X,Y) has the pmf $p_{Q_*}(0) = \frac{1}{2\log n}$, $p_{Q_*}(1) = 1 - \frac{1}{\log n}$, $p_{Q_*}(i) = \frac{1}{2n\log n}$, $i = 2,\ldots,n+1$, so that $C_{GK}(X;Y|Z) = H(Q_*|Z) = \frac{1}{\log n}$, thus achieving the SK rate.

In both the examples above, no assumptions have been made on the nature of the communication protocol (or its lack thereof) between Alice and Bob. For a non-communicative SK agreement model, i.e. a restricted key agreement model where no communication is allowed between Alice and Bob, let $S_{0-comm}(X;Y\|Z)$ denote the maximum attainable rate at which a SK can be extracted by Alice (knowing X^n) and Bob (knowing Y^n) about which Eve (knowing Z^n) has virtually no information. As usual, (X^n, Y^n, Z^n) are independent repeated realizations of the random experiment p_{XYZ}.

Conjecture 4. *For non-communicative SK agreement models,* $S_{0-comm}(X; Y\|Z) = C_{GK}(X;Y|Z)$. *Furthermore, if* p_{XYZ} *is conditionally resolvable, then*

$$S_{0-comm}(X;Y\|Z) = C_{GK}(X;Y|Z) = I(X;Y|Z).$$

4   Concluding Remarks

In summary, we have presented two results. The first result demonstrates the power of the framework of resource monotones for axiomatizing the general properties of upper bounds on the SK rate. We showed that $C_W(X;Y|Z)$ violates monotonicity under LO by Eve, which can be used to bootstrap the definition of the SK cost of simulating the triple (XYZ) up to a local degrading of Z. In the past, a similar approach has been put to direct practical use for deriving strong bounds on the SK rate [15]. Given many independent copies of a source distribution (q_{XYZ}) and a target distribution of a perfect secret bit $(p_{SS\Delta}^s)$, *reversible* conversion of q_{XYZ} and $p_{SS\Delta}^s$ is possible iff $R(q \to p^s)R(p^s \to q) = 1$, i.e., iff $S(X;Y\|Z) = I(X;Y \downarrow Z)$ and $I(X;Y \downarrow Z) = SK_c(X;Y|Z)$. In Theorem 3, we have given necessary and sufficient conditions for achieving the second equality.

More generally, monotones can be used to derive upper bounds on the asymptotic rate of conversion of q_{XYZ} to any other distribution $q_{X'Y'Z'}$ (e.g., one which is relatively less favorable to Eve). Thus, resource theories hold promise in capturing a general calculi of secret correlations.

In the second part, we constructed simple distributions for which the conditional Gács and Körner CI achieves a tight bound on the SK rate. The sequence of distributions $(q_{XYZ})_n$ in Example 2 was originally constructed by Renner and Wolf [3] to show that there exists sequences of distributions with asymptotic bound information, i.e., asymptotically non-distillable correlations with positive SK cost. This is the best that has been shown so far for the bipartite case. For more than two parties, the possibility of creating different bipartitions across the honest parties immensely simplifies the problem and, indeed, multipartite bound information has been shown to exist [17]. Constructing distributions that can show the existence of bipartite bound information remains an open problem and a scope for future work. Another problem of independent interest is to consider single shot versions of the SK cost of formation and intrinsic information.

Acknowledgments. PKB wishes to thank Amin Gohari for valuable comments and Paul Cuff for short useful discussions over email. This work is based in part on PKB's master's thesis [19] and was supported in part by the AVLSI Consortium, IIT Kharagpur.

References

1. Maurer, U.M.: Secret key agreement by public discussion from common information. IEEE Trans. Inf. Theor. **39**(3), 33–742 (1993)
2. Maurer, U.M., Wolf, S.: Unconditionally secure key agreement and the intrinsic conditional information. IEEE Trans. Inf. Theor. **45**(2), 499–514 (1999)
3. Renner, R., Wolf, S.: New bounds in secret-key agreement: the gap between formation and secrecy extraction. In: Biham, E. (ed.) Advances in Cryptology-EUROCRYPT 2003. LNCS, vol. 2656, pp. 562–577. Springer, Heidelberg (2003)
4. Winter, A.: Secret, public and quantum correlation cost of triples of random variables. In: Proceedings of the IEEE International Symposium on Information Theory (ISIT 2005), pp. 2270–2274 (2005)
5. Chitambar, E., Hsieh, M.H., Winter, A.: The private and public correlation cost of three random variables with collaboration (2014). arXiv preprint arXiv:1411.0729
6. Horodecki, K., Horodecki, M., Horodecki, P., Oppenheim, J.: Information theories with adversaries, intrinsic information, and entanglement. Found. Phys. **35**(12), 2027–2040 (2005)
7. Gács, P., Körner, J.: Common information is far less than mutual information. Prob. Control Inf. Theor. **2**(2), 149–162 (1973)
8. Wyner, A.D.: The common information of two dependent random variables. IEEE Trans. Inf. Theor. **21**(2), 163–179 (1975)
9. Cuff, P.: Distributed channel synthesis. IEEE Trans. Inf. Theor. **59**(11), 7071–7096 (2013)
10. Bennett, C.H., Devetak, I., Harrow, A.W., Shor, P.W., Winter, A.: The quantum reverse Shannon theorem and resource tradeoffs for simulating quantum channels. IEEE Trans. Inf. Theor. **60**(5), 2926–2959 (2014)

11. Csiszár, I., Körner, J.: Information theory: coding theorems for discrete memoryless systems. Cambridge University Press, Cambridge (2011)
12. Ahlswede, R., Körner, J.: On common information and related characteristics of correlated information sources. Preprint. Presented at the 7th Prague Conference on Information Theory (1974)
13. Christandl, M., Renner, R., Wolf, S.: A property of the intrinsic mutual information. In: Proceedings of the IEEE International Symposium on Information theory (ISIT 2003), pp. 258–258 (2003)
14. Christandl, M., Ekert, A., Horodecki, M., Horodecki, P., Oppenheim, J., Renner, R.S.: Unifying classical and quantum key distillation. In: Vadhan, S.P. (ed.) TCC 2007. LNCS, vol. 4392, pp. 456–478. Springer, Heidelberg (2007)
15. Gohari, A.A., Anantharam, V.: Information-theoretic key agreement of multiple terminals-Part I. IEEE Trans. Inf. Theor. **56**(8), 3973–3996 (2010)
16. Cerf, N.J., Massar, S., Schneider, S.: Multipartite classical and quantum secrecy monotones. Phys. Rev. A **66**(4), 042309 (2002)
17. Masanes, L., Acin, A.: Multipartite secret correlations and bound information. IEEE Trans. Inf. Theor. **52**(10), 4686–4694 (2006)
18. Liu, R., Trappe, W. (eds.): Securing Wireless Communications at the Physical Layer. Springer, New York (2010)
19. Banerjee, P.K.: Synergy, redundancy, and secret common randomness: Some intriguing links. M.S. thesis, Dept. E & ECE, IIT Kharagpur, India (2014)

Exploiting Domination in Attack Graph for Enterprise Network Hardening

Ghanshyam S. Bopche[1,2]([⊠]) and Babu M. Mehtre[1]

[1] Center for Information Assurance and Management (CIAM),
Institute for Development and Research in Banking Technology (IDRBT),
Castle Hills, Road No.1, Masab Tank, Hyderabad 500 057, India
{ghanshyambopche.mca,mehtre}@gmail.com
[2] School of Computer and Information Sciences (SCIS),
University of Hyderabad, Gachibowli, Hyderabad 500 046, India

Abstract. Attack graph proved to be a tool of great value to an administrator while analyzing security vulnerabilities in a networked environment. It shows all possible attack scenarios in an enterprise network. Even though attack graphs are generated efficiently, the size and complexity of the graphs prevent an administrator from fully understanding the information portrayed. While an administrator will quickly perceive the possible attack scenario, it is typically tough to know what vulnerabilities are vital to the success of an adversary. An administrator has to identify such vulnerabilities and associated/enabling preconditions, which really matters in preventing an adversary from successfully compromising the enterprise network. Extraction of such meaningful information aid administrator in efficiently allocating scarce security resources. In this paper, we have applied a well known concept of domination in directed graphs to the exploit-dependency attack graph generated for a synthetic network. The *minimal dominating set (MDS)* computed over the generated attack graph gives us the set of initial preconditions that covers all the exploits in the attack graph. We model the problem of computing *MDS* as a *set cover problem (SCP)*. We have presented a small case study to demonstrate the effectiveness and relevancy of the proposed approach. Initial results show that our *minimal dominating set-based approach* is capable of finding the sets with minimal number of initial conditions that need to be disabled for improved network security.

Keywords: Attack graph · Network security and protection · Security metric · Graph domination

1 Introduction

As computer networks continues to grow, there is an urgent need for automating the process of detecting network vulnerability to cyber attacks. While assessing the security of computer networks, it is hardly enough to look at the isolated vulnerabilities present in the system. Today's cyber attack combines multiple

© Springer International Publishing Switzerland 2015
J.H. Abawajy et al. (Eds): SSCC 2015, CCIS 536, pp. 342–353, 2015.
DOI: 10.1007/978-3-319-22915-7_32

isolated vulnerabilities based on their cause-consequence relationship in order to get incremental access to network resources. Even most diligent administrators may miss such security holes in an enterprise network. In order to assess the security posture of an enterprise network, administrator must consider the effect of interaction between isolated vulnerabilities. To assist administrator in finding such security holes, *attack graphs* [1–7] have been proposed.

Attack graph a well known formal model used in the context of network attacks. It gives a bird's-eye view of all plausible attack scenarios that can result in a severe security breaches in an enterprise network. Each attack scenario is a sequence of steps taken by an adversary that typically end up in an appropriate goal state. An adversarial goal may be an access to a particular database/host or disruption of mission-critical services running over the networked systems. Even though recent advances allow us to generate an attack graph efficiently, the size and complexity of the graphs generally prevent an administrator from fully understanding the information portrayed. Administrator can easily get over- whelmed by such a big volume of information represented in an attack graph. While administrator will quickly understand possible attack scenario, it is essen- tially hard to know what sort of privileges and which vulnerabilities are vital to the success of an adversary. Administrator can not patch all the vulnerabilities since it costs scarce human and financial resources. Again, not every vulnera- bility is equally important to an adversary. Most of the times, vulnerabilities are after-effects of successful exploitation of other vulnerabilit(y)ies and hence it is trivial to patch them. From the defender's standpoint, administrator has to identify the vulnerabilities and associated preconditions, which really matters in securing enterprise networks. Extracting such information is vital for the optimal placement of the security resources and hence for efficient network hardening.

There is a plethora of research work available on attack graphs and network hardening in the literature. The graph-assisted metrics proposed in literature, for e.g. shortest path metric [1], the number of paths metric [8], mean of path lengths [9], and others [10,11] can be used to identify attack scenarios of special interest. Such metrics measure different aspect of network security, computed by different mathematical operations viz. mean, standard deviation (SD), median, and mode etc. Such severity values do not have great significance and hence hardly support decision making. Network hardening solutions in terms of minimal critical set of exploits is proposed by [2,3,12]. The downside of the above approaches is that they fail to consider the complex relationships among exploits and network configuration elements. Noel et. al. [4] tried to harden the network at the level of initial conditions. Several other approaches [13–17] are also proposed to harden the network by disabling initial conditions. The proposed solutions suffers from one or more drawback for e.g. (1) exponential solution space, (2) unable to consider the cost factor while selecting the initial conditions, and (3) unable to consider available vulnerability patches as one of the options during network hardening. The problem of identifying the minimal number of initial conditions that cover all the exploits in an attack graph motivates our work. The added advantage of identifying such initial conditions is that these conditions can be disabled independently. We have applied a well known concept of domination in directed graphs to the exploit-dependency attack graph for the computation of minimum dominating set (MDS) of initial conditions.

The method we proposed for computing network hardening solutions in terms of the minimum number of initial conditions is inspired from the concept of domination in directed bipartite graphs. In such graphs, the subset of vertices is computed that in turn both *independent* and *dominating* in nature. Such vertex set acts as *solution* of the graph and can be used in real time enterprise networks to plant scarce security resources (for e.g. IDPS, Firewall, etc.) in order to monitor and secure all other network entities. The same analogy we have used for network hardening. Our goal is to compute the minimal number of initial conditions that covers all the exploits in an attack graph. By disabling these initial conditions, an administrator can make the network more secure.

The rest of the paper is organized as follows. Section 2 first reviews the attack graph model and establish a basis for using a well known domination theory for network hardening. Basic definitions concerning domination in directed graphs are also presented in Sect. 2. In Sect. 3 we will discuss the heuristics of computing the minimal dominating set for the attack graph. A case study is presented in Sect. 4 to confirm/validate the usefulness of our approach. Section 5 closes with conclusions and suggestions for future work.

2   Preliminaries

"An attack graph of the enterprise network is a directed graph representing prior knowledge about vulnerabilities, their dependencies, and network connectivity" [18]. In this paper, we have used an *exploit-dependency* representation of an attack graph that is based on the concept of monotonicity (having polynomial time complexity). Exploits and security conditions are the kind of nodes in the exploit-dependency graph. An exploit represents adversarial action on the network host in order to take advantage of the vulnerability. Security conditions represent properties of system/network vital for vulnerability exploitation. Existence of a host vulnerabilit(y)ies, network reachability, attacker privilege-level and trust relationship between communicating hosts are the kind of security conditions required for successful exploitation of vulnerability on a remote host.

Exploits and security conditions are connected by directed edges. No two exploits or two security conditions are directly connected. Therefore, an attack graph is a *directed bipartite graph* where the set of vertices is divided into two disjoint sets, namely *Exploits* and *Conditions* such that no edge has both endpoints in the same set. Directed edge from security condition to an exploit represent the *require relation* and it states that for successful execution of an exploit all the security conditions need to be satisfied. A directed edge from an exploit to the security condition indicates the *imply relation* [13]. Successful execution of an exploit leads to the generation of few more security conditions called *postconditions*. Such postconditions may act as a precondition for other exploits. With the perception of an attack graph discussed above, Wang et. al. [13] formally defined an attack graph as exploit-dependency graph as follows:

Definition 1 (Attack Graph). *"Given a set of exploits e, a set of conditions c, a require relation $R_r \subseteq (c \times e)$, and an imply relation $R_i \subseteq (e \times c)$, an attack graph G is the directed graph $G(e \cup c, R_r \cup R_i)$, where $(e \cup c)$ is the vertex set and $(R_r \cup R_i)$ is the edge set" [13].*

Attack graph consists of two kinds of security conditions. The first kind of them appears in an attack graph as an *exploit preconditions only* and it is possible only when such conditions are true/present in the network from the beginning and these conditions are not postconditions of any of the exploit. One can call them *initial conditions* and must consider for network hardening because such conditions represent network misconfiguration or vulnerabilities present across the network. The second kind of security conditions appears as a both exploit preconditions and postconditions. Such security conditions are not true/present in the network from the beginning, but are generated as a post-effect of successful exploitation of one or more vulnerabilities. So, the administrator should not consider such conditions for network hardening because they are not under her control and despite network hardening efforts adversary make them true.

In general, the relationship among initial conditions and exploits is of type *many-to-many* (M:N) and hence one initial condition could control execution of many of the exploits. In other words, one initial condition could be enabling precondition for many of the exploits and its true or false state in the network could control the execution of those exploits. Given the set of initial conditions $S = \{x, y, z\}$, condition x is said to be dominating other initial conditions y and z if and only if x is a required/enabling precondition for all the exploits, where as y and z are preconditions for less number of exploits. As evident from the Definition 1 the *require relationship* should be always conjunctive and hence removal of the dominating initial condition (here x) could stop most of the exploits from executing.

Let $G = (V, E)$ be the directed bipartite attack graph consists of finite set of vertices V and finite set of directed edges E, where $E \subseteq V \times V$. An edge $(u, v) \equiv u \to v$ is said to be directed from u to v, where u is said to be a predecessor of v, and v is successor of u. Throughout the paper, we consider G in the same meaning unless stated otherwise.

Definition 2 (Dominating Set). *In a digraph $G = (V, E)$, the set of vertices $S \subseteq V$ is a dominating set of G if every vertex $v \in (V - S)$ is covered by atleast one vertex in S.*

Definition 3 (Minimal Dominating Set). *A minimal dominating set S_m is a dominating set with no proper subset $S' \subseteq S_m$ as a dominating set [19].*

Definition 4 (Minimum Dominating Set). *A dominating set of minimum cardinality [19] and it is denoted by set S_M.*

So, the central idea of this paper is to compute the minimal dominating set (MDS) for an attack graph G in terms of initial conditions that covers/enables all the exploits in the graph and then disabling those conditions for efficient network hardening. In order to do this, we model the problem of computing *MDS* for a given attack graph G as a classical set cover problem (SCP). As each initial condition in G covers one or more exploits, hence we assume the total number of exploits "m" in G are partitioned into "n" subsets where each subset contains the number of exploits covered by the particular initial condition. So, our goal is to compute *optimal set cover* that covers all the exploits in an attack graph G. Such set cover represents the minimum number of initial conditions that covers all the exploits in G. More precisely, let $\mathcal{E}, |\mathcal{E}| = m$ be the universal set of exploits, and C be the family of subsets (i.e. initial conditions) $C \subseteq 2^{\mathcal{E}}$. A sub collection $X(X \in C)$ covers the universal exploit set $\mathcal{E}$, if $\mathcal{E} = \bigcup_{X \in C} C$.

3 Domination in Attack Graph

An attack graph we have generated contains no loops (i.e. an edge of the form (u, u)) or multiple edges (i.e. more than one copy of an edge (u, v)). For each kind of vertex in an attack graph G, we have *inset* and *outset*. The *indegree* and *outdegree* of those vertex type is as follows:

1. **Initial Conditions:** Let $pre \subset V$ be the finite set of initial conditions in an attack graph G available to an adversary. Let $u \in pre$ be the initial condition. Then $I(u) = \{w : (w, u) \in E\}$ be the inset of an initial condition u. As we all know, $\forall u \in pre, (\nexists w : (w, u) \in E)$ and hence $I(u) = \phi, \forall u \in pre$. Therefore, indegree $id(u) = 0, \forall u \in pre$. The outset of an initial condition be the set $O(u) = \{v : (u, v) \in E\}$. As we know, each initial condition when satisfied successfully leads to an exploitation of one or more vulnerabilities. In other words, each node $u \in pre$ in G covers one or more exploit nodes. Therefore, the outdegree $od(u) \geq 1, \forall u \in pre$. In case of directed graphs, the inset and outset of a vertex u can also be open or closed just like the open neighborhood and closed neighborhood concept of vertex in an undirected graph. Therefore, $id[u] = 1$ and $od[u] \geq 2, \forall u \in pre$.

2. **Exploits:** As evident from the Definition 1, let $e \subset V$ be the finite set of exploits in the attack graph G, where $e = \{e_1, e_2, \ldots, e_m\}$. The inset of an exploit e_i is the set $I(e_i) = \{w : (w, e_i) \in E\}$, where w is the precondition. For the successful execution of an exploit all its required preconditions need to be satisfied conjunctively. Therefore, $I(e_i)$ is never be an empty set and it consists two or more preconditions. In other words, indegree $id(e_i) \geq 2, \forall e_i \in e$. Successful execution of an exploit e_i creates few more conditions disjunctively and hence outdegree $od(e_i) \geq 1, \forall e_i \in e$. The newly created security conditions i.e. postconditions act as a precondition for other exploits. Similarly, $id[e_i] \geq 3$ and $od[e_i] \geq 2, \forall e_i \in e$.

3. **Postcondition:** Let $pst \subset V$ be the finite set of postconditions produced in an attack graph G after the successful execution of $|e|$ exploits. Let $u \in pst$ be the postcondition. Then, $I(u) = \{w : (w, u) \in E\}$ be the inset of a postcondition $u \in pst$. Each successful execution of an exploit results in a generation of one or more postconditions. Further, different exploits when

executed successfully on a target host may generate same postcondition and hence indegree $id(u) \geq 1, \forall u \in pst$. Newly generated postcondition may act as a precondition for other exploits. Therefore, the outdegree $od(u) \geq 1, \forall u \in pst$ except the final target postcondition, since adversary already achieved her goal. Similarly, $id[u] \geq 2$ and $od[u] \geq 2, \forall u \in pst$. Table 1 shows the indegree and outdegree for each type of vertices in an attack graph.

Table 1. Indegree and Outdegree for each vertex type in an attack graph G

Vertex u	$id(u)$	$od(u)$	$id[u]$	$od[u]$
Initial condition	0	≥ 1	1	≥ 2
Exploit	≥ 2	≥ 1	≥ 3	≥ 2
Post-condition	≥ 1	≥ 1	≥ 2	≥ 2

The exploit-dependency attack graph (G) generated for any vulnerable computer network consist of heterogeneous nodes, namely *preconditions, exploits,* and *postconditions* as shown in Fig. 1(a). Unlike domination in directed graphs where the nodes are homogeneous, finding MDS in an attack graph is difficult. Furthermore, computation of the dominating set for any graph is computationally challenging task as there is no known algorithm that runs in polynomial time. In order to reduce the complexity/hardness of the problem, here we have taken conservative approach. The nodes of type exploit and initial condition are the most important nodes in the attack graph, whereas postconditions are the result of successful exploitation of an exploit. As our goal is to compute the MDS of initial conditions that covers all the exploit, we have removed the postconditions from the attack graph. The resultant attack graph (as shown in Fig. 1(b)) contains the nodes of types exploit and initial conditions and edges directing from the initial conditions to the exploits. The resultant attack graph is also a *directed bipartite graph.* The MDS computed over such bipartite graph gives the set of initial conditions that covers all the exploits in an attack graph. As the computed set of initial conditions is both independent and dominant (covers all the exploits in G) and hence it acts as a solution of the attack graph.

The procedure for computing the MDS is given in Algorithm 1 (i.e. $findMDS$). First, all the vertices in the graph G are identified (line 1) and then classified (line 2–10) into vertex categories, namely *initial conditions, exploits, and postconditions* based on the indegree and outdegree criteria defined in Table 1. As we considered initial conditions for network hardening, we computed the number of exploits covered by each initial condition (line 11–13). Exploits covered by each initial condition represents the subset of the exploits present in the attack graph G. Each subset in the collection C (line 14) covers at least one exploit present in the attack graph G. Our objective is to find a sub collection of sets $X \subseteq C$ that covers all

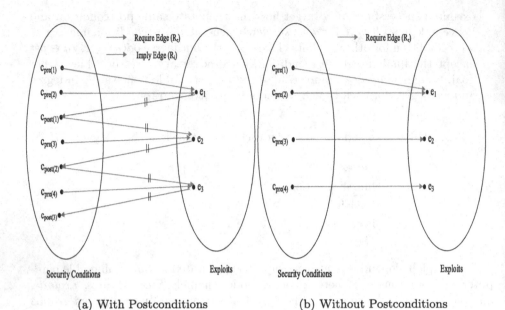

(a) With Postconditions   (b) Without Postconditions

Fig. 1. Attack graphs as a directed Bipartite graph

Algorithm 1. $findMDS$: Compute *Minimum Dominating Set (MDS)* in terms of initial conditions that covers all exploits (i.e. full coverage constraint imposed) in an Attack Graph G

Input:
$G = \langle V, E \rangle \rightarrow$ attack graph for the enterprise network
Output:
$MDS \subseteq InitialCondn \rightarrow$ Minimal Dominating Set (in terms of Initial Conditions) that covers all exploits in the Attack Graph G.

1: $\langle V, E \rangle \leftarrow$ MST (G) ▷ Apply minimum spanning tree algorithm (MST) on G to identify all the nodes and edges in G
2: **for all** $u \in V$ **do**
3:    **if** $\Big(id(u) = 0\Big) \wedge (od(u) \geq 1) \vee \Big(id[u] = 1) \wedge (od[u] \geq 2\Big)$ **then**
4:       $InitialCondn \leftarrow u$
5:    **else if** $\Big(id(u) \geq 2\Big) \wedge (od(u) \geq 1) \vee \Big(id[u] \geq 3) \wedge (od[u] \geq 2\Big)$ **then**
6:       $Exploit \leftarrow u$
7:    **else**
8:       $PostCondn \leftarrow u$
9:    **end if**
10: **end for**
11: **for all** $u \in InitialCondn$ **do**
12:    $c_i \leftarrow O(u)$
13: **end for**
14: Compute collection of sets $C = \bigcup_{i=1}^{n} c_i$; *where* $n = |InitialCondn|$
15: $MDS(G) \leftarrow GREEDY - SET - COVER(Exploit, C)$

Algorithm 2. $GREEDY - SET - COVER(\mathcal{E}, \mathcal{S})$: An algorithm for computation of set cover

---

Input:
Collection $\mathcal{S}(i) = S_i, (1 \leq i \leq n)$ of subsets over universe of exploits $\mathcal{E}$
Output:
Set cover D
1: $U \leftarrow \mathcal{E}$
2: $\mathcal{D} \leftarrow \phi$
3: **while** $U \neq \phi$ **do**
4:     Select $S(j) \in \mathcal{S}$ that maximizes $|S(j) \cap U|$ *where* $j \leq n$
5:     $U - S(j)$
6:     $\mathcal{D} = \mathcal{D} \cup S(j)$
7:     $S(i) = S(i) - S(j), 1 \leq i \leq n$
8: **end while**
9: Return $\mathcal{D}$

---

the exploits in G. *GREEDY-SET-COVER* (Algorithm 2) is used to find a sub collection of subsets that covers all the exploits in G. Such minimal sub collection of sets that covers all the exploits in an attack graph acts as a MDS. Dominating in the sense that these minimum number of initial conditions cover all the exploits in G and hence proves dominancy over other initial conditions.

4   Case Study

Test network identical to [20] has been used as the test network (Fig. 2).

Here $Host_3$ is the attackers target machine and $MySQL$ is the critical resource running over it. The attacker is an malicious entity and her goal is to obtain root-level privileges on $Host_3$. The job of a firewalls is to separate internal network from the Internet. Firewall policies that limits connectivity in the network configuration are given in Table 2. Table 3 shows the system characteristics for the hosts available in the network. Such kind of data is available in public vulnerability databases viz. *NVD, Bugtraq, OSVDB* etc. Here external firewall allows

Table 2. Connectivity-Limiting firewall policies

Host	Attacker	$Host_0$	$Host_1$	$Host_2$	$Host_3$
Attacker	Local-host	ALL	NONE	NONE	NONE
$Host_0$	ALL	Local-host	ALL	ALL	Squid LICQ
$Host_1$	ALL	IIS	Local-host	ALL	Squid LICQ
$Host_2$	ALL	IIS	ALL	Local-host	Squid LICQ
$Host_3$	ALL	IIS	ALL	ALL	Local-host

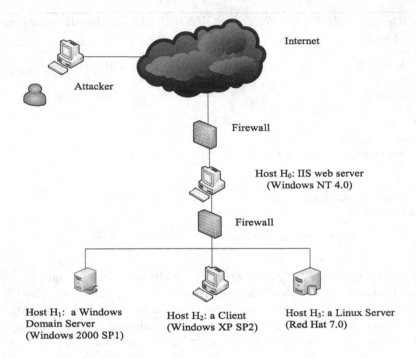

Fig. 2. Test network [20]

any external host to only access services running on host $Host_0$. Connections to all other services/ports on other hosts are blocked. Host's within the internal network have authority to connect to only those ports specified by the firewall policies as shown in Table 2. *ALL* specifies that source host may access all services running over the destination host. *NONE* indicates that source host is prevented from having access to any service on the destination host [20].

A goal-oriented exploit-dependency attack graph (Fig. 3) for the Test network (Fig. 2) is generated using model checking-based tool called SGPlan [7, 21]. Vulnerabilities in the Test network are logically combined to generate different attack scenario/paths. Attack graph is generated by collapsing all the attack paths for the same initial and goal condition and visualized using GraphViz (a graph visualization tool). Nodes in the attack graph (Fig. 3) are of type exploits, required preconditions and implied postconditions. Exploits are shown by a oval, initial conditions by a box and postconditions by a simple plain text. The ovals link preconditions (box) to post-conditions of each attack step.

As evident from the attack graph (shown in Fig. 3) there are total 17 exploits. Successful exploitation of each of these exploit requires preconditions that need to be satisfied conjunctively. Postconditions cannot be removed until actual causes responsible for their generation (for e.g. vulnerabilit(y)ies, unnecessary services/ open ports etc.) are removed from the network. Whereas, initial conditions can be independently disabled for network hardening. *findMDS* Algorithm 1 pro-

Table 3. System characteristics for network configuration [20]

Host	Services	Ports	Vulnerabilities	CVE IDs
$Host_0$	IIS web service	80	IIS buffer overflow	CVE-2010-2370
	ftp	21	ftp buffer overflow	CVE-2009-3023
$Host_1$	ftp	21	ftp rhost overwrite	CVE-2008-1396
	ssh	22	ssh buffer overflow	CVE-2002-1359
	rsh	514	rsh login	CVE-1999-0180
$Host_2$	netbios-ssn	139	netbios-ssn nullsession	CVE-2003-0661
	rsh	514	rsh login	CVE-1999-0180
$Host_3$	LICQ	5190	LICQ-remote-to-user	CVE-2001-0439
	Squid proxy	80	squid-port-scan	CVE-2001-1030
	MySQL DB	3306	local-setuid-bof	CVE-2006-3368

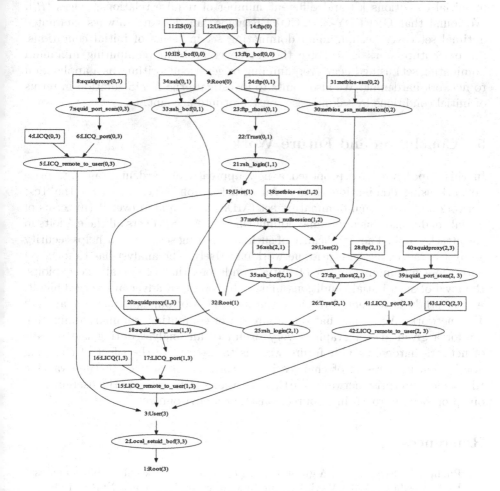

Fig. 3. Attack graph for the network configuration

posed in Sect. 3 detects the minimum dominating set (MDS) that covers all the exploits. It gives minimal dominating set $MDS = \{user(0), ftp(0,1), squid - proxy(1,3), LICQ(1,3), squid - proxy(0,3), LICQ(0,3), ftp(2,1), ssh(2,1), net- bios - ssn(0,2), squid - proxy(2,3), ssh(0,1), netbios - ssn(1,2), LICQ(2,3)\}$. Prioritizing and disabling one or more initial condition in MDS can stop attack in between and prevent the critical resource from being compromised. While disabling of one or more initial condition for network hardening, an administrator must consider the inherent cost associated with those conditions.

The complexity of the GREEDY-SET-COVER algorithm we used in this paper (i.e. Algorithm 2) is of $\mathcal{O}(mn)$ for an attack graph G having "m" exploits and "n" initial conditions. In general, set covering is the optimization problem. The limitation of our proposed algorithm lies in that it does not always guarantee the optimal set cover. To evaluate this, we tested the algorithm with different type of attack graph with different number of exploits $|\mathcal{E}|$, different number of initial conditions $|\mathcal{C}|$ and different number of require relations/ edges $|R_i|$. We found that GREEDY-SET-COVER algorithm does not always guarantee optimal set cover i.e. minimum dominating set in terms of initial conditions. So, our future work is to solve the set cover problem (computing minimum dominating set) using linear programming or genetic algorithms as a application to network hardening. We also wants to investigate the MDS solution in terms of initial conditions by taking cost constraint into account.

5   Conclusion and Future Work

In this paper, we have proposed a new approach of hardening an enterprise network using domination theory. An attack graph is generated for the Test network and a minimal dominating set (MDS) is computed over it (in terms of initial conditions). Such minimal dominating set (MDS) covers all the exploits in the attack graph. The significance of such dominating set is that it helps security analyst in hardening enterprise network effectively. The analyst has to focus on only those minimum number of initial conditions that covers all the exploits. Removal of such initial conditions makes the job of an adversary very difficult. A case study is presented to show the usefulness of our approach for a small Test network. We found that our approach of computing minimal dominating set for a given attack graph is very useful to an analyst during the process of network hardening. Our future work is to investigate the effect of changing domination as a result of changes in network attack surface in time varying (dynamic) enterprise network. Further, we wants to investigate the usefulness of our proposed approach in resource constrained environment.

References

1. Phillips, C., Swiler, L.P.: A graph-based system for network-vulnerability analysis. In: Proceedings of the Workshop on New Security Paradigms. NSPW 1998, pp. 71–79. ACM, New York (1998)

2. Sheyner, O., Haines, J., Jha, S., Lippmann, R., Wing, J.: Automated generation and analysis of attack graphs. In: Proceedings of the IEEE Symposium on Security and Privacy, pp. 273–284 (2002)
3. Ammann, P.: Scalable, graph-based network vulnerability analysis. In: Proceedings of the 9th ACM Conference on Computer and Communications Security, pp. 217–224. ACM Press (2002)
4. Noel, S., Jajodia, S., O'Berry, B., Jacobs, M.: Efficient minimum-cost network hardening via exploit dependency graphs. In: Proceedings of the 19th Annual Computer Security Applications Conference, pp. 86–95 (2003)
5. Ingols, K., Lippmann, R., Piwowarski, K.: Practical attack graph generation for network defense. In: 22nd Annual Computer Security Applications Conference, ACSAC 2006, pp. 121–130 (2006)
6. Ou, X., Boyer, W.F.: A scalable approach to attack graph generation. In: 13th ACM Conference on Computer and Communications Security (CCS), pp. 336–345. ACM Press (2006)
7. Ghosh, N., Ghosh, S.: A planner-based approach to generate and analyze minimal attack graph. Appl. Intel. **36**, 369–390 (2012)
8. Ortalo, R., Deswarte, Y., Kaaniche, M.: Experimenting with quantitative evaluation tools for monitoring operational security. IEEE Trans. Softw. Eng. **25**, 633–650 (1999)
9. Li, W., Vaughn, R.: Cluster security research involving the modeling of network exploitations using exploitation graphs. In: 6th IEEE International Symposium on Cluster Computing and the Grid, CCGRID 2006, vol. 2, p. 26 (2006)
10. Idika, N., Bhargava, B.: Extending attack graph-based security metrics and aggregating their application. IEEE Trans. Dependable Secure Comput. **9**, 75–85 (2012)
11. Noel, S., Jajodia, S.: Metrics suite for network attack graph analytics. In: CISR 2014, pp. 5–8 (2014)
12. Jha, S., Sheyner, O., Wing, J.: Two formal analyses of attack graphs. In: Proceedings of the 15th IEEE Workshop on Computer Security Foundations, CSFW 2002, Washington, DC, USA, pp. 49–63. IEEE Computer Society (2002)
13. Wang, L., Noel, S., Jajodia, S.: Minimum-cost network hardening using attack graphs. Comput. Commun. **29**, 3812–3824 (2006)
14. Man, D., Wu, Y., Wu, Y.: A method based on global attack graph for network hardening. In: 4th International Conference on Wireless Communications, Networking and Mobile Computing, WiCOM 2008, pp. 1–4 (2008)
15. Islam, T., Wang, L.: A heuristic approach to minimum-cost network hardening using attack graph. In: NTMS 2008, pp. 1–5 (2008)
16. Chen, F., Liu, D., Zhang, Y., Su, J.: A scalable approach to analyzing network security using compact attack graphs. J. Netw. **5**(5), 543–550 (2010)
17. Keramati, M., Asgharian, H., Akbari, A.: Cost-aware network immunization framework for intrusion prevention. In: IEEE International Conference on Computer Applications and Industrial Electronics (ICCAIE), pp. 639–644 (2011)
18. Wang, L., Singhal, A., Jajodia, S.: Measuring the overall security of network configurations using attack graphs. In: Barker, S., Ahn, G.-J. (eds.) Data and Applications Security 2007. LNCS, vol. 4602, pp. 98–112. Springer, Heidelberg (2007)
19. Pang, C., Zhang, R., Zhang, Q., Wang, J.: Dominating sets in directed graphs. Inf. Sci. **180**, 3647–3652 (2010)
20. Ghosh, N., Ghosh, S.: An approach for security assessment of network configurations using attack graph. In: 1st International Conference on Networks and Communications, NETCOM 2009, pp. 283–288 (2009)
21. SGPlan: 5. (http://wah.cse.cuhk.edu.hk/wah/programs/SGPlan/)

Modeling Dependencies of ISO/IEC 27002:2013 Security Controls

Anirban Sengupta[(✉)]

Centre for Distributed Computing,
Department of Computer Science and Engineering,
Jadavpur University, Kolkata, India
anirban.sg@gmail.com

Abstract. Security controls like policies, procedures, laws and regulations, or security tools and techniques help in mitigating risks to enterprise information systems. There are several security standards that provide guidance on the implementation of security controls. ISO/IEC 27002:2013 is one of the most widely accepted security standards; it has been adopted by the Indian government for implementation in critical sector enterprises. The controls of ISO/IEC 27002:2013 are inter-dependent and they consist of several types of implementation-specific tasks. Lack of proper research on these aspects makes it extremely difficult for enterprises to implement a comprehensive and correct control implementation programme. The present study analyses the controls of ISO/IEC 27002:2013, categorizes the implementation tasks and details the dependencies among controls and relationships among categories of tasks.

Keywords: Control dependence · ISO/IEC 27002:2013 · Security controls · Security standard

1 Introduction

Security controls are safeguards, or countermeasures, that help in mitigating risks [1] to enterprise information systems. Controls may be of different types like security policies, procedures, laws and regulations, or tools and techniques. Security policies [1] consist of sets of high-level statements of enterprise beliefs, goals, and objectives, and the general means for their attainment, in order to secure an enterprise. Security procedures [1] detail the steps needed to implement security policies. Usually, each security policy has a corresponding procedure. Laws and regulations are mandated by authorities; they usually vary from one nation to another, and from one business sector to another. For example, Indian banks and financial institutions are governed by the regulations of Reserve Bank of India [2]. Similarly, healthcare organizations in USA are bound by the norms of HIPAA [3]. Besides, different tools and techniques are also used to enforce security. Common examples include firewalls, Intrusion Detection/Prevention Systems, Anti-malware, and cryptographic techniques.

Over the years, several information security standards have evolved that prescribe security controls and contain compilations of industry best practices. These serve as indispensable reference manuals that are used by enterprises to identify, design, and

© Springer International Publishing Switzerland 2015
J.H. Abawajy et al. (Eds): SSCC 2015, CCIS 536, pp. 354–367, 2015.
DOI: 10.1007/978-3-319-22915-7_33

implement relevant security controls for mitigating risks. While some of these standards cater to the needs of specific business sectors, others are of a generic nature that can be used by almost all types of enterprises. Examples of sector-specific security standards are COBIT5 [4] for fiduciary organizations, MIL-Std [5] for military organizations, and TIA-942 [6] for Data-Centers. Some of the generic standards are ISO/IEC 27002:2013 [7], NIST SP 800-53 [8], and IT Baseline Protection Manual [9]. Among the generic information security standards, ISO/IEC 27002:2013 is most widely accepted, and it has also been adopted by the Indian Government to be mandatorily implemented by all critical-sector enterprises.

Decision to implement controls of ISO/IEC 27002:2013 poses a major challenge to an enterprise. It is crucial to identify *all* controls that are essential for mitigating the risks to the enterprise. This is challenging owing to the fact that almost all controls of ISO/IEC 27002:2013 are inter-dependent. This inter-dependence has not been specified by ISO, but it is implicitly embedded within the *implementation guidance* of controls. It is important to analyze each control and identify its corresponding dependencies. Absence of this exercise will lead to incomplete control implementation and expose the enterprise to security risks. This challenge persists owing to lack of proper research and guidance, making it difficult for enterprises to design and implement a comprehensive control implementation programme. Though there has been a similar study on the earlier version of the standard [10], namely ISO/IEC 27002:2005 [11], hardly any major effort has gone into the analysis of the current version of the standard [7], till date. This is all the more necessary since the current standard has undergone a major structural overhaul to keep pace with the changing ICT scenario in enterprises.

This paper attempts to fill this research gap by providing a systematic study of the inter-dependence of security controls of ISO/IEC 27002:2013. It also analyzes the components of each security control and categorizes them into specific *tasks*. This will enable an enterprise to formulate and implement a suitable control implementation programme, which will help in mitigating all identified information security risks without opening up newer ones.

Rest of this paper is organized as follows. Section 2 presents a survey of related work. Section 3 details the components of ISO/IEC 27002:2013 and classifies its implementation tasks. The control dependency model is described in Sect. 4. Section 5 discusses the benefits of the proposed methodology. Finally, Sect. 6 concludes the paper.

2 Related Work

The *Implementation guidance* sections in ISO/IEC 27002:2013 [7] contain some references of related controls. However, this is not an exhaustive reference list. Moreover, the standard has not categorized the controls, making it difficult for an enterprise to comprehend the means of implementation.

Though there has been some studies on measuring the effectiveness of security controls of ISO 27002 [12–16], to the best of the author's knowledge, there has not been any exhaustive research to categorize the controls and detail their inter-dependencies. Kaushik et al. [10] had presented a study on the dependencies of controls of ISO/IEC 27002:2005 [11], which was an earlier version of the standard. However, the current standard [7] has undergone major changes in both structure as well as content. For example, two new clauses have been introduced in the current standard, namely *Cryptography* and *Supplier Relationships*. Also, the clause *Communications and Operations Management* of the earlier version of the standard has been decomposed into two clauses, namely *Operations Security* and *Communications Security*. Several implementation-specific controls of the earlier standard (e.g. *Remote diagnostic and configuration port protection*, *Network routing control*, etc.) have been removed, while newer controls have been included (e.g. *Information security in project management*, *System security testing*, etc.). Besides, critical analysis of the standard shows a significant shift in the basic approach to implementing an Information Security Management System (ISMS) [17]. More emphasis is now being laid on governance of information security; in other words, major responsibility for design, monitoring, and evaluation of ISMS will rest with the senior management of an enterprise.

These changes have necessitated fresh in-depth research into the implementation aspects of ISO/IEC 27002:2013. The study presented in this paper addresses this research problem and proposes a comprehensive inter-dependency list of the security controls of ISO/IEC 27002:2013. It also categorizes the components of the controls for ease of implementation and management.

3   Components of ISO/IEC 27002:2013

ISO/IEC 27002:2013 [7] consists of 14 clauses as shown in Table 1. Each clause consists of several *main security categories*. Each main security category contains:

(a)   a control objective stating what is to be achieved; and
(b)   one or more controls that can be applied to achieve the control objective.

Table 1. Clauses of ISO/IEC 27002:2013.

Clause no.	Clause name
5	Information Security Policies
6	Organization of Information Security
7	Human Resource Security
8	Asset Management
9	Access Control
10	Cryptography
11	Physical and Environmental Security
12	Operations Security
13	Communications Security
14	System Acquisition, Development and Maintenance
15	Supplier Relationships
16	Information Security Incident Management
17	Information Security Aspects of Business Continuity Management
18	Compliance

The control structure of ISO/IEC 27002:2013 is illustrated in Fig. 1, where a *main security category* is shown along with its controls. The standard consists of 114 security controls grouped into 35 main security categories (the list of controls can be viewed on ISO's Online Browsing Platform [18]). The implementation of a control entails performance of a set of *tasks*. A task can be defined as a particular activity that is listed within the *implementation guidance* for a control. Analyses of control tasks show that they can be categorized into four distinct classes: governance, managerial, technical, and legal. This categorization is aimed at identifying the activities that can be assigned to different classes of users of an enterprise. Governance tasks refer to implementation techniques that are either supervisory in nature or deal with critical business or policy decisions. These tasks have to be initiated and controlled by the senior management of an enterprise. They are the drivers of all other types of tasks. For example, Control 5.1.1: *Policies for information security* "sets out the organization's approach to managing its information security objectives" [7]. Security policies need to be defined, approved, published, and communicated to stakeholders of the enterprise. As is obvious, these tasks can only be carried out by senior management of the enterprise, and hence they are categorized as *governance tasks*.

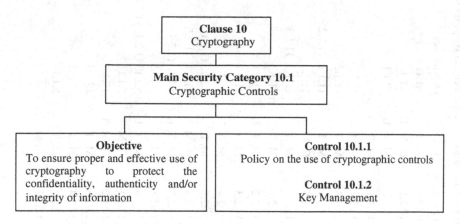

Fig. 1. Control structure of ISO/IEC 27002:2013.

Managerial tasks are operational activities that are non-technical in nature. Most of the controls of ISO/IEC 27002:2013 need some sort of managerial tasks for implementing them. These can comprise of one or more of the following: (i) preparation of operational procedures; (ii) enforcement of policies and procedures; (iii) conducting and attending awareness and training sessions; and (iv) maintenance of records. For example, the control *Use of secret authentication information* can be implemented by making users aware of the need and procedures for using such information, and regularly monitoring user activities. Such non-technical operational activities are categorized as managerial control tasks. It may be noted that almost *all* governance tasks need a set of managerial tasks to support their implementation. This is owing to the fact that governance implies establishment of organizational objectives, monitoring, and evaluating the fulfillment of

Table 2. ISO/IEC 27002:2013 control tasks and dependencies (G-governance, M-managerial, T-technical, L-legal).

Control no.	Tasks	Dependency	Control no.	Tasks	Dependency	Control no.	Tasks	Dependency
5.1.1	G, M, L	None	9.4.5	M, T	9.1.1, 9.4.1	13.2.4	G, M, L	5.1.1, 13.2.1
5.1.2	G, M	5.1.1	10.1.1	G, M, L	5.1.1	14.1.1	G, M, L	5.1.1, 6.1.5
6.1.1	G, M	5.1.1	10.1.2	M, T, L	10.1.1	14.1.2	G, M, T, L	13.1.1, 13.1.2, 14.1.1
6.1.2	M, T	6.1.1	11.1.1	M, T	9.1.1	14.1.3	G, M, T, L	14.1.2
6.1.3	G, M, L	6.1.1	11.1.2	M, T	11.1.1	14.2.1	M, T	5.1.1, 6.1.5
6.1.4	M	6.1.1	11.1.3	M, T	11.1.2	14.2.2	M, T	12.1.2, 14.2.1
6.1.5	G, M	6.1.1	11.1.4	M, T	11.1.1, 11.1.2	14.2.3	M, T	14.2.2
6.2.1	G, M, T, L	5.1.1	11.1.5	G, M, T	11.1.3	14.2.4	M, T	14.2.2
6.2.2	G, M, T, L	5.1.1	11.1.6	M, T	11.1.2, 11.1.3	14.2.5	M, T	14.2.1
7.1.1	G, M, L	5.1.1	11.2.1	M, T	11.1.3	14.2.6	M, T, L	14.2.1
7.1.2	G, M, L	5.1.1	11.2.2	M, T, L	11.2.1	14.2.7	G, M, T, L	14.2.1
7.2.1	G, M	6.1.1	11.2.3	M, T	11.2.1	14.2.8	M, T	14.2.1
7.2.2	G, M	7.2.1	11.2.4	M, T, L	11.2.1	14.2.9	M, T	14.2.1, 14.2.7
7.2.3	G, M, L	7.1.2, 7.2.1	11.2.5	M, L	5.1.1, 11.2.1	14.3.1	M, T	9.1.1, 14.2.8, 14.2.9
7.3.1	G, M, L	7.2.1	11.2.6	G, M, T	11.2.1, 11.2.5	15.1.1	M, L	5.1.1, 6.1.5
8.1.1	M	None	11.2.7	M, T, L	5.1.1, 11.2.1	15.1.2	M, L	15.1.1
8.1.2	M	8.1.1	11.2.8	M, T	11.2.1	15.1.3	M, T	15.1.1, 15.1.2
8.1.3	M, T	5.1.1, 8.1.1	11.2.9	M, T, L	5.1.1, 11.2.1, 11.2.8	15.2.1	G, M, T, L	15.1.1, 15.1.2
8.1.4	M, T, L	8.1.3	12.1.1	G, M	5.1.1	15.2.2	G, M, L	12.1.2, 15.1.1, 15.1.2, 15.2.1
8.2.1	G, M, L	8.1.1	12.1.2	G, M, T	12.1.1	16.1.1	G, M	5.1.1, 6.1.1
8.2.2	G, M, T, L	8.2.1	12.1.3	M, T	12.1.1	16.1.2	M	16.1.1
8.2.3	M, T	8.1.3, 8.2.1	12.1.4	M, T	12.1.1	16.1.3	M	16.1.1
8.3.1	M, T	5.1.1	12.2.1	M, T	5.1.1	16.1.4	G, M	16.1.1, 16.1.2
8.3.2	M, T	8.3.1	12.3.1	G, M, T, L	5.1.1	16.1.5	G, M, T, L	16.1.1, 16.1.4

(Continued)

Table 2. (*Continued*)

Control no.	Tasks	Dependency	Control no.	Tasks	Dependency	Control no.	Tasks	Dependency
8.3.3	M, T	8.3.1	12.4.1	G, M, T, L	5.1.1	16.1.6	M	16.1.1, 16.1.4
9.1.1	G, M, L	5.1.1	12.4.2	M, T, L	12.4.1	16.1.7	G, M, T, L	16.1.1, 16.1.4, 16.1.5
9.1.2	M, T	9.1.1	12.4.3	G, M, T, L	12.4.1	17.1.1	G, M	5.1.1
9.2.1	M, T	9.1.1	12.4.4	G, M, T, L	12.4.1	17.1.2	G, M, T	17.1.1
9.2.2	M, T	9.2.1	12.5.1	G, M, T	5.1.1	17.1.3	G, M, T	17.1.2
9.2.3	M, T	9.2.2	12.6.1	G, M, T	5.1.1	17.2.1	M, T	17.1.2
9.2.4	M, T	9.2.1	12.6.2	M, T, L	5.1.1, 9.2.3, 12.6.1	18.1.1	G, M, L	5.1.1, 6.1.5
9.2.5	M	9.2.2	12.7.1	G, M, T	5.1.1	18.1.2	G, M, T, L	18.1.1
9.2.6	M, T, L	9.2.2	13.1.1	M, T	5.1.1	18.1.3	G, M, T, L	8.2.1, 18.1.1
9.3.1	M, T	9.2.4	13.1.2	M, T, L	13.1.1	18.1.4	G, M, T, L	8.2.1, 18.1.1
9.4.1	T	9.1.1	13.1.3	M, T	13.1.1	18.1.5	G, M, T, L	10.1.1, 18.1.1
9.4.2	T	9.1.1	13.2.1	G, M, T, L	5.1.1	18.2.1	G, M	5.1.1, 5.1.2, 6.1.1
9.4.3	M, T	9.1.1, 9.2.1, 9.4.2	13.2.2	G, M, T, L	13.2.1	18.2.2	G, M, T	5.1.1, 18.1.1, 18.2.1
9.4.4	M, T	9.1.1, 9.2.3	13.2.3	G, M, T, L	13.2.1	18.2.3	G, M, T	5.1.1, 18.2.1

those objectives; simultaneously, managerial tasks are needed to realize the established objectives. For example, considering the earlier example, though senior management will define, approve, publish, and communicate *Policies for information security*, the tasks of documenting the policies and maintaining relevant records are managerial in nature and need to be carried out by operational personnel.

Technical tasks refer to operational activities that are technical in nature. These usually require specific tools and techniques for implementation. For example, Control 6.2.2: *Teleworking* needs technical infrastructure like virtual desktops, Virtual Private Networks (VPN), anti-malware, etc. for establishing secure connection between the teleworking site and the enterprise office building. Another example is Control 9.4.1: *Information access restriction* which requires physical and logical access control mechanisms (virtual Local Area Network, access tokens, etc.) for implementation.

Legal tasks are those that are mandated by relevant laws, statutes and regulations. Several controls of ISO/IEC 27002:2013 contain references to such legal documents. If an enterprise implements such controls, it is essential to identify the actual requirements of relevant laws and regulations and implement them to achieve compliance. For example, controls 13.2.4: *Confidentiality or nondisclosure agreements* and 18.1.2: *Intellectual property rights* contain legal tasks. Like governance tasks, legal tasks also need corresponding managerial tasks to support their implementation. For example, Control 18.1.2: *Intellectual property rights* needs managerial procedures to ensure compliance with legislative, regulatory and contractual requirements related to intellectual property rights and use of proprietary software products [7].

Table 2 lists the types of tasks (governance, managerial, technical, and legal) that are needed for implementing the controls of ISO/IEC 27002:2013 in an enterprise. It may be seen that only nine controls (out of 114 controls) contain tasks of a single type. These are Control Nos. 6.1.4, 8.1.1, 8.1.2, 9.2.5, 9.4.1, 9.4.2, 16.1.2, 16.1.3, and 16.1.6; among them, 7 are purely managerial controls, while 2 are technical controls. The remaining 105 controls contain tasks of multiple types; hence, they may be referred to as *hybrid* controls. This implies that about 92 % of the controls of ISO/IEC 27002:2013 are hybrid in nature, signifying the importance of coordination among multiple task forces to achieve security in an enterprise.

Table 2 highlights certain interesting facts. 53 controls contain governance tasks; 112 controls consist of managerial tasks; 81 controls have technical tasks; and 47 controls contain references to laws and regulations. Thus, over 98 % of controls need managerial tasks for their implementation (Fig. 2). This is expected as implementation

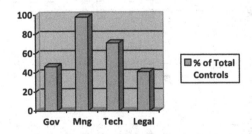

Fig. 2. Task categories of ISO/IEC 27002:2013 controls.

of a security control usually requires the enforcement of relevant procedures, and maintenance of documentation, which are, in essence, managerial tasks that are performed by operational personnel. Another vital statistic is the relatively high number of governance tasks (about 46.5 % of controls have governance tasks) within ISO/IEC 27002:2013. This signifies the emphasis of the standard in delegating major security responsibility to senior management of an enterprise. Specifically the ownership of risk, and its mitigation, is with the senior management who has to demonstrate leadership and commitment towards implementation of an Information Security Management System (ISMS) [17].

The following section discusses the dependencies among security controls of ISO/IEC 27002:2013.

4 Control Dependencies

Analyses of the controls of ISO/IEC 27002:2013 reveal that only 2 out of 114 controls (Control Nos. 5.1.1 and 8.1.1) are *independent*. All other controls are inter-dependent. The dependencies of controls of ISO/IEC 27002:2013 are shown in Table 2. In case of 24 out of 35 *main security categories*, the presence (or absence) of the first control of the *category* determines the need of all other controls in that *category*. In other words, if the first control of a *main security category* is *not required* for a particular enterprise, then none of the other controls in that particular *category* are needed. This includes transitive dependencies as well: for example, *Main security category* 17.1 consists of three controls; Control 17.1.2 is dependent on 17.1.1, while Control 17.1.3 depends on 17.1.2 for its existence. In other words, if 17.1.1 is not needed, then 17.1.2 and hence, 17.1.3 will also not be required. This is illustrated in Fig. 3. The reasons for the above dependencies are obvious: information security continuity cannot be implemented (Control 17.1.2) without proper planning (Control 17.1.1); likewise, it is impossible to verify, review, or evaluate information security continuity (Control 17.1.3) if it has not been implemented at all (Control 17.1.2).

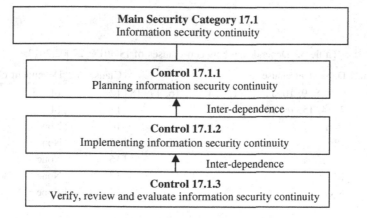

Fig. 3. Transitive dependency between controls of ISO/IEC 27002:2013.

Among the remaining 11 *main security categories*, 8 categories contain single controls (Table 3), while 3 categories contain controls that do not follow the pattern stated above. These categories are 6.2: *Mobile devices and teleworking*, 7.1: *Prior to employment*, and 9.4: *System and application access control*.

It is interesting to note that unlike the earlier version of the standard [11], some controls of ISO/IEC 27002:2013 [7] are dependent on controls of other *main security*

Table 3. Main security categories of ISO/IEC 27002:2013 containing single controls.

Main security category	Control
7.3: Termination and change of employment	7.3.1: Termination or change of employment responsibilities
9.3: User responsibilities	9.3.1: Use of secret authentication information
12.2: Protection from malware	12.2.1: Controls against malware
12.3: Backup	12.3.1: Information backup
12.5: Control of operational software	12.5.1: Installation of software on operational systems
12.7: Information systems audit considerations	12.7.1: Information systems audit controls
14.3: Test data	14.3.1: Protection of test data
17.2: Redundancies	17.2.1: Availability of information processing facilities

categories and *clauses* as is evident from Table 2. This implies that some of the main security categories have *objectives* that are related to each other. For example, Control 9.4.2: *Secure log-on procedures*, belonging to Main security category 9.4: *System and application access control*, depends on Control 9.1.1: *Access control policy*, that is included in Main security category 9.1: *Business requirements of access control*. Similarly, there are dependencies between clauses owing to dependencies among controls belonging to different clauses. Specifically, all other clauses of ISO/IEC 27002:2013 are dependent on Clause 5 since, implementations of several controls

Table 4. Dependency between clauses of ISO/IEC 27002:2013.

Clause no.	Dependent clause no.	Clause no.	Dependent clause no.
5	6, 7, 8, 9, 10, 11, 12, 13, 14, 15, 16, 17, 18	12	14, 15
6	7, 14, 15, 16, 18	13	14
7	None	14	None
8	18	15	None
9	11, 12, 14	16	None
10	18	17	None
11	None	18	None

depend on the contents of Control 5.1.1: *Policies for information security*. All such inter-clause dependencies are listed in Table 4.

4.1 Dependencies Between Control Implementation Tasks

The implementation tasks of a *hybrid* control are dependent on each other. As defined in Sect. 3, a hybrid control requires more than one type of task for its complete implementation. It has also been seen that *all* governance and legal tasks need corresponding managerial tasks for fulfilling their requirements. Another aspect is the relationship between managerial and technical tasks – they are mutually dependent on one another. The above dependencies can be illustrated with the help of a hybrid control, say 6.2.1: *Mobile device policy* that contains all four types of tasks. The identification of relevant business requirements and specification of the mobile device policy are *governance tasks*. These lead to the documentation and implementation of the policy that comprise of *managerial tasks*. Identification of relevant laws pertaining to the use and safety of mobile devices constitute *legal tasks*. These necessitate the establishment of additional *managerial tasks* like preparation of specific safety procedures and conducting training and awareness sessions for employees and third parties. Finally, *technical tasks* like installation of physical locks, security software, and access control mechanisms are needed to support the implementation of the above policies and procedures (*managerial tasks*). On the other hand, managerial tasks like review of the technical controls and providing training on their proper usage complement the technical tasks.

The above discussion leads to the formulation of the following intra-dependence rules for tasks of hybrid controls:

(R1) If a hybrid control, say CH, consists of a governance task, say CH_g, then there must exist a non-empty set of managerial tasks, say CH_m, that depend on CH_g. This means that

$$\exists\ CH_g \Rightarrow \exists\ CH_m \text{ s.t. } CH_m \neq \emptyset \tag{1}$$

(R2) If a hybrid control, say CH, consists of a legal task, say CH_l, then there must exist a non-empty set of managerial tasks, say CH_m, that depend on CH_l. Hence,

$$\exists\ CH_l \Rightarrow \exists\ CH_m \text{ s.t. } CH_m \neq \emptyset \tag{2}$$

(R3) If a hybrid control, say CH, consists of both managerial as well as technical tasks, say CH_m and CH_t, then they are mutually dependent on each. This implies

$$CH_m \Leftrightarrow CH_t \tag{3}$$

These rules are illustrated in Fig. 4 above.

Hybrid Control

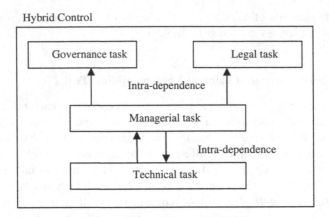

Fig. 4. Intra-dependence of tasks of hybrid controls.

5 Discussion

As stated earlier, in order to secure its information systems, an enterprise needs to implement ISMS (information security management system). ISO/IEC 27001:2013 provides the requirements for establishing, implementing, maintaining and continually improving ISMS within an enterprise [17]. It also contains a list of 114 security controls in an annexure, which may be implemented to mitigate risks. ISO/IEC 27002:2013 [7] provides detailed guidance on the implementation and maintenance of these controls. After implementing ISMS and security controls as per ISO/IEC 27001:2013 and 27002:2013, an enterprise may opt for a formal security certification. Certifying authorities check whether the enterprise has correctly identified all controls of ISO/IEC 27002:2013 that are necessary to mitigate the risks to its information systems. The documentation for control identification is technically referred to as the Statement of Applicability (SoA). The SoA is prepared in the form of a table with 114 rows (each row corresponding to a security control of ISO/IEC 27002:2013). Each row states whether a particular control of ISO/IEC 27002:2013 is required for the enterprise information system, along with a justification for the same. A sample SoA consisting of 5 controls is shown in Table 5.

Successful implementation of ISMS depends primarily on correct identification and implementation of security controls. Implementation of irrelevant controls will result in unnecessary investment; besides it may give rise to newer risks to the enterprise information system. On the other hand, ignoring necessary controls may lead to security breaches and attacks. Moreover, incorrect control identification will result in an enterprise failing to get ISO/IEC 27001:2013 certification.

Often, lack of knowledge of dependent controls leads to erroneous control identification and, consequently, preparation of an inaccurate SoA. The proposed control dependency model will help to eliminate such errors. This can be illustrated with the help of the following example: the branch offices of a critical-sector enterprise need the security controls 5.1.1: *Policies for information security* and 13.2.1: *Information transfer policies and procedures*, along with all dependent controls. However, the data

Table 5. Sample statement of applicability based on the controls of ISO/IEC 27002:2013.

Control no.	Control name	Applicable (Y/N)	Justification
5.1.1	Policies for information security	Y	The enterprise handles sensitive information and hence, needs information security policies
6.2.2	Teleworking	N	The enterprise does not allow teleworking
8.2.1	Classification of information	Y	The enterprise needs to classify its information assets in terms of business, security, and legal requirements
12.2.1	Controls against malware	Y	The enterprise needs to ensure that information and information processing facilities are protected from malware
14.2.1	Secure development policy	N	The enterprise does not develop (in-house or outsourced) any software or systems

centre of the same enterprise does not need Control 13.2.1 as "information exchange" is not allowed within the data centre. Hence, as shown in Table 2, the controls dependent on 13.2.1, namely 13.2.2, 13.2.3, and 13.2.4 will also not be needed for the data centre. Thus, the proposed control dependency model helps an enterprise to identify the controls that are applicable and necessary for its information systems. This leads to the preparation of an accurate SoA, and the implementation of a proper control implementation programme and ISMS.

6 Conclusion and Future Work

This paper presents an in-depth analysis of the security controls of ISO/IEC 27002:2013. It begins by categorizing the implementation components of controls into governance, managerial, technical and legal tasks. The inter-dependence of controls has been studied in detail. It has been shown that in most cases, the applicability of the first control of a *main security category* determines whether other controls in that *category* are needed for an enterprise ISMS. This pattern has some exceptions, which have been stated in Sect. 4. Besides, the dependencies between control implementation tasks of a *hybrid* control have also been described. The paper ends with a discussion on the benefits of the proposed control dependency model.

It may be noted that the *administrative tasks* [10] of the earlier version of the standard [11] have now given way to *governance tasks*, thus signifying greater involvement of senior management in ISMS implementation. Also, the new standard [7] contains dependencies between different *clauses* (and *main security categories*); this was absent in the earlier version [11]. Hence, though some portions of the earlier work [10] were applied in the current analysis, the changes stated above have necessitated significant enhancements in this study. Moreover, introduction of new controls and modifications in the *implementation guidance* of older ones have led to further changes in the study.

The analysis of controls presented in the paper will help security managers to design and implement a precise control implementation programme, which correctly identifies all *applicable* controls. Incomplete or missing controls allow risks to remain within enterprise information systems, which may lead to breach of information security. Often, this occurs due to the implementers' inability to determine *all* dependent controls. This paper tries to address this important aspect of enterprise information system security.

Future work is geared towards integration of the proposed methodology with security requirements engineering techniques. A tool may be developed that will first identify the information security requirements of an enterprise (e.g. via questionnaire, automated analysis of enterprise architecture, etc.). Based on these requirements, the tool will generate a comprehensive list of security controls (along with dependent controls), and suggest the implementation tasks that are needed to secure the enterprise.

Acknowledgments. Most of the concepts presented in this paper have evolved during the execution of a couple of R&D Projects at the Centre for Distributed Computing, Jadavpur University, sponsored by the Department of Electronics & Information Technology, Govt. of India.

References

1. ISO/IEC: ISO/IEC 27000:2014. Information technology – Security techniques - Information security management systems – Overview and vocabulary. Edition 3, Switzerland (2014)
2. Reserve Bank of India. http://www.rbi.org.in
3. Department of Health and Human Services: Health Insurance Reform: Security Standards; Final Rule. 45 CFR Parts 160, 162, and 164, Pennsylvania (2003)
4. ISACA: COBIT5. A Business Framework for the Governance and Management of Enterprise IT. ISACA, Illinois (2012)
5. Department of Defense: MIL-STD-882E. Department of Defense Standard Practice: System Safety. DoD, Ohio (2012)
6. TIA: TIA-942. Telecommunications Infrastructure Standard for Data Centers. Edition A, Virginia (2014)
7. ISO/IEC: ISO/IEC 27002:2013. Information technology – Security techniques - Code of practice for information security management. Edition 2, Switzerland (2013)
8. NIST: NIST SP 800-53. Security and Privacy Controls for Federal Information Systems and Organizations. Revision 4, Maryland (2013)
9. Federal Office for Information Security: IT-Grundschutz Catalogues. Germany (2007)
10. Kaushik, A.K., Sengupta, A., Mazumdar, C., Banerjee, P.: On the inter-dependence of security controls of ISO/IEC 27002:2005. IMS Manthan **VI**(1), 15–20 (2011)
11. ISO/IEC: ISO/IEC 27002:2005. Information technology – Security techniques - Code of practice for information security management. Edition 1, Switzerland (2005)
12. Huijben, K.: A lightweight, flexible evaluation framework to measure the ISO 27002 information security controls. Master's Thesis, Software Improvement Group (2014)

13. Bandopadhyay, S., Sengupta, A., Mazumdar, C.: A quantitative methodology for information security control gap analysis. In: International Conference on Communication, Computing and Security, pp. 537–540. ACM, USA (2011)
14. Karabacak, B., Sogukpinar, I.: A quantitative method for ISO 17799 gap analysis. Comput. Secur. **25**, 413–419 (2006)
15. Wright, S.: Measuring the effectiveness of security using ISO 27001. Whitepaper, SANS Institute (2006)
16. Praxiom ISO/IEC 27001:2005 Information Security Gap Analysis Tool. http://www.praxiom.com/iso-27001-gap.htm
17. ISO/IEC: ISO/IEC 27001:2013. Information technology – Security techniques - Information security management systems - Requirements. Edition 2, Switzerland (2013)
18. ISO/IEC 27002:2013 Online Browsing Platform. https://www.iso.org/obp/ui/#iso:std:iso-iec:27002:ed-2:v1:en

Secure Cluster Based Routing Scheme (SCBRS) for Wireless Sensor Networks

Sohini Roy[(✉)]

Indian Institute of Engineering Science and Technology (IIEST) Shibpur,
Howrah, India
roysohini266@gmail.com

Abstract. Wireless sensor network consists of micro electromechanical sensor nodes which are operated by battery power. Sensor network has emerged as an important supplement to the modern wireless communication systems due to its wide range of applications. The modern researchers are facing the various issues concerning sensor networks more graciously. However, offering security to an energy constrained network of sensor nodes is still a challenge. The proposed scheme named as Secure Cluster Based Routing Scheme (SCBRS) for Wireless Sensor Networks adopts a hierarchical network model coupled with low weight security mechanisms in order to conserve energy as well as offer security to the network. Elliptic Curve Cryptography (ECC) based public key cryptography, Elliptic-Curve Diffie-Hellman (ECDH) key exchange scheme, nested hash based message authentication codes (HMAC) and RC5 symmetric cypher are the light-weight security methods used by the proposed scheme. Simulation results prove that SCBRS performs better than Tree Based Protocol for Key Management in Wireless Sensor Networks in terms of energy efficiency and security. SCBRS also performs better than Secure Hierarchical Routing Protocol (SHRP) in fields where security is the most important issue.

Keywords: Wireless sensor network · Secure routing protocol · Cluster based · Level formation · Cluster head · One-way hash chain · Trust value · Data aggregation · Energy efficiency · Network lifetime

1 Introduction

A large number of micro electromechanical sensor nodes are deployed over a large area to form a wireless sensor network. These sensor nodes are responsible for sensing events occurring within their sensing zone and inform the base station about the occurrence of the event. Such events can be devastating environmental phenomena like earthquake, forest fire etc. In such cases, where a sensor network is created to monitor such devastating occurrences of events, time plays a very important role. The information should be delivered to the base station in minimum time such that a necessary action is taken. To minimize the time requirement, sometimes the security of data is sacrificed to some extent. However, in situations like military surveillance security of data is the first and foremost need. So, a wireless sensor network deployed for such an application must focus on the security needs of the network.

© Springer International Publishing Switzerland 2015
J.H. Abawajy et al. (Eds): SSCC 2015, CCIS 536, pp. 368–380, 2015.
DOI: 10.1007/978-3-319-22915-7_34

Sensor nodes are low-powered devices and they are deployed in a region where replacement of battery is also not easy. The nodes also have very limited computational capability and low storage. Thus, energy conservation is an inevitable challenge in a wireless sensor network. In a hierarchical routing, each and every node of the network does not need to forward the data to the base station individually as in flat routing schemes like SPIN [1] etc. This saves a lot of battery power and thereby prolongs the network lifetime. In the proposed scheme SCBRS, a level-based clustered network is created and also an optimum number of cluster heads for each level is selected to prevent extra energy drainage.

The proposed routing protocol SCBRS is designed especially for applications where security of data is more important than anything else. It is true that the time taken to secure the data is a bit more than forwarding of unsecure data. However, SCBRS compromises with time for the sake of offering data security. Thus, together with energy conservation, SCBRS aims in securing the data to be transmitted over the network. To avoid energy depletion, light-weight security methods like Elliptic Curve Cryptography (ECC) based public key cryptography [2], Elliptic-Curve Diffie-Hellman (ECDH) [3] key exchange scheme, nested hash based message authentication codes (HMAC) and RC5 symmetric cypher [4] are used by SCBRS. Both the upstream and downstream flow of data in the network is secured in SCBRS. Together with securing the data to be forwarded to the base station, the data forwarded by each member nodes to their respective cluster heads is also secured in this approach. Therefore, the main goals of SCBRS are energy conservation, both-way data security, detection and avoidance of malicious nodes present within the network region and lastly bypassing most of the common attacks in a sensor network like Sybil attack, Hello Flood attack, Wormhole Attack, Spoofing, Sinkhole Attack, Selective Forwarding, Denial of Service attack [5] etc.

The structuring of the remainder of the paper is done in the following way: Sect. 2 reviews the hierarchical secure routing schemes designed so far. In Sect. 3 the assumptions, network framework and threat model concerning SCBRS is discussed. Section 4 details the working of the proposed scheme. Performance analysis of SCBRS and simulation results is given in Sect. 5. Finally, Sect. 6 concludes the paper.

2 Related Works

In this section, different works done in the area of secure hierarchical routing in wireless sensor network is reviewed. Each and every work has its own pros and cons. However, none can guarantee complete security of data. Moreover, the focus of most of the protocols is on securing the upstream flow of data. Some of the protocols ignore the energy constraints and some focus on time optimization. All the variations are discussed in this section.

A Key Management Scheme for Cluster Based Wireless Sensor Networks [6] uses public key management scheme based on ECC and Diffie-Hellman key exchange scheme. The key preloading phase adopted by this scheme includes assigning an id to each gateway and preloading of public keys of sensor nodes, their own public keys and the public key of the Base station into the gateways. Each sensor node is loaded with a private and a public key and also with the public keys of the gateways of the network. A low cost ECDSA signature is used for the broadcast authentication of the gateways. Encryption and decryption of messages exchanged between the gateways and the sensor nodes is done using the public key of the gateways. Each sensor node requests for a session key using LCP routing algorithm to the gateway of that cluster and communicates with the other nodes by securing their message with the help of the session key provided by the gateway. The encrypted pair-wise session key provided by the gateway is generated using ECC. Tree Based Protocol for Key Management in Wireless Sensor Networks [7] minimizes memory occupation, ensures scalability and resists node compromise attack which is overlooked by most of the secure routing protocols. In this scheme each node is preloaded with three keys. The base station initiates the spanning tree construction by broadcasting a hello message. After the tree construction is complete each node shares a symmetric key with the base station, a symmetric key with its father and a common key with all the nodes of the network. The base station periodically sends a refresh message to the son nodes in order to launch a rekeying process and includes the ID of the nodes that are compromised. The nodes receiving the refresh message regenerates their common key and forwards the refresh message to their son nodes thus regenerating a new global key. If a father node detects that a son node is being suspicious, it removes that node from the list of sons and generates a refresh message and sends upwards until it reaches the base station. If a son node finds the father node to be suspicious it searches its list of neighbors to find another father node and thereby finds another way to reach its message to the base station. SHRP [8] uses ECDH key exchange scheme to set a secure channel of communication between the cluster heads and the base station. This conserves energy as well as minimizes time to complete the key set up phase. However, the data forwarded to the cluster heads by the member nodes do not follow any data encryption method to maintain the privacy of data. Blowfish symmetric cipher is used for encryption and decryption purposes by the cluster head nodes and the base station. However, symmetric key ciphers are always more prone to attacks compared to asymmetric key ciphers. Though most of the common security threats are avoided by SHRP, the level of security can be enhanced by means of stronger security mechanisms. Thus, SCBRS is proposed.

3   Network Framework and Threat Model

A network size of 100×100 m^2 is considered for simulating the performance of SCBRS and the number of nodes range from 100 to 150. The following assumptions are made in designing the network architecture of SCBRS.

1. The base station is of high configuration and it is assumed to be trust worthy. Although it requires authenticating itself to the nodes of the network in order to prevent flooding attacks. It is placed in a controllable place within the sensing zone of the nodes of first level.

2. Each node shares a global key G_k with the base station that is used to avoid outsider's attack. It is also assumed that even if a node gets compromised the global key is not revealed to the attacker.
3. The nodes agree upon all the domain parameters of the elliptic curves with the base station for the purpose of ECC based cryptographic mechanisms.
4. The member nodes and their cluster heads also agree upon all the domain parameters of the elliptic curves so that ECDH [3] based key exchange can be done.

There can be a number of security threats in the network area. A compromised node of the network may pretend to be the base station and forward bogus messages to the nodes of the network thereby launching a flooding attack. A flooding attack may turn into a denial of service attack if the nodes get overloaded with bogus messages. Sybil attack can be launched by a compromised node of the network making an illusion to the other nodes that it is present in more than one location at a particular time. It can compel a node to forward its data to a fake node. Node compromise attack can be induced by physically capturing a node and reprogramming it. However, it is assumed that this attack requires a minimum time to be launched. Compromised nodes of the network can launch a wormhole attack on the messages exchanged between a node and its neighbors. These nodes can also overhear the packets exchanged between a cluster head and its neighbors. Packet eavesdropping can be done by an intruder's node while sending the aggregated data to the base station. Sinkhole attack can be launched by a laptop-class attacker by advertising its high quality link and a high weight value based on which next-hop nodes are selected in SCBRS. All these threats are considered and mitigated by SCBRS.

4 Proposed Work

The algorithm is divided into seven modules, namely–Pre-deployment phase, Level Formation, cluster head selection, cluster formation, key exchange and set up, data sensing and aggregation phase and data sending to base station phase.

4.1 Module 1: Pre-deployment Phase

The first phase of SCBRS is completed before the nodes are deployed and before the network life starts. In this phase, the base station generates a key chain or one-way hash chain using a hash function like MD5 or SHA-1. A one-way hash chain is a sequence of keys generated using a hash function $HF(x)$ such that $y = F(x)$ can be calculated easily but it is computationally infeasible to generate $x = HF^{-1}(y)$ within a finite time. The base station uses the hash function to generate a chain of numbers in the fashion: $S_n \rightarrow S_{n-1} \rightarrow \ldots \ldots \ldots \rightarrow S_4 \rightarrow S_3 \rightarrow S_2 \rightarrow S_1 \rightarrow S_0$, where $S_{n-1} = HF(S_n)$ and so on. S_n is a random number selected by the base station. After the key chain is generated by the base station, each of the nodes is provided with same hash function as used by the base station and the last key of the key chain (S_0). Later these keys are used by the base station for authenticating itself.

Each node and the base station are also configured with a set of elliptic curves for Elliptic Curve Cryptography (ECC) based key generation and the global key (G_k) is also provided. Since all the procedures of this phase takes place before the nodes are actually deployed, no energy consumption of this phase is considered.

4.2 Module 2: Level Formation Phase

The second module of SCBRS is Level Formation. This phase takes place only once in the lifetime of the network. Once, the network is divided into levels, this process is not repeated. To perform the level formation, the base station forwards a request message (REQS) to the nodes within two-hop distance from itself. In order to authenticate itself, the base station randomly selects a key S_i from the key chain and appends that with the REQS as a sequence number (OHC). The format of the message forwarded by base station is: BS→*: REQS∥BS∥OHC∥HMAC (G_k; REQS∥BS∥OHC) where, BS is the ID of the base station, * denotes any node of the network, ∥ denotes concatenation and OHC is the one-way hash chain sequence number. A Hash based Message Authentication Code (HMAC) is generated over the whole message using the global key (G_k) and appended with it for the purpose of authentication and prevent the message from being eavesdropped. The nodes of the network after receiving the message from the base station, first verifies authenticity of the message by generating the HMAC using the same global key and matching it with the one appended to the message. If the message passes the authentication checks, next the base station is verified. The node receiving the request message performs i times execution of HF(S_i) on the sequence number S_i appended by the base station. If the node gets S_0 after the execution is complete, the base station is authenticated and the request is accepted. Otherwise, the request is discarded. Once a key S_i from the key chain used by the base station, it is stored as a used key by base station and all the nodes of the network and it is not reused in the lifetime of the network. Any further message appended with a used key is rejected. This prevents flooding attack. The nodes accepting the request from the base station mark themselves as nodes of first level and send back an acknowledgement (ACK) to the base station.

The base station then acts as the SUPERVISOR and calculates the initial trust value ($TV_{initial}$) of the nodes of first level by passing a number of test messages through them. The initial trust values of each node i is calculated using the following equation:

$$TV_i = \left(\frac{M_{delivered}}{M_{delivered} + M_{sent}} \right) * 100 \qquad (1)$$

where, $M_{delivered}$ is the number of messages actually delivered by the node i and M_{sent} is the number of messages sent to node i for forwarding. If TV_i of a node is less than 20 % it is marked as a suspicious node by the SUPERVISOR and it is avoided in the subsequent phases. The nodes of first level now calculate a PRESTIGE value (PV_i) from them using the following equation:

$$PV_i = E_{Ri} * N_{ng} * TV_i \qquad (2)$$

where, E_{Ri} is the remaining energy of node i, N_{ng} is the number of nodes of next higher level node i can sense and TV_i is the trust value of node i. After calculating the PV_i for each node, the nodes of level one rebroadcast the REQS to the nodes within their sensing radii and whose level value is not yet assigned. While forwarding the REQS, the nodes of level one append their PV_i values with the REQS. The message format is as follows:

$node_i \rightarrow * : REQS||PV_i||ID_i||OHC||HMAC(G_k; ID_i||OHC||(HMAC\_of\_parent))$

where, PV_i is the PRESTIGE value of the node forwarding the message and ID_i is the node ID of that node. A nested HMAC is generated over the HMAC of the parent. The nodes receiving the REQS from one or more nodes of level one checks the authenticity of the source of the message using the same procedure as followed by nodes of level one and then accept the REQS. The nodes accepting the message mark themselves as nodes of level two and the sender with highest PRESTIGE value as their parent. Thus, any two nodes of level two may have same or different parent node of level one. The parent node plays the role of SUPERVISOR for the nodes of level two and assigns them their initial trust value following Eq. (1). This process continues till the last level is formed. Base station forwards REQS to nodes of first level and again each node of first level forwards REQS to nodes of second level and so on. Thus level formation module runs in $O(N^2)$ time where N is the number of nodes.

4.3 Module 3: Cluster Head Selection Phase

In the next phase of cluster head selection, the number of clusters required in each level is determined first. The number of required cluster heads in a level is directly proportional to the average distance between the nodes of that level; since if the nodes are scattered through a large area, it will be difficult for a smaller number of cluster heads to sense them all. The required number of cluster heads is also directly proportional to the total number of living nodes. When there is more number of living nodes, more cluster heads are needed. However, the required number of cluster heads is inversely proportional to the average distance of the nodes from the base station. The cluster head nodes near the base station are the only connecting links with the base station. Thus, those nodes are always included in any route from a sender cluster head of any level. If the lower most level of the network has lesser number of cluster heads then the same nodes will be selected over and over again for communicating with the base station. Therefore, by selecting more cluster heads in the lower levels will evenly distribute the load among them. The following equation gives the required number of cluster heads in a level.

$$C_{req} = k * \left\{ (D_{avg}/D_{Bavg}) * N_{living} \right\} \qquad (3)$$

where C_{req} is the required number of cluster heads in level i, k is a constant, D_{avg} is average distance between the nodes of level i. D_{Bavg} is the average distance of the nodes of ith level from the base station and N_{living} is the number of alive nodes which have a battery power, greater than a given threshold. This threshold is the minimum battery power needed to send or receive a signal.

As the C_{req} value for each level is determined, the selection of cluster head starts on the basis of a competition bid value calculated by every node of each level. The competition bid value (CV) is calculated as:

$$CV = E_{Ri}/D_i \qquad (4)$$

where

$$D_i = \sum_{j=1}^{n} \frac{d_{ij}}{n} \qquad (5)$$

where d_{ij} is the sum of the distances of node i from each of its neighbor nodes j lying in the same level, n is total number of neighbor nodes of that node in that layer. E_{Ri} is remaining energy of the ith node.

In each level, C_{req} numbers of nodes with the highest competition bid values (CV) are chosen as cluster head nodes. However, no node even with high CV can be chosen as cluster head if it is too close to any already selected cluster head of that level. If there is a node with the highest value of CV but lying in the sensing radius of an already chosen cluster head, then the node with second highest CV is selected. When the residual energy of a selected cluster head goes beyond the average residual energy of the cluster, a new set of cluster head nodes is selected for that level following the same procedure. C_{req} number of nodes can be selected from the total number of nodes in each level in O(N) time.

4.4   Module 4: Cluster Formation Phase

After the completion of cluster head selection phase, the phase of cluster formation starts. In this phase, the selected cluster head nodes send a join request to the nodes of the same level, within one-hop distance from them. The format of the request is: $CH_i \rightarrow *$: join_REQ||ID_i||level_value||CV_i||HMAC(G_k;join_REQ||ID_i||level_value||CV_i).

The non-cluster head nodes join the cluster head node from which they receive the request if the CV of the sender is higher than a given threshold. If a non-cluster head node receives a request from more than one cluster head node, it accepts only the first request and discards the rest. The cluster formation phase is repeated only when new nodes enter the network. Otherwise, the role of the cluster head is rotated among the nodes of the cluster when the residual energy of the current cluster head goes beyond the average residual energy of the cluster. Now, the cluster heads of each cluster take up the role of the SUPERVISOR and periodically monitor the associated nodes to assign them their current trust value. The cluster head of each cluster re-assigns the trust value of each node i as:

$$TV_i = (TV_{initial} + TV_{current})/2 \qquad (6)$$

where $TV_{current}$ is calculated in the similar way as $TV_{initial}$. When the TV_i is re-calculated the last calculated trust value is taken as $TV_{initial}$ and the newly calculated trust value is taken as $TV_{current}$. The average of both the initial and the current trust value is the newly assigned trust value for a node. The member node having the highest TV_i assigns the new trust value of the cluster head. The process of both-way supervision avoids assuming any node to be trust worthy. Trust value of each node is calculated in constant time and the time required to forward join_REQ to each of the member nodes is O(N).

4.5   Module 5: Key Exchange and Set up Phase

The key exchange and set up phase starts as the cluster formation phase completes. In this phase, the cluster head of each cluster uses Elliptic Curve Diffie Hellman (ECDH) key exchange scheme to set up a shared secret key with each of the member nodes. ECDH is a key-agreement protocol that allows two nodes, each having an elliptic curve public and private key pair to establish a shared secret over an insecure channel. This shared secret can be used as a key for encryption-decryption purpose using a symmetric key cipher. Each cluster head node first generates a public-private key pair (Q_{Ci}, d_{Ci}) using Elliptic Curve Cryptography (ECC). The cluster head then unicasts the public key (Q_{Ci}) to each of its member nodes. The message format is:

$$CH_i \rightarrow *, : Q_{Ci}||ID_i||CV_i|| \ HMAC(G_k; Q_{Ci}||ID_i||CV_i)$$

The member nodes receiving the public point of the cluster head, uses ECC scheme to generate a private and public key pair (d_i, Q_i) and send back the public key (Q_i) to the associated cluster head node. The message format is:

$$node_i \rightarrow CH_i : Q_i||ID_i||TV_i|| \ HMAC(G_k; Q_i||ID_i||TV_i)$$

Each member node i also computes $(x_k, y_k) = d_i Q_{Ci}$. This x_k (the x coordinate of the point in the elliptic curve) is the shared secret or the session key between that member node i and the cluster head CH_i. The shared secret calculated by both the parties is equal since, $d_{Ci}Q_i = d_{Ci}d_iG = d_id_{Ci}G = d_iQ_{Ci}$; where G is the generator of the elliptic curve. This session key is used as a symmetric key by the member nodes to encrypt data and send them to the cluster head. This session key is regenerated after a particular time gap when the session expires. Session key is also regenerated when new cluster heads are selected.

In energy constrained networks like wireless sensor network public key cryptography is always avoided to save energy. However, ECC based schemes are energy conserving and thus can be used. To maintain the privacy of communication between the base station and the cluster head nodes, the base station generates a pair of keys (Q_B, d_B) using ECC. It then forwards the public key to all the cluster heads in the network. The message format is given as:

$$BS \rightarrow CH_i : Q_B||BS||OHC||HMAC(G_k; Q_B||BS||OHC)$$

where OHC is the newly generated One-way hash chain sequence number. The cluster heads receiving the public key uses it for encrypting the data, which is to be forwarded to the base station. Thus the public key Q_B of the base station acts as the encryption key (EK) for the cluster heads. ECC based encryption technique is used here. Whenever a new cluster head is selected, the base station re-generates the key pair and broadcast the public key to all the cluster heads. ECC runs in $O\ (e^{\frac{1}{4}\ln n})$ time and the key forwarding takes place in $O(N)$ time where N is the number of cluster head nodes.

4.6   Module 6: Data Sensing and Aggregation Phase

The next phase of SCBRS comprises of data sensing and aggregation. This module is initiated only when an event takes place within the network region. After completion of the previous phases, comprising of level formation, cluster head selection and cluster formation, key set up and exchange the nodes in the network periodically check for events within their sensing radius. If no event is detected, they remain idle. Otherwise, the nodes start sensing of data relevant to the event. Data sensing phase may not start at the same time for all the clusters in the network. Only nodes which sense some event within their sensing radii start this phase in their clusters. Nodes of other clusters may remain idle at that time. When each node of a cluster where this phase is initiated, gathers a certain amount of data, the sensed data is encrypted using the session key x_k established between that particular member node and the cluster head of that cluster. RC5 symmetric cypher [4] is used by the member nodes to encrypt the sensed data using the session key. The encrypted data is then forwarded to the cluster head of that cluster. A node waits till a certain amount of data is collected and encrypted before forwarding it to the cluster head. This is done, so that less communication overhead takes place. A nested HMAC using the global key as well as the session key is generated over the total message before forwarding it. The format of the messages forwarded by the member nodes to the cluster heads is:

$$v \rightarrow CH_x : ER_v||ID_v||HMAC(G_k; HMAC(x_k; R_v||ID_v||C_v))$$

where ER_v is the encrypted reading of the member node v, ID_v is the id of node v, C_v is a counter value that is incremented each time a new message is forwarded to the cluster head in order to avoid replay attack.

The cluster head nodes receive the sensed data from their member nodes. First the cluster heads generate the HMAC over the received message and match it with the HMAC appended with the message. If match is found, the received encrypted reading from the ith member node is decrypted using the session key for that node. The similar process is followed by the cluster head for all the received data from different member nodes. Redundant data from the received data is then removed by the cluster head and they are aggregated and compressed to be forwarded to the base station. The sensed data from all the nodes is forwarded to the cluster head in $O(N)$ time and data is aggregated in $O(N)$ time. HMAC calculation is completed in constant time.

4.7   Module 7: Sending of Aggregated Data to the Base Station

The last phase of SCBRS is routing of aggregated data to the base station. The aggregated and compressed data is then encrypted using the encryption key EK forwarded by the base station to the cluster heads of the network. ECC based public key cryptography [2] is used to encrypt the aggregated data by the cluster heads. The cluster heads then send the encrypted and aggregated data to the base station following a route, in which the next hop node is selected on the basis of weight values (W_{i_2}). Weight value for each cluster head is calculated in two steps. First each cluster head node of all the levels excepting the highest level, calculate a weight value W_{i_1} for themselves. The Weight value W_{i_1} is calculated as–

$$W_{i_1} = k_1 * \left(\frac{ER_i * N_i * TV_i}{DB_i^2 * CR_i * load_i} \right) \tag{7}$$

where k_1 is the constant of proportionality taken as $= 1$; ER_i is the residual energy of cluster head i, N_i is number of cluster heads adjacent to cluster head i; DB_i is distance between cluster head i and the base station, CR_i is the rate of energy consumption of cluster head i which is calculated as: $= \frac{\Delta E}{\Delta T}$; $load_i$ is the number of messages already sent to cluster head i by other cluster head nodes and TV_i is the current trust value of the cluster head node i.

The calculated W_{i_1} is then HMAC-ed using the global key G_k and is forwarded to the cluster heads of the next higher level, they can sense. The message format is:

$$CH_x \rightarrow CH_y : W_{i_1}||ID_{CHx}||HMAC(G_k; W_{i_1}||ID_{CHx}||C_x))$$

The cluster heads of the adjacent higher level, after receiving the W_{i_1} value for each cluster head within their sensing range in the next lower level, calculate the weight values W_{i_2} for them. W_{i_2} is calculated in the following way:

$$W_{i_2} = \left(\frac{W_{i_1}}{D_{N^2}} \right) \tag{8}$$

where, D_N is distance of the current cluster head from the cluster head i of the next lower level to which it can send data. The format of the message forwarded by each cluster head to the base station is:

$$CH_x \rightarrow BS : ARG_x||ID_x||Suspectlist||HMAC(G_k; HMAC(EK; ARG_x||ID_{CHx}||C_x))$$

where ARG_x is the aggregated and encrypted data from cluster head CH_x, ID_{CHx} is the id of that cluster head, EK is the public key or encryption key and C_x is a counter value. Suspect list contains the IDs of the member nodes of the cluster head CH_x whose trust value decrease considerably due to malicious behavior. The base station verifies the authenticity of the message received from cluster head CH_x and then uses ECC based decryption technique to decrypt the message using the private key of the base station. Once a route is established between a cluster head and the base station, the subsequent packets are forwarded by that cluster head to the base station following the same route. The route is re-selected when any of the levels select a new set of cluster heads or if the public key of the base station is regenerated. This module also takes O(N) time to complete. Therefore, time complexity of all the modules of SCBRS is given as:

$$O(N^2) + O(N) + O(N) + O(e^{\frac{1}{2}\ln n}) + O(N) + O(N) + O(1) + O(N) + O(N).$$

Thus the algorithm SCBRS runs in $O(N^2)$ time to complete all the phases or one round.

5   Simulation Results

The parameters used to simulate the performance of SCBRS are given in Table 1.

Simulation of the proposed scheme is done using NS2.2 simulator. The simulation results of SCBRS are compared with SHRP [8] and Tree based protocol [7] and is given below.

Table 1. Parameter list

Parameters	Description
Network size	100 nodes
Initial energy	50 J per node
MAC protocol	IEEE 802.15.4
Sensor node	Imote2
Radio frequency	13 MHz

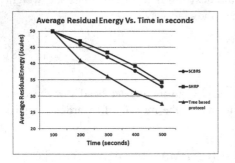

Fig. 1. Average residual energy vs. time   **Fig. 2.** Number of malicious nodes vs. packets dropped

Figure 1 shows the graph of average residual energy versus time in seconds. It is observed that even after 500 s SHRP [8] and SCBRS have more average residual energy compared to Tree based protocol [7]. However, it is observed that SCBRS consumes more battery power when compared with SHRP. This is due to the extra security measures adopted by SCBRS like ECC based public key cryptography for cluster head nodes and ECDH based key exchange between cluster heads and their member nodes. Although, SCBRS lags behind SHRP in terms of energy conservation, the difference of average residual energy in both the schemes is not huge in any point of time.

Figure 2 shows the graph of number of malicious nodes present in the network versus number of packets dropped by SCBRS, SHRP [8] and Tree based protocol [7]. It is observed that even in presence of 25 malicious nodes, the number of packets dropped by SCBRS is much less compared to SHRP and Tree based protocol. Thus, it can be concluded that though SCBRS drains a little more battery power than SHRP, it gains in terms of security. The use of ECDH based key exchange between the member nodes and the cluster head and also the use of a strong encryption method based on ECC by the cluster heads decreases the number of packets drop and the chances of data being snooped in case of SCBRS.

6 Conclusions

The hierarchical approach taken by Secure Cluster Based Routing Scheme (SCBRS) not only helps in conserving energy but also aids in area-wise monitoring of the intent area. Energy efficiency is targeted by SCBRS as much as possible however the main emphasis is given on securing the data. Thus SCBRS is highly suitable for applications like military surveillance where data privacy, integrity and authenticity are highly required. The strong ECC based data encryption technique followed by the cluster heads and RC5 based data encryption followed by the member nodes maintains privacy of data. HMAC generated by MD5 or SHA-1 is responsible for maintaining the integrity of data and the OHC attached with a message checks the authenticity of the sender. The common attacks like sinkhole, wormhole, Sybil attack, packet eaves-dropping and flooding attack are all alleviated to the maximum extent by SCBRS. This protocol is unique in its approach as it does not consider any party of the network to be trusted excepting the base station. Still, the authenticity of the base station is checked and also both way trust value calculation is performed by a cluster head and its member nodes.

References

1. Kulik, J., Heinzelman, W.R., Balakrishnan, H.: Negotiation based protocols for disseminating information in wireless sensor networks. Wirel. Netw. **8**, 169–185 (2002)
2. Mishra, A.R., Singh, M.: Elliptic curve cryptography (ECC) for security in wireless sensor network. Int. J. Eng. Res. Technol. (IJERT) **1**(3), 1–6 (2012)
3. Kumar, S., Girimondo, M., Weimerskirch, A., Paar, C., Patel, A, Wander, A.S.: Embedded end-to-end wireless security with ECDH key exchange. Published in: Circuits and Systems, 2003 IEEE 46th Midwest Symposium, vol. 2, pp. 786–789 (2003)
4. Rivest, R.L.: The RC5 encryption algorithm. In: Preneel, B. (ed.) FSE 1994. LNCS, vol. 1008, pp. 86–96. Springer, Berlin (1995)

5. Karlof, C., Wagner, D.: Secure routing in wireless sensor networks: attacks and counter-measures. Ad Hoc Netw. **1**, 293–315 (2003). Elsevier Journal, doi:10.1016/S1570-8705(03)00008-8
6. Azarderakhsh, R., Reyhani-Masoleh, A., Abid, Z.-E.: A key management scheme for cluster based wireless sensor networks. In: 2008 IEEE/IFIP International Conference on Embedded and Ubiquitous Computing (2008)
7. Messai, M.-L., Aliouat, M., Seba, H.: Tree based protocol for key management in wireless sensor networks. In: Hindawi Publishing Corporation EURASIP Journal on Wireless Communications and Networking, vol. 2010, Article ID 910695
8. Roy, S., Das, A.K.: Secure hierarchical routing protocol (SHRP) for wireless sensor network. In: Proceedings of Second International Symposium on Security in Computing and Communications (SSCC 2014), CCIS, vol. 467, pp. 20–29. Springer, Berlin, Heidelberg (2014)

A Pareto Survivor Function Based Cluster Head Selection Mechanism (PSFCHSM) to Mitigate Selfish Nodes in Wireless Sensor Networks

PL. Rajarajeswari[1][(✉)] and N.K. Karthikeyan[2]

[1] Department of Computer Science and Engineering,
Sri Krishna College of Technology, Coimbatore 641042, Tamil Nadu, India
pl.rajarajeswari@skct.edu.in
[2] Department of Information Technology,
Sri Krishna College of Engineering and Technology,
Coimbatore 641008, Tamil Nadu, India

Abstract. In Wireless Sensor Networks (WSNs), co-operation among sensor nodes plays a significant role for reliable data delivery by prolonging the lifetime of the network. Taking this aspect into account, a Pareto Survivor Function based Cluster Head Selection Mechanism (PSFCHSM) is proposed for electing the new cluster head under selfish attack. In this approach, the detection of selfish attack is achieved through a conditional probabilistic approach which monitors events that purely depends only on the continuous network parameters. The proposed strategy not only identifies the selfish attack in sensor networks but also elects a new sensor node as a rehabilitative Cluster Head (CH) based on Pareto Survivor Function (PSF). The preeminence of the proposed approach is evaluated through evaluation parameters like Packet Delivery Ratio (PDR), Energy Consumption Rate and Throughput by varying the number of sensor nodes and the transmission range. Further, the incorporation of this conditional survivability co-efficient mechanism detects and mitigates selfish nodes at a rapid rate of 32 % than the benchmark mechanisms like Fuzzy Ant Colony Optimization Routing (FACOR) and Genetic Algorithm Inspired Routing Protocol (GROUP) considered for comparison. The proposed approach not only isolates the selfish nodes that causes Denial of Service (DoS) attack but also reduces the cost incurred in communication. Furthermore, the simulation results show that PSFCHSM outperforms GROUP and FACOR by enhancing the network lifetime by 28 %.

Keywords: Selfish nodes · Conditional survivability co-efficient · Pareto Survivor Function (PSF) · FACOR · GROUP · Node lifetime

1 Introduction

Wireless Sensor Network (WSN) is defined as a collection of sensor nodes deployed in a random manner or uniformly in a smaller or larger geographical area for gathering data from a source area to another through a Base Station (BS) [1]. The sensor nodes

© Springer International Publishing Switzerland 2015
J.H. Abawajy et al. (Eds): SSCC 2015, CCIS 536, pp. 381–391, 2015.
DOI: 10.1007/978-3-319-22915-7_35

distributed in a sensor field have to cooperate with each other in a coordinated manner to confirm reliable data delivery to the sink environment [2]. Due to the unique characteristics of sensor networks, it may lead to various issues in the deployment of the network which includes dynamically changing and untrustworthy environment, irregular or random deployment of sensor nodes, restricted battery and other hardware resources. One of the major factors which have to be considered while designing mitigation mechanisms for sensor networks is the scarce resource availability [3].

Clusters are formed in WSN by grouping certain number of sensor nodes. From each cluster, a particular node is elected as a leader/coordinator. It becomes the Cluster Head (CH) and is responsible for sensing, gathering, processing the sensed information and also transferring it to the destination node. Hence, it is clear that the energy-consumption of a CH is higher than other sensor nodes. Therefore, CH selection will affect the survivability of a network. In this paper, the factor of energy consumption is considered in determining the CH.

The rest of the paper is organized as follows. Section 2 presents some of the related works on mitigating malicious nodes. Section 3 elaborates on the Pareto Survivor Function based Cluster Head Selection Mechanism (PSFCHSM) for detecting selfish nodes in WSNs. The detailed simulation and investigation conducted are discussed in Sect. 4. Section 5 concludes the paper with scope for future works.

2 Related Work

A number of CH selection mechanisms have been proposed for detecting and mitigating selfish nodes in WSNs. Some of those approaches are enumerated with their pros and cons as below.

A reputation based trust system was first proposed by Ganeriwal et al. [4] that use Bayesian formulation, specifically beta reputation system, reputation representation, updates and integration. A watch-dog mechanism was employed to compute reputation, in which each node on receiving the packets is calculated based on the secondhand information. The main drawback of this scheme is that the trust evaluation depends on a node's QoS property and is suitable for only non-scalable flat WSN architecture.

Momani and Challa [5] has propounded a trust mechanism that involves more than one trust component that possess the capability of adding a deleting a trust component. It introduces both data trust and communication trust since one trust component may not be sufficient for the data trust and communication trust. This approach also computes the trust based on beta reputation methodology which is the addition of first hand and second hand parameter.

Further, an aggregated trust scheme was designed to deal with the selfish nodes that try to malfunction in the network and distort the data integrity by appending false data during aggregation and disturbing the transmission of cumulative data as proposed by Ozdemir [6].

Alzaid et al. [7] have designed a data aggregation scheme for WSN that incorporates aggregation functionality. It is also based on beta reputation methodology and improves the network lifetime and the integrity of the aggregated data. It uses symmetric secret keys to assign keys to sensor nodes based on their locations. It is similar to watchdog mechanism and uses a reputation table that consists of sensing, actuating, forward based reputation values.

Another, energy efficient trust based algorithm is proposed by Taghikhaki et al. [8], where aggregation and energy are considered for detection and mitigation. The concepts of functional reputation and trust are used to select aggregators based on the quality of the node. To find the best path from every sensor node, the link availability and residual energy of the nodes are taken into account. ETA introduces some delay in the network but it outperforms other schemes in terms of reliability and lifetime.

Boukerche and Ren [9] have designed a reputation management system, where a trust management model is developed with predefined roles and capabilities. It is a flexible hybrid model combining certificate based and behavior based approaches. It enables controlled trust evolution and trust revocation.

Furthermore, Aivaloglou and Gritzalis [10] proposed a trust model based on entropy model to detect selfish and malicious nodes. It presents a trust propagation model to measure trust and to defend trust evaluation from attacks. It gives a clear understanding of trust metrics, mathematical properties of trust, dynamic properties of trust and trust models. It uses both entropy and Bayesian models. Possible attacks against the proposed system have been identified and various remedial techniques have been applied. This system improves the routing techniques and improves the throughput of network.

Hongjun et al. [11] proposed a trust evaluation scheme for ah-hoc networks. The trust value is found using novel entropy based model and evaluation methods. Entropy based trust calculation model is found to get the trustworthiness between two nodes. To compute the trust value from one node to another, a probability action [0,1] is followed. The trust is established between nodes using recommendations and a directed graph is used to describe the trust values.

In addition, a distributed and adaptive reputation mechanism is proposed for wireless ad hoc networks by Luo et al. [12] that blacklists the falsely perceived selfish nodes and the cooperation is restored between the nodes. This model brings out two distinct modes to learn and predict the deterministic and random behavior of the neighbors. The deterministic mode is generic and aids in finding out the behavior of the network for standard patterns. The random mode uses randomized analysis based on Genetic Algorithm (GA). The game theory gives a suggestion about how the participants have to behave in a crucial situation.

Agah et al. [13] proposed a game between a sensor node and three factors namely cooperation, reputation and quality of security based on cooperative game theory. Cooperation between nodes shows that the data communication between nodes is reliable. In addition, the reputation of a node increases and the misbehavior is easily detected. By combining these factors, the trust value is calculated.

Since, most of the CH election mechanism proposed for mitigating selfish nodes in WSNs considers either discrete or continuous events into account. Hence, we propose a Pareto Survivor Function based Cluster Head Selection Mechanism (PSFCHSM) that purely depends only on the conditional probability based on continuous network parameters.

3 A Pareto Survivor Function Based Cluster Head Selection Mechanism (PSFCHSM)

In this section, we present a Pareto Survivor Function based Cluster Head Selection Mechanism (PSFCHSM) that elects the new cluster of the WSN under selfish attack. In this approach, the detection of selfish attack is achieved through a conditional probabilistic approach which monitors events that purely depends only on the continuous network parameters.

Consider a WSN in which the path from the source to the sink is categorized into 'r' distinct routes. For each route 'i', the lifetime of the sensor node is exponentially distributed with parameter 'λ_i' and let 'y' denote the life time of a distinct route and 'x' denotes the lifetime of each wireless sensor nodes participating in the routing activity.

Then, the distribution function of each routing path 'i' of a sensor network within its lifetime 'y' is given by Eq. (1).

$$f_{Y/X}(y/i) = \lambda_i e^{-\lambda_i y}, \ y > 0 \tag{1}$$

Further, the density function of lifetime for a sensor node existing in a routing path at a particular instant of time 't' is given by Eq. (2).

$$p_X(i) = \alpha_i \tag{2}$$

Where, $\sum_{i=1}^{r} \alpha_i = 1$

Then, the joint density function that incorporates both the lifetime of a route and lifetime of the sensor nodes within the route stability 'y' into account for identifying selfish nodes is given by Eq. (3).

$$f(i, y) = f_{Y/X}(y/i)p_X(i) \tag{3}$$

Meanwhile, the Marginal Density Function (MDF) that quantifies the resilience of the entire network under selfish nodes is given by Eqs. (4) and (5).

$$f_Y(y) = \sum_{i=1}^{r} f(i, y) \tag{4}$$

$$= \sum_{i=1}^{r} \alpha_i f_{Y/X}(y/i) \tag{5}$$

In this scenario, the conditional survivability co-efficient that identifies whether a cluster head node is selfish or normal is given by (6) as

$$F_i(y) = \sum_{i=1}^{r} \alpha_i \lambda_i e^{-\lambda_i y}, \ y > 0 \tag{6}$$

Thus, the Conditional Survivability Co-efficient (CSC) quantifies the intensity of selfish nodes behavior on the routing path. Based, on the intensity of impact, the selfish CH is mitigated by electing a new CH that is determined based on Pareto Survivor Function (PSF).

Election of Cluster Head (CH) Based on Pareto Survivor Co-efficient. When a CH of a sensor network is compromised by the selfish attack, then a Pareto survivor function is calculated in each and every sensor node, except the compromised CH using Pareto distribution. Thus, the PSF that decides whether a specific sensor node may be elected as the new CH is given by Eq. (7). 'φ' is the Survivability Co-efficient.

$$R_{i(t)} = \left(\frac{\varphi(i)}{\varphi(i) + t} \right)^{\alpha} \tag{7}$$

where, 'α' is the scalability factor of the network that is determined based on the conditional probability of number of sensor nodes joining a cluster and the failure rate of node behavior at a point of time 't' as given by Eq. (8).

$$\alpha = \lambda_i e^{-\lambda_i t} \tag{8}$$

Further, the hazard failure rate (λ_i) towards selfishness of the CH is given by Eq. (9).

$$\lambda_i = e^{-\int_0^t H(t) dt} \tag{9}$$

where, the hazard failure rate depends on the non-cooperative probability '$H(t)$', which is defined as the ratio of total amount of energy present in a sensor node after drain 'E_{drain}' to the total amount of energy available in that sensor node as given by Eq. (10).

$$H(t) = \frac{E_{drain}}{E_{avail}} \tag{10}$$

Hence, a new CH is elected for replacing the compromised CH when it is above a threshold of $RT_{i(t)}$. The threshold Pareto survivor function value used for this mechanism is 0.4, since maximum selfish nodes are identified and mitigated at this point (as per simulation conducted).

In addition, the proposed PSFCHSM approach incorporates the energy model contributed by Heinzelman et al. [14] for calculating the amount of energy utilized by the sensor nodes. This mechanism also utilizes channel models of multipath fading with d^4 powerless and free space of d^2 power loss. Based on the distance from the threshold parameter, context switching of multipath or free space model are used. Thus, the equation to calculate the cost of transmission and receiver cost for transmitting m-bit information at distance 'd' is given by Eq. (11).

$$E_{TC}(m, d) = \begin{cases} E_{ec} + m + 8f_{sd} * m * d^2, & if(d < d_t) \\ E_{ec} + m + 8t_{mp} * m * d^4, & if(d \geq d_t) \end{cases} \tag{11}$$

where,

Threshold parameter, $d_t = \sqrt{\frac{\text{sfsd}}{\text{stsp}}}$ and $E_{TC}(m, d)$, t_{mp} and E_{ec} represents the energy required for transmission, time required for multiple packet transmission and energy required for packet generation.

Here, energy utilized by the amplifier of a transmitted for larger distance transmission is stop = 0.0016p J/bit/m^4, while the energy utilized by the transmitted for shorter disagree transmission is fsd = l^2 J/bit/m^2.

4   Simulations and Experimental Analysis

In this section, the performance of PSFCHSM under selfish node attacks is evaluated through ns-2 simulations. The superior performance of the proposed PSFCHSM approach is identified by comparing it with two benchmark mechanisms viz., Fuzzy Ant Colony Optimization Routing (FACOR) [15] and Genetic Algorithm Inspired Routing Protocol (GROUP) [16].

In case of sensor networks, the reliability of data transfer depends on the CH of each cluster group formed through local clustering. Hence, the presence of compromised CH decreases the packet delivery, throughput, whereas increases the total energy consumption and packet drop rate. Hence, the detection of selfish nodes and the election of new CH for data dissemination are needed to be evaluated based on the parameters like Packet Delivery Ratio (PDR), Throughput and Total Energy Consumption. The simulation parameters used for comparative analysis are described in Table 1.

Table 1. Simulation parameters

Parameter	Value	Description
No. of sensor nodes	100	Simulation node
Network size	100 × 100 m	Terrain area of the network
Distance threshold	65 m	Optimal distance set for transmission
Initial energy	2.5 J	Energy availability in a sensor node before transmission
Simulation time	50 m	Maximum simulation time
Data packets size	2000 bits	Maximum size packets used in simulation
Base station location	(60 m, 180 m)	Minimum and maximum distance of the base station from sensor nodes

Comparative Analysis for PSFCHSM. The performance of PSFCHSM is studied based on two experiments with respect to Packet Delivery Ratio (PDR), Throughput and Total energy consumption through experiments. In the first experiment, the number of sensor nodes is varied, while in the second experiment, the transmission range is varied.

Experiment 1-Performance Analysis for PSFCHSM Obtained by Varying the Number of Sensor Nodes

Packet Delivery Ratio (PDR). Figure 1 illustrates the comparative analysis of PSFCHSM with the benchmark CH selection mechanisms like GROUP and FACOR based on PDR. The proposed mechanism, PSFCHSM shows increase in the PDR than GROUP from 13 % to 19 % and from 23 % to 28 % over FACOR.

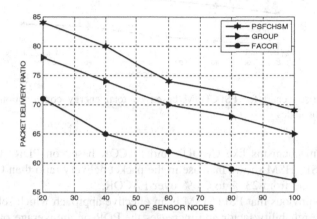

Fig. 1. Comparison chart for PSFCHSM based on packet delivery ratio with varying number of sensor nodes

Hence, it is obvious that PSFCHSM is an effective approach which selects the CHs through Kappa reliability factor and increases the PDR on an average of 32 %.

Total Energy Consumption. Figure 2 illustrates the comparative analysis of PSFCHSM with GROUP and FACOR based on total energy consumption. The proposed mechanism, PSFCHSM shows a decrease in the total energy consumption than GROUP from 18 % to 23 % and from 27 % to 33 % over FACOR.

Hence, it is obvious that PSFCHSM is an effective approach which reduces the total energy consumption on an average by 29 %.

Throughput. Figure 3 illustrates the comparative analysis of PSFCHSM with GROUP and FACOR on Throughput. The proposed mechanism, PSFCHSM shows an increase in the Throughput than GROUP from 20 % to 28 % and from 25 % to 31 % over FACOR.

Hence, it is obvious that PSFCHSM is an effective approach which maximizes the throughput on an average by 31 %.

Experiment 2-Performance Analysis for PSFCHSM Obtained by Varying the Transmission Range

Packet Delivery Ratio (PDR). Figure 4 illustrates the comparative analysis of PSFCHSM with Genetic Algorithm (GA) and Ant Colony Optimization (ACO) based

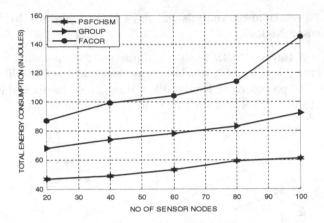

Fig. 2. Comparison chart for PSFCHSM based on total energy consumption with varying number of sensor nodes

CH selection mechanisms like GROUP and FACOR based on PDR. The proposed mechanism, PSFCHSM shows increase in the packet delivery ratio than GROUP from 13 % to 19 % and from 23 % to 28 % over FACOR.

Hence, it is obvious that PSFCHSM is an effective approach which selects the CHs through Kappa reliability factor and increases the PDR on an average of 14 %.

Total Energy Consumption. Figure 5 illustrates the comparative analysis of PSFCHSM with GROUP and FACOR based on total energy consumption. The proposed mechanism, PSFCHSM shows a decrease in the total energy consumption than GROUP from 18 % to 23 % and from 27 % to 33 % over FACOR.

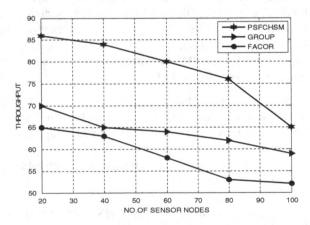

Fig. 3. Comparison chart for PSFCHSM based on throughput with varying number of sensor nodes.

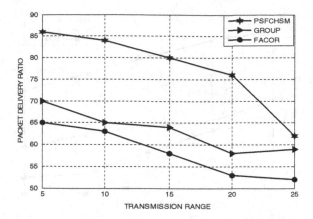

Fig. 4. Comparison chart for PSFCHSM based on packet delivery ratio with varying transmission range.

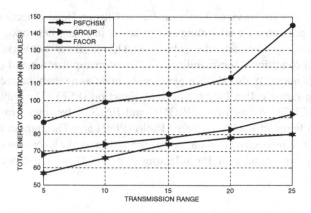

Fig. 5. Comparison chart for PSFCHSM based on total energy consumption with varying transmission range.

Hence, it is obvious that PSFCHSM is an effective approach which reduces the total energy consumption rate on an average by 23 %.

Throughput. Figure 6 illustrates the comparative analysis of PSFCHSM with GROUP and FACOR based on Throughput. The proposed mechanism, PSFCHSM shows an increase in the throughput than GROUP from 20 % to 28 % and from 25 % to 31 % over FACOR.

Hence, it is obvious that PSFCHSM is an effective approach which maximizes the throughput on an average by 27 %.

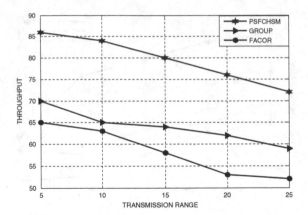

Fig. 6. Comparison chart for PSFCHSM based on throughput with varying transmission range.

5 Conclusion

In this paper, a Pareto Survivor Function based Cluster Head Selection Mechanism (PSFCHSM) is presented for mitigating selfish attack in sensor networks. The proposed strategy significantly identifies the selfish attack in sensor networks through the incorporation of conditional survivability co-efficient manipulated based on present and past behavior of nodes. It also elects a new sensor node as a rehabilitative CH based on a quantification factor called Pareto Survivor Function (PSF). The simulation results show that PSFCHSM outperforms GROUP and FACOR by improving the network performance in terms of Packet Delivery Ratio (PDR) and Throughput on an average by 27 % and 24 % respectively. As a part of the future work, Kappa co-efficient based mitigation may be formulation for selecting a new CH which depends purely on discrete events.

References

1. Liu, K., Abu-ghazaleh, N., Kang, K.D.: Location verification and trust management for resilient geographic routing. J. Parallel Distrib. Comput. **67**(2), 215–228 (2007)
2. Shaikh, R.A., Jameel, H., d'Auriol, B.J., Lee, H., Lee, S., Song, Y.J.: A group-based trust management scheme for clustered wireless sensor networks. IEEE Trans. Parallel Distrib. Syst. **20**(11), 1698–1712 (2000)
3. Komathy, K., Narayanasamy, P.: Trust-AODV routing against selfishness. J. Netw. Comput. Appl. **31**(4), 446–471 (2008)
4. Ganeriwal, S., Balzano, L.K., Srivastava, M.B.: Reputation-based framework for high integrity sensor networks. ACM Trans. Sensor Netw. **4**(3), 1–37 (2008)
5. Momani, M., Challa, S.: Bayesian fusion algorithm for interfering trust in WSN. J. Netw. **5**(7), 123–131 (2010)
6. Ozedemir, S.: Functional reputation based reliable data aggregation and transmission for wireless sensor networks. Comput. Commun. **3**(1), 3941–3953 (2008)

7. Alzaid, H., Foo, E., Nieto, J.: RSDA: Reputation-based secure data aggregation in wireless sensor networks. Int. Conf. Parallel Distrib. Appl. Technol. 1(1), 456–462 (2008)
8. Taghikhaki, Z., Meratnia, N., Havinga, P.J.: Energy efficient trust based aggregation in WSN. In: INFOCOM WKSHPS 2011, vol. 1, no. 1, pp. 584–589 (2011)
9. Boukerche, A., Ren, Y.: A trust based security system for ubiquitous and pervasive computing. Comput. Commun. 3(18), 189–197 (2008)
10. Aivaloglou, E., Gritzalis, S.: Hybrid trust and reputation management for sensor networks. Wirel. Netw. 16(5), 1493–1510 (2010)
11. Hongjun, D., Zhiping, J., Xiaona, D.: An entropy based trust modeling and evaluation for wireless sensor networks. In: International Conference on Embedded Software systems, vol. 1, no. 1, pp. 124–132 (2008)
12. Luo, J., Liu, X., Fan, M.: A trust model based on fuzzy recommendations for MANET. Comput. Netw. 5(3), 2396–2407 (2009)
13. Agah, A., Das, S.K., Basu, K.: A game theory based approach for security in WSN. In: IEEE International Conference on Performance, Computing and Communication, vol. 1, no. 1, pp. 259–263 (2005)
14. Heinzelman, W.B., Chandrakasan, A.P., Balakrishnan, H.: An application-specific protocol architecture for wireless microsensor networks. IEEE Trans. Wireless Commun. 1(4), 660–670 (2002)
15. Amiri, E., Keshavarz, H., Alizadeh, M., Zamani, M., Khodadadi, T.: Energy efficient routing in wireless sensor networks based on fuzzy ant colony optimization. Int. J. Distrib. Sensor Netw. 2014, 17 (2014). Article ID 768936
16. Chakraborty, A., Mitra, S.K., Naskar, M.K.: A Genetic algorithm inspired routing protocol for wireless sensor networks. Int. J. Comput. Intell. Theor. Pract. 6(1), 1–8 (2011)

Vehicle Brake and Indicator Detection for Autonomous Vehicles

R. Sathya[✉], M. Kalaiselvi Geetha, and P. Aboorvapriya

Department of Computer Science and Engineering,
Annamalai University, Chidambaram, India
{rsathyamephd,geesiv,aboorvapriya31cse}@gmail.com

Abstract. Automated detection of vehicle lights can be used as a part of the systems for forward collision avoidance and accidents. This paper presents automatic vehicle detection and tracking system using Haar-Cascade method. The threshold collection is HSV color space in the vehicle light representation and the segmentation selection of light area. The extracted vehicle brake and turn indicator signals are morphologically paired and vehicle light candidate information is extracted by identifying the Region of Interest (ROI). The canny edge light intensity of the vehicle is extracted and a novel feature is called Edge Block Intensity Vector (EBIV). In this experiment, traffic surveillance system is developed for recognition of moving vehicle lights in traffic scenes using SVM with polynomial and RBF (Radial Basis Function) kernel. The experiments are carried out on the real time data collection in traffic road environment. This approach gives an overall average higher accuracy 95.7 % of SVM with RBF kernel by using 36 EBIV features compared to SVM with Polynomial kernel by using 9, 16, 25, 36, 64 and 100 EBIV features and SVM with RBF kernel by using 9, 16, 25, 64 and 100 EBIV features for recognizing the vehicle light.

Keywords: Support vector machine · Driver assistance system · Vehicle detection and vehicle light recognition

1 Introduction

Recognizing and classification of the vehicle lights is an important area for intelligent automated vehicles. The vehicle signals have been used as significant cue for driver assistance systems. Vehicle light detection and classification in videos has been receiving increasing attention of computer vision. Intellectual Vehicles with the human resources are appearing to be hopeful to avoid the accidents. However, involuntarily recognizing vehicle light detection in videos is difficult. The autonomous vehicle systems are suitable for all environmental conditions, during daytime and at night time. Although Recognizing and classification of the vehicle reduced the death in vehicle crashes, accident prediction and prevention would be the ultimate solution for maximizing driving safety. This paper focuses on vehicle detection, vehicle light detection and classification.

© Springer International Publishing Switzerland 2015
J.H. Abawajy et al. (Eds): SSCC 2015, CCIS 536, pp. 392–401, 2015.
DOI: 10.1007/978-3-319-22915-7_36

1.1   Related Work

Robust and efficient vehicle light detection (VLD) [1] algorithm is used for vehicle and vehicle light detection. Detection of automatic vehicle and tracking system using Haar-cascade which can be applied to traffic environment. Traffic surveillance system [2] is developed for detecting and tracking moving vehicles in night time traffic scenes using SVM classifier. Vehicle detection and classification [3] was done by locating their head lights and tail lights in the night time road environment using SVM classifiers. Detecting vehicles [4] in front of a camera-assisted vehicle during night time driving conditions in order to automatically change vehicle head lights between low beams and high beams avoiding glares for the drivers and vehicle classified using SVM classifiers. [5] proposed feature extraction and classification for rear-view vehicle detection. The appearance based hypothesis verification step verifies using Gabor features and SVM.

The rest of this paper is organized as follows: Sect. 2 describes a proposed approach. Section 3 discusses the Feature extraction. Section 4 presents the experimental results. Finally, Sect. 5 concludes the paper.

2   Proposed Work

The datasets are collected for 30 min approximately for experimental purpose. The input video is processed at 25 frames per second. The video series is converted into frames in .jpg format. The haar cascade method is used to detect the vehicle and vehicle extraction. The HSV color feature is used to detect the vehicle light. The Edge Block Intensity Vector (EBIV) feature is extracted and fed to SVM classifier. The overall block diagram of the proposed approach is shown in Fig. 1.

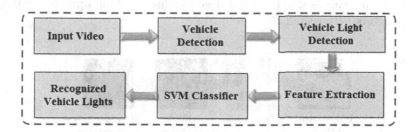

Fig. 1. Block diagram of the proposed approach.

2.1   Vehicle Detection

The automatic vehicle detection and extraction [1,6] has an significant importance in surveillance system. The traffic video sequences afford rich information regarding direction of the road, vehicle, pedestrian, traffic signs and lamps within its field of view as shown in Fig. 2(a). In this paper focal point is only vehicle and vehicle signals. First, the vehicle is detected using Haar cascade method [1]. Haar cascade [7] is used to find the vehicles shown in Fig. 2(b). The positive images contain vehicles and negative images did not contain vehicles. These set of samples are stored to XML files. Haar cascade XML file is used to detect the vehicles. Most of the detected vehicles are different size. Hence in order to minimize the computation, image size is reformed. The extracted vehicle regions are resized to image of size 240×240. pixels as shown in Fig. 2(c).

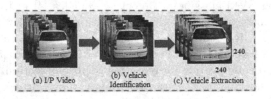

Fig. 2. Vehicle detection and extraction.

2.2 Vehicle Light Segmentation

The vehicle light segmentation is one of the mainly important features of vehicles. It is the major element which differs from other parts of the vehicles. The initial task of vehicle light detection is to convert RGB color image into HSV color image. The input RGB color format can represent any pattern color or intensity using a mixture of Red, Green, Blue components as shown in Fig. 3(a). RGB values could not represent the desired color range. In comparison, HSV is greatly improved than the RGB color at computer visualization and unproblematic to understand the color value. HSV is predictable and expedient color space. To adjust the parameter color region to real-world images convert it into the HSV color space as it is more sensitive to adjust and manipulate the threshold parameters better than RGB [8,9].

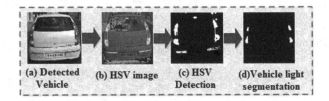

Fig. 3. Vehicle light segmentation.

Vehicle brake light, left and right indicator crave to be segmented out, while retaining the vehicles. The detected area is considered as yellow light only if the minimum and maximum values of HSV thresholds are in the range as mentioned in Table 1. The vehicle light is segmented using the HSV space vehicle light segmentation and small point of noise is affianced the image shown in Fig. 3(c). The operations of morphological erosion and dilation [10] used to remove the noises without changing meticulous light area. The morphological erosion course is to shrinks the pixels in the object boundary. The morphological dilation is to add the pixels in the object boundary as shown in Fig. 3(d).

Table 1. HSV space color values for vehicle brake and indicator lights.

	Minimum	Maximum
Hue(H)	64	178
Saturation(S)	80	253
Value(V)	98	256

2.3   Vehicle Light Detection

The prevalence of vehicle light detection systems for intelligent driver assistance system using video information is expanding rapidly in recent trends. Region of Interest (ROI) is used to detect the vehicle lights. ROI approach [11] is obtainable and it is utilized. The height and width of $ROI_{(light)}$ is calculated. ROI is identified as

$$ROI_{(light)} = Height_{(t)}/Width_{(t)} \tag{1}$$

where, $Height_{(t)}$ is the $ROI_{(light)}$ of height at time 't' and $Width_{(t)}$ is the $ROI_{(light)}$ of width at time 't' for the video sequences.

Fig. 4. Example frames for brake and indicator detection.

The height is calculated using,

$$Height_{(t)} = H_{(t)}/H_{(max)} \tag{2}$$

where $H_{(t)}$ is the height of the frame at time 't', $H_{(max)}$ is the maximum contour value at time 't' in video sequences. Width of the bounding box is calculated using,

$$Width_{(t)} = W_{(t)}/W_{(max)} \tag{3}$$

where $W_{(t)}$ is the width of the frame at time 't', $W_{(max)}$ is the width of max-imum contour at time 't' in video sequence. Region of Interest (ROI) is found in the original frame which identifies all type of vehicle lights. Fig. 4 shows the located vehicle light using Region of Interest (ROI) for brake light, left and right indicator detection.

3   Feature Extraction

A novel feature called Edge Block Intensity Vector (EBIV) is proposed in this work. One of the most essential features of visual system is edge features, and using such edge orientation information is feasible to express shapes. For this reason, canny edge detection is utilized to identify the edges. The work is divided the vehicle light region into various size blocks such as 9, 16, 25, 36, 64 and 100 blocks shown in Fig. 5(b). In reason, vehicle lights are installed in centred position of the left and right corner. The vehicle light image is size of 240×240. In order to minimize the computation, extraction of EBIV features as 3×3, 4×4, 5×5, 6×6, 8×8 and 10×10 blocks and each Block of size is 80×80, 60×60, 48×48, 40×40, 30×30 and 24×24 as shown in Fig. 5(c). The average intensity value of pixels in each block is calculated as Edge Block Intensity Vector (EBIV). In this work 9, 16, 25, 36, 64 and 100 dimension EBIV features are presented.

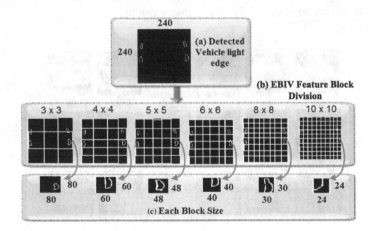

Fig. 5. Edge Block Intensity Vector (EBIV) feature extraction.

4   Experimental Results

In this section, proposed method is evaluated using real collection road environment datasets. The experiments carried out in C++ with OpenCV 2.2 in Ubuntu 12.04 operating system on a computer with Intel $CORE^{TM}$ I5 Processor 2.30 GHz with 4 GB RAM. The obtained EBIV features are fed to SVM with Polynomial and RBF kernel for vehicle brake and indicator recognition. Each incident of the input vehicle light from an input video sequence is represented as a feature vector. Classically the dimension of the feature vector is between a few and several tens. In this experiment used 9, 16, 25, 36, 64 and 100 EBIV feature vectors for vehicle light recognition.

4.1   Dataset

Vehicle light recognition plays an essential role in traffic surveillance system. The dataset created during daylight in real road environment, is used for experimental purpose. The video is processed at 25 frames per second. The video is converted into frames in .jpg format. The sample images are shown in Fig. 6.

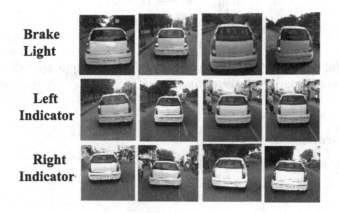

Fig. 6. Example frames for real collection dataset.

The collected dataset is listed in Table 2. In this work, the images are taken into a training set at 30 min video and testing set at 16 min video.

Table 2. Dataset description.

S.No	Vehicle signal type	Video duration in minutes
1	Brake signal	10:20
2	Left indicator	11:57
3	Right indicator	14:64

4.2   Support Vector Machine

Support Vector Machine (SVM) is a popular technique for classification in visual pattern recognition [12]. The SVM is most widely used in kernel learning algorithm. It achieves reasonably vital pattern recognition performance in optimization theory [13,14]. Classification tasks are typically involved with training and testing data. The training data are separated by $(x_1, y_1), (x_2, y_2), ...(x_m, y_m)$ into two classes, where $x_i \in \Re^n$ contains n-dimensional feature vector and $y_i \in \{+1, -1\}$ are the class labels. The aim of SVM is to generate a model which predicts the target value from testing set. In binary classification the hyper plane $w.x + b = 0$, where $w \in \Re^n$, $b \in \Re$ is used to separate the two classes in some space Z [15]. The maximum margin is given by $M = 2/||w||$. The minimization problem is solved by using Lagrange multipliers $\alpha_i (i = 1, ...m)$ where w and b are optimal values obtained from Eq. 5.

The non-negative slack variables ξ_i are used to maximize margin and minimize the training error. The soft margin classifier obtained by optimizing the Eqs. 6 and 7.

$$\min_{w,b,\xi} \frac{1}{2} w^T w + C \sum_{i=1}^{l} \xi_i \tag{4}$$

$$y_i(w^T \phi(x_i) + b) \geq 1 - \xi_i, \xi_i \geq 0 \tag{5}$$

If the training data is not linearly separable, the input space mapped into high dimensional space with kernel function $K(x_i, x_j) = \phi(x_i).\phi(x_j)$ is explained in [14].

4.3   Performance Evaluation

To compute F-measure,

$$F - measure = 2PR/(P + R) \tag{6}$$

where, P and R are precision and recall. The F-Measure computes some average of the information retrieval precision and recall metrics. Precision is calculated using following equation,

$$Precision = TP/(TP + FP) \tag{7}$$

where, TP and FP are True Positive and False Positive. Recall is calculated using the equation,

$$Recall = TP/(TP + FN) \tag{8}$$

where, TP and FP is True Positive and False Positive. TP is total number of correctly detected vehicles light. FP is total number of in-correctly detected vehicles light. False Negative (FN) represents the total number false detections.

4.4   Experimental Result for Vehicle Light Detection

The moving vehicle detection is very important for video surveillance. In this work, 3000 frames are taken into training set for each vehicle signals frame as 1000 and 1200 frames are taken into testing set for each vehicle signals frame as 400. In this experiment, the proposed approach utilized SVM with polynomial and RBF kernels. While, analyzing the performances of RBF kernels gives high

Table 3. Confusion Matrix for vehicle brake and indicators using SVM polynomial kernel with 36 EBIV feature (94.4 %).

	Brake Light (%)	Left Indicator (%)	Rigth Indicator (%)
Brake Light	**95.1**	3.3	1.3
Left Indicator	1.4	**90.2**	8.1
Rigth Indicator	0	2.0	**98.0**

accuracy compared with polynomial kernel. Table 4 shows the confusion matrix for vehicle brake and indicators using SVM Polynomial kernel with 36 dimension EBIV feature.

Table 3 shows the confusion matrix for vehicle brake, left and right indicator using SVM RBF kernel with 36 EBIV feature.

Table 4. Confusion Matrix for vehicle brake and indicators using SVM RBF kernel with 36 EBIV feature (97.4 %).

	Brake Light (%)	Left Indicator (%)	Rigth Indicator (%)
Brake Light	**97.3**	1.9	0.8
Left Indicator	1.8	**97.2**	1.0
Rigth Indicator	1.3	0.8	**97.9**

Table 5 shows the Precision and Recall value for vehicle brake, left and right indicators using SVM Polynomial kernel with 36 EBIV feature.

Table 5. Precision and Recall value using SVM Polynomial kernel with 36 EBIV feature.

	Precision (%)	Recall (%)
Brake Light	95.2	93.6
Left Indicator	93.8	92.0
Rigth Indicator	93.8	97.3

Table 6 shows the Precision and Recall value for vehicle brake, left and right indicators using SVM RBF kernel with 36 EBIV feature.

Fig. 7 shows the overall performance of the F-measure using SVM Polynomial and RBF kernel with EBIV feature. SVM with RBF kernel gives better accuracy 97.4 % for vehicle brake and indicators recognition compared to SVM with Polynomial kernel by using 9, 16, 25, 36, 64 and 100 EBIV features and SVM with RBF kernel by using 9, 16, 25, 64 and 100 EBIV features.

Table 6. Precision and Recall value using SVM RBF kernel with 36 EBIV feature.

	Precision (%)	Recall (%)
Brake Light	97.2	97.3
Left Indicator	97.2	97.2
Rigth Indicator	98.1	97.9

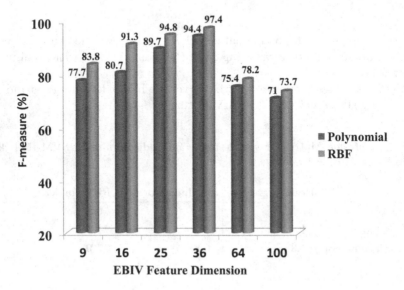

Fig. 7. The overall F-measure using SVM Polynomial and RBF kernel with EBIV feature.

Table 7. Comparative study of existing methods.

S. No	Traffic Scenes	Dataset	Method	Accuracy (%)
1	**Vehicle brake and indicator**	**Daylight in real road environment**	**EBIV Features and SVM (Proposed Approach)**	**97.40**
2	Vehicle head light	complex urban streets	Gabor Features and SVM	91.00
3	Traffic Lights	Highway traffic scenes	SVM Classifier	90.00
4	Head light	Caltech 1998	SVM Classifier	89.00
5	Vehicle lights	Highway traffic scenes	Rule Based Classifier	86.00
6	Vehicle tail lights	Highway traffic scene	SVM Classifier	85.00

4.5   Comparative Study

Table 7 provides comparative study of various vehicle light detection methods using SVM classifiers and various types of datasets. The proposed brake and indicator light EBIV feature method is no directly similar to compare existing method.

5   Conclusion

Vehicle light detection and recognition systems have a wide applications in video surveillance. This paper proposed efficient vehicle tracking and recognition system for identifying and classifying moving vehicle lights for traffic surveillance using SVM classifier. The Edge Block Intensity Vector (EBIV) features are evaluated and fed to multiclass SVM with polynomial and RBF kernel. This approach gives a excellent classification accuracy of 97.4 % for 36 EBIV feature using SVM (RBF) kernel. Experimental results and comparison with existing methods are shown that the proposed system is effective and offers advantages for traffic surveillance in various environments. In future work, be going to improve the flexibility of this features are used in another classifier and recognize the vehicle brake and indicators.

References

1. Aboorvapriya, P., Geetha, M.K., Sathya, R.: Detection and tracking of brake and indicator signals for automated vehicles. Int. J. Appl. Eng. Res. **9**(21), 5007–5013 (2014). Research India Publication
2. Raj Kumar, N., Saravanan, B.: SVM classifier for vehicle surveillance under night-time video scenes. Int. J. Comput. Sci. Inf. Technol. Secur. (IJCSITS) **2**, 11–20 (2012)
3. Sutar, V.B., Admuthe, S.: Night time vehicle detection and classification using support vector machine. Transp. Res. Appl. **1**, 01–09 (2009)
4. Alcantarilla, P.F., Bergasa, L.M., Jimenez, P., Sotelo, M.A., Parra, I., Fernandez, D.: Night time vehicle detection for driving assistance lightbeam controller. In: IJESAT, pp. 1–7 (2008)
5. Gokulakrishnan, R., Arun, R.: Object detection and tracking for android mobile devices using haar cascade classifier. IFET, pp. 1–6 (2012)
6. Sivaraman, S., Trivedi, M.M.: Looking at vehicles on the road: a survey of vision-based vehicle detection, tracking, and behavior analysis. IEEE Trans. Intell. Transp. Syst. **14**(4), 1773–1795 (2013)
7. Yong, X.: Real-time vehicle detection based on haar features and pairwise geometrical histograms. Information and Automation Technology, pp. 390–395 (2011)
8. Radha, R., Lakshman, B.: Retinal image analysis using morphological process and clustering technique. AIRCCASE, vol. 6, pp. 55–69 (2013)
9. Garg, S., Thapar, S.: Feature extraction using morphological operations. ASPRS, vol. 2 (2012)
10. Bai, M.R., Krishna, V.V., Devi, J.S.: A new morphological approach for noise removal cum edge detection. IJCSI **6**, 187–198 (2013)
11. Sathya, R., Geetha, M.K.: Vision based traffic personnel hand gesture recognition using tree based classifiers. In: Jain, L.C., Behera, H.S., Mandal, J.K., Mohapatra, D.P. (eds.) Computational Intelligence in Data Mining. Smart Innovation, Systems and Technologies, vol. 2, pp. 187–200. Springer, India (2015)
12. Cristianini, N., Shawe-Taylor, J.: An Introduction to Support Vector Machines and Other Kernel-Based Learning Methods. Cambridge University Press, Cambridge (2000)
13. Vapnik, V.: Statistical Learning Theory. Wiley, New York (1998)
14. Lewis, J.P.: Tutorial on SVM. CGIT Lab, USC (2004)
15. Chang, C.C., Lin, C.J.: LIBSVM: a library for support vector machines. ACM Trans. Intell. Syst. Technol. **2**, 1–27 (2011)

Secure Multipoint Relay Node Selection in Mobile Ad Hoc Networks

Jeril Kuriakose[1](✉), V. Amruth[2], and R. Vikram Raju[3]

[1] Department of Information Technology,
St. John College of Engineering and Technology, Palghar, India
jeril@muj.manipal.edu
[2] Department of Information Science and Engineering,
Bearys Institute of Technology, Mangalore, India
[3] School of Computing and IT, Manipal University, Jaipur, India

Abstract. MANETs has become a broad area in wireless networks, because of its reduced deployment cost, ease of use, and deliverance from wires. MANETs uses a decentralized and infrastructure-less network, thus making the nodes to route its messages / data with the help of intermediate nodes. Routing in MANETs is carried out with the help of broadcasting schemes, among which MPR is found to be the effectual and uncomplicated scheme. The MPR scheme broadcasts its messages only to the selected MPR nodes. The selected MPR node may be any node in the network, and there are no obligatory and adequate conditions that provides assurance about the selected node's integrity. In this paper, we have proposed a novel approach in the MPR node selection, by adding a security feature prior to the MPR node selection. We have verified the time constraints and efficiency with the help of localization techniques. Future events are also been discussed.

1 Introduction

A large consideration is being given to the mobile ad hoc networks (MANETs) these days, because of their self-organizing and infrastructure-less capabilities. MANET is a collection of mobile nodes that exchange the messages / data via wireless links with the help of intermediate nodes [1] to form a dynamic network. A network can formed anywhere and at any time without any additional requirement in MANETs; whereas this would not be possible in a cellular or wired network. Routing in MANETs is generally initiated using few broadcasting schemes, and multipoint relay (MPR) broadcasting scheme [2] is believed to be the effectual and uncomplicated scheme. As MANETs are infrastructure-less network, the messages / data is transferred with the help of intermediate nodes. During the routing process a broadcast message is sent from the sender node through the intermediate nodes to the network, for identifying the destination node. A broadcast message consumes more energy and floods the network [3], and this can be overcome by using MPR broadcast scheme. The MPR scheme broadcasts the message only to the selected MPR nodes, which in turn broadcast

© Springer International Publishing Switzerland 2015
J.H. Abawajy et al. (Eds): SSCC 2015, CCIS 536, pp. 402–411, 2015.
DOI: 10.1007/978-3-319-22915-7_37

to other MPR nodes or intermediate nodes to identify the destination node, thus reducing flooding and conserving energy.

Any of the neighboring nodes can be selected as the MPR node during MPR node selection, and does not provide any obligatory and adequate conditions for the integrity of the nodes. In this paper, we have added an additional security alternative during the node selection. Prior to the MPR node selection, the intermediate nodes are analyzed for integrity using trilateration technique [4]. Trilateration technique uses location coordinates and distance measurements to identify the vulnerable intermediate node. In MANETs, each mobile node is equipped with special hardware to identify its location reference, and by using trilateration technique in our work, a need for additional hardware for security is not required.

Global Positioning System (GPS) [5] is mostly used in identifying the location coordinates of a mobile node. The deployment cost of a dense network would become more expensive if each node is installed with a GPS receiver, and GPS would not perform effectively in an indoor and underwater environment [6]. To maintain a harmonious location identification of the mobile node, distributed localization schemes came into existence. Distributed localization schemes can overcome the drawbacks of GPS in an indoor and underwater environment. The mobile node that wants to find out its location reference starts by acquiring its range from three or more intermediate nodes, which then estimate the current location using trilateration technique.

The integrity of a network is a significant issue in MANETs. Any node that enters the network is used in the routing process with an assumption that the node is not malicious. The integrity of the network fails once a malicious node enters the network. When a MPR node is under Sybil attack [7], the attacker can create various arbitrary identities or imitate other nodes identities in the network / MAC layer. A MPR node under black hole attack [8] makes the nodes to magnetize all the traffic in the network, it does that by publicity advertising that it has the shortest path to the destination. A wormhole attack [9] makes the MPR node to distract the route from one section of network to a different section by using a wormhole link (tunnel) between two parts of the section.

In this paper, we had made an effort to seal the security problems faced during MPR node selection, by establishing the essential and adequate conditions. Whenever a new node enters a network it first identifies its current location reference. The conventional location identification process has been modified by adding a security feature to it. Our modified location identification process has been explained in the next section. The nodes that are found to be safe are only considered for MPR node selection. Finally, we verified our work using NS-2 network simulator. In this paper, we have referred the unknown node (the node that does not know its location coordinate or the node that wants to finds its location coordinate) as the node that does not know its location coordinates.

The rest of the paper is organized as follows: Sect. 2 briefs the modified location identification process Sect. 3 discusses the mathematical scheming of trilateration technique, Sect. 4 demonstrates how a MPR node is selected. Section 5 shows the results and Sect. 6 concludes the paper.

2   Modified Location Identification Process

Distributed localization is achieved with the help of beacon nodes. Beacon nodes are some special nodes in a network which knows its location reference. The nodes that want to identify its location does it with the help of three or more beacon nodes. Whenever a node wants to find its location reference, it starts by sending a localization request to the neighboring beacon nodes. The beacon nodes replies with the RSSI [10], ToA [11], or TDoA [12] measurements, which in turn is used by the unknown node to identify its location coordinates. Figure 1 shows a typical location identification process and the process is explained as follows:

  i. The unknown nodes send requests to the neighboring beacon nodes.
 ii. The neighboring beacon nodes replies with the distance measurements along with the beacon nodes location reference.
iii. The unknown node identifies its location with the help of trilateration technique (explained in the next section). Once the unknown nodes identify its location coordinates, it can also act as a beacon node if static.

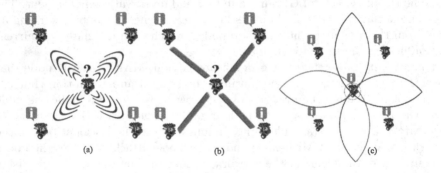

Fig. 1. Typical location identification process.

The beacon nodes that assisted the unknown node to identify its location coordinate, verifies the integrity of the unknown node by asking its newly identified location coordinates. Trilateration technique is again carried out with the obtained location coordinates, to identify whether any false location information is given by the node. In case of vulnerability, the node will not be eligible for an integrity credential scoring by the beacon nodes. Each beacon node provides an integrity credential score of 1 point, and a node to qualify for MPR node selection and to assist in localization must have a minimum integrity credential score of 3 points. More the integrity credential score more the upright.

2.1   Integrity Credential Scoring

Initially, all the beacon nodes are given an integrity credential score of 10 points. The 10 points are given to distinguish the beacon nodes from the other nodes.

A beacon node that assists in localization will be given an integrity credential score of 1 point, but only after it has completed assisting 10 unknown nodes. Vulnerable beacon node will not be eligible for the integrity credential score from the beacon nodes; whereas a negative integrity credential score is given. More the integrity credential score more is the integrity of the node. Due to the integrity credential scoring a malicious node will not be able to endure in a network for a longer duration.

3   Trilateration Technique

Trilateration technique uses the geometry of triangles and sphere to identify the current location of a mobile node. This technique does not require any additional hardware or space apart from the typical requirements of a MANET node. The mathematical computation of trilateration technique is as follows:

Consider three circles or spheres with centre S_1, S_2 and S_3, radius M_1, M_2 and M_3 from points B_1, B_2 and B_3 (beacon node location), refer Fig. 2.

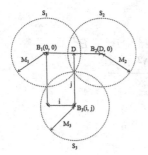

Fig. 2. Trilateration measurements.   **Fig. 3.** Initial MPR selection.

The general equation of the sphere is:

$$\sum_{k=1}^{3}(B_k - S_k)^2 = L^2$$

The following is the modified equation of three circles / sphere:

$$M_1^2 = B_1^2 + B_2^2 + B_3^2 \qquad (1)$$
$$M_2^2 = (B_1 - D)^2 + B_2^2 + B_3^2 \qquad (2)$$
$$M_3^2 = (B_1 - i)^2 + (B_2 - j)^2 + B_3^2 \qquad (3)$$

Subtracting Eq. (2) from Eq. (1), we get

$$M_2^2 - M_1^2 = (B_1 - D)^2 + B_2^2 + B_3^2 - B_1^2 - B_2^2 - B_3^2 \qquad (4)$$

Substituting we get,

$$B_1 = \frac{M_1^2 - M_2^2 + D^2}{2D} \tag{5}$$

From the first two circles we can find out that the two circles intersect at two different points, that is

$$D - B_1 < B_2 < D + B_1 \tag{6}$$

Substituting Eq. (5) in Eq. (1), we can procure

$$M_1^2 = \left(\frac{M_1^2 - M_2^2 + D^2}{2D}\right)^2 + B_2^2 + B_3^2 \tag{7}$$

Substituting we get the solution of the intersection of two spheres / circles:

$$B_2^2 + B_3^2 = M_1^2 - \frac{(M_1^2 - M_2^2 + D^2)^2}{4D^2} \tag{8}$$

Substituting Eq. (1) with Eq. (3) and (8), we get

$$M_3^2 = (B_1 - i)^2 + (B_2 - j)^2 + M_1^2 - B_1^2 - B_2^2 \tag{9}$$

$$B_2 = \frac{M_1^2 - M_2^2 - B_1^2 + (B_1^2 - i)^2 + j^2}{2j}$$

$$= \frac{M_1^2 - M_2^2 + i^2 + j^2}{2j}$$

$$B_2 = \frac{i}{j} M_1 \tag{10}$$

From Eqs. (5) and (10) we get the values of B_1 and B_2 respectively. From that we can find out the value of B_3 from Eq. (1),

$$B_3 = \pm\sqrt{M_1^2 - B_1^2 - B_2^2}$$

From the above equation we can say that, B_3 can have either positive or negative value. If any one circle intersect the other two circles precisely at one point, then B_3 will get a value zero if any of the circles intersect the other circles exactly at one point. If it intersects at two or more points, outside or inside it can get either a positive or a negative value, respectively.

Initially during deployment each beacon node carries out the trilateration process with all of its neighboring beacon nodes. During the process every beacon node is sanctioned with two or more trilateration points for security reasons. The trilateration point is where the coverage area of the three beacon nodes intersect. Each beacon node shares the trilateration point information to its immediate or one hop beacon nodes. This way we have reduced the chances of beacon nodes to become vulnerable. Precaution is taken that no beacon node

Data: Location infomration of the requesting nodes
Result: Detecting cheating nodes
Start;
Trialteration process is carried out with the unknown node to identify its
location coordinates ;
After location identification, the node that determined its location information
is asked to share its location information with the assisted beacon nodes ;
Correlate the obtained location information with the stored location reference
(L_1);
while *comparison not fullfilled* **do**

> The node is marked malicious and is not given any integrity credential
> scoring;
> **if** *a node is suspected to be malicious* **then**
>> Separate the mismatched nodes location and save the new location in
>> L_n;
> **end**

end
If comparison fulfilled, no cheating nodes found;
Stop;

Algorithm 1. Detecting cheating nodes

reveals the trilateration information about its neighbors, thus protecting the
beacon nods from clone attack [13,14].

The malicious nodes are not given any integrity credential scoring by the
beacon nodes, and a node that does have a integrity credential score of 3 is
considered for MPR node selection.

4 MPR Node Selection

The selection of MPR nodes is begun by choosing a random node r (or the node
that want to transfer any message). To select the MPR nodes for the node r,
the set of all one hop proximity nodes are taken as $P(r)$, and the set of all
two hop neighboring nodes of the node r are taken as $P^2(r)$. All the two hop
neighbors of the node r is represented with out-degree $O(s)$, where s is the one
hop neighbor of r. Figure 3 shows initial flooding problem. The selection of MPR
node is carried out as follows: [2]

- Initially MPR is an empty set $MPR(r)$, where r is the random node.
- For each node in P(r), the out-degree $O(s)$ is calculated.
- The nodes in $P(r)$ are added to the $MPR(r)$ set, which are the only node by
  which the nodes in $P^2(r)$ can be reached to r.
- If some nodes are not covered in $P^2(r)$ through $P(r)$, in the set $MPR(r)$:
  - Select the unselected node in $P(r)$, through which the uncovered node in
    $P^2(r)$ can be reached.
  - The node in $P(r)$ which covers the maximum uncovered node in $P^2(r)$, is
    added to the $MPR(r)$ set. If multiplicity occurs, out-degree is fetched into
    action to select the node.

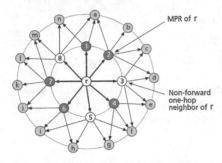

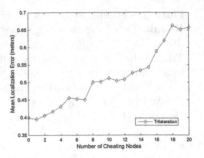

Fig. 4. Network after MPR node selection.

Fig. 5. Mean localization error.

- The nodes in $MPR(r)$ are again checked with all the covered two hop neighbours, which can be covered by another node in $MPR(r)$. In case of multiple choices, one node is removed from $MPR(r)$ using out-degree, thus optimizing the $MPR(r)$ set. Figure 4 shows the selected MPR nodes.

4.1 Determining Out-Degree

The calculation of out-degree $O(s)$ for the one hop neighbors is carried out as follows:

A hello message is transmitted between the one hop neighbors on regular time intervals. A typical hello message in MPR scenario, contains informative data such as the selected MPR, node ID, and other information's relevant to the neighbors to update their information regarding MPR.

5　Results

Our simulation was carried out in a 100 meters x 100 meters space. Initially 25 nodes were made the beacon nodes and were fixed at different locations. In scenario 1, for every 15 min, 7 new nodes were introduced in the network in which 2 were malicious. During network deployment the trilateration technique was carried out with all the beacon nodes in the network, and their respective trilateration points were saved. These trilateration points are exclusively used to identify the malicious beacon nodes.

Whenever a new node enters the network, the trilateration process is carried out with the new node, and the trilateration process is repeated for every 15 meters movement of the node. Authentic nodes are given an integrity credential scoring by the beacon nodes which assisted for its localization. Figure 5 shows the mean localization error occurred during the trilateration process and Fig. 6 shows the time take for trilateration process.

For MPR node identification, the sender node broadcasts a trilateration request message to all of its one hop neighbors. The one hop neighbors replies

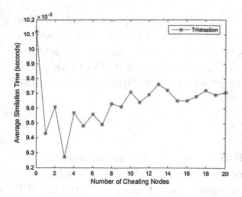

Fig. 6. Average time taken for the trilateration process.

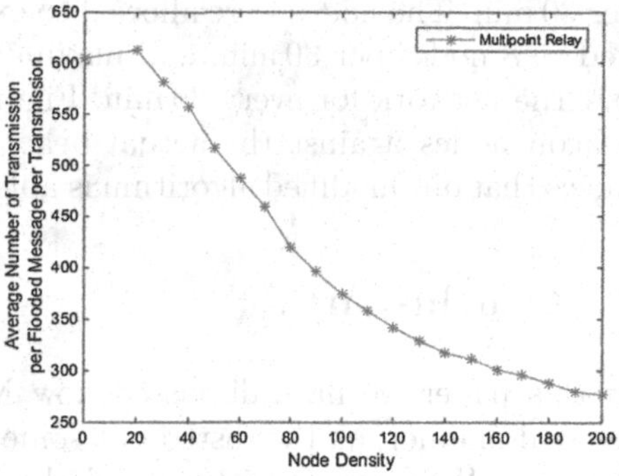

Fig. 7. Transmissions during MPR node selection.

with their integrity credential scoring, and the nodes that do not have an integrity credential score of 3 or more are not eligible for the MPR node selection. The total number of transmissions taken to select the MPR node is listed in Fig. 7. As the density of the network increases, the number of transmissions decreases.

For every 15 min, 7 new nodes were introduced in the network in which 2 were malicious. Figure 8 shows the total number of malicious nodes detected against the actual number of nodes. At one particular time (i.e. 180 min) the detected malicious nodes and the actual malicious were same, and this was due to the very less movement of the nodes in the network. More deviation was seen at 300 min due to the high mobility of the nodes, which increased the localization error. In scenario 1 no nodes were allowed to leave the network.

In our next scenario we added nodes in a random manner with a maximum threshold of 10 nodes per 30 min. The malicious nodes were also chosen at random and the maximum threshold for that was set to 5 malicious nodes

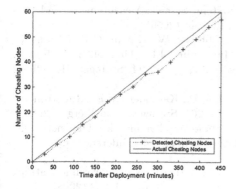

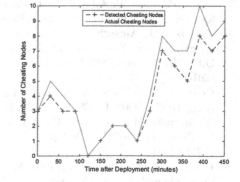

Fig. 8. Actual cheating nodes vs detected cheating nodes scenario 1.

Fig. 9. Actual cheating nodes vs detected cheating nodes scenario 2.

per 30 min. The nodes were allowed to exit the network at any time and was limited to 8 nodes per 30 min, and maximum of 4 malicious nodes were allowed to exit the network for every 30 min. Figure 9 shows the total number of detected beacon nodes against the actual beacon nodes in scenario 2. Figures 8 and 9 shows that our modified algorithm is able to give more than 80 % accurate results.

6 Conclusion

In this paper we have discussed how MPR node selection is carried out in a secured manner, and we listed out some of the attacks that happen during node selection. We came up with a novel idea to reduce the attacks faced during MPR node selection. We were able to get 80 % accuracy in identifying the malicious nodes. Although there is a trade-off in the time taken, we were able to achieve reasonable results in terms of security. We would be considering other alternate techniques, and a dense network for trilateration process in our future work.

References

1. Liu, K., Deng, J., Varshney, P.K., Balakrishnan, K.: An acknowledgment-based approach for the detection of routing misbehavior in manets. IEEE Trans. Mob. Comput. **6**(5), 536–550 (2007)
2. Liang, O., Sekercioglu, Y.A., Mani, N.: A survey of multipoint relay based broadcast schemes in wireless ad hoc networks. IEEE Commun. Surv. Tutorials **8**(4), 30–46 (2006)
3. Williams, B., Camp, T.: Comparison of broadcasting techniques for mobile ad hoc networks. In: Proceedings of the 3rd ACM International Symposium on Mobile ad hoc Networking & Computing, pp. 194–205. ACM (2002)
4. Kuriakose, J., Joshi, S., Raju, R.V., Kilaru, A.: A review on localization in wireless sensor networks. In: Thampi, S.M., Gelbukh, A., Mukhopadhyay, J. (eds.) Advances in Signal Processing and Intelligent Recognition Systems, pp. 599–610. Springer, Heidelberg (2014)
5. Misra, P., Enge, P.: Global Positioning System: Signals, Measurements and Performance, 2nd edn. Ganga-Jamuna Press, Lincoln (2006)
6. Kuriakose, J., Amruth, V., Sandesh, A.G., Abhilash, V., Kumar, G.P., Nithin, K.: A review on mobile sensor localization. In: Mauri, J.L., Thampi, S.M., Rawat, D.B., Jin, D. (eds.) SSCC 2014. CCIS, vol. 467, pp. 30–44. Springer, Heidelberg (2014)
7. Douceur, J.R.: The sybil attack. In: Druschel, P., Kaashoek, M.F., Rowstron, A. (eds.) IPTPS 2002. LNCS, vol. 2429, pp. 251–260. Springer, Heidelberg (2002)
8. Al-Shurman, M., Yoo, S.-M., Park, S.: Black hole attack in mobile ad hoc networks. In: Proceedings of the 42nd Annual Southeast Regional Conference, pp. 96–97. ACM (2004)
9. Khalil, I., Bagchi, S., Shroff, N.B.: Mobiworp: mitigation of the wormhole attack in mobile multihop wireless networks. Ad Hoc Netw. **6**(3), 344–362 (2008)
10. Viani, F., Lizzi, L., Rocca, P., Benedetti, M., Donelli, M., Massa, A.: Object tracking through rssi measurements in wireless sensor networks. Electron. Lett. **44**(10), 653–654 (2008)

11. Cheung, K.W., So, H.-C., Ma, W.-K., Chan, Y.-T.: Least squares algorithms for time-of-arrival-based mobile location. IEEE Trans. Sig. Process. **52**(4), 1121–1130 (2004)
12. Gardner, W.A., Chen, C.-K.: Signal-selective time-difference-of-arrival estimation for passive location of man-made signal sources in highly corruptive environments. i. theory and method. IEEE Trans, Sig. Process. **40**(5), 1168–1184 (1992)
13. Wang, D., Li, P., Hu, P., Xing, K., Wang, Y., Huang, L., Rong, Y.: On the performance of TDD and LDD based clone attack detection in mobile ad hoc networks. In: Wang, X., Zheng, R., Jing, T., Xing, K. (eds.) WASA 2012. LNCS, vol. 7405, pp. 532–539. Springer, Heidelberg (2012)
14. Kuriakose, J., Sisodia, P.S., Amruth, V., Kumar, A., Sushanth, K.J., et al.: A comparative analysis of mobile localization and its attacks. In: Proceedings of the 2014 International Conference on Information and Communication Technology for Competitive Strategies, p. 3. ACM (2014)

Human Activity Recognition Based on Motion Projection Profile Features in Surveillance Videos Using Support Vector Machines and Gaussian Mixture Models

J. Arunnehru$^{(\boxtimes)}$ and M. Kalaiselvi Geetha

Speech and Vision Lab, Department of Computer Science and Engineering,
Annamalai University, Annamalainagar, Chidambaram, Tamilnadu, India
{arunnehru.aucse,geesiv}@gmail.com

Abstract. Human Activity Recognition (HAR) is an active research area in computer vision and pattern recognition. The area of human activity recognition, attention consistently focuses on changes in the scene of a subject with reference to time, since motion information can sensibly depict the activity. This paper depicts a novel framework for activity recognition based on Motion Projection Profile (MPP) features of the difference image, representing various levels of a person's interaction. The motion projection profile features consist of the measure of moving pixel of each row, column and diagonal (left and right) of the difference image and they give adequate motion information to recognize the instantaneous posture of the person. The experiments are carried out using UT-Interaction dataset (Set 1 and Set 2), considering six activities viz (handshake, hug, kick, point, punch, push) and the extracted features are modeled by Support Vector Machines (SVM) with RBF kernel and Gaussian Mixture Models (GMM) for recognizing human activities. In the experimental results, GMM exhibit effectiveness of the proposed method with an overall accuracy rate of 93.01 % and 90.81 % for Set 1 and 2 respectively, this outperforms the SVM classifier.

Keywords: Human activity recognition · Frame difference · Feature extraction · Gaussian mixture models · Support vector machines

1 Introduction

In recent years, the visual surveillance system is an important technology to ensure security and safety in both public and private sectors like airports, railway stations, petrol/gas stations, bus stands, banks, and commercial buildings due to terrorist activity and other societal problems. The analysis of human activity recognition have been broadly utilized in the area of computer vision and pattern recognition [1], whose point is to consequently segment, keep and distinguish human activity progressively and maybe to anticipate the progressing human activities.

© Springer International Publishing Switzerland 2015
J.H. Abawajy et al. (Eds): SSCC 2015, CCIS 536, pp. 412–423, 2015.
DOI: 10.1007/978-3-319-22915-7_38

The habitual recognition of human activities opens a number of fascinating application areas such as automatic visual surveillance, health care activities, content based retrieval, human-computer-interaction (HCI), robotics and gesture recognition with conceptual information from videos [2,3]. Actions performed by humans are reliant on many factors, such as the view invariant postures, outfits, lighting changes, occlusion, shadows, changing backgrounds and camera movements. A human activity can be represented by short video sequences showing a distinct cycle of the corresponding motion of the body. Recognizing and classifying the strange and suspicious activities from natural actions will be obliging in envisioning the threats and terrorist attacks. Human interaction consists of more than one person's actions such as a handshake, hug, push and fight [4].

1.1 Outline of the Work

This paper deals with human activity recognition, which aims to identify activity from the video sequences. The proposed approach is evaluated using UT-Interaction dataset. Difference image is achieved by subtracting the successive frames in order to obtain the motion information. Thus, the motion projection profile (MPP) features are extracted from the difference image as a feature set. The extracted features are modeled by SVM and GMM classifiers for training and testing. The rest of the paper is structured as follows. Section 2 reviews related work. Section 3 provides an overview of the proposed approach. Section 4 describes the proposed feature extraction method and experimental results evaluating its performance on UT-Interaction dataset are presented in Sect. 5. Finally, Sect. 6 concludes the paper.

2   Related Work

The vision based activity recognition becomes the most significant goal to distinguish the activity automatically. The motive is to build a general framework for the representation and recognition of multifarious group activities. Despite the fact that recognition of group actions have been compensated by smaller amount of attention, there has been an immense quantity of prior work and survey on human action recognition [1–4]. This section discusses the various previous work on human action recognition. Computer vision and pattern recognition methods, comprise object detection, feature extraction, feature selection and classification and it is being effectively used in many activity recognition systems. Image-processing techniques such as analysis and detection of motion, shape, texture, color, optical flow and interest points [5], have also been found to be efficient. Bobick and Davis [6] proposed a method of motion energy images and motion-history images based on Hu moments to produce action templates represented by the mean and covariance matrix of the moments. The Mahalanobis distance measure is used to compute the distance between the moment descriptions of the input action for recognition. Wang et al. [7] proposed a novel method based on motion boundary histograms, which have shown excellent performance by classifying various actions. Moreover, Chundi Mu et al. [8] proposed an improved method for extracting histogram of motion vectors from high definition video sequences. Syed Ahmar Qamar used temporal approach for the history of motion in a sequence of images, and then motion vectors of the history images have been used to recognize suspicious behavior [9]. Iglesias-Ham, et al. [10] presented a method based on 2D binary projections of the shape over the time and human actions is recognized by fast matching algorithm which considers the spatial distribution of the 2D projection of the shape. Vezzani et al. [11] presented a method for action recognition based on projection histograms of the foreground mask which provide sufficient information to understand the dynamic posture of the person then HMM framework have been used for action recognition. Janez Pers et al. [12] presented a novel method for efficient training of human body motion from image sequences based on optical flow field and it is divided into six segments containing a flow field of a person. The two dimensional, eight-bin histogram is calculated from segmented part of the flow field. J. Arunnehru and M. Kalaiselvi Geetha [13] proposed a novel framework for automatic activity recognition based on maximum motion patterns extracted from the temporal difference image by selecting the Region of Interest (ROI) and the experiments were carried out on the publicly available datasets like KTH and Weizmann. Lu, Guoliang and Mineichi Kudo [14] proposed a novel framework for action representation based on Local Temporal Self-Similarities (LTSSs) pattern which is directly derived from the difference images (temporal difference) and does not require location of the human body in each frame. The bag-of-words framework is then employed for action classification to achieve performance.

3   Proposed Approach

The workflow of the proposed approach is shown in Fig. 1. The videos are smoothed by the Gaussian filter with a kernel of size 5×5 and variance $\sigma = 0.5$. It is essential to pre-process all video sequences eliminate noise for fine feature extraction and classification. The motion information is identified by subtracting the successive frames. The Motion Projection Profile (MPP) features are extracted from the difference image, representing various levels of a person interaction. The motion projection profile features determine the measure of moving pixel of each row, column and diagonal (left and right) pixels of the difference frame and they give adequate motion information to recognize the instantaneous posture of the person as discussed in Sect. 4. Then extracted motion projection profiles of row, column, left diagonal and right diagonal features are re-sampled to a fixed number of bins, where bin value is empirically fixed to 8 and the values are concatenated into a distinctive vector, in order to obtain a 32-dimensional feature vector for each frame in an activity video sequence. The extracted features are modeled by SVM and GMM for activity recognition. In this work, SVM with RBF kernel and GMM are used in order to evaluate the effectiveness of these two classifiers on the UT- Interaction dataset.

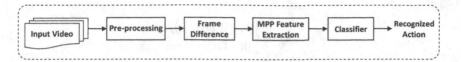

Fig. 1. Overview of the proposed approach

4   Feature Extraction

The extraction of discriminative feature is most essential and vital problem with human activity recognition, which represents the momentous information that is vital for further study. The ensuing sections present, the representation of the feature extraction method used in this work.

4.1   Frame Difference

To identify the moving object across a sequence of images, the current image is subtracted either by the previous frame or successive frame of the image sequences called as temporal difference. The difference images are obtained by applying thresholds to eliminate pixel changes due to camera noise, changes in lighting conditions, etc.

This method is extremely adaptive to detect the motion region corresponding to moving objects in dynamic scenes and superior for extracting momentous feature pixels. The temporal difference image obtained by simply subtracting the previous frame t with current frame is at time $t+1$ on a pixel by pixel basis.

(a)   (b)   (c)

Fig. 2. (a), (b) Two consecutive frames from kick activity (c) Difference image of (a) and (b)

The extracted motion pattern information is considered as the Region of Interest (ROI). Figures 2(a) and (b) illustrate the consecutive frames of the UT-Interaction dataset. The resulting difference image is shown in Fig. 2(c). $D_t(x, y)$ is the difference image, $I_t(x, y)$ is the pixel intensity of (x, y) in the tth frame, h and w are the height and width of the image correspondingly. Motion information D_t or difference image is considered using

$$D_t(x, y) = |I_t(x, y) - I_{t+1}(x, y)| \tag{1}$$
$$1 \le x \le w, 1 \le y \le h$$

$$T_k(x,y) = \begin{cases} 1, & \text{if } D_k(x,y) > t; \\ 0, & \text{Otherwise}; \end{cases} \tag{2}$$

4.2 Motion Projection Profile (MPP) Features for Activity Recognition

The procedure for extracting the features is explained in this section. To recognize the human interaction activity, motion information is an important signal generally extracted from video sequences. Projection profiles are compact representation of images, since much valuable information is retained in the projection. The projection profiles are extracted from the difference image that consists of motion information only [15]. The row (horizontal), column (vertical), left diagonal and right diagonal projection profiles are obtained by finding the number of white pixels for each bin in row (horizontal), column (vertical), left diagonal and right diagonal four directions respectively, as shown in Figs. 3 and 4. The projection $H[i]$ along the rows and the projection $V[j]$ along the columns of a difference image are mathematically defined by Eq. 3

$$H[i] = \sum_{j=0}^{n-1} T[i,j] \; ; \; V[j] = \sum_{i=0}^{m-1} T[i,j] \tag{3}$$

where T is the difference image and n and m are the height and width of the difference image respectively.

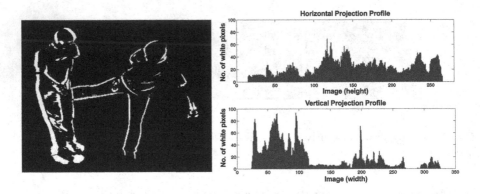

Fig. 3. Horizontal and Vertical projection profile of the kick action

For diagonal projections of an object requires only the area moments, the position can be computed from the horizontal and vertical projections are defined by Eqs.4 and 5

$$A_m = \sum_{j=0}^{m-1} V[j] \; ; \; A_n = \sum_{i=0}^{n-1} H[i] \tag{4}$$

$$\overline{y} = \frac{\sum\limits_{i=0}^{n-1} iH[i]}{A_n} \; ; \; \overline{x} = \frac{\sum\limits_{j=0}^{m-1} jV[j]}{A_m} \tag{5}$$

where A_m and A_n are area of the difference image. The diagonal projection profile is to compute the index for the histogram bucket for the current row and column. Let the row and column be denoted by i and j, respectively. Suppose that the dimensions of the image are n rows and m columns, so i and j range from 0 to $n-1$ and 0 to $m-1$, respectively. The diagonal projection will require $n+m$ buckets. The affine transformation should map the upper left pixel into the first postion of the diagonal projection, and the lower right pixel into the last position for left diagonal projection profile feature. For right diagonal profile feature, the affine transformation should map the upper right pixel into the first postion of the diagonal projection, and the lower left pixel in the last position as shown in Fig. 4. The motion projection profiles $H[i]$, $V[j]$, $D_L[\overline{x},\overline{y}]$ and $D_R[\overline{y},\overline{x}]$ are represented as four feature vectors $\{f_H, \; f_V, f_{D_L}, \; f_{D_R}\}$ to depict the difference frame. Then the feature set is re-sampled to a fixed number of bins, where bin value is empirically fixed to 8. The row, column, left diagonal and right diagonal projection profile bin values are concatenated into a distinctive vector, in order to obtain a 32-dimensional feature vector. The extracted features are modeled by SVM with RBF kernel and GMM classifier for activity recognition.

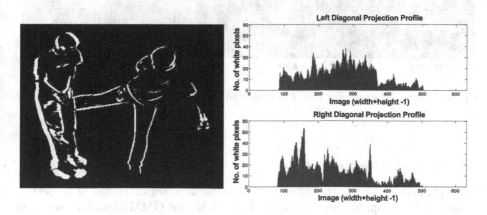

Fig. 4. Left diagonal projection profile and Right diagonal projection profile of the kick action

5   Experimental Results

The following six activities are considered for activity recognition: handshake, hug, kick, point, punch and push from UT-Interaction dataset. The experiments are carried out using MATLAB 2013a in Windows 7 Operating System on a computer with Intel Core i7 Processor 3.40 GHz with 8 GB RAM and using two types of classifiers for recognizing the activity, namely Support Vector Machines (SVM) with RBF kernel and Gaussian Mixture Models (GMM).

5.1   UT-Interaction Dataset

The UT-Interaction dataset [16] consists of a sequence of continuous executions of six classes of person-person interactions: handshake, hug, kick, point, punch and push. In total, 20 video sequences having an approximate length of one minute and each video consist of at least one execution per interaction. Nine persons with more than 15 different clothing conditions are present in the video. The videos are taken with the resolution of 720 × 480, 30 fps. The video is divided into two different sets. Set 1 consists of 10 video sequences that are captured on a parking lot with static backgrounds. The videos of Set 1 are taken with slightly different zoom rate, and with little camera jitter. The Set 2 (10 sequences) are captured in a lawn area on a windy day with non static backgrounds (e.g. tree moves), and contains more camera jitters. Example frames of UT-Interaction dataset (Set 1 and Set 2) are shown in Fig. 5.

Fig. 5. Sample frames of the UT-Interaction dataset: Set 1 (top row) and Set 2 (bottom row)

5.2   Quantitative Evaluation

As explained in Sect. 4, the 32-dimensional features are extracted. The performance of the proposed feature method on SVM and GMM classifiers is tested using 10-fold cross-validation approach. The quantitative evaluation is done with statistical metrices like Sensitivity (Recall), Specificity, Precision, F-measure and Accuracy, The classification accuracy can be evaluated by computing the number of correctly recognized class samples (true positives), the number of correctly recognized samples that do not belong to the class (true negatives), and samples that either were incorrectly assigned to the class (false positives) or that were not recognized as class samples (false negatives). Sensitivity or Recall(R) gives how good an activity is identified correctly. Specificity (S) gives a measure of how good a method is identifying negative activity correctly. Precision (P) is a measure of exactness and F-measure is the harmonic mean of

Precision and Recall. Finally, Accuracy (A) shows the overall correctness of the activity recognition. The statistical measures of Sensitivity (Recall), Specificity, Precision, F-measure and Accuracy is defined as $R = tp/tp + fn$, $S = tn/tn + fp$, $P = tn + tp/tp + tn + fp + fn$, $F - measure = 2P \times R/P + R$, $A = tp + tn/tn + fp + tp + fn$.

	A	B	C	D	E	F
A	88.18	2.20	4.01	1.80	2.20	1.60
B	1.85	92.15	2.31	0.92	2.00	0.77
C	1.70	1.31	92.02	1.18	1.70	2.09
D	0.74	1.73	3.46	91.60	1.48	0.99
E	1.37	5.27	4.30	0.78	86.13	2.15
F	1.41	1.61	3.02	0.20	0.81	92.94

(a) Set 1

	A	B	C	D	E	F
A	86.03	8.56	1.58	0.00	1.58	2.24
B	5.34	89.08	3.40	0.00	1.21	0.97
C	5.88	7.63	76.25	0.00	2.18	8.06
D	0.28	0.00	0.00	98.86	0.00	0.85
E	2.42	3.35	2.60	0.00	83.27	8.36
F	0.59	0.00	1.33	0.00	2.95	95.13

(b) Set 2

Fig. 6. Confusion matrices (%) for MPP features on Set 1 and Set 2 using SVM with RBF Kernel, where A = handshake, B = hug, C = kick, D = point, E = punch, F = push

5.3 Results Obtained with SVM with RBF Kernel

Support Vector Machines (SVMs) is a popular approach for data classification, that has recently gained attention within visual pattern recognition [17]. A classification process typically involves separating data into training and testing sets. In each occurrence, the training set contains one class labels and several observed variables. SVM is to build a model based on the training data to predict the target values of the test. $(x_i, y_i), i = 1, ..., l$ where $x_i \in \Re^n$ is a feature vector and $y_i \in \{+1, -1\}$ is a class label. The purpose of SVM is to separate the data with the hyperplane using a kernel trick [18]. The distance between the adjacent points on hyperplane to origin can be established by maximizing the x on the hyperplane. The hyperplane $w.x + b = 0$ is used to isolate the two classes in feature space, where w is the coefficient of the vector and b is the scalar. Such that $y_i(w.x_i + b) \geq 1$, $\forall i$. The maximum margin between two classes is given by $M = 2/||w||$. SVM theory is discussed briefly in [18]. The results obtained with SVM with RBF kernel are found to be satisfactory. While analyzing the performance of the RBF kernel for the MPP features, a grid search method has been utilized to identify the finest parameters for RBF kernel in parameter space using LIBSVM [19]. In UT-Interaction dataset (Set 1) the parameters are $C = 13.454$ and $\gamma = 0.000167$. For UT-Interaction dataset (Set 2) the parameters are $C = 32.0$ and $\gamma = 0.000398$, where C is the slack variable or error weight and γ is the curvature of the decision boundary, where these two parameters are used to obtain the optimal classifier performance. The confusion matrices of the SVM classifier on UT-interaction dataset Set 1 and Set 2 are shown in Figs. 6(a) and (b), where diagonal of the table shows that accurate responses of each activity. The average recognition rate of SVM with RBF kernel is 90.50 % for Set 1 and 88.11 % for Set 2. In Set 1, the activities are almost classified well, except for punch and handshake, that are mostly confused with a hug and kick activities respectively. In Set 2, handshake, kick and punch are misclassified as hug activity.

5.4   Results Obtained with GMM

Gaussian Mixture Models (GMM) is obtained by combining multivariate normal density components. Gaussian mixture models are frequently used for data clustering. Gaussian mixture modeling adopts an iterative method that converges to a local optimum value which is similar to k-means clustering. GMM is more suitable than k-means clustering, when clusters have various sizes and correlation within them. GMM is a mixture of numerous Gaussian distributions and represents various subclasses inside the one class. The probability density function is determined as a weighted sum of Gaussians. GMM algorithm is briefly discussed in [20].

	A	B	C	D	E	F
A	93.59	0.60	3.61	0.20	1.00	1.00
B	2.00	90.77	2.92	0.00	3.69	0.62
C	1.70	2.88	92.80	0.00	1.96	0.65
D	0.74	0.74	2.22	95.80	0.49	0.00
E	0.59	2.93	2.15	0.20	92.77	1.37
F	2.02	0.60	2.42	0.00	2.62	92.34

(a) Set 1

	A	B	C	D	E	F
A	88.41	7.51	2.90	0.00	0.53	0.66
B	7.40	87.74	3.16	0.00	1.33	0.36
C	3.70	3.70	89.54	0.00	1.31	1.74
D	0.00	0.28	0.57	99.15	0.00	0.00
E	2.60	3.53	4.83	0.00	85.32	3.72
F	0.59	0.74	1.33	0.00	2.65	94.69

(b) Set 2

Fig. 7. Confusion matrices (%) for MPP features on Set 1 and 2 using GMM classifier, where A = handshake, B = hug, C = kick, D = point, E = punch, F = push

Figures 7(a) and (b) shows the confusion matrices for the UT-Interaction dataset (Set 1 and Set 2) on GMM classifier, where diagonal of the table shows that accurate responses of each activity. The results obtained with GMM classifier shows promising results with an average recognition rate of 93.01 % for Set 1 and 90.81 % for Set 2. The majority of the activities are almost classified well in Set 1. The misclassification exists in a hug and push activities due to the similarities of the postures. In Set 2, handshake, kick, point and push activities are classified as well. From this, punch activity is confused as kick and push. Thus, it needs further attention.

The quantitative evaluation results are tabulated in Table 1, which shows that the proposed MPP approach has a higher recall, specificity, precision accuracy and F-measure for the GMM classifier on UT-Interaction dataset (Set 1 and Set 2), when compared to SVM with RBF kernel classifier.

5.5   State of the Art

Table 2 compares the activity recognition results of the proposed approach with the state of the art approaches for the UT-Interaction dataset Set 1 and Set 2

Table 1. Performance measure of the UT-Interaction dataset (Set 1 and Set 2)

Classifier	UT-Dataset	Sensitivity	Specificity	Precision	F-measure
SVM	Set 1	0.905	0.980	0.908	0.906
	Set 2	0.881	0.975	0.889	0.884
GMM	Set 1	0.930	0.985	0.932	0.931
	Set 2	0.908	0.979	0.908	0.907

Table 2. State-of-the-art recognition accuracy (%) for the UT-Interaction dataset (Set 1 and Set 2)

Method	Year	Set 1 (%)	Set 2 (%)
Proposed Method	-	93.0	90.8
M. S. Ryoo [21]	2011	85.0	78.0
S. Mukherjee et al. [22]	2011	85.0	73.3
D. Waltisberg et al. [23]	2010	88.0	77.0
A. Yao et al. [24]	2010	88.0	80.0

respectively. Based on the comparison, it is seen that the proposed MPP feature method shows good results on the UT - Interaction dataset (Set 1 and Set 2) on GMM classifier.

6 Conclusion and Future Work

This paper proposed a method for activity recognition for surveillance video using MPP as a feature. Experiments are conducted using UT-Interaction dataset (Set 1 and Set 2). The MPP feature was obtained from difference image, which represent a motion and posture information of a person. This approach evaluates the performance of MPP feature in video sequence using SVM with RBF kernel and GMM classifiers. From the experimental results, it is observed that GMM shows a classification accuracy of 93.01 % and 90.81 % for Set 1 and Set 2 respectively, and demonstarted that the proposed MPP feature method performs well and achieved good recognition results for various activities and outperforms the state of the art. It is observed from the experiments that the system could not distinguish punch and hug with high accuracy and is of future interest.

References

1. Vishwakarma, S., Agrawal, A.: A survey on activity recognition and behaviour, understanding in video surveillance. Vis. Comput. **29**(10), 983–1009 (2013)
2. Weinland, D., Ronfard, R., Boyer, E.: A survey of vision-based methods for action representation, segmentation and recognition. Comput. Vis. Image Underst. **115**(2), 224–241 (2011)

3. Hassan, M., Ahmad, T., Liaqat, N., Farooq, A., Ali, S.A.: A Review on human actions recognition using vision based techniques. J. Image Graph. **2**(1), 28–32 (2014)
4. Poppe, R.: A survey on vision-based human action recognition. Image Vis. Comput. **28**(6), 976–990 (2010)
5. Laptev, I.: On space-time interest points. Int. J. Comput. Vis. **64**(2–3), 107–123 (2005)
6. Bobick, A.F., Davis, J.W.: The recognition of human movement using temporal templates. IEEE Trans. Pattern Anal. Mach. Intell. **23**(3), 257–267 (2001)
7. Wang, H., Klaser, A., Schmid, C., Liu, C.L.: Action recognition by dense trajectories. In: IEEE Conference on CVPR, pp. 3169–3176 (2011)
8. Mu, C., Xie, J., Yan, W., Liu, T., Li, P.: A fast recognition algorithm for suspicious behavior in high definition videos. Multimedia Systems. 1–11, (2015)
9. Qamar, S.A., Jaffar, M.A., Habib, H.A.: A supervisory system to detect suspicious behavior in online testing system. In: Proceedings of International Conference on Machine Learning and Computing (ICMLC) (2009)
10. Iglesias-Ham, M., GarcaReyes, E.B., Kropatsch, W.G., Artner, N.M.: Convex deficiencies for human action recognition. J. Intell. Rob. Syst. **64**(3–4), 353–364 (2011)
11. Vezzani, R., Baltieri, D., Cucchiara, R.: HMM based action recognition with projection histogram features. In: Ünay, D., Çataltepe, Z., Aksoy, S. (eds.) ICPR 2010. LNCS, vol. 6388, pp. 286–293. Springer, Heidelberg (2010)
12. Pers, J., Sulic, V., Kristan, M., Perse, M., Polanec, K., Kovacic, S.: Histograms of optical flow for efficient representation of body motion. Pattern Recogn. Lett. **31**, 1369–1376 (2010)
13. Arunnehru, J., Geetha, M.K.: Automatic activity recognition for video surveillance. Int. J. Comput. Appl. **75**(9), 1–6 (2013)
14. Lu, G., Kudo, M.: Learning action patterns in difference images for efficient action recognition. Neurocomputing **123**, 328–336 (2014)
15. Arunnehru, J., Geetha, M.K.: Human activity recognition based on projected histogram features in surveillance videos using tree based classifiers. Int. J. Appl. Eng. Res. (IJAER) **9**(21), 4950–4954 (2014)
16. Ryoo, M.S., Chen, C.-C., Aggarwal, J.K., Roy-Chowdhury, A.: An overview of contest on Semantic Description of Human Activities (SDHA) 2010. In: Ünay, D., Çataltepe, Z., Aksoy, S. (eds.) ICPR 2010. LNCS, vol. 6388, pp. 270–285. Springer, Heidelberg (2010)
17. Cristianini, N., Shawe-Taylor, J.: An introduction to support vector machines and other kernel-based learning methods. Cambridge University Press, Cambridge (2000)
18. Mitchell, T.: Machine Learning. Computer Science Series. McGraw-Hill, Boston (1997)
19. Chang, C.C., Lin, C.J.: LIBSVM: a library for support vector machines. ACM Trans. Intell. Syst. Technol. (TIST) **2**(3), 27 (2011)
20. McLachlan, G., Peel, D.: Finite Mixture Models. Wiley, New York (2004)
21. Ryoo, M.S.: Human activity prediction: early recognition of ongoing activities from streaming videos. In: IEEE International Conference on Computer Vision (ICCV), pp. 1036–1043 (2011)
22. Mukherjee, S., Biswas, S.K., Mukherjee, D.P.: Recognizing interaction between human performers using 'key pose doublet'. In: Proceedings of the 19th ACM International Conference on Multimedia, pp. 1329–1332. ACM Chicago (2011)

23. Waltisberg, D., Yao, A., Gall, J., Van Gool, L.: Variations of a hough-voting action recognition system. In: Ünay, D., Çataltepe, Z., Aksoy, S. (eds.) ICPR 2010. LNCS, vol. 6388, pp. 306–312. Springer, Heidelberg (2010)
24. Yao, A., Gall, J., Van Gool, L.: A hough transform-based voting framework for action recognition. In: IEEE Conference on Computer Vision and Pattern Recognition (CVPR), pp. 2061–2068 (2010)

Analysis of Accountability Property in Payment Systems Using Strand Space Model

Venkatasamy Sureshkumar[✉], Anitha Ramalingam, and S. Anandhi

Department of Applied Mathematics and Computational Sciences,
PSG College of Technology, Coimbatore 641004, India
sand@mca.psgtech.ac.in, anitha_nadarajan@mail.psgtech.ac.in,
san@amc.psgtech.ac.in

Abstract. Nowadays payment protocols are facing difficulties in its implementation, as the parties involved in the execution deny their performed actions. In this context, there should be a provision to link the action to the concerned party, which is addressed by the accountability property. In this paper, a new framework in strand space model for the analysis of accountability property is proposed that can overcome the drawbacks of the existing models. Strand space model is improved so that the analysis of accountability property of a payment protocol that is designed under symmetric key cryptosystem can be done. As a test example, symmetric key based BPAC, a bill payment protocol ensuring accountability is used. Fine-grained analysis of accountability property of BPAC protocol is carried out and proved its correctness using the automated support provided by CPSA along with the strong mathematical proof.

Keywords: Accountability · Strand space model · Knowledge-domain · Payment protocol

1 Introduction

As the payment protocols are widely used in electronic commercial transactions, there is a requirement in offering accountability for engaging parties in the protocol. The accountability analysis of payment protocol concerns about the ability to show that particular parties involved in the protocol are responsible for their transactions [1]. In particular, the accountability involves the ability of a party(prover) to convince another party(verifier) that the concerned party is responsible for a particular action, without disclosing any secret information to the verifier. Strand space model is a formal method, recently used for the analysis of RFID and electronic voting protocols [3,10]. This model is enhanced in our study to analyze the payment protocols designed in Symmetric Key Infrastructure(SKI).

The rest of the paper is organized as follows. Section 2 discusses the related work. The two phases, bill payment and bill presentment of BPAC protocol

© Springer International Publishing Switzerland 2015
J.H. Abawajy et al. (Eds): SSCC 2015, CCIS 536, pp. 424–437, 2015.
DOI: 10.1007/978-3-319-22915-7_39

are described in Sect. 3. Section 4 presents the improved strand space model. Section 5 details the BPAC space and attacker model. The analysis of BPAC protocol against accountability property is given in Sect. 6 with an automated support and mathematical proof. Finally, Sect. 7 concludes this paper with future work.

2   Related work

Several formal methods were proposed to analyze the accountability property. Kailar [6] proposed a logical method for the analysis of accountability. Kailar's logic reason about the accountability of signed messages, which is insufficient for the analysis of the payment protocol that involves cryptographic multifaceted messages. Moreover, Kailar's logic reason about the prover's knowledge alone. The KN logic [7] presents to reason about the verifier's knowledge. However, it fails to prove accountability without disclosing secret information. The KP logic [8] was introduced as a modification of KN logic. This logic can be used for the analysis even in the presence of cryptographic multifaceted messages. Furthermore, it presents to reason the verifier's knowledge and proves the accountability without disclosing any secret information. However, the KP logic can only analyze the accountability property of protocols which are designed in the Public Key Infrastructure(PKI). Recently, KP logic was modified and proposed as KSL logic [9], which can analyze the protocol that involves cryptographic multifaceted messages designed in SKI. Nevertheless, the KSL logic fails to reason about the knowledge of each engaging parties and fails to distinguish the sender from the creator. For the analysis of accountability property of the payment protocol which is designed under the PKI, reasoning about the knowledge of prover and verifier is sufficient whereas to perform the analysis in the SKI reasoning about the knowledge of all the parties involved in the protocol is essential. Because when the verifier considers only the evidences provided by the prover to take a decision, it leads to a biased judgment. In order to provide an unbiased verdict, the verifier needs to consider the knowledge of all the parties involved in the protocol.

In this paper, we present an improvement in strand space model to overcome the limitations of the KSL logic. To the best of our knowledge, this is the first framework in strand space model for the analysis of accountability property. The proposed work provides a model that formulates the knowledge of each principal so that the messages known to each principal can be recognized by the prover and verifier. Also, our model distinguishes sender from the creator of a message. To show the applicability of the proposed model, BPAC protocol is considered.

3   BPAC: A Bill Payment Protocol

BPAC protocol is a symmetric key based payment protocol introduced in [9].

Table 1. Notations used in BPAC protocol

Notations	Description
TID	Transaction ID or invoice ID that is created by the merchant
OD	Order descriptions that notify the client what he/she needs to pay for
price	Price of products or services
date	Date and time of the transaction
K_{BM_j}	Session key shared between the banker and the merchant for the jth session
K_{CB_j}	Session key shared between the client and the banker for the jth session
K_{CM_j}	Session key shared between the client and the merchant for the jth session
ID_C	Identity of the client
$conf_{bill}$	Confirmation to the merchant notifying that the bill is received by the banker and passed it on to the client
$conf_{pay}$	Confirmation to the client notifying that the merchant has received the payment
h_1	$h(TID, K_{MB_j})$
h_2	$h(TID, OD, price, date, h_1, K_{CM_j})$
h_3	$h(conf_{bill}, TID, K_{MB_j})$
h_4	$h(TID, price, date, K_{CM_{j+1}})$
h_5	$h(TID, price, date, K_{CB_{j+1}})$
h_6	$h(conf_{pay}, TID, price, date, K_{CM_{j+1}})$
h_7	$h(TID, price, date, K_{MB_{j+1}})$

3.1   Description of the Protocol

For the analysis, we have used some notations which are given in Table 1.

Bill Presentment Protocol. The three steps involved in the bill presentment protocol are shown below:

Step I: Credit request to banker
$M \to B : m_1 = \{ID_C, TID, price, date, h_2\}_{K_{MB_j}}$

Step II: Invoice to client
$B \to C : m_2 = \{TID, price, date, h_1, h_2\}_{K_{CB_j}}$

Step III: Acknowledgment to merchant
$B \to M : m_3 = conf_{bill}, h_3$

The merchant sends banker the encrypted bill that the client needs to pay. In reception to the bill from merchant, banker forwards the invoice to the client and sends a confirmation message to merchant intimating that he received the invoice and sent it to the client.

Bill Payment Protocol. The payment process can be carried out as follows:

Step IV: Debit request to banker
$C \rightarrow B : m_4 = \{TID, price, date, h_4\}_{K_{CB_{j+1}}}$

Step V: Credit response to merchant
$B \rightarrow M : m_5 = \{h_4, h_5, date, price\}_{K_{MB_{j+1}}}$

Step VI: Payment receipt
$M \rightarrow B : m_6 = conf_{pay}, \{h_6\}_{K_{MB_{j+1}}}$

Step VII: Payment receipt to client via banker
$B \rightarrow C : m_7 = conf_{pay}, \{h_6, h_7\}_{K_{CB_{j+1}}}$

When the client receives the invoice, he makes payment to the merchant via the banker by sending the debit request to the banker. Upon the receipt of debit request banker deducts the requested amount from the client's account and transfers this amount to the merchant's account and intimating the same to the merchant by sending the credit response. After receiving the credit response, the merchant creates the payment receipt to the client and sends it via the banker. Finally, banker forwards the payment response sent from the merchant to the client.

4   Strand Space Model

In this section, the formal method strand space is enhanced to carryout the accountability analysis. Readers are recommended to refer [4] in order to get deeper understanding of strand space, basic terminologies and definitions.

4.1   Improved Strand Space

We define the following primitives for the proper analysis of accountability property using strand space model.

Definition 1 (Protocol). *A protocol in strand space Σ is a 6-tuple $Pr = (N, E_\Rightarrow, E_\rightarrow, \mathscr{A}, T, K)$ where*

- *N is the set of nodes in Σ;*
- *$E_\Rightarrow$ is the set of edges formed by the causal relation $\Rightarrow$;*
- *$E_\rightarrow$ is the set of edges created by the causal relation $\rightarrow$;*
- *$\mathscr{A}$ is the message algebra;*
- *T is the set of texts (representing the atomic messages);*
- *K is the set of cryptographic keys.*

We consider the following two subsets for the purpose of defining the most appropriate terminologies. A subset P of T which consists of the names of all principals involved in the execution of the protocol Pr. A subset N_X of N is the set of all nodes at which the principal X can send or receive messages in the execution of the protocol Pr.

Definition 2 (Construal). *The construal of a message m at a node n, denoted by $cons_n(m)$ and defined inductively as*

- *If $m \in T$, then $cons_n(m) = m$;*
- *If $m = gh$, then $cons_n(m) = cons_n(g)cons_n(h)$;*
- *If $m = \{t\}_{K_A}$, then $cons_n(m) = cons_n(t)$ iff $n \in N_A$;*
- *If $m = \{t\}_{K_{AB}}$, then $cons_n(m) = cons_n(t)$ iff $n \in N_A$ or $n \in N_B$.*

Definition 3 (Knowledge-Domain). *Knowledge-domain of a principal $X \in P$ at node n_k, denoted by $kd_{n_k}(X)$ and is defined as the set of construal of messages that are sent or received at all nodes $n_i, i = 1, 2, ...m$ such that (n_1, n_2), $(n_2, n_3), ..., (n_{m-1}, n_m) \in E_\Rightarrow$.*

Since a principal's knowledge always increases, the knowledge-domain of a principal X at a node n is $kd_n(X) = \bigcup_{i=1}^{n} kd_i(X)$, if the principal X has moved from node 1, 2...to node n. Therefore, the knowledge-domain of principal X is given by $KD(X) = \{kd_i(X)|\ i$ *is a node in the strand of* $X\}$.

Lemma 1. *If a sequence of nodes in a strand of an arbitrary principal $X \in P$ are in the partial order under causal relation, then there exists a knowledge-domain relation (denoted by $\leq_{kd}$) which is a totally ordered relation defined on $KD(X)$.*

Proof: Consider a sequence of nodes $n_i, i = 1, 2, 3, ...m$ in a strand that are in the partial order under the causal relation $\Rightarrow$. From the definition of the knowledge-domain, we have $kd_{n_{i-1}}(X) \subseteq kd_{n_i}(X)$. Moreover, the subset($\subseteq$) relation is a partial ordering. Also, from the fact that $kd_n(X) = \bigcup_{i=1}^{n} kd_i(X)$, any pair of nodes in this strand is connected by this $\subseteq$ relation that is the required knowledge-domain relation($\leq_{kd}$) and hence it is a totally ordered relation. $\square$

Definition 4. *Let X be an arbitrary principal involved in the execution of the protocol Pr. $Gen(X)$ is the set of messages that X alone can create during the protocol execution.*

$Gen(X) = \{x|x$ *is a message created by X alone in the protocol execution*$\}$.

This definition can be extended to any number of principals in P.

Definition 5. *Let $X_1, X_2, ..., X_n$ be n number of arbitrary principals involved in the execution of the protocol Pr. $Gen(X_1X_2...X_n)$ is the set of messages which can be created by $X_1, X_2, ...$ or X_n .*

$$Gen(X_1X_2...X_n) = \{x|x \ \text{is a message created by } X_1, \ X_2, ... \ \text{or } X_n \\ \text{in the protocol execution}\}.$$

The following results can directly be derived from the above definitions

1. $Gen(X) \subseteq Gen(XY)$ for some $X, Y \in P$.
2. If $x \in Gen(X)$ at node i of the strand of X then $x \in kd_i(X)$.

Lemma 2. *Let* $x \in Gen(XY)$ *and* $y \in Gen(X)$. *If* $y \sqsubset x$ *and* $y \notin kd_i(Y)$ *then* $x \in Gen(X)$.

Proof: By the definition of Gen, as $x \in Gen(XY)$ implies that the message x can be generated by X or Y. Similarly $y \in Gen(X)$, the message y can only be generated by X alone. Given that y is a subterm of x, from the definition of subterm, it is clear that x is derivable from y. Therefore to create x it requires the knowledge of y, but by hypothesis $y \notin kd_i(Y)$. That is, x is not created by Y at node i. Which implies that x can be generated only by X.   □

4.2   Notion of Correctness

Accountability requires that if a protocol execution fails or does not achieve some goal, then it is possible to determine which participant involved in the protocol execution misbehaved or did not follow the protocol. In simple words, the verifier(Judge) should able to associate the message with the creator, in order to achieve the accountability property. We model the accountability property using improved strand space that can be discussed in twofold with respect the sender as a creator and not a forwarder.

Let X and Y be two arbitrary principals in the execution of the protocol. Assume that Y sends a message x to X. The intention of the sender Y can be to create a new message and send or just forward what he/she received. Y is the creator of the message x if and only if $x \in Gen(Y)$. By considering the knowledge-domain and the trace of Y's strand at that instance, it is possible to determine whether Y is a forwarder or not. Y holds accountable for the sent message x if and only if $x \in Gen(Y)$ and x is not a forwarded message.

5   BPAC Space

In this section, we model the two phases of BPAC protocol, using the proposed framework and the attacker ability is also formulated to strengthen the analysis.

Definition 6 (BPAC Bill-Presentment Space). *In a BPAC Bill-presentment space set of merchant strands denoted by* $Merc(ID_C, TID, price, date, confirm_{bill}, h_2, h_3)$ *with trace of the form* $\langle +m_1, -m_3 \rangle$, *set of banker strands denoted by* $Bank(ID_C, TID, price, date, confirm_{bill}, h_1, h_2, h_3)$ *with trace of the form* $\langle -m_1, +m_2, +m_3 \rangle$ *and the set of all client strands denoted by* $Clie(TID, price, date, h_1, h_2)$ *with trace of the form* $\langle -m_2 \rangle$.

Definition 7 (BPAC Bill-Payment Space). *In BPAC Bill-payment space set of merchant strands denoted by $Merc(price, date, confirm_{pay}, h_4, h_5, h_6)$ with trace of the form $\langle -m_5, +m_6 \rangle$, set of banker strands denoted by $Bank(TID, price, date, confirm_{pay}, h_4, h_5, h_6, h_7)$ with trace of the form $\langle -m_4, +m_5, -m_6, +m_7 \rangle$ and the set of all client strands denoted by $Clie(TID, price, date, confirm_{pay}, h_4, h_6, h_7)$ with trace of the form $\langle +m_4, -m_7 \rangle$.*

Definition 8 (BPAC Space). *The sets $Merc, Bank$ and $Clie$ are mutually disjoint. The strand space of BPAC protocol is denoted by Σ and defined as $\Sigma = Merc \cup Bank \cup Clie \cup Pen$, where Pen is the set of penetrator strands.*

Definition 9 (Penetrator Strand [4]). *A penetrator trace is one of the following:* M. *Text message:* $\langle +t \rangle$ *where* $t \in T$

F. *Flushing:* $\langle -g \rangle$
T. *Tee:* $\langle -g, +g, +g \rangle$
C. *Concatenation:* $\langle -g, -h, +gh \rangle$
S. *Separation into components:* $\langle -gh, +g, +h \rangle$
K. *Key:* $\langle +k \rangle$ *where* $k \in K_P$
E. *Encryption:* $\langle -k, -h, + \{h\}_k \rangle$.
D. *Decryption:* $\langle -k^{-1}, - \{h\}_k, +h \rangle$.
H. *Hashing:* $\langle -m, +h(m) \rangle$.
KH. *Keyed-Hash:* $\langle -m, -k, +h(m, k) \rangle$.

Our theorems characterize a penetrator with just the abilities we have described. The bundles in BPAC space which represent the single run of the entire protocol are shown in Fig. 1.

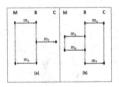

Fig. 1. An arbitrary bundle in (a) BPAC bill-presentment space, (b) BPAC bill-payment space

For an arbitrary run of the BPAC protocol, the knowledge-domain of each principal at their nodes are described as follows.

Merchant:

$kd_1(M) = \{ID_C, TID, price, date, h_1, h_2\}$
$kd_2(M) = \{ID_C, TID, price, date, h_1, h_2, confirm_{bill}, h_3\}$
$kd_3(M) = \{ID_C, TID, price, date, h_1, h_2, confirm_{bill}, h_3, h_4, h_5\}$
$kd_4(M) = \{ID_C, TID, price, date, h_1, h_2, confirm_{bill},$
$h_3, h_4, h_5, confirm_{payment}, h_6\}$

Banker:

$$kd_1(B) = \{ID_C, TID, price, date, h_2\}$$
$$kd_2(B) = \{ID_C, TID, price, date, h_2, h_1\}$$
$$kd_3(B) = \{ID_C, TID, price, date, h_2, h_1, confirm_{bill}, h_3\}$$
$$kd_4(B) = \{ID_C, TID, price, date, h_2, h_1, confirm_{bill}, h_3, h_4\}$$
$$kd_5(B) = \{ID_C, TID, price, date, h_2, h_1, confirm_{bill}, h_3, h_4, h_5\}$$
$$kd_6(B) = \{ID_C, TID, price, date, h_2, h_1, confirm_{bill},$$
$$h_3, h_4, h_5, confirm_{payment}, h_6\}$$
$$kd_7(B) = \{ID_C, TID, price, date, h_2, h_1, confirm_{bill},$$
$$h_3, h_4, h_5, confirm_{payment}, h_6, h_7\}$$

Client:

$$kd_1(C) = \{TID, price, date, h_1, h_2\}$$
$$kd_2(C) = \{TID, price, date, h_1, h_2, h_4\}$$
$$kd_3(C) = \{TID, price, date, h_1, h_2, h_4, confirm_{payment}, h_6, h_7\}$$

Using this knowledge-domain and trace of each principal, it is possible to determine whether the message received is sent by the originator of the message or it is forwarded by an entity. Also, this will be useful for the verifier to classify the knowledge obtained by each principal at each node and by this way we model the ability of the verifier's knowledge.

The following axioms are formulated based on the BPAC protocol and definitions 4 and 5 in the Sect. 4.1.

Axioms: As the hash value h_1 is created using the shared secret key between the banker and the merchant, we have

$A_1.h_1 \in Gen(MB)$.

Similarly, we have

$A_2.h_4 \in Gen(CM)$, $A_3.h_5 \in Gen(CB)$, $A_4.m_1 \in Gen(MB)$, $A_5.m_2 \in Gen(CB)$, $A_6.m_4 \in Gen(CB)$, $A_7.m_5 \in Gen(MB)$, $A_8.h_2 \in Gen(CM)$.

6 Analysis of BPAC protocol

The analysis starts with identifying the existence of possible issues in dispute. They are,(i) the invoice received from banker mismatches with the amount client supposed to pay, in this situation banker should be able to prove that merchant hold accountable for his sent credit request, (ii) the payment is not credited to merchant's account, at this dispute merchant should be able to prove that banker is accountable for his sent credit response, (iii) client claims that the amount debited from his account is incorrect, at this instance banker should be able to prove that the client is accountable for his sent debit request, (iv) the payment receipt mismatches with the invoice, in this regard client should be able to prove that banker hold accountable for the sent invoice.

The protocol analysis is carried out using an automated tool Cryptographic Protocol Shape Analyzer (CPSA) which is working under the basis of strand space model [2,5] and scenarios with respect to the accountability issues mentioned above are reported.

6.1 Scenarios

The scenario usually contains a regular strand for just one of the roles, in which the test node and its term namely critical-term are identified to form an initial skeleton. The originator of critical-term is to be authenticated in order to frame a realized skeleton, if no such a realized skeleton exists in the scenario then it means that there is no entity authentication. The authentication goal is achieved if for every receiving node in a regular strand there exist a unique strand that has a matching sending node as they agree with significant data such as keys and identity of the parties.

As the banker receives message m_1 from the merchant, he needs to know the existence of one such a merchant. In the CPSA results, we wish to confirm an authentication goal, there was a regular merchant strand agreeing on the name of the principal and the data exchanged between them.

Scenario 1 (Banker Strand in BPAC Bill Presentment Space). CPSA finds a shape, an initial skeleton in Fig. 2(a) with banker's strand and the critical-term m_1 is recognized at the test node. Using encryption test [2] the merchant strand is added with height 1, in which the test node and the critical-term m_1 are realized. In this way, CPSA constructs a realized skeleton from the initial skeleton and the critical-term origination is confirmed. Figure 2(b) depicts that the entity authentication at the test node is achieved.

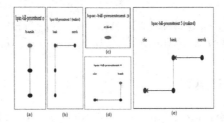

Fig. 2. Bill presentment phase: Initial skeleton to realized skeleton in banker's view and client's view

In the second scenario, CPSA analyzes the protocol in the client point of view. The client receives the message m_2 from the banker and it needs to have an entity authentication.

Scenario 2 (Client Point of View). In this scenario, CPSA finds a shape with the client strand of the full length shown in Fig. 2(c). As the critical-term

m_2 in the test node is recognized, the test node is realized by adding banker's strand in Fig. 2(d) followed by adding merchant's strand in Fig. 2(e) using the encryption test. Thus, the authentication for m_2 is achieved and the existence of unique banker strand is also realized.

The next two scenarios 3 and 4 describes the protocol analysis using CPSA for the authentication goal while receiving m_4 and m_5 by the banker and merchant respectively in the BPAC bill payment space.

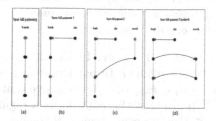

Fig. 3. Bill payment phase: Initial skeleton to realized skeleton in banker's view

Scenario 3 (Banker Strand in BPAC Bill Payment Space). CPSA finds a shape of an initial skeleton with the banker strand of full length, shown in Fig. 3(a). The critical-term m_4 and m_6 are recognized at their test nodes simultaneously. The critical-term m_4 is realized in Fig. 3(b) by adding the client strand. Also, the critical-term m_6 is realized by adding the merchant strand in Fig. 3(c) using encryption test. In this way, CPSA finally produces a realized skeleton in Fig. 3(d) from the initial skeleton.

Scenario 4 (Merchant Point of View in Bill Payment Space). In this scenario, CPSA finds a shape of an initial skeleton with the merchant strand of the full length shown in Fig. 4(a). The critical-term m_5 is recognized at its test node. The test node is realized by adding banker's strand in Fig. 4(b) followed by adding the client strand in Fig. 4(c).

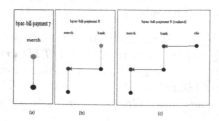

Fig. 4. Bill payment phase: Initial skeleton to realized skeleton in merchant's view

CPSA does not recognize that, this is not possible in a state-history, and thus provides only an approximate analysis. Showing the correctness of the protocol requires a more refined analysis that is carried out in the following subsection.

6.2 Mathematical Proof for the Correctness

In order to provide the correctness of BPAC protocol against accountability property, the following theorems are established and proved.

Theorem 1. *Suppose Σ is a BPAC Bill-presentment space and $\mathcal{B}$ is any arbitrary bundle containing a banker's strand s in $Bank(ID_C, TID, price, date, confirm_{bill}, h_1, h_2, h_3)$ with trace of the form $\langle -m_1, +m_2, +m_3 \rangle$ and $K_{BM_j} \notin K_P$, then there exists a unique regular strand t in $Merc(ID_C, TID, price, date, confirm_{bill}, h_2, h_3)$ containing a node n_0 such that $term(n_0) = m_1$, $m_1 \in Gen(M)$ and m_1 is not a forwarded message.*

Proof: Let us take the node $\langle s, 1 \rangle$ as n_1. In Fig. 2(b), CPSA shows that the existence of unique merchant's strand t. In particular there exists a positive node $n_0 = \langle t, 1 \rangle$ such that $n_0 \to n_1 \in E_\to$. In order to prove that t is not a penetrator strand, it is sufficient to prove that the node n_0 is a regular node. Except the trace for M-strand of $p \in Pen$, no other traces in the list of penetrator strands match with the one shown in Fig. 2(b). Since $n_0 \to n_1 \in E_\to$ and $term(n_1) = m_1$, implies that $term(n_0) = m_1$. Therefore, the node n_0 does not lie on M-strand because M-strand of p of the form $\langle +t \rangle, t \in T$ emits a text message t but m_1 is an encrypted message. Thus n_0 is a regular node. Axiom A_4 shows that $m_1 \in Gen(MB)$ and also we have $h_2 \sqsubset m_1$. Moreover, $h_2 \notin kd_0(B)$ because $h_2 \in Gen(CM)$ by axiom A_8 and hence it is not initially in the knowledge-domain of B. By using Lemma 2, we can prove that message m_1 cannot be created by B and it can only be created by M. Hence $m_1 \in Gen(M)$. By Lemma 1, nodes in the strand of merchant are related by the totally ordered relation $\leq_{kd}$ and the minimal node is n_0. Therefore $term(n_0) = m_1$ is not a forwarded message.   □

Thus, the banker can prove that the existence of merchant and he is the creator of the message m_1 to the verifier. Moreover, it is proved that this message is not a forwarded message. This proof can be used to assure that the credit request m_1 is sent by the merchant and he cannot deny it later.

As the banker sends m_2 to the client, the following theorem is to ensure that it is prepared and sent by the banker.

Theorem 2. *Suppose Σ is a BPAC Bill-presentment space and $\mathcal{B}$ is any arbitrary bundle containing a client's strand u in $Clie(TID, price, date, h_1, h_2)$ with trace of the form $\langle -m_2 \rangle$ and $K_{BC_j} \notin K_P$ then there exists a unique regular strand s in $Bank(ID_C, TID, price, date, confirm_{bill}, h_1, h_2, h_3)$ containing node n_2 such that $term(n_2) = m_2$, $m_2 \in Gen(B)$ and m_2 is not a forwarded message.*

Proof: Let us take the node $\langle u, 1 \rangle$ as n_3. CPSA finds a unique banker's strand s and the existence of the positive node n_2 such that $n_2 \to n_3 \in E_\to$ which is shown in Fig. 2(d). As no trace in the list of penetrator strands matches with the banker's strand in Fig. 2(e), n_2 does not lie on the penetrator strand. Thus, the banker's strand cannot be a penetrator strand. By axiom A_5, $m_2 \in Gen(CB)$ and hence $m_2 \notin Gen(M)$. Also h_1, h_2 are the subterms of m_2. By the axiom

$A_1, h_1 \in Gen(MB)$. Since $TID \in kd_1(B)$, we have $h_1 \in Gen(B)$. Moreover to create h_2, the knowledge of h_1 is essential but h_1 is not in the knowledge-domain of client initially and hence $h_2 \notin kd_0(C)$. Using Lemma 2 , $m_2 \notin Gen(C)$ and this implies that $m_2 \in Gen(B)$. By Lemma 1, the nodes in the banker's strand are related by the totally ordered relation $\leq_{kd}$ and there exist a minimal node n_1 such that $n_1 \leq_{kd} n_2$. The knowledge-domain at these instances shows that $term(n_2) = m_2$ is not a forwarded message .   □

By this way, the client can prove to the verifier that the banker is accountable for the sent invoice m_2.

Theorem 3. *Suppose Σ is a BPAC Bill-payment space and $\mathcal{B}$ is any arbitrary bundle containing a banker's strand s in $Bank(TID, price, date, confirm_{pay},$ $h_4, h_5, h_6, h_7)$ with trace of the form $\langle -m_4, +m_5, -m_6, +m_7 \rangle$ and $K_{BC_{j+1}} \notin K_P$, then there exists a unique regular strand u in $Clie(TID, price, date, confirm_{pay},$ $h_4, h_6, h_7)$ containing a node n_4 such that $term(n_4) = m_4$, $m_4 \in Gen(C)$ and m_4 is not a forwarded message.*

Proof: Let us take the node $\langle s, 1 \rangle$ as n_5. In Fig. 3(b), CPSA shows that there exists a node n_4 in the client's strand u such that $n_4 \rightarrow n_5 \in E_\rightarrow$. However, the only penetrator's strand matches with the one shown in Fig. 3(d) is M-strand of p. Since $n_4 \rightarrow n_5 \in E_\rightarrow$ and $term(n_5) = m_4$, implies that $term(n_4) = m_4$. The node n_4 does not lie on M-strand because M-strand of p of the form $\langle +t \rangle, t \in T$ but m_4 is an encrypted message. Thus n_4 lies on a regular strand and hence u is a regular strand. By the axiom $A_6, m_4 \in Gen(BC)$ and hence $m_4 \notin Gen(M)$. The hash value $h_4 \sqsubset m_4$. By the axiom $A_2, h_4 \in Gen(CM)$ and $h_4 \notin kd_4(B)$. By the Lemma 2, $m_4 \notin Gen(B)$ and hence $m_4 \in Gen(C)$. By Lemma 1, nodes in the client's strand are related by the totally ordered relation $\leq_{kd}$ and the minimal node is n_4. Therefore $term(n_4) = m_4$ is not a forwarded message.   □

Thus, the banker can prove to the verifier that the client is accountable for the sent debit request m_4.

Theorem 4. *Suppose Σ is a BPAC Bill-payment space and C is any arbitrary bundle containing a merchant's strand t in $Merc(price, date, confirm_{pay}, h_4, h_5,$ $h_6)$ with trace of the form $\langle -m_5, +m_6 \rangle$ and $K_{BM_{j+1}} \notin K_P$, then there exists a unique regular strand s in $Bank(TID, price, date, confirm_{pay}, h_4, h_5, h_6, h_7)$ containing a node n_6 such that $term(n_6) = m_5$, $m_5 \in Gen(B)$ and m_5 is not a forwarded message $m_5 \in Gen(B)$.*

Proof: Let us take the node $\langle t, 1 \rangle$ as n_7. CPSA finds the existence of unique banker's strand s with a node n_6 such that $n_6 \rightarrow n_7 \in E_\rightarrow$ in Fig. 4(b). As no trace in the list of penetrator strands matches with the banker's strand shown in Fig. 4(c), the banker's strand cannot be a penetrator strand and hence it is a regular strand. By the axiom $A_7, m_5 \in Gen(MB)$ and hence $m_5 \notin Gen(C)$. However, $h_4 \sqsubset m_5$ and $h_5 \sqsubset m_5$. The knowledge-domain of B shows that $h_4 \in kd_4(B)$. By axiom $A_3, h_5 \in Gen(CB), h_5 \notin kd_3(M)$ and hence $h_5 \notin Gen(M)$. Thus by Lemma 2, $m_5 \in Gen(B)$. By Lemma 1, there exist a minimal node

n_5 such that $n_5 \leq_{kd} n_6$. The knowledge-domain at these instances shows that $term(n_6) = m_5$ is not a forwarded message.   □

Using this, the merchant can prove to the judge that the banker is accountable for the received credit response m_5.

Thus following the above theoretical proofs, it can conclude that the BPAC protocol satisfies accountability property

6.3   Comparative Analysis

The proposed model is compared with existing methods in Table 2.

Table 2. Comparative analysis with existing methods

Methods	Prover's knowledge	Verifier's knowledge	All engaging parties knowledge	Disclosing secret information	Distinguish creator and forwarder	Infrastructure
Kailar's logic [6]	Yes	No	No	Yes	No	PKI
KN logic [7]	Yes	Yes	No	Yes	No	PKI
KP logic [8]	Yes	Yes	No	No	No	PKI
KSL logic [9]	Yes	Yes	No	No	No	SKI
Proposed model	Yes	Yes	Yes	No	Yes	SKI

7   Conclusion

In this paper, we have enhanced strand space model in order to perform the analysis of accountability property of any payment protocol that is designed in the SKI for e-commerce and m-commerce applications. The proposed model deals with the knowledge of each engaging parties in the protocol and distinguishes sender from the creator of a message which are essential to identify the appropriate accountable party. Using the proposed model and the automated tool CPSA, the correctness of the accountability property for BPAC protocol has been proved. For the future work, this model has to be extended to carry out the analysis of accountability property within the delegation.

References

1. Bella, G., Paulson, L.C.: Accountability protocols: formalized and verified. ACM Trans. Inf. Syst. Secur. (TISSEC) **9**(2), 138–161 (2006)
2. Doghmi, S.F., Guttman, J.D., Thayer, F.J.: Searching for shapes in cryptographic protocols. In: Grumberg, O., Huth, M. (eds.) TACAS 2007. LNCS, vol. 4424, pp. 523–537. Springer, Heidelberg (2007)
3. Doss, R., Zhou, W., Yu, S.: Secure rfid tag ownership transfer based on quadratic residues. IEEE Trans. Inf. Forensics Secur. **8**(2), 390–401 (2013)

4. Fábrega, F.J.T., Herzog, J.C., Guttman, J.D.: Strand spaces: proving security protocols correct. J. Comput. Secur. **7**(2), 191–230 (1999)
5. John D.R., Joshua D.G.: Cpsa: A cryptographic protocol shapes analyzer (2010). http://hackage.haskell.org/package/cpsa. Accessed 4 March 2015
6. Kailar, R.: Accountability in electronic commerce protocols. IEEE Trans. Softw. Eng. **22**(5), 313–328 (1996)
7. Kessler, V., Neumann, H.: A sound logic for analysing electronic commerce protocols. In: Quisquater, J.-J., Deswarte, Y., Meadows, C., Gollmann, D. (eds.) ESORICS 1998. LNCS, vol. 1485, pp. 345–360. Springer, Heidelberg (1998)
8. Kungpisdan, S., Permpoontanalarp, Y.: Practical reasoning about accountability in electronic commerce protocols. In: Kim, K. (ed.) ICISC 2001. LNCS, vol. 2288, pp. 268–284. Springer, Heidelberg (2002)
9. Kungpisdan, S., et al.: Accountability of centralized payment systems: formal reasoning, protocol design and analysis. IETE Tech. Rev. **27**(5), 351 (2010)
10. Sureshkumar, V., Anitha, R.: Analysis of electronic voting protocol using strand space model. In: Pérez, G.M., Thampi, S.M., Ko, R., Shu, L. (eds.) Recent Trends in Computer Networks and Distributed Systems Security. Communications in Computer and Information Science, pp. 416–427. Springer, Heidelberg (2014)

Technical Aspects of Cyber Kill Chain

Tarun Yadav[✉] and Arvind Mallari Rao

Defence Research and Development Organisation, New Delhi, India
{tarunyadav,arvindrao}@hqr.drdo.in

Abstract. Recent trends in targeted cyber-attacks has increased the interest of research in the field of cyber security. Such attacks have massive disruptive effects on organizations, enterprises and governments. Cyber kill chain is a model to describe cyber-attacks so as to develop incident response and analysis capabilities. Cyber kill chain in simple terms is an attack chain, the path that an intruder takes to penetrate information systems over time to execute an attack on the target. This paper broadly categories the methodologies, techniques and tools involved in cyber-attacks. This paper intends to help a cyber security researcher to realize the options available to an attacker at every stage of a cyber-attack.

Keywords: Reconnaissance · RAT · Exploit · Cyber attack · Persistence · Command and control

1 Introduction

One of the leading problems faced by organizations is the emergence of targeted attacks conducted by adversaries who have easy access to sophisticated tools and technologies with an aim at establishing a persistent and undetected presence in the targeted cyber infrastructure. These multi-staged attacks are now becoming more complex, involving vertical and horizontal movement across multiple elements of the organization. The security research community has given this multi-stage chain of events culminating to cyber espionage a name: *The Cyber Kill Chain*. This paper aims on providing a primer on the cyber kill chain and surveys the recent trends and methodologies of the attacker at each stage of the cyber kill chain.

The paper talks about attacks in general irrespective of operating systems or application software since Cyber Kill Chain is a process rather than a technology. Technologies involved at each stage of the cyber kill chain process is explained without going into much details.

The paper is organized into 4 sections. Section 2 introduces the phases of cyber kill chain, Sect. 3 discusses the technical trends at each step of the cyber kill chain. The paper ends with concluding remarks in Sect. 4.

© Springer International Publishing Switzerland 2015
J.H. Abawajy et al. (Eds): SSCC 2015, CCIS 536, pp. 438–452, 2015.
DOI: 10.1007/978-3-319-22915-7_40

2   Cyber Kill Chain

Cyber kill chain is a model for incident response teams, digital forensic investigators and malware analysts to work in a chained manner. Inherently understanding, Cyber kill chain is modeling and analyzing offensive actions of a cyber-attacker [1]. So, for a security analyst who develops defensive counter measures [3], it is of utmost importance to study the cyber kill chain. This knowledge can help one think on the same lines of that of an attacker. Each phase of the kill chain in itself is a vast research area to tackle and analyze.

In recent years, cyber attacks have been more complex than it used to be and hence more destructive and dangerous [14,41]. Nowadays multiple redundant attack vectors are being exploited in cyber attacks to not only multiply the effect but also making it more difficult for the response team to analyze.

To analyze such attacks, cyber kill chain provides a framework to breakdown a complicated attack into mutually nonexclusive stages or layers. Such a layered approach will enable the analysts to tackle smaller and easier problems and at the same time it will also help the defenders to subvert each phase by developing defenses and mitigation for each of the phases. Cyber Kill chain mainly consists of 7 phases [5,6,8] as shown in Fig. 1.

There are many articles [2,4,7] which describe the *Cyber Kill Chain* in detail with respect to recent attacks but most of them do not discuss the tools and technologies used by the attacker at each stage of the cyber kill chain. In the next

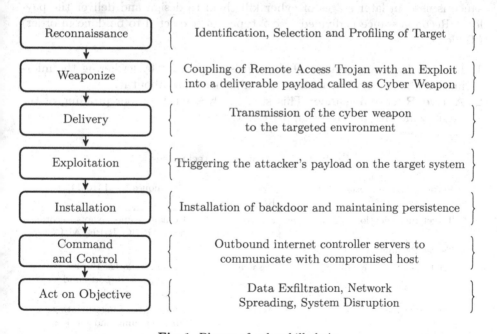

Fig. 1. Phases of cyber kill chain

section we will go through technical aspects involved at each step with respect to the attacker's perspective and will see the variety of tools and methodologies utilized by the attacker.

3   Technical Aspects of Cyber Kill Chain

As described cyber kill chain defines the flow of a cyber attack and in this 7-layer model each layer is critical. Studying the cyber kill chain will help cyber threats to be identified or mitigated at any layer of attack. Sooner the detection is done lesser is the loss to the organization under attack. This section broadly outlines the technical methodologies, implementation, research, and tools involved at each stage of the cyber kill chain with examples of famous cyber attacks and malware used in the bygone years.

3.1   Reconnaissance

Reconnaissance means gathering information about the potential target. A target can be an individual or an organizational entity. Reconnaissance can further be broken down to target identification, selection and profiling. Reconnaissance in cyber space mainly includes crawling World Wide Web such as internet websites, conferences, blogs, social relationship, mailing lists and network tracing tools to get information about the target. Information gathered from reconnaissance is used in later stages of cyber kill chain to design and deliver the payload. Reconnaissance is divided into 2 types [9] (expected to be done in order) (Table 1):

1. **Passive Reconnaissance:** This step is carried out by gathering the information about target without letting him/her know about it.
2. **Active Reconnaissance:** This step involves much deeper profiling of the target which might trigger an alert to the target.

Table 1. Reconnaissance Techniques

	Reconnaissance Methodology	Type of Reconnaissance	Techniques Used [10, 11]
1	Target Identification and Selection	passive	Domain Names, whois, records from APNIC, RIPE, ARIN
2	Target Profiling		
	(a) Target Social Profiling	Passive	Social Networks, Public Documents, Reports and Corporate Websites
	(b) Target System Profiling	Active	Pingsweeps, Fingerprinting, Port Scanning and services
3	Target Validation	Active	SPAM Messages, Phishing Mails and Social Engineering

Reconnaissance provides knowledge about potential targets which will enable the attacker to decide the type of weapon suitable for the target, the types of delivery methods possible (Table 3), malware installation difficulties and security mechanisms that need to be bypassed. We will now see how the information gathered by reconnaissance is used to develop sophisticated malware.

3.2   Weaponize

Weaponize phase of the cyber kill chain deals with designing a backdoor and a penetration plan, utilizing the information gathered from reconnaissance, to enable successful delivery of the backdoor. Technically it is binding software/application exploits with a remote access tool (RAT). Weaponizing involves design and development of the following two components:-

3.2.1   RAT (Remote Access Tool)

RAT is a piece of software which executes on target's system and give remote, hidden and undetected access to the attacker. RAT is usually called the payload of a cyber-weapon. The target system can be a computer, mobile [13] or any embedded device provided the RAT software is properly compiled for the architecture being targeted. The types of access provided by a typical RAT (Table 2) are system exploration, file upload or download, remote file execution, keystroke monitor, screen capture, webcam or system power on/off with limited or user level privileges. If by some mechanism the RAT gets administrator/root access then it could include network spreading [1], network data capture access or persistent installation of anti-detection module. A RAT again constitutes of two major parts:

Client. Client is the piece of code which is delivered to the target, executes and creates a network connection with the Command and Control infrastructure of the RAT. After establishing connection, the client receives the command from its controller. Client in turn executes the command and sends the results back. It is not always necessary to have all RAT functionalities in a single deliverable. There are many instances of RAT like Carberp [14], Ventir Trojan [15], Poison Ivy [42], etc. where RAT functions are delivered to the target in a modular manner by using a very basic stub. The compiled code can be deployed in the form of an executable binary or shellcode. Shellcode in simplistic terms is a position independent machine code generally compiled by assemblers. There also exists techniques [16] which use specially crafted C-language source codes to generate shellcode.

Server. Server is the other half of RAT which runs on the Command and Control infrastructure with a nice UI (User Interface) displaying the connection information from target's client part. Server typically has options of commands like gathering keystrokes, file browser, screen capture, etc. Based on the objective of a cyber campaign, the attacker gives an approproriate command or series of commands to the target using server interface which is executed by target's client side code and the output is returned back to the server. Depending on the execution permission level being allotted to the client part, these commands can be executed to get full access of target's system.

While developing RATs major constraints are size, anti-virus detection, extendibility, and scalability and user friendly interface. A big chunk of the RAT programing task is dedicated to UI design of server since ease of use of a RAT is defined by the server UI.

It is not necessary to code client and server in the same language. These days the servers are using either scripting languages(PHP, Javascript) for a web based UI [14,41] or C++, Java, delphi [17,42] for an application based interface.

Table 2. RATs and exploit kits

Famous RATs	Famous Exploit Kits [13,25]
Blackshades	Blackhole
DarkComet	Nuclear
Poison ivy	Styx
Bozok	Redkit
Njrat	Sweet Orange
Apocalypse	Infinity

3.2.2   Exploit

Exploit is the part of a weapon which facilitates the RAT to execute. Exploit acts as a carrier for the RAT and uses system/software vulnerabilities to drop and execute the RAT. The major objective in using exploits is to evade user attention while establishing a silent backdoor access using the RAT. Exploits can be of many forms like MS Office documents (.doc/ppt) [CVE-2010-3333, CVE-2014-4114] , PDF Documents [CVE-2014-9165, CVE-2013-2729], audio/video file [CVE 2013-3245] or web page [CVE-2012-1876, CVE-2014-6332] [18]. If a target opens any such file using the vulnerable software, RAT will be installed on targets system. After getting a RAT installed more exploits like privilege escalation exploits [CVE-2015-002, CVE-2013-3660] are used on the target to get higher privileges which can be used for spreading the RAT, persistent access and/or for destruction of the complete system.

There are methods to compromise the target using only RAT without using any exploit. But those methods are highly unreliable and not effective these days because of the increase in security awareness among the users. Embedding RAT in legitimate software executable, sharing via social engineering and faking RAT as genuine image/audio/video files are some of such methods which have been used in the wild in previous years [41].

3.3   Delivery

Delivery is the critical part of the cyber kill chain which is responsible for an efficient and effective cyber-attack. For any cyber-attack it is preferable to have target information to ensure a successful attack. In most of the cyber-attacks it is mandatory to have some kind of user interaction like downloading and executing malicious files or visiting malicious web pages on internet. This affinity comes from the information gathered during active and passive reconnaissance. There are some attacks which are performed without user interaction by exploiting network devices or services [CVE-2014-3306, CVE-2014-9583] [18].

Delivery is a high risk task for an attacker because delivery leaves traces. Therefore most of the attacks are performed anonymously using paid anonymous services, compromised websites and compromised email accounts.

While delivering the weapon multiple delivery methods are also used because no single method can guarantee 100 % success. Failed attacks sometimes are very useful to get basic information about the target's system information. Such types of information gathering mechanisms are very common in a browser based attack strategy, wherein a user visits the malicious web page which first tries to get user system information and then accordingly deliver the weapon [20].

Table 3. Delivery mechanisms

	Delivery Mechanism [1, 12]	Characteristics
1	Email Attachments	Email content is composed to entice the user by using appealing content
3	Phishing Attacks	Sensitive information like usernames, passwords, credit card details etc. are extracted by masquerading a trustworthy entity in communication [19].
4	Drive by Download	Target is forced to download appealing malicious content from internet. Malicious content could be a image file, pdf/word document or software setup file
5	USB/Removal Media	Infected files are kept in Removable media which afterwards silently infects other systems opening the files.
6	DNS Cache Poisoning	Vulnerabilities in DNS are exploited to divert internet traffic from legitimate servers to attacker controlled destinations

3.4   Exploitation

After delivering the cyber weapon, then as expected the target completes the required user interaction and weapon executes at the target side. On execution, the next step is triggering the exploit. The objective of an exploit is to silently install/execute the payload. To trigger the exploit there are certain conditions that need to be matched:

1. User must be using the software/Operating System for which exploit has been created.
2. The software/Operating System should not be updated or upgraded to the versions wherein an exploit does not work.
3. Anti-Viruses or any other security mechanism should not detect the exploit or payload neither in statically nor dynamically scan during run time.

If all these conditions are fulfilled then exploit is triggered and will successfully install/execute the payload in target's system. Payload will connect to its Command and Control counterpart to inform about successful execution and wait for further commands to execute.

It is clear that exploit is the most critical part of the chain technically. What is an exploit and how does an attacker find such exploits is the next question here.

Exploits are made using vulnerabilities in software publicly identified as CVE [18]. Vulnerability is the software bug which can result in a potential threat to the system. A software bug is an unexpected condition in which a program/software misbehaves. Usually, while programming an application, lots of effort is made to avoid such conditions by writing every possible use case, handling exceptions for all types of inputs, validating inputs, etc. But most of the times not all cases are covered because of vast variety of user input/interaction. Therefore such invalid or wrong input forces the program to misbehave and this misbehavior is defined as type of vulnerability as mentioned in Table 4.

Vulnerabilities are further analyzed by exploit writers to see the possibility to carry and execute a payload. Not all vulnerabilities are exploitable. Some of them are just crashes or DoS(Denial of Service) or limited execution of program. It means not all vulnerabilities result into exploitable crashes.

Regarding the interest that how these vulnerabilities are discovered, there are papers [22–24] that describe details about fuzzing. Fuzzing is a methodology to give customized input to the program and monitoring the output for abnormal behavior. This abnormal behavior is further analyzed with respect to given input to describe vulnerability and so to create exploits.

As mentioned in the Delivery section sometimes just one delivery method is not sufficient, in the same way not just one exploit is sufficient to attack multiple users specifically during mass attacks. Generally combination of exploits, called an Exploit Kit, is used for this purpose. As the name suggests Exploit Kit is a collection of multiple exploits for various versions of software. As an example for browser based attacks an exploit kit (Table 2) may have exploits for various versions of Google Chrome, Firefox and internet explorer. During delivery if target uses vulnerable version of any of listed browser for which exploit is available in exploit kit it will be delivered accordingly.

3.5   Installation

Host based security measures have grown leaps and bounds compared to other security mechanisms. This in turn has spurred innovation in procedures that circumvent host-based security controls to install, update and regulate the control of the malware installed upon the victims computing device. Traditionally, a computer would become infected by an infection vector like infected removable media, which in turn will leave a malware executable in some unusual location and modify registry/startup settings so that the malware executable is run everytime the computer boots up. Some user eventually will report [31] this executable to antivirus vendor, who in turn will analyze it and come up with a signature to detect it and in some cases a removal tool. Modern malwares are not that simple anymore [47]. Malware nowadays are multi staged and they heavily rely on droppers and downloaders to deliver the malware modules in a much more sophisticated manner.

- **Dropper** is a program that will install and run the malware to a target system. Before executing the malware code, dropper nowadays tries disabling host based security controls at the target and hides the installed malware.
- **Downloaders** were designed to perform the same actions as Droppers disabling the victims security and monitoring software, hiding core components and obfuscating the infection vector, etc. but tended to be smaller than Droppers because they did not contain the core malicious library components. Instead of unpacking an embedded copy of the core malware agent, the downloader would connect to a remote file repository and download the core components.

Today's installation life-cycle incorporates many checks, balances and resilience features as a means of maximizing the success of the installation, and protecting the participating attackers. Following are some techniques that malware authors use for covert persistent and anonymous installations.

Table 4. Vulnerabilities and Exploits

	Category of Exploits	Type of Exploit	Type of Vulnerability [21]
1	Operating System Level Exploits	Kernel Exploits, Device Driver Exploits	− Denial-of-Services − Remote or Local Code Execution
2	Network Level Exploits	Protocol exploits for FTP, SMTP, NTP, SSH, Router exploits,	− Privilege Escalation
3	Application/ Software Exploits	Browser Exploits, MS Office exploits, PDF Exploits, Java/Flash Exploits	Memory Corruption: − Dangling Pointer − Buffer Overflow [26] − Use-After-Free

- **Anti-Debugger and Anti-Emulation:** Dropper and downloader components are typically armored. Using a variety of packers, crypters and inspection-detection engines, malware authors can ensure that common debugger and emulation analysis techniques will not work. The addition of advanced anti-virtual machine analysis technologies also deters malware analysis to a high extent.
- **Anti-Antivirus:** Many malware packages include toolsets for automatically disabling host-based detection technologies disabling anti-virus and IDS products installed on the victim's computer, changing local DNS settings to ensure that no future updates to the operating system or packages are possible, and adding tools that recheck and re-disable protection settings frequently.
- **Rootkit and Bootkit Installation:** Rootkits are programs which hide the executed payload. Payload file hiding, process hiding are the core functionalities of rootkits like LRK, AFX and Mebroot [27]. Similarly Bootkits are malwares that are able to hook and patch system to get loaded into the system Kernel, and thus getting unrestricted access to the entire system. Bootkits like Stoned Bootkit [28] modify the MBR or boot sector for its execution to avoid protections from operating system.
- **Targeted Delivery:** By performing a quick inventory of the victim's machine at the dropper/downloader stage and submitting this information to the malware distribution site, the attackers can verify that the compromised computer is real (and not some analysis system) and respond accordingly. In some cases, upon discovering that the victim was faked or is an automated analysis system, the attackers would not serve the core malware.
- **Host-Based Encrypted Data Exfiltration:** Most malware does not encrypt outbound network communication. Critical data stolen from the victim's computer is typically packed and file-encrypted at the host-level before sending over a clear text network protocol such as HTTP and SMTP thereby evading anomaly detection systems and data-leakage prevention systems (DLP) [47].

3.6 Command and Control

An important part of the remotely executed cyber-attacks is the Command and Control(C&C) system. C&C system is used to give remote covert instructions to compromised machines. It also acts as the place where all data can be exfiltrated. Over the years, the architecture of C&C channels have evolved exponentially owing to the exponential development of defensive mechanisms, namely antiviruses, firewalls, IDSs, etc. [29,32]. There are mainly three type of C&C communication structures, namely the traditional centralized structure, the newer peer-to-peer decentralized architecture and the latest Social Networks based structure.

- **Centralized Structure:** Traditionally malware depended upon a classical client server model wherein a central server is used to command and control the infected machines. Since there is only one server, its easy to manage. Also there is no dependence on the infected machines to relay command control signals. Hence failure of random infected machines won't affect C&C architecture. But the number of bots that can be controlled depends is constrained by the hardware/software resources available to the C&C server. Also taking down the server strategically will shutdown the entire C&C infrastructure.

- **Decentralized Structure:** Owing to the fact that centralized architecture can be taken down easily and cannot control a large botnet [30], malware authors started using peer-to-peer P2P architecture for command and control. The main aims of using this architecture are scalability (infected machines are used as nodes, and each node in turn is responsible only for a subset of the total botnet), fault tolerance (redundant communication links can be formed to route information) and P2P nature (decentralized architecture removes the significant single point dependence of centralized architectures). Variety of options for P2P such as Bit torrent, Gnutella, LimeWire indicates the substantive depth of design possibilities. Eg. Storm [33]
- **Social Networks Based Structure:** Social networks now play a huge part in many peoples lives. Facebook has 1.35 billion registered users as of third quarter of 2014 [34]. Most of the social network services are free to use and these services are deemed to be benign in most organizational security policies. Owing to these reasons, social media has now become a viable option for malware authors. These high availability and reliable social networks are used to pass on information in a centralized/decentralized way to the infected machines. An example of such attacks is Taidoor [35].

C&C Communication Traffic analysis is a traditional technique to detect communication pattern among infected machines. As a result malware creators have adopted techniques to hide communication patterns. Anonymous communication techniques involve creating an unobservable communication channel that is resistant to traffic analysis. Unobservable communication channel refers to the communication capability that a third party cannot distinguish between a communication and non-communicating entity. It will be indistinguishable from legitimate traffic. Following is a review of techniques employed by the malware creators to achieve unobservable anonymous communication channel:

- **IRC Chats:** Internet Relay Chat(IRC) [36] was developed in 1988 and is a protocol used for text chat over the internet. Its primary function is to provide channels which are chat rooms allowing for public/private conversations. These channels were exploited by malwares to send and receive information once infection takes place.
- **TCP/HTTP/FTP:** Malwares relying on IRC as C&C channel were now easier to detect at network gateways. Malware authors circumvented this by employing TCP/HTTP/FTP [37–39] as C&C channels. Since majority of applications in all the operating systems use these channels for benign communication, malware traffic becomes indistinguishable. Examples: Zeus, Poison Ivy [41, 42]
- **Steganography:** Steganography technique involves hiding data inside images, video, audio or any such content which are hosted in attacker controlled harm-

less websites. The data is then hidden in specially constructed and encrypted inline annotations which are strewn randomly all over the page or extra spurious bytes of images. This hidden data can contain C&C commands like IP addresses of C&C server, shellcode commands to execute etc.

- **TOR:** Tor (originally The Onion Router) is a service used to provide anonymity over the Internet [40]. Tor directs Internet traffic through a free, worldwide, volunteer network consisting of more than six thousand relays to conceal a user's location and usage from anyone conducting network surveillance or traffic analysis. Apart from providing an anonymity network, Tor also has Hidden Service Protocol which makes it possible for users to hide their location while offering various kinds of public services. Hidden services work by setting up rendezvous points which are identified by .onion links. SDC Botnet [43] is a recent example of malwares employing TOR as C&C channel.

Attackers would like to stay undetected and covert for as long as possible. Following are 3 techniques commonly used by malware authors to hide their C&C server from the defense mechanisms of any organization:

- **DNS Fast Flux:** The Domain Name Service(DNS) [44] is a naming system of computers on the internet. DNS is not required to match hostnames to IP addresses in a one-to-one fashion. A single hostname may correspond to many IP addresses to facilitate fault tolerance and load distribution. Malware authors use a technique called fast-flux to hide C&C locations behind an rapidly changing(fast-flux) network of infected machines. This is achieved by setting a very short TTL(time-to-live) to DNS response which is known as single flux. Another technique called double flux is used which works by switching rapidly through multiple infected nodes addresses which in turn act as a proxy relay location to the original C&C site.
- **DNS as a Medium:** It is also possible to use DNS system as a communication mechanism rather than using it for setting up the channel. RDATA field of a DNS response can be of variable length and multiple formats. One of these is TXT, which can be used to transfer actual text. The commands are can be encoded into base64 and sent over the RDATA field. Feederbot [46] is one such example.
- **Domain Generation Algorithms:** Another method to stay under the radar is DGA. DGA programmatically generates pseudo random domain names which is used as address of C&C server. It is then upto the attacker to ensure he controls the domains that will be generated. Conficker malware for example, generates 250 domain names by using current UTC date as the seed of pseudo random DGA. The same domains are generated every 3 hours. All the 250 domain names are queried until one of them resolves successfully [45].

3.7   Act on Objectives

After getting the communication setup with target system, attacker executes the commands. The command used by attacker depends on interest of attack [48].

1. **Mass Attack:** Objective of mass attack is to get as many targets as possible. In mass attack more than a single system, multiple systems together are of interest. Most of such attacks aims at getting bank, email, social media and local system administrator credentials [49]. Bigger picture of mass attack is called BOTNets [50]. BOTNets are mainly used for DDoS attacks and virtual coin mining. Virtual coin mining harvest the system processors or GPU to generate virtual currency for the attacker.

2. **Targeted Attacks:** Targeted attacks are more sophisticated and carried with more caution. Most of such attacks are aimed to get confidential or secret information from target system. Data exfiltration and getting user credentials for online accounts are objectives of the attacks. Spreading through the network also becomes the primary goal when target is an organization.

In both types of attack if attack is intended for destructive purpose it may crash system hard drive or device drivers. Attacker may make CPU to use its maximum capability for long time to damage the processor hardware.

4 Summary

In this paper cyber kill has been discussed in detail with its technical aspects. The paper gives technical flow from attacker's perspective which may help security researcher to design prevention mechanisms.This paper explores the recent trends in malware development by reviewing weaponize and installation techniques. Delivery and Exploitation section gives an insight to the importance of software vulnerabilities, both from an attacker and security researcher's perspective, in the current cyberspace.Study of reconnaissance techniques and Command and Control infrastructure shows how benign features of network protocols are being misused to achieve nefarious end results.

References

1. Malware Risks And Mitigation Report. 1st ed. BITS - The financial services roundtable (2011). http://www.nist.gov/itl/upload/BITS-Malware-Report-Jun2011.pdf

2. Ranum, M.J.: Breaking Cyber Kill Chains. Tenable Network Security (2014). http://www.tenable.com/blog/breaking-cyber-kill-chains

3. Sager, T.: Killing Advanced Threats in Their Tracks: An Intelligent Approach to Attack Prevention. Sansorg (2014). http://www.sans.org/reading-room/whitepapers/detection/killing-advanced-threats-tracks-intelligent-approach-attack-prevention-35302

4. The Cyber Attack Cycle. http://www.eur.army.mil/vigilance/Cyber_Attack_Cycle.pdf

5. Hartley, M.: Strengthening Cyber Kill Chain with Cyber Threat Intelligence. iSIGHT Partners (2014). http://www.isightpartners.com/2014/09/strenghtening-cyber-kill-chain-cyber-threat-intelligence-part-1-of-2/

6. Hartley, M.: The Cyber Threat Kill Chain Part 2 of 2 - iSIGHT partners. iSIGHT partners (2014). http://www.isightpartners.com/2014/10/cyber-threat-kill-chain-part-2-2/

7. Davis, R.: Exploit Kill Chain with Controls — Critical Start. Criticalstartcom (2015). http://www.criticalstart.com/2014/01/exploit-kill-chain-with-controls/

8. Engel, G: Deconstructing the Cyber Kill Chain. Dark Reading (2014). http://www.darkreading.com/attacks-breaches/deconstructing-the-cyber-kill-chain/a/d-id/1317542

9. IT Security Reconnaissance. http://itsecurity.telelink.com/reconnaissance/

10. Pernet, C.: APT Kill chain - Part 3: Reconnaissance - Airbus D&S CyberSecurity blog (2014). http://blog.cassidiancybersecurity.com/post/2014/05/APT-Kill-chain-Part-3-Reconnaissance

11. Bhamidipati, S.: The Art of Reconnaissance - Simple Techniques. sans.org (2002). http://www.sans.org/reading-room/whitepapers/auditing/art-reconnaissance-simple-techniques-60

12. Security Threat Report 2013. 1st ed. SOPHOS. http://www.sophos.com/en-us/medialibrary/pdfs/other/sophossecuritythreatrep-ort2013.pdf

13. Security Threat Report 2014. 1st ed. SOPHOS. https://www.sophos.com/en-us/medialibrary/PDFs/other/sophos-security-threat-report-2014.pdf

14. Rodionov, E., Matrosov, A.: Defeating Anti-Forensics in Contemporary Complex Threats

15. Securelist.com.: The Ventir Trojan: Assemble Your MacOS Spy - Securelist. N.p (2015)

16. Anley, C., et al.: The Shellcoder's Handbook: Discovering and Exploiting Security Holes. John Wiley & Sons, New York (2011)

17. Research.zscaler.com.: Zscaler Research: Njrat & H-Worm Variant Infections Continue To Rise. N.p (2015)

18. CVE -Common Vulnerabilities and Exposures (CVE). https://cve.mitre.org/

19. Pernet, C.: APT Kill chain - Part 4: Initial compromise - Airbus D&S CyberSecurity blog 2014. http://blog.airbuscybersecurity.com/post/2014/06/APT-Kill-chain-Part-4-%3A-Initial-compromise

20. GitHub, DeviceFingerprint. https://github.com/dimalinux/DeviceFingerprint

21. CVE security vulnerability database. Security vulnerabilities, exploits, references and more. http://www.cvedetails.com/

22. Oehlert, P.: Violating assumptions with fuzzing. IEEE Secur. Priv. 3(2), 58–62 (2005)

23. Sutton, M., Greene, A., Amini, P.: Fuzzing: Brute Force Vulnerability Discovery. Pearson Education, Upper Saddle River (2007)

24. Godefroid, P., Levin, M.Y., Molnar, D.: SAGE: whitebox fuzzing for security testing. Queue 10(1), 20 (2012)

25. Contagio: An Overview of Exploit Packs (Update 24), March 2015. http://contagiodump.blogspot.in/2010/06/overview-of-exploit-packs-update.html

26. Chien, E., Szr, P.: Symantec Security Response: Blended Attacks Exploits, Vulnerabilities and Buffer-Overflow Techniques in Computer Viruses Virus Bulletin (2002). http://www.symantec.com/avcenter/reference/blended.attacks.pdf

27. Hardikar, A.: Malware 101 - Viruses. sansorg (2008). http://www.sans.org/reading-room/whitepapers/incident/malware-101-viruses-32848

28. Kleissner, P.: Stoned bootkit. In: Black Hat, USA, pp. 5–7 (2009)

29. Gradiner, J., Cova, M.: Shishir Nagaraja: Command and Control : Understanding, Denying and Detecting (2014)

30. Seenivasan, D., Shanthi, K.: Categories of botnet: a survey. Int. J. Comput. Control Quantum Inf. Eng. 8(9), 1589–1592 (2014)
31. Yen, T.-F., Heorhiadi, V., Oprea, A., Reiter, M.K., Juels, A.: An epiemiological study of malware encounters in a large enterprise. In: ACM SIGSAC Conference on Computer and Communications Security (2014)
32. QinetiQ. Command & Control: Understanding, Denying, Detecting, 36 February 2014. http://www.cpni.gov.uk/Documents/Publications/2014/2014-04-11-cc/qinetiq/report.pdf
33. Porras, P., Saidi, H., Yegneswaran, V.: A multi-perspective analysis of the Storm (Peacomm) worm. In: SRI Technical Report 10–01 (2007)
34. Statista. Facebook: figures of monthly active users 2014 — Statistic (2015). http://www.statista.com/statistics/264810/number-of-monthly-active-facebook-users-worldwide/
35. Fireeye.com. Evasive Tactics: Taidoor Threat Research — FireEye Inc. (2013). https://www.fireeye.com/blog/threat-research/2013/09/evasive-tactics-taidoor-3.html
36. Tools.ietf.org. RFC 1459 - Internet Relay Chat Protocol (2015). https://tools.ietf.org/html/rfc1459
37. Ietf.org. RFC 2616 - Hypertext Transfer Protocol - HTTP/1.1 (1999). https://www.ietf.org/rfc/rfc2616.txt
38. Ietf.org. RFC 959 - FILE TRANSFER PROTOCOL (FTP) (1985). https://www.ietf.org/rfc/rfc959.txt
39. Ietf.org. RFC 793 - TRANSMISSION CONTROL PROTOCOL (1981). https://www.ietf.org/rfc/rfc793.txt
40. Fox-IT International blog. Large botnet cause of recent Tor network overload (2013). http://blog.fox-it.com/2013/09/05/large-botnet-cause-of-recent-tor-network-overload. Accessed 24 March 2015
41. IOActive Inc. Reversal and Analysis of Zeus and SpyEye Banking Trojans (1st ed., p. 31). Seattle: IOActive, Incorporated (2012). http://www.ioactive.com/pdfs/ZeusSpyEyeBankingTrojanAnalysis.pdf
42. FireEye. Poison Ivy: Assessing Damage and Extracting Intelligence (1st ed., p. 33). California: FireEye Inc (2014). https://www.fireeye.com/resources/pdfs/fireeye-poison-ivy-report.pdf
43. ydklijnsma: Large botnet cause of recent Tor network overload 2013. http://blog.fox-it.com/2013/09/05/large-botnet-cause-of-recent-tor-network-overload/
44. Ietf.org. RFC 1035 - DOMAIN NAMES - IMPLEMENTATION AND SPECIFICATION (1987). https://www.ietf.org/rfc/rfc1035.txt
45. Porras, P., Saidi, H., Yegneswaran, V.: A foray into confickers logic and rendezvous points. In: Proceedings of the USENIX Workshop on Large-Scale Exploits and Emergent Threats (LEET) (2009)
46. Dietrich, C.J., Rossow, C., Pohlmann, N.: CoCoSpot: clustering and recognizing botnet command and control channels using traffic analysis. Comput. Netw. 57(2), 475–486 (2013)
47. DAMBALLA. Behind Todays Crimeware Installation Lifecycle: How Advanced Malware Morphs to Remain Stealthy and Persistent 10 (1st ed., p. 10). Atlanta: DAMBALLA (2015). https://www.damballa.com/downloads/r_pubs/WP_Advanced_Malware_Install_LifeCycle.pdf
48. A View From Front Lines. 1st ed. MANDIANT A FireEye Company (2015). http://www2.fireeye.com/rs/fireye/images/rpt-m-trends-2015.pdf

49. Pernet, C.: APT Kill chain - Part 5: Access Strenght-
    ening and lateral movements - Airbus D&S CyberSecurity
    blog (2014). http://blog.airbuscybersecurity.com/post/2014/11/
    APT-Kill-chain-Part-5-3A-Access-Strenghtening-and-lateral-movements
50. Naseem, F., shafqat, M., Sabir, U., Shahzad, A.: A survey of botnet technology
    and detectiion. Int. J. Video Image Process. Netw. Secur. IJVIPNS-IJENS 10(01),
    9–12 (2010)

Application Security

Detection and Mitigation of Android Malware Through Hybrid Approach

Kanubhai Patel[1]([envelope]) and Bharat Buddadev[2]

[1] CMPICA, Charotar University if Science and Technology, Changa, India
kkpatel7@gmail.com
[2] SS College of Engineering, Bhavnagar, India
bvbld@yahoo.com

Abstract. A good number of android applications are available in markets on the Internet. Among them a good number of applications are law quality apps (or malware) and therefore it is difficult for android users to decide whether particular application is malware or benign at installation time. In this paper, we propose a design of system to classify android applications into two classes i.e. malware or benign. We have used hybrid approach by combining application analysis and machine learning technique to classify the applications. Application analysis is performed by both static and live analysis techniques. Genetic algorithm based machine learning technique is used to create rules for creating rule base for the system. The system is tested with applications collected from the various markets on the Internet and two datasets. We have obtained 96.43 % detection rate to classify the applications.

Keywords: Malware analysis · Instrumentation · Rule-Based learning · Classification · Machine learning

1 Introduction

The number of mobile and smart phones' users has significantly increased in last few years. Android is the most predominant and popular platform for mobile and smart phone in the world. Because of this popularity, a good number of android applications are available in various markets on the Internet. More than 1,500,000 apps are available on Google Play Store alone. Among these a good number of applications are law quality apps (or malware). It is difficult for android users to decide whether particular application is malware or benign during installation time.

Mobile and Smart phones' users store their private and security related information in the devices. This results into information stealing through malwares and also misusing of it. There are many other side-effects of which most naïve users are unaware of.

We propose a design of system to classify android applications into two classes i.e. malware or benign. We have used hybrid approach by combining application analysis and machine learning technique to classify the applications. Application analysis is performed by both static and dynamic (or live) analysis techniques. Also machine learning technique is used to create rules for creating rule base for the system. We have

© Springer International Publishing Switzerland 2015
J.H. Abawajy et al. (Eds): SSCC 2015, CCIS 536, pp. 455–463, 2015.
DOI: 10.1007/978-3-319-22915-7_41

obtained 96.43 % detection rate to classify the applications. Also we have identified few weak points in our design that we need to rectify for better performance.

The remaining of the paper is organized as follows: Sect. 2 discusses related work. Section 3 presents the design of our system. Section 4 describes experimental study and results. Section 5 concludes our paper along with future directions.

2 Related Work

There are two types of Android application analysis viz., (i) static analysis, and (ii) dynamic (or live) analysis. A few researchers have used machine learning techniques to classify the apps into benign or malware [1] along with static analysis and dynamic analysis of apps.

2.1 Static Analysis

Few researchers have used static analysis approach alone for android [2–9]. Schmidt et al. [2] use static analysis approach for classification by using readelf command. To improve the performance of Android malware detection, Kang, Jang, Mohaisen, and Kim [3] use the creator's information, like serial number of certificate, as a feature to classify malicious applications. They use similarity scoring to increase detection accuracy.

Ded [4], CHEX [5], AppSealer [6], FlowDroid [9], Capper [7], and PEG [8] use static analysis of data flow to detect malicious code in Android applications.

2.2 Dynamic Analysis

Andro-profiler [10] and Crowdroid [11] perform system call classification based on dynamic analysis. Mulliner, Oberheide, Robertson, and Kirda [12] propose PatchDroid. It uses dynamic binary instrumentation to inject patches dynamically in Android application. Zhou, Wang, Zhou, and Jiang [13] proposed DroidRanger.

Grace et al. [14] propose an automated system called Risk-Ranker to analyze behaviors to detect root exploits. Pandita et al. [15] propose Natural Language Processing (NLP) based system called WHYPER TaintDroid [16], DroidScope [17], and VetDroid [18] have conducted dynamic taint-analysis to identify malicious code. Yan and Yin [17] present DroidScope, an android analysis platform that uses virtualization-based malware analysis.

2.3 Machine Learning Based Detection

A good number of reserchers have used machine learning techniques to classify Android malware [11, 19–29] automatically. Crowdroid [11] identifies trojan on Android smart phones using machine learning approach. Andromaly [19] uses behavior-based approach. MADAM [20] provides both kernal level and user level android malware detection using 13 features.

H. Peng et al. [26] classify permissions of android apps. Schmidt, et al. [21] extract features by monitoring smart phones. They detect anomalies using these features with machine learning algorithm. Enck, Ongtang, and McDaniel [23] and Ongtang, McLaughlin, Enck, and McDaniel [24] present Kirin security service, while Xie, Zhang, Seifert, and Zhu [22] propose pBMDS for Android smart phone.

Juxtapp [27] implemented feature hashing on the operation code sequence. Zhang, Duan, Yin, and Zhao [25] present DroidSIFT. DroidAPIMiner 28 use feature extraction at the API level. It also provides light-weight classifiers. While DREBIN 29 use feature extraction by considering both Android permissions and API calls.

3   Design

Our design uses static and dynamic (or live) analysis to analyze the apk and machine learning approach to derive rules to classify android apps into two classes. Figure 1 shows schematic overview of design of our system.

3.1   Feature Extraction

This module uses android application database and carry out on each apk serially. It converts apk to zip file and then unpack zip into different folders. Folder name is same as apk name. During static analysis, the module scans the manifest file of each apk. From this manifest file it generates comma separated values (CSV) file with various

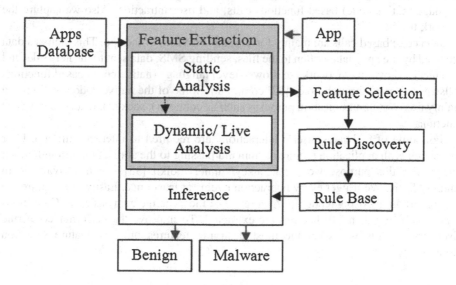

Fig. 1. Schematic overview of our system components

permission-based parameters. We use Android Asset Packaging Tool (aapt) which is part of the Android SDK.

More than 125 features are extracted related to permission of apk (android.permission). Some of the extracted features are as below:

ACCESS_WIFI_STATE	READ_OWNER_DATA	SEND_SMS
CHANGE_WIFI_STATE	READ_CONTACTS	RECEIVE_SMS
	READ_PHONE_STATE	CALL_PHONE
ACCESS_NETWORK_STATE	READ_SMS	VIBRATE
CHANGE_CONFIGURATION		WAKE_LOCK
	GET_ACCOUNTS	
MODIFY_PHONE_STATE	WRITE_EXTERNAL_STORAGE	NFC
MODIFY_AUDIO_SETTINGS	WRITE_SECURE_SETTINGS	INTERNET

Also, we extract information regarding intents, services, and broadcast receivers from the manifest file. After this, the classes.dex file is converted to smali [30] to get information regarding functions and methods. We are interested in the functions and methods which are commonly seen in malwares. For example, to get the country name of the smart phone user, apps are call getSimCountryIso(). Some of other functions and methods information retrieved from this smali are as below:

Name of methods/Functions	Purposes of methods/Functions
getPackageInfo()	To search for installed AV products
sendTextMessage()	To send SMS messages
Ljava/lang/Runtime;->exec()	To execute the particular command in a separate process. Malwares generally call su and chmod commands.
encryption libraries functions	To find use of encryption and obfuscation within the applications.

A partial CSV file is created as a result of the static analysis. Many kind of malicious behaviours can be observed during run time only. For this type of runtime behaviour observation, apps are executed on the Android emulator [31] and interact with them. Mainly we observed higher-level language (java) based calls, lower-level language (native code) based functions calls, and user intraction. Also we capture the network traffic.

Java code based calls are mainly for runtime activities of the app. This includes data accessed by the app, data written to the files, sending SMS, data sent to the networks and data received over the network etc. Lower-level language (native code) based functions calls are observed through ltrace [32] command. Some of the native code functions are mainly used for communication purposes such as connect(), socket(), read(), and write() functions.

For some of malwares, user's interactions are required to interact with app. User interaction with application requires command passing to the application through touch screen. For this purpose we use MonkeyRunner toolkit [33] which is available in Android SDK. We trigger every interaction events at least once. Lastly, we capture the network traffic by using tcpdump. As a result of the dynamic analysis a full CSV file is generated. More than 210 features are extracted. To improve the performance of rule discovery module we select the most desirable features only by feature selection module.

3.2   Feature Selection

We apply information gain technique to select most effective features only. This feature selection process make it possible to select only apprprite features which avoids over-fitting, reducing generality, misleading the learning algorithm, increasing model complexity, and descreasing run-time and there by it improves the performance. It is more needed in smart phones where there is resources constraints.

We use a normalized information gain, also known as asymmetric dependency coefficient (ADC), for estimation quality of each feature. ADC [34] is specified as

$$ADC(C,f) = \frac{MI(C,f)}{H(C)} \tag{1}$$

Where H(C) is class entropy, and H(f) is feature entropy. MI(C, f) is mutual information between class C and feature f. This is defined by Shanonna [35] as:

$$H(C) = -\sum_{i=1}^{C} p(Ci)\lg_2 p(Ci)$$

$$H(f) = -\sum_{x} p(f=x)\lg_2 p(f=x)$$

$$MI(C,f) = -H(C,f) + H(C) + H(f) \tag{2}$$

CSV file is generated by feature extraction and selection module. This CSV file contains permission related information alomg with behaviour related information of the app as well as class of the app i.e. 'Malware' or 'Benign'.

3.3   Rules Generation

Rule discovery module uses above CSV files and genetic algorithm to derive predictive rules to classify the applications into two classes i.e. Malware or Benign. It generates IF-THEN rules. We have used approach as described by us in Patel and Buddhadev [36]. Some of the rules generated are as below:

If apk does not have permission to send SMS message in manifest file and that apk try to send SMS messages then that apk may have malicious code.

IF Not (SEND_SMS) && CALL_sendTextMessage THEN Malware

If apk does not have permission to call (CALL_PHONE) in manifest file and that apk try to call on any premium number then that apl may have malicious code.

IF Not (CALL_PHONE) && Intent.ACTION_CALL THEN Malware

4   Experimental Results

To verify the design of the system we have implemented the system and carried out experiments.

4.1   Dataset Description

We have collected around 755 Android applications from various sources. Also we have used DroidKin [37] and ContagioDump [38] datasets. We have created a dataset from these android applications by extracting features. More than 251 features are extracted related to behaviour and permission of apk.

4.2   Implementation

The proposed technique is implemented in software using Java language. We have created classes for feature_extraction, feature_selection, individual, population, rule_evaluator (for fitness calculation), and breeder (for crossover and mutation). Feature_extraction module loads the apk one after other and scans it. Dynamic analysis loads the apk in to Google emulator and run the apk. Various commands are passed through the system to the apk to check the behavior of the apk. As a result of static analysis and dynamic analysis various features are extracted.

Feature_selection module use information gain technique and select the most appropriate features for rule discover. This results in to improvement of performance of the system which is desirable in mobile computing. Individual class describes chromosome representation and fitness value. Population class initializes the population. Rule_evaluator class is for to calculate the fitness using the the fitness function. Breeder class is for performing crossover and mutation to generate new population. In first phase, application uses above dataset to generate rule base. The system was trained by setting the parameters as below:

No of generations: 500
Cross over: one-point cross over
Probability of crossover: 0.7
Mutation rate: 0.01

In second phase, we test the system using this rule base and the testing datasets creating by us.

4.3   Results

This section presents the results of the experiments and system evaluation. We evaluated the system based on detection rate and performance of the system. In the testing phase, we have obtained 96.43 % detection rate as shown in Table 1. There is scope of

Table 1. Performance of the system

Parameter	Value	
Detection rate	96.43 %	
Scanning time	8 to 11 min	

improvement in term of the performance of the system, as it takes around 8 to 11 min to scan the application and extract the features of the single application alone.

5 Conclusion and Future Works

We attempt to explore the use of hybrid approach for classifying android applications into malware or benign in this paper. We use android application (static and live) analysis along with machine learning technique to extract the features and discover the classification rules. The proposed system is tested on collected android applications from open markets as well as DroidKin [37] and ContagioDump [38] malware datasets. Our system gives 96.43 % detection rate during testing phase. The weak point of our system is that it takes 8 to 11 min to scan the application. As future work, we would like to improve the performance of the system by performing various operations in parallel.

Acknowledgments. We are thankful to the management of Charotar University of Science and Technology for providing support for the research. Special thanks to Dr. Ajay Parikh and Dr. S K Vij for their support and help.

References

1. Spreitzenbarth, M., Schreck, T., Echtler, F., Arp, D., Hoffmann, J.: Mobile-sandbox: combining static and dynamic analysis with machine-learning techniques. Int. J. Inf. Secur. **14**(2), 141–153 (2015)
2. Schmidt, A., Bye, R., Schmidt, H., Clausen, J., Kiraz, O., Yuksel, K., Camtepe, S., Albayrak, S.: Static analysis of executables for collaborative malware detection on android. In: IEEE International Conference on Communications (ICC 2009), Dresden, pp. 1–5 (2009)
3. Kang, H., Jang, J.-w., Mohaisen, A., Kim, H.: Detecting and classifying android malware using static analysis along with creator information. Int. J. Distrib. Sens. Netw. **2015**, 9 (2015). Article ID 479174
4. Enck, W., Octeau, D., McDaniel, P., Chaudhuri, S.: A study of android application security. In: 20th USENIX Conference on Security (SEC 2011), p 21 (2011)
5. Lu, L., Li, Z., Wu, Z., Lee, W., Jiang, G.: CHEX: statically vetting android apps for component hijacking vulnerabilities. In: 2012 ACM Conference on Computer and Communications Security (CCS 2012), pp. 229–240 (2012)
6. Zhang, M., Yin, H.: AppSealer: automatic generation of vulnerability-specific patches for preventing component hijacking attacks in android applications. In: 21st Annual Network and Distributed System Security Symposium (NDSS 2014), San Diego, CA (2014)
7. Zhang, M., Yin, H.: Efficient, context-aware privacy leakage confinement for android applications without firmware modding. In: 9th ACM Symposium on Information, Computer and Communications Security (ASIACCS 2014), Kyoto, Japan, pp. 259–270 (2014)
8. Chen, K., Johnson, N., D'Silva, V., Dai, S., MacNamara, K., Magrino, T., Wu, E., Rinard, M., Song, D.: Contextual policy enforcement in android applications with permission event graphs. In: 20th Annual Network and Distributed System Security Symposium, (NDSS 2013), San Diego (2013)

9. Arzt, S., Rasthofer, S., Fritz, C., Bodden, E., Bartel, A., Klein, J., Traon, Y., Octeau, D., McDaniel, P.: FlowDroid: precise context, flow, field, object-sensitive and lifecycle-aware taint analysis for android apps. In: 35th ACM SIGPLAN Conference on Programming Language Design and Implementation (PLDI 2014), pp. 259–269 (2014)

10. Jang, J.-W., Yun, J., Woo, J., Kim, H.: Andro-profiler: anti-malware system based on behavior profiling of mobile malware. In: WWW Companion 2014 Proceedings of the Companion Publication of the 23rd International Conference on World Wide Web Companion, Seoul, Korea, pp. 737–738 (2014)

11. Burguera, I., Zurutuza, U., Nadjm-Tehrani, S.: Crowdroid: behavior- based malware detection system for android. In: ACM CCS Workshop on Security and Privacy in Smartphones and Mobile Devices (SPSM 2011), Chicago (2011)

12. Mulliner, C., Oberheide, J., Robertson, W., Kirda, E.: PatchDroid: scalable third-party security patches for android devices. In: 29th Annual Computer Security Applications Conference (ACSAC 2013), New Orleans, Louisiana, USA, pp. 259–268 (2013)

13. Zhou, Y., Wang, Z., Zhou, W., Jiang, X.: Hey, you, get off of my market: detecting malicious apps in official and alternative android markets. In: Network and Distributed System Security Symposium (2012)

14. Grace, M., Zhou, Y., Zhang, Q., Zou, S., Jiang, X.: RiskRanker: scalable and accurate zero-day android malware detection. In: 10th International Conference on Mobile Systems, Applications, and Services (MobiSys 2012), pp. 281–294 (2012)

15. Pandita, R., Xiao, X., Yang, W., Enck, W., Xie, T.: WHYPER: towards automating risk assessment of mobile applications. In: 22nd USENIX Conference on Security (SEC 2013), pp. 527–542 (2013)

16. Enck, W., Gilbert, P., Chun, B.-G., Cox, L., Jung, J., McDaniel, P., Sheth, A.: TaintDroid: an information flow tracking system for real-time privacy monitoring on smartphones. Commun. ACM **57**(3), 99–106 (2014)

17. Yan, L., Yin, H.: DroidScope: seamlessly reconstructing the OS and Dalvik semantic views for dynamic Android malware analysis. In: The 21st USENIX Conference on Security Symposium (Security 2012), pp. 29–29. USENIX Association, Berkeley (2012)

18. Zhang, Y., Yang, M., Xu, B., Yang, Z., Gu, G., Ning, P., Wang, X., Zang, B.: Vetting undesirable behaviors in android apps with permission use analysis. In: 2013 ACM SIGSAC Conference on Computer and Communications Security (CCS 2013), pp. 611–622 (2013)

19. Shabtai, A., Kanonov, U., Elovici, Y., Glezer, C., Weiss, Y.: Andromaly: a behavioral malware detection framework for android devices. J. Intell. Inf. Syst. **38**(1), 161–190 (2011)

20. Dini, G., Martinelli, F., Saracino, A., Sgandurra, D.: MADAM: a multi-level anomaly detector for android malware. In: Kotenko, I., Skormin, V. (eds.) MMM-ACNS 2012. LNCS, vol. 7531, pp. 240–253. Springer, Heidelberg (2012)

21. Schmidt, A.-D., Peters, F., Lamour, F., Scheel, C., Çamtepe, S., Albayrak, S.: Monitoring smartphones for anomaly detection. Mob. Netw. Appl. **14**(1), 92–106 (2009)

22. Xie, L., Zhang, X., Seifert, J.-P., Zhu, S.: pBMDS: a behavior-based malware detection system for cellphone devices. In: Third ACM Conference on Wireless Network Security (WiSec 2010), Hoboken, New Jersey, USA, pp. 37–48 (2010)

23. Enck, W., Ongtang, M., McDaniel, P.: On lightweight mobile phone application certification. In: CCS 2009 Proceedings of the 16th ACM Conference on Computer and Communications Security, pp. 235–245 (2009)

24. Ongtang, M., McLaughlin, S., Enck, W., McDaniel, P.: Semantically rich application-centric security in android. In: ACSAC 2009 Proceedings of the 2009 Annual Computer Security Applications Conference, Honolulu, HI, USA, pp. 340–349 (2009)

25. Zhang, M., Duan, Y., Yin, H., Zhao, Z.: Semantics-aware android malware classification using weighted contextual API dependency graphs. In: 2014 ACM SIGSAC Conference on Computer and Communications Security (CCS 2014), pp. 1105–1116 (2014)
26. Peng, H., Gates, C., Sarma, B., Li, N., Qi, Y., Poth, R., Nita-Rotaru, C., Molloy, I.: Using probabilistic generative models for ranking risks of android apps. In: 2012 ACM Conference on Computer and Communications Security (CCS 2012) (2012)
27. Hanna, S., Huang, L., Wu, E., Li, S., Chen, C., Song, D.: Juxtapp: a scalable system for detecting code reuse among android applications. In: Flegel, U., Markatos, E., Robertson, W. (eds.) DIMVA 2012. LNCS, vol. 7591, pp. 62–81. Springer, Heidelberg (2013)
28. Aafer, Y., Du, W., Yin, H.: DroidAPIMiner: mining API-level features for robust malware detection in android. In: Zia, T., Zomaya, A., Varadharajan, V., Mao, M. (eds.) SecureComm 2013. LNICST, vol. 127, pp. 86–103. Springer, Heidelberg (2013)
29. Arp, D., Spreitzenbarth, M., Huebner, M., Gascon, H., Rieck, K.: Drebin: efficient and explainable detection of android malware in your pocket. In: 21th Annual Network and Distributed System Security Symposium (NDSS), February 2014
30. smali. https://code.google.com/p/smali/
31. Android Emulator. http://developer.android.com/tools/help/emulator.html
32. Debian. http://www.debian.org/
33. MonkeyRunner Toolkit. http://developer.android.com/tools/help/monkeyrunner_concepts.html
34. Shridhar, D., Bartlett, E., Seagrave, R.: Information theoretic subset selection. Comput. Chem. Eng. **22**, 613–626 (1998)
35. Shannon, C., Weaver, W.: The Mathematical Theory of Communication. University of Illinois Press, Urbana (1949)
36. Patel, K., Buddhadev, B.: Predictive rule discovery for network intrusion detection. In: Third International Symposium on Intelligent Informatics (ISI 2014), Greater Noida, India, pp. 287–298 (2014)
37. Gonzalez, H., Stakhanova, N., Ghorbani, A.: DroidKin: lightweight detection of android apps similarity. In: International Conference on Security and Privacy in Communication Networks (SecureComm 2014) (2014)
38. Parkour, M.: ContagioDump. http://contagiodump.blogspot.in/

Malicious Circuit Detection for Improved Hardware Security

R. Bharath[✉], G. Arun Sabari, Dhinesh Ravi Krishna, Arun Prasathe,
K. Harish, N. Mohankumar, and M. Nirmala Devi

Department of Electronics and Communication Engineering,
Amrita Vishwa Vidyapeetham, Coimbatore, India
bharathr0705@gmail.com,
{n_mohankumar, m_nirmala}@cb.amrita.edu

Abstract. Hardware Trojans have become a major threat faced by most of the
VLSI fabrication houses. This paper proposes a non-destructive method for
Hardware Trojan detection. Since in many cases the golden chip is unavailable
and hence voting technique is adopted.This paper is an extension of the weighed
voting. A microcontroller based portable standalone system that will identify
any malicious activity in a circuit was designed and implemented. This standalone system performs the weighed voting to detect any malicious activity of the
Circuit under Test implemented in FPGA. The working of this standalone
system was tested and validated by using ISCAS '85 Benchmark circuits
implemented in Spartan 6 XC6SLX16 FPGA. The accuracy was around
93.93 % while testing the system. A novel hardware based solution for hardware
Trojan detection is attempted in this work.

Keywords: Hardware Trojan · Hardware security · Trojan detection

1 Introduction

Hardware Trojans can be simply termed as intentional malicious modification of
circuits, which can be used for various types of attack on the system. The Trojans are
mainly inserted during the fabrication process [5]. Hardware Trojans are of several
types based on their activation methods; Always on, internally triggered, externally
triggered [2, 6]. Since we are doing an exhaustive testing that is giving all possible
inputs to the circuit while determining the weights, we can detect all types of Trojans.
This is a non-destructive method of detection of hardware that is, while detection the
chip is not damaged [3].

2 Need for Hardware Trojan Detection

The effect of hardware Trojans can be visualized by everyone starting from a basic
mobile user to a national security. The working of the hardware Trojans is the similar to
that of software Trojans but, it is several folds severe [4]. And no antivirus software
would help. Since the Trojans are physically existing structures (in most cases).

© Springer International Publishing Switzerland 2015
J.H. Abawajy et al. (Eds): SSCC 2015, CCIS 536, pp. 464–472, 2015.
DOI: 10.1007/978-3-319-22915-7_42

With increasing demands and the financial benefits the companies are now moving on to third party fabrication. With the widespread use of fabless design houses and design reuse the circuits now are becoming more vulnerable to hardware Trojans.

3 Proposed Methodology for Hardware Trojan Detection

Various methods are available to detecting hardware Trojans most of them based on a simple method of comparing the suspicious chips with golden chips. Golden chips are chips which are considered accurate and give the correct output and are free from any malicious activity. But in many cases it is difficult to get golden chips. This leads to the proposed detection technique based on voting. This determines the malicious activity in circuits by cross checking the outputs of similar circuits [3].

PIC16f877a is used as the microcontroller which will act as the majority voter. PIC16f877a has 40 I/O pins which can be used as both-input as well at output pins. The program is suitable for multiple input circuits with up to 8 inputs. The weights of the circuits are displayed using 4 digit multiplexed seven segment displays. This PIC along with the display system acts as the microcontroller based standalone system (Fig. 1).

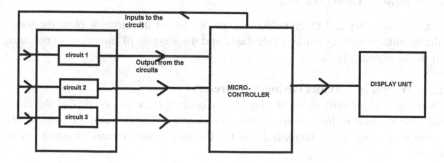

Fig. 1. Microcontroller based standalone system

Primarily there are three circuits. There may or might not be any malicious activity in these circuits. We initialize the weights of all circuits as zero. The inputs to these circuits are given from the microcontroller. Based on the given inputs each circuit produces an output. This output in fed into the microcontroller. Now voting is done to determine the accuracy of the circuits and the weights of the circuits are displayed by the display unit.

4 Voting

The simple voting technique is giving several inputs and getting the outputs of the chips under test. The output which is given by majority of the chips is considered as the correct output. The results obtained from these simple voters are like digital correct or wrong. But when we want a scale as to how correct the chip is we can go for weighed voting. The simple voting cannot perform properly when the number of circuits with Trojan is greater than the number of circuits without Trojans [3].

4.1 Weighed Voting

Weighed voting technique proposed by Hany A.M. Amin [3] is basically an improvement over the simple voting techniques. The method works by gradually building trust upon the circuits.

We initially assign weights to each chip and perform the voting. If the chip gives a correct input then its weight is increased and if it gives a wrong output we decrease the weight. This process is repeated several times and the final weight of the circuits are taken into consideration to determine if there is any hardware Trojan. So we now have a scale on the accuracy of the circuits. In this case even when the number of circuits with Trojans outnumbers the number of the Trojans without Trojans we can detect the Trojans by simple changes explained later in the inference section [1].

4.2 Weighted Voting Algorithm

The microcontroller first receives the outputs of each of the circuits. Now the weights of the circuits producing a one is calculated and the weights of the circuits producing a zero is calculated (Fig. 2).

4.2.1 Weight of Circuits Giving 1 is Greater
If the weight of the circuits producing one is greater than the weights of the circuits producing a zero then the correct output is considered to be one and the weights of the circuits producing one is increased and the weights of the circuits producing zero is reduced.

4.2.2 Number of Circuits Giving One is Greater
Else if the count of weights of the circuits producing zero is greater than the weight of the circuits producing one then the number of circuits producing one and number of circuits producing zero is calculated. Now if the number of circuits producing one is greater than the number of circuits producing zero then the correct output is considered to be one and similarly the weights of the circuits producing one is increased and the weight of the circuits producing zero is decreased.

4.2.3 Number of Circuits Giving Zero is Greater
In the other case when the number of circuits producing zero is greater than the number of circuits producing one then the correct output is considered to be zero and the weights of the circuits producing one is reduced and the weights of the circuits producing a zero is increased. This process is repeated for each possible input.

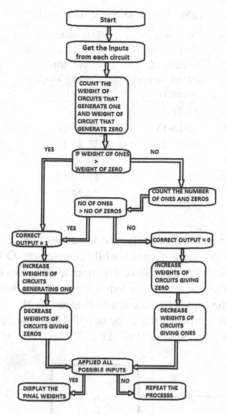

Fig. 2. Weighed voting algorithm [3].

5 Validation of the voter circuit

Now we have the stand alone microcontroller based weighed voter. We have to verify the working of this standalone system, if it is giving the desired results.

The testing of the voter circuit has been done using several circuits and the outputs have been verified. One of the circuits is a c17 benchmark circuit. We have considered benchmark circuits for standardization. We have implemented two c17 circuits one with a Trojan. The weight of the circuit with Trojan is lesser than the weight of the circuit without any Trojans. The exact weight depends on the number of iterations (Table 1).

The results were verified using benchmark circuit C17 using a stand-alone system for hardware Trojan detection built using pic16f877a microcontroller. Many samples were tested and the results were tabulated as follows

The very basic inference from the result is that the weight of the true circuits is greater than the weight of the circuits with Trojan. So we can easily determine which circuit has the Trojans and which circuit is Trojan free.

Table 1. Standalone system results

Combinational circuit	Trojan	Detection Trojan free (weight of circuit1-circuit2 circuit3)	Detection with one Trojan (true circuit-true circuit- Trojan circuit)	Detection with two Trojans (true circuit-Trojan-Trojan)
C17	XOR	31-31-31	31-31-29	31-29-29
C17	AND	15-15-15	15-15-11	15-11-11
MUX(8*1)	XOR	23-23-23	23-23-12	23-15-15
MUX(8*1)	AND	12-12-12	12-12-5	12-7-7
MUX(16*1)	XOR	17-17-17	17-17-12	17-12-12
MUX(16*1)	AND	24-24-24	24-24-21	24-21-21

C17 is ISCAS 85 benchmark circuit. We have considered benchmark circuits so that there can be standards and uniformity while comparison. Other ISCAS 85 circuits have inputs ranging from 32 to 200. Since PIC does not support these many inputs and physically putting up these circuits is a tedious process we have implemented these circuits in FPGA and the inputs to the circuits is given by the FPGA itself. Similar to the previous process the output of the circuits is fed into the pic and the weights are calculated by the stand alone system (Fig. 3).

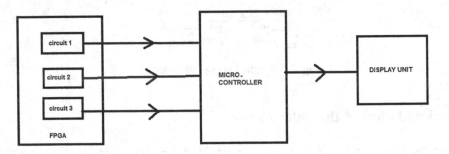

Fig. 3. FPGA based testing of the standalone system.

6 Results and Analysis

The algorithm was tested with and validated with the following ISCAS'85 benchmark circuits. The following Trojan circuits were embedded and tested. We were able to detect and distinguish Trojan infected circuits embedded with small Trojans, even made of single gate.

- Single EXOR
- Single AND
- Two EXOR
- Two AND
- EXOR and AND

The algorithm gave the expected results in almost all the cases. But in a few cases there were some discrepancies this arises due to the simple reason that the circuits with Trojan outnumber the Trojans with no Trojans. But this problem can be eliminated in the case of weighed voting (unlike in the case of simple voting). Let us consider the case initially the weights of all circuits is 0 (Table 2).

Triple redundant circuits having similar functionality and different implementation techniques were also tested and the difference was observed to be very clear. Several variations like one Trojan infected among the three and two Trojan infected among the three were also attempted and were able to distinguish the Trojan infected circuit attempting.

Table 2. FPGA based testing results.

Benchmark circuit under test	Weight with no Trojans	Weight with one XOR Trojan	Weight with one AND Trojan	Weight with two XOR Trojans	Weight with two AND Trojans	Weight with both XOR & AND Trojans
C17	9-9- 9	10-10-8	10-10-6	10-8 -8	10-6 -6	10-6 -6
C432	71-71-71	111-111-71	119-119-71	111-71-71	119-79-79	111-79-79
C499	71-71-71	103-103-71	103-103-71	103-71-71	103-71-71	103-71-71
C880	6-6- 6	6-6- 4	6-6- 4	4-6- 6	4-6- 6	4-6 -6
C1355	81-81-81	81-81-41	61-61-41	81-41-41	61-41-41	81-41-41
C1908	78 -78 - 78	78-78-41	71-71-7	71-7 -7	71-7- 7	71-7 -7
C2670	5-5- 5	7-7 -5	7-7- 5	7- 5- 5	7- 5- 5	7- 5- 5
C3540	6-6 -6	6-6 -4	6-6- 4	4-6 -6	6 -4 -4	6 -4 -4
C5315	6-6 -6	6-6- 4	6-6- 4	6- 4- 4	6 -4 -4	6 -4 -4
C6288	6-6 -6	6-6 -4	6-6 -4	6 -4 -4	6 -4 -4	4-6 -6
C7752	5-5- 5	7-7 -5	7-7- 5	7- 5- 5	7- 5- 5	7-5-5

6.1 CASE 1

With reference to Fig. 4

- In (I) all the circuits are producing the same output so all the weights are increased by 1.
- In (II) chip3 is giving an output 0.Now weights of circuits giving 1 as the output is equal to 2(chip1 + chip 2) and the weights of the circuits giving a output 0 (only chip 3) is 1. Since the weights of circuits giving an output 1 is greater. The correct output is considered to be 1 and the weight of the circuits giving 1 is increased.
- Similarly in (IV) chip2 is giving an output 0. Now weights of circuits giving 1 as the output is equal to 2(chip 1 + chip 3) and the weights of the circuits giving a output 0 (only chip 2)is 1. Since the weights of circuits giving an output 1 is greater. The correct output is considered to be 1 and the weight of the circuits giving 1 is increased.
- The final result is that the true circuit is having a greater weight that the malicious circuits. But considering this case

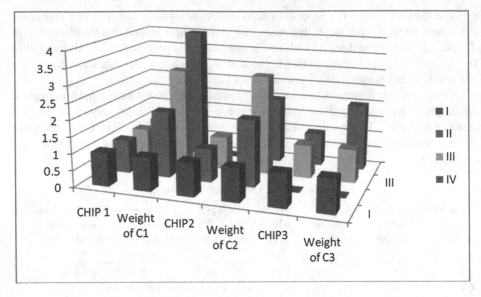

Fig. 4. Validating proper working of the system.

6.2   CASE 2

With reference to Fig. 5

- In (I) all the circuits are producing the same output so all the weights are increased by 1
- In (II) chip5 and chip6 is giving an output 0.Now weights of circuits giving 1 as the output is equal to 1(chip 4) and the weights of the circuits giving a output 0 (chip 5 and chip 6)is 2. Thus the weights of circuits giving an output 0 is greater. So now we check the number of circuits that give an output 1. It is equal to 1 and the number of circuits giving a value 0 is 2. So zero is considered to be the correct output (it is wrong) and the weights of the circuits giving 0 is increased and the weights of the circuits giving one is decreased.
- In (III and IV) all the circuits are producing the same output so all the weights are increased by 1
- The final result is that the true circuit is having a lesser weight than the malicious circuits.
- A simple method to overcome this problem is by gradually building trust in these circuits and this can be done by repeating the process again and again or by increasing the number of chips.
- Consider the case in which we use the chip 1 instead of the chip 4

6.3   CASE 3

With reference to Fig. 6

- In (I) all the circuits are producing the same output so all the weights are increased by 1

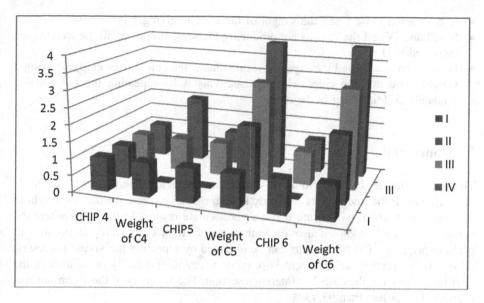

Fig. 5. Ambiguity in the working of the system.

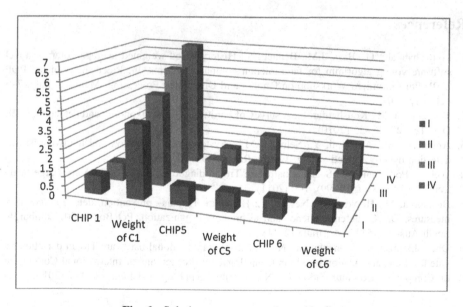

Fig. 6. Solution to overcome the ambiguity.

- In (II) the chips 5 and 6 produce a value of 0. Now weights of circuits giving 1 as the output is equal to 4(chip 1) and the weights of the circuits giving a output 0 (chip 5 and chip 6) is 2. Since the weights of circuits giving an output 1 is greater. The correct output is

- Is considered to be 1 and the weight of the circuits giving 1 is increased.
- In (III and IV) all the circuits are producing the same output so all the weights are increased by 1
- Now we have achieved the expected results that is the chip 1 (true chip) is having a weight more that the chips with Trojans. This is by repeating the process and gradually building trust in the chip 1.

7 Conclusion

The microcontroller based stand-alone system can act as a efficient detector for malicious circuits. If the true circuits is already known we can increase the default weight of the true circuit which will assure that we get accurate results. In the cases where the correct results are not known also like in the case of Trojans this voting algorithm will perform perfectly. The best results can be obtained by repeating the voting processes. Also 100 % accuracy achievement is possible when we gradually build trust in the circuits as shown in the case 3 in inference section. The accuracy of the algorithm was found to be not less than 93.93 %.

References

1. Latif-Shabgahi, G., Bass, J.M., Bennett, S.: History-based weighted average voter: A novel software voting algorithm for fault-tolerant computer systems. In: Proceedings of the PDP 2001: 9th Euromicro Workshop on Parallel and Distributed Processing, Mantova, Italy, 7–9 February 2001
2. Tehranipoor, M., Koushanfar, F.: A survey of hardware Trojan taxonomy and detection. IEEE Des. Test **27**, 10–25 (2010)
3. Amin, H.A.M., Alkabani, Y., Selim, G.M.I.: System-level protection and hardware Trojan detection using weighted voting. J. Adv. Res. **5**, 499–505 (2014)
4. Wei, S., Potkonjak, M.: Scalable hardware Trojan diagnosis. IEEE Trans. Very Large Scale Integr. (VLSI) Syst. **PP**(99), 1–9 (2011)
5. Beaumont, M., Hopkins, B., Newby, T.: Hardware Trojans– prevention, detection, countermeasures. DSTO, defense science and technology organization, PO Box 1500, Edinburgh, South Australia 5111, Australia (2011)
6. Dhineshkumar, K., Mohankumar, N.: Malicious combinational hardware Trojan detection by gate level characterization in 90 nm technology. In: Proceedings of International Conference on Computing, Communication and Networking Technologies, China, pp. 1–7 (2014)

Framework for Live Forensics of a System by Extraction of Clipboard Data and Other Forensic Artefacts from RAM Image

Rohit Sharma[✉] and Upasna Singh

Department of Computer Science and Engineering,
Defence Institute of Advanced Technology, Girinagar, Pune 411025, India
{rohit_mcse13, upasnasingh}@diat.ac.in

Abstract. In Memory Forensics, a variant of Live forensics, the acquired image of physical memory is analysed to find out crucial artefacts from the suspect's system. These artefacts include details of running processes, network connections, Clipboard data, Security Identifiers of users, Master File Table etc. which helps in providing an unprecedented visibility into the runtime state of the system. While there has been extensive work done for capturing processes, event logs, registry information and network activities, the focus towards Clipboard acting as another memory storage for evidential information has been limited. In this paper, a framework has been proposed to carry out Live forensics of a system by extraction of Clipboard data and other forensic artefacts from RAM image.

Keywords: Live forensics · Memory forensics · Clipboard data · Forensic artefacts

1 Introduction

Live Forensics, in which data is collected from running systems instead of permanent storage devices, has a variant known as Memory forensics. In Memory Forensics, first a bit stream copy of memory is acquired into a file and then this acquired image is analysed to find out crucial evidences from the suspect's system [2].

The evidences which can be extracted from image of RAM include details about processes and services which were running on the machine, security identifiers of users, network connections it had made including details of processes listening to the open ports, clipboard data, logged on users, commands written in command.exe etc.

Clipboard contents often provides valuable forensic data, including user passwords, copied sections of classified documents, path of the folders/files cut/copied or copied URLs [1]. All such information can provide vital evidence to investigating authorities because Clipboard will always have data pertaining to the last action on machine. The rest of the paper presents an overview of the related work already done in memory analysis. It then goes on to describing a proposed framework for Live forensics of a system by extracting the windows Clipboard data and other forensic artefacts. Finally, it concludes by applying the framework methodology to memory images from different Windows Operating Systems.

J.H. Abawajy et al. (Eds): SSCC 2015, CCIS 536, pp. 473–482, 2015.
DOI: 10.1007/978-3-319-22915-7_43

2   Related Work

There has been significant research into memory forensics and there have been tools written to capture process information, configuration information, network activity and clipboard data (Schuster's Ptfinder [16], Betz's Memparser [17], Walters and Petroni's Volatools [9] & CMAT for extracting clipboard data [1]). In CMAT Okolica and Peterson have first, identified functions in user32.dll or win32k.sys that accesses (Petzold, 1999) the Clipboard data then they have reverse engineered each function to identify the clipboard structures and finally they have added the ability to search for the structures into a memory analysis program [1].

What the above tools have in common is a limitation to a particular operating system (and in cases to a particular service pack) except CMAT that works only for Win XP, Vista and 7 [1]. Recently Volatility Framework, implemented in Python, has emerged very effective in extraction of digital artefacts from RAM images of different platforms [8].

While there has been extensive work done for capturing processes, event logs, registry information and network activities, the focus towards Clipboard acting as another memory storage for evidential information has been limited. Till date no methodology has been elaborated upon for sequentially using this Clipboard data along with other extracted artefacts for carrying out Live forensics of a system.

3   Proposed Framework

Some of the forensically relevant Executive objects in Windows OS are file, process, Window Station, desktop and key. When a kernel-mode component requests memory for storing any type of data, it is given from kernel pool range of memory. Each allocated block has a pool header that contains information about Pool Size, Pool type & Pool Tag. Pool tag is a four-byte value, which Microsoft created for debugging and auditing purposes [4, 11].

Pool scanning, refers to finding allocations based on the aforementioned four-byte tags. Executive object of importance for this work is Window Station object which contains the Clipboard [10]. In the structure of Window Station object, pClipBase points to an array of tagCLIP structures which provides handle to tagCLIPDATA structure that contains Clipboard data [6, 7, 11]. Window Station objects can be extracted by Pool tag scanning from all the sessions present in the memory image using functionality of Volatility framework. Procedure for pool scanning is as given in Fig. 1 [11].

Volatility framework is used to extract Window Station objects, MFT details, Clipboard data, details of session-wise processes, details of SIDs of users/groups and details of network connections the machine had at the time of creating the image of RAM [8].

In this proposed framework (Fig. 2), live forensics will start with carving out details of Window Stations objects. This will give information about number of users logged in (by seeing number of sessions found except session 0), frequency of clipboard usage by logged in users (by reading iClipSerialnumber field in Window Stations details)

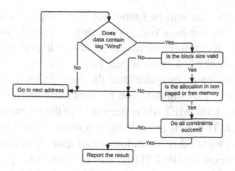

Fig. 1. Scanning memory pool for Window Station object

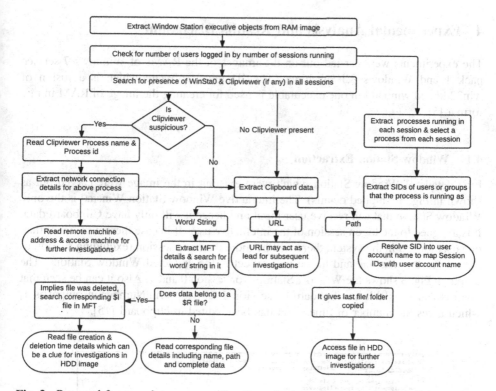

Fig. 2. Proposed framework to carry out live forensics by extracting and using clipboard data along with other forensic artefacts

and if any malicious executable is snooping on Clipboard (by reading spwndClip-viewer field in Window Stations details).

Next, sessionwise processes information is carved out and one unique process is selected from each session. Now SIDs of users or groups that the process is running as, is extracted which enables mapping of session IDs to user account. If in case a process is viewing the clipboard and trying to send the clipboard data to a remote machine, the address of remote machine will be found out. Next clipboard data is extracted from all user sessions. This data can be a URL or a string or a single word or a path. If it's a URL, it gives a starting clue to forensic investigator that the offender might have carried out any access to it or sent the link to someone. In case the data is a folder/directory path, it gives a direct evidence to investigator that the last file/folder copied or moved was accessed, and then further investigation can be continued in HDD image.

If it's a string or word, the MFT file is parsed from the memory image and extracted word/string is searched. This will provide the filename from which the data has been copied, user account to which this file belongs and time of access. Also if the file was deleted after the copy action, its $R & $I files can be searched in parsed MFT and time of creation and deletion of file can be found out. By the end of this process the investigator will have many valuable clues with him to proceed with further investigations.

4   Experimental Analysis and Results Discussion

The experiments were carried out on the images of the RAMs of Windows 7 service pack 1 and Windows 8.1 machines. The 'Dumpit' software which is a fusion of win32dd and win64dd in one executable is used for creating the image of RAM in raw format [5].

4.1   Window Station Extraction

First details of Window Station which were existing in the image were carved out as shown in Fig. 3 (snipped details). The interactive Window Station Winsta0 is the only Window Station that can receive user input and hence it will only have Clipboard data. It is assigned to the logon session of the interactive user. If in case there were more than one user logged in the system there will be more than one session (excluding session 0) running in the machine and hence will reflect in the extracted Window Stations. The output in Fig. 3 shows the Window Stations for session 0 and 1. Also it can be seen that there is data available in clipboard of session 1 as iClipserialNumber in output is 1, which gives the number of times data has been edited in clipboard [15].

```
WindowStation: 0x7418f508, Name: Service-0x0-3e4$, Next: 0x88daf2d8
SessionId: 0, AtomTable: 0x8cf80ba8, Interactive: False
Desktops: Default
ptiDrawingClipboard: pid - tid -
spwndClipOpen: 0x0, spwndClipViewer: 0x0
cNumClipFormats: 0, iClipSerialNumber: 0
pClipBase: 0x0, Formats:
**********************************************
WindowStation: 0x741af2d8, Name: Service-0x0-3e5$, Next: 0x891486a8
SessionId: 0, AtomTable: 0x9200a790, Interactive: False
Desktops: Default
ptiDrawingClipboard: pid - tid -
spwndClipOpen: 0x0, spwndClipViewer: 0x0
cNumClipFormats: 0, iClipSerialNumber: 0
pClipBase: 0x0, Formats:
**********************************************
WindowStation: 0x74200718, Name: WinSta0, Next: 0x0
SessionId: 1, AtomTable: 0x8cd59698, Interactive: True
Desktops: Default, Disconnect, Winlogon
ptiDrawingClipboard: pid - tid -
spwndClipOpen: 0x0, spwndClipViewer: 0x0
cNumClipFormats: 4, iClipSerialNumber: 1
pClipBase: 0xff8cc298, Formats: CF_UNICODETEXT,Unknown choice 0,Unknown choice 8192,Unknown choice 0
```

Fig. 3. Window Station executive objects: Session ID 0 and 1

4.2 Carving Out of Session Details and User Name

When a user log on to a computer system through the console or Fast-User Switching, kernel creates a fresh session, which is actually a container for session processes and other user logon objects. Now the details of processes running in each session are extracted. As seen below there was session 1 running in the system having 32 processes (Fig. 4).

```
Session(V): 8f633000 ID: 1 Processes: 32
PagedPoolStart: 80000000 PagedPoolEnd ffbfffff
  Process: 564 csrss.exe 2015-03-11 06:55:13 UTC+0000
  Process: 1268 winlogon.exe 2015-03-11 06:55:14 UTC+0000
  Process: 3064 taskhost.exe 2015-03-11 06:55:23 UTC+0000
  Process: 3156 dwm.exe 2015-03-11 06:55:23 UTC+0000
  Process: 3184 explorer.exe 2015-03-11 06:55:23 UTC+0000
  Process: 3248 taskeng.exe 2015-03-11 06:55:23 UTC+0000
  Process: 3576 igfxtray.exe 2015-03-11 06:55:25 UTC+0000
  Process: 3584 hkcmd.exe 2015-03-11 06:55:25 UTC+0000
```

Fig. 4. Session 1 processes details (snipped details)

One process from the session is selected and SIDs of users or groups that the process is running as, is extracted. This ultimately enables to determine the primary user account under which a process is running & map session IDs to user account [12].

As can be seen below, Pid 3184 was selected from the session 1. Its SIDs were extracted and resolved into user account names as mentioned in brackets in Fig. 5.

```
explorer.exe (3184): S-1-5-21-1415083519-4058233691-682063285-1000 (ROHIT SHARMA)
explorer.exe (3184): S-1-5-21-1415083519-4058233691-682063285-513 (Domain Users)
explorer.exe (3184): S-1-1-0 (Everyone)
explorer.exe (3184): S-1-5-32-544 (Administrators)
```

Fig. 5. Extraction of SIDs and corresponding user account name (snipped details)

4.3 Clipboard Snooping

A Windows 7 × 64 machine was installed with a Clipboard snooping software (Internet Download Manager) as many malware samples snoop on Clipboard operations to steal credentials. As can be seen in output in Fig. 6, PID 4104 IDMan.exe has registered as a Clipboard viewer in spwndClipviewer field [15].

```
**************************************************
WindowStation: 0x11b014120, Name: msswindowstation, Next: 0x0
SessionId: 0, AtomTable: 0xfffff8a003374a70, Interactive: False
Desktops: mssrestricteddesk
ptiDrawingClipboard: pid - tid -
spwndClipOpen: 0x0, spwndClipViewer: 0x0
cNumClipFormats: 0, iClipSerialNumber: 0
pClipBase: 0x0, Formats:
**************************************************
WindowStation: 0x11b4618d0, Name: Service-0x0-3e7$, Next: 0xfffff8a800891b320
SessionId: 0, AtomTable: 0xfffff8a001018a70, Interactive: False
Desktops: Default
ptiDrawingClipboard: pid - tid -
spwndClipOpen: 0x0, spwndClipViewer: 0x0
cNumClipFormats: 0, iClipSerialNumber: 0
pClipBase: 0x0, Formats:
**************************************************
WindowStation: 0x11b4d58e0, Name: WinSta0, Next: 0xfffff8008f09490
SessionId: 1, AtomTable: 0xfffff8a000f654e0, Interactive: True
Desktops: Default, Disconnect, Winlogon
ptiDrawingClipboard: pid - tid -
spwndClipOpen: 0x0, spwndClipViewer: 0xfffff900c0636b40 4104 IDMan.exe
cNumClipFormats: 6, iClipSerialNumber: 2
pClipBase: 0xfffff900c1a2a4c0, Formats: CF_UNICODETEXT,CF_TEXT,Unknown choice
```

Fig. 6. Window Stations details showing clipviewer presence

Now network connections details are extracted from memory image as shown below.

```
0x11f00bcf0   TCPv4   192.168.101.136:51160   173.194.138.10:80   ESTABLISHED   IDMan.exe
0x11f033cf0   TCPv6   ::1:50786               ::1:22350           CLOSED        CodeMeterCC.ex
0x11f0365e0   TCPv4   127.0.0.1:51173         127.0.0.1:7467      CLOSED        PublicWiFiServ
0x11f039910   TCPv4   192.168.101.136:51158   173.194.138.10:80   ESTABLISHED   IDMan.exe
0x11f085010   TCPv4   192.168.101.136:51157   173.194.138.10:80   CLOSED        IDMan.exe
0x11f39f010   TCPv4   127.0.0.1:51087         127.0.0.1:7467      CLOSED        PublicWiFiServ
0x11f3a1cf0   TCPv4   -:0                     56.235.144.3:0      CLOSED        PublicWiFiServ
```

Fig. 7. Carving out network connection details (snipped details)

It can be seen that the process IDMan.exe had established a connection with a remote machine with IP 173.194.138.10 on port 80 (Fig. 7). So if in case a malicious Clipboard snooping application is leaking Clipboard data to remote machine on a network, the details of the process and remote machine can be found out.

4.4 Extraction of Clipboard Data

Now the clipboard data is extracted from the image and this data can be any section of document or a password or a URL or a script which the user copied in his last activity. The case when only one user was logged in and he had copied a text string, the output of extraction is as shown in Fig. 8.

In the next example, a user selected a folder on the desktop and copied it to another directory. In this scenario the entire folder contents are not copied to the clipboard rather full path of the folder get copied to Clipboard, Fig. 9 [11].

```
Session     WindowStation Format              Object       Data
----------  ------------- ------------------  ----------   ---------------------------------
         1 WinSta0        CF_UNICODETEXT       0xffald9f0 Gigaset is a subsidiary ...
0xffald9fc  47 00 69 00 67 00 61 00 73 00 65 00 74 00 20 00   G.i.g.a.s.e.t...
0xffalda0c  69 00 73 00 20 00 61 00 20 00 73 00 75 00 62 00   i.s...a...s.u.b.
0xffalda1c  73 00 69 00 64 00 69 00 61 00 72 00 79 00 20 00   s.i.d.i.a.r.y...
0xffalda2c  6f 00 66 00 20 00 53 00 69 00 65 00 6d 00 65 00   o.f...S.i.e.m.e.
0xffalda3c  6e 00 73 00 20 00 63 00 6f 00 6d 00 6d 00 75 00   n.s...c.o.m.m.u.
0xffalda4c  6e 00 69 00 63 00 61 00 74 00 69 00 6f 00 6e 00   n.i.c.a.t.i.o.n.
0xffalda5c  20 00 70 00 72 00 69 00 76 00 61 00 74 00 65 00   ..p.r.i.v.a.t.e.
0xffalda6c  20 00 6c 00 69 00 6d 00 69 00 74 00 65 00 64 00   ..l.i.m.i.t.e.d.
0xffalda7c  00 00                                             ..
         1 WinSta0        0x0L                              ----------
```

Fig. 8. Clipboard data: String

```
Session     WindowStation Format              Object       Data
----------  ------------- ------------------  ----------   ---------------------------------
         0 WinSta0        0xc009L              0xe20c6598
0xe20c65a4  8a 00 01 00                                       ....
         0 WinSta0        0xc074L              ----------
         0 WinSta0        CF_HDROP             0xe1ba8c30
0xe1ba8c3c  14 00 00 00 00 00 00 00 00 00 00 00 00 00 00 00   ................
0xe1ba8c4c  01 00 00 00 43 00 3a 00 5c 00 44 00 6f 00 63 00   ....C.:.\.D.o.c.
0xe1ba8c5c  75 00 6d 00 65 00 6e 00 74 00 73 00 20 00 61 00   u.m.e.n.t.s...a.
0xe1ba8c6c  6e 00 64 00 20 00 53 00 65 00 74 00 74 00 69 00   n.d...S.e.t.t.i.
0xe1ba8c7c  6e 00 67 00 73 00 5c 00 41 00 64 00 6d 00 69 00   n.g.s.\.A.d.m.i.
0xe1ba8c8c  6e 00 69 00 73 00 74 00 72 00 61 00 74 00 6f 00   n.i.s.t.r.a.t.o.
0xe1ba8c9c  72 00 5c 00 44 00 65 00 73 00 6b 00 74 00 6f 00   r.\.D.e.s.k.t.o.
0xe1ba8cac  70 00 5c 00 64 00 61 00 74 00 61 00 00 00 00 00   p.\.d.a.t.a.....
         0 WinSta0        0xc0a7L              ----------
```

Fig. 9. Clipboard data: Folder path

4.5 Extraction of Master File Table (MFT) Details

The MFT has a record/entry for each file in an NTFS system [3]. The record has attributes and if file is small in size, most attributes are contained within the 1 KB MFT entry including $DATA attribute of 700 bytes which contains file data [3, 14].

```
Session    WindowStation Format                Object    Data
---------- ------------- ------------------- --------- ----------
        1 WinSta0       CF_UNICODETEXT        0xff9743a8 The sequence for visit w...m and
0xff9743b4  54 00 68 00 65 00 20 00 73 00 65 00 71 00 75 00   T.h.e...s.e.q.u.
0xff9743c4  65 00 6e 00 63 00 65 00 20 00 66 00 6f 00 72 00   e.n.c.e...f.o.r.
0xff9743d4  20 00 76 00 69 00 73 00 69 00 74 00 20 00 77 00   ..v.i.s.i.t...w.
0xff9743e4  6f 00 75 00 6c 00 64 00 20 00 62 00 65 00 20 00   o.u.l.d...b.e...
0xff9743f4  66 00 69 00 72 00 72 00 73 00 74 00 20 00 72 00   f.i.r.s.t...c.r.
0xff974404  79 00 70 00 74 00 6f 00 20 00 63 00 65 00 6e 00   y.p.t.o...c.e.n.
0xff974414  74 00 72 00 65 00 2c 00 20 00 63 00 6f 00 64 00   t.r.e.,...c.o.d.
0xff974424  65 00 20 00 70 00 72 00 6f 00 63 00 65 00 73 00   e...p.r.o.c.e.s.
0xff974434  73 00 69 00 6e 00 67 00 20 00 72 00 6f 00 6f 00   s.i.n.g...r.o.o.
0xff974444  6d 00 20 00 61 00 6e 00 64 00 20 00 74 00 68 00   m...a.n.d...t.h.
0xff974454  65 00 6e 00 20 00 73 00 74 00 72 00 6f 00 6e 00   e.n...s.t.r.o.n.
0xff974464  67 00 20 00 72 00 6f 00 6f 00 6d 00 2e 00 00 00   g...r.o.o.m.....
        1 WinSta0       0x0L                 ----------
```

Fig. 10. Clipboard data

In the experiment after the clipboard data is extracted from memory image (Fig. 10), MFT details were also extracted and clipboard data is searched in the parsed MFT (Fig. 11).

```
MFT entry found at offset 0x36e0c000
Attribute: In Use & File
Record Number: 120108
Link count: 2

$STANDARD_INFORMATION
Creation                  Modified                 MFT Altered              Access Date              Type
--------                  --------                 ----------               -----------              ----
2015-03-11 11:58:00 IST+0530 2015-03-11 12:01:49 IST+0530  2015-03-11 12:01:49 IST+0530  2015-03-11 11:58:00 IST+0530  Archive &
Content not indexed

$FILE_NAME
Creation                  Modified                 MFT Altered              Access Date              Name/Path
--------                  --------                 ----------               -----------              ---------
2015-03-11 11:58:00 IST+0530 2015-03-11 11:58:00 IST+0530  2015-03-11 11:58:00 IST+0530  2015-03-11 11:58:00 IST+0530  Users\ROHIT
SHARMA\Desktop\SEQUEN~1.TXT

$FILE_NAME
Creation                  Modified                 MFT Altered              Access Date              Name/Path
--------                  --------                 ----------               -----------              ---------
2015-03-11 11:58:00 IST+0530 2015-03-11 11:58:00 IST+0530  2015-03-11 11:58:00 IST+0530  2015-03-11 11:58:00 IST+0530  Users\ROHIT
SHARMA\Desktop\sequencedata.txt

$DATA
0000000000: 54 68 65 20 73 65 71 75 65 6e 63 65 20 66 6f 72   The.sequence.for
0000000010: 20 76 69 73 69 74 20 77 6f 75 6c 64 20 62 65 20   .visit.would.be.
0000000020: 66 69 72 73 74 20 63 72 79 70 74 6f 20 63 65 6e   first.crypto.cen
0000000030: 74 72 65 2c 20 63 6f 64 65 20 70 72 6f 63 65 73   tre,.code.proces
0000000040: 73 69 6e 67 20 72 6f 6f 6d 20 61 6e 64 20 74 68   sing.room.and.th
0000000050: 65 6e 20 73 74 72 6f 6e 67 20 72 6f 6f 6d 2e      en.strong.room.
```

Fig. 11. Master file table details (snipped details)

As can be seen, a MFT entry at offset 0x44b3ac00 has details about this string. The file which contained this data had the name sequencedata.txt, it was in user account Rohit Sharma & was accessed at 17:32:21 on 11Mar 2015.

When a file is deleted and moved to the Recycle Bin it generates two files in the Recycle Bin– $I and $R files. $I file maintains the original name and path, as well as the deleted date. $R file retains the original file data stream and other attributes like file creation time etc. [11, 13].

One such scenario is discussed here, in which after extracting clipboard data (Fig. 12), parsed MFT was searched for this data (Fig. 13) and it was seen that the file had been deleted as the file containing this data has $R beginning. Hence a forensic investigator knows the file from which last data was copied will be found in recycle bin in HDD image. Also by searching for $I file (Fig. 14), in parsed MFT, corresponding to this $R file investigator can get to know when file was deleted.

```
Session    WindowStation Format            Object    Data
---------  ------------- ------            ------    ----
        1 WinSta0      CF_UNICODETEXT      0xffa1d9f0 Gigaset is a subsidiary ...
0xffa1d9fc 47 00 69 00 67 00 61 00 73 00 65 00 74 00 20 00  G.i.g.a.s.e.t...
0xffa1da0c 69 00 73 00 20 00 61 00 20 00 73 00 75 00 62 00  i.s...a...s.u.b.
0xffa1da1c 73 00 69 00 64 00 69 00 61 00 72 00 79 00 20 00  s.i.d.i.a.r.y...
0xffa1da2c 6f 00 66 00 20 00 53 00 69 00 65 00 6d 00 65 00  o.f...S.i.e.m.e.
0xffa1da3c 6e 00 73 00 20 00 63 00 6f 00 6d 00 6d 00 75 00  n.s...c.o.m.m.u.
0xffa1da4c 6e 00 69 00 63 00 61 00 74 00 69 00 6f 00 6e 00  n.i.c.a.t.i.o.n.
0xffa1da5c 20 00 70 00 72 00 69 00 76 00 61 00 74 00 65 00  ..p.r.i.v.a.t.e.
0xffa1da6c 20 00 6c 00 69 00 6d 00 69 00 74 00 65 00 64 00  ..l.i.m.i.t.e.d.
0xffa1da7c 00 00                                             ..
        1 WinSta0      0x01                ----------
```

Fig. 12. Extracted clipboard data

```
MFT entry found at offset 0x26c35800
Attribute: File
Record Number: 56834
Link count: 1


$STANDARD_INFORMATION
Creation                Modified              MFT Altered           Access Date            Type
-----------             ---------             -----------           -----------            ----
2015-02-28 18:25:24 IST+0530 2015-02-28 18:27:03 IST+0530 2015-02-28 18:29:04 IST+0530 2015-02-28 18:25:24 IST+0530 Archive &
Content not indexed

$FILE_NAME
Creation                Modified              MFT Altered           Access Date            Name/Path
-----------             ---------             -----------           -----------            ---------
2015-02-28 18:25:24 IST+0530 2015-02-28 18:27:03 IST+0530 2015-02-28 18:27:03 IST+0530 2015-02-28 18:25:24 IST+0530 Boot\da-DK
\S-1-5-~3\$RJMXG2P.txt

$DATA
0000000000: 47 69 67 61 73 65 74 20 69 73 20 61 20 73 75 62  Gigaset.is.a.sub
0000000010: 73 69 64 69 61 72 79 20 6f 66 20 53 69 65 6d 65  sidiary.of.Sieme
0000000020: 6e 73 20 63 6f 6d 6d 75 6e 69 63 61 74 69 6f 6e  ns.communication
0000000030: 20 70 72 69 76 61 74 65 20 6c 69 6d 69 74 65 64  .private.limited
```

Fig. 13. Search for clipboard data resulted in deleted file : $R file

```
MFT entry found at offset 0x5430acd0
Attribute: In Use & File
Record Number: 1564
Link count: 1


$STANDARD_INFORMATION
Creation                Modified              MFT Altered           Access Date            Type
-----------             ---------             -----------           -----------            ----
2015-02-28 18:29:04 IST+0530 2015-02-28 18:29:04 IST+0530 2015-02-28 18:29:04 IST+0530 2015-02-28 18:29:04 IST+0530 Archive &
Content not indexed

$FILE_NAME
Creation                Modified              MFT Altered           Access Date            Name/Path
-----------             ---------             -----------           -----------            ---------
2015-02-28 18:29:04 IST+0530 2015-02-28 18:29:04 IST+0530 2015-02-28 18:29:04 IST+0530 2015-02-28 18:29:04 IST+0530 Boot\da-DK
\S-1-5-21-1415083519-4058233691-682063285-1000\$IJMXG2P.txt
```

Fig. 14. $I file corresponding to $R file

Hence by locating the data in parsed MFT it is found out from which file & user account the data was copied, when file was created/accessed and also if in case it was deleted after unauthorised access the time of such activity.

5 Conclusion and Recommendations

In this paper, a framework for carrying out the live forensics of a suspected system by extracting the Clipboard data and further using this data along with other forensically relevant artefacts has been put forward.

By the end, this framework will provide the investigator many important clues to proceed with further analysis of RAM or hard disk image. Investigator will be aware of how many users were logged in the suspected system (also the user account names), whether any malicious application was running in the system which was snooping the Clipboard along with IP address of remote machine to which application was communicating to transfer Clipboard data. Investigator would get the information about which all user accounts had undertaken the copy action and what was the last data copied i.e. the Clipboard data. Now if the Clipboard data extracted was a web address, it gives a lead that the user would have accessed the website or sent the URL to someone. If it's a folder path, it will give the folder name which user had moved last and hence same can be searched in hard disk image for further investigations.

Also if the data is a string or a word, after searching the extracted MFT, investigator can find out the name of the file to which the data belongs, file creation time, file data, file access time etc. and even if the cyber criminal has deleted the file after access (also from recycle bin), framework will confirm the same along with file creation time and deletion time if artefacts are existing in RAM image.

The experiments have been successful in extracting and using Clipboard data of text type belonging to Word document, Notepad file and Pdf file only, as per proposed framework. Also as $DATA attribute of MFT entry holds up to 700 bytes of data, for files bigger than this size, contents of the file could not be found in parsed MFT. Further work is required to address these limitations.

References

1. Okolica, J., Peterson, G.L.: Extracting the windows clipboard from physical memory. In: Proceedings of the 2010 Digital Forensic Research Workshop, pp. S118–S124 (2011)
2. Thomas, S., Sherly, K.K., Dija, S.: Extraction of memory forensic artefacts from windows 7 RAM image. In: Proceedings of 2013 IEEE Conference on Information and Communication Technologies (ICT) (2013)
3. Russinovich, M., Solomon, D.A., Ionescu, A.: Windows Internals, Part II, 6th edn. Microsoft Press, Redmond, Washington (2012)
4. Russinovich, M., Solomon, D.A., Ionescu, A.: Windows Internals, Part I, 6th edn. Microsoft Press, Redmond, Washington (2012)
5. Dumpit. http://www.moonsols.com/2011/07/18/moonsols-dumpit-goes-mainstream/
6. How Clipboard works Part I. http://blogs.msdn.com/b/ntdebugging/archive/2012/03/16/how-the-clipboard-works-part-1.aspx
7. How Clipboard works Part II. http://blogs.msdn.com/b/ntdebugging/archive/2012/03/29/how-the-clipboard-works-part-2.aspx
8. The Volatility Framework. https://github.com/volatilityfoundation

9. Walters, A., Petroni, N.: Volatools: Integrating volatile memory forensics into the digital investigation process. https://www.blackhat.com/presentations/bh-dc-07/Walters/Paper/bh-dc-07-Walters-WP.pdf

10. Window Stations. https://msdn.microsoft.com/en-us/library/windows/desktop/ms687096(v=vs.85).aspx

11. Ligh, M.H., Case, A., Levy, J., Walters, A.: The Art of Memory Forensics: Detecting Malware and Threats in Windows, Linux, and Mac Memory, 1st edn. Wiley, Hoboken (2014)

12. Event logs and Service SIDs. http://volatility-labs.blogspot.in/2012/09/movp-23-event-logs-and-service-sids.html

13. OS   Artefacts-Recycle.bin.   https://digital-forensics.sans.org/summit-archives/2010/12-larson-windows7-foreniscs.pdf

14. Reconstructing Master File Table. http://volatility-labs.blogspot.in/2013/05/movp-ii-24-reconstructing-master-file.html

15. Window Stations and Clipboard Malware. http://volatility-labs.blogspot.in/2012/09/movp-12-window-stations-and-clipboard.html

16. Schuster A.:Searching for processes and threads in microsoft windows memory dumps. In: Proceedings of the 2006 Digital Forensic Research Workshop (DFRWS), pp. 10–6 (2006)

17. Memparser Analysis Tool by Chris Betz. http://www.dfrws.org/2005/challenge/memparser.shtml

Anomaly Detection Through Comparison of Heterogeneous Machine Learning Classifiers vs KPCA

Goverdhan Reddy Jidiga[1]([✉]) and P. Sammulal[2]

[1] Department of Technical Education,
Government of Telangana, Hyderabad, India
jgreddymtech@gmail.com
[2] JNTUH College of Engineering, JNTU University,
Karimnagar, Hyderabad, India
sammulalporika@gmail.com

Abstract. The anomaly detection is applicable to wide range of critical infra-structure elements due to frequent change in anomaly occurrences and make sure to avoid all threats identified in regular. In this perception, we have to identify the abnormal patterns in applications and to model them by using a new adorned machine learning classifiers. In this paper we are investigating the performance by comparison of heterogeneous machine learning classifiers: ICA (Independent Component Analysis), LDA (Linear Discriminant Analysis), PCA (Principal Component Analysis), Kernel PCA and other learning classifiers. The Kernel PCA (KPCA) is a non-linear extension to PCA used to classify the data and detect anomalies by orthogonal transformation of input space into (usually high dimensional) feature space. The KPCA use kernel trick by extract the principal components from set of corresponding eigenvectors and use kernel width as performance parameter to determine rate of classification. The KPCA is implemented on taking two UCI machine learning repository sets and one real bank dataset. The KPCA implemented with classic Gaussian kernel internally. Finally KPCA performance compared with projection methods (ICA, LDA, PLSDA and PCA), other kernel (SVM-K) and non-kernel techniques (ID3, C4.5, Rule C4.5, k-NN and NB) applied on same datasets using training and test set combinations.

Keywords: Anomaly detection · Kernel · ICA · LDA · PCA · SVM · KPCA

1 · Introduction

The anomaly detection [2] is an emerging concept in the field of information security. The anomaly detection job is an abnormal pattern indicator (detect) and help to thwart the intrusive patterns or exploits which deviate to normal. The anomaly detection is subset of IDS (intrusion detection systems) primarily elaborated by Anderson [1]. He proposed an IDS based on two functional criteria: model based on events (i.e. Statistical anomaly detection [1, 18]), or rules generated from behavior (i.e. Rule based anomaly detection [2, 3, 18]). The two methods are fine in early inception of

© Springer International Publishing Switzerland 2015
J.H. Abawajy et al. (Eds): SSCC 2015, CCIS 536, pp. 483–495, 2015.
DOI: 10.1007/978-3-319-22915-7_44

applications; and these are working on execution of the program or system and prepare the model, form the rules. This process may raise an alarm if any instance deviates to model and behavior. The existing model and behavior based approaches [1] are suffering with a convergence time in learning. So the truly current anomaly detection systems must integrate with special features of the machine learning (ML) [4]. For this kind, we have many traditional and multilevel learning classifiers evolved in the ML. In ML, the algorithms are basically depends on learning profiles and similarity [5, 6]. In this paper we use a similarity based kernel classifier [15] to address the issues of abnormal data values in real world database. Many learning algorithms are kernel centric [15–17] generally a kind of similarity function of two arguments and proof that classification is to learn from example statistics for the applications of patterns, vectors, points and real world data analysis. The main objective to define the kernel is find the relation by mapping the input data (space) to feature space which has high dimensional to get better classification accuracy. The knowledge behind the kernel is to replace the dot product with a kernel function, so the learning classifier construct the high dimensional feature space and it is used to generate model to improve the performance of anomaly detection [15, 35]. The paper is organized as: the scope of anomaly detection, role of linear transformation and kernel classifiers importance given in this section, section two cover the traditional and latest work given to our paper in relative sequence, section three explained background work of Kernel PCA, section five given experimental work done on datasets, comparison of results and performance presented. The aim of our paper is to elaborate the role of kernel based machine learning classifiers is well contrast with others like PCA, ICA, SVM, LDA, other non-kernel based (ID3, C4.5, Rule C4.5, k-NN, NB) learning techniques compare with Kernel PCA to detect novelties.

1.1   Non-kernel vs Kernel Classifiers in Machine Learning (ML)

The ML [4, 5] classifiers are adapted with anomaly detection to decide on autonomous data instances whose behavior is not near to most probable class. Today the anomaly detection (ADS) is modernized with adorned ML classifiers [5, 16, 18] to get correct accuracy. The old classification is based on heuristics, normal rules, patterns (or signatures) and will detect anomalies (attacks) fall in the category of misuse (the regular system work flow and network operations). The ML gives better results, low false alarm rates, ability to detect novelty, scope to design well classifier against zero-day exploits in an application level behavior. In this paper we have used some projection methods (ICA, LDA and PCA) and explained in this section are competing with kernel and non kernel methods. The projection methods cover the fundamentals of principal components which help to design the kernels. So in this section we have given maximum scope on basics and the kernel PCA is explained in section three. The related concepts are given more in [6, 16].

Principal Component Analysis (PCA): The PCA is a basic linear approach on data (multivariate) and approximates a new kind of co-ordinates called principal components by use of eigenvector-value and orthogonal transformation of data [9]. It is popular statistical unsupervised method used in dimension reduction and also in anomaly detection. The PCA is mainly projecting data-instances along the principal coordinates (PCs) by maximum variance based on Gaussian process. The PCA is simply formulated by [32].

Let $W = [x_1, x_2, \ldots \ldots x_n]^T \in \mathbb{R}^{n \times p}$ for inputs as data instance x_i and n - no. of instances over p dimensions. Then PCA is by maximizing the variance using optimization problem.

$$\begin{matrix} Max \\ t, ||U|| = 1 \end{matrix} \sum_{i=1}^{n} U^T X X^T U \text{ Where } t = U \in \mathbb{R}^{p \times k}, X = x_i - \mu \tag{1}$$

Where U is a unit vector matrix contains k eigenvectors, μ is the mean. So the standard PCA can formulate by projecting data into large variation and use the reconstruction error (RE) [15]. Now PCA can optimize with objective function by minimize the RE as:

$$\begin{matrix} Min \\ t, ||U|| = 1 \end{matrix} RE(U) = \sum_{i=1}^{n} ||X - UU^T X||^2 \tag{2}$$

From above two formulations, to find the largest eigen-value, then use the Lagrange multiplier λ and select optimal principal components determined by $U^T X$. By deriving the above equations yields the corresponding eigenvalue formulation.

$\Sigma_W U = U \lambda$ Where $\Sigma_W = \frac{1}{2} \sum_{i=1}^{n} X X^T$ the co-variance matrix, λ is the eigenvalue and U is the eigenvector of Σ_W. Finally the necessary principal components calculated corresponding to k largest eigen-values respect to U.

Independent Component Analysis (ICA): The ICA is a kind of extension to PCA based on non-orthogonal transformation [28], which focus on minimizes both second-order and higher order non-Gaussian (components) dependencies in the input data and statistically independent in projecting data along directions [31]. An ICA basically supports for un-supervised features extraction. Let the data vector given as input X, $X = (X_1, X_2, \ldots X_n)^T$ and its components vector is S, $S = (S_1, \ldots S_n)^T$ after linear transformation of data X is S = WX, where W is the static transformation and then the independent components of S written as F: F $(S_1, S_2, \ldots S_n)$. The ICA is now defined as

$$X_i = a_{j1} S_1 + a_{j2} S_2 \ldots \ldots \ldots a_{jn} S_n \tag{3}$$

To give the generative model of ICA, use the latent variable in model with 'n' linear data points $S_1, S_2, \ldots S_n$ of S_k independent components sum for k = 1 ...... n, then the vector output of ICA generative model is

$$X = \sum_{k=1}^{n} S_k a_k \tag{4}$$

Linear Discriminant Analysis (LDA): LDA is similar to PCA [29, 30], but discriminate among classes by find the maximum variance between vectors in the underlying space is better. The LDA is supervised and its directions are computed (linear discriminants along axes) to form the multiple classes by maximize the separation. Let X_i is the set of data samples belongs to class i, N_i is the no. of samples (for training) in class i, D- no. of distinct classes. Then the class scatter matrix between classes S_B is formulate by

$$S_B = \sum_{i=1}^{D} N_i (x_i - \mu).(x_i - \mu)^T \tag{5}$$

Where μ is the mean for class i. and the class scatter matrix within the class S_W is

$$S_W = \sum_{i=1}^{D} \sum_{X_k \in X_i} (x_i - \mu).(x_i - \mu)^T \tag{6}$$

From the (5) and (6) extract eigenvectors of co-variance matrix is generalized by $A = S_w^i S_b$ then $A v = \lambda v$, where $A = S_w^i S_b$. Sort the generated eigenvectors values by order of decreasing and choose k eigenvectors (largest eigen-values) to form a $d \times k$-dimensional matrix W. Use this $d \times k$ eigenvector matrix to transform the data samples to the new subspace. The vector matrix transformation can formulate by the mathematical equation [29] $y = W^T \times x$.

The kernel is playing a discrimination role in ML (classification) algorithms used in anomaly detection by extracting key features which determine class variations. In this paper we referred some methods of popular kernels given in [15, 16] to model the data shown in Fig. 1. Generally the kernel can define as K: $X \times X \to R$, $K(x, y) = \Phi (x). \Phi (y)$, K is kernel used to measure similarity [17]. The kernel is based on principal basics shown in Fig. 1 (a) and (b), it shows the linear PCA of two dimensional input space (generally correlated). So while taking principal components and formulate the kernel, then mapping to high dimensional (probably un-correlated) shown in Fig. 1(c) and (d). Here we have given some mapping (Φ) formulations. Where (b) $\to$ (c) is mapping: $\Phi = R^2 \to R^3$ equal to

$$(x_1, x_2) \to (z_1, z_2, z_3) = x_1^2, \sqrt{2}x_1x_2, x_2^2) \tag{7}$$

From (7), the kernel is constructed by based on Mercer theorem (1909), from Fig. 1 (a) and (c),

$$\text{Kernel } K(x, y) = \Phi(x)^T\Phi(y) = (x_1^2, \sqrt{2}x_1x_2, x_2^2)^T (y_1^2, \sqrt{2}y_1y_2, y_2^2) \tag{8}$$

$$= x_1^2y_1^2 + x_2^2y_2^2 + 2x_1x_2y_1y_2 \tag{9}$$

$$= (x_1x_2 + y_1y_2)^2 = (x^Ty)^2 = K(x, y) \tag{10}$$

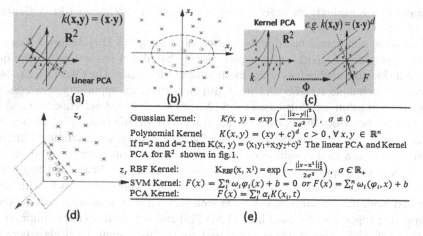

Fig. 1. Kernel motivation [17, 35]: (a) and (b) demonstrates example of two dimensional classifications; (a) shows linear-PCA and its extension shown in (c); (c) and (d) covers high dimensional feature space; (c) shows mapping criteria for KPCA; finally some popular kernels given in (e).

Where the kernel K is symmetric, positive and semi-definite shown in [16]. The popular kernels (K) [16] are given in Fig. 1 (e).

2   Related Work

The above section explained about the projection based classifiers. We can observe that all are robustly relate to each one in terms of basic functionality. Traditionally the PCA and ICA classifiers are learning equivalence in data distribution. The LDA is a supervised, but ICA and PCA are unsupervised having common feature of (dimension) reduction. The PCA is maximizes the variance (whereas ICA maximizes statistical independence) over finding the directions. Early days in the anomaly detection, the projection methods are popular and shown good results. The PCA [9, 32] is an approach used in dimension reduction initially for image analysis and later used in statistical applications. In security of information, the PCA play a vital task in [11] like the role of PCA is given to detect network anomalies. The PCA also used in [39] for spatial and temporal data to find anomalies and in [10] worked on distributed PCA. An ICA is also statistical method initially used in feature extraction applied first on study of blind source separation [28] and also use in speech processing and recognition [31], now it is also good in anomaly detection even class label not available. The LDA classifier is developed for pattern classification [30, 36–38] where training sets are large, also used in this field for better results sometime. But the drawback is more convergence time takes some times due large data volumes. All the above projection methods used in anomaly detection partially now, each one compare with others shown mixed results like in [37] claim that PCA is better than LDA and LDA is given good results as well as worse in some most of the experiments [38]. But little drawback of some projection methods are outer performs compared to SVM and KPCA shown in [13, 15, 35].

The other non kernel based classification algorithm ID3 [19] designed based on heuristics (top down, divide and conquer, greedy based and entropy-gain technique). But the ID3 is not suitable for current multi attribute databases. The C4.5 [20, 21, 24] is a posterior technique for ID3 and used still now in many applications successfully giving optimal solutions. Rule based C4.5 [22–24] is rule based induction tree and it is uses pruning heuristics to improve the accuracy by remedial strategy of derive, generalize, group and ordering the rules. The Partial least square discriminate analysis (PLSDA) [14] is a kind classification and regression problem generally used as alternate to PCA technique shows the proper relation between predictive and target variables. The k-NN classifier also improved by some simulation work with some extension work uses in intrusion detection well [12]. Later in anomaly detection, many are applying support vector machine (SVM) [13] and got good results to improve the efficiency of ADS. Also combine the classifiers and form multi level classifiers like SVM with NN, genetic algorithm with ID3 and ID3 with k-NN may chance to get good performance [23, 25, 27].

The KPCA, SVM kernels group, RBF kernels and CCA kernels are popular now in anomaly detection. The KPCA is generally based on non linear boundaries formed between classes of data instances and sound performance in anomaly (novelty) detection [15] and modeling data distribution in training data. The SVM kernel [13, 16] is uses well in multi-class classification and it is proved that use of SVM kernels better in anomaly detection on current applications. The RBF kernel is also frequently used in SVDD. Finally stationary kernels [16], multilevel kernels, or combination and cascading of different kernels used in anomaly detection for better improve in performance. Other traditional and well known techniques of linear and non-linear machine learning classifiers (including un-supervised and supervised techniques) are used in anomaly detection since many decades, but lack in performance [6, 12].

The projection methods are extended with kernels basics also used in anomaly detection and some authors are focusing well on KICA [34], KLDA [33], and KPCA. So our goal of this technique (KPCA) is here used in anomaly detection improve the performance when compared to others.

3 Proposed Work: Kernel PCA in Anomaly Detection

The PCA and other projection methods are not optimal always to ensure it as well classifier. The PCA is linear, so cannot classify the data better. The KPCA has mainly three advantages to use in anomaly detection: dimension reduction, classification and performance. So the goal classification by transforming the feature set into new one, which yields faster classification. Here the main criteria are extracts features may linear or non-linear after orthogonal transformation. So the KPCA [15] is an unsupervised learning classifier with idea of non-linear form of PCA used in anomaly detection. The KPCA is a functional extension to PCA, where PCA working details given in [10, 32] well. Now we need to integrate the kernel theorem into it and utilize to detect anomalies. In this paper the use of KPCA is not morally deviate any concepts with origin concepts given in [17], but problem analysis is integrate with extension scope to elevate how it useful to differentiate anomalies. Also the distribution of data into feature space gives scope to identify the boundaries between classes formed by evaluating reconstruction error [15, 35]. The logic and implementation steps are given in following steps.

The dataset taken as D, has $\{x_0, x_1 \dots x_n\}$ data instances; χ is subset of D projecting into high dimensional space called feature space on Hilbert context(space) $\mathcal{H}$, then mapping function $\Phi : \chi \rightarrow \mathcal{H}$, where x_i of χ is real: $x \in \mathbb{R}^d$, $\mathcal{H} \in \mathbb{R}^d$ and $d \ll D$. In order to calculate principal components, we first compute the co-variance matrix (Correlation) for $\mathcal{H}$.

$$C = \frac{1}{N} \sum_{i=1}^{N} \Phi(x_i) \Phi^T(x_j) \tag{11}$$

The principal components are calculated by evaluating original eigenvalue theorem where each eigenvalue $\lambda_i > 0$ and eigenvector $V \neq 0$ then $CV = \lambda V$. The eigenvector V (also called principal vector) can generally compute from the linear combination of features, then

$$V = \sum_{i=1}^{N} \alpha_i \, \Phi(x_i) \tag{12}$$

Then as per above theorem show the proof for V.

Proof. $CV = \lambda V$ or $\lambda V = CV$ in conventional Eigen problem, then

$$\lambda V = CV \rightarrow \sum_{i=1}^{N} \alpha_i \Phi(x_i) \cdot V \quad \text{Where} \quad V = \frac{1}{N\lambda} \sum_{i=1}^{N} \Phi(x_i) \Phi^T(x_j) \cdot V \tag{13}$$

$$\rightarrow \sum_{i=1}^{N} \left((\Phi^T(x_i)V) / (N\lambda) \right) \Phi(x_i) \rightarrow \sum_{i=1}^{N} \alpha_i \, \Phi(x_i) \tag{14}$$

So, as per eigenvalue theorem all Eigen-values are non negative and nonzero values in the vector V. Multiply the $\Phi(x_i)$ to both sides of $\lambda V = CV$ then

$$\lambda \Phi \cdot (x_i) \cdot V = \Phi \cdot (x_i) \cdot C.V \rightarrow \lambda[\Phi \cdot (x_k).V] = [\Phi \cdot (x_k).C.V] \tag{15}$$

$$\lambda \sum_{i=0}^{N} \alpha_i \, \Phi(x_k) \Phi(x_i) = \frac{1}{N} \sum_{i=0}^{N} \alpha_i \, \Phi(x_k) \sum_{j=1}^{N} \Phi(x_j) \Phi(x_j) \Phi(x_i) \tag{16}$$

Now we can define the kernel matrix K of size N × N, $K_{ij} = \left(\Phi(x_i) \Phi(x_j) \right)$ Then $N\lambda K\alpha = K^2\alpha \rightarrow N\lambda\alpha = K\alpha$, here the each α_i coefficient is depending Kernel K. Normalize the feature space: in KPCA always make sure that the mean value $\Phi(x_i)$ is zero by centered mean in feature space generally.

$$\widehat{\Phi(x_k)} = \Phi(x_i) - \frac{1}{N} \sum_{k=1}^{N} \Phi(x_k) \tag{17}$$

Finally normalize the Eigenvector (V) and here α used instead of V in original eigenvalue problem, solving the eigenvalue problem by imposing

$\|\alpha\|^2 = \frac{1}{\lambda_k}$ for k = 1, 2, ... d and where $\alpha_k^T \alpha_k \|\alpha\|^2$ here each λ_i is in non increasing order from λ_d by computing K. In the feature space the data to be centered by evaluating kernel matrix K with proper substitutions in $\lambda\alpha = K\alpha$ (V = α) with above equation.

$$\hat{K} = K - 2I_{1/N} + I_{1/N}K_{1/N} \quad \text{Or} \quad \hat{K} = K - I_n K - KI_n + I_n KI_n \quad \text{Where } 1/n = (1n)_{ij}$$

(18)

Principal Components extraction: if q is set of principal components extracted corresponding to Eigenvector α, then compute projections for new vector x (consider as test point) in new reduced feature space on to the α^k.

$$\alpha^k \Phi(x) = \sum_{j=1}^{N} \alpha_j^k \cdot \Phi(x_j)\Phi(x)) = \sum_{j=1}^{N} \alpha_j^k K(x_j, x)$$

(19)

Here x-new test data vector, α_j^k is the jth coefficient of α^k and it associate with the kth eigenvalue of matrix K Then Kernel K is: $K(x_i, x_j) = \Phi^T(x_i)\Phi(x_j)$

The selection of the no. of principal components in kernel-PCA is depending on the Eigenvectors (α) and evaluation of classification is depends on the selection on the kernel width. If the kernel matrix K is symmetric, then eigenvectors associated with different eigenvalue are orthogonal according to representation in eigenvalue decomposition of K.

4   Datasets as Case Studies

We have taken three identical datasets (1) Seeds Data (2) Banknote Authentication (3) Real time bank dataset. Both 1 and 2 from UCI ML repository.

Seed data [8]: The seeds dataset group is comprised of kernels of 3 kinds (Kama, Rosa and Canadian) of wheat and seventy instances each, selected for the experiment randomly. This dataset has seven attributes of multivariate data without missing values. For detecting structure of kernel they used a soft X-ray technique of high quality visualization and image was recorded by KODAK (13 × 18 cm X-ray).

Banknote authentication: This is available at UCI repository [8] and it is collection of bank specimen's feature data extracted from authenticated image and transformed into multivariate data (4 attributes and 1 class attribute). This dataset was actually digitized with 600 dpi with resolution of 400 × 400 pixel ratio. This dataset has 1372 instances. For this experiment the classification task is trained with 872 observations and tested on remaining samples with yes or no (1 or 0) basis.

Real time bank dataset: The bank database contains public bank transactions of 141261 records about transactions made during 2011 and 2013, Out of these 4221 unique records are identified and consider as training and test sets. The data set has eleven attributes, but three only consider which have highest information gain.

5   Experiments and Results

For this work, to carry out the experimental work, then similar kind of datasets consider as benchmark. The case studies are simulated on Intel Pentium(CPU 3 GHz speed), 2 GB RAM, Windows-XP OS, Matlab -32 bit version [7] and some performance benchmark values for case studies evaluated on SIPINA data mining tool [26].

The experimental work completed on 3 datasets shown in Table 1. The machine learning algorithms all are shown good performance in both datasets taken from UCI, but one dataset (real bank dataset) is not up to mark due large no. of duplicate records. The results which we got for seeds dataset by setting different parameters according to algorithms was very much satisfactory as equal to original contributor of dataset [8]. For seeds dataset, we have considered all attributes (7) and classify the kernels based on class data. By using non kernel algorithms such as ID3, C4.5, Rule based C4.5, NB, CART and K-NN how the performance is differentiate. The ID3 is identified 25 samples (kernels) are misclassified when five attributes considered, where as two samples are misclassified if all attributes taken. The ID3 shows 96 % detection rate (overall). In this category of algorithms the rule based C4.5 is performing well compare to K-NN, NB. The projection methods (PCA, LDA, PLSDA, ICA, and QDA) almost all are showing good performance compare with all non-kernel methods. Finally kernel based SVM and PCA shows excellent results for seeds dataset. From these observations SVM-K and KPCA performance is almost near to 100 %. So, the kernel based machine learning classifiers always well in anomaly detection to improve the DR and reduce the FPR as well as error rate.

The KPCA algorithm shows 99 % DR for dataset-1 due to small dataset, no data inconsistency and no missing values. Same process is not continuing for dataset-2 and

Table 1. Shows the performance of all algorithms tested on datasets. Here FPR-false positive rate, DR-detection rate, ER-error rate. DR is rounded for dataset-2, 3.

Datasets →	Dataset-1 (seed)			Dataset-2 (real bank data)			Dataset-3 (bank note)		
Method	D.R	F.P.R	E.R	D.R	F.P.R	E.R	D.R	F.P.R	E.R
PCA	98.05	1.03	1.50(± 0.52)	88	10.03	17.52(± 3.05)	90	9.03	7.52(± 0.82)
LDA	97.08	2.28	3.10(± 0.85)	79	16.45	23.28(± 5.05)	92	7.08	5.50(± 0.55)
PLSDA	97.35	1.83	2.82(± 0.49)	87	11.29	16.02(± 3.45)	91	8.83	6.52(± 0.71)
ICA	98.52	0.98	1.79(± 0.22)	89	10.13	11.12(± 2.65)	94	5.03	4.79(± 0.42)
QDA	96.38	3.73	3.89(± 0.62)	86	13.03	16.52(± 3.95)	90	9.73	8.59(± 0.22)
ID3	95.05	3.53	9.52(± 0.82)	78	18.38	20.52(± 4.05)	90	9.03	7.52(± 0.82)
K-NN	93.89	6.08	1.50(± 0.05)	89	09.45	10.23(± 2.05)	95	4.08	2.50(± 0.55)
C4.5	96.35	3.13	8.52(± 0.81)	80	17.23	16.02(± 2.45)	91	8.83	6.52(± 0.71)
RuleC4.5	97.65	2.03	7.79(± 0.62)	84	14.73	11.12(± 2.85)	94	5.03	4.79(± 0.42)
NB	96.23	3.13	3.59(± 0.22)	87	12.03	10.51(± 2.94)	93	3.73	3.59(± 0.22)
SVM-K	99.05	0.73	1.09(± 0.12)	95	3.03	08.02(± 1.95)	97	3.73	3.59(± 0.22)
KPCA	99.32	0.49	0.95(± 0.05)	95	2.97	07.39(± 1.28)	98	1.89	2.47(± 0.15)

dataset-3. For dataset-2, all algorithms are showing worse results due to lot of error data and un-structured. For the dataset-3, the algorithms are shown well in performance due to neat correlated dataset. The algorithms used in this paper, the experimental work done with different parameters and tested on different tools for verification of results. The PCA use with 3 and 7 principal components; LDA is work on 5-fold cross validation; PLSDA is work by 3 components with 5-fold cross validation; k-NN was use with Euclidian distance with 5-fold cross validation; finally non-kernel algorithms use with different variable combinations and confidence values.

5.1 Discussions

In our paper, we have focused efficient ML to anomaly detection and in that most important KPCA is adapted with simple and existing criteria to evaluate performance in all datasets. The results got from experiments with benchmark datasets shown in Table 1 and Fig. 2 are complete independent results for three similar datasets. We can observe those results of all standard and proposed KPCA has a little bit more performance than SVM and SVM-K in some cases. The results got in this paper are noted perfect. Here some standard algorithms are tested also on Matlab classification toolbox to identify the any changes in results. In all perspectives the evaluation of algorithm is depending on taking dataset, which is synthetic or real. So the score of algorithms are not same, because the real world database and latest cyber intrusions (anomalies) may affect on ADS and not sure that to achieve zero FPR with zero day attacks.

The overall performance of our algorithm is depending on selection of parameters for seed pair {kernel width, no. of eigenvectors}. The width of PCA kernel is always

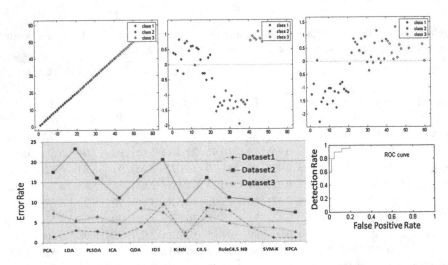

Fig. 2. The PCA classes with different combinations given for dataset-1 shown in Top figures, Bottom left shows error rate comparison for all classifiers given to the three datasets: (classification algorithm on X-axis and error rate on Y-axis to be taken. The ROC-curve is given for the dataset-1 in Bottom right of the figure

normal range and which leads to optimal performance will consider, for example taking small may not accurate [17]. Form Table 1 and above figures shown the comparative and brief investigation by using three bank datasets. The above results are evaluated at optimal selection of kernel width $\sigma = 0.2$ and no. of principal components $q = 20$ for datset-1 and dataset-3. Here the Gaussian kernel $\sigma = 0.2$ with non-linear extension PCA (KPCA) is well than SVM group one-class SVM.

The common computational complexity of a KPCA is to calculate easy for, but only difficult to extracting necessary principal components used in classification criteria. The KPCA is taking additional cost in high dimensional feature space to improve the performance by reducing reconstruction error. By KPCA we got better results and more than 95 % accuracy achieved, also recorded less error rate compare with all. In k-NN, PCA and PLSDA we have used five-fold cross validation and Euclidian distance used in k-NN. For PCA, KPCA the performance is depending on selection of kernel width and number of principal components. In this we have tested with {2, 4, and 7} principal components, but we got good results with 4, it shown in Table 1. For SVM, we have used LIBSVM and tested with only one-class SVM. The SVM-K and KPCA has very low false positives and error rate is also low for all datasets. The above performance details are tested on 60 instances with 150 training instances for dataset-1, tested on 500 instances with 872 training instances for dataset-3 and tested on 1000 instances with 3221 training instances for dataset-2.

6   Conclusion and Future Work

The most important point of our paper is to show some improvements on using kernel based ML classifiers. The paper gives brief details of popular machine learning approaches with some scope of work. The KPCA advantage is non-linear transformation, so we expected better results and those presented in this paper. In this paper we have concentrated on some projection methods, because of their motivations towards kernel designing. The KPCA and SVM-K are achieved equal results, but majority of people proved that SVM-K is better in classification. So in future, our work will extend towards the use of robust SVMs and multilevel machine learning classifiers to get effective results in critical database applications. Finally KPCA is selected and used after strong investigation of research work in machine learning.

References

1. Denning, D.E.: An intrusion detection model. IEEE Trans. Softw. Eng. 13(2), 222–232 (1987)
2. Axelsson, S.: Intrusion Detection Systems: A Survey and Taxonomy. Chalmers University, Technical report, vol. 99(15), March 2000
3. Lee, W., Stolfo, S.J.: Data mining approaches for intrusion detection. In: 7th USENIX Security Symposium, pp. 79–94, Berkeley (1998)

4. Lane, T., Brodley, C.E.: An application of machine learning to anomaly detection. In: Proceedings of the 20th National Information Systems Security Conference, pp. 366–377, October 1997
5. Breiman, L.: Random forests. Mach. Learn. **45**, 5–32 (2001)
6. Russell, S., Norvig, P.: Artificial Intelligence: A Modern Approach, 3rd edn. Prentice Hall, Saddle River (2009)
7. www.mathworks.in/products/matlab/
8. UCI Machine Learning Repository. http://archive.ics.uci.edu/ml
9. Hotelling, H.: Analysis of a complex statistical variable into principal components. J. Educ. Psychol. **24**, 417–441 (1933)
10. Bai, Z.-J., Chan, R.H., Luk, F.T.: Principal component analysis for distributed data sets with updating. In: Cao, J., Nejdl, W., Xu, M. (eds.) APPT 2005. LNCS, vol. 3756, pp. 471–483. Springer, Heidelberg (2005)
11. Lakhina, A., Crovella, M., Diot, C.: Diagnosing network-wide traffic anomalies. In: Proceedings of ACM Conference, Special Interest Group on Data Communication (2004)
12. Eskin, E., Arnold, A., Prerau, M.: A Geometric framework for unsupervised anomaly detection: detecting intrusions in unlabeled data. In: Applications of Data Mining in Computer Security (2003)
13. Lin, C.H., Chun Liu, J.. Ho, C.H.: Anomaly Detection Using LibSVM Training Tools. IEEE, Tunghai University, Taiwan. doi:10.1109/ISA.2008.12, ISBN-978-0-7695-3126-7/08 2008
14. Kleinbaum, D.G.: Applied Regression Analysis and Multivariable Methods, 3rd edn. Brooks/Cole Publishing Company, Pacific Grove (1998)
15. Hoffmann, H.: Kernel PCA for novelty detection. Pattern Recogn. **40**(3), 863–874 (2006)
16. Genton, M.G.: Classes of kernels for machine learning: a statistics perspective. J. Mach. Learn. Res. **2**, 299–312 (2001)
17. Scholkopf, B., Smola, A.J., Muller, K.R.: Nonlinear component analysis as a kernel eigenvalue problem. Neural Comput. **10**, 1299–1319 (1998)
18. Jidiga, G.R., Sammulal, P.: Foundations of IDS: focus on role of anomaly detection using machine learning. In: ICACM-2013 Elsevier 2nd International Conference. August 2013. ISBN No: 9789351071495
19. Quinlan, J.R.: Induction of decision trees. Mach. Learn. **1**(1), 81–106 (1986)
20. Quinlan, J.R.: C4.5: Programs for Machine Learning. Morgan Kaufmann, LosAltos (1993)
21. Quinlan, J.R., Rivest, R.L.: Inferring decision trees using the minimum description length principle. Inf. Comput. **80**, 227–248 (1989)
22. Polat, K., Güne, S.: A novel hybrid intelligent method based on C4.5 decision tree classifier and one against all approach for multi-class classification problems. Expert Syst. Appl. **36**, 1587–1592 (2009)
23. Yu, M., Ai, T.H.: Study of RS data classification based on rough sets and C4.5 algorithms. In: Proceedings of the SPIE Conference Series (2009)
24. Prema, R., Kannan, A.: An active rule approach for network intrusion detection with enhanced C4.5 Algorithm. In: IJCNS, pp. 285–385 (2008)
25. Ghosh, A., Schwartzbard, A.: A study using NN for anomaly detection and misuse detection. Reliable Software Technologies. http://www.docshow.net/ids/usenix_sec99.zip
26. http://eric.univ-lyon2.fr/~ricco/sipina.html
27. Daniel, L., Davis, J.: Improving Markov network structure learning using decision trees. J. Mach. Learn. Res. **15**, 501–532 (2014)
28. Comon, P.: ICA: a new concept. Signal Process. **36**, 287–314 (1994)
29. Fukunaga, K.: Statistical Pattern Recognition. Academic Press, New York (1989)

30. Haeb'h, R., Ney, H.: Linear discriminant analysis for improved large vocabulary speech recognition. In: Proceedings of ICASSP 1992, pp. 13–16, San Francisco, March 1992
31. Hyvarinen, A.: Fast and robust fixed-point algorithms for independent component analysis. IEEE Trans. Neural Netw. **10**(3), 626–634 (1999)
32. Jolliffe, I.J.: Principal Component Analysis. Springer, New York (1986)
33. Kocsor, A., Tóth, L., Paczolay, D.: A nonlinearized discriminant analysis and its application to speech impediment therapy. In: Matoušek, V., Mautner, P., Mouček, R., Tauser, K. (eds.) TSD 2001. LNCS (LNAI), vol. 2166, pp. 249–257. Springer, Heidelberg (2001)
34. Kocsor, A., Csirik, J.A.: Fast independent component analysis in kernel feature spaces. In: Pacholski, L., Ružička, P. (eds.) SOFSEM 2001. LNCS, vol. 2234, pp. 271–281. Springer, Heidelberg (2001)
35. Scholkopf, B., Smola, A.J., Muller, K.R.: Kernel Principal Component Analysis in Advances in Kernel Methods - Support Vector Learning, pp. 327–352. MIT Press, Cambridge (1999)
36. Siohan, O.: On the robustness of linear discriminant analysis as a preprocessing step for noisy speech recognition. In: Proceedings of ICASSP 1995, pp. 125–128, Detroit, May 1995
37. Beveridge, J.R., She, K., Draper, B., Givens, G.H.: A nonparametric statistical comparison of principal component and linear discriminant subspaces for face recognition. In: Proceedings of the IEEE Conference on CVPR, pp. 535–542, USA, December 2001
38. Martinez, A., Kak, A.: PCA versus LDA. IEEE Trans. Pattern Anal. Mach. Intell. **23**(2), 228–233 (2001)
39. Hang, Z., Greenberg, A., Roughan, M.: Network anomography. In: Proceedings of Internet Measurement Conference (IMC) (2005)

Android Users Security via Permission Based Analysis

Pradeep Kumar Tiwari[✉] and Upasna Singh

Department of Computer Engineering,
Defence Institute of Advanced Technology, Pune 411025, India
{pradeep_mcse13, upasnasingh}@diat.ac.in

Abstract. Android being the most popular mobile platform with nearly 80 % of global market share, attracts the mobile application developers to target end users for their private information such as contacts, GPS data, call logs, sending premium messages etc. through the use of application permissions. Android permissions are selected by the application developer and there is no check on whether asked permission is relevant for the application or not. Paper proposes a methodology for identifying the over privileged applications and then reducing the set of permissions used by these applications. The proposed work demonstrates that an over privileged application can be used with reduced set of permissions and thus successfully denying access to user's sensitive information.

Keywords: Permission system · Reverse engineering · Permissiongap · Smali · Over-privilege

1 Introduction

Android is most widely used mobile OS with soaring growth in its number of users. With increase in computation capability of the mobile hardware and open nature of application development, it attracts the nasty developers as well.

Whenever an android user installs an application, he is presented with the list of privileges, it asks for. User either accepts it, and gives the privilege to the application or doesn't install it. Android enforces permission system to guard access to privileged resources, including the Internet, GPS, and telephony. Though Android permissions ensures certain level of security, the existing permissions are often much more powerful than necessary. For example, the Flipkart shopping app must acquire "full Internet access" permission, enabling the app to send and receive data from any site on the Internet, not just flipkart.com. Similarly the other Android permissions are general in nature, which grants random access to a specific resource (e.g., the contacts list of user) or allowing numerous un-related privileges with a single permission (e.g., "modify system settings" permission). As a result of this, many apps violate the principle of least privilege [2], and the excessive privileges held by apps may be used to violate user privacy and security, e.g. by directly accessing sensitive resources or exploiting privilege escalation vulnerabilities. Least privilege is an important aspect of system design, benefiting system security and fault tolerance [4].

J.H. Abawajy et al. (Eds): SSCC 2015, CCIS 536, pp. 496–505, 2015.
DOI: 10.1007/978-3-319-22915-7_45

Existing work on android permissions to make it more fine grained requires modification at operating system level, which considerably reduces their potential or deters the user from installing them.

This paper explores how Android applications can be made more privacy friendly by permissions removal. The main emphasis of this paper will be on app permission removal using reverse engineering processes. Enhancement and novelty of the proposed work is as follows

- Detection of over privileged applications using the permissionmap, and
- Refining information stealing applications with anonymous data.

The paper is organized as follows: Sect. 2 discusses about the permission model and describes the literature already done in the area of android application security. Section 3 illustrates the proposed methodology. Section 4 shows the implementation of the proposed approach. Section 5 displays the results of the technique and its efficiency. And finally Sect. 5 concludes the work and talks about future scope.

2   Background

The Android platform (API 19) has about 79 application level permissions [10] which are requested during installation and enforced silently any time the application is executed [7, 9]. Unlike other privacy models, such as the iPhone, the user is not prompted when an application requests a resource during execution.

Android applications are poised of many different files, out of which two are most relevant. One is classes.dex file and the other is AndroidManifest.xml file. Classes.dex file is a zipped version of all the java files into one dalvik executable, which is similar to but light weight version of JVM. AndroidManifest.xml file contains information of the application package, including permissions.

TISSA [9], proposed a new privacy mode in android devices, through which users will have the option of selectively allowing the permissions. It also talks about keeping the permission of application but based on its nature, data will be fed to it in three forms: empty, returns absence of the asked resource, anonymized, provides random version of original information and bogus, provides fake result of the requested information. But it requires modification of OS itself. Having given such possibility we can provide user's security through application modification at OS level, not at application level.

Although android's access control policy is not well documented, especially mapping between the application code and the permissions need to be asked, it is possible to make a permissionmap for different versions (API Levels) of android [3, 10]. Having given with permissionmap we can apply least privilege concept on the applications, before asking for certain permissions and can also detect application against excessive privileges.

3 Proposed Approach

The proposed work was carried out by developing two algorithms, first algorithm detects the over privileged apps and second mocks the application with anonymous data. The approach first identifies if application is over-privileged and then makes it compatible with least privilege concept. The methodology used is static, where an application is received in either of two ways:

1. Through Google's PlayStore, but it doesn't allow downloading the APK (Android application package) directly. So with the help of APKDownloader [11] applications were downloaded.
2. Pull the application directly from the phone using adb (Android Debug Bridge)

After receiving the application, different reverse engineering techniques were applied to extract permissions and methods from the source files of the application and then using the permission map discussed by A.P. Felt [3, 14], over-privileged applications were detected.

3.1 Implementation

The implementation of how the data can be leaked from user's mobile phone to developer's site through the use of "INTERNET" permission, an innocent looking application ClipSniff was developed, which exploits the universal accessible nature of clipboard. It takes two arguments from user, concatenates and displays it but at the same time sends clipboard data to the remote server. It can be argued that app has no intention of using internet, still it is asking for INTERNET permission, but in order to use ClipSniff it should be given this permission. This proves that app developers can misuse permissions to collect user information for their purpose.

To prevent the misuse of application permissions, 1000 random applications were analyzed from PlayStore for proper permission invocation through their methods. Given application's APK file, we decompiled it using a popular tool apktool [10]. It disassembles the application into its constituents. The disassembled code is in SMALI format [12], which is less human understandable. As there is very less documentation available for smali, so to understand that, we developed some dummy applications, and decompiled them to see what is changing. We got to know that apktool generates smali files corresponding to every java file inside the application (Fig. 1).

We developed two functions *extractPermission() extractMethods()* to achieve the objective, first extracts all the permissions from the application and the other extracts all the methods used in that application. Then using the permission map [14] discussed by A.P. Felt [3] was converted to SQLite format (APIMap.db) and integrated with above two functions, to check the status of the application (Fig. 2).

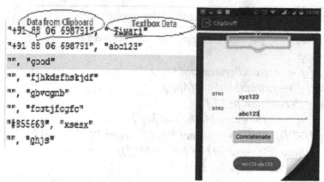

manifest android:versionCode='1' android:versionName='1.0' package='com.pradeep.clipsniff'>
<uses-permission android:name='android.permission.INTERNET'>

Fig. 1. ClipSniff secretly sending clipboard information to remote server in background

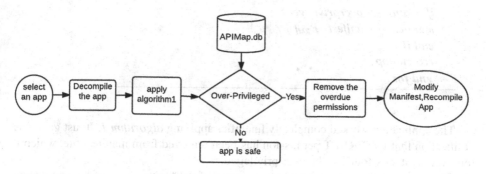

Fig. 2. Checking the status of the applications

Following pseudo code determines whether an application is over-privileged or not. If the status returned to be over-privileged, that permission will then be stored in P_{RM} (Permissions to remove) array and later removed from the manifest file of the application.

The variables used in pseudo code is defined below:

APIMap.db - > SQLite database of permission map for android jelly bean (API 19)
PM - > Permission Map Array of Table
P [] and M [] are the permission and method array of the application
Pa and Mb are the permission, method pair from the Permission map table.

Algorithm 1: Determining status of the application

PM← 2D array of permissionmap from APIMap.db
for every app
         P[ ] ← extractPermission(App$_i$)
         M[ ] ← extractMethods(App$_i$)
   for every Permission in P[ ]
                  for every Method in M[ ]
         If (P[i], M[j]) == (select Pa, Mb from PM
         where (Pa == P[i]) ^ (Mb==M[j]))
            status ← safe for P[i]
                     else
P$_{RM}$[ ] ← P[i]
            status ← overprivileged for P[i]
                  end for
   end for

   if (status == overprivileged)
   manifest = manifest −P$_{RM}$[ ]
   end if
   return app
   end for

The application worked completely fine after applying *algorithm 1*. It just gave one notification that INTERNET permission has been removed from manifest file, which it removed as it was found to be over-privileged.

The other possibility is, what if, user is aware of the functionality of the application and is able to decide the overdue permissions. So to investigate this, top 4 permissions of android framework were selected by analyzing 30 benign and 30 malicious

Fig. 3. Screenshot of the torch application [5], before and after applying *algrithm 1*.

application's manifest file. For experimentation, the selected permissions were INTERNET, WRITE_EXTERNAL_STORAGE, ACCESS_FINE_LOCATION and READ_PHONE_STATE permissions for our analysis. Then to make the application safer, below technique was applied to ensure user's privacy (Fig. 3).

Another algorithm was developed, which takes an application, and a suspicious permission, let's say P1, selected by user and results in application without that P1 and still functional (Fig. 4).

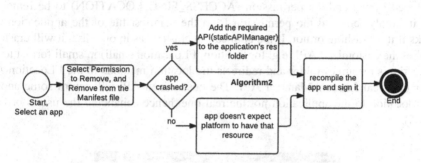

Fig. 4. Methodology followed to fix the application after removal of permissions

When below algorithm was applied to GetLocation app, developed by us, it successfully fixed the app which was crashing earlier, when LOCATION permission was removed.

Algorithm 2: Application of least privilege concept

$PM \leftarrow$ *2D array of permissionmap from APIMap.db*
for every app
select permission to remove, say P1
manifest = manifest − P1
$M_{PM}[\ ] \leftarrow$ (*select M_p from PM*
where permission == P1)
$\qquad M[\ ] \leftarrow$ *extractMethods(App_i)*
for every Method in M[ ]
$\qquad\qquad$ *for every Method in $M_{PM}[\ ]$*
$\qquad$ *If (M[i]) == ($M_{PM}[j]$)*
$\qquad\qquad M_R[\ ] \leftarrow M_R[\ ] + M[i]$
$\qquad\qquad$ *end if*
$\qquad\qquad$ *end for*
end for
$app \leftarrow app + APIa$
for every $M_R[\ ]$
$\quad M_R[i] \leftarrow$ *Ms from APIa*
$\qquad$ *end for*
$\qquad$ *end for*

The variables used in the pseudo code are as follows:

$M_{PM}[]$ - > *list of methods from APIMap.db where permission is Pi*
$M[]$ - > *list of methods available in application*
$M_R[]$ - > *list of methods to be replaced or removed, if the permission Pi is removed*
$APIa$ - > *API corresponding to that permission*
Ms - > *method from the APIa*

The above algorithm takes two arguments, app (GetLocation, a location based app developed by us) and the permission (ACCESS_FINE_LOCATION) to be removed. First it simply removed the permission from the manifest file of the application and checks if it is crashing or not. If the application crashes (as in our case, it will crash), it supplies the customized API (e.g. for location, FLoacation.smali) in smali format to the application's resources folder and redirects the location methods to the FLocation API rather than real LocationManager API. The customized API will return some anonymous location to the application not the real one, hence enhancing the user's privacy (Fig. 5).

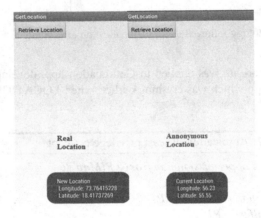

Fig. 5. Screenshot of the GetLocation app, before and after applying *algrithm2*.

4   Results

When technique of algorithm 1 was applied on 100 applications from PlayStore (applications were simply downloaded from the PlayStore for our project using apk-downloader), it effectively detects the over privileged applications using method-permission pair. It showed that 16.67 % of them are over-privileged i.e. they asked for certain permissions but the corresponding methods are not available. It has been happened because some developers ask for certain permissions; they think application will need in future.

Before applying our *algorithm 2*, when permissions were simply removed from AndroidManifest.xml of the application, they behave unexpectedly, some worked fine, while others crashed immediately. To investigate this, 5 most popular applications were selected and decompiled using *apktool* (Fig. 6).

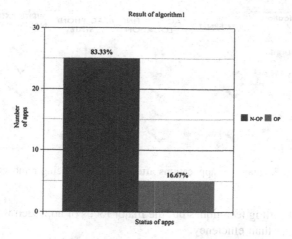

Fig. 6. Statistics of *alogorithm 1*

- Simply removing permission from the AndroidManifest only worked reliably with two of the permissions we wanted to investigate, INTERNET and WRITE_EXTERNAL_STORAGE.
- In case of INTERNET permission, application doesn't expect the user to always have data services enabled.
- And in case of WRITE_EXTERNAL_STORAGE permission, application doesn't expect user to have external SD card inserted, always.
- With all other permissions, removing them from the manifest is hit or miss. Some applications do fine while others crashed immediately.
- Hence, it was not enough to simply remove permissions from the manifest; we also needed to modify the source.
- After recompilation, apps were signed with our digital certificate and manually pushed back to phone.

So, *algorithm 2* ensures that, for those permissions to which, the application crashed, can be made to work successfully. For proof of concept, a location based application, GetLocation, was developed, which shows user's current location in the form of latitude and longitude and has the permission "android.permission. ACCESS_FINE_LOCATION". When the permission was removed from the manifest file, and later supplied the customized API to the decompiled application, it was fixed with anonymous location data. Following figure shows the application with and without that permission (Fig. 7).

Although the time and space complexity of algorithm is dependent on the number of applications being fed as input, the worst case time complexity for *algorithm 1* is O $(c*n)$, where n is the number of applications and c is a constant (because number of permissions and methods are constant for that application, typically permissions are < 134 and methods for each permission is <=34). For *algorithm 2* the time complexity is little high, it is $O(p^2 + n)$, where p is the number of rows in the permission map (APIMap.db) and n is number of applications. It can be further reduced by

Application	INTERNET	ACCESS_FINE _LOCATION	READ_PHONE _STATE	WRITE_EXTER NAL_STORAG E
FlashLight	✓	✗	✗	✓
Angry Birds	✓	–	–	✓
Instagram	✓	✓	✗	✓
Truecaller	✓	✓	✗	✓
Whatsapp	✓	✓	✗	✓

Fig. 7. Status of applications after permissions being removed

applying efficient sorting techniques but the major focus of approach was generation of methodology rather than efficiency.

5 Conclusion and Future Scope

As the popularity of android is on its peak, their user's security and privacy becomes essential part of the technology. Ensuring that users are safe to use applications of their choice without violating their privacy becomes necessary. Paper proposes two techniques, one of which ensures that, the application, users are using, is safe and the other restricts the application from accessing user's sensitive information.

As the proposed methodology is completely manual and based on static analysis of the application, it can be effortlessly automated. We targeted the Android API level 19, which has the maximum number of users [15], nearly 50 %. This work can be extended to higher API levels as well.

References

1. Brightest Flashlight Free. https://play.google.com/store/apps/details?id=goldenshorestechno logies.brightestflashlight.free. Accessed 26 February 2014
2. Saltzer, J.H.: Protection and the control of information sharing in Multics. Commun. ACM **17**(7), 388–402 (1974)
3. Felt, A.P., Chin, E., Hanna, S., Song, D., Wagner, D.: Android permissions demystified. In: Proceedings of the 20th ACM Conference on Computer and Communications Security (2013)
4. http://en.wikipedia.org/wiki/Principle_of_least_privilege. Accessed March 2014
5. Shin, W., Kiyomoto, S., Fukushima, K., Tanaka, T.: Towards formal analysis of the permission-based security model for android, pp. 87–92. IEEE (2009)
6. Shabtai, A., Fledel, Y., Kanonov, U., Elovici, Y., Dolev, S., Glezer, C.: Google android: a comprehensive security assessment. IEEE Secur. Priv. **8**(2), 35–44 (2010)
7. Ongtang, M., Butler, K., McDaniel, P.: Porscha: policy oriented secure content handling in android, pp. 221–230 (2010)

8. Saint, N.: 50 % of android apps with internet access that ask for your location send it to advertisers. http://www.businessinsider.com/50-ofandroid-apps-that-ask-for-your-location-send-it-to-advertisers-2010-10. Accessed October 2014
9. Zhou, Y., Zhang, X., Jiang, X., Freeh, V.W.: Taming information-stealing smartphone applications (on android). In: McCune, J.M., Balacheff, B., Perrig, A., Sadeghi, A.-R., Sasse, A., Beres, Y. (eds.) Trust 2011. LNCS, vol. 6740, pp. 93–107. Springer, Heidelberg (2011)
10. Au, K.W.Y., et al.: Pscout: analyzing the android permission specification. In: Proceedings of the 2012 ACM Conference on Computer and Communications Security. ACM (2012)
11. Smali, an Assembler/Disassembler for DEX format. https://code.google.com/p/smali/. Accessed 26 February 2014
12. http://apps.evozi.com/apk-downloader/. Accessed 26 February 2014
13. http://sourceforge.net/projects/dedexer/files/. Accessed 26 February 2014
14. https://developer.android.com/about/dashboards/index.html Accessed March 2015
15. http://pscout.csl.toronto.edu/results/jellybean_publishedapimapping Accessed June 2015

Data-Centric Refinement of Information Flow Analysis of Database Applications

Md. Imran Alam and Raju Halder$^{(\boxtimes)}$

Indian Institute of Technology, Patna, India
{imran.mtcs13,halder}@iitp.ac.in

Abstract. In the recent age of information, most of the applications are associated with external database states. The confidentiality of sensitive database information may be compromised due to the influence of sensitive attributes on insensitive ones during the computation by database statements. Existing language-based approaches to capture possible leakage of sensitive database information are coarse-grained and are based on the assumption that attackers are able to view all values of insensitive attributes in the database. In this paper, we propose a data-centric approach which covers more generic scenarios where attackers are able to view only a part of the attribute-values according to the policy. This leads to more precise semantic-based analysis which reduces false positives with respect to the literature.

Keywords: Information flow analysis · Dependence graph · Database application

1 Introduction

Protecting private data in computer systems is a promising field of research. While access control and encryption prevent confidential information from being read or modified by unauthorized users, they do not regulate the information propagation after it has been released from the source for execution. Confidentiality may be compromised during the flow of information along the control structure of any software systems [13]. For instance, let l and h be public (or *low*) and private (or *high*) variables respectively, an attacker can guess the sensitive value of h by observing l on the output channel in case of (i) assignment statements (*e.g.*, $l := h$) or (ii) iteration and conditional statements (*e.g.*, if $(h == 0)$ then $l := 20$; else $l := -20$;). The former is called a direct/explicit flow, whereas the later is called indirect/implicit flow. Language-based information flow security analysis [13] has emerged as a promising technique to identify such undesirable information flows in software systems and hence to prevent unauthorized leakage of confidential information.

1.1 Related Works

A series of works on language-based information flow have been proposed for various programming paradigms [8,10,12,15]. The first attempt to prevent

© Springer International Publishing Switzerland 2015
J.H. Abawajy et al. (Eds): SSCC 2015, CCIS 536, pp. 506–518, 2015.
DOI: 10.1007/978-3-319-22915-7_46

confidential information leakage is based on lattice theoretic model [4] where a partial order is defined among various security labels (*e.g.*, *high* $\geq$ *low*) and an upward information flow on lattice is allowed to ensure the confidentiality. In [13,14], authors proposed security type systems considering a set of security types and typing rules which guarantee secure information flow in programs. Type-based systems are not flow-sensitive and may produce false alarm [10]. As an improvement, dependence graph-based approaches [2,9,10,16] are flow-sensitive and they overcome the bottlenecks of security type systems [10]. Static analysis on all possible paths in dependence graphs identifies possible information leakage. An worth-mentioning approach is backward slicing *w.r.t. low*-variables [2]. The context-sensitivity and object-sensitivity are considered, as an improvement, in [10]. In practice, dependence graph-based security analysis is limited to realistic program of about 100KLOC [9]. Various formal methods, *e.g.* Abstract Interpretation, Model checking, Axiomatic Rules, etc. [6,11,18,19] are also applied in this direction. The non-interference principle [13] says that a variation of high input must not influence the low view of the applications, and this is the basis of security principle which must be respected by the proposed techniques.

1.2   Motivations

To the best of our knowledge, authors in [3,8] first proposed information flow analysis to the case of database query languages. The confidentiality of sensitive database information may be compromised due to the influence of sensitive attributes on insensitive ones during computations by database statements. The proposal in [3,8] uses the abstract interpretation framework to capture attributes dependences at each program points by combining symbolic domain of propositional formula and numerical abstract domain. However, the analysis may produce false alarms when we focus on the dependences based on values instead of attributes. More importantly, the analysis is coarse grained and makes the assumption that an attacker is able to view all values of public attributes.

1.3   Contributions

In this paper, we propose a fine-grained information flow analysis of database applications based on dependence graphs. The proposal covers generic scenarios where attackers are allowed to observe a part of insensitive database information (rather than all) corresponding to public attributes. To this aim, we propose a data-centric computation of dependences in database applications. This leads to a refinement of dependence graphs for database applications, giving rise to a more precise semantics-based analysis of information flow. The main contributions of the paper are:

- We propose a data-centric refinement of Database-Oriented Program Dependency Graph (DOPDG) in order to reduce a number of false data-dependences.
- We perform information flow analysis based on the refined DOPDG to identify possible information leakage in database applications.

The structure of the paper is as follows: In Sect. 2, we discuss in detail the notion of syntax-based DOPDG and its data-centric refinement. Information flow analysis of database applications based on the refined DOPDG is discussed in Sect. 3. The complexity and correctness of our approach is discussed in Sect. 4. Finally, we conclude our work in Sect. 5.

2   Database-Oriented Program Dependence Graph (DOPDG)

Willmor et al. [17] proposed the notion of dependence graph in case of database applications embedding query languages. This is an extension of traditional Program Dependence Graph (PDG) [7] considering two additional dependences defined below:

Definition 1 (Program-Database (PD) dependence). *A database statement Q is said to be Program-Database dependent on an imperative statement S if it uses a variable x defined by S such that there is no redefinition of x in between S and Q. A dual is also PD-dependence.*

Definition 2 (Database-Database (DD) dependence). *A database statement Q_1 is Database-Database dependent on another database statement Q_2 if Q_1 uses an attribute x which is defined by Q_2 and there is no redefinition of x and no roll-back operation of Q_2 between Q_1 and Q_2.*

The above definitions are syntax-based where dependences depend only on the presence of used and defined variables (either application variables or database attributes) in the statements. To illustrate the construction of syntax-based DOPDG, let us define the following two functions: DEF : $\mathbb{I} \rightarrow \wp(\mathbb{V} \times \text{Lab})$ and USE : $\mathbb{I} \rightarrow \wp(\mathbb{V} \times \text{Lab})$ where $\mathbb{I}$ is the set of statements (both imperative and database statements), $\mathbb{V}_{db}$ is the set of database attributes, $\mathbb{V}_{app}$ is the set of application variables, $\mathbb{V} = \mathbb{V}_{db} \cup \mathbb{V}_{app}$, $\mathbb{V}_{db} \cap \mathbb{V}_{app} = \emptyset$, and Lab = {full, partial}. The label "full", if associated with database attribute x, denotes that all the values corresponding to the attribute x is defined by database statement, whereas "partial" denotes that a subset of the values of the attribute is defined. For instance, an attribute is fully defined when there is no WHERE clause in INSERT, DELETE, UPDATE statements. Observe that, in case of application variable, the label is by default always "full".

Example 1. Consider the application program Prog and the database table Emp depicted in Figs. 1(a) and (b) respectively. The syntax-based DOPDG of P is depicted in Fig. 1(c). The data-dependences between imperative statements and the control dependences are computed following similar approach as in the case of traditional Program Dependence Graphs. To obtain DD- and PD-dependences, the defined- and used-variables are computed as follows:

$\text{DEF}(2) = \{(x, \text{full})\}$ $\text{DEF}(3) = \{(y, \text{full})\}$

$\text{DEF}(4) = \{(\text{ssn}, \text{full}), (\text{name}, \text{full}), (\text{salary}, \text{full})\}$

$\text{DEF}(5) = \{(\text{salary}, \text{partial})\}$ $\text{USE}(5) = \{(\text{salary}, \text{partial}), (\text{ssn}, \text{full}), (x, \text{full})\}$

DEF(6) ={(salary, partial)}   USE(6) = {(salary, partial), (ssn, full), (y, full)}
USE(7) ={(salary, partial), (ssn, full)}

Based on this information, we can easily compute DD- and PD-dependences. For instance, edges $4 \xrightarrow{\text{salary, ssn}} 5$, $5 \xrightarrow{\text{salary}} 6$, etc. represent DD-dependences, whereas edges $2 \xrightarrow{x} 5$, $3 \xrightarrow{y} 6$ represent PD-dependences.

Disadvantage of Syntax-Based DOPDGs. This is to be noted that the label "Lab" is not enough to remove all false dependences. For instance, in Fig. 1, although statement 7 is syntactically DD-dependent on statement 5, but semantically there is no dependence because the database-part defined by statement 5 is not used by statement 7. Therefore, we need a more precise semantic-based analysis.

2.1 Condition-Action Rules

In case of database applications, SQL statements define either a part of the values or all of the values corresponding to an attribute depending on the condition present in the WHERE clause. This may produce false dependence when the attribute-values defined by one statement does not overlap with the same attribute-values accessed by another statement. The presence of semantic

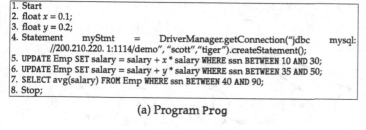

(a) Program **Prog**

(b) Table **Emp**

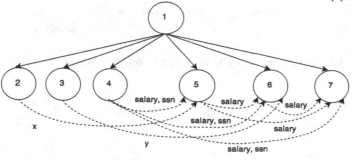

(c) DOPDG of Program **Prog**

Fig. 1. An example program and its syntax-based DOPDG.

independence, although syntactically dependent, can be identified by considering the Condition-Action rules as suggested by Elena and Jeniffer in [1].

Example 2. Consider the program Prog and its syntax-based DOPDG depicted in Figs. 1(a) and (c) respectively. Analysing dependences between each pair of nodes by applying Condition-Action rule [1], we get that the DD-dependences $5 \xrightarrow{\text{salary}} 6$ and $5 \xrightarrow{\text{salary}} 7$ do not exist. The refined DOPDG is shown in Fig. 2.

Various cases of overlapping of database information defined by Q_2 and subsequently used by Q_1 is depicted using Venn diagram in Fig. 3. Dependence occurs due to any of the followings: (i) both pre-defined and post-defined values are in the use; (ii) pre-defined values are not in the use whereas post-defined values are, (iii) pre-defined values are in the use whereas post-defined values are not. This makes the computational complexity of dependence computation exponential *w.r.t.* the number of defining statements.

Disadvantage of Condition-Action Rules. The Condition-Action rules [1] can be applied only on a single def-use pair at a time. If more than one database statements (in sequence) partially define an attribute which is then used by another statement, the Condition-Action rules fail to capture semantic independences. Example 3 depicts this.

Example 3. Consider the database application depicted in Fig. 4. The DOPDG, applying Condition-Action rules on each pair of def-use (*i.e.* $\ell_1 \xrightarrow{a} \ell_2$, $\ell_1 \xrightarrow{a} \ell_3$, $\ell_1 \xrightarrow{a} \ell_4$, $\ell_2 \xrightarrow{a} \ell_3$, etc.), is depicted in Fig. 5(a). However, observe that, since

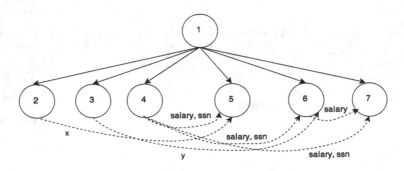

Fig. 2. Refined DOPDG applying Condition-Action rules [1]

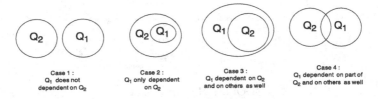

Fig. 3. Overlapping of data defined by Q_2 and used by Q_1

ℓ_1. Statement myStmt = DriverManager.getConnection("jdbc mysql: 200.210.220.1:1114/demo", "scott","tiger").createStatement();
ℓ_2. UPDATE t SET $a = a + 5$ WHERE a BETWEEN 20 AND 50;
ℓ_3. UPDATE t SET $a = a + 1$ WHERE a BETWEEN 10 AND 55;
ℓ_4. SELECT a FROM t WHERE a BETWEEN 10 AND 60;

(a) Program code P

id	a	b
1	10	5
2	50	9
3	30	15
4	20	40
5	60	30
6	70	10

(b) Table t

Fig. 4. Program P and database table t

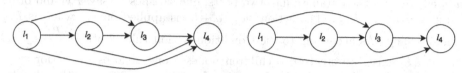

(a) Dependences by applying Condition-Action rules [1]

(b) More precise dependences

Fig. 5. Refinement failure by Condition-Action rules

ℓ_4 uses the values within the range 10 to 60 of 'a', no values defined by statement ℓ_2 can directly affect the observing range of ℓ_4, because ℓ_3 redefines the values. Therefore, the dependence $\ell_2 \xrightarrow{a} \ell_4$ does not exist. A more precise semantics based DOPDG is shown in Fig. 5(b).

2.2 Data-Centric Refinement of DOPDG

The proposed algorithm is based on data-centric approach to find dependences between database statements. The proposal consists of the following five phases: (i) Building of Action Tree, (ii) Computing traces, (iii) Backwards with pre-condition, (iv) Product of traces and observational-window, and (v) Identifying dependences. Let us describe in details each of the phases.

Building of Action Tree. Given a database statement Q, the abstract syntax is denoted by $Q = \langle A, \phi \rangle$ where A and ϕ denote the action-part and condition-part of Q respectively [1]. For instance, the query "SELECT b_1, b_2 FROM tab WHERE $b_3 \leq 30$" is denoted by $\langle A, \phi \rangle$ where A represents the action-part "SELECT b_1, b_2 FROM tab" and ϕ represents the conditional-part "$b_3 \leq 30$".

This phase is based on the partitioning of database states using condition-parts present in the defining database statements (*e.g.*, INSERT, DELETE and UPDATE). Given an application containing a set of defining database statements in an order, the partitioning of database information (in the same order) using the condition-parts generates a tree-like structure. We call it *Action Tree*. The nodes of the Action Tree denote actions involved in the defining statements, whereas edges are labeled with the conditions appearing in the condition-parts. The following example illustrates its construction in detail.

Example 4. Let us consider the program code P shown in Fig. 4(a). Analyzing the application, the sequence of definitions of attribute 'a' can be represented in a fixed order: $\ell_1 \to \ell_2 \to \ell_3$.

At program point ℓ_1, the statement acts as a defining statement for the values of all attributes in DB. We denote this definition as action part and this is represented by a child node "ℓ_1 : DB"connected with the root node by an edge. As there is no condition-part involved, the edge is labeled by "ℓ_1 : true".

Consider the next defining statement at ℓ_2. The condition-part "$\phi = 20 \le a \le 50$" divides the database into two parts: one satisfies ϕ (say, P_ϕ) and other satisfies $\neg\phi$ (say, $P_{\neg\phi}$). The action "$a = a + 5$" is applied on P_ϕ, whereas $P_{\neg\phi}$ remains same. As according to the Condition-Action rules, both $\ell_1 \xrightarrow{P_\phi} \ell_2$ and $\ell_1 \xrightarrow{P_{\neg\phi}} \ell_2$ exist, we create two children nodes – one denotes the action "ℓ_2 : $a' = a + 5$" (the edge labeled by ℓ_2 : ϕ *i.e.* ℓ_2 : $20 \le a \le 50$) and other denotes the action "ℓ_2 : $a' = a$ (the edge labeled by ℓ_2 : $\neg\phi$ *i.e.* ℓ_2 : $a < 20 \wedge a > 50$)[1]. Similar is done for the subsequent statement at ℓ_3 on the result just obtained.

Observe that as $\ell_2 \xrightarrow{P_{\neg\phi}} \ell_3$ (where $\neg\phi = a < 10 \wedge a > 55$) does not exist according to the Condition-Action rules, there is no child node corresponding to the action $a'' = a'$. The resulting Action Tree is depicted in Fig. 6.

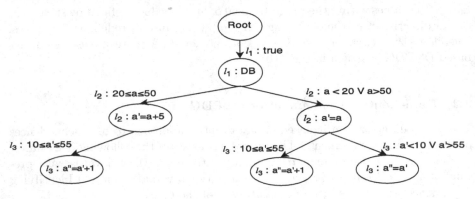

Fig. 6. Action tree of program code P

Computing Traces. A trace in an Action Tree is a sequence of labels from the root node to a leaf node. Given an Action Tree, we compute all traces from its root node to all leaves nodes.

Formally, a trace is defined as $\langle\, (\ell_i : \phi,\ \ell_i : A)\, \rangle_{i \ge 1}$ where $\phi \in \mathbb{W}$ (set of well-formed formulas) and $A \in \mathbb{A}$ (set of actions).

Example 5. Given the Action Tree in Fig. 6, the traces are:

$\tau_1 = (\ell_1 : true,\ \ell_1 : DB)(\ell_2 : 20 \le a \le 50,\ \ell_2 : a' = a + 5)(\ell_3 : 10 \le a' \le 55,\ \ell_3 : a'' = a' + 1)$

$\tau_2 = (\ell_1 : true,\ \ell_1 : DB)(\ell_2 : a < 20 \vee a > 50,\ \ell_2 : a' = a)(\ell_3 : 10 \le a' \le 55,\ \ell_3 : a'' = a' + 1)$

$\tau_3 = (\ell_1 : true,\ \ell_1 : DB)(\ell_2 : a < 20 \vee a > 50,\ \ell_2 : a' = a)(\ell_3 : a' < 10 \vee a' > 55,\ \ell_3 : a'' = a')$

---

[1] Note that we rename the attributes after an action is performed to distinguish the values before and after the action.

Backwards with Precondition. Hoare logic [5] is a deductive system whose axioms and rules of inference provide a method of proving statements of the form $\{P\}S\{Q\}$, where S is a program statement and P and Q are assertions about the values of variables. This is known as Hoare triple which means that Q (the "postcondition") holds in any state reached by executing S from an initial state in which P (the "precondition") holds. For instance, $\{j = 3 \wedge k = 4\}j :=$ $j + k\{j = 7 \wedge k = 4\}$.

As our objective is to find all semantics-based dependences for the use of an attribute on all previous definitions of it, we assume the condition-part of the used-statement as an observational-window (the viewing range). For instance, in the running example (Fig. 4), the observation window is the condition part of the used-statement at ℓ_4, *i.e.* $10 \leq a'' \leq 60$. Considering the observational-window as postcondition, we apply Hoare logic to compute weakest precondition at each program point appears before. Our aim is to determine the flow of definitions and to verify whether it affects the observational-window. Let us illustrate using running example.

Example 6. Consider the program P shown in Fig. 4. The observational-window is $(10 \leq a'' \leq 60)$ at ℓ_4. Let us denote it as $w_4 = \ell_4 : 10 \leq a'' \leq 60$. Applying Hoare logic, we get

$$\{w_1\}\,\ell_1 : \ DB\ \{w_2\}\,\ell_2 : \ a' = a + 5\ \{w_3\}\,\ell_3 : \ a'' = a' + 1\ \{w_4\}$$

where $w_3 = \ell_3 : \ 9 \leq a' \leq 59$, $w_2 = \ell_2 : \ 4 \leq a \leq 54$ and $w_1 = \ell_1 : \ 4 \leq a \leq 54$. This is depicted pictorially below:

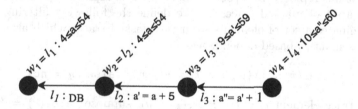

The sequence of these assertions forms an observational trace

$$\tau_o = w_1 w_2 w_3 w_4 = (\ell_1 : \ 4 \leq a \leq 54)(\ell_2 : \ 4 \leq a \leq 54)(\ell_3 : \ 9 \leq a' \leq 59)(\ell_4 : \ 10 \leq a'' \leq 60)$$

Formally, an observation trace is defined as $\langle\, (\ell_j : \phi)\, \rangle_{j \geq 1}$ where $\phi \in \mathbf{W}$ (set of well-formed formulas).

Product of Action-Tree Traces and Observational Trace. Given an action-tree trace τ and an observational trace τ_o, we perform production operation defined as: $\tau \times \tau_o = \langle\, (\ell_i : \phi',\ \ell_i : A')\, \rangle_{i \geq 1} \times \langle(\ell_j : \phi'')\rangle_{j \geq 1} = \langle\, (\ell_x : u,\ \ell_x : v)\rangle_{x \geq 1}$, where

$$(\ell_x : u, \, \ell_x : v) = \begin{cases} \text{if } \exists i, j: \; i = j \text{ and } \phi' \wedge \phi'' \neq \emptyset \\ \quad (\ell_i : \phi', \, \ell_i : A') \times (\ell_j : \phi'') = (\ell_i : \text{true}, \, \ell_i : A') \\[2ex] \text{if } \exists i, j: \; i = j \text{ and } \phi' \wedge \phi'' = \emptyset \\ \quad (\ell_i : \phi', \, \ell_i : A') \times (\ell_j : \phi'') = (\ell_i : \text{false}, \, \ell_i : A') \\[2ex] (\ell_j : \phi'', \, \ell_j : \text{observe}) \qquad \text{if } \not\exists i : \; j = i \end{cases}$$

Example 7. Consider the running example. The product of the action-tree traces (τ_1, τ_2, τ_3) and observational trace (τ_o) results the following:

Table 1. Product of action-tree traces and observational-window trace.

$\tau_1 \times \tau_o$	$(\ell_1 : \text{true}, \, \ell_1 : DB)(\ell_2 : \text{true}, \ell_2 : \; a' = a + 5)(\ell_3 : \text{true}, \ell_3 : \; a" = a' + 1)(\ell_4 : \; 10 \leq a" \leq 60, \ell_4 : \text{observe})$
$\tau_2 \times \tau_o$	$(\ell_1 : \text{true}, \, \ell_1 : DB)(\ell_2 : \text{true}, \ell_2 : \; a' = a)(\ell_3 : \text{true}, \ell_3 : \; a" = a' + 1)(\ell_4 : \; 10 \leq a" \leq 60, \ell_4 : \text{observe})$
$\tau_3 \times \tau_o$	$(\ell_1 : \text{true}, \, \ell_1 : DB)(\ell_2 : \text{true}, \ell_2 : \; a' = a)(\ell_3 : \text{true}, \ell_3 : \; a" = a')(\ell_4 : \; 10 \leq a" \leq 60, \ell_4 : \text{observe})$

Identifying Dependences. In this phase, a conversion of the traces is performed by masking the actions by either "**yes**" or "**no**". An action which may change states is replaced by "**yes**". Otherwise, it is replaced by "**no**".

Given a set of masked traces $\mathbb{T}$. We define the following filtering function which eliminates a set of elements from the masked traces which are irrelevant *w.r.t.* the semantics-based dependences:

$$\text{Filter}(\tau) = \tau \backslash \{(\ell_k : \; x, \ell_k : \; y) \mid x = \text{false} \vee y = \text{no}\} \tag{1}$$

Given a trace element $e = (\ell_k : \; x, \ell_k : \; y)$, suppose $\text{Label}(e) = k$ returns the label in e. The following function extracts the semantics-based dependences from the refined traces as follows:

$$\text{DEP}(\tau) = \text{DEP}(\langle e_1 e_2 e_3 \ldots \ldots e_n \rangle) = (\text{Label}(e_{n-1}) \rightarrow \text{Label}(e_n))$$

Example 8. In our running example, consider the set of traces obtained after performing product operation in Table 1. The set of masked traces is shown in Table 2(a). The result of applying **Filter** on the masked traces is shown in Table 2(b). Applying the function **DEP** on the filtered masked traces, we get the semantics-based dependences depicted in Table 2(c).

Table 2. Identifying semantics-based dependences

$\tau_1^m = (\ell_1 : \text{true}, \ell_1 : \text{yes})(\ell_2 : \text{true}, \ell_2 : \text{yes})(\ell_3 : \text{true}, \ell_3 : \text{yes})(\ell_4 : 10 \leq a'' \leq 60, \ell_4 : \text{observe})$
$\tau_2^m = (\ell_1 : \text{true}, \ell_1 : \text{yes})(\ell_2 : \text{true}, \ell_2 : \text{no})(\ell_3 : \text{true}, \ell_3 : \text{yes})(\ell_4 : 10 \leq a'' \leq 60, \ell_4 : \text{observe})$
$\tau_3^m = (\ell_1 : \text{true}, \ell_1 : \text{yes})(\ell_2 : \text{true}, \ell_2 : \text{no})(\ell_3 : \text{true}, \ell_3 : \text{no})(\ell_4 : 10 \leq a'' \leq 60, \ell_4 : \text{observe})$

(a) Masked traces

$\text{Filter}(\tau_1^m) = (\ell_1 : \text{true}, \ell_1 : \text{yes})(\ell_2 : \text{true}, \ell_2 : \text{yes})(\ell_3 : \text{true}, \ell_3 : \text{yes})(\ell_4 : 10 \leq a'' \leq 60, \ell_4 : \text{observe})$
$\text{Filter}(\tau_2^m) = (\ell_1 : \text{true}, \ell_1 : \text{yes})(\ell_3 : \text{true}, \ell_3 : \text{yes})(\ell_4 : 10 \leq a'' \leq 60, \ell_4 : \text{observe})$
$\text{Filter}(\tau_3^m) = (\ell_1 : \text{true}, \ell_1 : \text{yes})(\ell_4 : 10 \leq a'' \leq 60, \ell_4 : \text{observe})$

(b) Applying `Filter` on masked traces

$\text{DEP}(\text{Filter}(\tau_1^m))$	$\ell_3 \rightarrow \ell_4$
$\text{DEP}(\text{Filter}(\tau_2^m))$	$\ell_3 \rightarrow \ell_4$
$\text{DEP}(\text{Filter}(\tau_3^m))$	$\ell_1 \rightarrow \ell_4$

(c) Semantics-based dependences

3 Information Flow Security Analysis

In this section, we extend dependence graph-based information flow security analysis to the case of database applications. Given two nodes x and y in a DOPDG, a path $x \xrightarrow{*} y$ denotes that an information flows from x to y. If there is no such path, then there is no information flow.

As first step of the analysis to catch illegal flow of secure information, the attributes and program variables are assigned to various security levels according to their sensitivity. For simplicity, we assume only two security levels: *high* (for private attributes/variables which contain sensitive values) and *low* (for public attributes/variables which contain insensitive values). The finite set of security levels forms a complete lattice with partial order $\leq$ ($x \leq y$ represents x is of lower security level than that of y).

We consider a fine grained scenario where observers are able to see a part of values corresponding to the public attributes. Let us assume that the output statements (imperative or database statements) are considered as hotspots in database applications, *i.e.* the security levels of the variables in output statements are *low*. In order to find the possibility of information leakage, (i) we perform a refinement of DOPDG based on the observable range of the public attributes in the output statements, and then (ii) we compute a backward slice *w.r.t.* slicing criterion. Slicing criteria include a set of public attributes/variables along with the program point of the output statement. If an attribute or a variable presents in the slice with *high* security level, the analysis reports a possible information leakage.

Example 9. Let us consider the database application AP in Fig. 7(a) which interacts with a relational database whose schema is Customer(ID, CustName, Address, TransAmt, OfferAmt). Suppose the attributes ID, CustName, Address and OfferAmt have *low* security level, whereas TransAmt has *high* security level. The data-centric DOPDG of AP is shown in Fig. 7(b). The backward slicing of the DOPDG *w.r.t.* slicing criterion $c = \langle\ 35,\ \{\text{ID, CustName, OfferAmt}\}\rangle$ produces

1. Start;
2. $Identity = input( ), $AvailOffer=input( );
3. $PurchaseAmt = getPurchase( );
4. Statement myStmt=DriverManager.getConnection("jdbc mysql://.../demo","X","Y").createStatement();
5. ResultSet rs=myStmt.executeQuery("SELECT TransAmt, OfferAmt FROM Customer WHERE ID =$identity");
6. if($AvailOffer == "yes" and rs.OfferAmt > 200 and rs.TransAmt > 10000)
7. $discount = rs.OfferAmt * 0.02;
8. else if ($AvailOffer == "yes" and rs.OfferAmt > 200);
9. $discount = rs.OfferAmt * 0.01;
10. else $discount = 0;
11. $PurchaseAmt = $PurchaseAmt − $discount;
12. UPDATE Customer SET TransAmt = rs.TransAmt + $PurchaseAmt WHERE ID = $Identity;
13. if ($discount = = 0)
14.   UPDATE Customer SET OfferAmt = rs.OfferAmt + $PurchaseAmt WHERE ID=$Identity;
15. else UPDATE Customer SET OfferAmt = $PurchaseAmt WHERE ID = $Identity;
          -
          -
35. SELECT ID, CustName WHERE OfferAmt > 150 AND OfferAmt < 200;
36. Stop;

(a) Application Program AP

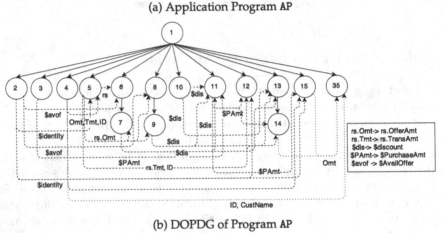

(b) DOPDG of Program AP

Fig. 7. Information flow analysis on DOPDG of AP.

following slice of the code: $BS(c) = \{4, 5, 6, 7, 11, 15\}$. As the result includes statement 5 which involves *high* variable "TransAmt", this means that there exists
a path $5 \xrightarrow{*} 35$ indicating a flow of secure information about "TransAmt" to the
output channel. Therefore, the program is not secure.

4   Complexity and Correctness

Complexity Analysis. The worst-case time complexity to construct action-tree,
assuming n defining statements for an attribute, is $O(2^n)$. Extending this for all
m attributes defined by the program, the worst-case time complexity is $O(m \times 2^n)$. Trace generation in the second phase can also be done during the first phase
while constructing the action-tree, reducing the extra computational overhead.
In the third phase, pre-condition computation based on the Hoare-logic uses

Theorem Prover which requires exponential time with respect to the length (say, l) of the conditions. However, we assume that database statements involve simple form of conditions which makes the analysis practically feasible. The time complexity of the remaining phases are linear, $O(n)$. Therefore, the overall worst-case time complexity of the proposed method is $O(m \times 2^n)$, assuming $l \ll n$.

Correctness. Let DB be the database state. Let $D \subseteq DB$ and $U \subseteq DB$ be the *defined* database-part (by statement S_d at program point l) and *used* database-part (by statement S_u at program point k) respectively. The correctness of the proposed method states that if $D \cap U = \emptyset$ then there is no dependence between S_d and S_u i.e. $l \nrightarrow k$. We prove this by contrapositive. Let us assume that the proposed method determines a dependence between S_d and S_u for attribute x, i.e., $l \xrightarrow{x} k$. This means that our method results a trace $t = e_1 e_2 \ldots e_{n-1} e_n$ such that $\mathrm{DEP}(t) = \mathrm{DEP}(e_1 e_2 e_3 \ldots \ldots e_{n-1} e_n) = \mathrm{Label}(e_{n-1}) \rightarrow \mathrm{Label}(e_n) = l \rightarrow k$ where $e_{n-1} = (l : \text{ true}, l : \text{ yes})$, $e_n = (k : \phi, k : \text{ observe})$ and ϕ is the observational-window. If we move backward along the phases of the proposed method, "true" and "yes" in e_{n-1} indicates the following: $\exists\, t_a \in$ action-tree traces and $\exists t_o \in$ observational-trace such that $\pi_l(t_a) \times \pi_l(t_o) = (\phi_a, A_a) \times (\phi_o) = (l : \text{ true}, l : A_a)$ where π_i is the projection operation of ith element from the trace, and $\phi_a \wedge \phi_o \neq \emptyset$. For $j > l$, $\pi_j(t_a) \times \pi_l(t_o) = (x, y)$ where either $x = $ "false" or $y = $ "no" or both, meaning that there is no re-definition of the part which is defined by S_d at l and is used later by S_u at k. Since $\phi_a \wedge \phi_o \neq \emptyset$, therefore $D \cap U \neq \emptyset$.

5   Conclusions and Future Plans

Computation of dependences in database applications is challenging than imperative programs, as variables consider a set of values instead of a single value. Dependence-graph based information flow analysis is a promising technique as it is flow-, context- and object-sensitive. As an extension to database applications, traditional DOPDG may act as flow-insensitive for database information and may give false alarm. Our proposed method is data-centric which reduces false dependences, leading to a more precise semantics-based analysis and covering more generic fine grained scenarios. Although the computational complexity is exponential, this can be reduced significantly by considering Binary Decision Diagram (BDD) as most of the nodes and edge-levels are repeated in the action-tree. This is our future aim. As the method is based on state space partitioning, this is comparable to the state explosion problem as in the case of model-checking. We are also investigating the possible use of abstraction to cope with such problems.

References

1. Baralis, E., Widom, J.: An algebraic approach to rule analysis in expert database systems. In: proceedings of VLDB (1994)
2. Cavadini, S.: Secure slices of insecure programs. In: Proceedings of the ACM Symposium on Information, Computer and Communications Security, pp. 112–122. ACM Press, Tokyo, Japan (2008)
3. Cortesi, A., Halder, R.: Information-flow analysis of hibernate query language. In: Dang, T.K., Wagner, R., Neuhold, E., Takizawa, M., Küng, J., Thoai, N. (eds.) FDSE 2014. LNCS, vol. 8860, pp. 262–274. Springer, Vietnam (2014)
4. Denning, D.E.: A lattice model of secure information flow. Commun. ACM 19(5), 236–243 (1976)
5. Dijkstra, E.W.: A Discipline of Programming, vol. 1. Prentice-hall, Englewood Cliffs (1976)
6. Dimitrova, R., Finkbeiner, B., Kovács, M., Rabe, M.N., Seidl, H.: Model checking information flow in reactive systems. In: Kuncak, V., Rybalchenko, A. (eds.) VMCAI 2012. LNCS, vol. 7148, pp. 169–185. Springer, Heidelberg (2012)
7. Ferrante, J., Ottenstein, K.J., Warren, J.D.: The program dependence graph and its use in optimization. ACM Trans. Program. Lang. Syst. (TOPLAS) 9(3), 319–349 (1987)
8. Halder, R., Zanioli, M., Cortesi, A.: Information leakage analysis of database query languages. In: Proceedings of SAC 2014, pp. 813–820. ACM (2014)
9. Hammer, C., Krinke, J., Snelting, G.: Information flow control for java based on path conditions in dependence graphs. In: IEEE International Symposium on Secure Software Engineering, pp. 87–96 (2006)
10. Hammer, C., Snelting, G.: Flow-sensitive, context-sensitive, and object-sensitive information flow control based on program dependence graphs. Int. J. Inf. Secur. 8(6), 399–422 (2009)
11. Joshi, R., Leino, K.R.M.: A semantic approach to secure information flow. Sci. Comput. Program. 37(1), 113–138 (2000)
12. Pottier, F., Simonet, V.: Information flow inference for ML. ACM Trans. Program. Lang. Syst. 25, 117–158 (2003)
13. Sabelfeld, A., Myers, A.C.: Language-based information-flow security. IEEE J. Sel. Areas Commun. 21(1), 5–19 (2003)
14. Smith, G.: Principles of secure information flow analysis. In: Christodorescu, M., Jha, S., Maughan, D., Song, D., Wang, C. (eds.) Malware Detection. AIS, vol. 27, pp. 291–307. Springer, Cambridge (2007)
15. Smith, G., Volpano, D.: Secure information flow in a multi-threaded imperative language. In: Proceedings of the POPL 1998, pp. 355–364. ACM (1998)
16. Taghdiri, M., Snelting, G., Sinz, C.: Information flow analysis via path condition refinement. In: Degano, P., Etalle, S., Guttman, J. (eds.) FAST 2010. LNCS, vol. 6561, pp. 65–79. Springer, Heidelberg (2011)
17. Willmor, D., Embury, S.M., Shao, J.: Program slicing in the presence of database state. In: Proceedings of the 20th IEEE International Conference on Software Maintenance, pp. 448–452. IEEE (2004)
18. Zanioli, M., Cortesi, A.: Information leakage analysis by abstract interpretation. In: Černá, I., Gyimóthy, T., Hromkovič, J., Jefferey, K., Královič, R., Vukolić, M., Wolf, S. (eds.) SOFSEM 2011. LNCS, vol. 6543, pp. 545–557. Springer, Heidelberg (2011)
19. Zanioli, M., Ferrara, P., Cortesi, A.: Sails: static analysis of information leakage with sample. In: Proceedings of the SAC 2012, pp. 1308–1313. ACM (2012)

Detection and Diagnosis of Hardware Trojan Using Power Analysis

Eknadh Vaddi, Karthik Gaddam, Rahul Karthik Maniam[(✉)],
Sai Abhishek Mallavajjala, Srinivasulu Dasari, and Nirmala Devi M.

Hardware Security Laboratory
Department of Electronics and Communication Engineering,
Amrita Vishwa Vidyapeetham, Coimbatore 641112, India
rahulkarthik2012@gmail.com

Abstract. Intended malicious modification in the integrated circuits is referred to as Hardware Trojans, which has emerged as major security threat. The earlier approach, to keep check to these threats, like logic testing also known as functional testing is proved to be no longer effective for detecting large sequential Trojans which are very rarely triggered. Side channel analysis has been an effective approach for detection of such large sequential Trojans but the increasing process variations and decreasing Trojan size resulted in the reduction of Trojan detection sensitivity using this approach. All these approaches also require golden IC. In this paper, we propose leakage power analysis approach which does not require golden IC and the issue of process variations does not affect the detection sensitivity.

Keywords: Hardware Trojan · Side channel analysis · Time based power · Leakage power · Golden IC

1 Introduction

Outsourcing the fabrication process may reduce cost but increases the threats to chip security. The possibility of Trojan insertion in an IC by third party vendors is more. Hardware Trojan leads to the degradation of system performance and results in the leakage of confidential information which becomes a serious threat to security concerned applications like military, space and defence [1]. This is unlike software threat (virus) which is well known and many techniques have been proposed (anti-virus) to counter those types of threats but this hardware threat to security is new and contemporary. In order to ensure trust over the third party IC, it has to be tested for Trojan free.

Hardware Trojans can be of two types: combinational and sequential [2]. Combinational Trojans are triggered by rare occurrence of logic values whereas sequential Trojans (Counters and shift registers) are triggered by rarely generated sequence. Combinational Trojans can be detected by logic testing as they can be made activated easily [3]. An intelligent adversary can inject Trojan in such a way that they turn up once in a million cycles. To detect such sequential Trojans logic testing can no longer be an effective approach [4]. Using the fact that Trojans also affect parameters like delay, power and current signatures, side channel approach is used to detect complex Trojans.

J.H. Abawajy et al. (Eds): SSCC 2015, CCIS 536, pp. 519–529, 2015.
DOI: 10.1007/978-3-319-22915-7_47

In this paper we deal with sequential Trojans so we use side channel approach. The side channel signals based on timing information, heat analysis and electromagnetic analysis are less sensitive in detecting sequential Trojans [5]. The side channel approach using power parameter is effective in detecting such sequential Trojans. In [6] differential power analysis is used but intra die and inter die process variations can mask the Trojan behaviour if the power difference is too small. In [7], Banga et al. proposed a technique which magnifies the power consumption difference by keeping the vector intact multiple times. Existing side channel approaches need the Golden IC in order to compare with CUTT (Circuit under Trojan test).

The Golden IC is obtained by destructive approach of ICs of same family which is difficult to obtain.In this paper we will overcome the need of Golden IC by time based leakage power analysis, constraining CUTT to combinational circuits and the Trojan to be of sequential type.

2   Previous Work

For a random input vector, total average power is calculated for the golden IC. Giving the same input vector to all the other ICs belonging to the same family, total average power is monitored. The existence of any power difference between golden IC and CUTT, it assures the presence of Trojan. The Trojan infected IC will have higher power than that of golden IC. This additional power is assumed to be consumed by the Trojan. If the Trojan affected CUTT is small circuit, it gives a good variation when compared to the golden IC. But when this method is applied to complex circuits, they give very small variation in the presence of Trojan which can possibly be masked by process variations. In this approach, both intra die and inter die process variations can mask the presence of Trojan. This problem can be easily overcome by segmentation [8] and by comparing the power of each segment of CUTT to that of the same segment from the golden IC [9]. This reduces the effect of process variations and increases the power variation in case of Trojan presence. We can make use of switching power by giving a vector pair as input to increase the power variation. But there are cases in which Trojan may not react to the random input vector pairs. Finally, the approach has two drawbacks:

(i)   Even for the Trojan free IC because of process variations, power measured for the same input pattern set will be different from that of golden IC.
(ii) Random input vector pairs may not generate transitions in hardware Trojans.

3   Motivation

The idea of this paper is originated from the example: c432 with 3bit counter as Trojan. ATPG patterns (stuck at faults) are generated for the circuit. The sequential Trojan shown in Fig. 1 is activated when 'pq' = 11 so that the output of AND gate is '1' and it needs to be toggled to run the counter.

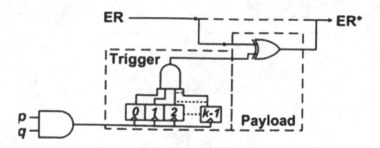

Fig. 1. Sequential Trojan

In order to toggle the input of counter, '*pq*' needs to be changed from 11 to 00, 01 or 10 (to make AND gate output '0').

The input vector pair is given continuously such that '*pq*' toggles between 11 and 00 (complemented form) which makes the counter run continuously.

Trojan activated vectors (like '*pq*' = 11) will be generated by ATPG considering only stuck at faults since to activate a sequential Trojan like 3 bit counter, it will be preceded by simple logic gates like AND, NAND, OR, NOR to which test patterns are generated for their rare occurrences (stuck at faults). Hence ATPG patterns are generated considering stuck at faults. It infers that at least one vector from the test set generated by ATPG will definitely trigger the sequential Trojan. Similar Trojan as in Fig. 1 but 3 bit counter is inserted in c432 and ATPG patterns for the circuit are grouped into vector pairs. If the Trojan activated vector pair is given multiple times, then the time based power profile of Trojan infected IC looks like in the Fig. 2(a). The highlighted portion in the plot shows abnormal variations. These variations in the graph from time to time even if the same vector pair is repeated multiple times is due to the presence of counter (sequential). But these variations become difficult to notice when dealing with complex circuits. This methodology avoids the need for golden IC and also mitigates the effect of process variations. The only limitation is that it becomes difficult to observe the variation since the power that changes will be in μW which becomes quite negligible when compared to the total power which will be usually in mW for complex circuits.

4 Methodology

The proposed approach is organized in two steps.

(1) To detect the presence of HT in the CUTT.
(2) To determine the Trojan prone gates

4.1 Trojan Detection

In this step, ATPG test patterns for CUTT are generated considering stuck at faults. Each test vector, from the ATPG test set, along with its complemented form is considered as a vector pair. This complementary test vector pair is given multiple times to

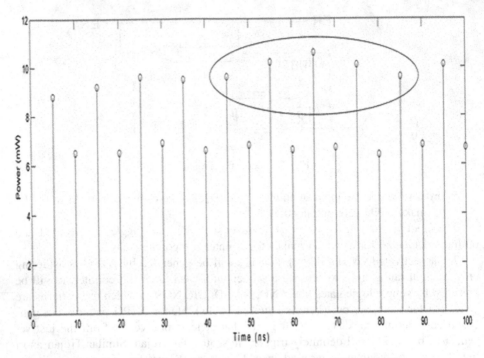

Fig. 2. (a) Time based power profile of Trojan infected c432

make the sequential Trojan active by keeping the rest of the circuit to toggle in a known manner. Each test vector in test set is applied similarly in complementary manner. Instantaneous power profile of CUTT is generated for each applied test vector pair. The obtained power profile is observed for all the test patterns. If the plot has abnormally drastic variations as shown in Fig. 2(a), it can be concluded that the CUTT is most likely affected with sequential Trojan. These variations in plot are due to the influence of sequential Trojan like counter.

The time based power plot of the Trojan free circuit when test set is applied in complementary manner multiple times looks like Fig. 2(b). For complex circuits (having more number of gates), the power may not vary too much. This behaviour is because the switching of the output of payload occurs once in many cycles and hence the contribution of Trojan towards switching power is less. Time based power analysis takes total power into consideration which would be in μW and change in power contributed by Trojan would be in nW which is really negligible. Hence time based power analysis is effective only for smaller circuits.

Considering the fact that an additional circuit changes the total leakage power of CUTT and also since the leakage power is dependent on input vector, we find leakage power for each vector pair given multiple times n_1, n_2, n_3. If the leakage power is same for all the three cases n_1, n_2 and n_3 then we can conclude that there is no Trojan or Trojan is not in activated state. The logic here is that if the Trojan is activated by any vector pair, then the leakage power changes continuously as the input of payload (output of counter) changes continuously.

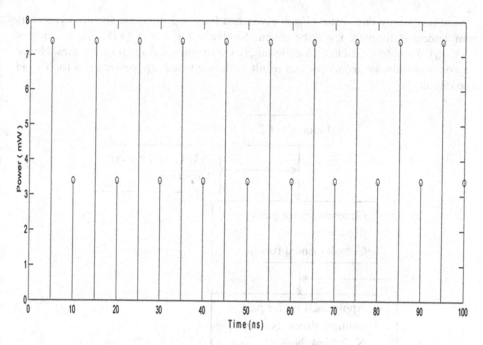

Fig. 2.   (b) Time based power profile of Trojan free c432

The leakage power is calculated by repeating the same vector pair multiple times like n = 2, 4, 6, 8 or n = 3, 6, 9, 12 or n = 5, 10, 15.... The reason for choosing this sequences is since we are calculating average leakage power with two test vectors (complementary pair) given multiple times continuously, even for Trojan free circuit, the average leakage power would be different if we calculate for n = 1, 2. Because in case of n = 1 only one vector (V_1) is given and for n = 2, both the vector (V_1) and its complemented form (V_2) will be given. Similarly for n = 3 ($V_1V_2V_1$), for n = 4 ($V_1V_2V_1V_2$) and so on. In that case, definitely the average leakage power varies. Hence we consider only the sequences that result in the same leakage power even for Trojan free circuit.

Considering the fact that an additional circuit changes the total leakage power of CUTT and also since the leakage power is dependent on input vector, we find leakage power for each vector pair given multiple times n_1, n_2, n_3. If the leakage power is same for all the three cases n_1, n_2 and n_3 then we can conclude that there is no Trojan or Trojan is not in activated state. The logic here is that if the Trojan is activated by any vector pair, then the leakage power changes continuously as the input of payload (output of counter) changes continuously.

The leakage power is calculated by repeating the same vector pair multiple times like n = 2, 4, 6, 8 or n = 3, 6, 9, 12 or n = 5, 10, 15.... The reason for choosing this sequences is since we are calculating average leakage power with two test vectors (complementary pair) given multiple times continuously, even for Trojan free circuit, the average leakage power would be different if we calculate for n = 1, 2. Because in case of n = 1 only one vector (V_1) is given and for n = 2, both the vector (V_1) and its complemented form (V_2) will be given. Similarly for n = 3 ($V_1V_2V_1$), for n = 4 ($V_1V_2V_1V_2$) and so on. In that case, definitely the average leakage power varies. Hence we consider only the sequences that result in the same leakage power even for Trojan free circuit (Fig. 3).

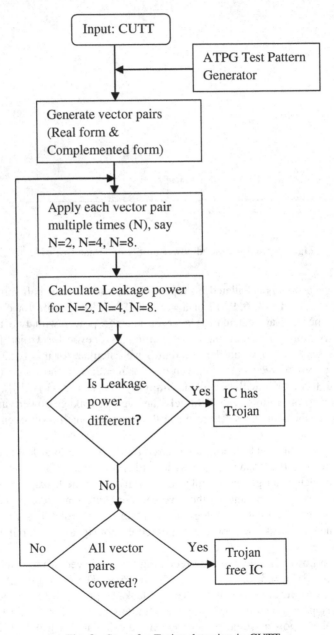

Fig. 3. Steps for Trojan detection in CUTT

The change in the leakage power indicates the presence of Trojan. The process is repeated for all the test patterns in the test set. If the leakage power is not varying for all the test patterns, then the circuit is Trojan free. Since there comes no process variations in the picture, even small change in power is also detectable increasing the detection sensitivity.

4.2   Trojan Diagnosis

If the CUTT is found to be Trojan affected, diagnosis is to be done to determine the segment in which Trojan is present in the circuit. All the nets in the circuit is determined and the test pattern for which the CUTT has shown aberrant behaviour in step 1 is given in complementary manner but multiple times (>1000). Simulation is done to check the unexpected toggles in the nodes and the nodes toggled in unusual manner are determined. The expected toggling could be one of these like..101010101....or...010101010...or 111111111...or...00000000. The unexpected toggling at Trojan affected nodes could be like 0101101010 or 1010110101 or 11111101111 or 0000010000... The gates corresponding to those abnormally toggled nodes are listed to be as Trojan prone gates.

5   Results

ISCAS'85 benchmark circuits have been chosen to validate our proposed methodology in detecting hardware Trojan. Three types of sequential Trojans are introduced into three benchmark circuits: c432, c1355, and c2670. Figure 3(a) shows the plot of time-based power analysis for c17 for the Trojan activated vector pair. The variations in the plot indicate the presence of sequential Trojan. Similar power profiles are plotted for all the ATPG test patterns using 90 nm technology. For the other vector pairs to which the Trojan is in dormant state, the plots are shown in Fig. 2(b). In time-based power analysis, energy for every event is calculated and it is distributed over specific time interval. In that way instantaneous power can be obtained for every clock cycle.

For the Trojan free combinational circuit, when this power profile is plotted, instantaneous power is expected to toggle between two values for the complementary vector pair given multiple times. As per the proposed technique, the variations in Fig. 2 (a) reflect the Trojan presence. The proposed leakage power analysis method is applied for some Trojan inserted benchmark circuits and checked for validation of our approach and the results are as shown in Tables 1, 2 and 3.

For c1355 nodes G_{29}, G_{30}, G_{34} are connected to a 3 input AND gate to trigger the 3 bit-counter which is made to affect the output node G_{657} only when counter output is 111. From Table 3, the patterns 1, 6, 8, 9, 10 triggered the Trojan where G_{29} G_{30} G_{34} must be either 111 or 000. Similarly for c432 Trojan is triggered when 'N_1N_4' is either 11 or 00. In the case of c2670 the triggering will occur when '$N_{95}N_{130}$' is either 11or 00.

All these Trojan affected benchmark circuits are diagnosed as per the step 2 in methodology. The unexpected toggling of Trojan affected nodes is to be observed.

Table 1. Leakage power for c432 when ATPG test patterns given multiple times

ATPG patterns for c432	N = 2 (μW)	N = 4 (μW)	N = 8 (μW)	Is Trojan activated?
1	3.430	3.466	3.476	Yes
2	3.365	3.366	3.365	No
3	3.335	3.334	3.335	No
4	3.418	3.455	3.465	Yes
5	3.418	3.455	3.465	Yes
6	3.403	3.439	3.452	Yes
7	3.400	3.437	3.450	Yes
8	3.365	3.366	3.265	No
9	3.362	3.362	3.362	No
10	3.418	3.454	3.468	Yes

Table 2. Leakage power for c2670 when ATPG test patterns given multiple times

ATPG patterns For c2670	N = 2 (10^{-05} W)	N = 4 (10^{-05} W)	N = 8 (10^{-05} W)	Is Trojan activated?
1	1.218	1.217	1.217	No
2	1.226	1.227	1.228	No
3	1.215	1.218	1.220	Yes
4	1.228	1.229	1.230	No
5	1.225	1.226	1.227	No
6	1.232	1.233	1.234	No
7	1.219	1.222	1.224	Yes
8	1.223	1.224	1.224	No
9	1.224	1.225	1.226	No
10	1.221	1.224	1.226	Yes

Table 3. Leakage power for c1355 when ATPG test patterns given multiple times

ATPG patterns for c1355	N = 2 (μW)	N = 4 (μW)	N = 8 (μW)	Is Trojan activated?
1	9.632	9.624	9.610	Yes
2	9.624	9.625	9.624	No
3	9.629	9.630	9.630	No
4	9.625	9.625	9.624	No
5	9.629	9.630	9.630	No
6	9.634	9.623	9.617	Yes
7	9.624	9.623	9.624	No
8	9.627	9.621	9.619	Yes
9	9.627	9.621	9.619	Yes
10	9.632	9.626	9.610	Yes

For each CUTT, the Trojan activated vector pairs are noted from the results table. All the nodes in the CUTT are noted and their toggling is observed by applying the Trojan activated vector pair multiple times.

For the Trojan activated vector pair when repeated multiple times the following nodes $G_{657}, s, t, out, x_1, x_2$ show anomalous toggling as shown in Fig. 4(a). The highlighted part shows that the output node G_{657} is affected by Trojan and its value changes for every eighth cycle (3 bit counter). Hence the gates connected to these nodes in c432 are listed to be Trojan prone gates. Similarly, in Fig. 4(b) the nodes N_{432}, x_1, x_2 and x_3 toggle abnormally.

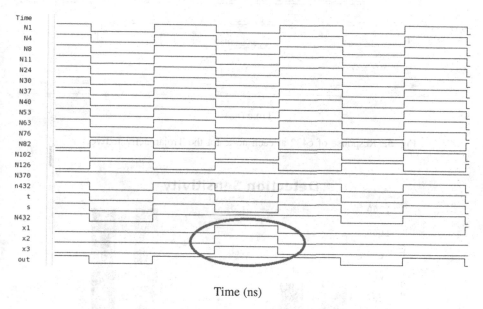

Time (ns)

Fig. 4. Response of c1355 at each node for the Trojan activated vector

The gate count of the Trojan inserted circuits c432, c1355 and c2670 is calculated to ensure that the proposed approach is effective in detecting even smaller Trojans which is reflected in the Fig. 5.

Detection sensitivity = ((Gate count of CUTT- Gate count of Golden IC)/ (Gate count of Golden IC))*100

For c432, detection sensitivity = ((167−160)/160)*100 = 4.375
For c1355, detection sensitivity = ((552−546)/546)*100 = 1.0989
For c2670, detection sensitivity = ((1197−1193)/1193)*100 = 0.3352

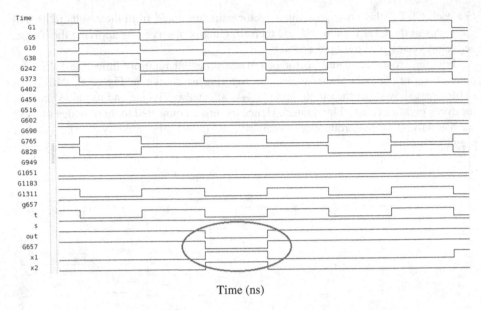

Fig. 5. Response of c432 at each node for the Trojan activated vector

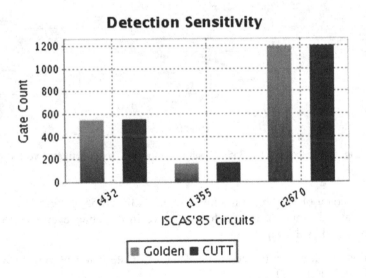

Fig. 6. Detection sensitivity of the proposed approach

6 Conclusion

We have presented a methodology based on leakage power which is very effective in detecting sequential Trojans in combinational circuits. Detecting sequential Trojans had been a herculean task which now has become simple with this approach. In earlier approaches the Trojan detection had been sensitive to many factors like process variations, Trojan size and requirement of golden IC. As Trojan size decreases power variation can easily be masked by process variations. Many proposed techniques required golden IC which is very difficult to obtain. The proposed side channel analysis approach based on leakage power avoids the need of golden IC and mitigates the effect of process variations. Detection sensitivity remains same and will not be reduced by any factor like Trojan size or process variations.

This approach has many advantages like no need of golden IC, no problem of process variations and can detect Trojan of any size. This work helps the further researchers to extend the detection technique to all types of hardware Trojans without the need of golden IC. Instead of using average power analysis considering total power of the circuit, leakage power analysis can be taken into account in all the earlier proposed approaches. This helps in increasing the detection range and detection sensitivity of all the techniques which uses power as a side channel parameter in detecting hardware Trojans.

References

1. Narasimhan, S., et al.: Hardware Trojan detection by multiple-parameter side-channel analysis. IEEE Trans. Comput. **62**(11), 2183–2195 (2013)
2. Mukhopadhyay, D., Chakraborty, R.S.: Hardware Trojans. In: Hardware Security: Design, Threats and Safeguards, 4th edn., Chap. 5, Sect. 1, pp. 341–345. CRC Press (2014)
3. Tehranipoor, M., Koushanfar, F.: A survey of hardware Trojan taxonomy and detection. IEEE Des. Test Comput. **27**(1), 10–25 (2010)
4. Chakraborty, R.S., Narasimhan, S., Bhunia, S.: Hardware Trojan: threats and emerging solutions. In: Proceedings of the IEEE International High Level Design Validation Test Workshop, pp. 166–171 (2009)
5. Rad, R., Plusquellic, J., Tehranipoor, M.: A sensitivity analysis of power signal methods for detecting hardware Trojans under real process and environmental conditions. IEEE TVLSI (2010)
6. Bhunia, S., et al.: Hardware Trojan attacks: threat analysis and countermeasures. IEEE Des. Test Comput. **102**, 1229–1247 (2014). Version 8
7. Banga, M., Hsiao, M.: A novel sustained vector technique for the detection of hardware Trojans. In: Proceedings of the 22nd International Conference on VLSI Design, pp. 327–332 (2009)
8. Dinesh Kumar, K., Mohan Kumar, N.: Malicious combinational hardware Trojan detection by gate level characterization in 90 nm technology. In: Proceedings of 5th International Conference on Computing, Communication and Networking Technologies (ICCCNT), China (2014)
9. Du, D., Narasimhan, S., Chakraborty, R.S., Bhunia, S.: Self-referencing: a scalable side-channel approach for hardware Trojan detection. In: Proceedings of the 12th International Conference on Cryptographic Hardware Embedded Systems Workshop, pp. 173–187 (2010)

A Low Overhead Prevention of Android WebView Abuse Attacks

Jamsheed K.(✉) and Praveen K.

TIFAC CORE in Cyber Security, Amrita Vishwa Vidyapeetham, Coimbatore, India
mail@jamsheed.me, praveen.cys@gmail.com

Abstract. WebView, an Android component to load and display web content, has become the center of attraction for attackers as its use increases with the increased trend of hybrid application development. The attackers mainly concentrate on abusing the JavaScript interface and accessing the native code. Since most of the developers do not go for HTTPS secure connections to decrease processing overhead, injection attacks becomes easy. The attacker looks for the JavaScript interface implementation in well known libraries like ad-provider libraries or hybrid application wrapper libraries and try to inject code that uses them. This paper presents a low overhead solution to use public key cryptography for ensuring integrity over data transferred and thus prevent such attacks.

1 Introduction

Android dominates the smartphone market by 76.6 % of smartphone sales in Q4 2014 [1]. Due to this, Android is the most targeted platform by cyber criminals. It is also harder to release patches for everyone because most of the devices does not run pure Android, but vendor modified version of it, and most of the time the vendor does not take the effort to deliver the patch to their users. A recent example is the Android Webview vulnerability, and the Google's decision to leave Android version 4.3 and former ones unpatched for the same reason.

WebView is an Android component that enables applications to embed web content in them. They are being used to create a full fledged application developed in web languages, which is commonly referred to as hybrid application development. It is also used by ad providers like inMobi to serve the advertisements. Android also provides the option for the content inside WebView to communicate with the native code using a JavaScript interface. Attackers try to modify the content that is to be loaded into the WebView to run malicious code or to access data through these open JavaScript interfaces.

2 WebView and Attacks

Android's WebView class, an extension of View class enables developers to show web content inside a native app. A native app makes use of a WebView to load

© Springer International Publishing Switzerland 2015
J.H. Abawajy et al. (Eds): SSCC 2015, CCIS 536, pp. 530–537, 2015.
DOI: 10.1007/978-3-319-22915-7_48

data that is frequently changed but does not want to update the application to deliver it to the user, like a End User License Agreement, as showing an older version of it may lead to problems. If a webview is used, irrespective of the version of the application, the same content will be fetched over the internet and shown to the user. This way the content will always be updated. In hybrid application development, the whole application is developed as a web application and is packaged as a native app. The native code launches a WebView at app start and shows the home page. If the web code wants access to some native components like camera or contacts, it does so through a JavaScript interface defined. There are frameworks like Phonegap and Appcelerator Titanium that provides users with predefined JavaScript interfaces that can be readily accessed from the WebView. Other popular use of WebView is by ad providers like inMobi, to load ads over the internet. Research shows that inMobi opens security vulnerabilities as they send data via HTTP, not HTTPS and this enables attackers to inject code which abuses the open JavaScript interfaces defined in the inMobi library like createCalendarEvent, makeCall, postToSocial, sendMail, sendSMS, takeCameraPicture, getGalleryImage, and registerMicListener. inMobi fixed it by adding user confirmation before doing any of the stuff mentioned above, but similar vulnerabilities exist in many of the applications using WebViews and JavaScript interfaces.

A WebView is declared as follows.

```
WebView myWebView = (WebView) findViewById(R.id.webview);
WebSettings webSettings = myWebView.getSettings();
webSettings.setJavaScriptEnabled(true);
```

The last line enables the execution of javascript inside the WebView. If WebView wants to invoke a Toast message, a JavaScript interface can be defined as follows.

```
public class WebAppInterface {
    Context mContext;

    /** Instantiate the interface and set the context */
    WebAppInterface(Context c) {
        mContext = c;
    }

    /** Show a toast from the web page */
    @JavascriptInterface
    public void showToast(String toast) {
        Toast.makeText(mContext, toast, Toast.LENGTH_SHORT)
        .show();
    }
}
```

Then, for the WebView to use the JavaScript interface, we have to add the interface to it.

```
webView.addJavascriptInterface(new WebAppInterface(this),
''Android'');
```

Now from the WebView, the interface can be invoked, like this.

```
Android.showToast(''Hello World!'');
```

The problem here is that, JavaScript access the native code by the name defined, in the above case, "Android". An attacker could either extract a packaged application and look for such interface names, which clearly appears in the script. What is even worse is that, applications that use frameworks like Phonegap which are well documented on how to access these interfaces are more vulnerable. Attacker could easily inject malicious JavaScript that access these interfaces as the attacker knows the interface names without any kind of reversing. Even if the interfaces are not defined, attacker could snoop the HTTP traffic and understand them.

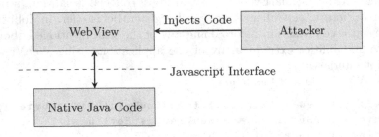

Fig. 1. Attack methodology

Figure 1 illustrates how most attacks happen. An attacker who could intercept the traffic poses as the server and serves malicious code, mostly javascript that abuses the javascript interface defined in the application to execute native code.

3   Related Works

There are several works related to WebViews on Android and the attacks related to them. Luo, et al. [5] explains about the various attacks possible in Android WebView, and does a statistical study on what applications are vulnerable to the attacks. The works provides us with an insight to the various types of attacks WebViews opens up to, and also introduces some new attacks. It also does a study on the usage of WebViews in applications and which category of applications do most of the vulnerable applications belongs to. It says says the attacks are a fundamental problem caused by the weakening the Trusted Computing Base and the Sandbox. Neugschwandtner et al. [6] also categorizes the WebView attacks and does a large scale evaluation of the threat map. Their work shows that about 25 % of applications that use WebViews have a simple implementation and uses non encrypted HTTP traffic and thus are vulnerable. They take into consideration the attacks due to Server compromise and traffic compromise. The work done by Chin et al. [3] is also on the same lines, finding and categorizing WebView vulnerabilities. They perform analysis based on a tool they created called the"Bifocals" and does a study on a set of apps for WebView vulnerabilities. They found that about 55 % of the applications in their test set that uses a WebView uses non encrypted HTTP traffic. They also measure the prevalence and impact of vulnerable WebViews, and suggest methods to mitigate the vulnerabilities. But the methods suggested are not effective enough or is restrictive compared to the normal usage of WebViews.

Stevens et al. [7] works on investigating user privacy on Android ad libraries and finds that failure to protect the integrity of the content transferred from the server to WebView is the main cause of the attacks. It also infers that most of the ad libraries implement a javascript interface and expose dangerous methods which an attacker could make use. Some of these interfaces enables sending of SMS, emails, getting contact information, modify users calender etc. They also obeserved that a lot of private data is being leaked due to careless design and implementation of libraries. The work by Wu et al. [9] shows how WebView vulnerabilities can be used to access users private files. They design an automated system to dynamically test 115 browser apps collected from Google Play and find that 64 of them are vulnerable to the attacks. Among them are the popular Firefox, Baidu and Maxthon browsers, and the more application-specific ones, including UC Browser HD for tablet users, Wikipedia Browser, and Kids Safe Browser. A detailed analysis of these browsers further shows that 26 browsers (23 %) expose their browsing interfaces unintentionally.There are many other researches [2,4,8,10] that does a comprehensive study or related attacks on an Android system.

4   Proposed System

All the studies have shown that the biggest reason for JavaScript abuse attacks are the use of insecure HTTP connections instead of HTTPS connection. A simple solution for the problem would be to use HTTPS connections. But this would cause a computational and network overhead as it requires a more complex connection establishment phase with key agreement in contrast to a normal HTTP connection. Further, getting an SSL certificate from a trusted certificate authority incurs recurring costs to the developer. Thus developers opt for an unsecured HTTP connection rather than a secure HTTPS connection.

This paper proposes an alternative to the scenario that would avoid JavaScript abuse attacks on WebViews. It proposes a technique where one could use public key cryptography to verify the integrity of the data transmitted. The key used in this methodology can be self generated and thus incur no additional costs to the development process. Keys could be generated using libraries like openssl. The example shows uses a 2048 bit RSA key generated using openssl.

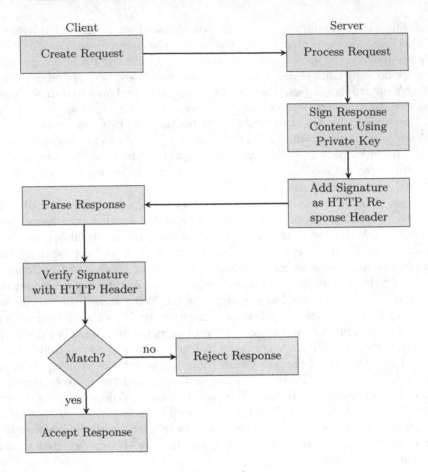

Fig. 2. Proposed system

Figure 2 illustrates the solution in which a public private key pair is used. The public key is packaged with the android application. The private key should be held securely in the web server. Every HTTP response should be signed using the private key by the server and is set as a custom HTTP header. The client on receiving the response, checks the header and verifies the signature using the public key packaged in the application. Further processing is done only if the verification is successful. This could be achieved by modifying JavaScript libraries like jQuery to callback an error if verification fails. Thus any code injection will be detected and the response will be discarded. The solution tries to protect the integrity, not the confidentiality of the data transmitted. This makes sense in cases where the confidentiality does not matter, for example, for ad networks to transmit their ads to the user. What matters is to avoid execution of any injected code in the response. The solution guarantees that.

4.1   Dealing with Attacks

The proposed system as such is viable to replay attacks. A smart attacker could get a malicious response signed and replay it for any client request and thus successfully attack the client device. The malicious code could override the script that verifies the signature and the attacker could now pose as the server and interact with the client as client now imposes no security measures. To avoid this, we could make slight changes in the system. Client could attach a request identifier with the request, and keep on incrementing it for every request. Response signature will also include that identifier making replay attacks harder. Request identified could also be generated randomly. Still, attacker could replay already captured responses with same request ids. The best option for the client would be to use UTC timestamp as the request identifier. This would be unique and the attacker cannot successfully replay packets as a timestamp would not repeat.

5   Result and Discussion

To study how the proposed solution fares compared to a normal HTTP or an HTTPS implementation, it was implemented on a node.js server and the results were observed. 2048 bit RSA keys were generated using the OpenSSL tool and used in the server for HTTPS transmission and for signing the message in our proposed solution. The server was benchmarked using Apache bench under varying conditions like number of requests, HTTP Keep Alive enabled and disabled and varying response length.

Average statistics for 10000 requests tested against the server with basic HTTP, HTTPS (with TLSv1.2, AES256-GCM-SHA384, 2048, 256 protocol), and our proposed solution with a 2048 bit RSA key is described below. In Table 1 we use the same response of all the requests.

Table 1. Statistics under fixed response length

	Time per request (ms)	Requests per second	Connection time (ms)
HTTP	0.755	1324.05	1.5
HTTPS	5.899	169.51	7.5
Proposed Scheme	4.187	238.84	4.7

Here it is observed that non encrypted HTTP traffic is atleast 3 times better than our method. Still our method fairs better than the HTTPS scheme in terms of performance overhead. But real life schemes are different than this, response length is substantially bigger than these tests and thus statistics may vary very much. To mimic a real life server behavior, we used different responses for different requests and the results were observed (Table 2).

Under variable response length we can see that there is no huge overhead between our method and non encrypted HTTP, whereas HTTPS is atleast 2.3

Table 2. Statistics under variable response length

	Time per request (ms)	Requests per second	Connection time (ms)
HTTP	4.450	224.74	4.8
HTTPS	10.715	93.33	12.5
Proposed Scheme	6.442	155.22	6.8

time slower than HTTP. This shows that, the proposed method will fare better in real life situations.

Figure 3 shows the average time taken to serve a request. It is about 40 % more efficient than using HTTPS scheme. Similarly, considering requests processed per second, the scheme is 1.6 times better than HTTPS and considering connection time, it is about 2 times better than HTTPS. Our scheme incurs substantial overhead over HTTP, but it is observably better than HTTPS and protects the integrity of the message.

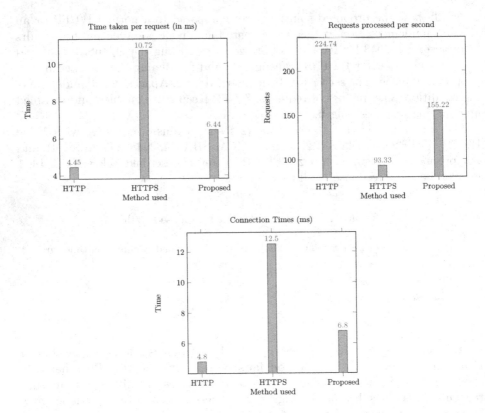

Fig. 3. Comparison of methods under variable response lengths

6   Conclusion

The solution proposed by the paper is not as secure as HTTPS, but it guarantees integrity of the transmitted content. Thus even if the attacker manage to modify the content and inject code, it would be rejected and will not be executed. The statistics observed show that this is better way for developers looking for a way with a performance overhead lower than HTTPS. While it does not prevent passive attacks like snooping, it is a good solution for purposes such as advertisement networks where confidentiality of the data transmitted does not matter.

References

1. Worldwide quarterly mobile phone tracker. Technical report, Q4 (2014)
2. Becher, M., Freiling, F.C., Hoffmann, J., Holz, T., Uellenbeck, S., Wolf, C.: Mobile security catching up? revealing the nuts and bolts of the security of mobile devices. In: IEEE Symposium on Security and Privacy, SP 2011, pp. 96–111. IEEE (2011)
3. Chin, E., Wagner, D.: Bifocals: analyzing webview vulnerabilities in android applications. In: Kim, Y., Lee, H., Perrig, A. (eds.) WISA 2013. LNCS, vol. 8267, pp. 138–159. Springer, Heidelberg (2014)
4. Fahl, S., Harbach, M., Muders, T., Baumgärtner, L., Freisleben, B., Smith, M.: Why eve and mallory love android: an analysis of android ssl (in) security. In: Proceedings of the 2012 ACM Conference on Computer and Communications Security, pp. 50–61. ACM (2012)
5. Luo, T., Hao, H., Du, W., Wang, Y., Yin, H.: Attacks on webview in the android system. In: Proceedings of the 27th Annual Computer Security Applications Conference, pp. 343–352. ACM (2011)
6. Neugschwandtner, M., Lindorfer, M., Platzer, C.: Webview exploitation. In: LEET A view to a kill (2013)
7. Stevens, R., Gibler, C., Crussell, J., Erickson, J., Chen, H.: Investigating user privacy in android ad libraries. In: Workshop on Mobile Security Technologies (MoST). Citeseer (2012)
8. Vidas, T., Votipka, D., Christin, N.: All your droid are belong to us: a survey of current android attacks. In: WOOT, pp. 81–90 (2011)
9. Wu, D., Chang, R.K.C.: Analyzing Android Browser Apps for file:// Vulnerabilities. In: Chow, S.S.M., Camenisch, J., Hui, L.C.K., Yiu, S.M. (eds.) ISC 2014. LNCS, vol. 8783, pp. 345–363. Springer, Heidelberg (2014)
10. Zhou, Y., Jiang, X.:. Dissecting android malware: characterization and evolution. In: IEEE Symposium on Security and Privacy, SP 2012, pp. 95–109. IEEE (2012)

An Automata Based Approach
for the Prevention of NoSQL Injections

Swathy Joseph[✉] and K.P. Jevitha

Department of Computer Science, Amrita School of Engineering,
Amrita Vishwa Vidyapeetham, Coimbatore, Tamil Nadu, India
swathyjoseph90@gmail.com, kp_jevitha@cb.amrita.edu

Abstract. The eminent web-applications of today are data-intensive. The data generated is of the order of petabytes and zetabytes. Using relational databases for storing them only complicates the storage and retrieval in the DB and degradation of its performance. The big data explosion demanded the need for a more flexible, high-performance storage concept the NoSQL movement. The NoSQL databases were designed to overcome the flaws of the relational databases including the security aspects. The effective performance and efficient storage criteria were satisfied by the non-relational databases. The attackers, as usual found their way into the NoSQL databases that were considered to be secure. The injection attacks, one of the top-listed attack type of the relational databases poses threat to the non-relational databases as well. MongoDB is one of the prominent NoSQL databases to which the application development trends are shifting. In this paper, we present the different injection attacks on the leading NoSQL database and an automata based detection and prevention technique for this attack. We also evaluate the effectiveness on different subjects with a number of legitimate as well as illegitimate inputs. Our results show that our approach was able to detect all the attacks.

Keywords: NoSQL injections · MongoDB · JSA · Automaton

1 Introduction

More than 75 % of world's total data has been produced within the last few years. The popularity of the social networking sites and the quest for research accounts for most of the data. Facebook alone produces terabytes of data on average per day. The scientific data produced as a result of subatomic particles-collision experiments are also in the range of terabytes per minute. To facilitate the storage of this challenging amount of data, we need some scalable, high-performance and flexible scheme. This need led to the idea of NoSQL databases. Currently there are over 150 NoSQL [1] flavors for us to choose from and each of them uses a different query language. The NoSQL databases are non-relational, easily replicated, distributed, open-source, schema-free and horizontally scalable. The injection is a method by which the attacker executes or injects his intended query on the backend database by manipulating the input to it. They inject queries through the points of interaction between the user and the database in such a way that syntactically valid query will be passed to the database. Unlike in relational

© Springer International Publishing Switzerland 2015
J.H. Abawajy et al. (Eds): SSCC 2015, CCIS 536, pp. 538–546, 2015.
DOI: 10.1007/978-3-319-22915-7_49

databases, there are no standard injection techniques that are applicable in common to all the NoSQL members. A few of the NoSQL databases use JSON and/or JavaScript for querying. There are also NoSQL databases that use their own query languages, e.g. CQL of Cassandra. But the fact is that, even with all these, the data security is still a matter of concern for the NoSQL family as it was for the SQL group.

The rest of this paper is structured as follows. In the next section, we present the related works. In Sect. 3 we give a brief introduction to MongoDB injection attacks and in the next section we mention our approach. In Sect. 5, we give a detailed description of our work. Section 6 presents the result and analysis and in Sect. 7 we conclude.

2 Related Works

Server-Side JavaScript Injection [2] is a work presented by Bryan Sullivan of Adobe labs, in BlackHat 2011. The NoSQL databases were crafted very carefully keeping in mind the security issues in relational databases. For a very long time, it was supposed that no injections were possible on them. However, this paper proved all of them wrong and showed that injections were possible on NoSQL databases also. The work is based on MongoDB and shows that MongoDB can be injected using time-based and boolean based blind techniques. The database can be put on hold as in the relational databases using JavaScript functions. Similarly the different methods provided by mongoDB for finding the details and for easy operation is used to exploit the database.

AMNESIA [3] is a model-based approach for countering SQL injections on java based applications. It combines the static approach as well as the dynamic approach. The static part of this approach deals with the code analysis and the automatic model building for queries that the application can generate. At runtime, the dynamically-generated queries are monitored and compared with the statically generated models. If the proposed technique detects a query that violates the model, it classifies the query as an attack, prevents it from accessing the database, and logs the attack information. It consists of three modules: analysis module, instrumentation and run-time module. An extensive evaluation was done and the effectiveness of the tool was evaluated using the real world SQLIA's. This technique was found to be very effective and hence important to us as we follow a similar approach. Diglossia [4] is a tool that detects SQL and NoSQL injections. Dual parsing technique is used in this approach. In this approach, the query is parsed one after the other with its shadow. It then checks if the two parse trees are syntactically isomorphic and also checks if all code in the shadow query is in shadow characters. An evaluation was done based on eleven applications and was found to detect all possible injections. Also performance was measured by enabling and disabling the database caches. The paper claims to be imposing low overheads. A limitation to this is pointed out. The ability of separating code and non-code depends on using the correct grammar for the query language.

The different works on SQL Injection attacks and their prevention [5–8] were also surveyed. [5, 6] classifies the SQL injection attacks extensively. It defines the different attack types and the intent of each attack type. [7] uses the concept of instruction-set randomization. The approach creates process specific randomized instruction sets. The keywords in a query are manipulated by randomizing an integer and then appending to them. The random integer should be chosen in such a way that it cannot be figured out easily. The manipulated query is inserted into the web application and sent to a proxy. The receiving proxy de-randomizes the query and then forwards it to the database after validating it. This method was also found to be effective.

3   MongoDB Injections

In this work, we propose a solution to MongoDB injection attack. The NoSQL injections are usually inferential and our work concentrates mainly on time based and blind based boolean injection attack. The NoSQL Databases were developed keeping in mind the different attacks possible on relational databases and have tried to eliminate them. However, in spite of all these efforts, injection attacks are still possible. We can use JavaScript functions to exploit the MongoDB. Our work mainly focuses on two injection types since we use java-based applications as testbed.

- Time-based: Similar to the time-based exploit in relational databases, the MongoDB is vulnerable to these injections. Along with a valid NoSQL token, the attacker appends a JavaScript function which puts the database on hold. The responses are observed and proper inferences are made from these. For example,

  ```
  - Bob',$where: 'function(){sleep(5000);
    return this.name =="Bob"}
  ```

- This query puts the MongoDB database on hold for 5000 ms, if it has a name entry as 'Bob'.
- Blind-based boolean: If the attacker does not have any knowledge of the contents of a collection, this type of attack is used. He can exploit the various functionalities provided by MongoDB to find the list of collections, the number of collections and so on. A few examples are noted below:

  ```
  - return(db.getCollectionNames().length == 1);
  - return(tojsononeline
    (db.collectionname.find()[0]).length == 1);
  - return(db.getCollectionNames()[0][0] == 'a');
  ```

4   Automata Based NoSQL Injection Detection

The entire input set to the mongoDB applications can either belong to two categories- the valid input set or the invalid input set. The valid inputs are those which are the acceptable queries. The invalid inputs are the attack queries or illegitimate queries. The finite automaton approach that we use, accepts a valid input and moves to the next state that could be a final or a non-final state. When we consider the final transition, if we arrive at the final state it means that the input is valid. If the last transition takes the input to some state that is not the final, then it is invalid.

Theoretically, the input that arrives at the final state is accepted by the automaton. We make use of this concept to categorize our inputs and proceed to the detection phase. We implement an automata based approach for the detection and prevention of MongoDB injections. A more specific explanation can be considered here with a sample query {"Age": "10"}. We take the input expected from the user to be a numerical value. In the valid input range we expect a number and allow regular expressions to handle it by using a regular expression [0-9]*. In our example we expect a value 10 as input. So if the user input is 10, we can classify it under the legitimate query class. Suppose the user input is:

```
10',$where : 'function(){sleep(5000);return this.Age=="10"}
```

The user tricks the legitimate structure by closing off the input with a single quote. He then enters the legitimate code for some illegitimate operation. Since the expected query is {"Age": "10"}, our approach creates an NFA model for this. Now when the attack-intended user input is received, another model is created. Since both of these models do not match, our approach blocks the attempt. The model checks if the user's input matches with the expected input. This is done by checking if the NFA for the expected input matches the NFA for the user given input.

Our proposed system consists of two stages.

Stage 1: To design a model to detect valid NoSQL queries.
Stage 2: If the user input does not match the model, the attempt has to be blocked and the input is rejected.

Both stages consist of two steps each. The first stage includes identification of points in source code from which calls are made to the database and building models for valid queries that can be generated in each hotspot. The second includes generation of dynamic query with the user inputs and query matching with the respective models. If the query matches the model, then the user is allowed to continue. Otherwise the

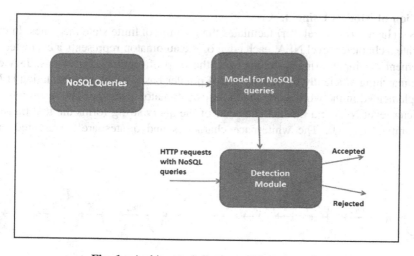

Fig. 1. Architectural diagram of the approach.

attempt has to be blocked and the input is rejected. The architectural diagram is given in Fig. 1.

5   Description

For building the query models we use a finite-automaton approach. An NFA (Non-deterministic finite automaton) that has transitions at character-level is obtained for each hotspot using JSA (Java String Analyzer) library [9]. NFA is preferred over DFA(deterministic finite automaton) as the number of states in NFA will be less than that of DFA which makes this model less complex. Moreover, NFA is capable of accepting everything that a DFA can accept. The first two modules in Fig. 1 belong to Stage 1. The queries are collected from each hotspot by static analysis. For each of these query models are built. The second stage comprises of the verification module and run time checking. When user inputs come in during runtime, the dynamically generated queries are passed into the verification module and verified against its corresponding model. If accepted, the user is allowed to proceed, otherwise the query is blocked from execution.

5.1   Stage 1: Building Query Models

The first step of our work needs the code to be scanned so as to find the hotspots. In MongoDB, find(), insert(), remove() and update() are considered as the places from which a call goes to the database. Once they are discovered, we analyze the query in the application at that point. For each of the input from the user, we estimate all the possible strings at that point and regular expressions are crafted. When a find is issued, a cursor pointing to the resulting documents is returned. This can be used to find the query issued to the database. These queries are used for building the query models using the JSA library.

Creation of Models Using JSA

JSA (Java String Analyzer) facilitates the creation of finite state machines. In order to create a character-level NFA, each edge of the automaton represents a character. We implement the input string matching with the help of regular expressions. JSA does string matching efficiently by making use of pointer-based graph representation [17]. It is implemented in the work using the dk.brics.automaton package. The result will be a character level NFA and the first character of the query string forms the first transition from initial state q0. The whitespace characters and quotes are represented in its

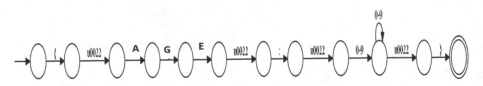

Fig. 2. Sample model for MongoDB query {"AGE": "β"}

Unicode format in the resulting NFA. A sample model for MongoDB is given in Fig. 2. This model corresponds to the query that returns a cursor to {"Age": "β"}, where β is user input which should be a numerical value.

If the entered input is invalid, even if the it is not attack-intended, it is flagged as injection and dropped out without allowing it to reach the database.

5.2 Stage 2: Verification

Now for the final step of our approach, we accept inputs from the user for MongoDB. Consider the sample query {"AGE": "β"}. The new database object is loaded with the required query. Now the cursor points to this particular result set in the document. The user inputs are used to construct dynamic queries at each hotspot and are now prepared to be verified. The JSA library is used to verify the automaton with the dynamically generated query. This converts the NFA to DFA by itself and checks whether the input is the expected one.

In Fig. 3, we have the model generated for an attack intended query or a sample illegitimate query. Observing the models in Figs. 2 and 3, we can see that the models are not matching. If any suspicious inputs are observed, we flag it as injection regardless of the complexity of the attack.

6   Results and Analysis

This section gives a description of the testbed we used, the application of the approach on the subjects and its effectiveness .We used five different test applications of varying sizes. The applications were Java based with MongoDB 2.2.7 as their back-end. These applications were deployed using tomcat on windows 7. All the four steps were performed on each of these applications and the evaluation was done on different metrics. The resulting models from the JSA 2.1-1 were taken in Dot representation and the GraphViz tool 2.38.0 [11] was used for the visualization purpose. The metrics used are

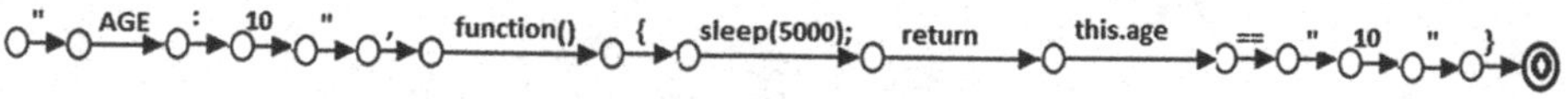

Fig. 3. Sample model for an attack intended user input

Table 1. Applications used for evaluation

Name of application	No. of pages	No. of injectable pages
Articles online	5	1
Bank	9	4
Classifieds	7	2
Employee directory	7	2
Events	5	2

the total number of pages, the number of injectable pages and successful detection rate for each application. The Table 1. lists out the various subjects used by the system. A brief description on the applications are given below:

- Banking: deals with online banking
- Articles: submit articles online
- Classifieds: online classifieds column
- Employee directory: details of employees
- Events: details of various events to be held/hosted.

A number of legitimate and illegitimate inputs were given to the subjects and the results were noted. The models do not accept anything other than the expected input. If the user enters an input that does not match, in the detection module mismatch occurs for expecting input model and the dynamically created model. Hence the input does not get accepted and the attempt for attack is blocked. The injection queries were application-specific. As specified earlier, the original query for the model in Fig. 2 is {"Age": "10"} if β is 10. A few possible injection queries that can be used instead as inputs are given below in Table 2.

Table 3 summarizes the evaluation of our approach. 13 application-specific injection queries were applied to each injection points of the test subjects. The queries consisted of time-based injection queries and blind based boolean injection queries. In addition to this, legitimate queries were also tested out. It can be observed that our approach was able to distinguish between legitimate and illegitimate queries and it effectively detected the illegitimate queries. Even though Diglossia [4] claims to be

Table 2. Sample legitimate and illegitimate inputs

Expected input	Illegitimate input
10	10' , $where : 'function(){sleep(5000);return this.Age=="10"}
10	10' , $where : 'function() {return(db.getCollectionNames().length == 1);}

Table 3. Evaluation table

Name of the application	Number of injectable pages	Number of injections on each injectable page	Injection detected successfully	% of detection
Articles online	1	13	13	100 %
Bank	4	13	13	100 %
Classifieds	2	13	13	100 %
Employee directory	2	13	13	100 %
Events	2	13	13	100 %

efficient, our approach is much simpler. They make use of Korean language in the shadow values which may be difficult to understand for people who don't know Korean.

7 Conclusion

This paper proposes an efficient mechanism for the detection and prevention of injection attacks in the most popular NoSQL database, the MongoDB. We have used an automaton-based approach for the same. NFA models are constructed at injection points and when the user input arrives dynamic query models are created with them. Both the models are then checked for similarity. Only if they match, the user is allowed to proceed. The use of the NFA's considerably reduced the number of states in the model. It does not affect the acceptance of the finite state machine as both DFA and NFA possess the same acceptance power. Since we used java-based applications for our study, the approach mainly focused on the time-based and blind-based boolean attacks. It was able to capture almost all the injection queries and blocks them all by issuing an injection warning. Also, this does not result in any false negatives. The quality of the approach will depend on how well the queries have been converted to the finite state models. Less ambiguous models easen up the work. However, the character-level automaton produced in our approach can be replaced with token-level automatons to further reduce the number of states in the corresponding finite state automaton. By reducing the number of states in the NFA, the complexity of our approach can be reduced.

References

1. NoSQL Databases. http://nosql-database.org
2. Sullivan, B.: Server-side javascript injection: attacking NoSQL and Node.js. In: BlackHat, USA (2011)
3. Halfond, W.G.J., Orso, A.: AMNESIA: analysis and monitoring for neutralizing SQL injection attack. In: Proceedngs of 20th IEEE/ACM International Conference on Automated Software Engineering, pp. 174–183. ACM, New York (2005)
4. Kindy, D.A., Pathan, A.-S.K.: Diglossia: detecting code injection attacks with precision and efficiency. In: Proceedings of SIGSAC. ACM (2013)
5. Halfond, W.G.J., Viegas, J., Orso, A.: A classication of SQL injection attacks and countermeasures. In: Proceedings of International Symposium Secure Software Engineering (ISSSE06). IEEE CS (2006)
6. Kindy, D.A., Pathan, A.-S.K.: A detailed survey on various as- pects of SQL injection in web applications: vulnerabilities, innovative attacks and remedies. Int. J. Commun. Netw. Inf. Secur. 5(2), 80–92 (2013)
7. Boyd, Stephen W., Keromytis, Angelos D.: SQLrand: preventing SQL injection attacks. In: Jakobsson, M., Yung, M., Zhou, J. (eds.) ACNS 2004. LNCS, vol. 3089, pp. 292–302. Springer, Heidelberg (2004)
8. Shar, L.W., Tan, H.B.K.: Defeating SQL injection. IEEE Comput. Soc. 46(3), 69–77 (2013)
9. Feldthaus, A., Miller, A.: Java String Analyzer. http://www.brics.dk/JSA/

10. Tiwari, S.: Professional NoSQL. Wiley India, Delhi (2012)
11. Graphviz-Graph Visualization Software. http://www.graphviz.org
12. Clark, J.: SQL Injection Attacks and Defence. Elsiever Inc., Waltham (2009)
13. Ullman, J., Hopcroft, J.: Introduction to Automata Theory, Languages, and Computation. Pearson Education, New Delhi (1979)
14. Sullivan, B.: NoSQL-But-Even-Less-Security. http://blogs.adobe.com/security/files/2011/04/NoSQL-But-Even-Less-Security.pdf
15. Testing for NoSQL injection. https://www.owasp.org/index.php/Testing_for_NoSQL_injection
16. Attacking MongoDB. http://2012.zeronights.org/includes/docs/Firstov%20-%20Attacking%20MongoDB.pdf
17. Hooimeijer, Pieter, Veanes, Margus: An evaluation of automata algorithms for string analysis. In: Jhala, R., Schmidt, D. (eds.) VMCAI 2011. LNCS, vol. 6538, pp. 248–262. Springer, Heidelberg (2011)

Author Index